Stanley Kubrick

Also by Vincent LoBrutto

Selected Takes: Film Editors on Editing
By Design: Interviews with Film Production Designers
Sound on Film: Interviews with Creators of Film Sound
Principal Photography: Interviews with Feature Film Cinematographers

STANLEY

Kubrick

A Biography

Vincent LoBrutto

DA CAPO PRESS

Library of Congress Cataloging-in-Publication Data

LoBrutto, Vincent.
   Stanley Kubrick: a biography / Vincent LoBrutto. —1st Da Capo
Press ed.
    p.   cm.
   Originally published: New York: D.I. Fine, c1997.
   Filmography: p.
   Includes bibliographical references and index.
   ISBN 0-306-80906-0 (alk. paper)
   1. Kubrick, Stanley. 2. Motion picture producers and directors—
United States—Biography. I. Title.
PN1998.3.K83L6 1999
791.43′0233′092—dc21   98-47434
[B]   CIP

First Da Capo Press edition 1999
2 3 4 5 6 7 8 9 10   02 01 00 99

This Da Capo Press paperback edition of *Stanley Kubrick* is an
unabridged republication of the edition first published in New York
in 1997, with several minor textual emendations. It is reprinted by
arrangement with Dutton Plume, a division of Penguin Putnam Inc.

Copyright © 1997 by Vincent LoBrutto

Published by Da Capo Press, Inc.
A Member of Perseus Books Group

All Rights Reserved

Manufactured in the United States of America

We gratefully acknowledge permission to reprint the following:

Tony Curtis: The Autobiography by Tony Curtis and Barry Paris, text copyright 1993 by
Tony Curtis and Barry Paris, used by permission of William Morrow & Company, Inc.

The Film Director as Superstar by Joseph Gelmis, copyright © 1970 by Joseph Gelmis.
Used by permission of Doubleday, a division of Bantam Doubleday Dell Publishing
Group, Inc.

"The Flower-Filled World of the Other Kubrick" by Valerie Jenkins, from the London
Evening Standard/Solo.

"Stanley Kubrick's Vietnam" by Frances X. Clines, copyright 1987 by The New York
Times Co. Reprinted by Permission.

"Cynic's Choice" by Ron Magid, courtesy of American Society of Cinematographers and
American Cinematographer magazine.

"Kubrick Does Vietnam His Way" by Lloyd Grove, copyright 1987, The Washington Post.
Reprinted with permission.

(The following page constitutes an extension of this copyright page.)

For Patrick McGilligan, patron saint of the small global family
who write about film

Contents

CONTENTS

PART THREE

1956–1960
Hollywood

PART FOUR

1960–1964
England

PART FIVE

1964–1987
Isolation / Solitude / Hermitage

PART SIX

Infinity

The Myth of the Reclusive Auteur

On February 25, 1996, Jim Coleman of Parryville, Pennsylvania, wrote to Walter Scott of *Parade* magazine, to the writer's Personality Parade column. Stanley Kubrick, the internationally renowned film director of *Paths of Glory, Dr. Strangelove, 2001: A Space Odyssey,* and *A Clockwork Orange,* had not released a film since *Full Metal Jacket* in 1987. Mr. Coleman exemplified many around the world who looked to the director as a cinematic messiah and waited with reverence for another opportunity to sit in front of a new Stanley Kubrick film. *"What has happened to the greatest director this country ever produced?"* Coleman wrote. Scott answered the question skillfully and directly by presenting an update of unrealized projects and hope for the coming summer when Warner Bros. announced that Kubrick would begin shooting a new project—but the question suggested deeper implications.

Like Greta Garbo, Howard Hughes, J. D. Salinger, and Thomas Pynchon, Stanley Kubrick is a celebrated recluse. Kubrick's notorious secrecy, obsessive perfectionism, and ever-widening chasm between films have created a torrent of apocryphal stories, producing a mythology more than a man.

The legend of Stanley Kubrick portrays an intense, cool, misanthropic cinematic genius who obsesses over every detail, a man who lives a hermetic existence, doesn't travel, and is consumed with phobic neuroses.

This book began with a search to understand the man who arguably may be the greatest living film director.

The journey began in 1964 when at age fourteen my friends and I went to the movies. I had been raised on television's Million Dollar Movie, repeated viewings of *King Kong,* Jerry Lewis, Elvis Presley, biblical spectacles, and Disney classics, and going to the movies meant seeing whatever was playing at the local theater. You went to the movies principally to pass the time and to be entertained. I can't say we knew what we were going to see as we approached the local theater in Sunnyside, Queens, New York, that day, but the marquee announced the feature as *Dr. Strangelove or: How I Learned to Stop Worrying and Love the Bomb.* As the black-and-white image of two military planes engaging in some sort of sexual misconduct crossed the screen, I knew I wasn't watching an Elvis Presley film. For that matter, this wasn't like any movie I had ever seen. Six years later, as a film student at the School of Visual Arts in New York, I saw *Paths of Glory* and have never forgotten those relentless tracking shots of Kirk Douglas as Colonel Dax, leading his doomed troops in the trenches. I caught up with the director's early work at a Museum of Modern Art retrospective and waited to see what Kubrick had in store for us. It was a screening of *2001: A Space Odyssey* at the Ziegfeld Theater in the early seventies that put me on the course that led to this book—I knew that neither the cinema nor I would ever be the same again.

This is the first full-scale biography of Stanley Kubrick. It is my intent that a narrative that traces Kubrick from his birth in the Bronx, New York, across decades of cinematic achievement, to the current larger-than-life public perception of him as a reclusive auteur living in oblivion will both shatter and inform the myths. After four years of intensive research and interviews with those who know and work with Stanley Kubrick, I have seen the myth crossfade into a man.

This is his story.

PART ONE

1928–1948
The Bronx

CHAPTER 1

"Stanley Was Only Interested in What He Was Interested In"

A s a cinematic voyager, Stanley Kubrick has witnessed three wars, an ancient slave revolt, and an absurdist superpower nuclear confrontation. He has traveled the bi-coastal noir landscape of urban cities, has explored the backroads of desire with a lust-filled professor and his nymphet, and has journeyed into and beyond our universe. He has visited an ultra-violent near future, time-traveled to the eighteenth century, and has experienced the now-and-then within a possessed hotel in Colorado, even though he has spent almost half of his personal and professional life in the countryside just outside London, England.

Stanley Kubrick arrived in Great Britain in the early 1960s as a filmmaker totally in control of his personal universe via the Bronx, New York City, and Los Angeles. His family's first pilgrimage to America began around the turn of the century, when his paternal great-grandparents, Hersh Kubrik and Leie Fuchs, emigrated from Galacia, Austria.

Born on April 4, 1852, Hersh Kubrik was a forty-seven-year-old tailor when he traveled from Austria via Liverpool to the United States on the *Lusitania,* the ship that was later, in 1915, torpedoed by a German submarine, leading the United States into World War I. The ship docked in New York on December 27, 1899.

The Kubrik household was established at 723 East Fifth Street in New York City. Hersh was the father of five children. Elias Kubrik, Stanley Kubrick's grandfather, was the oldest. Elias was born in Probuzna, Austria, on November 27, 1877, when Hersh was twenty-five years old. A daughter, Bela, followed on April 25, 1879. It is likely that Elias and Bela were the offspring of a first marriage of Hersh Kubrik's and that Leie was the natural mother of the remaining three children: Annie Kubrik, born in Austria on April 15, 1897, twenty years after the birth of Elias; Joseph, born July 21, 1900; and Hersh and Leie's youngest child, Michael, a native New Yorker, born on December 11, 1904, when Hersh Kubrik was fifty-two years old.

Grandfather Elias made his own way to America in 1902 on the *Statendam* when he was twenty-five years old. He traveled with his young Rumanian wife, Rosa Spiegelblatt, who was nineteen and pregnant with their first child. The trip took them through France, with their eventual arrival in New York City on March 11, 1902. They moved to 125 Rivington Street, where Elias, like his father, took work as a tailor. By the 1920s Elias had become a ladies' coat manufacturer in business with Jacob Maslen as Kubrick & Maslen, located in the garment district.

After Elias and Rosa had been in America for two months, Jacob Cubrick, as his birth certificate read, was born, on May 21, 1902. Jacob, who was also known as Jacques and Jack, with a middle name of Leonard or Leon, was the only male child of Elias and Rosa Kubrik. Two girls, Hester Merel and Lilly, were born on June 12, 1904, and August 11, 1906. The girls were also known as Ester and Lillian, and, as was common for the times, documents recorded their names with various spellings. It is not known precisely when the family appellation settled into its current spelling, but Jack Kubrick memorialized it on his medical degree and marriage license in 1927.

Stanley Kubrick's mother, Gertrude Perveler, was also the oldest child in her family and the only female. Social security records indicate Gertrude's date of birth as October 28, 1903, but her birth certificate, which records her first name as Sadie, shows a date of October 29, 1903. In either event, Gertrude was born to Austrian parents Samuel Perveler, a waiter, and Celia Siegel Perveler at 252 East Fourth Street in Manhattan. Twenty-five-year-old Sam and twenty-year-old Celia were married on June 15, 1902, and originally lived at 312 East Houston Street. Sam was the son of Israel and Brane Perveler. Celia was the daughter of Joseph and Gittel Siegel.

Gert's brothers, Joseph David and Martin, were born on May 27, 1906, and March 8, 1910, when the family lived on Hoe Avenue in the

Bronx. Martin Perveler, eighteen years Stanley Kubrick's senior, would become a pivotal figure in the financial solvency of Kubrick's early film career.

Gertrude Perveler and Jacques Kubrick were married on October 30, 1927, in a Jewish ceremony on Union Avenue in the Bronx just after Jack began his medical career by graduating from the New York Homeopathic Medical College and Flower Hospital, after attending New York University. They set up their household at 2160 Clinton Avenue in the Bronx.

Jacques sported the good looks of a silent movie idol, with a dashingly handsome face and well-groomed moustache. He was a popular med student and the vice president of his junior class, who charmed his thirty-one classmates with his mellifluous tenor voice.

The Bronx's preeminent film director, Stanley Kubrick, actually was born in the borough of Manhattan, at 307 Second Avenue, in the Lying-In Hospital on Thursday, July 26, 1928.

The birth of Stanley Kubrick was auspicious. The day was sunny, with cool summer temperatures in the high seventies. At twenty-six, Dr. Jacques L. Kubrick could feel comfortable that his firstborn was delivered under optimum circumstances at Lying-In, a well-established obstetric teaching hospital where medical students from his alma mater, Homeopathic Medical College, took course work to develop their obstetric skills for medical practice. (Four years later, the hospital became the Department of Obstetrics at New York Hospital.)

The events of the day were portents of things to come. The headline of the *New York Times,* which then cost two cents, read: "Tunney Scores Knockout over Heeney in Eleventh; Only 50,000 See the Battle—Champion Punishes Rival—Administers Such Severe Beating the Referee Is Forced to Stop Bout—Fight Nearly Ended in 10th—Tunney's Relentless and Powerful Punching Overcomes the Courageous New Zealander—Champion Always Master—His Superiority Evident Even When Challenger Made Best Showing in Early Rounds." The tabloid poetry on the day of Stanley Kubrick's birth would be echoed in his early work as a *Look* magazine photographer, when he took pictures of prizefighters Rocky Graziano and Walter Cartier—who would also be the subject of his very first film.

Napoleon, a career-long obsession of Kubrick's, was also in the news on July 26, 1928. A collection of extremely valuable Napoleonic manuscripts dating from 1793 to 1797 was discovered in the library of a Polish Count Zamoysk at his Kurnick estate. The papers related to the Italian campaigns and were written in Napoleon's hand. The article, shoehorned into a back page, was one that the adult Kubrick or his staff surely would never have missed. It had the required element—information—for the Kubrick data bank. During his career Kubrick would meticulously track down any knowledge that was connected to a project in development.

When Gertrude and Stanley were released from the hospital, the Kubricks went home to 2160 Clinton Avenue, a six-story brick apartment building with a courtyard located between East 181st and East 182nd Street in the Bronx. Dr. Kubrick began to develop his general practitioner's medical practice, and Gertrude attended to nurturing Stanley during his infancy and preschool years.

Stanley's school career was slated to begin at Public School 3 in the fall of 1934. That spring, on May 21, 1934, Dr. Kubrick was given quite a birthday present for his thirty-second year when Gertrude gave birth to their second child, Barbara Mary Kubrick. Stanley and his younger sister completed Jacques and Gert's family.

Dr. Kubrick's medical practice was set up on the northeast corner of 361 East 158th Street and Courtlandt Avenue. The office serviced the diverse, working-class community with general medical attention. For three decades J. L. Kubrick, M.D., practiced at this location, where patients could reach him at Melrose 5-8100 between the hours of eight and ten in the morning, one to two o'clock in the afternoon, and six to eight in the evening. When he wasn't in his office, Dr. Kubrick could be found at Morrisania City Hospital, practicing otolaryngology.

Stanley Kubrick's educational career had started off with a poor attendance record. He began grammar school at P.S. 3 in the Bronx on September 12, 1934, and remained at that school until the end of the fifth grade. The six-year-old Stanley was absent half of his first term, attending class for fifty-six days and missing class for the other fifty-six days. In 1935, while attending the 1B and 2A terms, Kubrick was absent for fifty-five days. His poor attendance record remained a constant for the major part of his limited academic career. In these first years, when he was there, his social habits and conduct were rated from A to C−.

From January to June 1936, Stanley, then eight years old, began to receive home instruction. It is unknown whether he was suffering from an illness that kept him from joining his schoolmates at P.S. 3 or whether the decision was made because of so called adjustment problems, but Stanley received tutoring in second grade grammar school subjects on at least four dates in the first half of the year. From September 1936 Stanley's attendance improved greatly, and through February 1938 he attained nearly perfect attendance.

During this period the family moved to a private two-family house on Grant Avenue between 163rd Street and 165th Street, an easy walk to the office for Dr. Kubrick. The Kubricks lived at two locations on Grant Avenue in practically identical two-story brick attached row houses, first at 1131, which connected to 1129, and then for a longer time at 1135, which was coupled to 1133 Grant Avenue.

In June 1938 Stanley began school at P.S. 90. His attendance from 1938 to 1940 was acceptable, but though he was present more often, the school found his behavior to be unsatisfactory in social areas. Stanley received U's in the areas of Personality, Works and Plays Well with Others, Completes Work, Is Generally Careful, Respects Rights of Others, and Speaks Clearly. His personal health habits were considered satisfactory by the school.

Gertrude Kubrick's brother, Martin Perveler, became a licensed pharmacist in California on October 22, 1938, when he was twenty-eight years old. He lived in the Southern Pasadena–San Gabriel area. Martin had married Marion Delores Wild on January 10, 1939, in Santa Ana, California. They had their first and only child, Patricia Ann, on November 25, 1939. Martin, exceedingly entrepreneurial, founded a string of pharmacies and engaged in other enterprises that ultimately made him a millionaire.

In June 1940, as Stanley Kubrick approached his twelfth birthday, he was discharged from P.S. 90 in the Bronx. Dr. Kubrick and Gertrude made the decision to give the boy a change of venue. Stanley went out to California to stay with his Uncle Martin and his Aunt Marion. The precise motivation for Jack and Gertrude's decision to send Stanley to Pasadena is not known, but the sister of a close family friend had the impression that Dr. Kubrick was concerned about his son's poor performance in school and thought some time on the West Coast would do him good. Stanley spent the fall term of 1940 and the spring term of 1941 in California. It was his first trip to the land of Hollywood. Later he would return three times in search of breaking into the big leagues of feature filmmaking. In September 1941 Stanley returned from California and reentered P.S. 90 in the eighth grade. He was back in the Bronx.

Stanley's mental ability otherwise showed potential, though his grades and social skills did not. From the period of May 1935 when he was seven, through November of 1941 when he reached thirteen, Stanley Kubrick took the standard reading and intelligence tests given throughout the New York school system. The results were above average. He continued to be a child of untapped potential, and the mounting absences did not help.

In hopes of stimulating Stanley with outside interests, Dr. Kubrick encouraged his son to use his Graflex camera. Jack enjoyed taking pictures as a hobby and thought that the Graflex could stir a passion in Stanley that would motivate him. Jack tried to instill in Stanley his love of literature and made his library of books available. Dr. Kubrick also taught his son how to play chess.

The Graflex was a high-speed, single-lens reflex American camera developed early in the century, the first to be used by newspapermen. The camera was portable, with a fast lens and focal plane shutter, which could freeze fast-moving action. The Graflex focused through the lens and produced a large-sized picture. Stanley Kubrick's first camera was not a child's toy but a professional tool and an invitation to a world of images.

Photography can be the most seductive of hobbies. Preteen boys growing up in the forties, fifties, and sixties often found fascination in the magic box of a still camera. A first camera could be used to explore a youngster's world, to document family activities, events, and rituals. An exposed roll of film sent to the lab via the local drugstore came back as moments in time preserved forever in positive photographic images. Some youngsters delved deeper into the hobby by working in makeshift darkrooms outfitted by a visit to the local photo shop, where they purchased their own equipment. Others worked in a school or club darkroom and saw the developing magic firsthand in the dim but alluring glow of a safety bulb, as absolute darkness protected the fragile emulsion from daylight and black-and-white images appeared on a special paper swimming in a chemical bath. To Stanley Kubrick, photography began as a hobby but quickly became a suitor and a muse.

Dr. Kubrick, Gertrude, Barbara, and Stanley continued to live in the Bronx in several locations. From 1942 through Stanley's graduation from high school, the Kubrick family moved several times. In 1942 they moved to 2715 Grand Concourse. By 1944 they lived at 1414 Shakespeare Avenue, and by the end of 1945 they had moved to 1873 Harrison Avenue. By age fourteen Stanley lived on the top floor of a six-story apartment building, the Majestic Court, located at 2715 Grand Concourse.

The Grand Concourse was lined with apartment buildings filled with Jewish, Italian, and Irish families. The structure at 2715 Grand Concourse was an elegant building near the corner of 196th Street, just a few blocks east of Jerome Avenue and the elevated IRT Lexington Avenue subway. A formal garden with benches connected 2715 with 2701. Across the spacious boulevard, on the other side of the Concourse, was

the underground IND Sixth Avenue line. At the entrance to the IND
was a newsstand operated by Al Goldstein, the neighborhood boxing
legend, who attracted adolescent boxing aficionados to his alcove. Goldstein proudly displayed a photo of himself when he was the lightweight
boxing champion of New York State in the twenties. "Al was a bit
punchy, but he had a brother who supervised things," recalled Donald
Silverman, who lived in Kubrick's building. "Inside the stand there were
fight pictures of Al with signatures. He was a very handsome guy when
he started fighting."

The main lobby of 2715 had a decorative marble floor. The elevator
operators knew where everyone lived, so Stanley could just enter and
travel to his floor while he remained occupied in his thoughts. The operators were on duty twenty-four hours a day. One of them, Ray, a thin
man who seemed to sustain himself mainly on ice cream, was often given
treats by the residents of the building. The superintendent lived in the
back, on the first floor facing the garden.

Kindred spirits have a way of finding each other. Marvin Traub, a boy
just four months older than Stanley, lived directly below him on the fifth
floor and had already been bitten by the shutterbug. Then entering his
teens, Marvin began processing black-and-white photographs in the sixth
grade. On his thirteenth birthday Marvin's grandfather gave him a twin-
lens reflex camera for his bar mitzvah. Marvin took pictures whenever
there were family occasions. At one Passover seder he joined the company of his relatives in front of the camera by using a time-release device
to trigger the shutter after he quickly ran to his front seat at the festive
table.

Once Stanley and Marvin met, they became close friends, bonded by
their budding passion for black-and-white still photography. Marvin
didn't go to the movies or share Stanley's attraction to chess, baseball, or
other sports, but he had a passion for building model airplanes. Stanley
liked to go to the movies, and Marvin and his cousin Cliff Vogel would
go to Van Cortlandt Park, on the east end of Moshulu Parkway, to fly
model airplanes. As a photographer Marvin possessed knowledge, experience, and his own darkroom. The home photographic lab was set up in
Marvin's bedroom across from his bed against the front entrance wall. A
table held trays of photographic chemicals and an enlarger given to Marvin by his father. Marvin had white and black shades on all the windows.
A red light protected the fragile images as they were developed. Stanley
Kubrick spent a lot of time in Marvin Traub's darkroom. The obsession
had begun.

The Traub apartment at 2715 Grand Concourse was the salon of the family. People were always coming in and out to visit. The living room was often converted into a bedroom, and at times several aunts and uncles joined the extended family. "It was like a hotel," Cliff Vogel, Marvin's younger cousin, recalls. Fourteen-year-old Stanley Kubrick was a very frequent visitor, always there for one purpose—Marvin's darkroom. Harriet Daniels, Cliff's sister who was a year older than Stanley and Marvin, remembers seeing the adolescent Kubrick in her aunt's home. "He would ring the doorbell every five minutes. I remember Aunt Edna was always saying, 'Oh, Kubrick the nudnik is here again.' He would come in and out several times in one day, quite often within five minutes of the time before."

"Aunt Edna was always saying, 'That Kubrick is always down here. Doesn't this kid have his own apartment? Why is he down here?' " Cliff Vogel recalls. Harriet Daniels remembers Stanley as a short, chunky boy with dark hair. Cliff recalls him as a flabby kid with a probing glare. "He had an aquiline face without the aquiline nose, sharp, piercing eyes—not warm and friendly but sharp, aggressive and intense."

Marvin and Stanley spent a lot of time together. Harriet would watch the boys skillfully develop the rolls of film they shot and spend hours printing their work through Marvin's enlarger. When they weren't inside the darkroom, they were out taking pictures and creating assignments for themselves as photojournalists. Stanley and Marvin were fascinated by the work of Arthur Fellig, the New York news photographer known as Weegee, who captured life on the streets in the city with the eye of a social caricaturist. His bold tabloid photographs evolved into an art form as he began to experiment with ways of contorting and distorting the photographic image to create a highly personal and wry view of his world. Weegee was an early and significant influence on the fledgling adolescent photographers.

Stanley and Marvin searched the streets for photographic subjects and walked the neighborhood business district. There was the Kingsbridge Movie Theater, and on the corner of Jerome Avenue and Kingsbridge Road was a Greek restaurant. Specialty stores featured smoked salmon, bins of candy, and giant kosher pickles in wooden barrels that could be purchased for just a few pennies.

Stanley navigated the streets of his Bronx neighborhood with his heavy wool mackinaw jacket, a style many of the boys wore. Stanley often donned his plaid jacket over a clashing-color patterned shirt. His hair ostensibly was combed with a center part, but in reality it was settled in lumps and bumps by hair tonic and natural oils, which glued it in place wherever it fell.

Many of the teenage boys in the Bronx were in SACs—Social Athletic Clubs. They met socially on Fridays, but their primary reason for existence was to play ball. In Stanley's neighborhood alone there were half a dozen SACs. The members all wore club jackets sporting the groups' names such as the Zombies, the Barracudas, and the Hurricanes. Gerald Fried, who would later be introduced to Kubrick by their mutual friend Alexander Singer and would become his first film composer, was a member of the Barracudas. Stanley Kubrick and Marvin Traub were not members of a social club—they were lone young men on a photographic mission.

Donald Silverman, who now runs a trademark licensing company, lived on the second floor of 2715 Grand Concourse. Donald was socially and athletically involved in the neighborhood and was Stanley and Marvin's contemporary. "Stanley was a very private person. He wasn't invited to play stickball with us. He wasn't invited to play roller hockey with us. He may not have wanted to, but he was so private that we never asked him. It was a very close-knit neighborhood. The fellas grew up on the Concourse. Everybody knew everybody else's parents. After coming back from Public School 46 or De Witt Clinton we would end up at different fellas' homes. There were different groups living within a five-block radius. Stanley and Marvin were really never in the group that I was in. I was friendly with Marvin Traub and Stanley Kubrick—I crossed boundaries. I was fairly close with Marvin and I'd been to Stanley's apartment many times, but we never really socialized—he was always busy studying photography or studying something. Marvin's keen interest in photography captivated Kubrick's interest.

"Stanley was very private, he never mixed with us as a group. He was not part of eight guys walking down the street or leaning against cars. There's no doubt there's a mystique about him. Kubrick was always a mystery. He never went to the same candy store at the time we were there. There were softball games on Sunday at Walton High School field. Whether you played or went to watch, that was a place where everybody was, and Stanley never showed up there."

The local boys also played stickball and baseball by their apartments. Often they played baseball against a wall with a "Spaldeen"—using the open space in the garden between the two buildings as a field. Touch football and roller hockey were played on the Concourse. "If we were playing ball and a car came to park, we would ask the driver, 'Could you move down a little ways—so not to block the field?' People did move their cars because there was ample space at the time," Silverman recalled.

Comic books were ten cents, and a bakery featured chocolate eclairs and freshly baked rolls. The streets were filled with stores. Around the corner from 2715 Grand Concourse was Guth's, a pharmacy that also served fresh ice cream, hand-packed for twenty cents a pint. Krum's was on the Concourse and Fordham Road. Jahn's, the legendary ice cream parlor, was on Kingsbridge Road and featured fake Tiffany lamps over wooden tables. Mammoth-sized ice cream desserts and the famed Kitchen Sink—an epic sundae that could serve a team of eaters—were the main attractions here. Nearby was the Valentine Movie Theater, the Castro Convertible showroom, and Bond's Clothing Shop. All the local bookmakers, with street names like "Joe Jalop," hung out at Bickford's Coffee Shop. The nearby Villa Avenue held an Italian enclave. The Villa Avenue Gang was a group of Italian American toughs who bullied the local kids and were to be avoided. On a vacant lot on the Grand Concourse between 203rd and 204th Streets, a vision of the Virgin Mary was spotted. Many arranged religious items at the holy site. The local priest from across the street drove a Lincoln Continental. Kingsbridge Road featured a tailor shop, a seafood store with live fish swimming in tanks, a Jewish bakery, and a Chinese restaurant.

The famed Loew's Paradise was on East 188th Street below Fordham Road on the Grand Concourse. The magical interior of the four-thousand-seat theater had a cloud-lit ceiling. The clouds moved across the imaginary sky, and it was like a movie unto itself. The movie palace designed in Italian Baroque by architect John Eberson and opened on September 7, 1929, was fully carpeted, with lots of hallways and statuaries worthy of a castle. Children loved to run around the spacious lobby, getting sweaty, having fun, and staging mock fights. They sat on the tall, Jacobean-style carved chairs wondering if their feet would ever touch the ground. The RKO Fordham was east of the Concourse at Valentine Avenue. Works of Hollywood art like John Ford's production of Steinbeck's *The Grapes of Wrath* graced the screens, along with commercial entertainments like *Casablanca*. The people of the middle-class neighborhood worked hard and shopped at Alexander's Department Store on the corner of Fordham Road and the Grand Concourse.

One day when Stanley, Marvin, and Cliff were walking down the Concourse, Marvin collected small change from the boys and went into a specialty store to buy a treat for the group. He came out and presented the boys with big, delicious kosher pickles. Stanley must have had his mind on something sweet and not sour. He grabbed the pickle and flung it into the air, where it went end over end like the ape Moon-Watcher's bone in *2001: A Space Odyssey*. In the film the bone turned into one of the most famous transitions in cinema history, but the pickle just plopped on the ground. Stanley, in a momentary burst of adolescent angst, said, "A pickle! Why did you buy a pickle?" while the younger Cliff enjoyed his delicacy, not understanding that the irrational burst of energy was part of Stanley's developing single-mindedness and fierce determination.

Frank Sinatra, from Hoboken, New Jersey, was a major singing idol driving bobby-soxers to hysteria as he performed at New York's famed Paramount Theater. Marvin and Stanley managed to get backstage passes to Sinatra concerts, where they would take pictures of the skinny Italian kid with the magnificent voice and snap photos of the screaming girls and adoring boys who dreamed of being Frankie. Before Elvis, the Beatles, and Michael Jackson, Frank Sinatra was whipping America's youth culture into a frenzy, and Stanley and Marvin were there—not to make snapshots for keepsakes but to document a cultural phenomenon that was unfolding in front of their lenses.

When it was time for Stanley Kubrick to go to high school, he went to William Howard Taft. The more ambitious took and passed the test to get into the Bronx High School of Science, but because of his unexceptional educational standing, Stanley simply attended the district school in his neighborhood. Taft was a new school, built in 1941, and rumors abounded that the building was sinking because the foundation had been built on unstable land.

Kubrick began at Taft during the World War II years, under the stewardship of principal Robert B. Brodie, and was required to sign a pink card known as a loyalty oath. The card, signed twice in pen in Kubrick's hand, pronounced: "I hereby declare loyalty to the government of the United States and State of New York and I promise to support their laws to the best of my ability."

Stanley did not have a good attendance record at Taft High School, but he did have a solid one at the local movie theaters. He religiously attended the Loew's Paradise and the RKO Fordham—twice a week to see double features. "One of the important things about seeing run-of-the-mill Hollywood films eight times a week was that many of them were so bad," Kubrick told Bernard Weinraub of the New York Times. "Without even beginning to understand what the problems of making films were, I was taken with the impression that I could not do a film any worse than the ones I was seeing. I also felt I could, in fact, do them a lot better." The rabid moviegoing was not a conscious attempt at a film education—nevertheless, it exceeded the normal habits of most Bronx teenagers, who went to the movies every Saturday. Stanley quickly developed a quite judgmental attitude. Rather than sitting in the dark and falling into the realm of fantasy that would allow the screen entertainment to take him from the Bronx to a magical place, young Stanley Kubrick actually had the audacity to think he could do at least as well as, if not better than, what was coming out of the Hollywood studio film factories. Young Kubrick could see himself making movies. An early subconscious choice told him he must see everything that was on film. His logical mind and growing curiosity taught him not to use emotionalism to select a film based on the star or the genre. He began to see everything, because it all had something to teach him.

The conventional academic program at Taft didn't attract Stanley's attention as well as the movie theaters did. R. I. Meeks, Stanley's math teacher, encountered behavior problems with the young man in Geometry class and gave him a character card that indicated his habit of talking during class and, in the teacher's view, disturbing the other students.

In February 1943, Stanley took a Saturday morning children's art class at the Art Students League of New York, on Fifty-seventh Street in Manhattan across from Carnegie Hall. He returned in April to be part of watercolorist Ann Goldthwaite's class. The seeds of art began to cultivate in Stanley.

Robert M. Sandelman, later creative director of a sales promotion advertising agency, which he owned, lived on Sheridan Avenue in the Bronx directly across the street from Taft High School.

In 1943, Bobby Sandelman played clarinet in the William Howard Taft orchestra. The orchestra comprised sixty to seventy high school musicians under the baton of conductor Harry A. Feldman, who had played first violin for maestro Leopold Stokowski. The percussionist of the ensemble was Stanley Kubrick.

"Stanley was a very quiet boy," Sandelman recalls. "He came to orchestra rehearsals with a 35mm camera around his neck, which was very unusual because not everybody had a camera in those days. He was very quiet. He played his percussion and had a very faraway, dreamy look in his eyes as if he wasn't with us. Very often Mr. Feldman, our conductor, would admonish Stanley to pick up the tempo. He was losing tempo, but he really wasn't with us, he was somewhere else. We assumed that photography was his all-consuming passion and not the tempo in the orchestra. He wasn't very good unless he concentrated, then he was okay."

The orchestra had a classical repertoire and played compositions like *Slavonic Rhapsody.* Practice was held by Mr. Feldman in the morning two to three days a week during first or second period. Stanley was a member of the Assembly Band in 1943 and 1944. In addition to rehearsing with the orchestra, Kubrick was in the band when they performed concerts in June 1943 and March and May 1944. Stanley also received extracurricular credit for performing in the Taft assembly program in March and May 1943.

Stanley and Bobby knew each other as orchestra members in their respective percussion and woodwind sections but were not friends until later, when they both became members of the Taft Swing Band.

The Swing Band was formed by leader Shelly Gold, who played the saxophone. The group consisted of seven to nine pieces. Bobby played clarinet and B-flat tenor sax in the three-man woodwind section. There were three trumpet players and Stanley played the drums. "I knew a female student who told me she could sing in the style of Betty Hutton. Her name was Edith Gorme. She was in my class, and she was also living across the street from my apartment house, so I knew her pretty well," Sandelman recalls. Eydie Gorme, who went on to become internationally famous in her own right, was the Taft Swing Band's female singer, performing forties pop hits like "Where or When" in what Sandelman describes as "the typical Betty Hutton jumping-around, energetic style." Eydie lived on East 168th Street and was co-captain of the cheerleader squad at Taft.

The Swing Band practiced its contemporary pop repertoire and played dances held in the school's gymnasium for bobby-soxers who were fueled by the sounds of Glenn Miller and Benny Goodman and the crooning of Frank Sinatra.

The demands a swing band makes on the drummer, along with the opportunity to express the music of his era, must have inspired the young Stanley Kubrick, because Sandelman remembers the fledgling Gene Krupa/Buddy Rich as an integral part of the band's swing. "He was very involved, came to practice and played. He was more focused when we played swing, jazz, or the music of the time. He didn't wear the camera at the band. We caught his attention, and we got all of Stanley Kubrick, not part of him. He was a good drummer. He was more than a timekeeper, he would take some drum solos," Sandelman recalled. Kubrick's participation in the Taft music program gave a boost to his low academic standing, earning him twelve extracurricular credits for the term ending in June 1943.

Stanley's interest in still photography continued to grow. He became a member of the Taft High School photography club, which was supervised by Mr. Sullivan, who was responsible for photographing the students and activities. A disciplined man with wire-rimmed glasses, slicked-back hair, and a tightly controlled facial expression, Mr. Sullivan ran his well-equipped photographic darkroom with a firm hand. The students were given assignments to document such school activities as basketball games and school plays, and their photographs were published in the Taft newspaper and magazine.

Bernard Cooperman, a member of the photography team, remembers helping Mr. Sullivan take pictures of the students with a fellow camera enthusiast named Stanley Kubrick. The boys were connected by their passion for still photography and spent hours together in the darkroom. The air was filled with the smell of the photobugs' sweet chemical elixirs. The photos in the school literary organs were credited to the individual photographer. One issue of the school's glossy-paged magazine accidentally reversed the credits for pictures taken individually by Bernard and Stanley, symbolically linking them as members of a larger community of photographers.

As their friendship grew, Stanley began to involve Bernard in the photographic projects that were dominating his imagination. "We went out to take photographs at a baseball game, and to me this was a sign that he had something," Mr. Cooperman recalled fifty years later from his backyard deck in Syosset, Long Island. "I had no idea of what to do. I mean, I was going to take pictures of a baseball game. What he did was he just sat in front of a group of three or four kids facing the camera. They made faces at him and he just sat there until they finally forgot that he was there and he got great pictures. I realize now at that age he knew what to do."

Despite Stanley Kubrick's ability in photography, at Taft his overall grades remained poor. In the spring of 1945 he was reported to the attendance bureau for excessive absences. From 1944 until 1946 Stanley Kubrick ran up a high absence rate at Taft. His family received notes informing them about the problem. The school criticized Stanley's behavior and social skills. He received low ratings in Courtesy, Dependability, and Cooperation—skills he later mastered and that served him well in his professional life. Later, as a film director, Kubrick would demonstrate his strength of character by commanding respect from those who worked with him, and he was recognized as a leader, but without the motivation of his art, Stanley Kubrick was perceived by Taft High School as an underachiever with less than acceptable socialization with his peers and teachers. The conventional education system was unable to bring Stanley Kubrick, like so many individuals in the arts, into the mainstream or to recognize and harvest his extraordinary talent.

Chess was more than a game to Stanley—it represented order, logic, perseverance, and self-discipline. The game embraced the young man's fascination with war and the military. Stanley inherited the chess player's persona, quiet but determined, intense and strong-minded, while he exerted his will on the other player. The game early became a mania and merged with his love of photography and movies. Kubrick let in only interests that would function with a single purpose. As he became experienced and skilled at the chessboard, he began to use it as a way of learning important life lessons. "Chess is an analogy," he later said. "It is a series of steps that you take one at a time and it's balancing resources against the problem, which in chess is time and in movies is time and money." As his instincts as an artist began to grow, they were shaped by the desire to explore all his choices and coolly weigh each decision, a lesson the long hours of playing chess taught him. "I used to play chess twelve hours a day. You sit at the board and suddenly your heart leaps. Your hand trembles to pick up the piece and move it. But what chess teaches you is that you must sit there calmly and think about whether it's really a good idea and whether there are other, better ideas."

On April 12, 1945, President Franklin Delano Roosevelt died. The beloved Commander-in-Chief had a cerebral hemorrhage, collapsing at his desk at the "Little White House" in Warm Springs, Georgia, as Elizabeth Schoumatoff, an artist, was painting his portrait. The President's passing brought on national grief. Roosevelt was in his fourth term, and his leadership had guided the country through an economic collapse and a world war. FDR's New Deal rebuilt the country and the national consciousness to pave the way for the prosperity of the fifties.

Stanley was a senior at Taft and was living the inner life of the photojournalist. He always had his camera around his neck, ready to capture life as it was unfolding. As he walked the street this day, he saw a photographic opportunity that reflected the dramatic history of the moment. Stanley saw a corner newsstand on the Grand Concourse and 172nd Street. A saddened and defeated-looking dealer sat, his hand at his face, his eyes downcast and full of the grief communally felt by the country. Stanley didn't just take the man's picture, he made the situation into a piece of photojournalism. As he looked through the viewfinder, he carefully composed the frame to tell a story. In front of the news seller were papers with headlines proclaiming Roosevelt had died, and the man's right hand lay lifelessly on them. Above his head was a newspaper heralding, "Truman Takes Office: Roosevelt Rites Tomorrow." The rectangular object was perfectly placed in the upper left of the frame above the man's head. On the right side of the frame were two papers with headlines that cried, "Roosevelt Dead," and below, the *Daily Mirror* said, "F.D.R. Dead." The two square shapes were on top of each other. The newsdealer was in a box within a box. He sat in the news unit perfectly framed by the hanging papers. This was not an amateur snapshot, not just a documentary moment caught haphazardly, but an early meeting between reality and a photographic artist.

Stanley quickly developed and printed the picture and with what Bronxites would call moxie, he proceeded to shop it around. He received an offer to buy the shot from the *New York Daily News,* a major city tabloid, then boldly parlayed the offer by going to *Look* magazine, where he sold it for twenty-five dollars, ten dollars more than the *Daily News* had offered. The photo ran in the June 26, 1945, issue of *Look* magazine in an article that photographically traced the careers of two Democratic presidents, Franklin Delano Roosevelt and Harry S. Truman. Stanley's picture was six times the size of the other pictures in the timeline article and was used to dramatically link the two men.

Look magazine was a national glossy photomagazine that rivaled the popular *Life* magazine. Helen O'Brian, the head of the photographic department, purchased the picture immediately—recognizing its power and simplicity of vision. She had discovered a talent. Stanley Kubrick was seventeen years old, but the Roosevelt picture had the qualities of a seasoned pro. The kid had an eye and technical skills. "There was an excitement in him—he was always going somewhere to photograph something," Donald Silverman recalls.

As the spirit of the artist burgeoned in Stanley Kubrick, he grew more distant from the academic standards of William Howard Taft High School and the judgmental views of many in his Bronx world. In the teachers' lounge he was labeled an underachiever, a bright boy from a good family who was not living up to his potential. Many couldn't see the unique qualities growing steadily in him, but at least two exceptional educators did.

Aaron Traister was Stanley Kubrick's English teacher at Taft. Part educator, part performer, and a teacher totally dedicated to all of his students, Traister inspired his unmotivated pupil by serving as a role model who demonstrated a fiery passion for literature and as a pictorial subject who stirred the young photojournalist's sense of drama.

Traister was born in Minsk and described his own arrival in America as "a bundle under his father's arm." As did so many immigrant Jewish families, the Traisters lived on the Lower East Side of Manhattan.

Aaron's father was a synagogue official sanctioned to perform weddings, and he also worked as a kosher meat inspector for the Armour Meat Company. When he reached thirteen, Aaron rebelled against his Orthodox Jewish background by refusing to be bar mitzvahed. The only one of seven children who survived to adulthood to go to college, Aaron Traister was forced to leave high school at age thirteen when his father made it clear that if their boy didn't accept his Judaism then he didn't need an education. For several years Aaron took jobs that would allow him time to study secretly for college entrance exams. He got into City College through open admissions, graduated in the mid-1920s, and went on in graduate studies to earn a master's degree in education.

Aaron Traister's teaching career began with an assignment to teach English at a Yiddish school in New Jersey. At the end of the twenties, he secured a position as an elementary school teacher in the New York City school system.

Traister's career as a high school teacher began in the mid-thirties at James Monroe High School. In 1941, when William Howard Taft High School opened, he was one of the first cadre of teachers to work at the new school.

Aaron Traister didn't just teach English at Taft; he lived it. Literature was a deep passion that went beyond words on a page. Traister instinctively knew that teaching was performing. His philosophy and approach to teaching literary works were to dramatize them by reading aloud, changing voices, adapting mannerisms, gestures, and movement, and bringing the characters to life in front of his audience. The classroom was his stage. He studied Shakespeare, coached and directed student theater, and performed humorous skits in faculty shows. Mr. Traister was highly regarded by his colleagues and adored by his students. A June 1947 Taft yearbook referred to him as "Doll Face."

Traister was always the teacher/actor. "At home he changed voices to tell stories, to act out characters. He had a long running story he would tell me and my sister," remembers his son, Daniel Traister, who teaches at the University of Pennsylvania. "I remember him as a reader of poetry and occasionally of prose. I remember him reading 'Sinners in the Hands of an Angry God,' a Jonathan Edwards sermon from the eighteenth century. It was a pretty fierce reading—he was very good at that."

Stanley Kubrick was in Mr. Traister's English class. The boy known to many teachers as an unanimated, lackluster student sat in the classroom as Traister fervently brought the drama and poetry of William Shakespeare's time to life.

Already a contributor to *Look* magazine, the young Stanley Kubrick was constantly looking for photojournalistic opportunities. The Bronx English teacher who performed *Hamlet* for his English class was a perfect subject. When Stanley approached Traister with the idea of photographing him for *Look* magazine, Traister saw it as a perfect occasion to motivate the student by merging the bard's legacy with Stanley's love for photography.

A series of photos was taken in Traister's English classroom as he stood in front of and among his students—a copy of *Hamlet* in his hand, his body always the thespian's tool. Kubrick's camera balanced the drama of the performer with his audience and environment. The pictures capture a dramatic reading—his teacher is an actor still on book, but not seated at the rehearsal table. On his feet, Traister used the volume to refer to Shakespeare's text while the pictures reveal how the pages became a dramatic prop to clutch and forcibly thrust at his audience even as he became one of the bard's many characters.

Taken individually, the pictures show an educational innovation frozen in time. As a series, they are a sequence, part of the photojournalist's art. They tell a story and communicate the unfolding of an event. The photo sequence sits at the door of the cinema. Stanley's ability to depict photographically what he was seeing in his world was already propelling him toward the cinematic experience. An inbred love of films, hours of sitting in the dark, and the lure of literature opened by the books in his father's library and from the soul of an impassioned educator continued to move him closer to the motion picture.

The pictures of Aaron Traister delivering Hamlet to his Bronx high school class appeared in the April 2, 1946, issue of *Look* magazine under the banner "Teacher Puts 'Ham' in *Hamlet.*" The four pictures depict Traister describing a desolate Hecuba, Hamlet brushing off Ophelia, Hecuba's dismay, and Hamlet's scathing comments on women. A brief text under each photo describes the action and contains the quote from the play's text. A simple paragraph identifies the teacher and school with a quote from Traister about his mission: "I try to put across the emotional content of the play." Writer and photographer are not revealed in the article, which ends, "Shown these candid pictures taken by a pupil, he exclaimed, 'Poor kids, how can they sit and take it?'" The photo credits for the issue reveal the pictures taken on pages 60 and 61 to be the work of Stanley Kubrick. The text itself could only have come from the pupil who found photographic and artistic inspiration in Aaron Traister.

Lou Garbus, a retired Bronx mailman who teaches and practices the art of photography, remembers his neighbor and friend Aaron Traister telling him about his former student. "Among his students was this guy Stanley Kubrick and he couldn't do anything with him. He was completely inattentive. 'What am I going to do with this guy?' So when Stanley suggested this project of photographing him while he was emoting Shakespeare, Aaron was delighted with the idea. Anything to bring this kid out of his indifference and boredom in the class. And the rest was history."

Over the years Aaron Traister went to see all of Stanley Kubrick's films. He was especially fond of *Paths of Glory*. "I can still remember his walking out after *Barry Lyndon,* which we saw together shortly before his death," remembers his son, Daniel. "He had seen the movie and commented on how as a young person Kubrick had always had extraordinary literary ambitions, which he saw this movie as encapsulating. He said that Kubrick was not a great student, it just wasn't what interested him, but the idea of literature and the reading of literature from a nonacademic, from a more human point of view, clearly was what interested him. He was a literary guy even as a young man, as a high school student, and that had stuck very clearly in my father's memory about him."

Throughout his life, Traister often spoke about the student who became the internationally famous film director. He talked about Stanley Kubrick to Daniel and his sister, Jane, and proudly showed them his pictures in *Look* magazine. Aaron talked to his friends and neighbors in their community, which was formed by socialists, intellectuals, and lovers of literature and the cinema.

Kubrick's photos of Aaron Traister were another lesson in the development of an artist. Kubrick would soon become a filmmaker born of the photographic spirit. The nature of photography itself—light, depth, space, composition, and seizing the reality perceived through the eye of the photographer—throbs at the heart of every Stanley Kubrick film. To his teacher and to those who admired Aaron Traister's zeal for literature and art, the publication of the pictures represented acknowledgment and recognition. The sentiments of those who remember the impact that Aaron Traister had on all of his students are best expressed by Lou Garbus. A Bronx philosopher, Lou said of the article, "Most of us would be delighted, it's our Academy Award in many ways. Who would notice that in a small classroom—who the hell would know that he was a great Shakespeare teacher—nobody, but here it was basically put on paper and in archives."

Rose Florio was the unofficial ambassador of her block in their Bronx community. The Florio home was often a meeting place for friends and neighbors. Gert Kubrick was a close companion of Mrs. Florio, and theirs was a friendship that lasted throughout their lives. Rose Florio's son, Danny, was likewise friends with Stanley.

A frequent visitor to the Florio residence was Rose Spano, Mrs. Florio's cousin, who remembers a day when Stanley was there and mentioned that he had sold one of his pictures to *Look* magazine. "He was very young. I was so proud of him. He was always with a camera, always with a camera."

Rose Florio shared with her cousin that Dr. Kubrick was disappointed with his son. "His father thought he wasn't going to make anything out of himself," Rose Spano recalled. "All Stanley wanted to do was go out with his camera. Dr. Kubrick wanted him to study a lot. Stanley had other dreams, which he showed in his moviemaking. Stanley was so within himself. Deep thinkers are in a world of their own. That must have been why he couldn't cooperate with his father."

Mrs. Spano remembers Dr. Kubrick as a respected neighborhood physician who had a practice on the ground floor of a new building located on the corner of Courtlandt Avenue with the entrance on 158th Street. She also remembers Stanley's mother. "Mrs. Kubrick was lovely. I remember meeting her a couple of times on the Eighth Avenue subway when she would go shopping. I was a single woman then and worked in the garment industry. She had had a mastectomy at the time, but she looked great. Mrs. Kubrick always looked so pleasant. She had that surgery and she did so well.

"Stanley and his mom were such regular people. They had no airs about them. They were very regular to me. In those days a lot of people who were doctors or professionals had some sort of airs about themselves, but no, not Stanley or his mother. His mother was so down to earth, she was lovely."

In acknowledgment of their friendship, when Gertrude Kubrick died in California in 1985 at the age of eighty-one, Kubrick's sister, Barbara Kubrick Kroner, sent Mrs. Florio two bedspreads her mother had crocheted so her longtime friend could have a keepsake.

At eighty-one Mrs. Spano still lives in the Bronx. Like many who knew the young Stanley Kubrick, she is proud of his achievements. "I am one person who will never miss an Academy Award show. I always looked forward to seeing what he looked like grown up. That was always my desire. I never did see him because he never did go to the Academy Award presentations but he got a lot of nominations. He had this natural ability to make such good pictures. I'm telling you, I was so proud."

Bernard Cooperman became a documented part of Kubrick's fast-growing career as a young photojournalist. This time, he appeared in front of the camera as the subject of Stanley the inquiring photographer. The photo article appeared in the April 16, 1946, issue of *Look* magazine with the headline "A Short Short in a Movie Balcony." On the first page is a sequence of three small black-and-white photos depicting a teenage boy and girl sitting in a movie theater. As the pictures progress, we see the boy contemplating an advance toward the girl. The caption reads, "To test a girl's reaction to advances of an amorous stranger a freelance photographer and friend recently visited a Bronx movie and selected a total stranger, and as the photographer's friend sat down beside her she was completely unaware that a photographer was recording the scene a few seats away on infrared film. See below for what he recorded." When the reader turns the page, he is greeted by a full-page photo of the girl slapping the boy in the face. The "freelance photographer" was Taft High School student Stanley Kubrick, the friend was Bernard Cooperman, and the "total stranger" was an attractive schoolmate Kubrick had selected as a model. The setup designed to look like a candid camera event was one of Kubrick's early directorial experiences. He arranged to bring his two friends to the Park Plaza Theater on University Avenue in the Bronx at twelve o'clock, when the theater was not yet open to the public. He also brought his younger sister, Barbara, to sit in another row, posing as an audience member; only the top of her head can be seen in the photo. Fully understanding what he wanted the pictures to look like before he shot them, Stanley took both of his young subjects aside and gave each private direction. "Here's the way he gave direction," Cooperman recalled as he looked at the article in an original copy of *Look* magazine he has preserved for half a century. "He told me, 'What I want you to do is to make a move on this girl.' I didn't know all of the directions at the time. What I didn't know was what he told her privately: 'When he goes too far, you really let him have it.' If you look at the next page, she's almost knocked my teeth out of my head. I mean, that wasn't a pretend slap. He was setting up the whole thing, but he wanted to get reality and this is what he did."

As a member of the Taft photography squad, Stanley Kubrick continued to photograph life at the high school. One of his assignments was to take pictures of the Taft cheerleaders. Claire Abriss was a member of the cheerleading squad who remembers the individualistic photographer. The cheerleaders were summoned to the gym in their uniforms to pose for a black-and-white school photograph. Stanley Kubrick walked into the gym in his official capacity as a Taft High School photographer. He was quiet and very professional as he composed and snapped shots of the cheerleaders while they posed in archetypal formations. There was however an unorthodox element in this photo session: The cheerleaders were not outdoors on a field, they were within the confines of the school gym, but the photographer was wearing a raincoat. "He was way out then, very different. He walked around with a raincoat and he did his own thing—he really was eccentric," Claire Abriss recalls. She remembers Kubrick as chunky, quiet, and sloppy. "He was his own person and didn't mingle too much," remembers the popular cheerleader who often went to the well-attended Taft swing band dances, where she jitterbugged. Claire has an unusual memento of her high school years. In addition to her yearbook, she has an original print of a Stanley Kubrick photograph taken at the inception of his career as an enfant terrible photojournalist.

Students typically see a photo of themselves taken on a sports team, in a cheerleading squad, or during a shop class in the school yearbook. Kubrick, however, after shooting his pictures of the Taft cheerleaders, developed the negative, blew up the image in an enlarger, and printed the shot on photographic paper. He then made prints for everyone on the squad and personalized each photo on the back with a rubber stamp he had made professionally with his name on it. The inked impression boldly stated: "Stan Kubrick Photo, 1414 Shakespeare Ave., N.Y.C." He also used a stamp to label the back of the prints he gave to Mr. Traister. The stamped imprint of the name of Stanley Kubrick was more than just an ego exercise. At seventeen he was a professional photographer published in *Look* magazine. To him this was not just a boyhood hobby or an extracurricular activity for high school good citizenship. He was a photojournalist documenting the world around him. The name stamped on the back of Claire's photo was destined for importance.

Kubrick did not have a lot of friends at Taft. His solitary demeanor closed him off to the majority of the student body, but he remained very open to those who would connect to his particular world. Many of the people Kubrick would meet in his early years became part of his independent quest to become a filmmaker. Among them was fellow Taftite Alexander Singer.

Alexander Singer, now an acclaimed director of hundreds of episodes of classic television series like *The Fugitive, Hill Street Blues, Cagney and Lacey,* feature films such as *A Cold Wind in August, Psyche '59,* and *Love Has Many Faces,* and—continuing into the nineties—TV shows like *Star Trek: The Next Generation* and *Deep Space Nine,* was a critical force in focusing Kubrick's destiny as a film director.

Alexander Singer and Stanley Kubrick first met at Taft, where they were both students more interested in pursuing their own dreams than in the prescribed curriculum. Alex was also interested in photography, but he was not on Mr. Sullivan's photography squad with Stanley and Bernard Cooperman. Alex was very involved with painting and drawing and was a member of the large art program at Taft, headed by Herman Getter. While he was planning to direct a new episode of *Star Trek: The Next Generation,* more than fifty years after first meeting Stanley Kubrick in a hallway at Taft, Alexander Singer thought back to a meeting that shaped and informed both of their lives.

"We were sixteen. Stanley is a staff photographer on the school's newspaper and he's taken a picture of a race that somebody from the school had won. Somebody pointed out to me that this was the fellow who had taken the picture, and I just introduced myself. We began to talk. I was interested in his photographic work. I had just become serious about photography at that time, and so somebody who was a photographer and pretty expert was useful and interesting to me. He was sophisticated in terms of the whole range of the photographic process. He had a darkroom at home and was able to develop his own pictures and print them pretty early on. He had that in his back pocket. There were a limited number of people in the school who were interesting to me, and both of us were, relatively speaking, kind of loners in the school pursuing our own growth and self-discovery. That was the source of the beginning of our interest in each other."

Stanley knew Alex as an art major who wrote stories and illustrated them for the *Taft Literary Art* magazine. The boys were attracted by mutual interests and had the innate feeling that they could lead each other to finding ways to express the inner creative forces that were driving them.

Stanley and Alex began spending a lot of time with each other, discussing artistic plans for future projects. Singer often went to the Kubrick home at 1873 Harrison Avenue and was impressed to see that his friend Stanley's family lived in a style well above the world Alex knew. "Stanley was the richest kid I ever knew," Singer recalls. "The people I knew who lived in my immediate neighborhood, in my own life, lived one paycheck away from being thrown out into the street. So a doctor who lived in his own house was almost unimaginably well off. I had never been in a house until then. We lived in apartments in the Bronx, and families generally tended to move pretty regularly because the rents would go up. So it was a way of avoiding paying the rent and moving on before they caught up to you. There was a lot of moving that went on. I didn't know anybody who lived in their own house. Stanley was the first one that I knew.

"His father had been an amateur photographer and supported him in his photographic adventures. He had gotten him a darkroom, so he had a good deal of support and help."

Singer, like Kubrick, had also lived in many locations in the Bronx. He lived on 196th Street near Kingsbridge Road when he first met Kubrick. The apartment was one of six places that the Singers lived in before they settled down on Kingsbridge Road during World War II.

Howard Silver lived in an apartment building across the street from the Kubrick private home on Harrison Avenue. "They had a large, rather vicious dark-colored dog. In their backyard there was a very high ledge, and behind all these homes was this water aqueduct that went along it," Silver recalled in reference to the Croton Aqueduct, which had been built in 1842. One of the first great modern aqueducts, it was constructed of masonry and lined with brick. Iron pipes carried water across the Harlem River over a viaduct. "You couldn't get to that upper part unless you walked a couple of blocks around, and occasionally if you were up in that area—and we used to play ball up there occasionally—to get back to our house it was often convenient to hop a fence and go through someone's backyard. I tried to go through Stanley's backyard once, and his father came out and set the dog after me. I had to run for my life and hop over, and then Dr. Kubrick gave me a lecture about never coming through his backyard again. Stanley used to play stickball in the streets with us—he was older than my group. After I left the neighborhood I didn't really connect him for many years thereafter to the movie director. It wasn't until many years later, when he became well-known for *2001*, that I made that connection that he was the guy who had lived on our block."

Howard Sackler was also a student at Taft. Howard was born in Brooklyn in 1929 and began his high school career at Stuyvesant before transferring over to Taft. Howard was a good student who was in the upper third of his class and excelled in English. Howard, who would go on to write the Pulitzer prize–winning play *The Great White Hope*, was a columnist for the *Taft Review* and a member of the school Literary Club. Stanley would later tap Howard's writing skills when he aspired to make his first feature film.

Herman Getter was in charge of the art program at Taft and was another encouraging influence on Stanley Kubrick's artistic nature. A teacher for forty-six years, Mr. Getter had begun his career at De Witt Clinton High School. He came to Taft when the school first opened in 1941. He taught there until he retired in 1972. Mr. Getter was also an accomplished mural painter and produced several films on art technique. Getter once held the patent rights to his invention, the Project-O-Slide, which allowed doctors and dentists to quickly review a photographic reference of medical techniques. The invention utilized frames of 16mm footage of a medical procedure to create slides so doctors could quickly review diverse aspects of the procedure in a nonlinear fashion. Herman Getter was a self-professed "lover and student of cinematography" and a man whose primary goal as an educator was to motivate and inspire.

In 1992, at age eighty-nine, after lunch at his neighborhood YMHA, where he dined daily and held court dressed in suit and tie, he reminisced about his encounters with Stanley Kubrick. "Stanley had a brilliant mind. Stanley was only interested in what he was interested in. In other words, he had a terrible record in math, in science, in physics, not because he couldn't do it if he wanted to, he had no interest. He came running to me one day—this kid. 'Mr. Getter, I was told by the program committee, I have to take a major to be able to at least get my diploma and graduate.' He needed a major not to go to college but to get out of high school. I said, 'Sure, that's all right. What do you do in art? Bring in some of your artwork, drawings, paintings, watercolors—whatever you want—so I can pass upon you as being eligible to take a major in art.' He said, 'Oh, I don't do that, I'm a photographer.' I said, 'Well, that's art.' When I said that, his eyes lit up! He suddenly found someone with whom he could talk."

Getter was an experienced teacher who concentrated on developing talents within his students rather than imposing a prescribed course on them. He created a stimulating environment for a young artist's mind. Alexander Singer was also a student of Mr. Getter's. In his class he produced drawings the teacher called "marvelous artwork." "Attending Getter's class certainly enabled me to graduate," Alexander Singer remembers. "I was a very poor student, and it not only didn't bother me, it was just another goad to remind me how individually I'd have to pursue my own muse. I was an inveterate learner and very hungry to learn. Either I didn't approve of what they were teaching me or their notion of what was important. So it was a case of precocious children who really need special attention, and in an ordinary school you're not going to get much of that. This was a working-class school and that was just fine for me. They bothered me as little as possible. I did my thing, so it was relatively easy to survive and prosper in some small measure."

Mr. Getter had many long talks with Alex and Stanley about motion picture photography. The teacher showed Stanley and Alex the 16mm films he had made to demonstrate art technique. "I was trying to show Stanley different motion picture techniques. I saw in him a certain eagerness, a certain feeling for the use of the camera as an art medium, like an artist uses his palette, his canvas, and a brush. The camera was his medium and he painted with it."

This was 1945. Motion pictures were made primarily in Hollywood. Students didn't have access to home 16mm or 8mm equipment as would the baby boomer generation of filmmakers who were just being born and would come of age in the sixties. Filmmaking wasn't part of the New York City school system. Mr. Getter looked fondly upon his talks about cinematic exploration with Alex and Stanley. Both boys were interested in still photography, so Mr. Getter encouraged them to look to the medium of cinematography, which was just half a century old. Stanley had spent hours and hours with his Graflex, experimenting with composition, lighting, and lenses, and in the darkroom, watching the pictures from his magic box take shape. A boy with big ideas and artistic aspirations, Stanley Kubrick talked to Herman Getter about a philosophy of filmmaking that was beginning to stir inside of him. "He had a very interesting viewpoint. This technique had to be almost an experiment to discover new vistas, new ideas that had never been seen before. So I suddenly thought to myself, 'Hell, this kid is the Picasso of cinematography.'" Stanley brought in his photographs and Mr. Getter continued to instill in the boy that photography was an art. As part of the course the students were shown slides of great paintings by Cézanne, Renoir, Seurat, Picasso, and others. Alexander Singer would create articulated drawings, while Stanley used the opportunity to express visual ideas. "He could draw and he could paint in a very free style that summed up his accumulated vision of what something should be. He didn't go into little details but, by golly, it was broad, it had an approach which hit you—visual kinetics is the best way I can describe it," Herman Getter recalled.

In May 1959, Mr. Getter wrote to Stanley Kubrick at Universal-International Pictures, where he was directing *Spartacus*. The teacher received a reply on June 17. Kubrick asked to be forgiven for being so late in replying to Getter's letter of May 7th. Kubrick explained he had been working on *Spartacus* seven days a week since February with another two months to go before shooting was completed. He told his former teacher that Alexander Singer was living in Los Angeles and working in films for Leslie Stevens, who had just formed his own production company. Kubrick told Getter that he and Alex often reminisced about the stimulating film discussions they had had in his art class. Kubrick closed by telling Getter to contact him if he ever vacationed in Hollywood. In a later correspondence, in January 1976, after the release of *Barry Lyndon*, Kubrick again responded to a letter from his former art teacher and told him that his memories of him and his art classes were amongst the best that he had of Taft High School. He told Getter that he was an inspiration to him at a time when it was most critical. This time Getter tantalized Kubrick's legendary curiosity by writing to his former student about seeing a 1929 silent film, *Cain and Artem*, directed by Pavel Petrov-Beytov, that had never left his imagination. The film, adapted from a work by Maxim Gorky, was given a soundtrack in 1932 by Abel Gance. Always the curious and total consumer of films, Kubrick wrote back that he would search the archive of the National Film Theater in London and would correspond again after seeing the film.

As his artistic qualities were taking hold, Stanley Kubrick's passions were developing on another level. Romantic feelings began to grow in the adolescent Kubrick. While the Kubricks lived at 1414 Shakespeare Avenue, he met Toba Metz. Toba Etta Metz was born on January 24, 1930, at 7:15 in the morning at Holy Name Hospital in Teaneck, New Jersey. The Metz family originally lived in Cliffside, New Jersey. Toba's brother, Henry, was six years older, born in April 1923. Toba's father, Herman Metz, was a jeweler who was born in Hasenpoth, Latvia, and was fifty years old when his daughter arrived. Toba's mother, Bessie Silverman Metz, was born in the United States. Herman Metz emigrated to the United States in 1912, from Bremen, Germany, on the ship *Kronprinzesin Cecilie* after living in Antwerp, Belgium. Stanley and Toba lived in the same apartment building on Shakespeare Avenue. Future Kubrick collaborator Gerald Fried called Toba "the prettiest girl in Taft High School."

Toba had gone to P.S. 104, where she was a fair student and maintained good conduct ratings. In junior high school Toba belonged to the Cartoon Club, the Portrait Club, and the Sketch Club and showed interest and promise in being an artist. She also was developing an affinity for literature. Toba took extracurricular courses in typing and reading for appreciation and considered drawing and reading as special interests.

Toba Metz entered Taft in February 1945, when Stanley had one more year to go in his high school career. She graduated in January 1948. Toba maintained a fair attendance record at Taft, where her early drawing talents continued to develop. She took Herman Getter's major art class, achieving an average of 80 percent in 1947 and 85 in 1948. Mr. Getter's legacy to his Bronx students was unconditional support to anyone who wanted to be an artist, and his definition of "artist" went beyond the traditions of the time. If you could draw, take a picture, or dreamed of making cinematic vistas, Mr. Getter was prepared to embrace you.

Alexander Singer graduated Taft in June 1945. He had been on the art staff of the yearbook and was following the calling of his inner voice. Alex intended to be an artist.

Kubrick's high school average historically has been stated as 68 in books and articles containing biographical information, but upon his graduation from William Howard Taft High School in January 1946 his actual high school average was 70.1. He was ranked 414 out of a senior population of 509, putting him in the last quartile of his graduating class. His Regents exam grades were 85 in Biology, 75 in Intermediate Algebra, 81 in Spanish, 85 in American History. At the time of Stanley's graduation, his family was still residing on Harrison Avenue.

Marvin Traub had gone to De Witt Clinton and graduated on the same timetable as his photobug buddy, Stanley. In preparation for applying to college, Stanley had his high school records sent to New York University's uptown campus in November 1945 and the downtown campus and CCNY's evening program in December 1945.

In his official high school record there was no reference or report about Stanley Kubrick's photographic initiatives. As a public high school student he had sold a photograph to a major national magazine at age seventeen. This was an enormous accomplishment, but the system at the time did not acknowledge such an achievement, judging success by academic standings and tests alone. The practice of evaluating behavior and good social citizenship didn't favor those with the temperament of an artist verging on obsession.

During his high school career, Kubrick's grades didn't reflect the intellect and ambition growing in the young man. As his interest in photography grew and his artistry expanded, there was no way for the conventional educational system to identify his actual potential in what would become his life's work. His interest and application of ideas and information crystallized when applied to his photographic and cinematic projects, but in class he remained uninspired and unmotivated and demonstrated little academic aptitude. Kubrick's lifelong fascination with and knowledge of literature was not in evidence in his grades in English class. He never received higher than a 75 average in the subject, his grades were as low as 55, and even in Mr. Traister's class he only received a 65. He was a self-taught student of history, and his scores remained in the 70 to 75 range in social studies. In the sciences they fluctuated wildly from 68 to 95. Foreign languages and math were not Stanley's high card. He maintained a 65 average in Spanish and ranged from 50 to 65 in Algebra.

The Taft yearbook in 1946 listed Kubrick as a member of the *Taft Review* for the term ending in June 1944 and also as a member of the school band. Under his picture, which revealed an adolescent boy moving through the awkward stage, the caption stated: "When he was on The Taft Review, you always found him in a stew." Stanley's graduation picture captured a young man, his hair neatly cut and combed. Stanley's eyes looked like they rarely blinked, his eyebrows strongly arching from the strain.

Kubrick found it difficult to gain acceptance at a New York college. It was 1946, and thousands of G.I.'s had returned home from World War II and were entering college on the G.I. Bill. His poor grades and academic standing placed him at the bottom of the list, and he was refused entry to the colleges he applied to.

Attending evening school did present him with an opportunity to qualify eventually for day school so he enrolled in evening classes at City College.

Eager to get on with his life, Kubrick turned to *Look* magazine. He was already a professional photographer who had sold his photos to a major national magazine. The avenues of higher education were not available to him, but the boulevards of self-education were wide open.

Stanley Kubrick's career as a film director begins with two convergent forces—his early love of the movies and his work as a professional still photographer. Like such diverse filmmakers as Jean-Luc Godard, François Truffaut, Martin Scorsese, and Quentin Tarantino, Stanley Kubrick is a cineaste, a self-ordained film historian, deeply knowledgeable and passionate about the past, present, and future of the cinema. Kubrick's technical and aesthetic knowledge of the art and craft of photography as a medium informs every shot in his filmography.

Film directors come from many roots. From the theater (Orson Welles and Elia Kazan), from film criticism (Godard, Truffaut, and Eric Rohmer), from film editing (Robert Wise and Robert Parrish), from acting (Paul Newman, Robert Redford, and Clint Eastwood), from commercials (Ridley Scott and Alan Parker), from cinematography (Victor Fleming, Haskell Wexler, and Nicolas Roeg), from writing (Woody Allen and James L. Brooks). Others come from dance, poetry, painting, the graphic arts, related arts, and every walk of unrelated, nonartistic life.

While cinematography has spawned many film directors, still photography has produced few, and Stanley Kubrick is the most prominent. Others include Gordon Parks, who worked for *Life* magazine for twenty-five years as a staff photographer; Ken Russell, who was a freelancer for *Picture Post* and *Illustrated*; and New York fashion photographers Jerry Schatzberg, Dick Richards, and Howard Zieff.

Stanley Kubrick's work as a staff photographer at *Look* magazine for a period of a little over four years helped transform the photographer into a filmmaker. Kubrick's coming-of-age is an excursion through countless rolls of Kodak black-and-white film, as he discovered his photographic identity, which gave him entrée to the bold cinematic experiments to follow. The commercial assignments and professional magazine deadlines developed and sharpened Kubrick's ability to deliver on call and meet the constant demand to think photographically in situations that ranged from trite to significant. He learned to direct his subjects, to control light and shade, to understand lenses, composition, exposure, and balance within the frame. Never more alive than when he was looking through the lens of a camera, Kubrick became self-sufficient at a tender age and blossomed from a Bronx underachiever into a legitimately confident New York professional.

Stanley Kubrick had sold several freelance photographs to *Look* magazine while he was still a student at William Howard Taft. When he found himself unable to go to college and was attending night school at City College of New York, Helen O'Brian, the head of *Look*'s photography department, offered the young photographer a staff position.

"I worked for *Look* magazine from the age of seventeen to twenty-one," Kubrick told Michel Ciment. "It was a miraculous break for me to get this job after graduation from high school. I owe a lot to the then picture editor, Helen O'Brian, and the managing editor, Jack Guenther. This experience was invaluable to me, not only because I learned a lot about photography, but also because it gave me a quick education in how things happened in the world."

Gardner Cowles was the news editor for the *Des Moines Register and Tribune*, a newspaper owned by his father. Gardner, who was known as Mike to all his friends, was educated at Exeter and Harvard, where he edited *The Crimson*. Cowles was impressed by reader response to news photos and the combination of pictures and text. He asked Dr. George Gallup to do a study on the subject for him, thus commissioning the very first Gallup poll. The findings supported Cowles's intuition, and he decided to form a picture magazine. *Life* magazine had not yet appeared. Cowles began *Look* magazine in January 1937 in Iowa and moved to

New York City in 1940. Cowles, a lifelong Republican with liberal ideas, was a friend of Nelson Rockefeller, Jock Whitney, the Aldriches, the Vanderbilts, Thomas E. Dewey, Earl Warren, and Bernard Baruch.

Look magazine's offices were at 511 Fifth Avenue. The magazine occupied several floors, which contained executive offices, the editorial department, and the photographic department. The photographic department did its own developing and printing. There were studios so the photographers could shoot under controlled lighting conditions. Kubrick was given an assignment, and his job was to go out and get the pictures his editors required. Eight thousand photographs were screened by the editors for a typical issue of the biweekly magazine.

For the January 8, 1946, issue Kubrick contributed a picture of a man reading a horoscope book to illustrate *Look*'s Personality Clinic column. This issue's subject was "Are You a Fatalist?" The quiz asked multiple-choice questions to test the reader's personality quotient, which upon completion was categorized and analyzed.

The June 11 issue ran a twelve-shot sequence titled, "A Woman Buys a Hat." The two-line caption credited "A *Look* photographer's candid camera" with the pictures of a woman trying on a series of hats at New York's Ohrbach's clothing store. The shots were all taken from the same camera position and remain similar in image size. The twelve pictures look like frames from a movie sequence, maintaining continuity and depicting movement as the woman reacts to the hat choices.

On July 23, 1946, Kubrick took portraits of Lee Bowman, Harry Cohen, Mario Mascolo, Vincent Costello, and Manning Halpert for a Meet the People feature, "How Many Times Did You Propose?" The pictures are workmanlike and professional. The regular *Look* feature sent an inquiring photographer out to snap man-on-the-street photos of both average and prominent people, who were asked to answer the question of the day.

For the August 20 issue Kubrick shot a series of three photos for the payoff of a two-page humorous spread. The first page features a picture of a chimpanzee with the caption "How a Monkey Looks to People." The pictures on the second page are taken from the point of view of the chimpanzee inside a cage at a zoo. The pictures are printed to look like a wide-screen CinemaScope film frame. The bars of the cage run up and down the frame and behind the bars people look up at the monkey.

Photoquiz was another regular *Look* feature. A series of twenty photos were used for a multiple-choice quiz. A revolving guest editor hosted the game, which was scored from 65 to 90, with 5 points for each correct answer. For the September 3, 1946, issue the guest editor was Bob

Hawk, the quizmaster from the CBS Monday night television program *The Bob Hawk Show*. Many photographers and sources were used for the pictures. Here Kubrick contributed a picture of a sign reading, BUY VICTORY BONDS with two arrows, one pointing right indicating Saks Thirty-fourth Street and one pointing left displaying the direction to Gimbel's. The caption says, "The sign indicates you're probably in a) Chicago, b) San Francisco, c) New York City or d) New Orleans."

Kubrick began to draw a lot of assignments for the Meet the People feature, for which he would go out and take a portrait of local and national personalities of the day. For the September 17 issue he shot eleven of the twelve pictures. The celebrities were asked, "What was your childhood ambition?" Among those photographed and interviewed were composer Sunny Skylar, radio announcer Art Ford, restaurateur D. L. Toffenetti, radio producer Martha Roudtree and harmonica virtuoso John Sebastian. Also in this issue Kubrick took a dramatic extreme-low-angle shot with high-key lighting of a woman opening a telegram for Ernest Dichter, Ph.D.'s psychoquiz "Do You Have Imaginary Illnesses?"

For the October 10 issue, Kubrick's spontaneous camera captured men, women, and children in the reception room of a dentist's office. The eighteen pictures are mini character studies of people waiting, preoccupied with pain, pondering their fate and wishing they were somewhere else. Unlike the posed portraits for Meet the People, the dental office photo study shows Kubrick's ability to capture people in an environment and to project their feelings and personal natures. Some of the photographs have the quality of a grabbed moment possibly snapped by a hidden camera. Others are carefully composed and demonstrate Kubrick's developing eye for light and space.

For the November 26 Meet the People assignment, twelve working Americans answered the question "How Would You Spend $1,000 in a Week?" Kubrick photographed his Taft High School buddy and fellow Bronx dreamer Alexander Singer. The picture ran next to one of accordionist Nikke Montan and identified Alexander Singer as a freelance photographer. Singer's answer to the question was, "I'd hire a terrific studio, engage a gorgeous Southern gal to model and take some color pictures for magazine covers. I'd triple my take in a week—I hope!"

In the same issue Kubrick continued to depict the world around him in the Bronx. In the tradition of the great documentary street photographers like Brassai, Kubrick took a series of photographs of two women examining the new hairdo of a friend. The four pictures selected ran with the caption "Bronx Street Scene." The camera catches an off-guard episode about a hairdo. From one camera position Kubrick captures a spirited sequence that again could be a moment in a film. In the first frame the woman tells her friends about the hairdo by gesturing with her hand. In the second, she is turned around and they examine the back of the hairstyle. In the third the woman, still turned around, lifts up her hair to reveal the back of her neck under her hair, and in the final picture she is gone—leaving the others to laugh and shrug their shoulders.

For the same edition Kubrick took a photo of twenty-three-year-old Johnny Grant, a radio interviewer who used a wire tape recorder to do location shows for WINS radio. The picture shows the young man known as Johnny on the Spot talking to New York's Latin Quarter chorines.

Kubrick took all twelve pictures for the December 10 Meet the People, which asked the question "What's Your Idea of a Good Time?" Two of the people interviewed played a significant role in Stanley Kubrick's personal life. Kubrick's darkroom mentor, Marvin Traub, was now in the Navy, where he became an official ship photographer. While Traub was home on leave, Kubrick snapped a profile shot of him in his uniform. Identified as "s 2/c Marvin Traub," Stanley's kindred spirit from 2715 Grand Concourse said, "I've changed. I used to like to spend my time at the movies. But since I've been in the Navy I'd rather go out and let off a little steam." On the next page, next to producer Harold Shaw, is a photo of Stanley's girlfriend, Toba Metz. Toba was identified as a musician and said, "It's amusing to caricature friends. Their reactions are a scream. No matter how attractive they are they're still afraid it's a true likeness."

Kubrick's fascination with the movies began to intensify. When he learned that *Look*'s photographic technical director, Arthur Rothstein, had an interest in the cinema and a large collection of film books, he began to borrow volumes to enhance his serious self-study of motion pictures. Kubrick was particularly interested in the theoretical writings of Russian master Sergei Eisenstein. After the young autodidact read his way through Rothstein's personal film archive, Rothstein noticed that Stanley had been making notes in many of the books, leaving him with an unauthorized collection of writings from the nascent filmmaker.

The March 4, 1947, issue of *Look* featured a six-page photo study of the New York underground called "Life and Love on the New York Subway." The lead picture was a full shot looking down on a Grand Central subway station packed with people who are surrounded by steel pillars and signs. In a series of photos candidly taken inside the trains, Kubrick captured New Yorkers from a broad spectrum: a fifteen-piece orchestra, their instruments, and girl vocalist ride to a gig; a young man carries flowers purchased for his girl over his head to protect them from a crushing standing-room-only crowd; four theater matrons ride in for a Saturday matinee; students do homework; a Talmudic scholar reads the Yiddish paper to a friend; a woman knits; two lovers stare into each other's eyes; a little boy peers out of the head car; a man sleeps on his feet; two girls sleep in evening gowns; a man lies prone on a seat; others sleep leaning, holding their heads; and two children slumber sprawled on their parents' laps. Under difficult photographic conditions, Kubrick nevertheless remained in control of the frame. The results demonstrate symmetry, balance, and compositional harmony. "Stanley operated the shutter of his camera, which hung in plain view from his neck by a leather harness, from a switch hidden in his pocket," G. Warren Schloat Jr., a reporter who worked with Kubrick, remembered. "The switch was connected to the camera's shutter by wires he had placed up his sleeve. Thus equipped, he could look at and talk to a passenger sitting next to him and at the same time snap a photo of a person sitting across the aisle without detection. He could sit there on the New York City subway and look at the guy on his left shoulder and talk to the guy, but he had already focused the camera to shoot across the aisle. He would take a picture of a woman nursing her baby without ever looking over there. So they never had any idea in the world they were being photographed." Kubrick continued to perfect his candid-camera technique. At times he hid a wire in a brown paper bag and operated the camera by tripping the shutter through a hole in the bottom.

The department heads at the magazine were the ones who ultimately made the decision on what stories were to be pursued and assigned them to writers and photographers. G. Warren Schloat Jr., now the author of twenty children's books, was working for *Look* magazine in 1947. *Look* had been impressed with a series of stories that Schloat had written while he was working for the Walt Disney Studio. Schloat and Kubrick were paired by assignment editors. "Both of us were newcomers at *Look* magazine," Schloat recalls. "Stanley was a quiet fellow. He didn't say much. He was thin, skinny, and kind of poor—like we all were." When Kubrick learned that Schloat had been connected to a film studio, he began to talk to him about his movie plans. "My feeling at the time was, 'Gee, this guy just doesn't have the personality to run around in Hollywood and direct movies.' He just seemed too quiet and too unassuming. If you're out there on a stage you've got an awful lot of guys to scream and holler at when you're making a movie. So I was always impressed that he was able to do what he did."

Schloat was credited as a department editor by *Look* and received a salary of ten thousand dollars a year. "We always said, 'They don't give us much money, so they give us a title of sorts,'" Schloat recalls.

March 18, 1947, brought "Baby Wears Out 205-lb. Athlete," a human-interest story in which Kubrick spent a day with Bob Beldon, a football player from Carleton College, who tried to keep up with fifteen-month-old Dennis Henry, the son of a Carleton physics professor. Kubrick snapped Beldon duplicating all of Dennis's maneuvers on the floor, couch, and lunch table to see if he could keep up with the toddler. The pictures are insufferably cute and crowd-pleasing. Beldon and the baby walk on all fours, squat, and crawl together.

Kubrick shot the cover photo for the August 5, 1947, issue, receiving the credit "Stanley Kubrick" at the bottom of the page. The picture is of a small boy taking a shower to cool off during the dog days of summer.

That same summer Kubrick satisfied his growing passion for aviation by obtaining a private pilot's certificate issued by the Federal Aviation Administration, on August 15, 1947. He was then permitted to fly a single-engine aircraft.

The January 6, 1948, issue featured a profile of entertainment personalities to watch in the coming year. The nineteen-year-old Stanley Kubrick photographed a twenty-three-year-old Doris Day performing a song next to a statue of an ancient goddess and used the frame to describe space and comment on his subject.

For the January 20 issue, Kubrick went on location to Wilkes-Barre, Pennsylvania, to the Kingston Armory, where the Bowman Gum Company and the Hamid-Morton Circus were sponsoring a bubble-gum contest for children. The lead picture shows a clown using a bubblemeter to measure a young girl's bubble. Featured was a four-shot sequence of a young boy in a sailor's hat blowing a bubble. The effect is similar to a zoom or tracking shot in a film. The first picture is a long shot of the boy starting to blow the bubble, framed by two children blowing bubbles to his left and right. The second picture is considerably closer, but from the same angle, and now the bubble is starting to grow. For the third, Kubrick is tight on the boy with the bubble covering the majority of his face. For the last picture in the sequence Kubrick got an extreme close-up of the boy with the bubble burst over his face and sadness in his eyes. The influence of cinematography is starting to show. Also in the issue was a large photo Kubrick had shot of an X ray taken by Dr. Charles Breimer of a patient with appendicitis.

In January 1948, Toba Metz graduated Taft. The Taft yearbook said of Toba: "Skating in winter, art the year round, are two happy pastimes,

Toba has found." Toba's interest in art continued and she performed in the senior show. Toba's high school records were sent to CCNY for evening school and also to NYU.

For a survey of life in the United States called "It Happened Here," in the March 2, 1948, issue, Kubrick photographed showgirl Nanette Fredries wearing a sandwich board on an East Side Manhattan street for the luncheon service at Roger Stearn's 1-2-3 Club.

For the March 16, 1948, issue Kubrick followed Miss America 1947, Barbara Jo Walker, to a Methodist Youth Conference in Cleveland, Ohio, for a photojournalist story. The pictures follow her to the front row of a youth address, a dormitory, an autograph signing, folk dancing, and the receiving of benediction.

Kubrick was sent to the Bignou Gallery for the March 30, 1948, issue to document the preview of an exhibition by surrealist painter Salvador Dali. He took pictures of the work itself, the reactions of the elite New York guests, social chatting, and the charismatic artist.

Kubrick went to Connersville, Indiana, for a photojournalist assignment to cover a meeting between Eric O. Johnson, general manager of American Central, a division of Avco Manufacturing Corporation, and his labor force of 2,500, which he talks to in groups of 100 at a time to bridge the problems of management and labor. Kubrick took pictures of Johnson addressing his workers, the reaction of the laborers, and a dramatic shot of the men filing out the door with the empty chairs and Johnson in the foreground—his back to the camera—watching as the men leave. To capture Johnson's approach to the men and his reaction to them, Kubrick held his camera in the same position and took a series of ten pictures of Johnson in front of a "Think" sign. Throughout the sequence, Johnson talks, listens, smiles, is serious, and runs a gamut of emotions—even holding his head in his hands at one point. The spread pushes the limits of the photo sequence—Kubrick is looking for the movies.

Kubrick spent some time in a self-service laundromat in a Greenwich Village neighborhood for an April 27 study of the locals doing their laundry. Actor John Carradine was captured sharing a newspaper with his wife and their son (not one of the three acting Carradines) as they waited for their clothes. Kubrick also did a sensitive photo study of childhood rheumatic fever for the issue.

For the May 11 issue of *Look*, Kubrick was sent to New York's Columbia University to do a nine-page feature on the institution, including a portrait of the school's new president, "Ike" Eisenhower—four years before he would become president of the nation.

The title page of the edition ran an article proudly profiling *Look*'s nineteen-year-old photographer, Stanley Kubrick. The piece explained that Kubrick had spent two weeks at Columbia getting his photo story. The young Kubrick is presented as a "quiet brown-eyed youngster" who "like any experienced photographer . . . knew exactly what he wanted."

Kubrick was described as a two-year veteran of the *Look* photographic staff. The professional team of photographers who worked for *Look* quickly took the boy under their wing. Technical director Arthur Rothstein and photographers Frank Bauman, James Chapelle, Bob Hansen, James Hansen, Doug Jones, Bob Sandberg, Sprague Talbott, Maurice Terrell, Earl Theisen, and darkroom manager Vincent Silvestri formed what they called the "Bringing Up Stanley Club," reminding him not to forget his keys, glasses, and galoshes.

Their biggest challenge was in sartorial matters. "The subtle influence of this loosely organized advisory group has also brought an apparent change in the young man's clothing tastes," the article stated. "Once given to wearing teenage trademarks—saddle shoes, lounge jackets and sport shirts—Stanley now leans toward glen plaid business suits and white shirts." The *Look* photogs were the first and last major influence on how Kubrick dressed. Never one to pay much attention to fashion, Kubrick was coming as close as he ever would to looking like he was part of the establishment.

The teenager's growing interest in filmmaking made itself known to the staff at *Look*. The article concludes with a gaze to Stanley Kubrick's cinematic future. "His preoccupation with photography is unchanged. In his spare time, Stanley experiments with cinematography and dreams of the day when he can make documentary films. The young fellow may go on forgetting his keys. But photographically, Stanley doesn't need any help in bringing himself up."

Kubrick went to the winter headquarters of the Ringling Bros. and Barnum & Bailey Circus to do a four-page article and a Meet the People spread for the May 25, 1948, edition. A picture of circus president John Ringling North barking orders is balanced in a composition featuring three aerialists and a bicycle. Kubrick was refining his documentary skills, shooting the performers practicing their athletic crafts and at rest. He was learning how to compose reality within the firm confines of the frame.

For the May 25 issue Kubrick also shot a photo study of the father of the motivational-speaker movement, Dale Carnegie. Visiting Carnegie at work training students in positive thinking, Kubrick photographed the positive-thinking guru addressing a group in a sequence filled with expressive arm and hand gestures, pictures of the students learning the skills of communication, and a three-picture sequence of Carnegie's wife watching and reacting to her husband criticizing student speakers. These character studies were good training for a future film director.

The May 25 issue was a big one for Kubrick. In addition to the Carnegie spread, it included his photojournalist story chronicling a party given by opera star Risë Stevens for deaf children who had been given hearing aids and trained in lip reading at a special program in New York Junior High School 47. Kubrick's unobtrusive camera had a special gift for reading the sensitivities and joys of the children. The candid pictures, which always maintained the traditions of good composition, revealed the naturalness of the children enjoying the party.

As the May 25, 1948, issue of Look magazine hit the newsstands Stanley Kubrick was preparing to leave the Bronx. He and Toba Metz were moving to Greenwich Village.

PART TWO

1948–1956
New York

CHAPTER 2

Photographed by Stanley Kubrick

At 10:30 A.M. on May 29, 1948, Stanley Kubrick married his high school sweetheart, Toba Metz, at the home of Acting Judge Harry Krauss, who performed the civil ceremony at 544 East Lincoln Avenue in Mount Vernon, New York. Mount Vernon was known as the City of Homes, a suburban community just a footstep out of the Bronx in Lower Westchester. Toba was eighteen years old and working as a secretary. Stanley was nineteen and noted his profession as photographer on their marriage certificate. They established a residence in Greenwich Village, a bohemian community of artists, performers, writers, and musicians.

The Kubrick family continued to live at 1873 Harrison Avenue, and Stanley's sister, Barbara, began Roosevelt High School in September 1948. As a teenager she had her own telephone, listed under the name of Bobbie Kubrick. After her graduation in June 1952, she entered Adelphi College, which she attended until 1954.

Kubrick continued his steady output at *Look*. The ability to portray childhood reality continued in a five-page pictorial study that Kubrick photographed for the June 8 *Look*, taken at a private preparatory and vocational school in Mooseheart, Illinois. Kubrick went to classes featuring farm skills, sculpture, and athletics to represent training the children were receiving at the school for *Look* readers. Ten pages later were two pictures of a Chicago model posing in the latest fashions, and three more pages revealed a full-page shot of the great Berlin painter George Grosz straddling a chair on a New York City street. Kubrick's assignments were running the gamut of the magazine's features, photojournalism, posed portraits, man-on-the-street inquiries, celebrity features and nuts-and-bolts pictures for the magazine's various needs.

For the summer issue of August 3, 1948, Kubrick had traveled to Portugal to document the two-week vacation of Bill Cook, a drug-firm executive, and his wife, Jan. Many of the photos in the five-page article were intended as a tourist guide to the picturesque land, but Kubrick included a six-shot series of the people of Nazare, an ancient Portuguese fishing village. The pictures depict the natives with a timeless documentary reality that reveals Kubrick's eye for serious photojournalism devoid of the glitter of magazine coverage for the masses. The pictures speak to the tradition of photography that explores and seizes the real world—past, present, and future.

The August 17 issue brought Kubrick back to his surprise camera technique—this time his camera was hidden behind a mirror at a clothing store where children were trying on fall fashions. Kubrick, with the freedom of being out of sight, catches the innocence and delight of kids trying on raincoats, cowboy outfits, and school clothes. Later in the couture-oriented issue, Kubrick took a series of men's fashion shots for a piece that encouraged readers to vote to determine the new style in men's fashions.

On October 12 *Look* ran a series of pictures of five-year-old Wally Ward, who was struck by infantile paralysis at two and was now, through physical therapy, able to play with a football and do a two-handed handstand. Kubrick also visited a celebrity art show at the gallery of the Associated American Artists, benefiting the Urban League, and took pictures of artworks created by Frank Sinatra, John Garfield, Joe Louis, Katharine Cornell, and Esme Sarnoff. Kubrick also shot a series of photographs of people looking up at something out of his frame under the headline, "What Makes Their Eyes Pop?" The reader is requested to turn to page 50, where there is a picture of the *Mona Lisa,* which was currently on display.

In January 1949 Stanley Kubrick came of age as a photojournalist with a mature study of a boxer titled "Prizefighter." Kubrick received the credit "Photographed by Stanley Kubrick" on the first page of the article. The assignment came his way because of his abiding passion for boxing. The forties were a vital time for the sport, and men like Joe Louis, Gus Lesnevich, Tony Zale, Rocky Graziano, Marcel Cerdan, "Sugar" Ray Robinson, Willie Pep, and Jake LaMotta were urban heroes. Kubrick saw great drama in boxing and aimed to investigate beyond the gloss of the sports pages. He wanted to penetrate the human and mythic areas that boxing occupied for many young men who idolized the warriors of the ring.

For the study, Kubrick chose Walter Cartier, a twenty-four-year-old middleweight, who also lived in Greenwich Village. Cartier was the ideal image of an American boxer, good-looking with soulful, deep-set eyes, the strong body of a gladiator, and a sense of identity well beyond his years. In the lead picture, which dominated the first page of the article, Cartier leans against a large brick wall as he sits on a bench, head back, gloved hands together at his lap. Light pours down from above, carving his chiseled features, his eyes in deep shadow. Next to Walter is legendary fight manager Bobby Gleason; the two men wait for the call to the ring. Gleason's arms are folded. He is looking off, eyes open but focused well beyond their apparent gaze. Walter is contemplative, serious, and ready as he ponders his mission. The photo story that follows is the backstory to this opening moment. A headline reads "The Day of a Fight," as a series of pictures takes the reader through a day in the life of a prizefighter. Walter wakes up at 9:30 as his twin brother, Vincent, sleeps on. Vincent appears in the lower third of the frame, and Walter is perfectly centered in the background. At breakfast, Vincent serves his brother as their Aunt Eva looks on. The picture is a real moment in time but controlled in composition, balance, and movement within the frame. Cartier weighs in and is examined by a doctor as Kubrick positions his lens to tell the story. Walter sits on his front stoop waiting, Vincent and a neighbor framing him on either side. In church, Walter prays—a study in repose. Kubrick follows Cartier out to a beach on Staten Island, where he enjoys an outing with a girlfriend. At Yankee Stadium, Walter cheers on his feet, hands clapping. In another study, he fixes a toy sailboat for his nephew. Gleason gives Walter final instructions, Vincent adjusts his brother's glove, Walter is deep in thought. Vincent rubs Vaseline on his brother's face in profile as Kubrick evokes the love and devotion of the twin boys for each other.

During a fight with Tony D'Amico at Jerome Stadium, Kubrick shoots from a low angle, capturing the men frozen in time. D'Amico has just thrown a punch, Walter readies his right arm for a fierce blow. In between rounds Gleason removes Walter's mouthpiece. On the phone, Gleason sets up an important match as Walter carefully watches his manager at work. Below, dominating the page, is a picture that demonstrates Kubrick's dramatic understanding of space. It is Roosevelt Stadium in Jersey City. Walter has just knocked out Jimmy Mangia in the first round with a slamming right to the jaw. The ropes of the ring run from right to left, left to right through the frame. Walter is standing full frame at the extreme left, victoriously moving forward in triumph. In the lower right foreground, Mangia is down flat on his stomach, and the referee looms over the downed fighter, counting him out to defeat. Black negative space dominates the distance between the two men and gives the photograph depth, drama, and a sense of hyperrealism. After the fight Walter and Vincent walk the streets of the Village. A street lamp backlights the men and causes long shadows. The photojournalist in Kubrick was developing into a mature artist. He applied his artistic photographic abilities to a subject that fascinated him. These were more than just professional assignment pictures, like much of his work for *Look* was. Kubrick was expressing the need to communicate atmosphere, environment—he was becoming a photographic storyteller.

For an April 26, 1949, photo feature on the radio show *Stop the Music,* Kubrick went to the ABC studio to photograph emcee Bert Parks at the microphone talking to a contestant on the phone.

In the May 10 issue, *Look* ran a nine-page photo story on the University of Michigan, a profile similar to the one Kubrick had done on Columbia University. Kubrick spent time on the campus taking posed portraits of the professors and taking candid pictures of the myriad areas of study throughout the university.

Kubrick photographed Armenian-born sculptor Koren der Harootian. Before landing a show at the Metropolitan Museum, when he couldn't get a gallery to represent him, the artist showed his work in an empty lot in Washington Square. Later Kubrick photographed the work of Swedish sculptor Carl Milles. He also captured low art by going to a Washington Gridiron dinner of the St. Louis Advertising Club, where he photographed skits ridiculing President Truman and local politics.

Assignments ranged from the sublime to the ridiculous, including a mundane display of the new sixteen-ounce look of tennis clothes exhibited on a court fence for the June 7 issue.

For the Father's Day issue in 1949, Stanley Kubrick visited the home of Mr. Television, "Uncle Miltie" Milton Berle. The layout included a sequence of four photos of the video comedian playing and mugging with his daughter.

For the July 19 issue, Kubrick contributed pictures of New York nightlife at the Riviera, Latin Quarter, Penthouse Club, and Ezio Pinza on stage in Broadway's *South Pacific* for a feature titled "Midsummer Nights in New York."

By mid 1949, Kubrick was beginning to get a lot of celebrity assignments. The July 19 issue also had a picture of Arthur Godfrey at his CBS microphone and a major "Look Picture Personality" photo spread of actor Montgomery Clift. Kubrick received a credit under the staff writer Jack Hamilton's name proclaiming, "Photographed by Stanley Kubrick." Kubrick spent time with the enigmatic star who was next to be seen in director William Wyler's *The Heiress*. He photographed Clift on the street, in bed reading a script, with actor friend Kevin McCarthy, and moodily looking out the window of his low-rent midtown apartment.

For the August 2 issue Kubrick did a pictorial spread on Mr. New Year's Eve, bandleader Guy Lombardo, showing the Lombardo family at home in their zebra-themed living room and on the bandstand playing "the sweetest music this side of heaven."

For a picture spread on the new musical *Miss Liberty*, Kubrick also spent a night on Broadway at the Irving Berlin–Robert E. Sherwood production, directed by Moss Hart.

Kubrick continued to take pictures of the New York City he lived in and loved. A picture of a Lexington Avenue subway station ran in the August 16, 1949, issue. He also followed bandleader Vaughn Monroe into the recording studio and onto the stage. The assignment desk also sent Kubrick to profile Masterpiece, a globe-trotting toy poodle who had won more than sixty international prizes.

For the September 13 issue Kubrick got to shoot a more bohemian assignment, the Beaux Arts Ball, to which artists and art students came dressed as figures from surrealist and classic paintings.

Kubrick received a lead photo credit for a six-page profile of *New Yorker* cartoonist Peter Arno. He photographed the sophisticated Arno at his Park Avenue home playing the piano, rising from bed, in the studio with a naked female model, and on the town dating twenty-one-year-old actress Joan Sinclair.

For the September 27 issue, Kubrick went to the Camden, New Jersey, offices of the *Courier-Post* to take pictures of teenage columnist Pat White, following her home, as she went shopping, and to a drawing class. He also went to the home of socialite adman John Davies, where celebrities came to angel the Jule Styne musical of *Gentlemen Prefer Blondes*. Kubrick snapped author Anita Loos and other celebrities, as well as a six-shot sequence of Styne performing and selling the show to potential backers. These sequences continued to show Kubrick's feel for movement and action. Kubrick would stake his ground in a fixed position, firing his still camera like frames out of a film.

Even the more mundane assignments, like the September 27 article on the World's Most Escape-Proof Paddy Wagon, tapped into Kubrick's interest in telling a story with images. He shot the exterior of the wagon, then the interior, a detective inspecting the new van, a profile close-up of a .38 revolver firing into the side of the impenetrable van, a complementary angle of a hand holding a gas gun, and finally a full view of a man with an acetylene torch testing the walls of the van.

The October 25, 1949, issue ran a Kubrick photo story on Lou Maxon, the head of an advertising agency in Detroit, as he was honored by a parade on Maxon Day in Onaway, Michigan. In the political arena, Kubrick also shot the chairman of the Republican Party, Guy G. Gabrielson, at his New Jersey home with his wife and sons.

For the November 8 deadline Kubrick shot pictures for a six-page human interest story, "A Dog's Life in the Big City," chronicling canines at the 21 Club, the ASPCA, in a convertible, at a dogsitter's house, at a butcher shop, and at a vet.

Kubrick and *Look*'s technical director, photojournalist Arthur Rothstein, went to the Wedgwood Ball at the Waldorf-Astoria for a society gala. The young photographer explored all strata of life. The lead picture for an article taken by Kubrick features socialite Nancy Oakes as she danced the polka for a benefit supporting the Lighthouse for the Blind. Oakes had recently won an annulment from Alfred de Marigny, who was acquitted of her father's murder in 1943.

The twenty-year-old magazine photographer continued to exhibit a flair for photographing children. The December 6 issue also ran a photoessay on seven-year-old Jere Whaley of Chattanooga, Tennessee, who won a trip to New York and tickets to the World Series as *Look*'s Junior Photographer for taking an action photo of soapbox racers with a camera he got for fifty-five cents and a Wheaties boxtop.

In between assignments that involved notable celebrities, *Look* continued to send Kubrick out for less-high-profile shots, dispatching him, for instance, to Grand Central terminal to shoot a model demonstrating new portable luggage. For the same issue, Kubrick shot a picture of Buffalo Bob Smith of the *Howdy Doody* show posing with his muse, two young fans, and official show merchandise.

Kubrick began the new decade of the fifties with a shot of actor Robert Montgomery at the mike for an ABC radio news commentary show. Also in the January 3 issue are two pictures that Kubrick took showing the effects on the brain of a blow to a boxer's head. The new decade was heralded as well with a feature called "The Mid-Century Look Is the American Look," in which Kubrick shot a photo spread of model Ann Klem as an example of the ideal American woman. Kubrick photographed her with her fiance, Bob, riding a horse, singing in a choir, and in profile, sporting her contemporary short haircut.

For the January 17 issue Kubrick again photographed Dwight Eisenhower, the president of Columbia University, who was emerging as the GOP's greatest hope for the 1952 presidential election.

At the end of the month, *Look* ran a two-page spread of Kubrick's pictures of Frank Sinatra and Dorothy Kirsten, who were on the Lucky Strike radio show *Light Up Time*. When Kubrick and Marvin Traub first photographed Frankie, Kubrick was an aspiring amateur—unaware that he would photograph Sinatra on assignment. He also shot a five-page photo profile of Ohio senator Robert A. Taft, who was running for reelection. The study followed Taft on the campaign trail and showed him meeting constituents and stumping for votes. The pictures catch the immediacy of the campaign, but Kubrick is always in control of the composition and the use of space relative to his subject. In addition, Kubrick contributed posed pictures of a couple having fun during a night out on the town for an article about enjoying middle age.

For the February 14 issue Kubrick photographed another "Day of a Fight" story—this time featuring Rocky Graziano coming back from a New York and Illinois suspension on his way to a middleweight title fight during the summer. The results continue to show Kubrick's love for boxing and his skill as a photojournalist. The opening picture is a portrait of the gutsy Brooklyn fighter after a tough workout. Graziano is covered in a robe and cowled by a towel, his face a road map of his stormy life, the negative space to the right defining him in the frame. A series of pictures documents his day as Rocky eats breakfast, talks by phone to his wife, promotes the fight on a radio broadcast, weighs in, walks to the arena, waits for the call to the ring, walks through the crowd, throws a punch, and sits in his corner between rounds. There is a full shot of Rocky stalking his opponent, and the study ends with Graziano talking to a *World-Telegram* reporter after the fight. The sequence synthesizes time, tedium, tension, and the drama of the day in a fighter's life.

In the March 14 issue *Look* ran a series of pictures that Kubrick had taken of maestro Leonard Bernstein with Serge Koussevitsky (the former conductor of the Boston Symphony), actress Stella Adler, and musicians Oscar Levant, Aaron Copland, and pianist William Kapell.

Kubrick spent a day at the ABC radio quiz show *Quick as a Flash* and shot the contestants, host Bill Cullen, and guest actresses Gene Tierney and Mercedes McCambridge for the March 28 issue.

A big baseball fan, Kubrick got the chance to shoot a pictorial for the April 11 issue on Brooklyn Dodgers pitcher Don Newcombe. The story begins with another Kubrick photo sequence—this time extreme close-ups on Newcombe's face as he throws a pitch—the ninth picture, a confident Newcombe as he watches the pitch reach home.

The May 9 *Look* had two Kubrick profiles—the first, of Ken Murray in search of seven beautiful girls for his CBS television show and the second, a study of Yankees shortstop Phil Rizzuto. The lead picture featured Rizzuto waiting for his turn at batting practice, standing next to Yankees legend Joe DiMaggio. Other pictures show Rizzuto playing cards with Yogi Berra and kidding with pitcher Vic Raschi.

In the May 23 issue Kubrick returned to the political scene for a smiling portrait of Theodore Roosevelt III. For the June 6 issue Kubrick contributed pictures for a photo study of another of his enthusiasms—jazz. Kubrick shot expressive pictures of jazz instrumentalists George Lewis, Eddie Condon, Phil Napoleon, Oscar Celestin, Alphonse Picou, Muggsy Spanier, Sharkey Bonano, and others in a nightclub setting.

Kubrick photographed another profile of a radio game show—*Double or Nothing,* an NBC show that selected two contest winners from its Chicago studio audience.

For the June 20 issue Kubrick went back to the ballpark to photograph Giants broadcaster Russ Hodges. In the July 18 issue Kubrick shot a pictorial study of eighteen-year-old debutante Betsy von Furstenberg as she auditions for producer Gilbert Miller, gossips with other debutantes, lounges with an old boyfriend under Picasso's *The Absinthe Drinker,* and plays tennis. The pictorial ends with a full-page shot of Betsy sitting in the window of her hotel reading a script by British playwright Christopher Fry. The low-key profile shot is classically centered with the window and curtains and the background of another New York hotel, as Betsy's long legs curve up to the side of the window frame.

Also for the July 18 issue Kubrick contributed two pictures for an article about children's cowboy outfits. The first is a shot of two young cowboys checking each other's outfits. The other is a photo of Roy Rogers showing two girls how to spin an official Rogers trick rope, which was available at the time in department stores.

In the August 1 issue Kubrick provided a series of posed pictures to illustrate an article called "What Every Teenager Should Know about Dating." The pictures demonstrate tips provided in an article by Evelyn Millis Duvall, a consultant for the National Council on Family Relations. Kubrick posed the teenage models in natural settings to show proper dating habits. Also for the issue Kubrick took several pictures of the singing cowboy Gene Autry, and made a four-picture study of jazz stylist Erroll Garner for *Look*'s Record Guide feature.

For the August 15 issue Kubrick snapped the cover picture and pictorial on TV star Faye Emerson for the *Look* Picture Personality.

As a *Look* magazine photographer Kubrick was part of the New York community of photographers. The staff of the magazine had embraced him because of his youthful talent. His work also caught the eye of photographer Diane Arbus, who often brought the twenty-two-year-old Kubrick to Saturday night charade games held at an actor's apartment in the Village. The gatherings were a place for show business folk from the theater, TV, and movies to meet and have fun trying to decipher the titles to old movies and Broadway plays as they were acted out by a participant.

At the time, Arbus and her husband, Allan, were very successful fashion photographers whose pictures graced the pages of *Vogue* and *Glamour*. Eventually, Diane began to move beyond commercial photography to become a serious artist obsessed with photographing the hidden world she saw through the lens. Arbus's disturbing portraits of both society's undesirables and the status quo had a tremendous impact on photographers and filmmakers. Her famous picture of identical twin girls standing side by side became the cover of an Aperture Monograph published for an exhibition of her work at the Museum of Modern Art after her suicide in 1971. Looking at the black-and-white photo of the not-quite-smiling, doe-eyed girls, standing straight, their arms stiff, it is difficult not to think of the doomed daughters of Grady in *The Shining*. "Nothing is ever the same as they said it was," Diane Arbus once said. "It's what I've never seen before that I recognize."

"It was tremendous fun for me at that age, but eventually it began to wear thin especially since my ultimate ambition had always been to make movies," Kubrick told Michel Ciment about his experiences with *Look* magazine. "The subject matter of my *Look* assignments was generally pretty dumb. I would do stories like 'Is an Athlete Stronger Than a Baby?' photographing a college football player emulating the 'cute' position that a fifteen-month-old child would get into. Occasionally I had a chance to do an interesting personality story. One of these was about Montgomery Clift, who was at the start of his brilliant career. Photography certainly gave me the first step up to movies. To make a film entirely by yourself, which initially I did, you may not have to know very much about anything else, but you must know about photography."

CHAPTER 3

"He Now Understands That It's Directing He Wants to Do"

Stanley comes in prepared like a fighter for a big fight, he knows exactly what he's doing, where he's going and what he wants to accomplish.

—Walter Cartier

After graduation from William Howard Taft High School in June 1945, Stanley Kubrick's friend Alexander Singer began a process of transition from artist to filmmaker.

Singer's yearbook testimonial read: "His ambition? Artist, author, musician, that's all; Alex really has something on the ball!"

Singer was interested in still photography, but his primary creative focus was on becoming an artist who would paint and illustrate his original stories. In addition to his art studies at Taft, Singer studied at the Art Students League in Manhattan, went to museums, and surrounded himself with an artist's milieu.

His standards in art were of the highest order. Ultimately, when he was in his senior year at Taft, Singer came to the decision if he couldn't be Rembrandt, he didn't want to be a painter. Filmmaking began to attract him. The medium was still in a relatively formative stage in comparison with the long tradition of painting. Energized to express his love of storytelling, music, photography, and art—a seed cultivated by his Taft art teacher, Herman Getter—Alexander Singer decided to become a film director.

Singer's decision had a significant influence on Stanley Kubrick, who was quietly watching his friend's metamorphosis. "At seventeen I decided to become a film director and the way I was going to become a film director was to write, direct, and produce my own picture," Singer recalls. "It was going to be a tough job, so I knew I better pick something I loved very much because I could spend years working on it. I picked Homer's the *Iliad*. I read five versions of it, a handful of reference books on Greek civilization and began writing a one-hundred-twenty-five-page treatment, which I completed. Then I did nine hundred continuity sketches on the fall of Troy. The embodiment of this project showed to Stanley was one of the things that turned him on to this process. It was as if to say, 'Yeah, you're a Bronx kid, you're a million miles away from this world, but so what? You can do it.' It was one of the dreams of glory, of teenagers stalking the streets of the Bronx dreaming about impossible dreams."

Animated-film creator Faith Hubley remembers the two young men walking through New York's film district in the Times Square area. Singer had his detailed notebook filled with ideas for a film adaptation of Homer's masterwork, and Kubrick had his own link with the written word. "Stanley would walk around with a book of abbreviated novels of classic literature. He would stop people at 1600 Broadway and say, 'Dostoyevsky, what do you think?' He couldn't pronounce the names."

Singer decided that MGM was the right studio for his production of the *Iliad*. Kubrick told his friend that he could get the script to Dore Schary, a production executive at MGM, through an editor he knew at *Look* magazine. The script was sent, and Singer did eventually get a letter back from Schary. "He was very polite," remembers Singer. "He said, 'Thank you for letting me see this, but we're doing *Quo Vadis?* this year and we do only one of these things every ten years.'"

Singer began to explore the art theater film scene in New York and discovered the work of Eisenstein, Pudovkin and early German filmmakers, as well as the surrealism developing in experimental film in France. Alex brought his friend Stanley with him, and the two young men moved from early interests in photography, art, and literature into the ultimate medium of the twentieth century—filmmaking. "I'd take Stanley to see these things," Singer remembers. "I'm an instrument of exposure to him and he's very excited and very turned on by all of this. I take him to *Alexander Nevsky* and we hear Prokofiev's score for the battle on the ice and Stanley never gets over that. He bought a record of it and played it until he drove his kid sister Barbara right around the bend. He played it over and over and over again and she broke the record in an absolute rage. Stanley is—I think the word 'obsessive' is not unfair."

Both Stanley and Alex had been brought up on a diet of Hollywood movies, but this initial exposure to the art of film had a divergent effect in shaping their immediate goals. Alexander Singer became determined to be a film director, and Stanley Kubrick, with his highly developed photographic skills and knowledge, wanted to become a cinematographer.

Kubrick was judiciously saving money from his *Look* magazine salary for his artistic future. He spent a lot of his time reading classic literature by Joseph Conrad, Fyodor Dostoyevsky, and Franz Kafka. Alexander Singer was developing his film career by landing a job as an office boy at Time Inc., where *The March of Time* newsreels were being produced. The Louis de Rochemont screen magazine series offered him practical insight into documentary filmmaking.

Created by Time Inc. in 1935, *The March of Time,* under the tutelage of producer Louis de Rochemont, drew on Roy Larsen's successful radio series of the same name and used the resources of *Time* magazine to revolutionize film journalism. The segments were conceived to be shown in movie theaters before a feature presentation and ran between fifteen and twenty-five minutes. They supplied news and informational programs to moviegoers. A cross between classic newsreel and documentary techniques, *The March of Time* films created a format that ultimately became a mainstay of television news. When TV incorporated this news pattern, the series ended in 1951. The impact of *The March of Time* can still be seen in network magazine shows such as *60 Minutes, Dateline,* and *20/20.* Orson Welles immortalized *The March of Time* blueprint in his debut film, *Citizen Kane,* by creating a newsreel that looked back on the life of Charles Foster Kane.

Alex and Stanley decided that they were going to make a short film. Alex was to be the director, Stanley the cinematographer. Singer, with his literary art magazine background from Taft, decided to write a short story that he could adapt to a short film. "It's about some teenagers at

the beach and a wistful love, a chance encounter that doesn't materialize. Very much a teenage experience," Singer recalls.

After completing the short script, Singer, as the director, sat down and
used his drawing skills to create a series of continuity sketches—today
more commonly called storyboards—that specified what was in the
frame for every shot. Director Singer clearly proclaimed that he would
decide where to place the camera for each moment in the film.

When the story and the cinematic presentation were ready, Singer and
Kubrick planned a meeting to discuss the teenage epic.

"I will never forget this because it's a rather momentous moment in
my development as an artist. We're now riding on the top deck of a Fifth
Avenue double-decker bus and we're having a deadly earnest talk. I have
just delivered the script and continuity sketches to him on the bus. I
have a premonition that Stanley may not take too comfortably to the
notion I have specified every single camera setup in the short. He reads
this thing and looks at the pictures and says, 'This is beautiful, Alex, you
should make it yourself. You've just taken away all of the choices from
me and what's left is to sort of fill the frame—and while that takes some
photographic knowledge and some doing, the real creativity and the real
choices have already been made.' And that is the last time there'll ever
be a question about who's in charge if the two of us are working together. From that point on it is, as we say, Stanley's ball, and it becomes
his ball on the basis that in fact he had not just the skills but the where-
withal to realize the dream. He now understands that it's directing he
wants to do. Not only directing but directing as a total control in which
the cinematography is also under his aegis—and not only the cinematography but the editing also."

Confident that he had the vision and desire for the control to make his
own film, Stanley Kubrick used Alexander Singer's presentation of a director's cinematic ideas as a catalyst to inspire him to create, direct, and
produce his first film.

It was 1950. Stanley Kubrick had come of age and was ready to put
behind him the role of wunderkind photojournalist for *Look* magazine.
He decided it was time to make his first motion picture.

Movies had always dominated Kubrick's dreams, stimulated by hour
upon hour of gazing at the Loew's Paradise silver screen. He had been
surrounded by great storytelling in his father's substantial personal library and was filled with well-composed and diversified images from his
work as a still photographer. He haunted New York's art house circuit,
the film program at the Museum of Modern Art and Amos Vogel's Cinema 16, an alternative venue for experimental and groundbreaking films.

Stanley Kubrick had no formal filmmaking education, and little was available. Film literature was minimal. Few productions originated in New York City at the time. Television was beginning to emerge, but it did not attract him. The New York theater scene was a training ground for nascent film directors, but Kubrick was not a man of the theater. He had taught himself to be a photographer by hands-on experience and by learning from the knowledge of others. There was no place on the East Coast to apprentice in filmmaking, and he didn't have a calling to head for Hollywood. Stanley Kubrick had the determination to be an autodidact, however. He would teach himself to be a filmmaker.

The always inquisitive Kubrick asked Singer to find out how much it cost to produce a *March of Time* segment. With his direct access, Singer was able to learn that de Rochemont spent up to $40,000 for an eight- or nine-minute film. Driven by the arrogance of youth, Kubrick announced that he could easily do it for $1,500 and planned on using his *Look* magazine nest egg to create the independent film's budget.

For the subject of his first film, Kubrick dipped into his photojournalist file and selected the story he had photographed on the middleweight boxer Walter Cartier, which had run as a pictorial called "Prizefighter" in the January 18, 1949, issue of *Look* magazine. The article was seven pages long and contained twenty black-and-white photographs telling Cartier's story. The pictures documented the fighter's preparation and served as a matrix for the short that became Kubrick's first motion picture. The plan was to independently produce a segment on the boxer and to sell the completed short film.

"We had a notion that you could get tens of thousands of dollars," explains Alexander Singer. "We were off by an order of magnitude. The truth was, they gave them away. They were not paid for at all. The shorts anybody paid for were the comic routines professional vaudeville characters did, not the sort of sports short we were contemplating—all of those were throwaways. But what we did know was that what passed for a sports short at this time was pretty low stuff; it was junk. There was no question in our minds that we could vastly exceed the impact and power. That everything about such a project could be masterfully done. Stanley's concept of using the photojournalist story on *Day of the Fight* was inspired. Not only were the drama elements of it marvelously compressed, but the subject himself, Walter Cartier, was a textbook hero. Walter Cartier was good-looking and able. He surely looked good—and his brother, Vincent, looked good—and the two of them together were really quite marvelous figures."

Kubrick chose the title *Day of the Fight* for his short film. The title comes from a headline, "The Day of a Fight," used to begin the *Look* photo story of Walter Cartier's day as he prepares to fight middleweight Tony D'Amico at Jerome Stadium that night. As recently as February 14, 1950, Kubrick had photographed a story for *Look* magazine on boxer Rocky Graziano called "Rocky Graziano, He's a Good Boy Now," which used the bold headline "The Day of the Fight Is a Long One."

The concept of the short would be to film the day in the life of a boxer as he prepared to step into the ring. Kubrick already had a good rapport with Walter and Vincent Cartier from the *Look* story. Walter took a liking to the young photographer and respected his professionalism and talent. In addition to being the focus of the film, Walter would also act as technical adviser on the project. Both Walter Cartier and Stanley Kubrick wanted the film to be accurate and to rise to the top of the genre.

Kubrick's high school friend Bernard Cooperman had followed an interest in electronics after high school and had just formed a company when he went to visit Kubrick and his wife Toba Metz at their 37 West Sixteenth Street apartment. "It was a small apartment on the ground floor with a fireplace," Cooperman remembers. "And he asked me to do sound recording on his first movie—it was about a prizefighter. Later, he was dropping me off someplace in a taxicab and he was still trying to talk me into it. I just wouldn't do it. I told him I couldn't take time away, but the real thing was I would have taken time away if I knew what the hell to do, I just had no idea."

Walter Cartier died on August 16, 1995, at age seventy-three. His identical twin brother, Vincent, a practicing lawyer for forty-five years, looked back on Walter's relationship with the burgeoning film director Stanley Kubrick. "Walter had a high regard for Stanley. He stated many times that *Day of the Fight* would go down as a classic fight documentary because Stanley was so conscientious and so prepared. Walter used to say, 'Stanley comes in prepared like a fighter for a big fight, he knows exactly what he's doing, where he's going and what he wants to accomplish. He knew the challenges and he overcame them.' Walter would praise Stanley, saying, 'Vincent, we're being a part of a classic fight picture. There's never going to be anything as good as this—because it's authentic and I'm assisting in making it authentic. I'm proud, we should be proud of our contribution.' Walter was the technical adviser of the integral parts of what should be in a fight film. Stanley would ask him questions, he wanted it to be authentic. Walter and Stanley were very good working together."

Kubrick had seen a fight film featuring the Bronx heavyweight Roland

LaStarza and thought he could do better. Cartier was a perfect subject, a good-looking, professional boxer with the manners of a gentleman. "Stanley was quiet, but he was always thinking." Vincent recalls, "Stanley saw a story, he visualized a young, handsome, well-built, very successful fighter, and he had Walter Cartier in mind—he was a mold."

Kubrick was twenty-one when he began *Day of the Fight,* Walter and Vincent Cartier were twenty-eight-year-old identical twins born in the Bronx on March 22, 1922. The boys gave boxing exhibitions at the Woodstock, Connecticut, Country Fair. The matches were refereed by their older brother. Often Walter would get knocked down in one round, Vincent would get knocked down in the next, and after the last round the fight would be called a draw. In the Navy the Cartiers gave fighting exhibitions at venues like the Chicago Pier. Walter began to do some tournament boxing. After serving in World War II Walter went back to Connecticut to train to be a professional prizefighter. Then their aunt invited them to live with her in Greenwich Village.

Walter originally fought under the name Wally "Twin" Carter. The Cartiers were Irish. Their grandfather was a violinist in the Boston Symphony Orchestra and changed the family name from McCarthy to Carter to Cartier. In New York City, Walter trained at his manager Bobby Gleason's place, the legendary Gleason's Gym in the Bronx.

When Stanley Kubrick first met Walter Cartier and approached him for the *Look* magazine story, Walter was a Main Event fighter who had worked himself up from four-round to six-round to eight-round to Main Event fights.

For the sequence of Cartier preparing for his fight with black middleweight Bobby James, Kubrick spent time with Vincent, who was present for all of his brother's fights, and Gleason. He observed the pre-fight rituals. Kubrick turned his powerful and insatiable curiosity on Walter Cartier and asked questions of the seasoned fighter while he organized the pre-fight sequence, breaking it down into a series of shots. He listened to his technical adviser. "Walter would say, 'Stanley, this would be a good shot, why don't you take this,'" Vincent remembers. "Stanley would think about it and make a quick decision, he was amiable to suggestions."

"Stanley was a very stoic, impassive but imaginative type person with strong, powerful thoughts," Vincent Cartier observed. "He commanded respect in a quiet, shy way. Whatever he wanted, you complied, he just captivated you. Anybody who worked with Stanley did just what Stanley wanted. He would say to our aunt, 'Miss Cartier, would you stand over here? Would you do this?' You did it, he commanded such a quiet, positive respect. He's got a calmness about him, there's no noise with Stanley. There's calmness and simple direction that's so clear there's no opposition to it, there's no objection. You could see he knew what he was doing. He knew what he wanted. He was very focused. Stanley was unobtrusive, he just walked around slumped and slouched over with a light meter and took classic black-and-white pictures. He took giant steps and walked around somewhat hunched over, but he moved around with a grace you cannot explain. He always wore a sports jacket, a pair of baggy slacks with things in both pockets, and rubber-soled shoes. He always wore a tie. He's quiet by nature. He would hold the light meter up, step back, and take the shot. He's just all business, he's not a jokester. He's very shy, but he's confident. Stanley's certain and sure of himself, but we would joke with him and get him to laugh once in a while. We'd hug him a little bit. 'Loosen up Stanley, loosen up,' and he would laugh and go along. Stanley was a person who was highly intellectual, highly secretive in his thoughts—it's hard to read Stanley. He never bragged, never boasted, never made claim to anything even when the *Look* magazine story came out. He never took praise or boasted about how great the story was. He was a very sincere, low-key person. Some geniuses boast about themselves, but he doesn't."

Kubrick spent time with Walter and Vincent Cartier and their aunt in their small Greenwich Village apartment on West Twelfth Street, capturing their daily routine. Kubrick was going for realism in putting Cartier's life on film, but he did add some human-interest touches of his own, which he learned from the years at *Look*. One of these was to give Walter a dog.

Kubrick directed the Cartier brothers through their normal morning rituals after talking to them about their habits. "He would get from you what your routine was. He would ask you questions. 'Walter, what's the first thing you do when you get up in the morning?' 'Well,' Walter said, 'we go in and have breakfast.' 'And how does that work?' 'Usually Vincent is the one who puts the water on for the oatmeal.' Stanley would say, 'Well, tomorrow morning we'll take that scene.' That's the way we would do it. It just flows. He didn't really rehearse it at all. It was just so quick. Once he did it, it was done. It wasn't retake, retake, retake. He was photographing—not manufacturing the day of a fight. He would set up a scene," Vincent remembers. "Stanley would say, 'Walter, we're going to put the scene on you waking up in the morning, I want you to get out this side of the bed, walk, stretch, and yawn."

Kubrick followed Walter to his favorite restaurant in the Village, the

Steak Joint on Greenwich Avenue, where the fighter would eat a steak for lunch while training.

Walter was a deeply religious man and attended mass at Saint Francis Xavier Church on Sixteenth Street and Sixth Avenue. Kubrick took his 35mm Eyemo motion picture camera to the neighborhood church to film the brothers worshiping before the fight. During the sequence where Vincent helps his brother to prepare for the fight in the arena dressing room, Kubrick shot footage of Vincent removing Walter's Saint Jude medal.

Walter and Vincent Cartier had a chessboard set up in their living room. Kubrick watched the boys play but never engaged in a game with them. A year or so after completing *Day of the Fight*, he saw the brothers again and told them he was playing chess in Washington Square Park and had joined a chess club in the Village.

Kubrick started his professional career in cinema as a complete filmmaker. "I was cameraman, director, editor, assistant editor, sound effects man—you name it, I did it. And it was invaluable experience, because being forced to do everything myself I gained a sound and comprehensive grasp of all the technical aspects of filmmaking," Kubrick told Joseph Gelmis for his 1970 book, *The Film Director as Superstar*. Working with an Eyemo, a daylight loading camera that takes one-hundred-foot spools of 35mm black-and-white film, Kubrick quickly learned that he had been overoptimistic about the budget; he covered the actual $3,900 cost with his savings. "I did everything from keeping an accounting book to dubbing in the punches on the soundtrack," Kubrick told writer Gene D. Phillips. "I had no idea what I was doing, but I knew I could do better than most of the films that I was seeing at the time."

The climax of *Day of the Fight* is the Main Event that Walter Cartier had been training for, a bout with middleweight fighter Bobby James. The sequence was shot live during the fight on April 17, 1950, at Laurel Gardens in Newark, New Jersey. The shoot came well into the process of making of the documentary. Kubrick had one opportunity to capture the fight—live in 35mm black-and-white cinematography. The actual fight was the only time during the documentary that more than one camera was employed. Alexander Singer operated the second camera, also a 35mm Eyemo shooting in black and white. Kubrick was hoping that Cartier would win, but he saw the drama in the story either way. The first Cartier match that Kubrick photographed for *Look* had been with Tony D'Amico and was stopped after Walter received a head butt that caused a viscous cut to his right eye. D'Amico won on a technical K.O. In the second fight, a preliminary to the Tony Zale–Marcel

Cerdan championship held at Jersey City's Roosevelt Stadium, Walter knocked out Jimmy Mangia in the first round with a right to the jaw.

For *Day of the Fight* Kubrick and Singer covered the Cartier–James fight with their Eyemos grinding away—each aware of the other trying to get the event on film so it could be structured in the editing room as a total live event. Kubrick shot the hand-held material, and Singer operated the second Eyemo positioned on a tripod. They both were shooting hundred-foot loads, which required constant reloading. With two cameras, one could be shooting while the other was reloading. A four-hundred-foot magazine was available at the time, but that required extra expense and extra bulk for Kubrick's hand-held camera.

"With me on one camera and Stanley on the other, it was pretty busy and pretty hectic. We had to get it. It had to be down on film—there was no picture without getting this fight," Singer emphasizes.

During the fight, the camera captured a close-up of a young woman cheering the fighters on. The woman was Alex's girlfriend, Judy, to whom he has now been married for forty-five years. Singer calls his wife, a novelist and screenwriter, "my buddy, my love."

One of the most impressive moments in the sequence was taken by Kubrick. The shot is from the point of view of the canvas—looking straight up at the two boxers, who punch at each other over the camera. The only reference point in the shot is a light coming from above, and full shots reveal there were several lights in the stadium ceiling—so it looks as if Kubrick was lying down in the middle of the ring while the fighters fought over him. The fight had to be filmed live with no chance of re-creation; thus when the fighters were within a reasonable distance of the ropes, Kubrick ran and extended his arm out and low to the canvas, pointing his Eyemo straight up at the fighters and shooting blind to capture the shot. This kind of shooting was commonplace to the photojournalist, who often had to shoot above crowds and other obstructions that blocked the camera lens.

When Walter Cartier landed the knockout punch, defeating Bobby James in the second round, Alexander Singer was there, getting the culminating moment of the documentary on film. "Stanley always credited me with capturing the knockout punch. During the fight itself, I was running and right where I should be to catch the punch—and in telling people about this, Stanley always would say that. It was a nice way of doffing your hat to another photographer, another professional—but what you saw watching Stanley at work in *Day of the Fight* was the Stanley Kubrick that everybody knows and the Stanley Kubrick who has received the recognition. He was fully formed, and that's a very rare thing."

The March of Time was going out of business. Kubrick turned down one offer for less than the original budget and eventually sold the completed sixteen-minute film to RKO-Pathé for $4,000, thereby making a total profit of $100. Unblinking, the enterprising Kubrick was able to secure a $1,500 advance for a second short for the studio. RKO-Pathé told Kubrick that $3,900 was the most money they had ever paid for a short film.

Stanley Kubrick was a good film student. From watching films and understanding the structure of the newsreel, he was able to work in the format of *The March of Time* style while developing a personal sense of film grammar. Hints of the film noir genre, which dominate Kubrick's first three feature films, have their genesis in *Day of the Fight*.

Day of the Fight opens with the marquee of New York's fight mecca—Madison Square Garden. "Tonite Boxing" is in bold letters and partially cut off by the dead-on close-up composition. The first four minutes and twenty seconds are a tabloid history of boxing synthesized through the eyes of a New Yorker schooled in the sports pages of the *Daily News* and the *Daily Mirror*. Boxers are portrayed as visceral animals who live for the K.O. We are told by our narrator, veteran newsman Douglas Edwards, that boxers come from all walks of life. They are stevedores, dockworkers, college graduates, gas station attendants, milk company lab technicians, and grocery store clerks.

The narration is crisp and lean, like that of a forties detective novel. "This is a fight fan," Edwards delivers in a no-nonsense tone. "Fan—short for fanatic. There's a legion just like him in the United States. Each year he shoves his share of ninety million dollars under the wicket for the privilege of attending places where matched pairs of men will get up on a canvas-covered platform and commit legal assault and lawful battery."

The text poses as documentary fact, but it is filled with noir poetry. "It's a living. For some, not much of a living. There are six thousand men like these in America—professional prizefighters. Only six hundred will make a living at all—and of these only sixty will make a good living. One out of one hundred."

Images of boxers working out in the ring and in the gym are structured together. Nat Fleischer, longtime boxing historian and publisher of the fighter's bible, *Ring* magazine, is shown looking through a boxing record book. There are pictures of Joe Louis and Jack Dempsey. A fighter is chosen at random so we can understand this life and profession. We are about to see one day in the life of middleweight Walter Cartier.

A fight poster announcing an upcoming match, "Walter Cartier versus Bobby James," is displayed on a street pole in Manhattan. It is early morning, the streets are deserted. In true noir fashion we are always reminded of the time. It is the day of the Cartier–James fight, to be fought at 10:00 P.M. It is now 6:00 A.M.

We meet Walter Cartier, who has just awakened in the bedroom of a three-room Greenwich Village apartment he shares with his aunt. His identical twin brother, Vincent, rises just seconds after him. Vincent is a lawyer who acts as Walter's fight manager. We are told he resides out of town but lives with Walter when he has a fight. They are twenty-four years old. Kubrick's narration represents the age Walter had been known as, four years younger than his actual age of twenty-eight. Vincent makes a fighter's breakfast for Walter, and then the two walk through old New York streets, past bars, to go to church for early mass. An exalted high angle picks them up as they enter the church, where they receive Holy Communion.

The clock advances. Walter eats a rare steak at the Steak Joint, where the actual owner, who looks to be straight out of central casting from a boxing B movie, smokes a cigarette and brags that one day Walter will be champ.

It is 4:00 P.M. Cartier lays out the tools of his trade on the bedspread: a towel, shoes, ice bag, Vaseline, a robe with his name stitched in script on the back. He takes a last look in the mirror in a shot that transcends the documentary reality, staring into the mirror in an existential moment that telegraphs many of Kubrick's future themes. "Before a fight there's always that last look in the mirror," Edwards says prophetically. "Time to wonder what it will reflect tomorrow." With Kubrick's dramatic composition, the reflection takes on greater significance than the real figure of Cartier.

The twins ride to the arena in a convertible. A moving point-of-view shot captures the sweep and ambience of New York. The brothers are inseparable. The film is about not only a boxer but also the indivisible connection of twins. We are told that when Walter is hit with a punch, Vincent feels the sting.

It is now 8:00 P.M. Walter is in his dressing room under the stands of the arena. There are two hours of waiting left. Kubrick visually compresses the time in a series of shots of Cartier waiting and preparing, but Douglas Edwards continues to tell us about the fighter moving through time, giving the short film weight and emphasizing the relentlessly slow passage of time. "In these hours he can feel his body tightening, but it's a tightness that does not come from lack of confidence, it's the pressure of the last waiting. Here in a place where the walls are so close a man can barely move his body around. If only the fight would come, then everything else would not be so bad—not really bad at all." The narrator enters the mental transformation occurring in Cartier. Kubrick has found a literary device that will coexist with his cinematic sense of storytelling. "Walter isn't concerned with the hands of the clock now, just his own hands. As he gets ready to walk out there in the arena in front of the people, Walter is slowly becoming another man. This is the man who cannot lose, who must not lose. The hard movements of his arms and fists are different from what they were an hour ago. They belong to a fierce new person. They're part of the arena man, the fighting machine that the crowd outside has paid to see in fifteen minutes."

At 9:00 P.M. Walter contemplates his opponent and continues to prepare and wait. Vincent covers Walter's face and body with Vaseline and goes through the fight ritual of getting his brother ready for battle. He takes Walter's religious medallion.

9:45. Walter makes the final transition from man to the fighting machine the crowd clamors for. He is called to the ring, the tip of his manager's cigar glows hot white.

10:00. The fighters are announced. Bobby James is a middleweight from Jamaica, Queens. The bell rings. Both men trade punches equally. Cartier gets James on the ropes. More sparring. Cartier sees his opening and knocks James out. Edwards proclaims the final narration—cementing the imagery of the boxer as both animal and professional. "One man has skillfully, violently overcome another—that's for the fan. But K.O., name of opponent, time, date, and place—that's for the record book. But it's more than that in the life of a man who literally has to fight for his very existence. For him, it's the end of a working day."

Kubrick's standard for his inaugural film was absolute, and he insisted from the outset that his fight film would have an original musical score and not the usual canned music used in most sports shorts.

Alexander Singer had met Gerald Fried, a talented musician living in his Bronx neighborhood, about a year and a half before meeting Kubrick in the halls of Taft. Gerald was a student at the prestigious Juilliard School, where he studied music and played the oboe. Alexander Singer encouraged his friend to consider composing music for film scores and introduced Fried to Kubrick.

"I was a handball partner with Alex," Fried recalled forty-five years later, having just returned from recording a film score with the Israeli

Philharmonic. "They asked me if I wanted to do the music. Why me? Because I was the only musician Kubrick knew. I happened to be an oboe major at Juilliard at the time and it never occurred to me that I might write film music or conduct anything like that. This sounded like a good idea for me, and I said, 'Sure Stanley, I'll do it.' I had ten months to a year to learn how the hell to do it. There were no courses. I went to a lot of movies and took notes. Stanley and I went to movies together and we would say, 'This is working, this is not working,' kind of self-help. We saw *The Creature from the Black Lagoon* and laughed so much. Some things worked, some things were ludicrous, some things were obvious and some things were on-the-nose in a good way. You had to make these definitions. What is on-the-nose and if it's on-the-nose, is that bad necessarily? When do you want to be on-the-nose? When are you subtle? When do you get internal? When do you just play bridges? It was exciting! We were in our early twenties, it was fun—it was a great adventure."

Time's *The March of Time* was a model for the sports short, but its episodes were scored with music from music libraries, and often the same music was heard from one short to the next. "It never occurred to us that there was something valuable there for our purposes," Fried remembers. "We were young and we knew everything. In our minds we were going to be Beethoven and Sergei Eisenstein.

"I decided on a fanfare as a main theme because fights are exciting and fanfares are exciting. My first job was with the Dallas Symphony. I was twenty years old. We played Debussy's *Three Nocturnes*, and what turned me on was that distant fanfare in the nocturne called *Festivals* where the trumpet fanfare in the distance gets louder and louder. So I said, 'Well, maybe we can do a fanfare here, fight, fanfare, announcement, excitement.' That was the main theme and that's how I built my composing bag of tricks. I would discuss it with Stanley. He was a sophisticated musician, he was a drummer in high school. He had a good feel for it."

Kubrick and Fried spotted the short together and decided that the fight that climaxes the film should not be scored. "That was a joint decision, we learned enough from going to movies to know what sound effects should carry and what music should carry," Fried explained.

The music for *Day of the Fight* was recorded at RCA Studios on Fifth Avenue in New York. Nineteen musicians were contracted for the session. Kubrick had budgeted for the music. Gerald Fried did the arrangements and his own copying work and conducted the orchestra. Playing in the session were several musicians who later came to prominence. The first horn player was jazz historian Gunther Schuller. Bernie Adelstein, who became the first trumpet of the Cleveland Orchestra, was also in the trumpet session. Los Angeles concertmaster Sidney Hass was a session musician playing the score written to dramatize a day in the life of prizefighter Walter Cartier.

As the story shifted from an overview of the world of boxing accompanied by fanfare to the story of New York and Walter Cartier, Fried chose music reminiscent of the Bernard Herrmann score of *Citizen Kane*. The legendary composer had a strong influence on the budding composer.

Kubrick was present for the scoring session and worked very closely with Fried. The final sound mix for the film was prepared by Ray Griswold, a mixer of considerable experience. Fried sat next to Kubrick as they strove to get the perfect blend of narration, sound effects, and music. "I had a big buildup before the fight, and the fight crowd was supposed to take over from the music," Fried recalls. "Ray did it and Stanley said, 'Good, that's fine,' and I said, 'No, there was a dip there. I want the music to come out of the sound effects as if there is no break,' and Ray said, 'Yeah, yeah, you're right, let's do it again.' I remember Stan looking over, 'Hmmmm, this guy knows what he's talking about.' I did have a sound in my head. We stuck to it and we got it."

Day of the Fight helped to start Gerald Fried on a long career in film music. His work on the short opened the door to several music jobs scoring films for RKO-Pathé.

To narrate *Day of the Fight* Kubrick considered actor Montgomery Clift, whom he had photographed for *Look* magazine, but ultimately Kubrick hired veteran CBS newsman Douglas Edwards to read the narration.

Day of the Fight is visually exciting. Kubrick's innate photographic sense and the passion he brought to the project result in a film devoid of the common pitfalls of novice filmmakers. A wonderful mimic in search of a personal stamp, Kubrick imitates the newsreel while freely experimenting with a vivid editing style. Images flow through direct cuts, jump cuts, wipes, and dissolves. Structure is controlled by compression, documentary real time, and fades-to-black.

Kubrick's camera eye captures many striking and unique shots of a sort not often seen in the newsreel-documentary style. An extreme high angle looks down on a boxing ring, as two beams of intense spotlight illuminate the canvas and ropes while the surrounding crowd falls into blackness. Kubrick often lights Cartier from above so that his deep-socketed eyes look like Jack Palance in Rod Serling's teleplay *Requiem for a Heavyweight*. Heavy shadows are more reminiscent of a forties policer than a boxing documentary. Cartier is silhouetted against his apartment window. In the dressing room the camera rack-focuses from Walter's taped fist to Vincent preparing a glove for his brother's hand. First Walter's fist is in sharp focus and the glove in Vincent's hand is in soft focus. Then the point of focus shifts dramatically, to the glove being readied for the warrior as Walter's hand gently blurs—contrasting and relating the two images without a cut. In the ring we see Walter waiting for the bell in an extreme low-angle shot through the legs of his opponent's stool. The fight is shot hand-held, a restless, moving camera peering outside the ropes, inside the ropes, and from the point of view of the canvas, looking up at the fighters as they flail at each other, a moment recaptured by Martin Scorsese in *Raging Bull*. It's hard not to think of *Raging Bull* while watching *Day of the Fight*, a film that looks back on the history of boxing in film and points toward its future.

For Alexander Singer, the experience was a lasting one. "I was very proud of my association with it and with Stanley. It was a triumph for me as well as for him. I had no question about it, it was the first real film I was involved in."

On October 16, 1951, Walter Cartier made boxing history by knocking out Joe Rindone in the first forty-seven seconds of a fight. The rocket punch, the first and only punch thrown by Cartier, ended the fight. It has remained the fastest knockout in Boston Garden history. *Day of the Fight* was Walter's entrée into show business. He appeared in Robert Wise's film bio of Rocky Graziano, *Somebody Up There Likes Me*, and Elia Kazan's *A Face in the Crowd*. He played Claude Dillingham on *You'll Never Get Rich* (the Phil Silvers Sergeant Bilko TV series), was on *Crunch and Des* with Forrest Tucker, and did guest spots on *The Ed Sullivan Show*.

When Walter's son, a high school track star who broke Jim Ryan's record, graduated college and was offered an opportunity on a film project, his father, the star of Kubrick's first film, contacted the world-renowned director for advice. Kubrick took the time to write Cartier and provide counsel from his vast personal and professional experience.

Although Kubrick has stated the final cost of *Day of the Fight* as being $3,900 and the sale to RKO-Pathé at $4,000, Alexander Singer remembers the budget being in the area of $4,500, with half the money coming from Kubrick's savings and the remainder borrowed from his father, Jack Kubrick. In any event, it was a remarkable feat. Kubrick was able to finance, produce, and direct a 35mm film and harness the reins of all the film crafts with a kind of filmmaking autonomy that had few precedents in the film community of the fifties.

In 1950, when, Alexander Singer prepared to marry Judy Singer, they, like all engaged couples, looked for a photographer to capture the milestone. Stanley Kubrick, the established *Look* magazine photographer turned film director, with *Day of the Fight* in the can, took the assignment. "He shot the wedding like a standard wedding job except it was Stanley Kubrick shooting it," Singer remembers. "They're the best wedding pictures I've ever seen. He shot it with a Rolleiflex. They were conventional wedding pictures but one cut above. It was his use of bounce flash, which looked like natural room lighting, a concept almost inconceivable in wedding shots. It was like a contradiction in terms. Usually you stared into the camera and said, 'Cheese,' and it looked like a blast of light. Well, Stanley was bouncing the light. It was so subtle you didn't know he shot it with a flash."

Day of the Fight became part of RKO-Pathé's *This Is America* series and opened at the Paramount Theater in New York on April 26, 1951, as a short subject in a program featuring *My Forbidden Past* starring Robert Mitchum, Ava Gardner, and Melvyn Douglas and directed by Robert Stevenson. The film was also an RKO release. Headlining in a live stage show was Frank Sinatra, whom Kubrick and his friend Marvin Traub surreptitiously photographed in the forties. The *New York Times* ad heralded that Frankie was back home and flanked by Joe Bushkin and Orchestra. The blond bombshell Dagmar was making an appearance on the stage. Stanley Kubrick had made his debut on the screen of the famed Paramount—his career as a film director had begun.

"He Was Like a Sponge"

Kubrick took the $100 profit from the sale of *Day of the Fight* and the $1,500 advance RKO gave him for a second film and made his second short, *Flying Padre.*

The eight-and-a-half-minute short released by RKO-Pathé as part of the *Screenliner* series is a human-interest documentary that follows two ordinary days in the life of a Southwestern priest, the Reverend Fred Stadtmueller, known as the Flying Padre.

When we meet him, Stadtmueller has been a priest at Saint Joseph's Church in Mosquero, in Harding County, part of northeastern New Mexico, for eight years. His parishioners are primarily Spanish-Americans who are modest farmers and ranchers. Six years earlier, Stadtmueller borrowed $2,000 from a friend and purchased a small, single-engine airplane in order to best serve his eleven-mission church jurisdiction, which was spread over four thousand square miles.

Stadtmueller spends his first typical day flying over land and cattle to conduct the funeral of a ranch hand. Two men wait on the makeshift airstrip to take him to the small mission church, which is alongside the cemetery where the man will be buried. Back in his plane named the *Spirit of St. Joseph,* Stadtmueller returns to his main parish in time to conduct the evening devotions.

The next day begins as the padre eats breakfast in the parish house. A young girl knocks on his door and asks Stadtmueller to speak to her young friend Pedro, who has been cruel to her. The priest immediately goes to talk to the boy, who confesses his wrongdoings and the two friends make up.

Later, Stadtmueller works on his plane to keep it in a constant state of readiness. A man runs up to give the priest the news that a mother on an isolated ranch fifty miles away needs help. Her husband is away on business, and her baby is sick and getting sicker. They must get to a hospital. The padre pilots the *Spirit of St. Joseph* to the ranch and flies the mother and baby to an airport, where an ambulance is waiting to take them to a nearby hospital. This is a typical day. Stadtmueller averages twelve thousand air miles a year.

Unlike *Day of the Fight, Flying Padre* is a rather typical human-interest newsreel documentary. Kubrick's filmmaking skills are assured but reveal less of the cinematic talent that lies within. The photography is evenly lit. Shots are composed in classic photojournalist style, pleasing and artful to the eye. The narration, spoken by Bob Hite, is smooth and comforting.

Kubrick's love of aviation is evident in a montage of the priest's trip to help the mother and baby. It details intercutting of Stadtmueller's hand on the throttle with many points of view, including aerial shots during the flight. Stadtmueller's single-engine plane was the kind of aircraft that Kubrick was familiar with from his own flying experience.

The one shot of note is the final view of the priest. As the narrator is bidding farewell to the Flying Padre, Kubrick operated his trusty 35mm Eyemo camera while secured in a vehicle that swiftly pulls straight back as Stadtmueller—looking proud and heroic—gets smaller and smaller.

For his second short, Kubrick just barely recouped his budgetary expenses and broke even on the project. The significance of *Flying Padre* is not in style or content but the confidence it gave Kubrick to make a life decision. "It was at this point that I formally quit my job at *Look* to work full time on filmmaking," he told Joseph Gelmis.

In 1952 Stanley Kubrick was looking for a production designer to design his future films. Richard Sylbert, one of Hollywood's finest production designers, who designed *The Manchurian Candidate, Chinatown,* and *Shampoo* and won Oscars for his work on *Who's Afraid of Virginia Woolf?* and *Dick Tracy,* was at the beginning of his career, working in television in New York as an art director on a television production of *Patterns,* starring Everett Sloane and Ed Begley, when he had a fateful encounter. "A guy comes to see me who's exactly my age, twenty-three," Richard Sylbert recalled from the *Mulholland Falls* art department. "He said, 'My name is Stanley Kubrick and I want you to design my movies. I'm going to raise some money and make a picture.' "

The men exchanged information and small talk. Sylbert went back to designing *Patterns*. In 1956 he designed his first feature film, *Crowded Paradise,* and went on to work with Elia Kazan on *Baby Doll* and *A Face in the Crowd* and with Sidney Lumet on *The Fugitive Kind*. But he didn't hear from Stanley Kubrick.

Stanley Kubrick's self-styled film school was located at 1600 Broadway, New York, New York. It was there that he learned film technique by asking technicians, salesmen, and craftspeople about the mechanics of filmmaking.

He spent a lot of time in Faith Hubley's cutting room, talking about his cinematic dreams and quizzing her about how films were made. Faith nurtured and encouraged the young film enthusiast by giving him lists of films to see. One day Kubrick asked Hubley to teach him how to match a 16mm work print to the original negative so he could prepare to cut the negative to make a print of a film. Kubrick was a quick study. "He was like a sponge," Faith Hubley remembers. Kubrick learned from the industry professionals he met in New York, voraciously watching every film he could, becoming a regular at the Museum of Modern Art's film program, and reading the small library of film books that was available at the time.

In 1953 Kubrick received a commission from the Seafarers International Union (SIU) to make an industrial film. In tone the project was an extension of the positive-spin material he had done for *Look* magazine. The assignment was to do a goodwill promotional film of the offices at the Atlantic and Gulf Coast District of the American Federation of Labor (AFL).

The thirty-minute film was written by Will Chasan and supervised by the staff of the *Seafarers Log,* the union's house organ. A self-contained Kubrick again photographed and directed the film, which was produced by Lester Cooper Productions in New York.

On casual viewing, *The Seafarers* has all the trademarks of a typical industrial film of the period. It opens with an on-screen narrator, Don Hollenbeck, reading from a script into the camera as he explains the function of the Seafarers and their union. During the fifties and sixties, thousands of these films were made as in-house training and promotional tools, often used as morale boosters for regional and national industry. The creators of such films were usually local production houses and independent film companies that specialized in corporate advertising.

Although these films served important social and business purposes, they rarely contributed greatly to the art of filmmaking. If *The Seafarers* had been directed by any of the hundreds of professionals working on these meat-and-potatoes films, it would probably be of little note to film history. But the short subject as directed contains the DNA to identify it as a Stanley Kubrick film.

The Seafarers was Kubrick's first color film, shot in June 1953. He would shoot four feature films in black and white before he had another opportunity to work in color, on *Spartacus*.

After a series of shots of ships in the harbor, Kubrick's camera goes into the headquarters of the New York City Atlantic and Gulf District of the union, home to the men who work at sea. A montage of machines is framed with Kubrick's exacting photojournalist eye and makes the point that machines serve man, a theme he would later confront head-on in *2001*. To show the cafeteria in action, Kubrick makes a continuous fifty-eight-second dolly shot tracking across the room and the food displayed. A cut produces the first example of nudity in a Stanley Kubrick film and shows the director's adolescent sense of sexuality. The screen is filled with a photograph of a young naked woman, a string of pearls draped above her breasts. The shot is there to entertain the hard-living sea-bound men who will be the main viewers of the in-house film and to arouse the perverse and devilish sense of humor tickling Kubrick. A full shot identifies the photograph as a nudie pinup calendar on the wall of the SIU barbershop, provided by Thorman, Baum & Co., Incorporated—sellers of fresh and frozen fruits and vegetables.

Though Kubrick was working on a shoestring budget and virtually alone, his cinematography is well executed and carefully composed. The color is warm, rich, and subdued, recalling the Kodachrome beauty of the fifties. Kubrick doesn't use the even, flat lighting often seen in industrials but models his light as he did in his *Look* magazine portfolio. Many shots employ a good use of contrast. A man works on a job chart in near silhouette. Kubrick's camera tours the Port-of-Call Bar and a gameroom where men play pocket billiards. Men playing cards are backlit. A room featuring artwork done by the members has two more discreet examples of the naked female torso rendered in pencil drawings and typical of work done by amateur artisans using art class models. Kubrick experiments with the grammar of film, utilizing dissolves to link the images and shooting a scene of a family receiving information about maternity benefits in a single take without cutaways. The tour continues to the Welfare Headquarters of Beefs & Dues and the office of the union newspaper—the *Seafarers Log*.

The Seafarers concludes with a dramatic scene saluting democracy in action during a union meeting. A speaker gives a fiery talk from the podium as a roomful of men listen and react. This sequence goes beyond the bland "show me, tell me" quality of the film up to this point. Kubrick approached the event in true documentary form, bringing realism to the conclusion in the tradition of Robert Flaherty and John Grierson. Kubrick frames the speaker right and left with union officials to his side. A questioner is centered in front of the speaker, with men in the audience to the questioner's right and left. The speaker builds to a crescendo, and Kubrick accelerates a montage of close-ups as the men react emotionally to him. As a director, Kubrick begins to express his talent in visual storytelling and the power of successive images in presenting a vision of a film. Intercutting the men and the speaker as the scene climaxes brings meaning to the apparently carefree and everyday events witnessed earlier. The skeleton of this dramatic interplay between a group of men in an audience and their presenter must have been buried in Kubrick's subconscious when he came up with a last-minute ending for *Paths of Glory*.

Gene D. Phillips uncovered *The Seafarers* for his 1975 book, *Stanley Kubrick: A Film Odyssey*. Phillips suggests that the overhead lighting and composition in the sequence where the men are shown in a grievance session with a union representative foreshadows the heist-planning sequence in *The Killing*. Kubrick may have been influenced by a similar sequence in John Huston's *The Asphalt Jungle* for both his short and his feature.

The Seafarers ends as we return to Don Hollenbeck for his closing remarks. The opening and closing titles feature rope letters and the SIU logo, which makes the film the official property of the Seafarers Union—but Stanley Kubrick was ready to create his own films, films that were beginning to emerge from his fertile mind.

CHAPTER 5

"It Took Stanley Kubrick, Is What It Took"

There have been no wasted people in my life. There's no time for waste if you're obsessed.

—Faith Hubley

ex·is·ten·tial·ism *n.* a philosophical theory emphasizing that man is responsible for his own actions and free to choose his development and destiny

—*Oxford American Dictionary*

Fear and desire are very close emotions.

—Bob Gaffney

More than three years before the ultimate March 31, 1953, re-lease of *Fear and Desire,* Stanley Kubrick walked into 369 Lex-ington Avenue, the New York offices of Richard de Rochemont, the younger brother of Louis de Rochemont, who created *The March of Time* series. At forty-six, Richard de Rochemont was just one year younger than Kubrick's father, Jacques. Kubrick was twenty-one, but he looked like a "mature eighteen" to the seasoned producer.

De Rochemont had occupied several floors of a building on Lexington

Avenue and Fifty-seventh Street. Dick de Rochemont had worked as a producer with his brother, Louis, on *The March of Time* series and took over as executive producer in 1943. Dick had had a colorful and varied career. He was a Harvard graduate who produced and directed documentaries. During World War II he was associated with General Charles De Gaulle and wrote reportage for *Life* magazine. As the leader behind the organization France Forever, de Rochemont was responsible for France's rallying around De Gaulle and against the Vichy government. De Rochemont was born in Massachusetts in 1903 and was highly decorated with honors in the country of his French Huguenot family. He went on to write two books with Waverly Root—*Eating in America,* about the history of food in the United States, and *Contemporary French Cooking.* "He was a *wonderful* man of great style and elegance," recalled Norman Lloyd, who worked with de Rochemont in television. "It just came to him like a great lord or aristocrat and yet he was so kind, sensitive, and understanding of people, he was just a wonderful man."

Kubrick handed de Rochemont a screenplay co-written by his high school friend Howard O. Sackler and asked him to read it. Kubrick described Sackler as a contemporary poet. De Rochemont interpreted that to mean that the twenty-year-old Sackler "was a poet, and a contemporary of Stanley's."

When Kubrick confidently departed the office, he left the impression on de Rochemont and his staff that they had just witnessed a "boy wonder producer," and his cocksure demeanor prompted one of Richard's associates to say, "That Stanley has a nerve."

De Rochemont read the screenplay (which would undergo many title changes) and described it as weighing "upwards of three pounds." He was impressed with this upstart named Stanley Kubrick.

"Dick was always interviewing people he thought were talented," remembers Dick's widow, Jane de Rochemont, who worked for *Life* magazine and as a photographic stylist for Irving Penn, Bert Stern, and others. "He thought Stanley had talent. Stanley looked very young and very skinny. Stanley felt quite a bit about himself, he was not exactly modest."

In the fifties there was virtually no New York independent film scene as we now know it, but Stanley Kubrick declared himself a New York independent filmmaker with his next move. In early 1951, at age twenty-two, with the short films behind him, Kubrick knew it was time to direct a feature-length film. He completely bypassed the conventional idea of going to Hollywood and decided instead to independently produce and direct his own film without traditional financial backing or a distribution deal. Kubrick was able to raise almost $10,000 from his friends, his father, and his uncle Martin Perveler, who would be credited as associate producer.

Perveler owned a string of drugstores in the Los Angeles area and by the mid-sixties, had acquired significant wealth. In addition to pharmacies, Perveler owned Bowling Romana, a bowling alley in Rome, Italy, a substantial stock portfolio, sizable real estate holdings in the San Gabriel–Santa Barbara area, a thirty-two-foot yacht, and a series of sports cars that included a Mercedes 190 SL, a Jaguar purchased in England and imported to the United States, a Porsche bought in Europe, and a Lamborghini.

Perveler had seen *Day of the Fight* and *Flying Padre* and was interested in investing in his nephew's first feature film. Perveler, clearly the entrepreneur, set the stipulation that Stanley Kubrick sign a contract guaranteeing that a sizable percentage be returned to the uncle for the term of his nephew's creative life.

Kubrick refused the deal, even though it meant putting his feature debut in jeopardy. He later told Alexander Singer that his uncle said, "Okay, that's the way you want it, you got it. I'm not going to put up money for one movie. I think you're going to be a big success over the years and I want a piece. I'm a businessman."

Kubrick said, "No" and departed for the Southern California airport to return to New York. Perveler followed Kubrick and caught up with his stalwart nephew as he was on the ramp to board the flight home. Stanley Kubrick, only in his early twenties, was already a steely businessman in a field filled with sharks. Perveler blinked, dropped his percentage clause, and promised to give his nephew a one-picture deal.

The subject Kubrick selected for his first feature was war, a theme he would return to throughout his career. Sackler and Kubrick's screenplay centered on four soldiers who were trapped behind enemy lines in an unnamed war.

Since he had left *Look* magazine, Kubrick had been committed to becoming a successful film director. At the time his only steady income was the $20 to $30 a week he made playing chess to comers in Washington Square Park. Always the strategist, during the day Kubrick would position his board under a street lamp so that as night fell his opponent had a hazy view of the board while the rays of the lamp dramatically illuminated Kubrick's view of the chess pieces.

On February 26, 1951, Stanley Kubrick signed an employment agreement with his uncle Martin Perveler for his first feature film. Kubrick formed Stanley Kubrick Productions and set out to become a one-man filmmaking unit to produce a project then known as *The Trap*.

A cold New York winter prevented Kubrick from using East Coast exterior settings, so the film was shot on location in the San Gabriel Mountains outside Los Angeles and at a river on the coast. The forest sequences were shot in Azusa, on the outskirts of Los Angeles. The West Coast location also suited his main backer, Uncle Martin, who could cast a watchful eye with the production in such close proximity.

For his cast Kubrick chose actor Frank Silvera, who had been in the Elia Kazan production of *Viva Zapata!*, starring Marlon Brando. Also in the cast was the twenty-year-old actor Paul Mazursky—who went on to become the bicoastal director of *An Unmarried Woman, Down and Out in Beverly Hills,* and *Moscow on the Hudson.* Rounding out the soldiers were Kenneth Harp and Steven Coit. For the part of a native girl captured by the soldiers Kubrick discovered Virginia Leith, a Cleveland woman who came to Hollywood to be a model at a fashion agency. Leith was not expecting to get into the movies when the young producer-director came upon her and told her she was going to be in his first feature film.

The bare-bones crew was made up of few more than the multi-hatted Stanley Kubrick. Dick de Rochemont referred to him fondly as "a one-man band." "The entire crew of *Fear and Desire* consisted of myself as director, lighting cameraman, operator, administrator, make-up man, wardrobe, hairdresser, prop man, unit chauffeur, et cetera," Kubrick told Alexander Walker, the author of *Stanley Kubrick Directs* and a friend. Kubrick's collegiate-looking friend Steve Hahn, an executive for Union Carbide who was knowledgeable about electricity, was credited as assistant director. Bob Dierks, a studio assistant from *Look,* functioned as a grip, helping to set up and break down equipment.

Kubrick's wife, Toba, used her secretarial skills to deal with paperwork and minor administration. Toba Metz wore dark clothing, her brunette hair long with short bangs cut over sharply drawn eyebrows. Her intense, brooding looks were typical of the native women who populated the clubs and coffeehouses of Greenwich Village where she and Stanley Kubrick relocated after they married. Toba could easily be described as a beat generation chick. She also had a sweetness retained from her sheltered childhood in a middle-class Bronx Jewish neighborhood.

Mexican laborers were employed to carry the equipment, their weathered faces reminiscent of characters in an early Luis Buñuel film. The man who would go on to direct the massive crews of *Spartacus* and *2001* set off with only a lucky thirteen.

Kubrick photographed the film himself for $9,000 without sync sound and in 35mm black and white with a Mitchell camera that he rented for

$25 a day. The plan was to add the soundtrack later during postproduction to save the cost of shooting with sync sound.

"The first time I used a Mitchell camera was on *Fear and Desire,*" Kubrick told Joseph Gelmis. "I went to the Camera Equipment Company, at 1600 Broadway, and the owner, Bert Zucker, spent a Saturday morning showing me how to load and operate it. So that was the extent of my formal training in movie camera technique. Bert Zucker, who has subsequently been killed in an airline crash, was a young man, in his early thirties, and he was very sympathetic. Anyway, it was a sensible thing for them to do. I was paying for the equipment."

Kubrick, still under the influence of his *Look* colleagues, sported a neatly cut and combed haircut, casually parted on the side, the sort inspired by European stylists and worn by New York professionals. He wore a dark sport coat, jeans, a white T-shirt under a white dress shirt without a tie, and a light meter around his neck. His intense photographer's eyes always revealed a young man immersed in deep thought.

Kubrick had a near catastrophe during production. To produce fog for a scene, he used a California crop sprayer. The insecticide mist was convincing in creating the look of a fog on camera, but it had the unwelcome side effect of nearly asphyxiating the cast and the crew.

Finishing the eight-reel film became a more costly undertaking than the careful director had planned for. Kubrick edited the feature himself and learned he had made a mistake in deciding to add the entire soundtrack of dialogue, effects, and music after shooting. The post-synchronization process of dubbing in all of the dialogue was time-consuming and costly, adding an additional $20,000 to $30,000 to the final budget, which was estimated at around $40,000.

The New York City film community was good to Kubrick. Alan Friedman of Deluxe Laboratories extended him a modest credit during the production of the film.

For musical scoring, the lofty intentions of the story created by Kubrick and Sackler were put onto the shoulders of twenty-four-year-old composer Gerald Fried, who wrote the music for *Day of the Fight.* Fried had gotten a few scoring jobs from Pathé after writing the music for the short. The music for *Fear and Desire* was a big challenge. "The music was supposed to mourn the world's innocence," Fried explained. "Fear and desire are the two dominant forces of our species. This movie was supposed to say everything. There were going to be no more movies after this. So I had to be sophisticated, profound yet empathic with the fate of us poor human beings. There were all these magnificent parables, killing a general and the name of the dog was Proteus. I mean, how many symbols can you get? So it had to be important, profound, meaningful, touching, despairing but yet triumphant. I thought it was pretty good at the time."

As with *Day of the Fight,* the music was recorded at RCA Studios in New York. There were twenty-three musicians. The final mix was done by Al Gramaglia, one of New York City's top re-recording film mixers.

Little film music was being composed and recorded on the East Coast at the time. Fried and Kubrick were guided by what they heard in other movies. This was on-the-job training in filmmaking. When *Fear and Desire* was finally released, Walter Winchell mentioned the music in his influential column.

On August 12, 1951, working out of his apartment at 37 West Sixteenth Street, Kubrick created the document "Kubrick—Financial Resume of Motion Picture," which detailed the costs for *Fear and Desire* to date—the film was about a month away from being mixed. The statement was sent to Richard de Rochemont's Vavin, Inc., office. At this point $29,000 had been spent on the first feature. There were no deferred bills to labs and vendors, but $9,500 in outstanding deferments to actors and crew were due and $5,000 was necessary to complete postproduction. This brought the total cost of *Fear and Desire* to $53,500. Twenty-one percent of the film was owned by investors and Kubrick owned 39.5 percent of the remaining 79 percent. As the resume was created, the sound effects, optical, and final mix remained to be completed.

Kubrick reported that the film was shot in five weeks at a cost of $5,000. The two-man camera crew was paid at $1,000 per week for a total of $2,500. The four grips were paid $500 a week for a total of $1,500, and the remainder of the crew was paid $25 a week at a cost of $1,000. This figure comprised the union settlement costs, which totaled $10,000.

The completion costs of $5,000 were made up of: editor's salary of $1,200, cutting room rental at $67 a week for a total of $400, a total of $900 to RCA Studios for the mix at $75 per hour. RCA raw stock costs for the mix totaled $300, sound effects costs were $500, opticals $250, screening to determine sync $150, a lab bill $700, and a miscellaneous figure of $600.

On August 31, de Rochemont began to deal with Local 802 of the American Federation of Musicians, who wanted to settle the outstanding payment due the union for the recording of the musical score.

Writing Al Knopf, the union's representative and a member of the executive board, de Rochemont sent a check for $500 in the name of

Vavin, Inc., for the Martin Perveler–Stanley Kubrick Production. De
Rochemont requested a receipt to indicate that the check was to be
applied to the outstanding balance and confirming a verbal promise to
delay final payment until September 18 and not take action against the
production.

On the same day, de Rochemont telegrammed Kubrick, who was at
the Palmer House in Chicago, advising him that he had placated the
musicians union. On September 4, de Rochemont received the receipt
from the musicians union and on the next day a letter arrived from Al
Knopf acknowledging the payment applied to the account of the Gerald
Fried Orchestra for the Martin Perveler–Stanley Kubrick production.
The letter stated the balance due as $1,039.36. It was due on or before
September 18 or the producers would be placed on the national unfair
list.

On September 19, Knopf wrote de Rochemont granting the production another extension of payment of the balance to October 2.

During this period Richard de Rochemont was in the process of producing a television series of five episodes on the life of Abraham Lincoln.
The shows were for the *Omnibus* series, were created by the TV Radio
Workshop of the Ford Foundation, and were written by James Agee and
directed by Norman Lloyd. The executive producer was Robert Saudek.

Lloyd had begun his prestigious career in the theater, television and
film in 1932. He had a strong background on stage as an actor in productions directed by Eva Le Gallienne, Joseph Losey, Elia Kazan, and Orson Welles. As a member of the Mercury Theater, he appeared in
Welles's legendary production of *Julius Caesar* and worked as an actor in
Hitchcock's *Saboteur* and *Spellbound, The Southerner* directed by Jean
Renoir, *A Walk in the Sun* directed by Lewis Milestone and *A Letter to
Evie* directed by Jules Dassin. In 1952 Lloyd began his work as a director at the La Jolla Playhouse and in television.

"I was brought East to direct these five episodes by James Agee on
Abraham Lincoln, and when I got to New York we began to look over
what had to be done at the beginning of the shooting," recalled Norman
Lloyd, who went on to direct and produce *Alfred Hitchcock Presents,*
star in TV's *St. Elsewhere,* and play roles in Martin Scorsese's *The Age of
Innocence* and *Dead Poets Society,* directed by Peter Weir. "The first
episode was going to be shot in New York at the Fox Studios over on
Tenth Avenue and Fifty-seventh Street and there was second-unit work
to be done for where Lincoln was born in Hodgenville, Kentucky. So
after I shot the first episode in New York it required my going out to
New Salem, Illinois, where Lincoln had lived as a young man and had

done a lot of his growing up. We were going to shoot in the New Salem Village that had been reconstructed and on the banks of the Sangamon River. It was clear that I could not be in both New Salem, Illinois, and Hodgenville, Kentucky, at the same time, so Dick de Rochemont said to me that the best idea would be to have a second unit, to which I agreed. He suggested that I look at the picture of a young still photographer whom he knew who worked for *Look* magazine. He felt that this young man could handle it, but he would not hire him unless I, as the director on the piece, approved of it. So I said, 'Fine.' He suggested that I look at this picture, *Fear and Desire*. So I looked at it and sitting rather darkly in the back of the projection room was twenty-three-year-old Stanley Kubrick. I ran the picture, which I thought was beautifully shot. It had some interesting scenes, a very good look, and a silly script in blank verse. The picture had unquestionable cinematic qualities, and it seemed that Kubrick was a very good choice. De Rochemont was not present at that running. I didn't talk to Stanley because I wanted first to talk to de Rochemont and tell him, 'Yes, fine, hire him.' I didn't want any complication of anything I might have said. I thought, 'Well, you better keep your mouth shut until a deal is made.' Being raised in Hollywood, one instinctively did that. I do recall walking up the aisle and seeing Stanley sort of hunched down, looking rather dark. Later I said to de Rochemont, 'Hire the guy.' "

The Lincoln series was photographed by Marcel Rebiere, a documentary cameraman from France who had worked on *The March of Time*. "Rebiere went down to Hodgenville with Kubrick and Marian Seldes, who was playing Lincoln's mother, Nancy Hanks, and Crahan Denton, who played Lincoln's father, Tom, to shoot a reconstruction of the Lincoln cabin. Apparently there were certain difficulties that Kubrick and Rebiere had between them," Norman Lloyd recalled. "I never could pinpoint what it was, but Rebiere said one thing about Kubrick when he came back: 'He shoots everything like it's through a Rolleiflex.'

"Kubrick shot silent material in Hodgenville, images of work at the cabin, slaves coming through in the wagon, and the family sitting outside the cabin at dusk—all beautifully shot. They brought a lovely flavor to the piece, a lovely ambience, and you saw where this boy came from. He was also down there because he had to cast the little boy Lincoln and Lincoln's older sister, Sarah. He took a very interesting angle in the cabin, he took it from up an attic, so to speak, and shot down so you saw the activity happening in this little cabin from a high shot. He shot an exterior of the cabin and the well. There was a lovely shot of the slaves in a horse and wagon going off into the distance that was very well done and a pastoral shot of the family sitting in front of the cabin at dusk. These were all good shots. Everything was used."

Kubrick was staying at the Kirk Cottages in Hodgenville, Kentucky. De Rochemont wrote Kubrick a letter of agreement to be used to engage children to appear in the production. He also sent a list of the lighting and electrical equipment being brought to the location shoot. Kubrick's experience in cinematography on the three shorts and the feature gave him an understanding of the detailed list, which included McAlisters, broads, inky-dinkies, photofloods, gobos, and reflectors.

On September 30, de Rochemont again wrote Kubrick in Kentucky, sending him a clip of a scene of the Knob Creek log cabin, which was reconstructed and shot at the Movietone Studio. Kubrick would use the clip to determine the angle from which to make his second-unit dolly shot into the window. Kubrick was also sent a still of the cabin used in the death of Nancy Hanks and blankets and other props to be used for the second-unit work. The photo determined what the bed and cabin walls should look like so the location would match the studio work. Bearskin rugs were rented and shipped to Kentucky to dress the set. The first episode of the series had been costly, so de Rochemont asked and trusted Kubrick to keep costs down and give him a full accounting.

To cast local children for Lincoln as a boy and his sister, Sarah, Kubrick searched the school in Hodgenville, Kentucky. "A couple of people came into the classroom and said they were picking out some people for a play, it didn't dawn on me that it was a movie," recalls Alice Brewer Brown, who met Stanley Kubrick when he entered her classroom. "I had a certain dress on that day that my mother had made and my hair was long. Later I found out the main reason why they picked me was because my hair was so long. I still have the dress to this day, I call it a lucky dress. I was very poor. We didn't have as much staying out on the farm as a lot of people in town had, so I was in the right place at the right time.

"Every one of them, Stanley, Marian Seldes, were very nice. A lot of times they wouldn't even eat in town at the hotels, they would come out there and eat out on the farm with us. They'd sit at the dining room table and just eat and set around. They were very, very nice people. They treated you nice. They had more class, more money. They didn't treat the people that was from the country any different. In fact they acted more country than town."

While Kubrick was directing the second-unit material, Lloyd was casting Joanne Woodward, Jack Warden, and other actors for the series. Later, Marian Seldes sent Norman Lloyd newspaper clippings of interviews that Kubrick had given local newspapers. "In these interviews you got the impression that he was directing the whole Lincoln series, all five shows," recalled Lloyd. "I read this and I must say I was amused because I said, 'There is no question in my mind that Stanley Kubrick is going to be a very big man in pictures because with this ego nothing will stop him,' and I was right.

"So he shoots all of this material, it's very good and we use all of it. Stanley comes out to New Salem, Illinois, and he offered to stay and help me. I said, 'Well, Stanley, I don't think so.' Then he watched me shoot one scene and said to me, 'You've got a lot of wasted footage in that shot. You don't need that long a pan.' And I said, 'Well, okay, but I'm going to leave it.' So that's one reason I knew he couldn't help me because it would always be a conflict of how the shots should be. He was starting as a motion picture director and he was hungry—that was great. That was it and I said, 'No, there's no reason for you to stay, Stanley.' Of course I had read those clippings by that time. He went back East and the rest is history.

"Stanley was a very dark, sort of a glowering type who was very serious. I would say I couldn't see any gleamings of humor. Not that I had spent that much time with him, but we had spent a little time."

The Lincoln assignment facilitated by de Rochemont gave Kubrick a financial boost during lean times.

After completing postproduction on *Fear and Desire,* Kubrick embarked on finding a way to have the film shown. The limited art house appeal made it difficult to sell. The film's existential nature and lack of B-movie-genre elements made it unattractive to distributors. Kubrick approached all of the major studios who turned it down out of hand.

Kubrick had backed off from the title *The Trap* for his first feature when de Rochemont wrote him telling him there were previous films with the same title. One was made in 1918 by Peerless World, two by Universal in 1919 and 1922, and the most recent released by Monogram in 1947. De Rochemont also supplied variants of the title, including *Trapped,* which were used to help guide Kubrick in finding a new title.

By June 1952, Kubrick was still negotiating for the release of his first feature. He told the *New York Times* that he had a few stories in mind that he would like to film, but, "There's no point in talking about my next picture until we see how *Shape of Fear* does both critically and financially." The new title was provocative but not to last.

Also in June, Kubrick got a strong endorsement from Mark Van Doren, the noted Columbia professor whose class Kubrick had audited several years earlier. Writing from Falls Village, Connecticut, Van Doren praised the director and his independent feature film. "*Shape of Fear* is a brilliant and unforgettable film using the simplest materials toward the most profound and surprising result—a fable that has the feeling of truth, a fairy tale that belongs to this world after all. The invention is delightfully free and many of the devices employed have a freshness we too often miss in current movies; but everything contributes to a total effect which is both serious and original, and to a suspense which nothing ever breaks. The incident of the girl bound to a tree will make movie history once it is seen; it is at once beautiful, terrifying and weird; nothing like it has ever been done in a film before, and it alone guarantees that the future of Stanley Kubrick is worth watching for those who want to discover high talent at the moment it appears."

On January 28, 1953, Martin Perveler and Stanley Kubrick signed an agreement with Richard de Rochemont to complete production on *Fear and Desire*. The agreement lists Perveler as the owner of the production with co-authors Howard O. Sackler and Stanley Kubrick. In the agreement, Perveler consented to repay the $500 to de Rochemont and give up first receipts from the sale or distribution of the film along with the other investors. De Rochemont was also to get 2 percent of Stanley Kubrick's share of the film.

Eventually Kubrick was discovered by motion picture distributor and entrepreneur Joseph Burstyn. Burstyn became enamored of the young director, proclaiming to many in the tight-knit New York film scene in his one-of-a-kind rendition of a Yiddish-Polish accent, "He's a genius, he's a genius." After one screening of *Fear and Desire*, Burstyn quickly made up his mind, calling the film, "an American art picture without any artiness."

Burstyn was a Polish Jew born in 1901. After emigrating to the United States in 1921, he worked in the jewelry business as a diamond polisher and then as a press agent and stage manager for the Yiddish theater in New York City. Under five feet tall and with a hunched back, Burstyn was a brilliant businessman with the gift to promote. His work as a motion picture distributor began in Chicago. In 1936 he formed a company with former Paramount publicity director Arthur Mayer, who sold out to Burstyn in 1949.

When he began to make a profit buying and selling movies, Burstyn moved to New York and set up an office at 113 West Forty-second Street. He ruled his business with a smile and an iron hand. Burstyn was a distributor and exhibitor responsible for creating the idea of art house cinema in the United States by distributing important foreign films such as Rossellini's *Rome, Open City*, *The Miracle*, and *Paisan*, De Sica's *The*

Bicycle Thief, and Renoir's *A Day in the Country.* Burstyn got the films shown in art theaters and fought hard against the dangers of censorship when the Catholic Church picketed and threatened to have many of them banned. Burstyn's legendary fight to have the American public view *The Miracle,* which had been given a Condemned rating by the Catholic Legion of Decency and was suppressed by the New York State Board of Regents, went all the way to the Supreme Court, where he eventually was victorious.

When he met the young Kubrick, Burstyn was in his early fifties, frail, with a shock of white hair, but sporting his ever-determined smile and dictatorial will. Joseph Burstyn took his juvenile genius under his wing and signed on as distributor of the director's pilot feature effort. He released the film with the provocative and sexy title *Fear and Desire.*

On February 25, 1953, Richard de Rochemont sent Stanley Kubrick a four-page, double-spaced essay about the director and his career. The piece was intended for publicity use and was written with admiration for the young independent filmmaker. De Rochemont requested only that neither Burstyn nor Kubrick change any of his words without permission. Coming from the distinguished producer of *The March of Time* and current president of Vavin, Inc., this endorsement, like Mark Van Doren's, was generous and essential in getting the word out on the young director, who was flying without a studio net.

De Rochemont was Kubrick's benefactor, boss, and father figure. Kubrick once told Dick's wife, Jane, "You know we're really Dick's children."

Fear and Desire received a Legion of Decency certificate on April 23, 1953. The Legion granted a class B classification, citing a suggestive scene, referring to the sequence when a soldier physically expresses sexual feelings to a tied-up woman who has been captured.

Fear and Desire was previewed in New York on March 26, 1953. *Variety* called it "a literate, unhackneyed war drama, outstanding for its fresh camera treatment and poetic dialogue."

The film ran at the Guild Theater in New York. The theater, located on Fiftieth Street in Rockefeller Center, specialized in showcasing foreign and art films. During its run Alexander Singer went to see his friend's first feature. "I was a snotty kid in terms of arrogance. I wanted to make films like the greatest things ever done, and if this wasn't the greatest, then it was of little importance. I gave it short shrift except I was aware of what an astonishing performance this had been from Kubrick. This was a polished work as a piece of professional filmmaking."

It was the marquee's sidebars outside the Guild Theater that gave Alexander Singer a glimpse into future expectations from Stanley Kubrick. "Out front there were still photographs, they were Stanley's still photographs," Singer remembers. "They were without question the best photographic record of a picture ever put on the front of a movie house. This was to me a mark of what this guy would do, that everything he touched would be special. There would be something about the way he did everything that would be outstanding. I didn't care whether other people recognized it or could put a quantification on it. I knew what it was and I knew how remarkable it was. I knew what it took to do that and that's what it took—it took Stanley Kubrick, is what it took."

Kubrick's tender age and giant ambition gained the attention of critics. Wallace Markfield writing in *The New Leader* called Kubrick, "a highly gifted beginner" who "takes delight in inch-by-inch close-ups and photographic excursions into underlighted forests that reveal lacey patterns of vegetation, leaf and splatters of sun." Markfield went on to chastise the young Kubrick for his symbolic excess and juvenilia themes but recommended the film to his intellectual, cinematic-minded readers.

Critic and screenwriter James Agee, who had scripted the *Mr. Lincoln* series, saw the film and had a drink with the young director at a Sixth Avenue bar in Greenwich Village. "There are too many good things in the film to call it arty," the dean of American film criticism and screenwriter of *The Night of the Hunter* and *The African Queen* told the eager novice.

Fear and Desire is the story of four soldiers: Mac (Frank Silvera), Corby (Kenneth Harp), Fletcher (Steve Coit), and Sidney (played by Paul Mazursky).

Kubrick and Sackler begin the film with an existential message directly delivered by the never-seen narrator, spoken by David Allen. "There is a war in this forest. Not a war that has been fought, nor one that will be, but any war. And the enemies that struggle here do not exist unless we call them into being. For all of them, and all that happens now is outside history. Only the unchanging shapes of fear and doubt and death are from our world. These soldiers that you see keep our language and our time, but have no other country but the mind."

The soldiers' plane has been shot down, stranding them in a forest several miles behind enemy lines—they are surrounded by the enemy, they have one revolver and no food. Lt. Corby convinces the men to head for a nearby river, where they can build a raft and float to safety.

At night they construct a raft but abandon the plan when they learn there is an enemy command post on the other side of the river. A plane spots them, forcing them back into the woods.

Later they overtake three enemy soldiers in a shack and acquire food and guns. The next day they return to the raft where they run into a girl (Virginia Leith), whom they hold hostage by tying to a tree. The girl is unable to communicate with them. Sidney is left alone with the young woman and has an emotional breakdown.

The other three men return to the raft, where they spot a general and his aides at the command post. Mac decides to kill the general.

Sidney loses touch with reality and begins to act out the story of Shakespeare's *The Tempest*. Mac tries to talk to Corby about the general, but Corby orders him back to Sidney, while he and Fletcher begin to camouflage the raft. Sidney gives the girl water and begins to caress and kiss her. He unties the woman, who tries to run away. Sidney shoots her and runs off into the forest in madness. Mac sees this and tells the others when they return.

At nightfall, Mac convinces Corby and Fletcher to kill the general. They plan to take the raft and draw the sentries from the post with gunfire while Corby and Fletcher execute the general. They will use the general's plane to escape.

Through his field glasses Corby sights the general, who is drunk, and his aide. The general and the aide are played by Kenneth Harp and Steve Coit—the same actors portraying Corby and Fletcher, who are coming to kill them. Ironically, Steve Coit, with his intense eyes and arched eyebrows, bears a strong resemblance to Stanley Kubrick.

Mac begins to shoot and the sentries run toward the gunfire. Fletcher shoots the general and his aide. The general crawls toward the door.

Mac is badly wounded by the sentries. The general gets through the front door. Corby fires, then recognizes his own face in that of the dead general. Fletcher and Corby run for the plane. Mac, fatally wounded, floats down the river. Sidney approaches him, now quite insane.

Corby and Fletcher, safe at their base, wait for the raft. Corby speaks of having escaped but is unable to return to himself. Fletcher feels free but no longer has plans or desires.

They hear singing as the raft floats into view. Mac is dead. Sidney is on all fours staring into the swirling fog, singing incoherently. The four men are together again.

In a letter written to Joseph Burstyn and printed in Norman Kagan's *The Cinema of Stanley Kubrick,* Kubrick attempted to explain the film to the distributor, to whom he looked as another father figure. "Its structure: allegorical. Its conception: poetic. A drama of 'man' lost in a hostile

world—deprived of material and spiritual foundations—seeking his way
to an understanding of himself, and of life around him. He is further
imperiled on his Odyssey by an unseen but deadly enemy that surrounds
him; but an enemy who, upon scrutiny, seems to be almost shaped from
the same mold. . . . It will, probably, mean many things to different
people, and it ought to be."

Fear and Desire premiered on March 31, 1953, and had booking dates
in California, Chicago, Detroit, and Philadelphia. On August 7, the film
came back to New York for an engagement at the Rialto Theater, where
it was sold as a sexploitation picture.

Soon after its release *Fear and Desire* dropped from sight. The film
went unseen for almost forty years. Stanley Kubrick's first feature film
was legend. Few had seen it, but many had expectations that it could
provide a glimpse into Kubrick's psyche. Cultists and Kubrick fanatics
saw it as a cinematic equivalent of the Rosetta Stone or the Shroud of
Turin. Prints of the film were not available for public screening.

The mistake to post-dub the entire soundtrack, a technique later used
almost exclusively by Federico Fellini, contributed to the film's failure to
make its money back for the investors.

Over the years Kubrick has not looked back on *Fear and Desire* with
much fondness, but he characterized it as a learning experience and
stated succinctly to Joanne Stang of the *New York Times,* "Pain is a good
teacher." He told Alexander Walker, "The ideas we wanted to put across
were good, but we didn't have the experience to embody them dramatically. It was little more than a thirty-five-millimeter version of what a
class of film students would do in sixteen millimeter.

"Particularly in those days, before the advent of film schools, Nagras,
and lightweight portable equipment, it was very important to have this
experience and to see with what little facilities and personnel one could
actually make a film. Today, I think that if someone stood around watching even a smallish film unit, he would get the impression of vast technical and logistical magnitude. He would probably be intimidated by this
and assume that something close to this was necessary in order to
achieve more or less professional results. This experience and the one
that followed with *Killer's Kiss,* which was on a slightly more cushy basis,
freed me from my concern again about the technical or logistical aspects
of filmmaking."

"I just didn't have enough experience to know the proper and economical approach," Kubrick told Joseph Gelmis. *"Fear and Desire*
played the art house circuits and some of the reviews were amazingly

good, but it's not a film I remember with any pride, except for the fact it was finished."

The film was never truly lost—a single print was at the George Eastman House in Rochester, New York.

In 1991 *Fear and Desire* played the Telluride Film Festival in Colorado, where it was highly anticipated but met with mixed reaction. In January 1994 the enterprising Film Forum in New York ran the film on a double bill with Kubrick's second film, *Killer's Kiss*, under the banner "The Young Stanley Kubrick."

Kubrick was unavailable for comment about the resurfacing of his first feature film but asked his longtime distributor, Warner Bros., to release a statement to the press, "He considers it nothing more than a 'bumbling, amateur film exercise,' written by a failed poet, crewed by a few friends, and 'a completely inept oddity, boring and pretentious.' "

Fear and Desire may not be *Citizen Kane* or even *Blood Simple*, the striking 1984 debut film by the Coen brothers, but it clearly reveals the raw beginnings of a major film talent. Thematically Kubrick is at work with the big theses he will tackle throughout his career: war and the cruel nature of man. Even in his early twenties Kubrick's work reveals that his vision is bleak and cold. Visually, considering the limited tools available on the shoestring project, *Fear and Desire* has remarkably textured cinematography tinged with the film noir style and dipped in absurdism. Here, Kubrick was more influenced by the literary existential thought of Albert Camus and Jean Paul Sartre than by the myriad Hollywood movies he absorbed. He emerged from his first effort as a visual director with a specific and grim view of his world.

CHAPTER 6

Guerrilla
Filmmaking

Black and white are colors. I could see more in the dark than I could in color. I could see in the dark.

—John Alton

Many people have asked me how it was working in film noir. As far as I know nobody had put a name to it at that time. I think after a great collection on the screen of film noir pictures, that is the name somebody decided to call them. I just thought it was interesting photography and it was a job.

—Marie Windsor

Stanley Kubrick's second wife, Ruth Sobotka, was a ballet dancer. She was born in Vienna in 1925, and at age fourteen emigrated to America with her mother, Gisela, and her father, a preeminent architect and interior designer, Walter Sobotka. Ruth studied at the American School of Ballet and danced with the New York City Ballet.

In 1950 David Vaughan, choreographer of *Killer's Kiss*, traveled from London to New York to study at the American School of Ballet. In the summer of 1951 Ruth Sobotka moved to 222 East Tenth Street in the East Village. She was looking for someone to share the apartment and asked David to be her roommate. The East Village neighborhood was quiet and populated by Ukrainians. "Ruth tried very hard to make that apartment into a very nice place," recalls David Vaughan, currently archivist for the Merce Cunningham Dance Company. "She certainly worked on the garden."

When Ruth met Stanley Kubrick, he was still married to Toba Metz. Sobotka was three years older than Kubrick. Sobotka and Kubrick soon became a permanent item, and David Vaughan moved out of the small apartment so Stanley could move in with Ruth. The three became good friends. "We used to go to the movies all the time because Stanley used to go to *every* movie. We used to go to terrible double features on Forty-second Street simply because Stanley wanted to see everything that was being put out. He was only interested in the way the film was made visually. If the actors started to talk too much, he would start reading his paper by whatever light he could until they stopped talking.

"He was *obsessed* with going to see every film and very critical of films. At the same time he would just see everything, that was all he really wanted to do. We would not only go to terrible films on Forty-second Street, we would go to important movies as well. We went to the Museum of Modern Art to see a special screening of Bresson's *Diary of a Country Priest*, which Stanley thought was wonderful.

"Ruth used to call Stanley 'Cupcake,' that was the pet name he was known by in the ballet company at the time when Ruth started her affair with him. Stanley used to go to performances to see her, and he hung out with the dancers at their parties.

"Stanley was very sardonic, extremely intelligent. He was certainly intense. He said very cutting things about other people. He didn't have a warm sense of humor, but quite a cruel sense of humor. I can never say that Stanley was a tremendously warm person, and I never found his films to be tremendously warm in that sense. He wasn't exactly a stylish dresser. He looked like somebody from a Jewish family in the Bronx. Ruth was an extremely stylish person. She used to make her own clothes a lot. It's a wonder she didn't make things for Stanley or take him shopping.

"I had the feeling Stanley really had a paranoia about the possibility of New York being obliterated by an atomic bomb. I remember at one point he said he wanted to go live in Australia because that was the place least likely to be the victim of an atomic bomb attack.

"Stanley was a great chess player. He had extreme concentration and a determination to win. Stanley would go play on Forty-second Street, Ruth and I would meet him there and then go to a movie. Typically, Ruth, of course, immediately learned to play chess just as she started to learn the technique of film editing. Stanley started teaching both of us editing one day. It didn't go anywhere because it wasn't something I was particularly talented for. Ruth really wanted to be his collaborator, not just his girlfriend or wife.

"In some ways Ruth was in tune with an aspect of Stanley's personality. She was the kind of person that anything she undertook she would become the best at it. There was a time after the ballet company where she was trying to become an actress. So she worked as a waitress in the Limelight, a coffeehouse in the West Village. Whichever waitress sold the most pastries would get a bonus, so Ruth got that bonus. She was going to be the best waitress, she would do it one hundred percent."

Valda Setterfield, who shared the Village apartment with Ruth Sobotka after her marriage to Kubrick broke up, remembers her first image of Ruth as that of an elegant and captivating woman. "She was wearing a ravishing bathrobe, which was red and full-length with a fur collar. She looked like something out of *Anna Karenina*," recalls Setterfield, a dancer and actress who was preparing for Woody Allen's *Fall Project 1995* and appeared in *Mighty Aphrodite*. "She was incredibly beautiful, with a very high forehead and a very mobile, articulate face. She had a musical voice that was light and lively and that gave it energy. She was interested in everything and was always wide open to the occasion and never tempered by any kind of rules or form."

Even as Kubrick was ending his relationship with Toba Metz and beginning another with Ruth Sobotka, his primary focus was his career. It was now 1954, and encouraged by the critical attention he received for *Fear and Desire*, Kubrick pressed ahead with self-determination to produce a second feature film.

The project had its genesis in 1953 while *Fear and Desire* was still playing at the Guild Theater. Kubrick started to string together a series of action scenes concerning a down-and-out boxer, which he planned to flesh out later when he wrote the screenplay.

Boxing was a profession he understood. His *Look* photo stories on Walter Cartier and Rocky Graziano and the making of *Day of the Fight* had taken him into the world of the prizefighter. The boxer was a key figure in the crime movies Kubrick had seen and was attracted to. The bleak view of life that surrounded the existentialist figure of a man fighting for his life was a perfect subject for a feature film. The formulaic doomed romance of a film noir and New York's underbelly would tie the film together.

For the financing Kubrick again approached friends and relatives.

Fear and Desire didn't make its money back, so he borrowed from different friends and relatives this time. The principal capital for the $40,000 budget came from Morris Bousel, a Bronx pharmacist. Kubrick gave Bousel a shared producer credit, abandoning alphabetical protocol and listing the name Stanley Kubrick first.

On April 22, 1954, Kubrick wrote a personal letter to Richard de Rochemont from Room 510 at 1600 Broadway, where he had set up his new production company, Minotaur Productions, Inc., to produce his second feature. Writing on Minotaur's stationery, Kubrick wanted de Rochemont to know the status of the producer's investment in *Fear and Desire*. Kubrick told de Rochemont that upon reflection he had come to the undeniable conclusion that the producer's investment in *Fear and Desire* should have been a loan because Kubrick could not repay the money in the foreseeable future, since the film was doing poorly at the box office. He closed with an assurance that he would repay him as soon as possible. Kubrick sent his benefactor good wishes and signed the handwritten note, "Stan Kubrick."

On April 28, de Rochemont wrote back to Kubrick at the apartment in the East Village where he lived with Ruth Sobotka. The producer thanked Kubrick for his note and sent assurances that he would "go along with whatever seems fair to you." De Rochemont expressed interest in Kubrick's second feature and requested an invitation to screen it when the film was completed.

For the screenplay, Kubrick again worked with Howard O. Sackler, but this time Sackler was not to receive screen credit. The opening credits read only "Story by Stanley Kubrick." The original story about a New York boxer developed by Kubrick and Sackler was called *Kiss Me, Kill Me*.

Norman Lloyd, the director of the Lincoln series, was directing at the La Jolla Playhouse in California, a theater founded by Gregory Peck, Dorothy McGuire, Joseph Cotten, Jennifer Jones, and Mel Ferrer, all of whom were under contract to David O. Selznick, when he was told he had a call from New York. "Stanley is on the phone. He's doing a picture about taxi dancers called *The Nymph and the Maniac* and would I come east and be in it," Lloyd recalled. "So I said, 'Well, Stanley, at the moment, I'm directing, when do you intend to do this?' He gave me the dates. Then I had a thought about something. I said, 'Stanley, is this a union picture?' and he said, 'No, no.' I said, 'Well, I can't do a non-union picture, I'm in the Screen Actors Guild,' and he said, 'Well, Frank Silvera's going to do it, he doesn't give a damn.' I was a great admirer of Frank Silvera's. I think he was one of the best actors in the business, but at that time Frank was breaking any rule he could break. So I said, 'Stanley, I just can't do this.' "

Production began in 1954 on location in New York City. Alexander Singer was on the set as the unit still photographer. Kubrick worked on the city streets, guerrilla-filmmaking style. Scenes of the main characters in their tenement apartment were shot in a small studio. All the camera equipment, laboratory, editing, and dubbing costs were arranged on a deferred-payment basis. The actors worked for a modicum, including Frank Silvera, who had appeared in Kubrick's first opus, *Fear and Desire.* Kubrick shot the film in twelve to fourteen weeks, a long schedule for a low-budget production. "Everything we did cost so little that there was no pressure on us—an advantage I was never to encounter again," Kubrick told Alexander Walker. Photography and postproduction were completed over a period of ten months. Not wanting to replicate the post-sync-sound fiasco of *Fear and Desire,* Kubrick set out to shoot the film in sync-sound. In the end, he was again forced to post-sync all of the dialogue and effects.

Soundman Nat Boxer was hired by Kubrick to record production sound for *Killer's Kiss,* but the job came to an abrupt end. "We were in some loft in New York's Greenwich Village, around Fourth Street, and he was lighting the back room for the first scene," Boxer told *Filmmakers Newsletter* in a 1976 interview. "He wouldn't let us in there, and then he finally did. It was very handsomely lit, but when we went in and placed the microphone where we normally would, there must have been seventeen shadows in the picture. What do still photographers know about the problems of a movie? Well, he looked at the set and said, 'Is that the way you do it? You mean you're going to put the microphone *there?* But that's impossible.' 'But that's the way we do it,' I said. And then the actor started moving and all the shadows started moving and Kubrick yelled, 'Cut! You don't make a movie that way. You guys are all fired!' Then he brought in a Webcor, a little school audiovisual tape recorder, and looped the whole picture because he didn't know how to light yet. On his next picture, *The Killing* with Sterling Hayden, he hired a professional lighting man, and it must have been a real education."

Kubrick went on to photograph the film himself in 35mm black and white using Mitchell and Eclair cameras. He had photographed *Fear and Desire* with little assistance, but on his second feature he did have his first experience working with a camera operator.

While shooting principal photography, Kubrick met Max Glenn at Titra Films, a company that did subtitles for foreign films and was located at 1600 Broadway, the local film haunt where Kubrick gathered much of his technical information. Glenn was a cinematographer who was a member of the New York cameramen's Local 644.

"I worked for Titra for a while and so I met Stanley," explained the seventy-seven-year-old Glenn from the projection booth of New York's Donnell Library, where he was working as a projectionist, retired after forty-five years as a cameraman. "He had to have someplace to edit. He was a loose, sloppy-looking guy, and so he came to ask the owner if he could use the cutting room where there were Moviolas. The owner looked at Stanley and said, 'Stanley, you look like a bum. Take a shave and I'll let you use the equipment.' He always looked like he needed a shave and a haircut. I just got the feeling he didn't shower very often.

"Stanley knew I was a cameraman. He was shooting a scene and he asked me to come down. He said, 'Would you like to work on this? I'll give you credits.' He promised that in advance. I didn't expect that I'd get credit on the picture. He also used my home, he came up and shot some scenes right off my television set. He handled the whole thing. It was part of a fight sequence, people watching the television set.

"We did an exterior sequence. He was down on Wall Street on a Sunday morning. Everything was dead, there was nobody around. A lot of cops came by and he was prepared for this. He had a whole flock of twenty-dollar bills in his pocket and everybody came to be paid off. Everybody got a twenty-dollar bill. One of the guys came back and said, 'Listen, the sergeant couldn't make it, he had to stay at the office.' Twenty to him too.

"I loaded and threaded the camera. I did the actual shooting, but he directed. He was right next to me. He knew the composition that he wanted and where the camera should be set.

"He borrowed a Bell and Howell Eyemo I owned, which is a hand-held camera that holds hundred-foot rolls of 35mm. He occasionally picked it up for hand-held shots for out of a car window. He called me one Saturday morning and said, 'Somebody broke into my car and stole the Eyemo.' I said, 'Okay, worse things have happened to me in my life.' So he quickly suggested he'd like to pay for it. He said, 'I want to make it up to you.' He had his lawyer write up a paper saying that he would give me the first receipts from the picture so I would be paid for the piece of equipment. He signed it and handed it over to me and that was it. The Eyemo was not a very expensive piece of equipment. I don't know if the picture ever made any money or not.

"Then I went out to Hollywood to shoot some stuff for the evangelist Oral Roberts. I called Stanley and he spent the whole day with me. He was very nice and took me around and showed me things there. He was ready to go to Europe on *Paths of Glory*. So he was standing around pissing in one of the urinals over at Universal, and I held the paper up and said, 'Hey, Stanley, what about this?' 'Aw,' he said, 'shove it up your ass, I'm not going to pay on that,' and we both laughed. I didn't expect much for working on *Killer's Kiss*." Kubrick didn't come through monetarily, but he did keep his word and credited Max Glenn as camera operator.

"My whole picture of Stanley is standing tall, wearing a sloppy kind of sweater outfit with the shirt hanging over, in need of a shave and his hair uncombed. I never thought he would make it. I didn't think what the hell he was doing made any sense to me, but then he made it and I didn't, so he was way ahead of me. I just had a general feeling that this guy was not going to be a wheel of any kind. But he knew photography. He had a general acquaintance with the whole thing, his compositions and so on, a feeling of competence of knowing what the hell he was doing."

As the unit still photographer, Alexander Singer was brought in to document Kubrick at work directing, producing, and photographing the New York independent film production. Kubrick was able to attract *Life* magazine, *Look*'s key competitor, to do a photo story on the making of his second feature film. *Life* photographer Alan Grant, a respected photojournalist, spent one day on the set to capture the young Kubrick at work. Singer continued to shoot behind and around Grant. Some of Singer's stills were shown to the *Life* picture editor, and several of the pictures ran in the article, along with the seasoned pro's work. The *Life* editor introduced Singer to playwright, screenwriter, producer, and director Leslie Stevens, who brought Singer out to the West Coast and helped launch his career. Irene Kane, the stage name of writer Chris Chase, the actress playing Gloria in the film, took some of Singer's work to *Modern Romance* magazine. There Singer did film noir–like still photography to illustrate the lurid tabloid tales in the magazine.

As a director, Kubrick was discovering all the tools available to him and was voracious about learning his craft. "He amplified and enlarged upon his skills with a ruthless energy, he devoured knowledge," remembers Singer, who watched closely as Kubrick directed his second feature. "He understood the value of a little light called an inky. His delight in discovering the power and flexibility and usefulness of this tiny light was extraordinary. Stanley said, 'It's the only light I ever want to use again!' He was very extreme in pronouncements. It was because it's a small cone of light which is very controllable, and control is the essence of cinematography. Control is also the essence of what filmmakers are about, they want to control the universe, and his explosive discovery was deliciously naive and so pure in spirit that it's hard to find its equal."

In developing the plot line of *Killer's Kiss*, Kubrick told David Vaughan he wanted to put Ruth Sobotka in the film and asked him to choreograph a ballet sequence.

In addition to asking Vaughan to take on the assignment of choreographer, Kubrick asked him to play one of the conventioneers who playfully steals the boxer's scarf as he waits in Times Square for his girlfriend, Gloria. Kubrick also asked Vaughan to do double duty as a person in a dance hall, in a scene taking place simultaneously to the one on the street. For Vaughan, this economy created a technical challenge. "I had to sit in the back where no one could see me," Vaughan relates, "because at one point it was when the action was going on in the street at the same time. He needed bodies, and everybody we knew was in that film, friends of Ruth and the ballet company and friends of mine. By that time I had started working in summer stock musicals, and various people I had met in those shows were also in the film just for fun."

The ballet sequence designed to feature Ruth Sobotka was shot at the Theatre de Lys on Christopher Street in Greenwich Village—presently the site of the Lucille Lortel Theatre. Kubrick told his choreographer David Vaughan the intent of the sequence. The scene was a flashback of Gloria's sister, a ballet dancer. Over the dance, Gloria told a complex and twisting story of her sister's tragedy. There was little money in the budget for the sequence. No other dancers could be hired, so Vaughan had to design the dance as a solo, for Ruth. The stage was small, with no real backstage area. "It had to be a solo, but it had to look like it was something from a ballet," Vaughan recalls. "Gerald Fried wrote special music for it. I didn't have any input about what the music was to be like, but I tried to make it look as if it could be part of a longer ballet and not just sort of a little solo number. So I put in a passage where she was doing a rather generalized mime as though there were some other characters that she might have been relating to."

The sequence was photographed by Kubrick in one morning—an achievement, considering the large amount of setups employed in the final scene. "He had one or two trick moments," Vaughan observes, "like when she pirouettes and it looks as if she's done more pirouettes, which is like what Moira Shearer does in *The Red Shoes*."

The Times Square sequence, where two conventioneers tease Jamie as he waits for Gloria, was shot on a cold New York night, but the actors had to dress for a warmer night as portrayed in the film. "It was a freezing cold night," David Vaughan recalls. "Stanley really kind of left the street scene to me. He told me afterwards he thought I was a great comic actor, but I was a little embarrassed by doing it. I wasn't used to doing that kind of improvised work out in public like that."

Alec Rubin, an old friend of Ruth's and now an actor and acting teacher, played the other conventioneer. As David and Alec kidded and danced around Times Square, the crowd on the street was unaware of the filming. As passersby turned around to watch Vaughan and Rubin clowning around, Kubrick's camera captured real-time reactions. "Alec was more of an actor than I was, but Stanley just told us what the situation was and let us do it," Vaughan remembers.

There were long breaks between shots as Kubrick thought out how he was going to shoot parts of the scene. Vaughan, Rubin, and Jamie Smith, who played boxer Davey Gordon, would take the opportunity to go to a Broadway luncheonette to drink hot coffee and to warm their underdressed bodies.

Kubrick and his actors had to be discreet while working on the street. "We had to not make what we were doing too obvious, since Stanley hadn't done anything about getting permission to shoot out on the street," David Vaughan recalls. "Everything had to be done sub rosa."

Kubrick shot the sequence himself, using an Eyemo, probably the one he had borrowed from Max Glenn. For the shot where the camera follows Vaughan and Rubin down Broadway during the stolen-scarf chase, Kubrick was concealed in a truck driving close to the curb to achieve a tracking shot.

During postproduction, money began to run out. Unable to afford an assistant editor, Kubrick edited the film himself. The post-synchronization process used to create the soundtrack to the silent picture was painstaking and time-consuming. It took Kubrick four months to cut in every sound effect and footstep.

Kubrick did his editorial work at Titra Sound Studios at 1600 Broadway where he had first met Max Glenn. While he was editing the film and creating the soundtrack he met Peter Hollander, a documentary filmmaker who produced and directed films for the United Nations.

Titra Films was owned by a European company and specialized in creating subtitling for foreign films. A respected film historian and one of the best known writers of subtitles, Herman G. Weinberg worked for Titra at the time. Next to Titra Films was Titra Sound, which had Moviolas and editing equipment and editing rooms for rental. "Titra was a very nice place, a very pleasant atmosphere, and they charged reasonable rates," Hollander recalls.

Kubrick and Hollander met while Peter was working on one of his first documentaries. "We kibitzed over each other's shoulder," Hollander remembers. Both Hollander and Kubrick were fascinated by the process Titra used to create subtitles. "Stanley and I used to watch them do it. They took release prints, coated them with wax, set the subtitles in type, and with a stamper impressed them frame by frame into the wax. The film was then sent through an acid bath which ate away the film emulsion not coated with wax, leaving white subtitles."

Titra Film and Titra Sound had a connecting door between them. In addition to separate editing rooms, they had a large and small sound recording studio to do sound transfers and sound mixes.

Kubrick told Hollander that his wife, Ruth Sobotka, was a war refugee, and the two men became close when Hollander told Kubrick he was a German Jewish refugee. Kubrick's marriage to Toba Metz had ended in a Mexican divorce. Ruth Sobotka and Stanley Kubrick were married in Albany, New York, on January 15, 1955. On September 11, 1955, Toba Kubrick married Jack Adler in North Bellmore, Long Island.

"One day Stanley came in clutching a rather large hardcover book," Peter Hollander remembers. "He was very excited at what he had found in a secondhand bookshop. Published in the very early days of motion pictures, it claimed to contain all the possible plots for a screenplay—*all* of them. Stanley took it very seriously. He clutched it in his hands like it was the most precious thing he had ever bought. He was very excited about it, as though he had found the key to filmmaking—that this was the answer that would solve every kind of problem.

"He was delightful, he was charming. We had a great deal of fun together. We used to horse around a great deal. Stan was a great one for that, but he worked hard, he spent hours at the Moviola. Coffee breaks was the time we had fun. We were in separate rooms but we'd step out after you had about three hours of heavy work and then kid around. There were mixers and sound recordists—everybody kibitzed on everybody else. Stanley was very witty.

"He was a very good technician. He knew what he was doing. He would edit there. Very often he wasn't doing anything and he would just sit around the front office and kid around. He wasn't constantly involved with something. I'd come back three months later and Stan was still there."

After the feature was completed, the final cost rose to $75,000 by the time he paid his deferred costs and union rates. Kubrick was able to sell the film to United Artists, which bought it for worldwide distribution and released it under the title *Killer's Kiss*. "To the best of my belief, no one at the time had ever made a feature film in such amateur circumstances

and then obtained worldwide distribution for it," Kubrick told Alexander
Walker. The film made a profit for the studio, which released it on the
bottom half of a double bill. For Kubrick the film did not break even,
but as with *Fear and Desire,* he ultimately paid back his investors. This
would be the last time Stanley Kubrick would have to be privately responsible for financing a film.

Kubrick has always referred to *Killer's Kiss* as an amateur undertaking,
a student film. The undernourished budget, largely no-name actors, the
absence of a technically experienced crew and post-synched dialogue
compromise this early effort, yet clearly it indicates a filmmaking talent
not only exploring and learning the craft but developing a cinematic
vision.

Like so many of his generation, Kubrick was greatly affected by a
rapidly changing world. The post–World War II years had brought the
constant threat of annihilation and the gnawing terror of the nuclear age.
As an artist, Kubrick found a means of expressing his gloomy and detached view in the film style that came to be known as film noir, literally
translated from the French as "black film." The term "film noir" was
derived from "roman noir," meaning "black novel" and used by French
literary critics in the eighteenth and nineteenth centuries to describe the
British Gothic novel. In the 1950s French critics observed a trend in
Hollywood films of the forties and early fifties that they labeled and
codified as film noir. A few examples of these bleak and dark-souled
films are *The Asphalt Jungle, The Big Sleep, Double Indemnity, The Lost
Weekend, The Lady from Shanghai, The Big Heat, Gun Crazy, Kiss Me
Deadly,* and *Pickup on South Street.* The films depict an underworld of
crime and corruption peopled by cynical, disillusioned, and fatalistic
loners. The visual style is bleak and unrelentingly dim. Scenes take place
principally at night, a nocturnal world of shadows and lurking evil. Som-
ber, realistic, shabby, and spare, the film noir camera captures light without hope—a stark, contrast-enveloped atmosphere with dark shadows
and glaring light from extreme angles. There is no hope, no way out of
the impending fate.

Filmmakers like Joseph H. Lewis and Edgar G. Ulmer and cinematographer John Alton defined their careers working in the film noir style.
Others, like Alfred Hitchcock, Orson Welles, Billy Wilder, Otto Preminger, and John Huston, experimented with the form as a way of exploring the terrain and then moving on. Kubrick was a new generation of
filmmaker not born out of the Hollywood system. Like Roman Polanski
in *Chinatown,* Robert Altman with *The Long Goodbye,* and Ridley Scott

with *Blade Runner*, Kubrick was using the film noir style as a way of evolving as a film director.

Killer's Kiss is filled with classic film noir elements and many innovative images that Kubrick had been cultivating since *Day of the Fight*. In the documentary of the middleweight Walter Cartier, Kubrick first examined the netherworld of the boxer. Many of the images in the short film are echoed and refashioned for this fictitious life of a prizefighter.

The doom-laden atmosphere of the noir is created by flashbacks, which descend into deep layers of the past, and the forward propulsion to the present. Kubrick's camera records gray, black, and white in effective compositions that engulf Davey Gordon in a dismal world. The repeated image of Davey in hopeless limbo at Penn Station has an odd rear-screen-projection quality to it. Although Kubrick photographed it directly at the New York station, he achieves his effect by having the background lit in a soft, even, gray light. Davey appears slightly more modeled, standing out from his environment. The constant time-shifting reminds us that the film is taking place in Davey's mind and that for him, the recent and earlier past coexist in concurrent time continuum.

In *Killer's Kiss*, Kubrick documents his New York environment, the city that shaped his consciousness as an artist and a person. Penn Station, deserted streets, fight posters, and the old barbershop in the opening capture the reality and resonance of New York City in the fifties. There is a Times Square montage: hot dogs sizzle on a grill, a neon photo shop sign glows, glaring signs on the Great White Way advertise Bond's and Canadian Club, ice cream sundaes rotate on a carousel, a plastic baby swims in a miniature pool of water.

Mirror shots appear throughout. Davey peers into his future before his fight, as did Walter Cartier. Rapallo seethes with self-loathing at his image. A symbolic, cinematic, and practical resource for expanding imagery economically, the mirror reflects and extends our view of the characters and their environment.

The arrogance of youth impelled Kubrick to create self-conscious but arresting images—Davey's face distorted through a tight close-up shot through a fishbowl, Davey's nightmare visualized in a series of jump-cut negative images of the camera moving down barren city streets. Kubrick designed strategies to get around the complexities of shooting sync-sound dialogue sequences—techniques that student filmmakers would follow for the next four decades. The narrative stays on course via voice-over from Davey and Gloria. An entire sequence in which Gloria tells of her father's death and her sister's suicide is told in voice-over while we see Iris dancing.

Visual effects are minimal and concise. Kubrick dissolves to a wavy screen to denote time-shifting in both directions. For a transition from Gloria's flashback to Rapallo roughing her up, Kubrick swirls the camera 360 degrees in the empty apartment to get back to Gloria in the first flashback.

Many of the images from *Day of the Fight* are echoed in *Killer's Kiss*. The short film created a library of New York visions for the director to transplant and explore in a feature film. The fight poster on a lamppost, the New York City streets, the boxer contemplating his existence in a mirror, and the milieu of Walter Cartier's fight day gave *Killer's Kiss* corporeality.

Concerns about box office potential weakened Kubrick's resolve for the film's conclusion. Doomed lovers of film noir never find happiness. The hero never finds peace. Violating the formula, *Killer's Kiss* closes quickly with an upbeat ending as hero and heroine come together to live happily ever after. The gloomy tone of the film was established but not sustained to its conclusion. Kubrick's film noir adventure was truncated.

For the score, Kubrick turned again to Gerald Fried. Two main musical themes recur throughout the film. One is the love theme from the song "Once," written by Norman Gimbel and Arden Clar, used here for a romantic link. The other is a fiery Latin-jazz piece that punctuates the criminal-element and action scenes. For the street chase at the end, Fried created a tension-producing percussion track that echoes the rhythmic sense of the War (Mars) movement of Gustav Holst's *The Planets,* a piece familiar to filmgoers from *Apocalypse Now.*

Kubrick heard the Gimbel and Clar love song and asked Fried to develop it as the love theme to *Killer's Kiss.* Fried arranged the song in every possible variation, using different instruments as a lead and interpreting the song in a variety of musical moods. The film was scored a section at a time with Fried determining where the different versions of the song would go.

For the action sequences and scenes that required a treatment that spoke to the underworld nightlife of New York City, Fried began working in a Latin motif. "I was working in a mambo band that summer and once again I said, 'What excites me?' Latin rhythms were irresistible to me, so I said, 'I've got to use this!' I never got tired of playing it, so I just put it in there."

The chase scene and confrontation in the mannequin factory that is the climax of *Killer's Kiss* were scored with a tension-provoking series of percussion sounds. Kubrick's high school experience as an orchestra and swing band drummer gave him a predilection for percussion. "Both

Stanley and I were drum happy," Fried recalled. "Nothing is as exciting as a heartbeat, and we had a lot of bass drum with a big beater with the mike close to the skin sounding like a heartbeat—this was before synthesizers. I figured if that's exciting, other percussion instruments just by themselves would be exciting."

Editing has always fascinated Kubrick. Here he uses intercutting to relate Davey and Gloria and complement the written-in structure with a brisk pace. Kubrick, as director and cinematographer, still retained the student's mark, but his work as an editor on the film is cleanly compressed and polished.

Max Glenn's Eyemo was put to good use for hand-held shots, particularly in the fight sequence, which uses some of the technique Kubrick explored on *Day of the Fight*. The brazen and innovative camera gets inside the fight to become an active participant in the scene. Low-angle shots, distorted wide-angle close-ups, and the glare and flare from overhead lights capture the heat of the fight.

Shooting from vehicles, Kubrick was able to create movement. Not being able to do a proper tracking shot, he improvised by using a hand-held camera from a moving car. The high-angle moving shot of Gloria crossing the street after the fight captures the almost ghostly quality of her walk. Breezing along Times Square, the fluid camera picks up the carefree spirit of the mischievous conventioneers.

The soundtrack was done completely in postproduction. Vivid sound effects create an artificial but highly effective sound design. Kubrick cut in every footstep and body sound with great pains to capture realism in every step and slide of a foot.

Kubrick had devoted all his energies to filmmaking, and almost everyone who came in contact with him was connected to this central purpose. He did, however, continue to be obsessed with chess. The chess world in New York was a universe unto itself. His forays to Washington Square Park and excursions to the city's many chess clubs connected him to an environment that fine-tuned his ability to make decisions, a principal task of the film director.

The Marshall Chess Club was located on West Tenth Street between Fifth and Sixth Avenues, just a crosstown trip from home at 222 East Tenth Street. Kubrick went to the Marshall Chess Club quite often, usually at night.

The club was the private home of Frank Marshall, one of America's great chess champions. Marshall started the chess club in his brownstone. After he died, his wife, Carrie, maintained the club. The Marshall Chess Club had a garden in the back and an open membership. Larry Evans, a U.S. chess champion at that time, frequented the Marshall.

In the early fifties, while he was a member of the Marshall Chess Club, Kubrick met Gerald Jacobson. Both men were also members of the United States Chess Federation. "We played a few times. We were about equal strength, perhaps he was a trifle stronger," remembers Jacobson, now a resident of Florida. "They had tournaments at the Marshall Chess Club. That's where I met Stanley for the first time. We were in the same tournament together. We played against each other. The chemistry was there, so we spoke quite often. He was a quiet loner. He always wore a corduroy jacket and he was a soft-spoken person. We'd play one or two games and then go to a restaurant or a bar to have beers and talk. We used to sit around and talk for hours. He was always frustrated that he couldn't get started in the film business. He was fairly young, but he was also having marital problems. Alton Cooke, the film critic for the *New York World Telegram and Sun,* was a member of the Marshall Chess Club. Someone mentioned to [Stanley], 'Why don't you speak to Alton Cooke?' He just said, 'I have talent, I know I'm good. I just can't get a backer or a producer.' " Later, Kubrick did encounter Cooke at the Marshall, and he was impressed by Kubrick's audacity and confidence at the board.

Washington Square Park was a mecca for chess players. "There were tables for chess and checkers and a whole group of coffeehouse players who played very fast and sometimes for money. They would take out their clocks and play five-minute games," Gerald Jacobson explains. "They were very familiar with certain moves and knew all the traps, but if they would go against a really good player they couldn't beat them, they were street-smart."

Gerald Jacobson didn't see Stanley Kubrick for a while. Then one day he took his son to Washington Square Park to watch some exciting chess action, and there was Stanley Kubrick watching a match. "He said, 'I'm going to California,' " Jacobson remembers. "The next thing I remember he was making *Spartacus.* He just shot up like a rocket!"

PART THREE

1956–1960
Hollywood

CHAPTER 7

Harris-Kubrick

Alexander Singer was in the Signal Corps for his stint in the army during the Korean War. There he met James B. Harris, a young man with whom he shared a mutual interest in filmmaking. From 1950 to 1952 Harris and Singer were both in the photo unit, making training films.

Harris entered the film business in 1949 when he became one of the founders of Flamingo Films, a motion picture and television distribution company. Flamingo Films was set up with Harris's school buddy David L. Wolper and Sy Weintraub, who was in the army with James's brother Bob. The venture was financed by James B. Harris's father.

As part of their R and R, Singer and Harris, along with another Signal Corps buddy, developed a fifteen-minute detective script. They were going to shoot the script on weekends. Singer thought that Harris-Singer would make a good team.

Singer told Harris about a friend of his from Taft High School days named Stanley Kubrick, who had been a photographer at *Look* magazine and was now the kind of independent filmmaker they envisioned becoming themselves.

Harris and Singer put their script into production, scheduling a weekend shoot at the Harris family home, which was doubling as a production facility and set for their detective story. The project would serve as an experiment in fictional filmmaking. James B. Harris was the director and Alexander Singer was the cameraman. Harris's cousin was cast in one of the roles, and another army buddy, James Gaffney, was enlisted to be the film editor. Singer invited his friend Stanley Kubrick, who was working on his second feature film, *Killer's Kiss,* to the set. "I was a little nervous," Harris recalls, "because it was like performing in front of someone who was already an established professional. He was telling me about the two short films he had made, *Day of the Fight* and *Flying Padre.* He had just completed his first feature film, *Fear and Desire,* which he had done all by himself."

Kubrick met another future longtime associate, Jimmy Gaffney's brother Bob, during a subsequent filmmaking experiment. "My brother Jimmy was conned into being the cameraman, and Alexander Singer was directing. Alex read some book on the 'Russian School,' and he put kraft paper on the floor with marks for the camera angles and where people's feet would go. I wound up being the electrician because they were shooting in some transvestite nightclub in the Village. Stanley came by, and that was the first time I met Stanley," Bob Gaffney explains.

Bob Gaffney was working with Louis de Rochemont Associates, which had a three-picture deal with Columbia. De Rochemont was doing East Coast location movies, like *The House on 92nd Street* and *Walk East on Beacon.* They had finished *The Whistle at Eaton Falls* and *Walk East.*

Alexander Singer saw in James B. Harris a potential producer who could help launch his directorial career. "I realized Jimmy was potentially valuable as a financier," Singer recalls. "It was the first time I had met anybody that could finance or partially finance a feature film, and ideally I would have kept him to myself. But Jimmy is also very shrewd, very much a businessman, very solid. Despite his early years—we must have been about twenty-two or twenty-three when we met—Jimmy was also pretty fully formed, and he would not have backed a film that I proposed because I did not have two movies to my credit. Stanley had done two feature films by this time, *Fear and Desire* and *Killer's Kiss.*"

After being discharged from the army, James B. Harris ran into Stanley Kubrick one day on the street. The two young men reintroduced themselves, and Kubrick invited Harris to a screening of the just-completed *Killer's Kiss.*

Since his first meeting with Kubrick, Harris had seen *Day of the Fight, Flying Padre,* and *Fear and Desire,* and he was most impressed with Kubrick's talent and individualistic spirit. Seeing *Killer's Kiss* confirmed it. "I was very impressed with this guy. I was very impressed that somebody could do it all. It had a beginning, middle, and end. It seemed to be very professional. I thought it was a hell of an accomplishment and said, 'This guy is really going to be a great, great director!' "

Kubrick remembered Harris's connection to Flamingo Films and asked if he could meet with him about getting *Fear and Desire* into television distribution. Harris said, "Sure, come into the office."

They met at the offices of Flamingo Films at 509 Madison Avenue. Kubrick was not able to clear the rights to *Fear and Desire* for television, and Harris advised him that he could assist him only if Kubrick had the distribution rights. When the formal part of their discussion concluded, Harris asked Kubrick what he was going to do next. "He said, 'I really don't have anything scheduled to do. I wish I could make another movie.' So I said, 'I would love to produce pictures. What do you think about maybe we could team up. You direct and I produce. Possibly I could bring to you a lot of things you didn't have the advantages of when you were doing these other two, like maybe acquiring a story from a book so you have something more substantial to work with—and sort of run interference for you so you would not have to do everything for yourself.' So he said, 'It sounds great to me!' "

James B. Harris had an eye for literary properties. Kubrick had the vision and genius of a natural-born filmmaker. Stanley Kubrick and James B. Harris were born six days apart under the sign of Leo the Lion. Both were ambitious, had nerves of steel, confidence, chutzpah, and the will to succeed.

Harris moved ahead to close the deal. "I said, 'The first thing we should do is form a company. Let's call it Harris-Kubrick Pictures, and he said, 'Terrific!' He was all for it a hundred percent." Harris incorporated the new company. They found an office on the west side of Fifty-seventh Street, which consisted of an outer office and one executive office, which they shared. Harris-Kubrick was just that, Harris and Kubrick. They both agreed to look for material for their inaugural production. "I immediately went to Scribner's Bookstore on Fifth Avenue and went through the books," Harris remembers. "In what today would be called the mystery section I found a book called *Clean Break,* by Lionel White. I looked at the dust cover—'Gee, the robbery of a race-track—it sounds exciting!' "

Harris bought the hardback and instantly read it. He liked the structure. The story was told in a series of flashbacks, which intrigued him. "I called Stanley and said, 'I think I found something that would make a helluva movie.' Kubrick read the book in a matter of hours and said, 'It's terrific, let's see if we can't get the rights to this thing.' " They were attracted to the time-shifting qualities intrinsic to the way White told the story of a racetrack heist.

Harris traced the rights to *Clean Break* to the Jaffe Agency in Los Angeles and called to inquire about obtaining the book. " 'I'm glad you called,' they said. 'It just happens to be available, but we're negotiating with Frank Sinatra.' I said, 'Well, has the deal been made?' They said, 'No, not yet, and he's taking his time about it and it bothers us a little bit.' I said, 'What makes the deal right now?' He says, 'If you send me a telegram with a firm offer for ten thousand dollars for the rights to the book, it's yours.' So I said, 'You got it!' I knew Stanley wanted to do it, I loved it. What was there to think about?"

The literary agent for the Jaffe Agency was Bob Goldfarb. The powerful agency also had agents Ronnie Lubin and Phil Gersh. Harris-Kubrick did not have agents at the time and was fielding and executing its own deals.

Harris made out a check for ten thousand dollars, sent it to the Jaffe Agency, and received a telegram confirming that Harris-Kubrick were now the proud owners of the rights to *Clean Break*, by Lionel White. The two self-styled movie moguls ran to United Artists to make a deal.

They made an appointment to meet Bob Benjamin, who along with Arthur Krim had left the powerful theatrical law firm of Nizer, Phillips, Benjamin, and Krim to run United Artists. Harris informed Benjamin that Harris-Kubrick had acquired the rights to *Clean Break*. Benjamin said, "That's impossible, we're going to do that with Sinatra." UA had done *Suddenly* with the crooner-actor, an assassination drama that had an eerie portent for the murder of President John F. Kennedy. United Artists wanted a reprise with Sinatra doing another thriller. Harris explained that Sinatra's foot-dragging with the agency enabled Harris-Kubrick to secure the rights. "Benjamin said, 'Oh, that's terrific, it's a terrific property—good luck with it.' We said, 'Well, don't you want to do it?' They said, 'Yes, show us a script and we'll let you know.' " Benjamin knew that UA had nothing to lose by encouraging the hungry filmmakers.

"We decided we weren't going to raise the money to make this without a screenplay," Harris recalled. "So Stanley said, 'Did you ever hear of a novelist named Jim Thompson?' and I said, 'No.' He said, 'Let me educate you about Jim Thompson. Here's a list of books I want you to look at.' " One of the novels was *The Killer Inside Me*, a book Kubrick would later blurb on the cover, calling it "Probably the most chilling and believable first-person story of a criminally warped mind I have ever encountered." Harris began reading the work of the legendary hardboiled novelist. Kubrick said, "Let's see if we can't get Jim Thompson to work with us on the screenplay." Harris-Kubrick found Thompson and hired him to write his first screenplay, an adaptation of Lionel White's *Clean Break*.

Thompson did not know screenplay format. Kubrick worked closely with him, concentrating on developing the dialogue. The physical screenplay was not conventional. It was written on legal-size paper instead of the standard eight and a half by eleven and was bound on the top, so the reader had to turn the pages over bottom to top rather than the usual right to left.

Thompson was ultimately credited with "Additional Dialogue," a common credit at the time. The Thompson family has expressed dissatisfaction with Thompson's credit, protesting that he should have received full screenwriting credit for the film. The structure was basically transposed from the book. Kubrick organized the scenes, and Harris also made contributions to the screenplay.

Upon completion of the screenplay, Harris and Kubrick quickly returned to United Artists, which read the script and was amenable to making the picture.

"Boy, we were excited," Harris remembers. "They said, 'What you guys do is go out and get an actor, and if you can get an actor, we'll make the picture.' " Benjamin concluded by giving them a list of actors.

"I said, 'Boy, we've got a deal to make this movie, all we have to do is get an actor.' So I told my father about it. I said, 'We're off to a great start!' He said, 'What's the deal?' I told him what it was and he says, 'That's like me sending you out in the street to look for money and promising I'll give you half of whatever you find.' He said, 'You mean you're going to go out and bring them an actor. If you can get the actor that they'll accept, you could have taken that actor anywhere. What do you need them for? What are they doing? Are they helping you get the actor? No, but they like the screenplay.' "

Harris and Kubrick filled a large box with copies of their script and put in a list of actors they had selected. They shipped the package to Bob Goldfarb at the Jaffe Agency in Los Angeles so the agent could send out the scripts to potential stars. Sterling Hayden was just one of the names on the list.

Harris tried to get a few actors on his own. After learning that Jack Palance was doing Shakespeare up in Connecticut, he jumped in his car and drove to the theater so he could personally put a copy of the script on the tough-jawed actor's dressing table. "I called him in an appropriate amount of time—which I thought was a week. I figured everybody is like us, we would read it immediately. He didn't even know who I was and never had read it," Harris recalled.

Several weeks later Harris received a call from agent Bill Shiffren, who said, "I represent Sterling Hayden. We like your script a lot, but who is Stanley Kubrick? It's not Stanley Kramer you're talking about?' I said, 'No, it's Stanley Kubrick.' He said, 'Well, who is he, what has he done?'" Harris proceeded to recite Kubrick's self-made résumé, and Shiffren replied, "I never heard of him or the two films, but we like your script a lot." "I said, 'Well, Kubrick is terrific and so you're saying that Sterling would like to do the film?' He said, 'You know if you make an offer . . .' He sort of backed off this who's Kubrick business and I said, 'What's Sterling's price?' He said, 'He gets $40,000.'"

Harris and Kubrick again ran to Benjamin at United Artists with the good news that they had secured a star. The rugged actor had been in more than thirty films, including *The Asphalt Jungle, Johnny Guitar,* and *Suddenly,* the film UA had done with Sinatra. "We said, 'Guess what, we've got Sterling Hayden,' and they said, 'So, Sterling Hayden, we're selling his films for flat rentals for twenty-five dollars,'" Harris remembers. "We said, 'But what about *The Asphalt Jungle,* he's terrific, he'd be great, he's good enough for John Huston!' They said, 'Listen, we have a deal with Victor Mature, he's available in eighteen months—why not wait for Victor Mature?' They're telling two kids to wait eighteen months for an actor who hasn't even read the script yet or anything. We said, 'No, we've got Sterling, he wants to do the picture, he gets $40,000.' They said, 'Okay, boys, you want to make this movie that bad, we'll give you $200,000 to make the movie, and that's it. If it costs you any more, you've got to pay for it yourself. And if you do pay for it yourself and it costs more, we get our $200,000 back first and you're going to have to get in line to get your overages back, but that's the deal. Now our advice to you is wait for Victor Mature or make it for $200,000, but don't go spending a penny more.' Stanley is coming off pictures that were made for pretzels, he made them for nothing. I said, 'We should be able to make the picture for $200,000. If it costs more—that's my end of this business. Let's not lose this deal, let's grab it while we can and see how close to it we can make the picture and take it from there, but let's not lose the deal. I'll have to worry about what we do.'"

Harris and Kubrick forged ahead with production on *The Killing.* First they began to research production locations. Although Kubrick was a New York filmmaker and Harris had learned the business on the East Coast through television distribution, they decided to shoot their first film together in L.A., the City of Angels, where the majority of films were still made under the studio-controlled system. UA was supplying some of the money, but for all intents and purposes this was an independent production—Harris-Kubrick was on its own. By doing the film in

California, they thought they could save travel and per diem costs associated with transporting a West Coast cast back east.

Sets had to be built. A good portion of the story took place at the racetrack, and although they found they could get some cooperation from the Golden Gate Racetrack in San Francisco, no racetrack would allow them to use its facility for a film about the robbery of a racetrack. Most of the scenes in the script were interiors. The old Chaplin Studios was available, and they could build sets there. Kubrick's wife, Ruth Sobotka, eager to function in a role as collaborator, was signed on as production designer. She had designed for the theater and ballet, and she had been a student at Carnegie Tech, where she studied stage design. She had designed several ballets for the New York City Ballet, including Jerome Robbins's *The Cage*. She had also designed several ballets for David Vaughan, the choreographer from *Killer's Kiss*. Alexander Singer was brought aboard as associate producer. "In 1956, Stanley brought me out to the West Coast as his associate producer on *The Killing*. It was a kind of repayment for having introduced Jimmy Harris to him," Singer says.

On the massive set depicting the betting area of the racetrack, part of one wall had betting windows. Sobotka and Kubrick created nameplates for the cashiers that were in-joke references to some of their friends. One cashier was given the name David Vaughan. Another was named after one of Sobotka's friends from the ballet company, Shaun O'Brien.

The film was budgeted at $330,000. This was a low budget compared to what Hollywood was spending but a small fortune to two kids from New York City who were working on sheer gall and their own resources. They had UA's $200,000. Harris had saved up $80,000. That made the working capital $280,000. To round out the budget, Harris asked his father to invest $50,000. "I knew before we started shooting that it was going to be a hardship. I'd have to find a way—and I was putting up all the money, but I interpreted it as we were buying a future. We were investing in a future. A picture made for $200,000 would take a lot of days off the schedule, and Stanley would have to rush through it. Mind you, with the $330,000 we only had twenty-four days to shoot—which is what they do television movies in now. We figured for $200,000 it would look like a real cheap picture, and that wasn't what we wanted to do. If we were going to have a future, we'd have to show something that looked like pretty good quality. So I just took a deep breath and said, 'Okay, let's do it,' and I came up with the $130,000."

Kubrick's deal was to direct *The Killing* for no salary. His fee was deferred 100 percent. Kubrick lived on loans from Harris.

Up until now the twenty-seven-year-old Kubrick had personally photographed all the films he directed. The cameraman's union would not
allow Kubrick to shoot *The Killing* himself, so he chose Lucien Ballard
as his director of photography.

Ballard was a forty-seven-year-old Hollywood veteran who had been
married to Merle Oberon. He had worked as an assistant cameraman for
Lee Garmes on *Morocco,* which starred Marlene Dietrich and was
directed by Josef von Sternberg. He went on to become director of
photography on von Sternberg's *The Devil Is a Woman* and *Crime and
Punishment.* Ballard was a master of black-and-white film, and his work
on *Al Capone, The Rise and Fall of Legs Diamond,* and *Pay or Die* made
him the perfect choice for Kubrick's caper film. In 1960, Ballard photographed *Ride the High Country* for cinematic desperado Sam Peckinpah
and went on to lens *The Wild Bunch, The Ballad of Cable Hogue, Junior
Bonner,* and *The Getaway* for the man who came to view Kubrick as his
chief rival.

Kubrick proudly screened his first two features, *Fear and Desire* and
Killer's Kiss, for Ballard, who politely watched the films that featured a
raw but imaginative low-budget cinematography shot by the director
himself.

Just before principal photography was to begin, Kubrick, Harris,
Singer, and Ballard had a meeting concerning footage for the opening
titles of the picture. Harris and Kubrick knew that getting permission to
shoot a film about the robbery of a racetrack at an actual track would be
impossible, so sets were being designed and built for the interior sequences. Other exterior sequences could be achieved using second-unit
footage and rear-screen projection. The Bay Meadows Racetrack in San
Francisco had agreed to allow the production to film second-unit material of a race in progress. It was decided that Ballard and his camera
crew would go to the track and shoot material to be used for the opening
titles.

Ballard, who was used to working on conventional Hollywood films,
brought several cameras and a crew of ten to Bay Meadows, where they
exposed thousands of feet of film. Kubrick remained at the studio to
continue the preproduction work.

After Ballard and his crew returned, the material was developed and
screened for Kubrick, Harris, and Singer. The result of the screening
was the beginning of a parting of the photographic ways between the
seasoned Hollywood pro and the fledgling director. "Stanley and Jimmy
looked at it," Alexander Singer recalls. "And Stanley gets up at some
point and says, 'I'll fire him!' The stuff was terrible. We tried to under-

stand how it could be terrible, because we'd seen several pictures Lucien had done and he was very good, but this was just wretched. The problem was that he was sent out like a documentary film man. He had no control, he had a few lights and reflectors, but essentially Lucien had none of the tools of control that conventional cameramen require, and control is everything in cinematography. He was shooting at crowds in a major racetrack, he couldn't control anything, and it looked it.

"You can imagine the despair of three youngsters where you have your best man out there. He goes up with all these guys and all this equipment, comes back, and it's useless. You say, 'Well, what do we do now?' Because we still need the footage. Stanley says to me, 'Either you go up or I go up alone. It's either one or the other of us. I can't go because I have to work on the script, so you're going to go.' "

Singer was sent to Bay Meadows, but not with ten men or with standard Hollywood Mitchell cameras. Singer arrived at the track with a trusty Eyemo, the camera that had served him well filming Walter Cartier knocking out Bobby James for *Day of the Fight* and no more than two lenses and pocketsful of hundred-foot loads of black-and-white 35mm film. That was it.

Lucien Ballard was not told about the plan to send Singer to get the second-unit footage. Kubrick was very pleased with the results, and the material was later used not only for the opening title sequence but also to link the time-shifting elements of the story, to provide the viewer with a reference point. By repeating and evolving the sequence of shots photographed by Singer's Eyemo, Kubrick was free to create the nonlinear story inherent in Lionel White's novel.

Singer completed his work over a weekend. Utilizing the skills developed in the Signal Corps and as a photojournalist, he was able to get realistic documentary material while maintaining the tenets of good photography in his use of composition and light. The shots depicted the ritual of bringing the horses to the starting gate and the details of the approach to the race.

Singer planned to save the most critical shot—the horses actually leaving the starting gate—for the end of the last day. It would be the last shot he was to take and for good reason. "I preset my exposure and prefocused and waited until exactly the right moment," Singer recalled. "I walked out into the middle of the track when the actual race was about to happen, laid face down in the dirt, pointed the camera, and simply started it rolling. I knew what was going to happen. I figured the cops would be on me before the horses came and I would die, that they would haul me out of the way. That was the way to get the shot. The world exists in the viewfinder, period, it doesn't exist outside the view-finder. The photographer stops thinking about the world and lives through the viewfinder."

After getting the footage, Singer phoned Kubrick back at the studio, telling him, "I got the footage. I think you'll like it. Things worked out." Singer was excited about his work but wanted to remain low-key about it until he was back in the screening room with Kubrick and Harris.

The next day, Harris, Kubrick, and Singer screened the weekend shoot. "I couldn't wait because what he saw was this rather remarkable shot from ground level. You saw the horses coming up to the starting gate. What you continued to see was some feet walking into the frame and a hand reaching down and then the frame turns upside down because I was dragged, lifted off the field, and told to never come back again. The crowd of about twenty thousand people howled with laughter when this idiot goes out on the track and starts rolling a camera. I got the shot, and I figured the cops wouldn't beat me with clubs in front of twenty thousand people."

The relationship between director and director of photography was strained. Commenting on Stanley Kubrick and explaining his contribution to the photographic style of *The Killing*, Ballard told Leonard Maltin for his 1971 book *Behind the Camera*, "It was just my own style of contrasty black and white. I didn't think Kubrick was much of a director at that time, but I was impressed with his screen treatment."

Kubrick pushed Ballard with his unconventional photographic ideas. Kubrick insisted on a 25mm lens for the panning and tracking shots, which give *The Killing* a powerful cinematic drive. In 1956, the 25mm was one of the widest motion picture lenses available. Ballard feared that moving the camera with this lens would cause distortion. Of course, it was the distortion and heightening of reality that Kubrick was after. The daring tracking wide-angle shots make a bold statement throughout the film. Kubrick was unflinchingly confident in what he knew about cinematography, which was both too much and not enough for the seasoned Ballard. Nonetheless, their ill-matched collaboration yielded the startling look of *The Killing*.

Breaking the Hollywood rules at the time involved confronting the director of photography. Associate producer Alexander Singer was on set when Kubrick laid out a tracking shot played early in the film. The shot moved through several rooms in an apartment. Kubrick had the set built with open walls so the camera could track from room to room following the characters as they walked through the apartment. The technique has influenced countless movies. Four decades later, the Hughes brothers included this approach in *Menace II Society* and *Dead Presidents* after director of photography Lisa Rinzler screened *The Killing* for them.

Singer watched as Kubrick confidently proceeded to call the shot, the movement, and the lens. "Stanley set up the first shot with a viewfinder. The viewfinder on the old Mitchell BNC camera was a parallax correcting finder and it was detachable from the camera. It was not uncommon for a director who was very involved in composition and camera setups to pick up a finder and walk around with it and in effect choosing the setup and making the appropriate adjustments in the finder for the kind of lens the director wanted. This particular shot was early in the picture and was going to define a certain stylistic quality. It was a very long dolly shot. I hesitate to say a 'Kubrick dolly shot,' but it was. Other people have done it, but this became characteristic of a lot of what he did and would do at other times. It dollied past the rooms in the apartment. It goes one room to the next, and as it passes the room you would simply go past the doorway and the boundaries of the walls as if they didn't exist. We just moved through them.

"Stanley was, needless to say, very specific about this particular setup, as he was with all setups. He adjusted the finder to the lens he wanted, and it was a 25mm lens. At that point in time the 25mm was the widest lens currently available to the Mitchell BNC. So there's the 25mm lens and there's a long dolly shot. Stanley goes from one end of the set to the other and the set has been designed to do this. So it's all been pre-planned. Then he gives the finder to Lucien Ballard, and Lucien has watched him and says, 'I see, it's going to be a very nice shot.' Lucien gets to work, Stanley walks off the set to do some piece of business. He comes back a few minutes later and Lucien has indeed set up the dolly track but he set it up at a considerable distance from where Stanley's position had to be—in terms of the proximity to the set. Now Stanley said, 'Wait a minute, Lucien, what are you doing, Lucien?' 'Well, I took your dolly shot and instead of the 25mm, I'm just going for the 50mm, but I'm at a distance where you would get the same image size for the distance as that. So everything is the same size, but I prefer to work at this distance. It's a little easier to light, it won't make any difference.' "

"Well, it's all the difference in the world," Singer explains. "As soon as you back up, you can hold the same image size, but the entire perspective changes. The trick of doing it with a wide-angle lens is you have a sense of intimacy with the set and the lines are more clearly defined and more powerful graphically—it's a dynamic effect. It was a dynamic lens and a dynamic application of it. Lucien had simply dismissed that and assumed Stanley wouldn't know the difference or wouldn't care about the difference. You're talking about a man who, aside from being one of the reigning masters of the time, is married to Merle Oberon and who looks like a beautifully dressed movie idol. Stanley looks like the Bronx kid who is still wiping his nose on his sleeve and looks all of eighteen, maybe.

"Stanley looked up at Lucien Ballard and said, 'Lucien, either you move that camera and put it where it has to be to use a 25mm or get off this set and never come back!' There's a long silence and I'm waiting for Lucien to say the appropriate things in two or three languages to dismiss this young snotnose, but no, he puts the camera where it has to be and there is never an argument about focal length and lenses again. To me it was a defining moment. I don't think Stanley did it casually and it cost him something, but it was done without hesitation. It was done calmly, unhysterically, and in deadly earnest. It marked the kind of control and icy nerve he brought to the job at the very beginning."

Kubrick opted for hand-held-camera shots and personally operated the camera on the hand-held shot that pans over all the dead bodies of the heist crew after a big shoot-out. The shot brings an immediacy and a cinematic vitality to the action.

Kubrick cast *The Killing* with veterans of the Hollywood crime film: Sterling Hayden, Jay C. Flippen, Elisha Cook, Jr., Ted de Corsia (who was in noir classics *The Naked City* and *The Big Combo*), Joe Sawyer, and femme fatale Marie Windsor. For other roles Kubrick selected Coleen Gray, Vince Edwards (before he hit international fame as TV's Ben Casey), New York–born actor Joseph Turkel, and Timothy Carey (a character actor who had just been in Kazan's *East of Eden* and became noted for his maniacal characters). For the role of a wrestler hired to be involved in the stickup, Kubrick chose Kola Kwarian, a chess buddy from a Forty-second Street chess hall in New York.

Vince Edwards got the part of Val, the gigolo boyfriend, while he was acting in *Hit and Run*, which was shooting at Chaplin Studios, where *The Killing* was being made.

"I knew Jimmy Harris through David Wolper," Edwards recalled. "Stanley and I used to play cards a lot, and he just said, 'You'd be good for this guy' and that was it. Stanley was a great poker player in those days. We used to play with Everett Sloane, Lee Cobb, and Marty Ritt." Novelist Calder Willingham, who worked with Kubrick on the screenplay for *Paths of Glory*, occasionally would take a seat at the poker table. "Stanley's so meticulous," Edwards remembered. "He gave all the players a book to buy—Yardley's *Education of a Poker Player*, where we could figure the percentages. We all had little index cards with all the

percentages so we'd know when to pull with two jacks and a queen—
that's Stanley. He sure moved the camera a lot and was knowledgeable."
Edwards often went to the movies with Kubrick, who continued to see
every movie he could. "We once looked at *High Noon* together on Wil-
shire Boulevard after everybody raved about it," Edwards recalled. "He
said, 'You know, this is not such a good movie.' I'll never forget that line.
He's a meticulous guy."

Vince Edwards completed his role in about a week out of the twenty-
four-day shooting schedule. Kubrick was self-assured and comfortable
with his actors. "He let you alone a lot. He didn't get into the patina of
the scene and all of your imagery like Marty Ritt. He would have you
read it and tell you, 'That's good' or 'A little more intensity' or 'Play it
off-the-shoulder a little more,' but he tried to get your personality in it."

Marie Windsor, who played Sherry Peatty, was a former Miss Utah
who was trained as a theater actor under Maria Ouspenskaya and had
been playing featured and lead roles in crime dramas and westerns since
1947. "Stanley saw a movie I made, *The Narrow Margin,* and said to
Jimmy Harris, 'That's my Sherry!' " Windsor recalls. "They negotiated
and set me for the part. Unfortunately, my agent had committed me to
Swamp Women, a Roger Corman movie, and we found out that the
schedule overlapped *The Killing.* Everybody got together, and Kubrick
and Harris said they could arrange for me to be two days late and
Corman let me off two days early, so I was able to come right from
Louisiana and jump into this."

In the two weeks it took for Windsor to complete the role of Sherry
Peatty, she observed the young director to be very different from any
other she had worked with in almost ten years as a film actress. "He was
a very gentle man, very quiet. I never had a director that didn't speak
out on the set when he was giving an actor a direction. Kubrick wasn't
like that. If he had something to say, whether it was a big point or a little
point, he'd call an actor off to the side and say, 'I think if you did this, it
would be better' and 'I'd like you to try this in a certain spot.' Then, we
would walk back onto the set and do it, but he didn't direct in front of
the crew, which I thought was very interesting.

"In his quiet way he had great authority. I remember the cinematographer Lucien Ballard, who had many, many pictures under his belt and
I guess practically more experience than anybody on the set, and Stanley
wanted things done a certain way. I remember a couple of times when
Lucien disagreed with him, Stanley held his own. He wanted it his way
and that was it. It was mostly discussions about angles and where to cut

that I was in on. They weren't heated discussions, just where one didn't agree with the other. Stanley sure acted like a cameraman.

"You just had a feeling that these were important people you were working for and this was an important director. There was his sense of authority. He was comfortable and secure in every move he made.

"I never had any deep conversations with him, I was too busy memorizing my lines and he was too busy making a movie to do that, but he did come up to the house once for dinner with members of the cast."

Kubrick was also unconventional in the way he dressed on the set. "The vivid thing I remember mostly about Stanley was he always wore those funny beige work pants that the working guys buy," Windsor recalled. "He dressed very odd. He wasn't a beatnik, but he was way ahead of his time. He sort of dressed like the sixties and he was such a free thinker. He was sort of like the sixties people, except not that destructive."

This was Kubrick's third feature film, and he had yet to work with an experienced film production designer. As a self-taught filmmaker, Kubrick utilized whatever information and data he could compile from books and from his endless inquiries to all industry insiders he could meet. Still working outside of the Hollywood system, he was driven by his strong personal visual style and his interpretation of filmmaking methods. Marie Windsor remembers seeing what added up to a storyboard of *The Killing*. "Ruth Sobotka was a very fine artist. Stanley had her do all these wonderful charcoal drawings of every single scene he wanted to shoot, and they were all around his office on the walls in sequence."

The story told in *The Killing* is little more than a typical crime potboiler, but the complex narrative structure of the novel reached back to *Citizen Kane* and catapulted Kubrick into cinematic storytelling and time-shifting that would influence generations of noir-crazed filmmakers. From Kubrick's perspective, this audacious little crime picture became his first film, even though he had directed three shorts and two features. The amateur had become a professional.

When Kubrick and Harris were finished with their cut of *The Killing*, they held a preview for the film. They invited all their friends and as many industry insiders as they could. "Bill Shiffren, Sterling Hayden's agent, was the first one out of the theater, telling us that we substantially hurt his client," James B. Harris remembers. " 'This movie is all mixed up,' Shiffren said. 'What is all this business of back and forth, back and forth? Just when you're getting to the crux of the robbery, you cut. You're going to irritate the audience. I'm very disappointed in you guys.'

What a terrible thing to say to us. It was our first showing of the film and my first picture. This was Stanley's third feature, but his first real exposure to Hollywood. We were really devastated by a star's agent having that kind of negative attitude about the picture. A lot of our friends seriously advised us to re-edit the picture as a straight-line story."

The Killing is now considered a classic for its daring cinematic storytelling and its use of nonlinear structure (just the sort of thing that made Quentin Tarantino's career in the early nineties), but at the time many found it baffling. Flashbacks had been used since D. W. Griffith, but *The Killing* took several steps past the idea of a simple backstory to reveal dramatic information. In Kubrick's cinematic world, time could be visited and revisited, like tripping with H. G. Wells's time machine. "It was very hard for me to follow reading the script," Marie Windsor remembers, speaking about when she first read the screenplay. "I hadn't seen a script that was involved in those flashbacks before, and I had a hard time keeping track of it. Now that's sort of the normal thing, but at that time I had never had a script like that in my hand, but it sure came alive when I saw it on the screen."

Harris and Kubrick believed in the structure. "The book was that way really, and that's what did it for us," Harris explains. But the negative criticism from so many friends, agents, and other insiders got to the deflated filmmakers. "If enough people tell you you're sick, maybe you should lie down," Harris said.

Disappointed, Harris and Kubrick flew back to New York. Before they turned in their final cut to United Artists, they decided to see if everyone was right about the structure. Kubrick brought the picture to Titra Films, where he had cut much of his earlier work. He took the picture apart and began to re-edit the film as a straight-line story.

Harris and Kubrick's filmmaking instincts served them well. Taking the complex cinematic structure apart and trying to make the film into a conventional narrative made them trust their original vision. "We couldn't get ourselves to abandon it, in spite of what friends and agents told us," Harris explains. "In most cases we had straight-cut from one scene to another and not much of that had been done before. So Stanley and I said, 'For Chrissakes, the whole thing about the book that had intrigued us was its structure. In our view the thing that makes this picture stand out beyond any caper movie—and there's been so many of them—is the structure, which follows the book. We've got to go with what got us involved to begin with.' So we put it back the way we had it at the preview and delivered it that way to United Artists."

Back in its original nonlinear structure, *The Killing* was scored by

Gerald Fried. The main theme is full of bold, brassy horns and a stag-
gered rhythm that kicks off the caper movie with a bang. "We call it a
dogfight between three and four," Fried explains. "The strings play a
four/four feel, and the brass goes over that. That's the main theme—
clashing themes. I figured the most exciting thing was to get back to
what excited me—like Stravinsky's *Rites of Spring*. What's more primal
than three fights four? That's the main theme of that movie.

"I wanted to give it size. It wasn't just the story of a racetrack robbery,
it was the story of the quality of life. At the end Sterling Hayden's girlfriend says to him that he has a chance to run, and he says, 'What's the
difference.' This was a large statement, which Stanley makes continually.
So I wanted it to sound large—and brass to me was exciting. Our aesthetic was the forward thrust. This movie had gotten started and, like a
runaway train, it just never let up."

The score was recorded in Los Angeles at the Goldwyn Studios. "It
was the best scoring stage in history and Vint Vernon, the music recorder, was probably the best music recorder in history," Fried recalls.
The orchestra comprised forty musicians. "None other than André
Previn was on piano, Pete Candoli was in the trumpet section, and
Shelly Manne was on drums. I was conducting them, that was a big
moment—it was exciting," Fried remembers.

After the film was put back into its original nonlinear structure, Harris
and Kubrick brought it to Max Youngstein at United Artists. "We
proudly showed him the picture, and at least he didn't say make it a
linear, straight-line story, at least he liked it for what it was," remembers
Harris. As they left the screening room the twenty-seven-year-old filmmakers followed Youngstein down the hall, trying to get him to commit
to a future with Harris-Kubrick. "It was pretty much, 'You bring us a
project that we like,' and I said, 'We could do that anywhere,'" Harris
recalled. "It was the feeling, 'What did you do for us today? Okay, you
delivered the picture, it's terrific, I hope you can get your $130,000 back
and leave us alone.' We said, 'Yes, but you have other people who have
deals here, these people are making movies.' I remember Stanley asking
him, 'How do you rate us with all the filmmakers that you have?' Youngstein said, 'Not far from the bottom.' That's the line we got, 'Not far
from the bottom.' It was like, 'We have to get another project and come
to you?' 'Yes, the door is always open, kids, I'll see you later.'"

Harris and Kubrick left the meeting determined to continue on their
own. It was time to get an agent to represent them. So they contacted
Ronnie Lubin at the Jaffe Agency, where they first bought the rights to
Clean Break. They decided to take out trade ads and promote them-

selves, using *The Killing* as a calling card. They designed a trade ad. Kubrick had maintained his contacts with his former employers at *Look* magazine, so he was able to use one of *Look*'s photo studios to take a publicity picture for the ad. Kubrick and Harris posed sitting next to each other in director's chairs, with a Goldberg can presumably filled with a spanking-new print of *The Killing* next to them. When they were ready to strike the right attitude of confidence and youthful arrogance, Kubrick ran over to his camera and set off the time exposure—a technique that his boyhood friend Marvin Traub used to take family pictures and one that Kubrick had used many times as a professional still photographer. When the ad was laid out, they included the copy "The new UA team James B. Harris, Stanley Kubrick, the new suspense film of the year—all through United Artists" and brought the concocted trade advertisement to Max Youngstein. Harris recalls Youngstein's tirade: " 'Are you guys crazy? You must be nuts! First of all *we're* the new UA team! Bob Benjamin, Arthur Krim, Roger Lew, who is the head of advertising and publicity, and myself, *we're* the new UA team! What is everybody else who makes pictures here going to say? They're all going to want trade ads! You kids are really starting to get me crazy now!' " My comeback was, " 'Well, okay, we'll do it ourselves, you don't have to pay for it, Max. It's all right, we'll do it ourselves.' He said, 'No, no you don't get it, I don't care who pays for it. *Don't run these ads!*' "

Harris-Kubrick ran the ads, verbatim. They took out a full page in *Weekly Variety* and another in the *Hollywood Reporter* and went out to the West Coast to promote the film. The ads came out. Youngstein tracked Harris down from his office at the old Goldwyn Studios. "He screamed at me," Harris recalls. " 'You doubled-crossed me! I told you not to do this! You're not running this ad anymore, are you?' " We said, 'Well, it's going to be in *Variety*.' He said, 'If you run this again you're just going to antagonize UA to the point where they're not going to give a shit about your picture and your future certainly will not be here!' So we didn't take the next ad."

Despite their enthusiasm, James B. Harris and Stanley Kubrick were not able to get the special handling *The Killing* required. Kubrick saw his film as a sleeper and wanted it to be opened at art houses so it could be discovered by critics and sophisticated audiences—but that was not to happen.

After Harris and Kubrick had been out in L.A. for a couple of months trying to gather momentum for their film, Harris got an emergency call from United Artists. The studio had decided to open the picture—within the week. It needed to pull one of its films from a Broadway theater in

New York because it had failed to perform, and product was needed. UA requested that Harris and Kubrick fly back with *The Killing* and do publicity for the film. The team obliged, but the odds of success were strikingly against them. There was little time to mount an effective campaign in just a few days, and the film was to play second on a double feature with *Bandido,* starring Robert Mitchum. The double billing had earnings implications, since it meant the film would receive flat rentals and not play the kind of engagements in which Harris-Kubrick would receive a percentage of the house.

The Killing didn't receive public adoration or a shower of box office riches, it didn't make its money back, but the ingenious caper film did succeed as a reputation builder for Harris-Kubrick Pictures. The film began to be screened in Hollywood's in-crowd circles.

The Killing is the first mature Kubrick film. Working with a largely professional crew, he was able to clearly display his directorial talents. The film's design and structure are cleanly thought out and executed. The high-key, contrasty, low wide-angle shots mimic the noir style, but the complex story structure pushes the film well beyond the goals of a B-movie potboiler. For the first time, Kubrick demonstrates his bold use of camera movement—tracking the camera left, right, forward, and back. A connection with Orson Welles is apparent—the multiple points of view, extreme angles, and deep focus.

The Killing was released on May 20, 1956. On June 4, a *Time* magazine article titled "The New Pictures" stated: "At twenty-seven, writer-director Stanley Kubrick, in his third full-length picture, has shown more audacity with dialogue and camera than Hollywood has seen since the obstreperous Orson Welles went riding out of town on an exhibitor's poll." The ever elusive King-of-the-Hollywood-hill scepter was now in Stanley Kubrick's hands.

Kubrick was beginning to develop a philosophy about how his films looked cinematographically. His deep love for filmmaking had its genesis in the symmetrically balanced photographic images that obsessed him since his early teens. He regarded the shorts and his first two features as adolescent experiments. *The Killing* was his first big-league production. Kubrick began to approach all of his cinematic tools as means for seizing a photographic vision. The themes were developing subconsciously. In his heart Kubrick was a fatalist, an existentialist, and he was attracted to literary material, which spoke to his growing dark vision. Photographically he was on a quest to take the implements of cinematography and reinvent them for his own purposes.

The viewfinder he used to determine and plan shots became an important bridge between his inner eye and the final light-struck result on film. This device allowed the camera operator to compose and view images before and during the filming. Kubrick did a lot of thinking about what he was seeing through the viewfinder and began to develop an ideology. "The Mitchell viewfinder had an extraordinary property because the optics of the finder and the ground glass were roughly the equivalent of looking at a right-side-up ground glass on a view camera, that's the way the image was formed as it was focused on the ground glass. The quality was quite striking," Alexander Singer explained about the focusing system where light hits an etched or "ground" pane of glass, which allows the viewer to focus an image if it appears to be fuzzy. "At one point Stanley said, 'I'm not going to look through the viewfinder. I'm going to get a finder with cheap optics and a rotten image because when you look through the Mitchell viewfinder everything looks wonderful.' With the viewfinder you cut out a segment of the world and surround it by the darkness of the perceived image—the concentration of light and color surrounded by darkness and, thereby, intensified produces an effect of drama that by the nearest move and angle suddenly is amplified to something really quite special. He was forever wanting to say, 'I have to do more, it's not just taking a pretty picture. I've got to push the limits more. If I start out already perceiving what looks to be a pretty picture, I will be less effective.' To me it was a mark of extraordinary visual sensibility. He knew the difference of the perceived effect, of the one thing against the other. That sense that he could control his world was really very special."

By 1958, after the completion of *Paths of Glory*, Kubrick had synthesized his lighting credo. "We are all used to seeing things in a certain way, with the light coming from some natural source. I try to duplicate this natural light in the filming. It makes for a feeling of greater reality," he told Joanne Stang for the *New York Times*.

In the fall of 1955 David Vaughan had returned to England for a visit. In the summer of 1956 he went to Paris to see the New York City Ballet on tour. Vaughan met Sobotka there. "I gathered from her at the time that her marriage with Stanley was not in a very stable state," he recalls. In October 1956 Vaughan returned to New York and called Kubrick and Sobotka in Los Angeles. "They said, 'Oh, why don't you come out?'" Vaughan remembers. "A friend of mine was driving out, so I drove out with him because Stanley said, 'I'll get you a job here.' I don't know what sort of a job it was, but he felt he could get me a job in the studios. So I went out there and found that things were in a terrible state between them. Stanley was going off to the studio. He would leave every morning and Ruth was left alone at home. Ruth always feared she'd be like her mother. Her father was a professor at the University of Pittsburgh and a very distinguished architect. He had a girlfriend out there, but he would come back to New York and be with Gisela, Ruth's mother, and her mother was perfectly content, she just accepted this not-very-good situation. Ruth really didn't want to be left at home and have a dinner ready for Stanley when he came home—which is what he seemed to want. So it was an unhappy time."

Vaughan found the tension between the couple unnerving, so he called the only other person he knew in Hollywood, Gavin Lambert, to get away from the marital strife. Sobotka decided to return to New York. The ballet company was about to go into rehearsals. Kubrick told David Vaughan, "You don't have to stay here if you don't want to" and lent him the money for the airfare to return to New York.

Vaughan and Sobotka remained good friends. In 1964 she told Vaughan, who was in India on tour with the Merce Cunningham Dance Company, that an apartment was available in their old building. Sobotka forged her friend's name on the lease so he could obtain the apartment.

As *The Killing* was beginning to solidify his career, Kubrick's second marriage was unraveling.

CHAPTER 8

"This Is
Stanley Kubrick"

The opening looked like a monochromatic painting painted in mud.
—Keir Dullea

I'd call Stanley a movie scientist. He's always interested not only in technology but in people's motives.
—Richard Anderson

As *The Killing* was attracting the eyes and ears of those in Hollywood who were looking for new trends and vital talent, the film came to the attention of Dore Schary, then head of production at MGM. Schary had worked for David O. Selznick and RKO and was in the slim minority of studio executives who tried to resist the blacklist during Senator McCarthy's reign of anti-Communist hysteria.

Schary saw *The Killing* before United Artists made its abrupt decision to hastily release the picture. He was enthusiastic about the film and the filmmakers and inquired as to whether the film was going to be released. At the time, *The Killing* was still in distribution limbo, sitting on the proverbial "shelf." Harris told Schary that UA was eventually going to release the film. "I'd like MGM to have this picture," Schary told Harris, who went back to UA and tried to negotiate buying *The Killing* back so it could be sold to MGM for proper treatment. "We're not in the business to make movies and then sell them" was the studio's response. Even though he couldn't get *The Killing*, Schary was still interested in Harris-Kubrick, the new kids on the block. So the compact mini-production company moved to MGM under Schary's aegis. The deal was made by Phil Gersh of the Jaffe Agency, who continued to be supportive of Harris-Kubrick and *The Killing*.

Now positioned at MGM, Harris and Kubrick set out to look for their first project for Leo the roaring lion. They started talking about subject matter. Both men were attracted to literature and good writing. Harris and Kubrick could work with writers but knew their own limitations as creators of an original story. They both agreed they wanted to do a film about war. Harris had been in the military; Kubrick had not, but he had always had a fascination with war and the military. It fit in with his attraction to chess, one of the oldest games of battle, and with his innate sense of organization. He was fascinated by the strategy of great generals.

The futility of war and man's bleak destiny to destroy occupied his imagination and had inspired him on his first feature—the existential *Fear and Desire*. Kubrick observed in 1958, "The soldier is absorbing because all the circumstances surrounding him have a kind of charged intensity. For all its horror, war is pure drama, probably because it is one of the few remaining situations where men stand up for and speak for what they believe to be their principles." The subject was to be war, and Kubrick remembered a book he had read in his teens in high school, *Paths of Glory* by Humphrey Cobb, which remained in his imagination. "It was one of the few books I'd read for pleasure in high school. I think I found it lying around my father's office and started reading it while waiting for him to get finished with a patient."

The novel had been published in 1935 and was later adapted into a Broadway play. Humphrey Cobb fashioned his bitter and searing story of three World War I soldiers executed for cowardice in France to cover up the maddening actions of a general who was willing to fire on his own men to further his ambitions.

The title was inspired by Thomas Gray's *Elegy Written in a Country Churchyard* in which the poet cautions, "The paths of glory lead but to the grave." The book had made a lasting impression on Kubrick. He reread the novel and declared it was to be his next project. After putting the book down in New York, Kubrick immediately sent a copy to James B. Harris, who was in Los Angeles. Harris read the book and gave an emphatic thumbs-up to his partner. He moved quickly to secure the rights. Harris and Kubrick agreed they would bring it to Dore Schary.

Schary was less than enthusiastic about *Paths of Glory*. "He said after

The Red Badge of Courage he had enough of downbeat antiwar stuff," Harris recalls. "I'm sorry, I know that book, it's great but not here," Schary told the disappointed duo. "Anything you want to do that we own, we'll discuss." Schary then told them to go to MGM's literary department to go through the studio's archive of books.

While they were going through hundreds and hundreds of titles, they came upon the novel *The Burning Secret* by Stefan Zweig. Kubrick had remembered the story of a child who protects his mother when his father finds out she has had an affair. He was animated about selecting it for their first MGM project. Harris was less excited, but they agreed to present it to Schary, who green-lighted the project.

The deal at MGM was for Harris-Kubrick to write, produce, and direct a film in forty weeks for a fee of $75,000, less their agent's fee. Schary was interested in developing new talent, but he also was a good executive. Kubrick had a writing credit on *The Killing* and had directed the film. Harris had produced. The deal was a neat package, but James B. Harris and Stanley Kubrick knew they had to work with writers. Kubrick had educated his partner about Jim Thompson; now he tapped another intriguing writer, Calder Willingham.

Calder Willingham was a thirty-three-year-old novelist who had written *End as a Man, Geraldine Bradshaw, Reach to the Stars, Natural Child,* and *To Eat a Peach,* which had just been published in 1955. A Southerner born in Atlanta but raised in Rome, Georgia, Willingham left the South as a young man to seek his literary fortune in New York City. In 1953 he settled into the lakes region of New Hampshire with his wife and children. His sense of irony, savagery, and dark knowledge of the military mind made him an ideal Kubrick collaborator.

Schary at first balked at hiring a writer. He pointed to their triple-threat deal, but eventually Harris and Kubrick convinced him that Willingham was the right person to adapt *The Burning Secret.* At the time Calder Willingham was in Ceylon script-doctoring *The Bridge on the River Kwai* for producer Sam Spiegel and director David Lean, so Harris and Kubrick had to wait for him to return. The forty-week clock was ticking.

While at MGM Harris-Kubrick continued to be a production entity that consisted only of James B. Harris and Stanley Kubrick. They were given an office and a secretary and were expected to comply with the corporate nine-to-five mentality of the studio. Stanley Kubrick had never been a nine-to-five guy. He was attuned to little sleep and constant work, work that didn't always take place at the office. "I remember being called in by one of the executives, who said, 'Where's your partner?

Where's Kubrick?' " Harris recalls. "I said, 'He's home working on the script. What do you think, we are at the racetrack or something?' They said, 'But he doesn't come to the studio.' I said, 'So what, he's working on the script.' They said, 'How do we know that?' I said, 'Because I'm telling you, that's how you know. I'm not a liar. We want to make movies—what would be the advantage in us goofing off?' "

Calder Willingham came back from Ceylon and began to work on the adaptation of *The Burning Secret,* with Harris-Kubrick halfway through the forty-week deal. Concurrently, they put Jim Thompson on assignment adapting *Paths of Glory,* even though MGM had given a firm no to their first selection.

The weeks continued to pass. The script for *The Burning Secret* was nowhere near completion, and it was clear to Harris and Kubrick that they were not going to fulfill the obligations of their contract deal. They turned in a first draft and were waiting to do revisions. Then corporate politics signaled trouble. Dore Schary was immediately summoned to New York for a big board meeting. After Schary left for the East Coast, MGM executive Benny Thaw called James B. Harris into his office. Back in New York during a tense board meeting, Dore Schary was fired, he was out as head of production for MGM. The Harris-Kubrick deal was no longer in his control. At the Los Angeles office, Thaw said to Harris, "We would like to cancel out the contract. We don't particularly think this is going to make a movie. The script isn't anywhere near ready in our view. Why don't we just call it off?"

"I was not ready to quit," remembers Harris. "So I said, 'Well, I have to discuss this with my partner.' " Harris thought about the cash flow of Harris-Kubrick—they were relying on the income from MGM. "There's nothing to discuss. This is it," Thaw proclaimed, ending the meeting and the arrangement.

Not knowing about Schary's fate, Harris ran to the phone and called the MGM executive offices in New York. "I got him out of a board meeting. I said it was an emergency," Harris recalls. "I tell him my sob story, we're his boys, so to speak, he brought us over. He said, 'Jimmy, right now I've got my own troubles here.' "

Harris found out that Schary was out of MGM. Harris-Kubrick received a registered letter from MGM informing them that they were in default of their contract. Somehow the studio had learned that Harris-Kubrick was working on *Paths of Glory* at night. Working on the second project wasn't a flagrant violation of the deal, but it handed MGM the excuse they needed to terminate *The Burning Secret* (which eventually

was made into a film). That was the end of the Harris-Kubrick relationship with MGM.

Kubrick had been moonlighting with Jim Thompson to write a draft of
Paths of Glory. Now the focus became getting *Paths of Glory* made.

When the script was finished Kubrick came up with an idea to help
sell the project. He and Harris gathered up several of their male friends,
dressed them in rented French World War I uniforms, and went out in
the woods for a photo shoot. They had done some photographic research
and found several World War I photos they liked. Kubrick used his photojournalist skills and staged the picture, re-creating the atmosphere and
reality of the actual World War I photos. "It was funny to see a head-
waiter and a friend of mine who was a violinist under contract to Universal as French soldiers."

The photo was put on the cover of the script, and like the trade ad for
The Killing that featured the young filmmakers in director's chairs, it was
a sign that for their time Harris-Kubrick were innovative rogues—an
independent production company long before Cannon, Carolco, New
Line, or Miramax.

Harris approached United Artists with *Paths of Glory*. Management
executive Max Youngstein told the young producer he would not accept
the project until the script was rewritten or a top star was attached.

The script by Kubrick and Jim Thompson was significantly rewritten
by Calder Willingham and resubmitted to United Artists. UA again rejected the project, telling Harris-Kubrick they felt strongly that the film,
if made, would surely be banned in France. Then UA's first requirement
became a reality. A star was interested in *Paths of Glory*. In Youngstein's
words a top, top star.

It was 1956. Kirk Douglas was a major Hollywood star. The handsome, well-built, intense actor with the dimpled, jutting chin and a voice
that could crack with fiery passion at any time, had been nominated for
the Oscar for his work in *Champion, The Bad and the Beautiful,* and
Lust for Life (in which he played tortured painter Vincent van Gogh).

Douglas's production company, Bryna Productions, named after his
mother, had been formed in 1955 to produce starring vehicles and films
with other stars. He was always looking for properties and talent.

Harris and Kubrick wanted Kirk Douglas to play Colonel Dax, the
lead role in the film. Their agent, Ronnie Lubin, sent the actor the
script.

Douglas had seen *The Killing* that year and was so taken with the film
that the forty-year-old actor arranged to meet its young twenty-eight-
year-old director. During their meeting, Douglas asked Kubrick if he

had any projects in the offing. Kubrick mentioned *Paths of Glory* and told Douglas that he and Harris were having trouble getting the picture set up at a major studio.

Kubrick got a rapid-fire response from Douglas about the script: " 'Stanley, I don't think this picture will ever make a nickel, but we *have* to make it,' " Kirk Douglas recalled in his autobiography, *The Ragman's Son.*

Kirk Douglas was enthusiastic and interested in doing the film, but he was unavailable at the time because of a prior commitment to do a play.

Not wanting to wait, Harris and Kubrick moved on to find another star to play Colonel Dax. While brainstorming over casting, they received a call from director William Wyler and actor Gregory Peck. The two Hollywood stalwarts were developing a caper picture and were so impressed with *The Killing* that they wondered whether Harris and Kubrick could inject a little of their magic into the Wyler-Peck script. Harris and Kubrick were both flattered by the overture. "We were so complimented and really loved the idea that we went over there," Harris recalls. "But what was really on our minds was, How can we get Gregory Peck to do *Paths of Glory*? We know he likes us, he respects us; let's show him the script, maybe we can make a trade deal. If they want us to fool around with their script and bring a little Harris-Kubrick into Wyler's style, maybe we can get Gregory Peck."

They did manage to get Peck to read the script, but despite the desire to do the film, Peck, like Kirk Douglas, was committed to several projects and couldn't offer a start date.

Harris and Kubrick continued searching for a star to create a package for the tough-sell project. The story was about World War I, not World War II. There were no women in it, and it was downbeat. "It's not what the studios dream about as their Christmas picture," Harris states. "There were agents who wouldn't even let their actors read the script. We tried and we couldn't get anybody to do this movie, we really couldn't."

When it seemed like Harris-Kubrick would never find their Colonel Dax, Kirk Douglas came back on the scene. There was a change in plans concerning the play he was to do. Douglas contacted Harris and Kubrick asking if the part was still available. He wanted to star in *Paths of Glory*.

Kirk Douglas's agent was Ray Stark, a former literary agent who represented Ben Hecht and was presently a powerful talent agent for Famous Artists—he had Marilyn Monroe and Richard Burton in his stable of stars. Stark was in his last days as an agent, about to form the Seven Arts Production Company with production executive Eliot Hyman. "This was like his last deal and he's going to make it a killer of a deal to make him go off with some style," Harris remembers.

A meeting was called on a Saturday in Palm Springs with James B. Harris, Stanley Kubrick, their agent Ronnie Lubin, Kirk Douglas, and Ray Stark. Harris and Kubrick wanted to make *Paths of Glory*. They had the ability and the resolve but little political power, so Stark made the terms tough and very much in favor of his star client. The film had to be a Bryna production. Douglas was to get a salary of $350,000. The deal was layered with many details, including first-class accommodations, a staff for location work, and the delivery of a 16mm print of the film. "The killer was Harris-Kubrick had to sign a deal with Bryna for five movies," recalls Harris, "two of which he would be in and three of which he did not have to be in. So we were going to work for Kirk Douglas at this point for our future."

The deal was tough, but Harris and Kubrick felt Douglas could get the film made. And he did. The powerful actor brought the project to United Artists, who told him they weren't interested in *Paths of Glory*. But Douglas's political stature paid off. He reminded UA that he had *The Vikings* scheduled to shoot for them in the summer and told them he had other studios vying for *Paths of Glory*. In reality Harris had already been turned down by all the major studios. Douglas made UA an offer it couldn't refuse—either make *Paths of Glory* with *The Vikings* and its box office potential, or he would go elsewhere. Under those circumstances United Artists agreed to make *Paths of Glory*. Harris-Kubrick moved into Bryna's offices in Beverly Hills.

Kubrick immersed himself in research about World War I. He spent hours carefully going over the extensive World War I photo collection at the Los Angeles Library and studying the details of trench warfare.

Paths of Glory now had the backing of a major studio and a top star, but Harris-Kubrick were still dealing with a low budget. UA agreed to finance the film up to a cash cost of $850,000. The total cost of the film was between $935,000 and $954,000. Kirk Douglas was getting $350,000, more than a third of the whole budget. That left $20,000 to $25,000 for director and producer fees. Harris and Kubrick would benefit from profits if the film were to make money. After the film broke even, the profits were to be divided 60 percent to Harris-Kubrick and 40 percent to United Artists.

Bryna and Harris-Kubrick decided to shoot the film in Munich, Germany. The anti-French sentiment made it problematic if not impossible to shoot in France, but Munich had the right architecture and terrain for the story.

Kubrick and Harris went ahead to Europe to begin preproduction. When Kirk Douglas arrived in Germany, he was surprised to see that the screenplay had been changed from the one he originally read—the revised version by Calder Willingham. "When I arrived at the Hotel Viejahrzeiten in Munich, I was greeted by Stanley and a completely rewritten script," Douglas recalled in his autobiography. "He had revised it on his own, with Jim Thompson. It was a catastrophe, a cheapened version of what I had thought had been a beautiful script. The dialogue was atrocious. My character said things like: 'You've got a big head. You're so sure the sun rises and sets up there in your noggin you don't even bother to carry matches.' And 'And you've got the only brain in the world. They made yours and threw the pattern away? The rest of us have a skullful of cornflakes.' Speeches like this went on for pages, right up to the happy ending, when the general's car arrives screeching to halt the firing squad and he changes the men's death sentence to thirty days in the guardhouse. Then my character, Colonel Dax, goes off with the bad guy he has been fighting all through the movie, General Rousseau, to have a drink, as the general puts his arm around my shoulder.

"I called Stanley and Harris to my room. 'Stanley, did you write this?' 'Yes.' Kubrick always had a calm way about him. I never heard him raise his voice, never saw him get excited or reveal anything. He just looked at you through those big, wide eyes. I said, 'Stanley, why would you do that?' He very calmly said, 'To make it commercial. I want to make money.' I hit the ceiling. I called him every four-letter word I could think of. 'You came to me with a script written by other people. It was based on a book. I love *that* script. I told you I didn't think this would be commercial, but I want to make it. You left it in my hands to put the picture together. I got the money, based on *that* script. Not this shit!' I threw the script across the room. 'We're going back to the original script, or we're not making the picture.' Stanley never blinked an eye. We shot the original script. I think the movie is a classic, one of the most important pictures—possibly the *most* important picture—Stanley Kubrick has ever made."

Egos clashed. Douglas had signed Kubrick to a multipicture contract to Bryna Company, which was producing *Paths of Glory*, but Kubrick continued to put up Harris-Kubrick signs everywhere to claim ownership to the film. Douglas didn't confront Kubrick, but he boiled at the implication that the film was a Harris-Kubrick production.

Actor Richard Anderson had just completed his contract at MGM, where he had appeared in more than thirty films. One of Anderson's friends had met Kubrick and told the director he knew the actor. With his voracious appetite for screening movies, Kubrick had seen all of Anderson's work at Metro and told the friend he would like to meet the actor. "He came up to my apartment and we talked for two hours, mainly about movies, not of actors particularly, but just pictures," recalled Anderson, who went on to appear in *Compulsion, Seven Days in May,* and *Seconds,* as well as playing government agent Oscar Goldman in television's *The Six Million Dollar Man* and *The Bionic Woman.* "I had always dreamed of eventually going into production and making pictures, so we had a lot to talk about. He was very curious about my six years at Metro. So that was it. Then one night about eleven o'clock, I got a telephone call from Jimmy Harris. He said, 'How would you like to go to Germany?' Then Stanley got on the phone and explained the story to me. I said it sounded interesting and they sent me a script."

Anderson remembers Kubrick as an avid reader who could stay home all day surrounded by stacks of books. "He read a lot of Immanuel Kant," Anderson said. "He used to have this apartment off of the strip and he just stayed home all day. All he would do was read, read, read, read and smoke. Read and smoke."

When Anderson arrived on the set in Germany before shooting began, Kubrick asked him to be his dialogue coach on *Paths of Glory.* In addition to playing the important role of Saint-Auban, the officer who prosecutes the doomed men, Anderson worked with the cast, running lines and rehearsing with them to help them learn their parts. Anderson was on the film from the first to the last day and had the opportunity to watch Kubrick direct the masterful *Paths of Glory.*

Kubrick had individual meetings with all of his cast, but he never talked with Anderson. Apparently he had confidence in the seasoned actor in his conception of the character of Saint-Auban and trusted him to work effectively with the other actors.

Kubrick continued not to give Anderson any notes during his performance of the early scenes in the film. During the court-martial sequence the judges were seated at a table. Kirk Douglas was seated at the defense table, and Anderson was opposite him at the prosecution table. Anderson had been playing Saint-Auban in a laid-back manner, as the second to the mad General Mireau—played brilliantly by George Macready—and he felt this was the time for his character to take charge. Anderson stood up and walked toward the first defendant, firing his interrogation. "Stanley said, 'Wait a minute, just stand by your table,' " Anderson recalled. "I said, 'Just a minute, Stanley, watch this.' He was marvelous because from then on there was not a word out of him. He saw what I was doing and that gave him the opportunity to put the camera behind the judges, which he loved. He just had the best time when we got onto the set with the sound of the boots on the marble floor and the whole thing."

Kubrick took full advantage of the production sound, capturing the echo of the château and preserving the actual performances that he filmed, without any significant dubbing or looping during postproduction.

The marble floor in the court-martial scene is a chessboard. When the camera is placed in a high position, the viewer can see that the three men are standing in a human chess game and they are the pawns. Kubrick continued to find metaphors for the game that so pervaded his imagination and shaped his view of the world.

The day of filming for the opening scene, in which General Broulard, played by Adolphe Menjou, cajoles General Mireau into taking on the Ant Hill attack, Kubrick had preplanned moving the camera in a dance-like choreography that follows the two men as the web of the film's plot line is being spun. Kubrick had been a longtime lover of the films of Max Ophuls. He had spoken to James B. Harris and others about the fluid camera movements the director had achieved in films like *The Earrings of Madam De . . . .* Kubrick arrived on the set. Before a camera was turned, he walked over to Richard Anderson and said stoically, "Max Ophuls died today—this is in honor to him." Kubrick inherited the mantle of the moving camera from Ophuls, but when combined with his own bleak vision the dance became not Ophuls's dance of elegance and humanity but a Kubrick dance of doom.

Anderson's first day of work as Saint-Auban in the film was the scene where Mireau goes to Dax's underground quarters to give him orders to take the Ant Hill. "After a couple of takes I turned to Stanley and I said, 'Well, this is really exciting,' " Anderson recalls. "And Stanley said to me, 'What do you mean exciting? It's just like Hollywood. You've done a lot of movies, Richard, and this is no different from what you did in Hollywood.' I was a little stunned and didn't answer him because I really couldn't answer him. I couldn't specifically say to him this was different—because you're just making a movie. You don't know what it's going to turn out to be like, but I sensed that it was quite different from anything I had ever done before working in the studio system. It was different. It was more offhand, less people, less autocratic, less front-office."

The interiors were shot at the Bavarian Film City in the old Geiselgasteig Studios on the outskirts of Munich. Once very active, the studio was not used during World War II and had been in disuse in the postwar years. The locations for the battle site and the château used as a base for the French military were within forty minutes of the studio by car.

For the battle scenes the company employed nearly eight hundred German policemen to play the French soldiers. In the early fifties German police were given three years of strict military training, and so were able to perform the tasks of the fighting soldiers in the film. The men were well trained but at first did not understand that they were playing battle-weary troops under constant bombardment. The script called for the infantrymen to be beaten down and tired. The spirited German policemen wanted to perform feats of valor to show their bravery and patriotism for their country. Eventually Kubrick was able to get them to understand the danger that the characters were in and the moral desperation that overcame them. His film was about the futility of war.

Kubrick enjoyed working with the German crew, who barely spoke English, and he told Alexander Walker, "The Germans were superb technicians, totally work-oriented." For director of photography Kubrick chose George Krause, a German cameraman who had photographed *Man on a Tightrope* for Elia Kazan four years earlier. Working in Germany allowed Kubrick to operate the camera himself and get back to the hands-on control of his films that he had had before *The Killing*.

Kubrick operated the hand-held camera on *Paths of Glory* as he had on *The Killing*. His hand-held work with the motion picture camera was an extension of his photojournalist background and brought documentary reality to his fictional films. As James Monaco observes, "Kubrick's cinema is a laboratory in which the various contrasting elements of still and movie aesthetics are rigorously tested. . . . [C]onsidering the close technological parallels between still photography, it's surprising that so few still photographers have had any success with movies. . . . But for many years Stanley Kubrick stood alone as the only director to have successfully bridged the gap between stills and movies."

Originally Kubrick had intended to use the flat lands behind the Bavaria studios lot for the battle scene depicted in the film. The lot had been the setting for many great German war films, but Kubrick needed a larger area to create the no-man's-land between the French trenches and the German wire at the Ant Hill.

Production manager John E. Pommer scoured the area and eventually found a proper location for the battlefield, but the land was owned by at least sixteen different landholders, each of whom made insurmountable demands on the production company.

Two weeks before cameras were to roll, Pommer discovered a fertile country pasture owned by a single proprietor. The man was reluctant to have his cultivated farm field destroyed, but he was convinced to rent the land to the production.

The art department, headed by art director Ludwig Reiber, began to transform the peaceful pasture of 1957 into a 1915–16 Western Front battlefield. Reiber began his career in 1923. *Paths of Glory* was his 106th film. Working closely with Reiber and Kubrick, who demanded complete accuracy, was Baron Otto von Waldenfels, one of Europe's preeminent authorities on World War I, who was the film's technical adviser.

The transformation from pasture to World War I battlefield took three weeks and up to sixty laborers working around the clock in shifts. Eight cranes were employed to excavate crater holes and trenches. Kubrick wanted a barren wasteland for the sake of both realism and metaphor. Once the ground was prepared, authentic World War I shells, abandoned equipment, and weapons were spread over the vast expanse. Rolls of barbed wire were strewn across the terrain, forming grisly patterns. In the distance was the Ant Hill, the French objective staunchly held by the Germans. In front of the Hill was a crashed 1915 World War I airplane, a grim reminder of the futility of the situation. Kubrick wanted the plane to be smoldering as a result of a recent crash. Special-effects wizard Erwin Lange created a liquid chemical that could be sprayed on the plane. When the chemical made contact with the air, it gave the visual impression of a smoldering fire.

Having worked on many outstanding European war films, Lange was up to the many challenges presented to him by his meticulous young director. He began as a professional chemist and in 1930 was creating special effects at the legendary German film studio Universum Film Aktien Gesellschaft, known as UFA.

Kubrick insisted that he did not want the conventional war film explosions that produced clouds of dust and sand raining down on the battlefield. He wanted verisimilitude on film. A shell explosion threw mud, stones, and shrapnel into the air, which tore into the ground.

The production demanded such large quantities of smoke, fireworks, and other explosives that Lange had to go before a special German governmental commission before obtaining permission to amass the immense quantities of explosives dictated by Kubrick's penchant for absolute authenticity. Lange quickly learned that this was not a routine assignment.

Lange spent long hours experimenting with untried techniques to simulate a shell explosion. Eventually he came up with a solution that involved filling cone-shaped craters lined with metal sleeves with fine dirt and a composition of blackened, pressed cork. The craters were dug at precise and strategic coordinates across the expanse of the battlefield. When detonated, the cork emerged as a hard, heavy, and brittle rubble mixing with the shards of dirt spitting into the air and into the ground.

To explode the charges, a team of electricians lined the field with miles of electrical wire. Timing the explosions required precision accuracy and steely nerves, as Kubrick repeated movements of the battle up to as many as thirty times until he was satisfied. In the first week alone, Lange estimated he disbursed more than a ton of explosive material.

Kubrick invested a lot of time and effort in detail to create the atmosphere of a real battlefield. "We worked for a month preparing that field—500 yards wide and 300 feet long," Kubrick told *Newsweek* in 1957. "After we'd dug and blasted up the field, we put a great many little props around—ruined guns scattered in different holes, and bits of soldiers' tunics. You couldn't see them, but you could feel them. . . . Most of the time was spent in planting explosive charges and timing them so they'd go off right. It took a half a day to set up, and thirty seconds to do."

For the hopeless attempt to take the Ant Hill, Kubrick employed multiple cameras and devised a grid system to coordinate how the French infantrymen would die as they were slaughtered by the barrage from behind the German wire. Six hundred extras were used for the sequence. "We had six cameras, one behind the other on a long dolly track which ran parallel to the attack," he told Alexander Walker. "The battlefield was divided into five 'dying zones' and each extra was given a number ranging from one to five and told to 'die' in that zone, if possible near an explosion. I operated an Arriflex camera with a zoom lens and concentrated on Kirk Douglas." "The men in zone five went all the way," Kubrick told *Newsweek*.

The most memorable images in *Paths of Glory* are the relentless tracking shots in the French trenches. Before shooting began Kubrick took Richard Anderson out to the field where he was planning to shoot the trench sequences. "He said, 'Here's where we're going to dig the trench,'" Anderson remembers. "And that's just what they did, they dug a trench and put in wooden planks." Kubrick wanted his camera to dolly through—tracking forward and back. Tracks could not be laid because Kubrick wanted the frame to capture the bleak sky above and the dirt below the men's feet. He ordered that the trenches be dug six feet wide in order to allow the camera and dolly to pass through freely. Technical adviser Otto von Waldenfels protested vigorously that the French World War I trenches were narrow and that Kubrick was not being historically correct. Kubrick pressed on and had the art department lay duckboards on the dirt floor. This was historically accurate, the boards protected the men from walking on the sinking mud that developed, and it was the solution to creating smooth long-take moving shots. The camera dolly moved along the duckboards as the lens disclosed the beaten-down, bat-tle-weary soldiers devoid of all hope.

"The trench was gruesome," Anderson recalls. "It just reeked, and then the weather was so lousy—it was cold, it was freezing and overcast and gray. We were all sick. We all had colds, we were all sick from the first week. We all looked awful and it certainly added to the movie."

Kubrick sat on a stool placed on the dolly and called for take after take. Crew members kept putting pieces of wood under the duckboards to even out the path of the dolly as it tracked in front of and behind Kirk Douglas, Richard Anderson, and George Macready, with Kubrick lead-ing the camera's thrusting force.

When Mireau and Saint-Auban tour the trenches to connect with the battle-weary men, they are under a ferocious bombardment. Anderson, who had served in World War II and has long been a student of history, understood that Saint-Auban wanted to set a good example for the men in front of his general and therefore would barely react to the explosions as they went off around them. "Stanley said, 'Dick, you've got to ac-knowledge that the explosions are going off there,'" Anderson remem-bers. "I said, 'I will.' When he saw what I was doing he left it alone. A good director will leave you alone if it satisfies him. He is an audience. Once they have confidence in you as an actor they leave you alone, but if you try something they don't understand or if you're shaky they'll drive you crazy through the whole movie and they may keep going after you."

Kubrick totally immersed himself in the world of *Paths of Glory*. To understand the full scope of what he was putting on film, Kubrick de-manded to know the answers to questions that multiplied with each new answer: What brand of cigarettes did the French soldiers smoke? What newspapers did they read? What songs were sung? How did they trim their beards? What pinups were tacked to their trench walls? What did they talk about?

A medieval château was selected for the general's headquarters. *Paths of Glory* was about class distinction. The fighting men lived under the ground—their blood spilled. The officers lived in splendor—the wine flowed.

During the filming of the execution scene, which was staged in front of a castle and took several days to shoot, Kubrick spent time experi-menting with long lenses, shooting the three men walking to their death. The compression of the lenses caused the castle in the extreme background to overwhelm the foreground action, so he backed off using the full effect.

When Saint-Auban walks up to the men and reads them their death sentence just before they are to die, Richard Anderson felt it was an opportunity to reveal Auban's humanity and his displeasure at his half-mad superior. "Stanley said to me, 'Dick, just read it off, this is almost a vindication of what you've been attempting to do. Just read it off,'" Anderson remembers. "Okay, I said, 'I'll do it.' I did it and then I said, 'Alright, will you let me try what I originally wanted to do?' He says, 'Okay,' and then I did that and I remember the German script girl said, 'The first one's better because at the end you just knocked the guys off.' Well, this was just a choice, so he had them both. He was smart—he didn't just say, 'Do it.' He had enough confidence in the actor. Stanley said, 'Let's shoot it two ways.' He hadn't made up his mind what to do with it. What I had in mind was, The guy's a human being and when he actually sees the enormity of this crime, it overwhelms him—but Auban still has to say, let's do it. So my sense was to show the audience that this is lunacy. Menjou says just to shoot a couple of them, it's good for discipline. We had to do something—we couldn't blame the general. The enormity of a man like Saint-Auban who's intelligent—brought up in the French military system, but he's intelligent—he suddenly sees this as a catastrophe and that's how I played it."

During Easter, Anderson decided that he wanted to go to Paris for the weekend. "Stanley heard that I was going to Paris and he didn't like that," Anderson recalled. "He said, 'Here I am working on a goddamn soundstage and you're going to Paris.' I said, 'I'm going to take a train and stand up and go to Paris. For God's sake, I've never been to Paris and I'm twenty-six years old. I wanted to go see what Paris was like.' So he says, 'All right, go ahead.' And then he asked me a question. It wasn't a serious question, it had nothing to do with me personally, but it had to do with a lady I knew. I said, 'Stanley, if I answer this question will you use the second take?' and he said, 'Yes.' And I answered the question and he used the second take. Now that's integrity. Now he might have asked sixty people which one do you think? But he did exactly what he said he would do."

Paths of Glory demonstrates Kubrick's technical virtuosity and his bleak, cold vision. The high-key, wide-angle shots of the château interior are contrasted against the bleak, gray, constantly tracking shots of the men. Kubrick learned lessons from the masters. The fluid tracking shots he so admired from Max Ophuls and the deep-focus, low wide-angle shots that became Orson Welles's signature are articulated through Kubrick's geometric, symmetrical, photographer's eye. Kubrick drains the humanity and theatrical drama out of the images. This is a human chess game, an overwhelming metaphor that obsesses Kubrick. The battle through no-man's-land is choreographed with long takes and accented with long lenses, which push Dax into a surreal state as he is surrounded by the reality of war. The effectiveness of Kubrick's use of the camera during the battle scene incited film critic Peter Cowie to say that Kubrick handled the camera "unflinchingly like a weapon." The film's finale is a masterful example of the power of film editing, as Kubrick builds a sentimental but powerful montage of battle-worn faces tired of war. The rhythm of the scene is dictated by the sweet German girl's singing voice.

Kubrick elicited strong performances from his male cast. As Dax, Kirk Douglas gives a seething but controlled portrayal exploding with the passion of his convictions at the injustice leveled at his men. Adolphe Menjou was a casting coup that Kubrick used to his advantage. Menjou was sixty-eight years old, near the end of an illustrious career after appearing in scores of films since *The Man Behind the Door* in 1914. An extreme conservative, Menjou had gone to a military academy, served in World War I as a captain in the Ambulance Corps, and in 1944 was among the founding members of the Motion Picture Alliance for the Preservation of American Ideals. Ten years before *Paths of Glory* Menjou was a "friendly" witness for the 1947 hearings of the House Un-American Activities Committee. Kubrick worked very closely with Menjou, convincing the actor that Broulard was an important and great general who was the real hero of the story. Broulard kept the power-hungry Dax and Mireau at arm's length. Menjou was an experienced and skilled film actor. When he worked with Charlie Chaplin in *Woman of Paris* in 1923, Chaplin defined screen acting by saying, "Menjou, this is how an actor works in movies. You're in a bedroom and a camera is like a person looking through a keyhole at you."

When Menjou first started on the film, he turned to Richard Anderson and said, "I'll be very interested to see how *this picture* turns out." After the film was released, Anderson ran into Menjou in Beverly Hills. The two actors had a leisurely chat, but *Paths of Glory* and Stanley Kubrick were never introduced into the conversation.

Menjou did talk to the press at the time about working with Stanley Kubrick, saying, "The greatest director who launched me on my career was Chaplin. Stanley works more like him than anybody I've ever seen—

in that the actor is always right and the director always is wrong. . . . He'll be one of the ten best directors. When? It usually takes three pictures, so I guess the next one."

Kubrick used his indomitable patience to succeed in getting Menjou to perform take after take until the director was satisfied that the actor had explored all the terrain of a scene. This was a formidable accomplishment with a powerful actor of Menjou's stature in the film industry.

This process was not without tests for the young director. As the producer of *Paths of Glory,* James B. Harris remembers an incident that occurred during a scene early in the film between Menjou and George Macready as Kubrick called, "Go again," for take after take. Harris recalls Adolphe Menjou getting really upset with Kubrick about the number of takes and saying, 'Why again?' Kubrick very calmly told him that 'It was not quite right' and that 'We're going to stay with it until we get it right and we can get it right because you guys are so right and it's working beautifully. What's there to be excited about, it's going great.' Usually you get defensive when somebody screams at you," Harris explains. "The first thing is to yell back to defend yourself, but Stanley handled it so beautifully. He may not have everybody love him while making a movie, but he gets what he wants because he earns it out of respect. When he wants something he usually can justify it."

Kubrick may have revealed his motive behind casting Adolphe Menjou by telling *Newsweek,* "You let the character unfold himself gradually before the audience. You hold off as long as possible revealing the kind he is. He comes in like a nice guy, and when the audience finds him out, they're trapped. You cast a person as the opposite of what he's really trying to do, so the audience will find out only later."

The scene when the three men are served their last meal racked up an enormous amount of takes due to the unorthodox acting methods of Timothy Carey, who continued to surprise the camera with unexpected gestures and facial manipulations. The shot in which the men grab at the duck dinner that is to be their last, took up to sixty-eight takes. If the take was aborted before the duck was ripped apart by the desperate men it could be used for the next take. If it had already been destroyed, a new duck was readied for the next take. "Timothy Carey just couldn't do the same thing twice, either deliberately or unconsciously," Kubrick told *Rolling Stone.* "He had to eat this meal in a prison cell and every take required an untouched duck."

The scene where the men sit in the prison and discuss their fate was shot on a Saturday morning that became Saturday afternoon. When the official shooting day had exhausted itself, the slate read Take 63 and

Kubrick was still not satisfied with the results. James B. Harris came down to tell Kubrick that they were beginning to get into overtime, which was not allowed in Germany. Kubrick continued to shoot take after take. The production manager came down and was very worried about the extended hours. The director, rarely known to express anger or any extreme emotion on the set, broke through his ice-water temperament. When Harris reminded him of the overtime situation by saying, "Stanley, we're in a lot of trouble," Kubrick shouted in anger, "I haven't got it yet!" The producer and production manager left and by Take 74 Kubrick had gotten his scene.

Outbursts like this are rare with Kubrick. Under tremendous stress and pressure he manages to maintain a flat, calm demeanor and the ability to transcend the temperamental nature of those around him, rarely reacting to a situation. With the nerve of a chess master or a general in the heat of battle, he is propelled by his icy calm and lack of emotion until he achieves his goal.

The film is nearly stolen by an outstanding performance by George Macready as General Mireau. A cultured gentleman who once owned a Los Angeles art gallery with another civilized screen villain, Vincent Price, Macready made his Broadway debut in 1926 playing Arthur Dimmesdale in *The Scarlet Letter,* and he made several stage appearances with Katharine Cornell. In the forties he became known for his portrayal of screen villains. Macready's theatrically trained voice and dynamic screen technique brought the maniacal General Mireau to life. A deep scar that Macready had gotten on his right cheek during a car accident gave a frightening reality to his heinous presence as the power-mad general. The film is filled with sharply drawn characterizations—especially by Ralph Meeker, Joe Turkel, and the irrepressible Timothy Carey as the doomed soldiers. The ensemble cast was rounded out with solid backing by Richard Anderson, Peter Capell, Wayne Morris, Bert Freed, Emile Meyer, and Jerry Hausner.

For the role of the German girl who sings to the shell-shocked men Kubrick chose Susanne Christian, whom he had seen on German television, a woman who was to become his third wife and permanent partner.

Christiane Susanne Harlan was born into a family of musicians, actors, and playwrights on May 10, 1932, in Braunschweig, Germany. The proud parents, Ingeborg de Freitas and Fritz Harlan, were both opera singers.

As a girl, Christiane was given dancing lessons and passed many hours playing in an old-fashioned opera house in Karlsruhe while Ingeborg and Fritz rehearsed the classics.

The Harlans lived in Karlsruhe, an artist's town, where little Christiane sketched and created craft objects. The family shared a house with artist Paul Kusche. Later, when Christiane's brother, Jan, was born, Kusche's old painting studio became her bedroom, and she began to paint, inspired by hours spent watching Kusche paint at his easel.

As Christiane was developing an artistic persona and talents during her earliest years, the hate-filled dread of the Nazi Party, led by Adolf Hitler, was gaining terrifying velocity, ready to sweep terror throughout Europe. Like so many German children, Christiane was forced to be part of the Nazi youth movement. "I remember we had lovely uniforms with great pockets and we loved to stride around in them," Christiane Kubrick told Ann Morrow of the *Times* of London. "But all this Heil Hitler thing was really tongue-in-cheek, even with the most emotionally committed Nazis. I saw Hitler once when I was a little girl. I could hear that insane voice. I remember thinking he didn't raise his hand as high as I'd expected."

In 1941, when Christiane was nine years old, she was separated from her parents and she and Jan were evacuated to a brick factory in Reihen, a small village near Heidelberg. She worked in the fields harvesting peas and potatoes and lived with destitute families from surrounding coal-mining towns, prisoners of war, Frenchmen, and Ukrainian women. Christiane's fertile imagination gave her strength and developed her character. She created costumes out of what she could find, invented stories, and charmed the other children with her finesse. Christiane entertained with a puppet show all of her own creation. She conceived and constructed all of the puppets, drew all the tickets by hand, and played all the roles during the performances. She made toys and other decorations from clay she collected from the brick factory. The creative child also gathered scraps around the factory to construct scarecrows, which would remain in her emotional memory and later appear in her work as a mature painter.

Christiane drew the world around her, which enveloped the trappings of war. Her sketches of barbed wire and American airplanes became her diary of history. "It added up to a child's view of war. I was the little girl who moved in where Anne Frank was pushed out," she told Valerie Jenkins of the *Evening Standard*. The drawings of war-ravaged Germany were later lent for a Russian exhibition after World War II but were never returned. The childhood experience of growing up in Nazi Germany tormented Christiane with nightmares as a child and continued into her adult years.

Christiane turned thirteen as World War II was coming to a close, and her parents sent her to Salem, a prestigious boarding school near Lake Constance. The school had been founded by Kurt Hahn, who believed in the wholeness of humanity and a reconciliation of action and contemplation. "When I was at Salem, Kurt Hahn was teaching us democracy, I knew he'd had this skull injury and had a piece of silver going from his head into his jaw," Christiane Kubrick told Ann Morrow of the *Times* of London. "I spent the whole time during his classes with my head on one side trying to see if he had a silver plate—so much for democracy." Salem had been shut down by the Nazis, forcing Hahn to flee to England where he formed Gordonstoun, one of Britain's best-known schools. While at Salem Christiane designed and supervised the construction of sets for theater pieces performed at the school. After she had attended Salem for three years, the Harlans were forced to take her out of the school because of financial difficulties caused by the long and brutal war, which left Germany in ruin. In 1948 currency reform gave all German citizens forty marks to rebuild their lives with a new start. Fritz Harlan became a professor of music and taught opera at the Musikhochschule in Freiburg im Breisgau and struggled to support his family along with fellow West Germans. After leaving Salem, Christiane was compelled to earn a living. The sixteen-year-old changed her name to Susanne Christian and entered the world as an actress, joining thirty-nine members of her family, spanning three generations, who had worked in the theater as distinguished musicians, writers, actors, and directors.

Christiane first played roles in operetta and ballet productions and then moved into radio, theater, television, and films.

In 1952, Christiane married German actor Werner Bruhns, and in 1953 she gave birth to a daughter, Katharina Christiane, when she was twenty-one. The marriage to Bruhns ended four years later. Christiane spent much of her free time painting and drawing.

Stanley Kubrick discovered the beautiful and vulnerable actress one day while he was watching a television show that she appeared in. As soon as Stanley met Christiane he knew he wanted her in *Paths of Glory* as the only female in the film. He also knew that he was head over heels in love with her.

Once again, Kubrick got Gerald Fried to score his film. Fried and Kubrick relied on percussion, as they had for *Killer's Kiss*. *Paths of Glory* was about war, so the military snare drum became a key motif. A Johann Strauss waltz, *Artist's Life*, was used for an officers' dress ball. The sheet music to the classic waltz was rented, and Fried conducted an original recording of the piece. Fried was instructed to compose two main title themes. One featured the French national anthem, the "Marseillaise," which was used for the release of the film in the United States and other parts of the world. For French-sympathetic countries, the "Marseillaise" was removed and a percussion track was used for the main title.

The score was conducted by Fried and recorded at Geigelistag, the Bavarian Film Plaza, on a sound stage near where the film was produced. The musicians were members of the Bavarian Philharmonic and were contracted by Kurt Granker, who was the conductor of the Bavarian State Orchestra.

Kubrick and Fried screened *Paths of Glory* and carefully decided exactly where there would and would not be music. To achieve a full dramatic effect, they used percussion in key moments of the film while leaving many scenes without music. "There are certain places that just begged for music, like when the patrol went out the night before," Fried recalled. "That seemed like a perfect place for underscoring and for a percussion solo."

The music for the execution scene is chillingly scored with snare and bass drum, a minimalist approach that creates tension devoid of the sentimentality of a lyrical theme. "The execution is a six- or seven-minute segment, which was tough to score because it was not cut to rhythm," Fried explains. "I had to cheat on the beat to make it work. So when you cut to a guy drumming, you actually see him drumming right."

The ending of the film, where the young German girl sings to the men, was not the original ending of *Paths of Glory*. When Kubrick decided on the scene he turned to his composer and said, "Fried, I swear I didn't put it in because of Christiane, I really wanted it in there!" Fried remembers Kubrick at the last minute coming up with an old German folk song for Christiane to sing mournfully to the men. The song was "La Troeyer Hussar" (The Faithful Hussar). The folk song, well known to German schoolchildren at the time, was about a faithful Hussar in love with a maiden.

The song was selected and Christiane sang it live during the shooting of the scene. During the music scoring session nearly forty male singers were brought in to dub the voices of the men singing along with the girl. The music track was slowly developed, with Fried conducting the voices one at a time, then two at a time, building until the room in the film is filled with the men singing. "I had earphones and was listening to her while I conducted and brought in the musicians," Fried remembers. "There were a few mistakes, so we had to choreograph the mistakes to match what was on the picture."

James B. Harris remembers that when Kubrick selected the men to be used for the ending, he chose to use the actor whose character was killed earlier while on patrol by Lieutenant Roget, played by Wayne Morris. In order to have enough soldiers to effectively stage the scene, the actor was given a different makeup appearance and put in the bistro—back from the dead—to sing with the other men.

Fried arranged a symphonic march version of "La Troeyer Hussar" to play over the end credits of the film, which features portraits of the cast in the spirit of Orson Welles' *Citizen Kane*.

Paths of Glory was the last Kubrick film to be composed by Gerald Fried. It was the last Kubrick film to be scored by a single composer without using previously recorded music—called needle drops in the industry—and the last in which Kubrick would work one on one with a composer. Over the years his use of music would become controversial and influence the nature of film scoring itself. Gerald Fried had the distinction of being there at the beginning. About Kubrick's later use of needle drops, he jokes, "Either I was so good that he couldn't replace me or I was so bad he lost faith in contemporary composers." Alex North would score his next film, *Spartacus*, but he worked outside the control of the director.

Fried reflects, "I was rather in awe of the fact that this guy was a friend of mine who absolutely dazzled Hollywood, he also antagonized them as well. It was fun, people would be sitting around at a dinner party and someone would say, 'What are you doing?' 'Well, I just wrote the music for one of Kubrick's pictures.' 'What!' There was kind of an electricity. The only two directors you could talk about with him were Fellini and Bergman—that was fun, it was kind of neat. We were really good friends. He used to give my first baby his bottle, we were that good friends."

Simon Bourgin was the *Newsweek* magazine bureau chief in Los Angeles in the late fifties. Bourgin had worked for the U.S. Information Agency and was an expert in foreign affairs. He provided the New York office of *Newsweek* with weekly interviews and stories about leading Hollywood film directors and had covered George Stevens, Orson Welles, John Ford, Lewis Milestone, Cecil B. DeMille, George Cukor, Max Ophuls, Jean Renoir, and others.

Bourgin had seen *Paths of Glory* at a studio screening and described the experience as witnessing "an almost perfect motion picture, if you had to edit the goddam picture you couldn't take anything out of it." Bourgin arranged an interview with Kubrick and found him to be outside the nature of the film directors he had spent so much time knowing. "He was very young, he talked to me in short sleeves without a tie, he was very sober and not inclined to laugh or make small talk. Almost everything he said came out of a well-organized mind, it was in a straight line. He didn't hem and haw or hesitate. He had a strong personality and knew exactly what he wanted to say. I just really took it all down and there was my story. It was a very economical interview, I used almost everything he told me. I was very impressed—he was just a young man but I knew he had stature. I was interested in him for the things that he didn't say as much as for what he said. He was a man who, if you could know him and draw him out, would have a good deal to say about a lot of things. He wasn't an intellectual, but he had intellect. He was highly articulate, wrapped up totally in moviemaking to the point where nothing else very much interested him. He dressed very casually and not fashionably. Obviously, clothes meant nothing to him. He was one of those people who functions totally in relation to pictures. I've known a couple of them since and they exist for movies, they're loners even though they're married and have lives."

The article ran in *Newsweek* on December 2, 1957, and was filled with Kubrick's philosophy on filmmaking. "Intuition is the thing," Kubrick told Simon Bourgin. "A director has to work with so many elements in a film that he has to operate three quarters on intuition. The best ideas always come on the set when you see what's happening. I suppose most directors and writers find the reason why afterward. Feelings are more important than intellect. The audience responds to a film by its feeling not through any conscious analysis of what it has seen. . . . People go to movies in order to have some kind of intensive experience, whether it's comic, tragic, or horror and the biggest sin is to deprive them of it."

Joseph Laitin, a World War II war correspondent and former ombudsman for the *Washington Post,* was a freelance writer in Hollywood from 1952 to 1962, writing on film and entertainment for *Collier's* magazine, *The Saturday Evening Post,* CBS radio, and others. In 1957 Laitin saw *Paths of Glory* and was quite taken with the film. "I wrote and narrated a one-hour documentary for CBS radio called *The Changing Face of Hollywood,* an examination of whether the motion picture studios would survive TV, which at that time was only a remote threat to the movie industry. But the coaxial cable was snaking its way across the continent at that time and aimed at the heart of a slumbering industry and they were panicking. Kubrick was one of the upstarts, with no credentials and no studio backing who was the second most threatening specter to the moguls, although they wouldn't acknowledge it. I had seen *The Killing* and that impressed me enough to think he might be a good subject for a magazine piece."

After seeing *Paths of Glory* at a screening at the Screen Writers Guild,

Laitin arranged to meet Kubrick for coffee at the famed Schwab's drug-store—home of real and apocryphal stories of movie star discoveries. Kubrick chose the meeting place. Laitin had not seen Kubrick at the Guild screening, and he waited at Schwab's for half an hour past their scheduled appointment. "He finally arrived, physically shaking," Laitin recalled. "He apologized, saying he'd been stopped by a cop while he was driving to meet me." "I've always been terrified by cops. I don't understand it but I'm pretty shaken up and I can't even remember what the cop said I did wrong," Kubrick told Laitin.

Kubrick did not look like the typical Hollywood type to Laitin, who has interviewed a who's who of Hollywood from Fred Astaire to Adolph Zukor. "He dressed like a newspaper photographer," Laitin recalls. "In those days newspaper photographers dressed like blue-collar types."

Laitin was not able to sell the idea of a story on Stanley Kubrick. He tried *Collier's* magazine, *The Saturday Evening Post,* the *St. Louis Post-Dispatch* and *Coronet* magazine. None was interested in a story about Stanley Kubrick, at least not yet.

Laitin, a newspaperman with keen instincts who had the ear of Washington players from President Lyndon Johnson to Colin Powell, felt strongly that Stanley Kubrick was representative of a new wave in American filmmaking. He asked Kubrick to give him a taped interview for his radio documentary on the future of Hollywood.

After taping the interview, Laitin invited Kubrick to his studio at CBS Radio to listen to a rough cut of the program.

The radio program aired in late December 1958. The one-hour overview of Hollywood in transition at the end of the fifties contained interviews with Sam Goldwyn, Stanley Kramer, Kirk Douglas, Samuel Z. Arkoff, Joanne Woodward, Yul Brynner, and others.

Kubrick is introduced after an interview with the Duke of Hollywood, John Wayne. Laitin wrote a crisp lead-in heralding the young director. "Some younger people have managed to enter the field of moviemaking in the last few years, most of them recruited from television," Laitin pronounced over the air. "But one young man, still in his twenties armed only with faith in himself and the motion picture, came to Hollywood uninvited. Hardly anyone showed up at the preview of his first film but word did get around that it was an exciting low-budget movie." Laitin was referring to *The Killing* (which was Kubrick's third feature film—a sign of how little Hollywood had heard about his early work). "And when he followed this up with a film entitled *Paths of Glory,*" Laitin continued, "which was a courageous and effective undertaking, the town begrudgingly began to take notice of him. Here he is."

In the company of the Hollywood elite, Kubrick's voice sounded cool, confident, and self-assured. Speaking in a quiet, thoughtful manner, in a clean but clearly Eastern accent, Kubrick gave his views on the industry he had infiltrated on sheer talent, nerve, and ambition.

"This is Stanley Kubrick," he began. "I think that if the reigning powers had any respect for good pictures or the people who could make them that this respect was probably very well tempered by the somewhat cynical observation that poor and mediocre pictures might just as well prove successful as pictures of higher value. Television has changed this completely and I think that despite the unhappy financial upheaval that it has caused in the movie industry, it has also provided a very invigorating and stimulating challenge, which has made it necessary for films to be made with more sincerity and more daring. If Hollywood lacks the color and excitement of its early days with Rolls-Royces and leopard-skin seat covers I think, on the other hand, it provides the most exciting and stimulating atmosphere of opportunity and possibilities for young people."

On December 29, 1958, Kubrick wrote to Laitin on Harris-Kubrick Pictures stationery from their office at 250 North Canon Drive in Beverly Hills to tell him he enjoyed the show. Kubrick had reservations about the show's conclusion that the Hollywood old guard would rally in the face of crisis, a notion he found a bit sugarcoated, but he otherwise praised the broadcast as the most accurate assessment of the film industry that he had ever heard. Written in his own hand and signed "Stan Kubrick," the letter shows Kubrick's skill at promoting his work with diplomacy and directness.

Back on the East Coast, Stanley Kubrick's parents, Jacques and Gertrude, were now living on Castle Drive in Englewood Cliffs, New Jersey. Jacques was earning $500 a week from his medical practice in the Bronx and drove a 1957 DeSoto.

The European reaction to *Paths of Glory* was swift and outraged. The French military establishment was so riled at the film's portrayal of the French army that it launched an all-out assault to ban the film throughout Europe. The notion that the French military command would sacrifice innocent lives to maintain national glory infuriated the European community.

In Brussels protests forced the film to be withdrawn from first-run theaters. *Paths of Glory* was later put back in theaters in Brussels after the State Department and the French Foreign Ministry negotiated a special foreword to be added to the film, which stated: "This episode of the 1914–1918 war tells of the madness of certain men caught in its

whirlwind. It constitutes an isolated case in total contrast with the historical gallantry of the vast majority of French soldiers, the champions of
the idea of liberty, which, since always, has been that of the French
people."

François Truffaut, who had completed his first short film, *Une Visite*,
in 1954 but was better known as a film critic for André Bazin's *Cahiers
du Cinema*, remarked that the film would never be released in France as
long as the ministry of war had anything to say about it. Truffaut had
deserted from military service and received a prison sentence and a dishonorable discharge.

When the film was ready for international release, UA decided not to
present the film to the French censorship board, fearing that the government would never give approval of a film so brazenly critical of the
French military.

In June 1958 *Paths of Glory* was shown in Berlin. During the running
of the premiere at Marmorhaus, a group of around fifty Frenchmen
dressed in civilian clothes loudly protested the showing of the film. The
film ran at numerous local theaters in Berlin but not in the French
sector, the districts of Wedding and Reinickendorf. Former French commander general Geze declared that the film discriminated against the
French army. Allied Orders Numbers 501 and 504, which dated back to
the time of Allied Control in 1948, allowed French military authorities to
inform exhibitors in the area to ban showings of the film. Allied Occupation Statute 501 forbade any action that might harm the reputation of
one of the occupying powers of Berlin. Geze informed the Berlin senate
that the French would pull out of the Berlin Film Festival if United
Artists continued showing *Paths of Glory*. Under pressure, the film was
withdrawn from the festival. The film was allowed to be shown only in
the U.S. and British sectors of Berlin and in West Germany. French
soldiers created a disturbance during a screening of the film in the British sector of Berlin by throwing stink bombs into the audience.

In July 1958 the U.S. military banned *Paths of Glory* from the Army
and Air Force Military Motion Picture circuit in Europe.

By December 1958 the government of Switzerland had banned *Paths
of Glory*. The ministry of the interior called the film, "Subversive propaganda directed at France . . . highly offensive to that nation." The
Swiss government threatened to confiscate all prints of the film unless
United Artists immediately exported them from the country. The Swiss
ban continued for twelve years, until German television announced in
1970 that it was considering showing the film.

The Italian film critics showed their support for *Paths of Glory* by voting it the best foreign film of 1958 and awarding it the Silver Ribbon. Winston Churchill commended the authenticity of the film. Luis Buñuel was also among the film's admirers.

By 1974, *Paths of Glory* still had not been released in France. Late in the year, after French president Valéry Giscard d'Estaing proclaimed there would be no political censorship, plans were announced to release the film in both subtitled and original versions in four Paris first-run theaters.

Paths of Glory did not make a profit, so as with *The Killing*, Kubrick did not personally make any money from the film. "As I had predicted, it made no money," Kirk Douglas lamented in his autobiography, *The Ragman's Son*. "A picture can't make money unless people pay to see it, and people can't see it if it's been banned in their country."

Harris and Kubrick talked to many actors about working with their independent production company. In addition to Gregory Peck they had informal talks with Richard Widmark and Tony Curtis. The discussions didn't result in specific projects, but they were a sign that the young filmmakers were taken seriously by the Hollywood film community and were continuing to gain attention. The talks with Gregory Peck concerned a film about the Civil War based on the life of John Singleton Mosby.

In 1957 Harris and Kubrick went to see *Operation Mad Ball*, starring Ernie Kovacs. They both loved the movie, and the idea of a television series based on the character played by Kovacs tickled their fancy. The proposed series would follow the exploits of a commandant of a boy's school. Harris and Kubrick met with Kovacs and began to research the project. Producer, director, and star actually had a meeting with a real commandant of the Black Fox Military Academy. Harris and Kubrick tried to play it straight to get background for the show, in which they were planning to send up the staid institution. During the meeting Kovacs kept cracking up the partners, who kept getting up to turn away from the commandant so he would not see the tears of laughter streaming down their faces. The project never was realized.

Writers were critical to Harris-Kubrick, which needed them to create and adapt material to develop into film projects. They had talked to Civil War expert Shelby Foote, satirist and cartoonist Jules Feiffer, and Marlon Brando's friend Carlo Fiore, who had ambitions to become a writer. Korean War veteran Richard Addams wrote a script titled *The German Lieutenant* for Harris-Kubrick. The script was eventually sold but not put into production by Harris-Kubrick.

Another project that was to follow *Paths of Glory* was *I Stole*

$16,000,000. A script was developed with Kubrick and Jim Thompson. Bryna Productions purchased the autobiography of Herbert Emerson Wilson, a safecracker who served twelve years in San Quentin. The book was written in collaboration with Thomas P. Kelly.

On January 7, 1958, Kubrick received a letter c/o Bryna Productions located at 9235 West Third Street in Beverly Hills. The correspondence was from A. Joseph Handel, Richard de Rochemont's attorney on Fifth Avenue in New York City. Handel indicated that he and de Rochemont were pleased with the recent acclaim for *Paths of Glory* and went on to remind Kubrick about the $500 that de Rochemont had lent him to complete *Fear and Desire.* Handel suggested that now that Kubrick was doing well he should do the right thing and repay the $500 to de Rochemont.

The next day Kubrick wrote back to Handel from 250 North Canon Drive in Beverly Hills. Kubrick opened by expressing regret that his past circumstances required Handel to write his January 7 letter. Kubrick told the lawyer that he had not ever forgotten his obligation to de Rochemont and how grateful he was for his past assistance. Kubrick did not want de Rochemont to think of him as an ingrate and went on to explain that *The Killing* had still not turned a profit for Harris-Kubrick and that *Paths of Glory,* while critically acclaimed, was made for a percentage. Harris-Kubrick received 60 percent of the producer's share and waived all salary. He explained that if and when the profits came in, it would be the first time in his career that he would be ahead of a long line of his creditors. Expressing embarrassment and goodwill, Kubrick sent a check for $100 toward the $500 he owed and asked Handel to give de Rochemont his apologies and thanks.

On January 15, Handel wrote back after having a telephone conversation with de Rochemont, telling Kubrick that he and Dick understood the situation and assuring him that they never considered him an ingrate or thought he was avoiding his obligations. He closed with their hopes that *Paths of Glory* would be the first in a series of critical and commercial successes.

On August 10, 1958, Kubrick sent the remaining $400 to de Rochemont and a heartfelt handwritten note. Kubrick acknowledged de Rochemont's friendship and patience and said he would use the producer as a role model when he was in a position to give similar assistance to a deserving young filmmaker. Thinking back, Kubrick told de Rochemont that his $500 loan was a brave investment, considering the vagaries of the film industry.

On August 18, de Rochemont wrote back, thanking Kubrick and saying he almost regretted no longer having a wager on America's hottest young film director. De Rochemont was gratified at how quickly Kubrick had learned his craft. The producer told Kubrick he was trying to do something more with the *Lincoln* series, possibly focusing on the middle years. An MGM East story department friend advised against it on the theory that no Lincoln picture had ever made money and suggested that the only thing that paid off was sex. Thus he closed by advising Kubrick to consider *Lolita* as his next picture. De Rochemont was an admirer of Vladimir Nabokov's novel and told Kubrick that it was a project he should consider. "Dick liked the novel very much and told Stanley to do it," remembers de Rochemont's wife, Jane. The book had been recommended to Kubrick by others as well.

During the making of *Paths of Glory* Kubrick wrote a letter to David Vaughan in New York. "Stanley wrote to me and said he would like me to pay back the money he had lent me for the fare back to New York," Vaughan remembers. "At the time I was living on very little money, doing temp work between acting jobs, which paid nothing or very little, so I wrote back to him and said, I would be prepared to pay him in installments, but that's the way I would have to do it. I said, I had as much hope of paying him the whole thing now as I had of ever receiving the fee I was supposed to get for the choreography of *Killer's Kiss*. There was a letter of agreement that I was to be paid. I don't think anybody ever got any of those delayed payments. He sent back the check I sent him and said, 'Forget it.' "

CHAPTER 9

"This Isn't Working, Stanley"

After *Paths of Glory* Harris-Kubrick began to attract attention from key Hollywood insiders. *The Killing* had brought Gregory Peck and Kirk Douglas to them. Now, with *Paths of Glory,* they caught the eye of Marlon Brando, who wanted to pursue a relationship with Harris-Kubrick Pictures. Carlo Fiore, Brando's friend and associate from his Pennebaker production company, set up a screening of both films for the actor at the offices of MCA in Beverly Hills. Brando thought *The Killing* was one of the most original pictures he'd seen, and he liked *Paths of Glory.* After seeing *The Killing,* Brando said he was amazed that Kubrick "could project such a completely distinctive style with so little previous filmmaking experience. Here was a typical, episodic detective story—nothing unusual in the plot—but Stanley made a series of bizarre and interesting choices which buttressed and embellished an ordinary story into an exciting film."

In Pennebaker's first four years of existence, Brando had developed a story about the United Nations and a Western based on the plot of *The Count of Monte Cristo.* Neither of the projects got past the developmental stage. Brando continued to develop ideas for a western. At one point he called the project *Ride, Commanchero,* but the story had similarities to Arthur Penn's *The Left-Handed Gun,* starring Paul Newman, which forced Brando to scrap it.

Harris-Kubrick and Brando were searching for project material. Kubrick and Brando were both very interested in making a boxing film together, but the weekly meetings didn't get specific enough to create a project that could be realized.

Brando read the 1956 novel *The Authentic Death of Hendry Jones,* by Charles Neider, which he thought would make a good western. The novel used the Billy the Kid legend. Neider had researched historic materials on Billy the Kid in New Mexico and changed the name of the men to Dad Longworth for Pat Garrett and Hendry Jones for Billy the Kid. The title is a reference to Pat Garrett's memoir, *The Authentic Life of Billy the Kid.* In early 1957, producer Frank Rosenberg had approached Sam Peckinpah, who was working in television Westerns like *The Rifleman,* to write a script of the novel. Peckinpah was paid in the neighborhood of $4,000 and completed the script in six months, handing it in by early October 1957. Peckinpah told Rosenberg to send the script to Brando, who then bought it for Pennebaker.

Brando continued to meet with James B. Harris and Stanley Kubrick. One day Brando invited Kubrick to dinner. Kubrick notified his partner that Brando wanted to see him and reported back to Harris that night. During dinner, Brando told Kubrick that he had a commitment at Paramount to do a western and offered him the director's chair. After discussing the situation, Harris and Kubrick decided it was a good career move. Marlon Brando was one of the world's most gifted and powerful actors. The assignment would bring in money, and when completed, it would clear the way for a Harris-Kubrick-Brando production.

Kubrick signed on as the director of the project on May 12, 1958, for a six-month probation period. He was also hired to revise Peckinpah's screenplay. Pennebaker was under fire from Paramount's Y. Frank Freeman. Paramount was tired of supporting Pennebaker without results and wanted to get the project under way.

Brando called up Sam Peckinpah and told him that he had hired Kubrick to direct the film. Peckinpah was excited and told Brando Kubrick was an excellent choice. Brando and Kubrick found a low-rent apartment in Hollywood near Gower and Melrose where they could work undisturbed and away from Paramount's eagle eye. However, many of the distractions came from Brando, who kept engaging Kubrick in games of chess, dominoes, poker, and imbibing to avoid serious work on the screenplay. Several of Brando's associates, including his father, George Glass, and Walter Seltzer were becoming unhappy with Kubrick, who had promised to shoot the original script in three weeks, only to announce after three weeks that the screenplay needed work.

Brando thought very highly of the young director at the time. "Stanley is unusually perceptive," Brando told Joanne Stang of the *New York Times*, "and delicately attuned to people. He has an adroit intellect and is a creative thinker—not a repeater, not a fact-gatherer. He digests what he learns and brings to a new project an original point-of-view and a reserved passion."

After six weeks of work and play Kubrick suggested to Brando that Calder Willingham come on board as a screenwriter. Brando was impressed with Willingham's work and especially admired his novel *End as a Man*, about a cruel military school that reminded the actor of the Shattuck Military Academy he had been forced to attend as a boy.

Kubrick and Willingham began to carve out a new draft while James B. Harris held the Harris-Kubrick fort at Kirk Douglas's Bryna Company.

Harris negotiated with Douglas, who eventually agreed that the five-picture commitment that Harris-Kubrick Pictures had with Bryna Company was too much. The new agreement called for Harris-Kubrick to give Kirk Douglas the major share of their next production.

As the screenplay progressed, Brando fired Sam Peckinpah from his team after three weeks. The termination caused a lot of tension. "One night we were home and Sam got a telephone call," Peckinpah's wife, Marie, told biographer David Weddle. "His voice was very excited because it was Marlon. I went out of the room and came back a little while later and Sam was just sitting there on the bed, staring into space. I asked him what was wrong and he said Kubrick had wanted to bring his own writer onto the project to do a rewrite of the script. Sam had been fired just like that—it was over. He was devastated."

Brando had reversed the story based on the Billy the Kid legend so that the Kid killed Pat Garrett in the end. Later Peckinpah was to say, "Marlon screwed it up. He's a hell of an actor, but in those days he had to end up as a hero, and that's not the point of the story. Billy the Kid was no hero. He was a gunfighter, a real killer." Walter Seltzer and Frank Rosenberg liked Peckinpah's script and were disturbed that Brando, Kubrick, and Willingham were working to the exclusion of everyone else on the project. For Sam Peckinpah it was the beginning of his long war with the powers-that-be in Hollywood as he continued to struggle to become a film director. He later told actor James Coburn, "Marlon taught me how to hate." For Peckinpah, who along with Stanley Kubrick would become a major filmmaking force in the sixties and seventies, it was also the beginning of long competition with the Bronx renegade. "There was an article in *Esquire* about Stanley Kubrick. I remember Sam being mad that they were paying so much attention to Kubrick and not to him," Judy Selland, Peckinpah's former sister-in-law, later recalled to biographer Marshall Fine. "He felt he was just as good if not better than Kubrick and clearly as important." In 1973 Peckinpah would finally reclaim the novel by adapting *The Authentic Death of Hendry Jones* into *Pat Garrett and Billy the Kid.*

As Kubrick, Brando, and Willingham began to work on what eventually became *One-Eyed Jacks,* Harris came across a literary project that caught his eye. One day while reading the Kirkus Service, Harris learned about a new novel, *Lolita,* by Vladimir Nabokov, a Russian writer who was teaching at Cornell University. Harris contacted Putnam in New York, which was publishing and representing the book, and asked to see a copy. Excited by the prospect, Harris told Kubrick about the book. Kubrick told his partner that he also had heard of the book through Calder Willingham.

When *Lolita* arrived at the Harris-Kubrick office, both men were brimming with enthusiasm to read it. "It was a hardback and we only had one copy, so we both couldn't read it at the same time," Harris recalls. "I cracked the book, began to read it, and passed the pages to Stanley. I was reading it and passing the pages, that's how anxious we were. After we finished it we said, 'Well, what's to talk about, this is terrific. What's there to talk about—we've got to do this!' "

Kubrick went back to Brando and his western. Over the summer of 1958 the script conferences were moved to Brando's house on Mulholland. Brando required that anyone entering the house take off their shoes so as not to damage his teakwood floors. Kubrick took it one step further and removed his pants as well, often working in only his underwear and a dress shirt. Brando conducted the meetings sitting in modified lotus position on the floor and struck a four-foot gong with a leather mallet when he felt the discussions were getting off his track. The sound of the gong was reported to be so powerful that it caused the dishes to rattle in Brando's kitchen.

Harris proceeded to acquire the rights to Nabokov's *Lolita.* He began by calling Putnam in New York, which asked Harris how much he was prepared to offer. Harris explained he had paid $10,000 each for the last two books Harris-Kubrick had bought, *Paths of Glory* and *Clean Break.* Once the Putnam representative was clear that this was a serious offer, he told Harris that the representation of *Lolita* had been assigned to legendary Hollywood literary agent Irving "Swifty" Lazar.

Lewis M. Allen, an Off-Broadway producer who later produced *The Connection, The Balcony, Lord of the Flies,* and *Fahrenheit 451,* had put in a bid for the screen rights to *Lolita* within two weeks after its publication. Nabokov rejected the offer. In September 1958 Nabokov wrote to his publisher about his feeling toward Allen's offer, saying, "His offer does not appeal to me at all. For one thing, my supreme, and in fact only, interest in these motion picture contracts is money. I don't give a damn for what they all call 'art.' Moreover, I would vet the use of a real child. Let them find a dwarfess."

Kubrick and Willingham produced a new story outline for the western, but it was poorly received by Frank Rosenberg, who told them it wouldn't work as a shooting script. Frustrated, Willingham slapped a book of matches down on Brando's coffee table and in his Southern accent said, "You've gotta have faith in ma God-given gifts as a writer." Brando pulled Rosenberg behind a Chinese screen he had set up in the house and convinced him to let Willingham and Kubrick continue their work.

Harris and Kubrick met with Lazar, who told them he wanted them to purchase *Lolita* because the studios were afraid of the controversial subject matter. Lazar thought Harris-Kubrick was the team to make this film, but they would have to pay for it. This was not a $10,000 deal. Lazar's asking price was $150,000.

Harris began to work on the deal. Because Lazar felt Harris-Kubrick was the right team to do the film and the Hollywood community was tempted but too timid to commit, he worked out an option deal rather than sticking to a firm single purchase price.

The deal was for two years. Harris-Kubrick was to pay $75,000 up front, which bought an option for one year. If they wanted to purchase the screen rights to *Lolita*, they would pay the remaining $75,000. If at the end of the year they weren't ready to go into production, they could buy a new option. If the film got made, the deal called for 15 percent of the profits from Harris-Kubrick to go to Vladimir Nabokov.

Kubrick and Willingham continued to work on the western script, based on their outline, but hit a dead end on page 52, realizing that the story indeed wasn't working—as Rosenberg had feared.

Harris and Kubrick said okay to Lazar, but they didn't have the $75,000. In order to finance the *Lolita* purchase, they decided to sell their rights to *The Killing* to United Artists, which wanted to air the film on television earlier than the original contract called for. Harris was eager to make his money back for *The Killing*. He was still in the red for more than $90,000 of his $130,000 investment. UA negotiated to get Harris his money back, but the price was—all rights and interest in *The Killing*. The film had not been performing at the box office, but as soon as the deal was made and UA owned *The Killing* outright, with the machinations of studio accounting, the film began to make profits. UA guaranteed Harris-Kubrick its money back. The studio promoted the film heavily, exploiting television and distribution areas, and it quickly turned a profit. Kubrick was pleased that his partner got his money back, Harris was glad to get his investment back, and Harris-Kubrick now owned the hottest property in the film business—the rights to Vladimir Nabokov's *Lolita*.

Preproduction began on Brando's western. Brando hired actress Pina Pellicer, who starred in the Mexican television version of *The Diary of Anne Frank*, and moved forward to cast the other female roles.

Lolita hit number one on most best-seller lists—until another Russian novelist, Boris Pasternak, usurped that position with *Dr. Zhivago*. *Lolita* remained in the number two slot for months while gathering a storm of controversy across the country. The novel was an account of a middle-aged man named Humbert Humbert and his sexual obsession with a twelve-year-old girl named Lolita. The *scandale* was good for business. After a year on the best-seller lists, *Lolita* had sold 236,700 copies in bookstores and 50,000 copies through book clubs. By the mid-eighties, Nabokov's novel had sold 14 million copies worldwide.

The starting date for Brando's western was pushed back again, this time to September 15. Kubrick and Brando were not getting along well. Brando had hired Kubrick because he wasn't a yes man. Kubrick admired Brando as an actor but was used to having complete artistic control. The arguments and disagreements accelerated. Carlo Fiore tended to agree with Brando, who was paying his salary.

Brando had given his promise to Karl Malden, who had worked with him in *A Streetcar Named Desire* and *On the Waterfront*, that the actor could have the part of Dad Longworth in the film. Kubrick disagreed and pushed to have Spencer Tracy in the role because he felt that Malden was associated with characters who were losers. Kubrick felt that Brando and Tracy would present a heroic struggle in the film. Brando told Kubrick that the decision was his to make. The film was already three months behind its original shooting schedule. Malden had been signed earlier and was collecting a salary that ultimately totaled almost $400,000 before the film was finally made. The unusually large sum for the time bought Malden and his family the west Los Angeles home he stills lives in.

As Calder Willingham saw his ideas being abandoned, he became increasingly silent at the story conferences lorded over by Brando and his gong. Willingham recalls that he resigned from the project, but Carlo

Fiore reports that Brando took the writer out and fired him over dinner, giving him an inlaid rosewood chess table for his troubles.

In November 1958 Rosenberg was considering rehiring Sam Peckinpah. He later decided to hire screenwriter Guy Trosper, with whom he got along well. The western was now called *One-Eyed Jacks* and a starting date was set. The name on the slate was changed from Kubrick to Brando. The working collaboration between Stanley Kubrick and Marlon Brando was not to be.

Brando claims that just before shooting was to commence, Kubrick told him he didn't know what the film was about. Brando told him that he had already paid Karl Malden $300,000 and had to begin. Brando says Kubrick bowed out at that point. The actor stated that he called Elia Kazan, Sidney Lumet, and several other directors to take over the helm, but they all turned down the project. According to Brando, he had no recourse but to direct the film himself to stop the economic bleeding caused by being so far behind schedule.

Frank Rosenberg's recollection of the parting was that Brando wanted his character, Rio, to fall in love with a Chinese girl because there was a growing Chinese community in Monterey, California, where the story took place. At a meeting with Rosenberg and Kubrick, Brando told the director he wanted France Nuyen for the part. Kubrick disagreed and said, "She can't act." Brando quietly signaled Rosenberg to follow him into the kitchen, where he told him, "We've gotta get rid of Kubrick." Brando then decided to direct the picture himself.

On November 21, 1958, Walter Seltzer called Kubrick into the Pennebaker offices at Paramount and told him, "This isn't working, Stanley."

Kubrick told the press that his contract with Brando did not allow him to discuss the reasons for leaving the project. He issued a statement saying he resigned "with deep regret because of my respect and admiration for one of the world's foremost artists, Marlon Brando. Mr. Brando and his assistants have been most understanding of [my] desire . . . to commence work on *Lolita*."

Kubrick later told Carlo Fiore that he was glad that Brando was directing the film himself, saying, "If he had hired another director, it might have appeared that I was lacking in talent or temperament, or something. But if Marlon directs it, it gets me off the hook."

Guy Trosper polished off the draft. Marlon Brando moved ahead to direct himself in *One-Eyed Jacks*. Stanley Kubrick never turned a frame on the film. *One-Eyed Jacks* was released in 1961. Two scenes remained from the Peckinpah script, but he was not given a screen credit.

As 1959 began, Stanley Kubrick and Christiane Harlan had settled into domestic life at 316 South Camden Drive in Beverly Hills. Kubrick didn't have a swimming pool, but he had acquired a little black Mercedes brought back from Germany after *Paths of Glory*. Katharina was now six years old, and Christiane was expecting her first child with Stanley Kubrick.

CHAPTER 10

"He Never Really Would Agree to the Concept That This Was His Movie"

Stanley is very monastic. He's a great beard scratcher. He thinks, he rubs his beard. He expresses himself quietly. He's not a yeller. I found working with him terrific. I can't say he's reasonable, I can only say that he's obsessive in the best sense of the word—because reasonableness doesn't make anything good. There has to be a certain unreasonableness in any serious creative work and he is that way.

—Saul Bass

He'll be a fine director some day, if he falls flat on his face just once. It might teach him how to compromise.

—Kirk Douglas

After Stanley Kubrick departed from *One-Eyed Jacks*, Harris-Kubrick began to channel all its energies into *Lolita*—until Kubrick got a call from Kirk Douglas.

As 1957 came to a close, Edward Lewis, who had been associated with

Kirk Douglas and Bryna Company since 1949, brought Douglas the novel *Spartacus*, written by Howard Fast. Fast, an American Communist, served prison time for his association with the Party and was known for his books on American patriots George Washington and Thomas Paine. Spartacus was a real-life historical figure, a slave who formed an army of gladiators, revolted, and ultimately conquered the majority of Southern Italy by defeating two Roman armies.

Douglas, always looking for heroic characters in socially conscious stories, was immediately attracted to the material and had Lewis secure the rights to the book. Douglas paid for the option with his own money, confident he could get United Artists to finance the film. Douglas approached Arthur Krim, then head of United Artists, and pitched his idea for a film about Spartacus. He was given an immediate no. Krim followed up in mid-January of 1958 with a telegram that explained that the studio was committed to *The Gladiators*, based on a book by Arthur Koestler, that covered the same territory as the Howard Fast story. *The Gladiators* was to be directed by Martin Ritt and would star Yul Brynner.

Ritt, who was in the process of developing the screenplay for *The Gladiators*, called Kirk Douglas and tried to get him to abandon his *Spartacus* project. Lewis and Douglas discussed the matter and decided to propose joining forces, but Brynner told Ritt in no uncertain terms that he was not amenable. Within days *Variety* ran an ad that featured Yul Brynner costumed as Spartacus and the line *"The Gladiators*, Next from United Artists." The film was budgeted at $5.5 million.

The competitive actor decided he was going to fight. Douglas sent Krim a terse telegram that stated, "We are spending five million, five hundred and two dollars on *Spartacus*. Your move."

Douglas went to other studios but was rejected in turn; no one wanted to challenge UA. The option on *Spartacus* was about to run out, so Douglas renegotiated for a sixty-day extension, which Fast agreed to for the sum of one dollar, but his quid pro quo was a clause that allowed him to write the screenplay. Douglas and Lewis were disinclined, but they had no leverage.

Douglas was encouraged by his agent, Lew Wasserman, the future head of Universal Studios, to get a top-notch director attached to the project. David Lean was one of several to pass on the venture.

Howard Fast began to send pages of his script to Bryna, and it quickly became apparent to Douglas that his screenplay would be unusable. The script was lacking in the dramatic power that Douglas saw in the book. Convinced that he needed a solid script to launch the project, Douglas hired Dalton Trumbo, one of the Unfriendly Ten who in 1947 went to jail for a year after refusing to cooperate with the House Un-American Activities Committee. Trumbo, who had written the anti–World War I novel *Johnny Got His Gun* and the screenplays for *Kitty Foyle, A Guy Named Joe,* and *Thirty Seconds over Tokyo,* had been on the blacklist for almost ten years and was barred from all of the studios. He had been forced to work under many pseudonyms, the most infamous being Robert Rich, with which he won an Academy Award for writing *The Brave One* in 1956.

By 1958 the blacklist had been in place for more then ten years. Individuals working in the motion picture industry who had been named as members of the Communist Party during the witch-hunts launched by Senator Joseph McCarthy and the House Committee on Un-American Activities (HUAC) or labeled by self-professed patriots who thrived during this period were not able to gain employment in the major studios that controlled the film business. Screenwriters were especially damaged by the scourge of the blacklist. Pseudonyms were created so the listed writers could continue to work. Even after ten years and the support of many in the industry who despised the practice, the blacklist had not yet been broken.

Dalton Trumbo did not like Howard Fast. In their only face-to-face meeting, Fast berated the screenwriter for not holding Marxism classes while in prison. Douglas decided Dalton Trumbo had to write the screenplay outside the knowledge of everyone except him and Edward Lewis, and a plan was devised. Edward Lewis was to be the front for Trumbo, using his name for anything written by Trumbo. The process of "fronting" was common during the blacklist and was the subject of the 1976 film *The Front,* directed by Martin Ritt and starring Woody Allen. Bryna would pay Edward Lewis, who would then get the money to Sam Jackson, the pseudonym chosen by Trumbo for the *Spartacus* project.

Trumbo, Douglas, and Lewis met in secret, and all memos were signed "Sam Jackson." Fast continued to be difficult. He insisted on holding a meeting with the department heads of the production staff, where he lectured pedantically on the righteousness of his views on the project.

During his years as a blacklisted writer, Trumbo learned to work rapidly. He moved briskly through the epic *Spartacus* script and worked easily with Douglas and Lewis.

While working on *The Devil's Disciple,* Douglas gave Laurence Olivier a copy of the novel *Spartacus.* Olivier liked the book and was interested in directing the film and playing the title role.

The two rival screenplays, *Spartacus* and *The Gladiators*, continued to be developed at a breakneck pace. Martin Ritt and United Artists commissioned another blacklisted screenwriter, Abraham Polonsky, who had written *Body and Soul* and directed *Force of Evil*; he was now working under the name of Ira Wolfert. By August of 1958 Dalton Trumbo completed the first-draft screenplay of *Spartacus*.

Douglas, Lewis, and Trumbo had only modest success keeping their secret. Lew Wasserman learned the true identity of the screenwriter on his own, as did many other Hollywood insiders. Throughout the blacklist era many knew of the sub rosa methods to which writers were forced to resort, but the dreaded blacklist persisted. Wasserman sent the first draft to Olivier, Charles Laughton, and Peter Ustinov. Douglas and Lewis went to London and visited Laughton backstage at a play he was appearing in. Laughton dismissed the script out of hand, but an appointment with Olivier found the actor enthusiastic, his reservations connected to the stature of the part. Lewis was becoming uncomfortable with getting praise for something he hadn't written.

Back in Hollywood, Wasserman told Douglas that Laughton had—after all—accepted the role. At the end of August, Peter Ustinov signed on, and by the beginning of the next year, they had enlisted Olivier, who turned down consideration as director because of a commitment to *Coriolanus* at Stratford-upon-Avon. He was still prepared to play Crassus if the role could be brought up to the weight of the parts played by Douglas, Ustinov, and Laughton.

By this time the United Artists production had a director, Martin Ritt, and actors, Yul Brynner and Anthony Quinn, in position. Locations in Europe had been scouted. Ritt called Douglas and told him he had reconsidered and wanted the two productions to join forces. Douglas was dismissive and ready to deal the death blow to *The Gladiators*. Confident that he had the better script and a blockbuster cast, Douglas also knew that Ritt couldn't begin shooting in Europe until the summer weather made conditions tolerable. Douglas made the bold choice to commence shooting in Hollywood, where weather permitted year-round exterior production, even though Trumbo's screenplay still needed work and his own role as Spartacus was subservient to the Laughton-Ustinov-Olivier triumvirate.

On October 27, 1958, the first battle of what Kirk Douglas calls in his autobiography "The Wars of *Spartacus*" was over. He received a telegram from United Artists stating, "Dear Kirk—At Arthur's [Krim] request Yul Brynner has agreed in the interest of good will to your use of the title *Spartacus*."

Douglas began to put the production together. Tony Curtis lobbied hard for a role in *Spartacus,* and one was created for him. Howard Fast hated the Trumbo screenplay and called Edward Lewis, the ersatz author of the script, "the world's worst writer."

Douglas's idea was to cast British actors to play the Romans in the film and have Americans play the slaves. He set out to find a foreign actress to play Varinia, the slave woman whom Spartacus marries. Elsa Martinelli, the stunning former model that Douglas had discovered for *The Indian Fighter* in 1955, was working in Italy and not available. Ingrid Bergman turned down the role, finding the film too violent for her taste. Jean Simmons, who had appeared in *Caesar and Cleopatra, Great Expectations, Hamlet, The Robe, Elmer Gantry,* and other films, coveted the role of Varinia, but she was born in London and had a pronounced British speaking pattern—so he moved on. Douglas flew to France to woo Jeanne Moreau, who had caught the actor's eye in Louis Malle's *The Lovers,* but the actress turned down the role because she was dually involved in a play and a new love affair.

Douglas screened countless films looking at foreign actresses and then decided to cast a little-known German actress, Sabina Bethmann. He flew her to Hollywood for a screen test. The results showed that Bethmann was strikingly beautiful on film but not a very good actress. Douglas hired dialogue coaches to tame her German accent and contracted blacklisted actor Jeff Corey, who was making a living as an acting teacher, to coach her as a performer.

Douglas wanted a distinctive look as Spartacus, so he hired famed Hollywood hairstylist Jay Sebring, who had a celebrity clientele (which included Steve McQueen), to design a look for the slaves. (Sebring later was slaughtered along with Sharon Tate by the Manson Family.) Sebring's hair design called a "cow-do" featured a crew cut on top, long hair in the back, and a ponytail, a style quite ahead of its time.

The second battle in "The Wars of *Spartacus*" began over the director of the film. Universal Studios committed to the film's being executive-produced by Douglas and produced by Edward Lewis for Bryna Productions, but they were unilateral in their choice of Anthony Mann as the director of *Spartacus.*

Mann was a seasoned Hollywood director in his early fifties and had begun his career as a Broadway theater actor. In 1938 he joined the Selznick Company and later became an assistant director working with Preston Sturges on *Sullivan's Travels.* As a director he became known for his distinctive Westerns, *Bend of the River, The Naked Spur, The Far Country, The Man from Laramie,* and *Man of the West,* which highlighted both outdoor splendor and inner conflicts. Universal had had financial success with Mann and felt that his command of capturing exterior vistas and the inner life of his characters, along with his sense of craftsmanship, made him perfect for *Spartacus*. The director was adored by Jimmy Stewart—the star of many Anthony Mann films—Jean-Luc Godard, the *Cahiers du Cinema* crowd, and American cult critics like Andrew Sarris, who elevated Mann to the ranks of auteur status. Nevertheless, he was not what Kirk Douglas had in mind for his Roman epic.

Saul Bass was hired to devise the title sequence. Bass was a graphic designer who revolutionized feature film credit sequences by utilizing animation and live action to set the theme of a film. He had designed the striking titles for several films directed by Otto Preminger: *Carmen Jones, Saint Joan, The Man with the Golden Arm, Bonjour Tristesse,* and *Anatomy of a Murder*. He also title-designed *North by Northwest, Vertigo,* and *Psycho* for Alfred Hitchcock and numerous other films, including *Around the World in 80 Days* and *The Big Country*.

Kirk Douglas and Edward Lewis both knew Saul Bass, and Douglas asked the designer to create the titles for *Spartacus*. Bass had no previous relationship with Anthony Mann, but the director was agreeable to working with him.

Bass's responsibilities exceeded title design. He was also involved in scouting locations for *Spartacus*. For the mine sequence that opens the film, he ultimately found an ideal location in Death Valley. The producers asked Bass to find a location in the United States to film the staging area for the Roman army when they position themselves for the final battle. He also designed the gladiator school. Douglas and Edward Lewis gave Bass carte blanche to work on any design aspect of the film that attracted him. For the gladiator school, Bass used the metaphor of a circus—with the slaves performing for the Roman audience. He storyboarded the scene in which the slaves break down the fence of the gladiator school and originated the concept of the slaves' using the fence as a weapon. The major sets were built and ready for production under the aegis of production designer Alexander Golitzen, who was the prestigious head of Universal's art department.

The cameras began to roll on January 27, 1959, in Death Valley. Mann directed the opening sequence. The scene depicted the slaves working in mines as they were selected by the Romans to be trained as gladiators. Shooting went well for three weeks, but as production moved to the sequences concerning the gladiator school run by the Romans, Anthony Mann began to lose control of the film. Kirk Douglas felt that the director was allowing Peter Ustinov to direct himself by his docile acceptance of many—if not all—of the actor's suggestions.

Douglas reports that Universal finally agreed to remove Mann from the helm but demanded that the star and executive producer personally fire him. At the end of the day of shooting on Friday the 13th in February 1959, Douglas gently fired Anthony Mann, paid him $75,000 in full, and removed him as the director of the film.

At the beginning of the *Spartacus* project, when Universal was insisting on Anthony Mann, Douglas's choice for director had been Stanley Kubrick, whom he considered a young genius after the brilliant results on *Paths of Glory*. Now the cameras had begun to roll, the clock was ticking, and the money flowing. Douglas again pressed for Kubrick and the studio relented.

Stanley Kubrick had not directed a film since *Paths of Glory* and was recovering from his protracted mental duel with Marlon Brando on preproduction for *One-Eyed Jacks*. One night during a regular poker game attended by Kubrick, James B. Harris, Calder Willingham, Martin Ritt, Vince Edwards, and Everett Sloane, Kubrick received a phone call telling him he was now the director of *Spartacus* and that his start-up time was twenty-four hours. Richard Anderson, who had played Saint-Auban in *Paths of Glory*, was at the gaming table that evening when Kubrick returned to finish the hand. "I'm starting tomorrow and I haven't even seen the sets," he told the actor.

Kubrick was brought in over the weekend. He read the script, sat in on meetings, and was ready to shoot first-up on Monday February 16. The sets had been built and were ready for production. Some of the personnel hired by Anthony Mann were discharged. Saul Bass was in the process of storyboarding the final battle. "I was the only one, as I recall, that survived that process and Stanley asked me to just keep going on the battle because he had his hands full," Bass recalls. "I mean, he was really coming from behind at that point and he seemed to be very pleased at the notion that I was working on it and Stanley said, 'For God sakes, keep going.'"

Bass had done a lot of research on the battle before Kubrick's appearance on the project. The budget was at $4 million to $5 million. Douglas and Lewis told Bass to create a symbolic battle that could be executed on a modest budget without employing large troops. Later, when the budget was increased, Douglas and Lewis came back to Bass and asked him to increase the scope of the battle. He began to re-storyboard the sequence. Bass researched Caesar in Gaul and the nature of the mechanics of the Roman army and their vehicles and weapons. "I simply took the position that the Roman army was a highly mechanized and disciplined force and I wanted to suggest a certain precision, a mechanization and geometry. I created geometric patterns and had those patterns shift. So what you saw was like a moving painting, where forces would open up from the checkerboard form and would unite as a solid mass. The slaves had a lack of precision. They had no precise uniforms, they lined up but were never straight. We were trying to project the soulless Roman army against the soulful slave army."

Saul Bass screened any film that had a battle: *War and Peace, Friendly Persuasion,* and *Alexander Nevsky.* The crew was shooting at this point, but Bass posted a notice announcing the battle film festival he ran every day. There were probably days where Kubrick would rather have been at a screening of *Alexander Nevsky* and listening to his cherished Prokofiev score, but he and the rest of the cast and crew were busy. Only Peter Ustinov was not needed on set at the time and sat in on the cinematic battles with Bass.

Bass continued to develop the storyboards gauging geometric patterns used to form the Roman army. Rather than working small, as he usually did, the designer created large sketches numbering as many as five hundred full-size drawings. This process was separate from Alexander Golitzen's art department contribution. Kubrick reviewed all of Bass's work and absorbed the details into his directorial plan for the epic film. Golitzen and his art department were occupied with the large number of sets and historical details.

The finished film employed some of the fundamental geometric patterns Bass had designed, some ideas were dropped, and others—like the flaming rolling logs used by Spartacus's army—were an invention and departure from historic accuracy but were audience-pleasers.

When Bass was first hired, his initial deal was to be credited as design consultant. When the title was made known, Edward Muhl, in charge of production at Universal, came to see Saul Bass and said, "Look, Golitzen feels uncomfortable with 'design' because he is the production designer, and he feels like it diminishes his role. We would prefer if you used the term 'visual consultant,'" Bass recalls. "I said, 'Well, I have no objection to that.' Then I got a call from Stanley in which he indicated that he was uncomfortable with 'visual consultant.' A man with such a strong visual sense, he felt it seemed to impinge upon his area. I totally agreed and was empathetic to it, and I said, 'Fine, then it's going to be design consultant.' Then I got called to Eddie Muhl, who said to me, 'It must be visual consultant.' And I said, 'No, I'm sorry, Mr. Muhl, I can't do that because I have to respect and support the director's position. I must support the creative force in this picture, not the production requirements. Mr. Kubrick is uncomfortable with that, and I therefore will have to insist upon your adherence to the credit that was part of our deal.' I was a lot younger and I was talking to a very powerful man. I'll never forget this, Eddie Muhl looked at me and said, 'Saul, there's an awful lot we have in mind here for you at Universal.' And I said, 'Well, I'm pleased to hear that, but I'm sorry to say I must stick with my position.' "

Harris and Kubrick decided that Kubrick's involvement on *Spartacus* would be beneficial for their production company. Harris tried to get Douglas to consider the loan-out of Kubrick as director as satisfying the Harris-Kubrick obligation. Harris asked Douglas to wave off *Lolita* as the single project they owed to Bryna. When Douglas learned it was an adaptation of the notorious novel, he agreed to let them do the film without him because he was convinced the film would never get made.

The cast and crew of *Spartacus* was in place to shoot the gladiator school sequences as Kirk Douglas brought Kubrick into the middle of the arena and announced, "This is your new director." Although Kubrick was thirty, he looked much younger and was a far cry from the macho persona of a Hollywood director familiar to most of the cast and crew. The majority of cast and crew were underwhelmed, and Kubrick did little if anything to become part of the team. Many thought that Kubrick was in Douglas's pocket, but they were quickly disabused of the notion by Kubrick's iconoclastic way of making a movie.

Anthony Mann's only representation in the film was Spartacus's introduction—the opening sequence of the slaves working in the mines, which was not reshot.

After the director was replaced the next major change in the production involved the leading lady, Sabina Bethmann. Douglas was concerned about her lack of emotion, which went against his idea of the role and his philosophy of passion-charged performances. Kubrick suggested they conduct an improvisational scene with Bethmann to see if there was any untapped emotional base. Kubrick proposed that he, Lewis, and Douglas tell the actress she had just been fired from her starring role in the film to see if her reaction would reveal something he could work with. Lewis and Douglas considered this a cruel manipulation. Lewis chose to leave. Douglas stayed to watch Kubrick conduct his improvisation. Bethmann immediately froze in silent pain when she heard she had lost the coveted role. She left the production after working on camera for two days and was paid her salary of $35,000. Douglas dropped what he called his "linguistic scheme" and phoned Jean Simmons at her ranch in Nogales, Arizona—she was now Varinia.

Injuries caused the production to shoot around actors. Shortly after starting work on the film, Jean Simmons needed emergency surgery and was out for more than a month. Tony Curtis severed his Achilles tendon playing tennis at Douglas's home one Sunday and was in a hip cast and a wheelchair for a period. Studio production was shut down when they could no longer shoot around the disabled actors, and Laurence Olivier was sent to the Hearst castle in San Simeon for some exterior shots. For the first time in his career, even Kirk Douglas couldn't work after being struck with the flu.

Douglas tried to cultivate a friendship with Kubrick, who continued to direct the film with an aloof, perfectionist attitude. The actor was even willing to open his psyche to the director by bringing him to his psychiatrist of four years to give Kubrick more insight into Kirk Douglas.

The session might not have produced major spiritual revelations, but the actor and star talked about using music to set the tone for actors, a technique both men fondly admired from the days of silent moviemaking. They tried the technique on MOS sequences (scenes shot without sync sound) that were to be scored later, and they enjoyed the results. On the whole, Douglas respected the sense of detail and commitment to precision displayed by Kubrick. Many discussions, disagreements, meetings, and picayune arguments were observed by the crew. Douglas reported saying no to Kubrick when the director demanded that the ceiling of a stage set be raised by two feet.

Saul Bass originally met Stanley Kubrick at a screening of *Paths of Glory*. Bass had great regard for the film. Kubrick was very aware of Bass's graphic design in films. "I talked to him afterwards," Bass, whose credits mounted with films like Scorsese's *Cape Fear, Goodfellas*, and *Casino*, recalled. "He was excusing the typography he used. 'I really wanted to use a Bodoni but they didn't have the right Bodoni.' He was saying, 'So I want you to understand that it isn't *exactly* what it should have been.' Stanley is really very knowledgeable in all these visual areas, surprisingly so. Most directors or producers who are really wonderful filmmakers have no real sense of things like typography and certain graphic issues. He is one of the exceptions."

Kubrick was pleased to have Saul Bass as part of the mammoth production. Bass's preproduction work was helpful in getting the director up to speed on the one film on which Kubrick had no involvement in preplanning.

A team of six stuntmen was hired and put on salary for almost three months before principal photography began. The stuntmen doubled for major characters and also played on-screen roles. One of the stuntmen was Richard Farnsworth, who began in film stunts in 1936, when he was sixteen. He later became the acclaimed actor of *The Grey Fox, Comes a Horseman, The Natural,* and many other films. Another of the stunt team was Loren Janes, veteran stuntman of five hundred films and over one thousand television programs. Janes was a stunt double for Steve McQueen for twenty-five years, worked with Michael Landon and Jack Nicholson, and is an upstanding member in the Hollywood film community. Sol Goras, who had doubled for Errol Flynn, was also on the team. The stunt coordinator was Johnny Dayheim, who worked directly with Stanley Kubrick, Kirk Douglas, and the first assistant director, Marshall Green.

The six stuntmen were originally selected when Anthony Mann was the director of *Spartacus.* The selection was made by Kirk Douglas, who walked down a line of forty stuntmen with Johnny Dayheim. Douglas was looking for men who matched the principal actors in size and build. As he surveyed his troops, Douglas pointed and touched his selections, saying, "You stay, you stay." When he was finished, his team of six men was left.

The stunt team spent the three months developing period weapons to be used in the film and practicing for the grueling gladiator training and battle sequences. They worked out battle choreography and trained Kirk Douglas to fight like a gladiator and rebel fighter. Actors also went through physical training to evolve the right look for the camera and to be up to the strenuous demands of the film. Period and historic research was done, and the stuntmen advised Golitzen's art department during construction of the gladiator school set.

The six stuntmen played slaves for the opening, filmed in Death Valley. Later they played gladiators, then generals in Spartacus's slave army, and for the conclusion of the film they were crucified on the road by the Romans.

A large group of extras was employed for background scenes of Spartacus and his people, and another fifteen to twenty stuntmen were hired to fight around the key team.

Actor Woody Strode didn't have a stunt double. There were black stuntmen available, but none who matched his physique. So the stuntmen worked with Strode, who was a fine natural athlete. For the fight to the death between Strode and Douglas, the stuntmen worked with both actors, teaching them how to fight. Spartacus fought with a sword, and Draba—played by Strode—used a trident. At one point Draba scores a hit on Spartacus, tearing the trident blades across Douglas's chest. The trident was made of hard rubber and filled with movie blood. As the rubber trident went across Douglas's chest, a button was pressed to spurt artificial blood across the actor's body.

When stunts were worked out by the team, they would show the routine to Kubrick, who accepted most of their work without changes. He had inherited the team of professionals and had not yet directed a film that involved this complexity of stunt work. The stuntmen also offered suggestions of the best camera angles to show a particular stunt or fight move. Kubrick often took their suggestions and covered the action from many camera angles. He shot in Super Technirama 70mm, with two or three cameras and sometimes as many as six.

The stuntmen, who had worked with the gamut of experienced Hollywood directors, were astonished at the amount of coverage called for by Kubrick. When they thought a scene was covered by every possible angle, they began to bet against each other to guess what new angle Kubrick could come up with to cover a scene. In addition to the massive coverage, Kubrick would shoot a high take ratio on many of the camera angles, requesting to print all of the takes. Kubrick would take suggestions about where to put the camera to best photograph an action, and he also would shoot an angle he planned even if the stunt team mentioned that it wouldn't capture the action to full effect.

In the midst of the pressured, massive production of *Spartacus* Stanley Kubrick became a father when Christiane gave birth to a baby girl, Anya Renata Kubrick, on April 6, 1959, at Cedars of Lebanon Hospital.

The extensive shooting ratio that Kubrick used became more common in the late sixties and early seventies, but it was anathema to the studio system supporting *Spartacus*. The crew was dumbfounded by the director's methods.

One piece of action in the gladiator school involved a training apparatus that spun a sword blade around and around so the slaves could practice jumping over the attacking weapon. Kubrick covered the action with angle after angle. At one point stuntman Loren Janes was standing next to director of photography Russell Metty, and the two perplexed Hollywood professionals tried to figure if there was any angle that could possibly be left. "Russ said, 'Loren, what other angle could we cover this with?'" Janes remembers. "I said, 'Well, the only way would be shooting straight up and putting the camera on the ground. He'll probably come and dig a hole and put the camera down in the hole to shoot up,' and just as I said this, five guys walked by with shovels and started digging a hole. Kubrick loved weird and unusual camera angles."

The crew also witnessed a lot of discontent on the set. The film was over budget and over schedule and Douglas, Edward Lewis, and Kubrick were often in an office working out disagreements.

A camaraderie was quickly formed among actors like John Ireland, Woody Strode, Nick Dennis, and Kirk Douglas and the stunt team and crew. Kubrick remained quiet and kept to himself, choosing not to commit to being one of the guys or not caring to be a leader who was respected or feared. He remained an enigma throughout the process because of his perceived indifference and laborious working methods. He was neither well liked, feared, nor respected. The family of *Spartacus*, which embraced the cast and the crews of special effects, props, and all of a film's myriad crafts, looked upon him as a loner. Kubrick was thirty years old, but to those on the set he looked like a baby-faced kid surrounded by athletic, tanned, outgoing men in sunny California. He looked out of place and sounded affected to people used to the likes of John Ford and Henry Hathaway. He was perceived as a know-it-all and a boy genius. Kubrick's detached, intellectual approach to his work gave *Spartacus* its shining intelligence on film, but it did not make for a happy set.

Dealing with the egos of the likes of Charles Laughton and Olivier was quite a challenge for the young director. The actors were highly competitive and did not get along well. Peter Ustinov, who was a witness to the constant infighting, gave Norman Lloyd a sense of the verbal jousting that was going on while Kubrick was trying to keep the epic project under control. "Ustinov told me of a time when Laughton and Olivier and the whole cast were reading the script," Lloyd recalled. "Every time anyone read, Olivier would step in and tell the actor what to do right over Kubrick. He did this over a long speech that Laughton read, and Olivier turned to Laughton and said, 'No, no, no, Charles, that speech should be thus and so.' And Charles said, 'Well, I don't quite understand what you are saying.' Olivier said, 'Would you like me to read it for you?' And Charles said, 'Do, please.' Olivier read it, and Laughton said, 'If I only understood it a little bit before, I understand it not at all now.' Now this is what Kubrick was having to put up with. You're dealing with guys who are bigger than any director."

During the making of *Spartacus*, Lloyd had a bungalow on the Universal lot while he was working with Alfred Hitchcock on his TV series, *Alfred Hitchcock Presents*. When he went to visit his former second-unit director, he noticed that in the anteroom to Kubrick's office were stacks of scientific magazines. Kubrick's interest in science and high-tech matters would express itself in future films.

Stanley Kubrick certainly didn't dress the part of a film director. He wore the same shirt, same pants, and same coat for what seemed to the crew to be weeks on end. Kirk Douglas was aware that the crew was not responding to Kubrick, and he called a group of them together to try to rally a spirit around his young director. When the actor-producer asked why they weren't relating to Kubrick, someone politely asked if Douglas had noticed the director wore the same clothes for long periods of time. Douglas excused himself and went out to ask Kubrick about his sartorial habits, and the next day the director came in with a new outfit, which he proceeded to wear for the next duration.

The opening to the battle sequence was shot on location in Spain. Alexander Golitzen remembers being in Spain for about four months. The scene itself was shot in a week, according to the stunt crew. The Spanish army was employed to portray the slave army led by Spartacus and the Roman forces. Russell Metty didn't go on the trip to Spain. The Spain footage was photographed by Clifford Stine, who was credited with additional photography. The crew in Spain also included makeup man Bud Westmore, the head property master, and a few others. The Spanish military leaders took the information furnished by Saul Bass's storyboards and Kubrick's direction and created a phalanx of the mighty Roman army moving in platoons toward Spartacus's slave army. Just the scenes of the Roman army approaching took a week to shoot.

The battle between the slave army and the Romans was shot on the Universal backlot. Stuntmen were enlisted to play both armies. The sequence involved such dangerous stunts as the slaves rolling burning logs at the Romans. Men with missing limbs were hired and fitted with prosthetic arms and legs filled with movie blood, which could be severed when hit by a sword.

Loren Janes doubled for Kirk Douglas throughout the shooting and also played one of his soldiers. Stuntmen would switch from playing a slave to playing a Roman, depending on what was needed. In the battle Janes doubled for Spartacus for dangerous and involved fighting maneuvers, and in other shots he played a Roman fighting Spartacus so he could protect the actor and make him look like the fearless warrior he was portraying.

The aftermath of the battle was a sequence showing the hundreds of slaughtered slaves strewn on the hills of the battlefield. The sequence was originally planned to be shot on the backlot but Kubrick called for it to be created inside on the soundstage. Three stages were used to re-create the exterior location in the interior space. Alexander Golitzen's art department created hills and terrain to stage the massive scene. Several hundred extras were brought in and placed by the assistant directors. Kubrick ordered that each extra be assigned a large card with a number so he would know where to return after Kubrick carefully designated where he would lie dead. Dummies were laid in the background sur-rounding the extras to create the massive grave of bodies.

On the day scheduled to shoot the scene, Kubrick walked in, looked at the hundreds of extras playing dead as Spartacus's fallen slave army on hills created by Golitzen's artisans, and before a camera could roll he announced, "I don't like it, I want to do it outside."

The Hollywood regulars on the set were stunned. The production took the loss for the construction, labor, and precious time. The sequence was now to be done out on the backlot as originally planned.

Kubrick continued to use his method of assigning numbers to the extras to maintain control and continuity. After a lunch break, each of the hundreds of extras would know exactly where to lie dead for the scene.

The opening was shot in Death Valley, the full shots of the troops forming were shot in Spain, the horseback caravan on the beach was shot on location, but all of the other exterior scenes were staged and photographed on the Universal backlot. The battle scene, the Appian Way, the hills strewn with the dead of Spartacus's army were all filmed on what is now the Universal Tour at Universal City in Los Angeles.

The revolt of the slaves was an intricate action sequence. The art department created storyboards for the whole film and Saul Bass worked independently on storyboarding the sequence. Alexander Golitzen had two storyboard artists on the project, Claude Gillingwater and Johnnie Peacock. Kubrick would review the boards for the key action scenes, but his extensive coverage went well beyond the boundaries of the drawings, at times employing as many as thirty camera positions.

The storming of the gates of the Roman gladiator school was a partic-ularly impressive and dangerous stunt to perform, especially when the slaves climb the high fences, which collapse, crush the Romans, and then are used as a weapon against them. "Those were our six stunt guys on the fence," Loren Janes recalls. "I doubled Kirk on that. We had the fence rigged so it would go down and stop at about six feet and they had the real guys playing Romans there. Then we took them out and put in dummies dressed as Roman soldiers holding their spears, and we would crush the dummies. The dummies kept the fence from going down and smashing our knuckles and actually hitting the ground, it gave a little cushion."

For the scenes involving the crucifixion of the slaves, stuntmen were put up on the large wooden crosses created by the art department and held by a footstop and their hands tied to the crossbeam. The long takes, high shooting ratio, and multiple camera angles taxed the experienced stuntmen to the limit. When they got too tired, sore, hot, and thirsty in their uncomfortable positions Kubrick would call, "Okay, get them down for ten minutes and then we'll go back up again."

The night scene after Spartacus and Antoninus have been captured and talk about their imminent crucifixion was shot at the foot of a big hill on Barham Boulevard and the 101 Freeway. Kubrick worked the cast and crew from nine at night to six o'clock the next morning. Kirk Douglas and Tony Curtis sat in front of the camera and performed the scene. Behind them was a row of the slaughtered slave army corpses that went up the hill fifteen hundred feet past the actors. In the background were crucified slaves on crosses. Kubrick's camera position took in the entire scene. The director insisted that all the bodies be played by extras and stunt personnel because he wanted continuous groans and writhing during the dialogue.

In *Tony Curtis: The Autobiography,* Curtis recalls a particularly rigorous night shoot. After everything was in place Kubrick began to make takes of the scene. " 'Spartacus, what is the meaning of life?' Antoninus asks. The extras moan and groan. 'Life is not a bowl of cherries, Antoninus,' Spartacus replies. Kubrick called cut and said, 'On the cherries line, the man on the third cross on the left is supposed to move, you didn't move,' " Tony Curtis recalled. The man apologized. This went on for take after take. Kubrick never lost his temper but continued to find fault with the reactions of the extras while Douglas and Curtis worked in front of the camera.

The assistant director Marshall Green was assigned to *Spartacus* by Universal Studios to watch over the young director and to keep him on schedule. The all-night shoot was wearing the AD down. At one point in the wee hours Kubrick again called cut because of the background action. He called for Marshall Green and said, "Marshall, the guy up there on the twentieth cross on the left is supposed to struggle, but he didn't move at all. I want you to go up there and tell him that on the 'cherries' and the handkerchief signal from you, he's got to move. I can't use the megaphone to tell him during the shot because it'll screw up the dialogue."

"Green gave Kubrick a dirty look, turned around and walked up to the highest point on the hill," Curtis writes. "It took him three minutes to get to the cross right near the end. There were about thirty-five crosses on either side and this was one of the farthest ones." Curtis watched Green looking up at the cross. It seemed like he was having a conversation with the extra. "Marshall turned around and walked slowly back down the hill just looking at his feet and took another three minutes. He walks straight up to Kubrick and says, 'It's a fucking dummy.' Kubrick displayed no surprise or regret and gave a calm reply like, 'Oh, then put on wires and wiggle it.' "

The stunt team was originally scheduled for five to six months for preproduction and production. When *Spartacus* finally wrapped, the six stuntmen had put in close to a full year on the project.

Kubrick's old friend Alexander Singer was around to give support to the director, who for the first time was up against opposition that clawed at his fierce sense of artistic control. Kubrick complained about back problems and asked Singer, who was now working as an associate producer to Leslie Stevens, to drive him to the studio lot. During the drives Singer learned that each morning Kubrick was barely aware of what he was to shoot that day. Dalton Trumbo was furiously rewriting the script, and Kubrick did not have the total command his psyche required.

Singer did get to observe Kubrick directing on the set of *Spartacus* and witnessed the experiments with utilizing music on the set. When a scene did not require dialogue, Kubrick played music on the set as had been customary in the silent film days. Rather than talk them through it, this was an alternate means of evoking emotion from his actors, a methodology that Kubrick and Douglas embraced. Singer watched as Kubrick shot the scene in which Kirk Douglas and Woody Strode are waiting to fight each other to the death for the pleasure of Laurence Olivier and his friends. "Woody Strode was a man of innate dignity," Singer notes. "When you just turned the camera on him there was something rather special. Stanley needed a very curious performance out of him. It was the sense of a man turning inward and asking some profound questions of himself. 'Is this what I do in my days, kill my friend for the luncheon pleasures of the masters?' It's turning over in his head. Well, there's not much point in telling Woody Strode to do that and I don't think Stanley had any intention of doing that. There's a limit to what Woody Strode would have been able to render, but what Stanley did was to play some music. I'll never forget the power of the music and what happened to Strode's face as the music proceeded. I was near the camera and I could watch his face while it was happening. The music was a Prokofiev concerto, a passage which is haunting—not clashing. It was filled with infinite longing—a kind of love story, and the effect on Strode was visible."

Ultimately, Kirk Douglas had to decide what to do about the screenplay credit for the film. Both Edward Lewis and Douglas had long detested the blacklist. The shooting script was credited "By Eddie Lewis and Sam Jackson."

Douglas called a meeting with Lewis and Kubrick to deal with the matter. Lewis was against having the credit stand or having it with his name alone. This left only the choice of having the fictitious Sam Jackson as the sole writer. Douglas felt that using a pseudonym, as the producers of *The Brave One* had been forced to do, fooled no one and was also morally wrong.

Kubrick then suggested that the credit read, "Screenplay by Stanley Kubrick." Douglas and Lewis were aghast at the suggestion. Douglas turned to the director and said, "Stanley, wouldn't you feel embarrassed to put your name on a script that someone else wrote?" Kubrick replied, "No," Douglas recalled in his autobiography.

The meeting came to an abrupt end, and Douglas and Lewis were catapulted into making a courageous decision. The next morning Kirk Douglas phoned the security gate at Universal Studios and simply said, "I'd like to leave a pass for Dalton Trumbo." The blacklist was getting a final death knell. Otto Preminger, who had contracted Trumbo to write the screenplay to his own epic, *Exodus,* soon publicly announced that Dalton Trumbo was also receiving full screen credit. In his autobiography Douglas insists he wasn't being a hero in breaking the blacklist but was reacting on impulse to Kubrick's declaration about taking credit for a screenplay he didn't write.

The film moved into the postproduction phase. When Kubrick and film editor Robert Lawrence were ready with the director's cut of *Spartacus,* the screening was poorly accepted. Trumbo sat down and personally typed a critique of the film that ran more than eighty pages and was divided into two sections, "The Two Conflicting Points of View on Spartacus" and "Scene-by-Scene Run-Through." Douglas called it "the most brilliant analysis of movie-making that I have ever read" and ordered the film to be reshot and restructured.

Douglas asked for and received additional money to shoot battle scenes that were originally indicated but had not been developed in the first draft of the screenplay. It was at this point that Kubrick went to Spain to photograph the broad expanse of the armies in full shots. The original intention was to then dissolve to a bloody aftermath. The Trumbo critique led Kirk Douglas to conclude that more money was

needed for reshoots and that more battle material would need to be shot
when Kubrick returned from Spain, where the production had the cooperation of the government to use the Spanish army as Roman soldiers.

After reshoots, the film went back to Kubrick and Lawrence in the
cutting room. The editorial department also felt the upheaval of the
project. After Anthony Mann was fired, the original film editor, Robert
Swink, left with his assistant, Hal Ashby, who was to become the director
of *Harold and Maude, Bound for Glory, Coming Home,* and *Being
There.* Irving Lerner took on editorial responsibilities. Kubrick had been
involved with Lerner during the time he was working with Brando on
One-Eyed Jacks. Faith Hubley, the film editor and animated film creator
whom Kubrick had known from 1600 Broadway in New York, knew the
inside Hollywood circles and had given Kubrick Lerner's number, telling
him, "If you ever get into trouble—see Irving." Kubrick brought Lerner
onto *Spartacus* as editor and second-unit director. But as they continued
to get into disagreements, the principal editing went to Robert Lawrence, who had worked as an assistant editor on *Shane* and *A Place in
the Sun.* Lawrence had worked with Lerner in the past and was an editor
on *Murder by Contract,* which Lerner had directed. Lerner had other
projects in the fire while he was on *Spartacus,* and that prompted him to
bring in Lawrence, who would cut under his supervision. Lerner began
spending less time in the *Spartacus* cutting room and more time arguing
with the young director. Eventually, Lawrence found himself cutting
Spartacus and working closely with Stanley Kubrick. "There was a lot of
film, some of it had been cut," Lawrence, the editor of *El Cid, 55 Days
at Peking,* and *Fingers* recalls. "I looked at it and said, 'Why would anybody want to change this, this looks good?' But that didn't work with
Stanley. When Stanley was doing this picture he was already thinking
about *Lolita* because he never really would agree to the concept that this
was his movie. He would have done it differently, and there was so much
politics. We got along very well. One of the great experiences of my life
was knowing him, but he made everybody a lot of trouble by kidding
around a lot. His big ambition when he was young was to be a baseball
player. He'd work Saturdays—it was all overtime. He'd bring in a whole
crew and he wanted to go out and play stickball out in the backlot on the
Universal New York Street. He had the bat and the ball. I would say,
'Stanley, I've got those changes' and I'd go out on the street, and he
would say, 'Wait a minute, wait a minute, I've got two outs, I've got to
get this guy out.' This was on overtime. The treasurer at Universal used
to say, 'Stanley, you're on overtime, everybody's on overtime and you're
playing baseball. What are you doing playing baseball?' He'd say, 'Listen,

Saturday is not all that expensive. Think of it. The interest you're paying on this money, if we get so much and so much done you know how much I save you?' By the end of the day, of course, he was saving Universal money every Saturday.

"I used to pick up Stanley to drive him to the studio and we had to stop off at Merrill Lynch. He'd check out the stock market. Those mornings were the joy of all time, we laughed all the time all the way to the studio.

"Stanley used to be behind me in the cutting room and he'd be throwing a ball up against the wall over my head. He could turn on and turn off—and not do anything with such intensity that you would mistake it for profundity—but he would say, 'Why don't you try putting this over here?' and it was right. I'd say, 'Why didn't I think of that?' At times he could be very, very generous and friendly. Once in desperation I tried something which I was afraid to show him. When Spartacus is being inspected by Olivier and he says, 'You are Spartacus, aren't you?' Kirk spits in Olivier's face. Then Olivier slaps him. Well, the slap went so quick that you never saw it. I used a double slap. I used a big, wide, long shot the second time. I didn't say anything about it. I showed it to him and he didn't say anything, but later on he said, 'Hey, that was nice.' He liked it very much and he was wonderful."

During the production and postproduction of *Spartacus* James B. Harris continued to work out of Kubrick's bungalow on the Universal lot, developing *Lolita*. In addition to working on the next Harris-Kubrick production, Harris was also there to support his director and friend during the singular experience when he did not have absolute directorial prerogative.

Howard Fast would come into the cutting room demanding to see the cut material and complaining about what he saw. "What's this! Where did these words come from!" Fast would remark about the rewritten and redirected dialogue.

Lawrence observed that Kubrick was not at all affected by the antagonism of the crew. "Stanley and Russ Metty the cameraman had a terrible time. Whether it was in jest or serious, Russ used to say, 'Let's get that little Jew-boy from the Bronx off the crane.' It didn't bother Stanley one bit—never."

In his autobiography Tony Curtis recalls Russell Metty as a "boisterous, red-faced man—been around for years. He always had a coffee cup loaded with Jack Daniel's." Curtis describes Metty as "gregarious and friendly," a man twenty years older than he who mentored the young actor like an older brother but who detested Stanley Kubrick. "To Russ

Metty, Kubrick was just a kid, barely shaving. 'This guy is going to direct this movie? He's going to tell me where to put the camera? They've got to be kidding.' That was his attitude," Curtis explained. "We were on Stage Twelve at Universal doing the scene where Kirk makes a deal with Herbert Lom, the merchant, to get the ships for Spartacus's people to escape. We rehearsed it three or four times, and then the stand-ins went in so Metty could do his lighting. When that was finished, Marshall Green said, 'We're ready,' and in came Kirk, me, and Herbert. Kubrick was sitting on the side, and Metty was in his big high chair with his coffee cup, watching. Kubrick never said anything, and I wasn't quite sure what his attitude was. With Kubrick it was hard to tell because his mind was always popping all over the place. Finally he got up, looked over the shot, and went over to Russ Metty and said, 'I can't see the actors' faces.'

"Russ Metty, who was red-faced to begin with, got purple. He never said a word, but he was fuming in that high chair with his name on the back.

"By chance, next to his high chair, there was a little light no larger than the circumference of, say, a beer bottle—a little thin-necked spotlight with shutters on it, about five feet tall, on a tripod. Russ Metty just lifted up his foot and gave it a big kick, and it skidded its way onto the set and into the scene.

"That light just went rolling in and came to a halt there. When it stopped, Metty looked at Kubrick and said, 'Now is there enough light?' Kubrick just looked at it, looked back at Russ, and said, 'Now there's too much light.'

"Almost everybody treated Kubrick that way. They had no idea who they were dealing with. Later on they'd lionize and canonize him at Universal and everywhere else, but not in those days."

Although Kubrick was under the enormous pressure of an epic production and having to cope with ubiquitous power struggles, his disengagement from a film that wasn't really his and his inbred sense of dark humor helped move him through the project.

Saul Bass began work on the title sequence for *Spartacus*, which ranks among his best work in a superb career. Bass worked very closely on the sequence with his wife, Elaine, with whom he has often collaborated. They found a store on Formosa Avenue across from the Goldwyn studio. The place had copies of Roman statuary, which they painted. They used heads, body parts, and swords to create a powerful opening to the film. The sequence utilizes symbols to relate to the main characters as they are introduced in type by name. It features the profiles of Roman heads and ends with a frontal shot of a head cracking into pieces, symbolizing the fall of Rome.

The images dissolve from one into the other, creating a layering of one image over another. Originally Bass ordered twelve-foot dissolves to create long periods of superimposition before one image faded and the next reached full strength, and the first version of the titles ran almost five minutes. Bass supervised the shooting and cutting of the sequence, producing a short finished film to begin *Spartacus*. Bass ran the sequence for Kubrick, and when the lights came up Kubrick looked at him and said, "Saul, five minutes?" Bass appreciated Kubrick's sweet tone, realizing he had gone too far, and proceeded to trim the dissolves to bring the sequence to its present length of three minutes and thirty seconds. Nothing was changed in the imagery. Sitting in the room with Kubrick and watching the five-minute version, Bass instinctively knew the sequence was right but needed to be compressed.

The score written by Alex North was recorded on the Goldwyn scoring stage. North had had close to a year to write it. "I had the greatest experience with him," North told Irwin Bazelon for his book *Knowing the Score: Notes on Film Music*. "I had the good fortune of writing a temporary score for two pianos and two percussionists to fit the battle scene, for example, so that the cutter, Irving Lerner, could cut the scene to fit the music, which is unusual. But that was not the final track!"

The constant flow of massive amounts of footage coming in from the set kept Robert Lawrence in the cutting room practically around the clock. "I used to sleep under the cutting table," he recalled. In the confines of the editing room, Kubrick reacted to the pressures of the project and his status as a hired hand with mischievous and rambunctious behavior. "Stanley used to draw all kinds of porno pictures on my shoes," Lawrence remembered. "We had a room that didn't have any windows, and the light came from a single overhead globe. Stanley used to stand on a chair and draw dirty pictures on the globe and nobody would notice it."

Kubrick, an avid baseball fan, gave his editor the advice most often given by Leo Durocher. "He was also very cynical—he used to tell me all the time, 'Don't forget, Lawrence, nice guys finish last.' "

Kubrick's love of baseball continued outside and inside the editing room. "He used to imitate the pitchers," Lawrence remembers. "He had a tennis ball and a glove and he'd wind up, throw, and the ball would come pounding back off the wall."

The practical jokes and baseball practice did not affect Kubrick's intense concentration and dexterity in the editing room. "He was a wonderful editor," Lawrence recalled. "He knew just where to stop. At first I resented it, because he'd say, 'Cut it here, cut it here and cut it here.' So I would cheat and cut it two frames ahead or two frames later, and most times he found me out. He would say, 'Is that where I wanted it?' "

Even in Kubrick's one experience as a hired hand, his obsessive modus operandi pervaded his filmmaking work method. "When the picture was finished and they were preparing to mix the picture I gave the sound editors copies of my code book," Robert Lawrence recalls about the log that contains a list of all the footage shot for the film and the corresponding code and edge numbers on the film. "Stanley said, 'How many of these do you have?' I said, 'One.' He said, 'Make me a copy.' I made him one, it was a lot of work to get it done. He said, 'So you have one and I have one and these guys have copies. Suppose you lose yours? Make two copies.' Pretty soon we had multiple copies of almost everything."

The sound editing for *Spartacus* was a daunting job. Kubrick applied his meticulous attention to craft and his growing knowledge of every aspect of the filmmaking process to the task. One of the sound editors was Frank Warner, who had begun working in sound effects for radio and television. Warner's career has included supervising sound editing on *Close Encounters of the Third Kind* and *Taxi Driver*. His contribution to *Raging Bull* is considered by industry insiders to be one of the finest achievements in film sound history. In the sixties and seventies Warner laid the groundwork for what became the advent of the sound designer—*Spartacus* was his first experience in feature filmmaking. "Stanley Kubrick was the first person to ever make me understand that film was an art form," Warner, now retired in Sedona, Arizona, said. "We'd go out to dinner and sit around the table and talk. *Spartacus* had images of thousands of soldiers, and his philosophy was to just concentrate on the foreground action. He taught me to be able to control that. He led me to the fact that we had an awful lot going on—to concentrate on the primary story that we were telling, that the sounding of the picture is part of the story. When you've got a battle going on and two characters are working together you can't have a CinemaScope screen full of the sound of ten thousand people."

Kubrick encouraged the sound editors to create sound effects that would help the viewer to enter the mind of the characters of *Spartacus*. Frank Warner would later employ the theory of a psychological use of sound to enter the tormented soul of Jake LaMotta in *Raging Bull*. "In the great scene when Spartacus is sitting waiting to go up and fight, he's sitting in the cell isolated, all by himself, and you hear the background sounds of his friends fighting. Kubrick wanted to get into what Spartacus was really thinking about, what his worries were. From then on if I was doing anything in my work, I began to learn from him."

Jack Foley, the legendary Universal soundman who invented the process of recording footsteps and other sounds performed live while watching a picture (now called Foley in his name), was part of the *Spartacus* sound team. Foley was intimately involved in creating sounds for the intricate battle scenes. The production track recorded during shooting was no more than a guide for the sound team, who removed the track that contained camera noises and the sound of artificial weapons. One of Jack Foley's key jobs was to bring the battle alive aurally. "The first time I met him was on *Spartacus*," Frank Warner recollects. "I remember walking on the stage, and six guys were walking around clinking rings they hang draperies on. Ten thousand men were walking on the screen and these six guys were going, *ching, ching, ching.*"

John Bonner, an engineering executive for Warner Hollywood Studios and recipient of the Cinema Audio Society Lifetime Achievement Award, was a full-time student at UCLA when he worked as a sound engineer on the team selected to do the re-recording mix of *Spartacus*. "I would start at six o'clock in the evening and we worked until two in the morning. Stanley would say, 'No, that was perfect, but let's try this.' And this is in the finals, we'd already gone through months of panning and combining sounds, so to try something new was difficult, but we would do that. He was very creative and genuinely interested in what we could do," Bonner recalled.

Kubrick continued to search for innovative ways of mixing the sound even if he eventually went back to an earlier version they had already tried. In 1960 it was not possible to go back and forth to rerecord a small section if there was a mistake or the director decided to change something. There was no insert recording—so thousand-foot reels had to be recorded in one take with no going back. Every time Kubrick revised something, the entire reel had to be redone. The revisions were complex and labor-intensive.

The sound team remained motivated and strived to give the director what he wanted during the grueling months of rerecording *Spartacus*. Veteran sound mixer Murray Spivak, who had worked on the original *King Kong*, was the lead mixer on the film and was mixing the John Wayne epic *The Alamo* during the day.

Don Rogers, who was selected by Samuel Goldwyn's sound director, Gordon Sawyer, to replace him at Goldwyn Studios, was a recordist on *Spartacus*. Rogers operated the tape machines, which were tested to the limit during the arduous mixing process. "We worked on that film for nine months," Rogers, a Warner Bros. executive and the recipient of the 1995 Academy of Motion Picture Arts and Sciences' Gordon Sawyer Award, recalled. "Stanley came into work at 11:00 at night. We were working nights. We were doing *The Alamo* in the daytime and *Spartacus* at night with separate crews. Murray Spivak mixed both films. We only had one rerecording department. They'd pre-dub effects on one movie and do a final reel of the other movie. So Murray would move at night to do a final and then a week later he would move to daytime to do a final on *The Alamo*. He was something else.

"We got there at 6:00 P.M., the day crew left at 6:30 P.M., but we had to prepare. So we'd work at 7:00 P.M., Stanley always came to work about 11:00 P.M. At 12 midnight we would be getting hungrier than heck, ready to eat, and Stanley wanted to start making a take. We never went to dinner until about 2:00 in the morning on meal penalty and you try to find a place around Hollywood at 2:00 in the morning. There were a few places to eat and you didn't want to go in them. So we all brought our own lunches. We were rerecording for nine months. I got to know Stanley real well.

"In those days everything was panned. They had a pan pot and every person on the screen had to be placed exactly where they were—the same thing with every effect, every footstep, every bang, every crash— everything! Everything was panned and it took hundreds of hours to pan this stuff—it was incredible," Rogers recalled. "Pan pot" is short for "panoramic potentiometers," a control that is two connected volume controls with a common knob, used to move a sound from speaker to speaker to pan or place a sound. "If you went down 750 feet and made a mistake you ate it and started at the beginning again," Rogers explained. "It was time-consuming. Stanley's a real perfectionist, a demanding perfectionist. He wants everything just exactly perfect. Nine months! It was the longest show that I worked on in my lifetime."

"We made a lot of changes on *Spartacus*. One day while we were mixing, Stanley wanted to make a change after the battle, with all of the dead," Robert Lawrence recalled. "So we took the work print off the projector into a little change room, and I said, 'What do you want to do that for?' Stanley said, 'Well, it will look better if . . .' Maybe it would have but we didn't do it. It would have meant changing so many sound units because we hadn't pre-dubbed anything. In running the film back and forth on the Moviola I got my finger caught in the sprockets. Stanley had put his foot on the pedal to go backwards or forwards. My finger was still in there and we couldn't get it out. We had to go backwards to get it out and I was in terrible pain. I finally got it out. There was blood on the bottom of the picture side of the Moviola, and Stanley said, 'Bob, you got this so dirty, you think we could ever get this blood off, we'll never be able to run any film through it.' He didn't give a shit. They took me to the hospital and stitched up my finger. I came back and he never said a word. For days, he never mentioned it. I was so glad I still I had my finger that I forgot to be angry about it. Then one day I said, 'You son of a bitch, one of these days you're going to get your balls caught in the Moviola and I'm going to drive it fast forward!' And he said, 'Listen, there's no point in giving you sympathy after it's done.' "

Although the musical score for *Spartacus* was being written by Alex North, Kubrick tried to introduce the use of previously recorded music during the editing process, an idea that in its fruition revolutionized the nature of film music in *2001*. For the sequence in which Marcus Crassus (Laurence Olivier) takes over the command of Rome, Kubrick asked that "The Battle of New Orleans" be inserted. "The Blue Danube Waltz" of *2001* fame was considered at one point.

For the concluding scene of the three-hour-and-eighteen-minute epic Kubrick played some mischievous tricks. First he asked his editor, Robert Lawrence, to score the last sequence when Spartacus is dying on the cross and Varinia shows him their baby with the theme from Chaplin's *Limelight*. Next, when he was preparing his first cut of the film, he said to Lawrence, "You know what would be a fun thing to do?" "And I said, 'No, what?' " Lawrence recalled. "He said, 'Let's never show Kirk. She holds up the baby and she says what she has to say—but you don't see him up there.' I said, 'You're crazy. You'll get us killed!' He said, 'No, it's worth a try, c'mon.' We ran the picture in a big room at Universal, and Kirk and Eddie Lewis were sitting up front. Stanley and I were in the back at the control center—he liked to fool around with the dials. We ran the whole picture without a stop and it felt like it was doing very well. When we got to the end you never see Kirk up on the cross. We drew the lines on the film for the big fade-out as the cart goes down the road, and then the lights went on. There had been a screening the night before and they had these folding chairs. Kirk grabbed a folding chair and threw it. He was beside himself with anger. 'You're fired—and you're fired, I want to talk to you!' They marched out, and Eddie Lewis was puffing on his pipe saying, 'Now wait a minute, Kirk, wait a minute.' I thought I was fired, but Stanley said, 'You know what, from now on— no jokes, no kidding around with him. Yes, sir, no, sir, Do you want this? Can we do this? Yes, I'll do it. No questions asked, no fooling around.' That was on a Friday. I didn't come in Saturday and Stanley didn't come in and I didn't work Sunday, which was strange, because we used to work Sunday. When I came in Monday, I went to the cutting room. The next thing I know, Stanley and Kirk walk in buddies. They made up over the weekend and I was the heavy. Stanley said, 'Listen, let's start on the last reel. What happened to those close-ups that I picked of Kirk on the cross?' "

For background voices the production went to a Michigan State–Notre Dame football game played in East Lansing, Michigan, in October 1959 to record the 76,000 screeching fans on three-channel stereo sound for voices used in scenes where men said, "I am Spartacus" and "Hail Crassus!" The sound elements later became part of the legendary sound mix that went on for months.

When Kirk Douglas first conceived of making *Spartacus* into a movie, Lew Wasserman was his agent at MCA. During production of the film, MCA purchased Universal. Now Douglas was working for Wasserman. MCA paid $11,250,000, three quarters of a million dollars less than the $12,000,000 budget of *Spartacus.*

As *Kubrick's Spartacus* ordeal was winding down, Christiane again gave birth to a baby girl, Vivian Vanessa Kubrick, on August 5, 1960, at Beverly Hills Doctors Hospital. Stanley Kubrick was the proud father of three daughters.

The Hollywood premiere of *Spartacus* was held at the Pantages Theater on Wednesday, October 19, 1960. For Kirk Douglas, *Spartacus* took three years from conception to completion. When *Spartacus* was released, the American Legion attacked Kirk Douglas by sending a letter to seventeen thousand posts imploring members not to see *Spartacus* and castigating the actor for hiring a Communist writer. The all-powerful Hedda Hopper condemned the film for its gore, telling her readers: "That story was sold to Universal from a book written by a Commie and the screen script was written by a Commie, so don't go see it." The attacks from patriotic groups continued on many fronts and were primarily aimed at Dalton Trumbo and Howard Fast. To show his support for the film, President John F. Kennedy ignored White House tradition, went to a public Washington, D.C., screening of *Spartacus* unannounced, and gave a good review to the press, an act that Dalton Trumbo greatly appreciated.

Surprisingly, *Spartacus* was not nominated for a best picture Oscar, but the film did win the award in four categories. Peter Ustinov garnered the Oscar for best supporting actor. Despite his antagonism for the young director, Russell Metty took home the trophy for best cinematography. Alexander Golitzen, Eric Orbom, Russell A. Gausman, and Julia Heron won for best art direction. Valles and Bill Thomas acquired an

Oscar for best costumes. Alex North was nominated for his magnificent score, and Robert Lawrence was nominated for his heroic efforts in editing the complex epic.

In his autobiography Tony Curtis called Stanley Kubrick his favorite director and a genius with the camera. "His greatest effectiveness was his one on one relationship with actors," Curtis wrote.

The supreme lesson that Stanley Kubrick learned from his experience on *Spartacus* was that he had to have autonomy on the films he directed. "*Spartacus* is the only film on which I did not have absolute control," Kubrick told writer Gene D. Phillips. "The film came after two years in which I had not directed a picture. When Kirk offered me the job of directing *Spartacus,* I thought that I might be able to make something of it if the script could be changed. But my experience proved that if it is not explicitly stipulated in the contract that your decisions will be respected, there's a very good chance that they won't be. The script could have been improved in the course of shooting, but it wasn't. Kirk was the producer. He and Dalton Trumbo, the screenwriter, and Edward Lewis, the executive producer, had everything their way."

Spartacus marked the end of the relationship between Stanley Kubrick and Kirk Douglas. In the fall of 1961 Kubrick and his lawyer, Louis Blau, met with Douglas at his Canon Drive home, requesting to be relieved of the contract with Bryna Company. After negotiations, Kubrick was released from his commitment on December 15, 1961. In his autobiography Douglas laments, "In the nearly thirty years since *Spartacus,* Stanley has made only seven movies. If I had held him to his contract, half of his remaining movies would have been made for my company." Douglas summarized his feelings about working on *Spartacus* with Stanley Kubrick with strong words: "You don't have to be a nice person to be extremely talented. You can be a shit and be talented and, conversely, you can be the nicest guy in the world and not have any talent. Stanley Kubrick is a talented shit."

PART FOUR

1960–1964
England

CHAPTER 11

How Did They Ever Make a Movie Out of *Lolita*?

In July 1959, Vladimir Nabokov and his wife, Vera, were in Arizona hunting butterflies, which was Vladimir's beloved hobby. He received a message from his agent, Swifty Lazar, telling him that James B. Harris and Stanley Kubrick, who had acquired the film rights to *Lolita*, were requesting that Nabokov come to Hollywood to pen the screenplay. To protect their *Lolita* investment, Harris-Kubrick also optioned Nabokov's *Laughter in the Dark*, which had a theme similar to that of *Lolita*: an older man's obsession for a young girl. Nabokov was intrigued by the monetary offer to write the script but troubled by the idea of adapting his own novel. When he found that in order to get the film past the censors it might be necessary to suggest that Humbert and Lolita were secretly married, Nabokov spent a week considering the dilemma at Lake Tahoe and decided to decline. Then he departed for Europe.

After Nabokov said no to writing the screenplay, Harris and Kubrick gave the assignment to Calder Willingham, who wrote a script, but it was rejected by Kubrick.

While touring England, France, and Italy, Nabokov had what he called in the foreword to the published screenplay of *Lolita* "a nocturnal illumination of diabolical origin," which gave him the idea of how to bring *Lolita* to the screen. As he was experiencing regret at having turned down the Harris-Kubrick offer, they sent him a telegram imploring him to reconsider.

In January 1960, Nabokov received a telegram from Lazar. Harris-Kubrick offered Nabokov $40,000 while he was writing the screenplay, with an additional $35,000 if he received the sole writing credit. The deal also included six months of expense money for Nabokov while he was in Los Angeles. Nabokov cabled Lazar with his acceptance of the offer the same day.

Nabokov had many flirtations with the cinema. In the twenties he wrote screenplays in Berlin. He dreamed of collaborating with Lewis Milestone. Later, after *Lolita* was released, he discussed working with Hitchcock, but nothing materialized.

Worldwide, others tried to jump on the *Lolita* bandwagon. A French film, *Les Nymphettes*, was announced, and an Italian film, *Le Ninfette*, was claiming to be a freely adapted version of *Lolita*. Pirated versions of the novel began appearing in Greece, Turkey, Latin America, India, and Arab countries. James B. Harris brought suit against *Les Nymphettes*, but it proved to be a flop and not a worthy competitor. Nabokov learned that Italian director Alberto Lattuada was developing his own interpretation of the *Lolita* story, called *The Little Nymph*, which never materialized. Unauthorized *Lolita* dolls began to show up in Italy.

The initial challenge for *Lolita*, the film, was getting it through the conservative censorship system that still controlled Hollywood.

Ronnie Lubin, agent for Harris-Kubrick, had Jack Warner and Steve Trilling titillated by *Lolita*. Warner Bros. agreed to pay Stanley Kubrick $1 million, an impressive sum for the time, to direct *Lolita* if Harris-Kubrick could deliver the precious Code Seal, which was obligatory before the film could be distributed to theaters and sold to television.

At the time there was no completed script. A Code Seal was given only upon approval of the finished film, but it was possible for the Motion Picture Association of America (MPAA) to consult with filmmakers about whether a script had the potential to pass code requirements.

Warner Bros. was prepared to strike a development deal with Harris-Kubrick to finance the writing of the screenplay. James Harris proceeded to set up a series of meetings with Geoffrey Shurlock, president of the MPAA.

On March 1, 1960, Vladimir Nabokov and Stanley Kubrick met at an office in Universal City Studios to trade suggestions and countersuggestions about a screen adaptation of *Lolita*. By the next morning, Nabokov sat on a public park bench not far from the Beverly Hills Hotel cottage Swifty Lazar reserved for him. He was already constructing the script in his mind.

On March 9, Kubrick introduced actress Tuesday Weld, who had been in *Rock Rock Rock* and *Rally Round the Flag, Boys!*, to Nabokov as a possible Lolita. The author found her unsuitable. By March 11, Kubrick had sent Nabokov a rough outline of the scenes they had agreed upon, which covered the first part of the novel. Nabokov began to feel that Kubrick was listening to him more than he was the censors, and he went on to write the remaining two acts. The two men were thirty years apart in age, but they were both chess players, understood the dark side of human nature, and used their intelligence to make their way through demanding professions. Nabokov certainly revealed his understanding of the unlit recesses of the id in his masterful *Lolita*, and artistically Kubrick lived on the dark side. From his first feature on, he explored the raw emotional and physical brutality of war and the greed and hopelessness of the inner-city underworld. Personally, beneath a quiet and polite demeanor, Kubrick was deeply cynical and pessimistic in his worldview.

During the next several months Nabokov and Kubrick met less often. Outlines stopped coming, criticism and advice diminished, and Nabokov was left to ponder whether Kubrick was serenely accepting or silently rejecting his work on the screenplay.

Nabokov spent from eight until noon each day butterfly hunting and mentally composing the screenplay. Lunch was prepared by a German cook. Then Nabokov sat in a lawn chair for four hours, writing down the morning's ideas for scenes on index cards. Some of the scenes introduced into the screenplay were based on unused material that Nabokov had saved after he destroyed the novel's original manuscript.

Swifty Lazar gave his client the full star treatment and introduced him to John Huston, Ira Gershwin, David O. Selznick, John Wayne, Gina Lollobrigida, and Marilyn Monroe.

In late April, Nabokov sent Kubrick the completed second act of his *Lolita* screenplay. Nabokov and Lazar had been engaged in a struggle throughout the year to get the rights for Nabokov to publish his completed screenplay. Kubrick's lawyer continued to stall the negotiations because the director wanted to avoid comparison between Nabokov's script and his finished film. Kubrick knew he was taking liberties with Nabokov's work. Kubrick rewrote the script, even though Nabokov would get the full screen credit.

By the end of June, Nabokov had more than a thousand index cards and a four-hundred-page typed script, which was sent to Kubrick. The

Nabokovs went to Inyo County for a much-needed rest to collect butterflies. When they returned to Mandeville Canyon, they received a visit
from Stanley Kubrick, who told Vladimir that his screenplay was too
long, had too many scenes, and would make a seven-hour film. "You
couldn't make it. You couldn't *lift* it," James B. Harris told Richard Corliss in 1993. Kubrick gave Nabokov a list of deletions and changes.
Nabokov made some of them, while creating new sequences.

In September 1960, Vladimir Nabokov delivered a shorter version of
the script, which Kubrick accepted. The script had taken six months to
write. On September 25, Nabokov met with Kubrick at the director's
house in Beverly Hills. Kubrick showed the writer photographs of Sue
Lyon, who had been signed to play the title role.

The trio of Nabokov, Stanley Kubrick, and James B. Harris was a
model of diplomacy and verbal acumen. Nabokov provided a brilliant
adaptation, Kubrick was able to shape it into his own cinematic vision,
and James B. Harris continued to move the project through the
minefield of moral opposition. All three men possessed persistence,
sheer will, and the ability to maneuver one another without the customary Hollywood strong-arm techniques featuring many threats and loud
voices. The process was convoluted but civil.

Harris and Kubrick had known from the outset that adapting *Lolita*
would be an awesome challenge. The book was considered a literary
masterpiece as well as provocative, and in some circles, even pornographic. They decided to give Vladimir Nabokov the sole on-screen
credit. With the exception of *Spartacus,* it is the only Kubrick film to
have an exclusive writing credit without acknowledgment of the director's hand. Nabokov was writing the screenplay and wanted his creation
to remain intact. Harris and Kubrick would work on the screenplay to
keep it to length, control the sensitive censorship issues, and to make it
cinematic. The sole Nabokov credit may have seemed an acknowledgment of Nabokov's mastery and an absence of Harris-Kubrick ego, but
the duo knew they would be roundly criticized if they tampered with a
masterpiece. Wisely, they did not want to put themselves on the firing
line, and they concluded that producer and director credits for *Lolita*
would be enough to go around. In the end, there would be some invention and intervention with Nabokov's original novel that darkly probed
Humbert Humbert's proclivity for very young girls, and a final reclama-
tion of part-ownership by putting in the opening credits: "MGM
Presents in association with Seven Arts Productions James B. Harris and
Stanley Kubrick's *Lolita.*"

Geoffrey Shurlock saw himself as a bridge between the film industry and the political and religious groups that served as watchdogs for the public. James B. Harris and Stanley Kubrick took a political stance as they set out to get the necessary Code Seal. Their argument to Shurlock was, If something is legal how can it be immoral?—noting that there were some states that would allow Lolita and Humbert to marry. To get the pressure off the focus of an older man sexually obsessed with a teenage girl, they tried to shape the story as an odd love affair.

When they were beginning to feel confident that the story could be told in a manner that would earn the seal, Harris-Kubrick moved forward with the Warner Bros. deal, and the studio proceeded to draw up the contracts.

The completed paperwork was sent to Harris-Kubrick attorney Louis Blau. After surviving *Spartacus*, Kubrick had vowed he would never again relinquish control on a Stanley Kubrick film, so he and his partner were dismayed to see that the contract called for consultation with Warner Bros., and granted the studio final approval on most areas of the production of *Lolita*—even the choice of composer, cameraman, and editor. Additionally, if agreement could not be reached between Warner's and Harris-Kubrick on any matters during the making of the film, control would stand with the studio. The deal offered $1 million plus 50 percent of the profits, guaranteeing a return on their initial investment.

Harris and Kubrick asked their attorney to advise Steve Trilling that the deal was off. There were to be no compromises on control this time.

Now that the Warner's deal was nixed, another tactic to raise money was to start the search for an actor to play Humbert Humbert. An early choice was James Mason. Kubrick called James Mason and offered him the role. Mason was keen on the idea, but he had signed on to appear in a new musical based on Arthur Schnitzler's *Anatole*.

While Kubrick was still on *Spartacus*, he had suggested to Harris that they ask Laurence Olivier about the role. During lunch at their Universal bungalow, Harris and Kubrick told Olivier about *Lolita*. The distinguished actor told them he would discuss it with his agent at MCA. Since their agent, Ronnie Lubin, was at MCA, they thought they would have an edge, but ultimately the agency counseled the renowned actor to move away from the quarrelsome project.

They continued to seek out an attractive star. If the actor playing Humbert was in any way vulgar or neurotic it would create an air of sexual depravity. They talked to the erudite David Niven, who also agreed to the movie when approached. A deal was made. Harris and Kubrick were summoned to the office of Abe Lasfogel, the head of the powerful William Morris Agency. The meeting, however, was not to sign papers but for the agency to apologize on behalf of David Niven. Niven had to withdraw. He was involved with *Four Star Playhouse,* and there was concern that its sponsors would frown on anything that smacked of controversy. At one point even Marlon Brando was interested in playing Humbert, but no one was able to give Harris-Kubrick a firm commitment.

Their next strategy to obtain capital to put the film into production involved pre-selling foreign territories. Harris flew to New York and had lunch with an old school chum, Kenneth Hyman, whose father, Eliot, ran Associated Artists. Harris told his friend about *Lolita,* and after lunch they paid a visit to the senior Hyman. "I knew Eliot from the old days when I was a kid and he said, 'What's up kid, what are you doing?' " remembers Harris. "So I told him and he said, 'How much do you need?' So I said, 'A million dollars.' Stanley and I had figured before I left that would be the number I would be looking for, because we could do it in some country where the costs were really cheap as possible, and we could do a picture that looked like millions. We'd get nothing and we'd put it all in the picture. So Eliot Hyman said, 'Is that all you want is a million? You got it.' That's how fast the meeting was."

The deal was made on a 50/50 partnership basis. Now that they had the money, Harris and Kubrick decided not to pre-sell the foreign territories, but to sell off the negative around the world. Associated Artists had a relationship with an Italian distributor, but all other territories would be open.

Harris brought their lawyer, Louis Blau, to New York to complete the contracts before the producer left for Europe. The European trip now had a new focus, not to pre-sell but to locate production facilities where *Lolita* could be made less expensively than in Hollywood.

Then a particular kind of luck struck a second time. As with Kirk Douglas on *Paths of Glory,* James Mason became available. When his wife, Pamela, and his friends learned he had turned down the role of Humbert Humbert in *Lolita,* they persuaded him to change his mind. Mason was a great admirer of Nabokov's novel and longed to play the part. He called Kubrick and accepted the role.

Now Harris-Kubrick had the money and a star. They then decided to do the film in England under the Eady plan, which allowed foreign producers to write off costs if 80 percent of the laborers were UK subjects. Mason was English, so deals were made to produce the film in England. Nabokov was not to be invited to Elstree Studios in England, where *Lolita* would be filmed. The project qualified under the Eady plan. Kubrick talked to Marie Windsor, who had played Sherry Peatty in *The Killing* about a part in *Lolita,* but the Eady plan limited the number of American actors he could employ in the production. What started as a pragmatic business arrangement would ultimately have a career-changing impact on Stanley Kubrick.

The search was then on for an actress capable of playing Lolita. Kubrick and Harris were barraged with potential Lolitas. The hopefuls included everyone from middle-aged women who came to auditions without makeup and dressed in middy blouses to nine-year-old girls wearing makeup and high heels.

"We had a desperate search for the right actress," Kubrick recalled to Jack Hamilton, senior editor at *Look*, in 1962, "but it wasn't because mothers kept their daughters away from us. We got thousands of applications. Some mothers even wrote to say their children were *born* Lolitas. I think this means that the public is more sophisticated and less shockable than the watchdogs give them credit for. After all, it is only a part, it's only a movie. It could obviously launch a career for a talented actress."

After almost a year of searching for what Vladimir Nabokov called "the perfect nymphet," Kubrick immediately responded to fourteen-year-old Sue Lyon. "From the first, she was interesting to watch—even in the way she walked in for her interview, casually sat down, walked out," Kubrick told *Look* magazine. "She was cool and non-giggly. She was enigmatic without being dull. She could keep people guessing about how much Lolita knew about life. When she left us, we shouted to each other, 'Now if she can only act!'"

Sue Lyon was from Los Angeles and started in show business by playing bits on TV's *Dennis the Menace* and *The Loretta Young Show.* She did hair commercials featuring her dyed-blond locks and was chosen Miss Smile of 1960 by the dentists of Los Angeles County. She had friends from Hollywood High. Her favorite movie star was Paul Newman. Her mother, Sue Karr Lyon, was a fifty-six-year-old widow who raised her five children by working as a hospital housemother.

Stanley Kubrick first saw Sue Lyon on an episode of *The Loretta Young Show* and gave her a screen test. He shot the scene where Humbert gives Lolita a pedicure while grilling her about where she's been spending her time.

Sue was offered the notorious part of Nabokov's prepubescent vixen. Mrs. Lyon went to her pastor for guidance about her daughter playing Lolita. The priest told her that Jean Harlow had been one of his parishioners and she had never been influenced by her roles. He encouraged Sue to take the part.

When production began, Sue Lyon was fourteen years and four months old. She was fourteen years and nine months old when shooting was completed. Lolita was twelve years and eight months old when she met thirty-nine-year-old Humbert and over seventeen when the novel concluded.

For the role of Clare Quilty, the mysterious playwright who in his own lustful quest for Lolita taunts Humbert while cloaked in a series of disguises, Kubrick tapped Peter Sellers. He was impressed with Sellers when he saw the comedian in *The Ladykillers* in 1955, *The Naked Truth* in 1957, and *Battle of the Sexes* in 1959. He also listened closely to *The Best of Sellers* album and was fascinated by Sellers' range. Peter Sellers had been on the BBC radio program *The Goon Show*, where he created voices and did impressions of Winston Churchill, the Queen, and Lew Grade. When Kubrick contacted Sellers about playing Clare Quilty in *Lolita*, the multifaceted actor was at a career low. Kubrick offered Sellers a small part in *Lolita*, telling him he would be on the screen for no more than five minutes.

Sellers' first reaction was that Clare Quilty, the flamboyant television playwright who tormented Humbert Humbert, was outside his experience, and he became jittery about playing the role. After several dinners at the Sellers home, Kubrick began to realize that the dominant manic state the actor achieved on the screen was less prevalent than the depressive one he observed.

In order to play Quilty with an American accent, Sellers told Kubrick, he needed a model. They decided on the voice of jazz impresario Norman Granz, who was born in Los Angeles and was connected to Verve Records and Jazz at the Philharmonic. Kubrick asked Granz to record sections of the *Lolita* script on a tape so Sellers could study them and develop his voice for the part. When Sellers was confident that he had Quilty's voice, the character began to form.

Sellers usually spent most of his creativity during the preproduction of a movie, but on *Lolita* Kubrick encouraged him to improvise and exhaust all the possibilities in playing a scene. Sellers and Kubrick began to elaborate on the multiple-disguised appearances Quilty made as a state trooper and a German psychologist.

Kubrick talked to Alexander Walker, who wrote *Stanley Kubrick Directs* and the authorized biography of Peter Sellers, about how the actor worked on the set of *Lolita*. "When Peter was called to the set he would usually arrive walking very slowly and staring morosely. I cleared the crew from the stage and we would begin rehearsing. As the work progressed, he would begin to respond to something or other in the scene, his mood would visibly brighten and we would begin to have fun. Improvisational ideas began to click and the rehearsal started to feel good. On many of these occasions, I think, Peter reached what can only be described as a state of comic ecstasy."

"The most interesting scenes were the ones with Peter Sellers, which were total improvisations," Oswald Morris, the cinematographer of *Lolita*, told *Film Dope* magazine. "They'd roughly block it out, go upstairs and leave me to light it, then come down with, for instance, the table tennis scene. There was nothing like that in the script, it was just off the cuff."

Sellers always relied on inspiration, not a preplanned strategy on how to play Quilty. He would start with the lines as written in the screenplay and then would begin to expand and develop the material as he performed. Sellers had the ability to repeat lines and routines that Kubrick liked.

Kubrick often used two or three cameras to capture the first take, when Sellers would hit the height of improvisation. By the second take, half of Sellers' energy was gone, and by the third it was time to move on.

Sellers found his relationship with Kubrick to be his most rewarding since his collaboration with director John Boulting on *I'm All Right, Jack*. Sellers trusted Kubrick, who he felt pushed him to the limits of Quilty's character. The two men were bonded by a growing cynicism about life. Kubrick especially prompted Sellers to probe the darker side of the comedy of *Lolita*. Sellers had feared that his interpretation of Quilty went too far, but Kubrick assured him that larger-than-life was the essential reality.

Peter Sellers was a brilliant impromptu talent, and Kubrick used the inspiration to fine-tune a scene by playing a key line or using the line to rewrite the sequence. The improvisation was a tool, and Kubrick's method both encouraged and controlled the volcanic hilarity so it always hit its target.

In October 1960, Kubrick wrote to actress Shelley Winters from England, asking her to read the novel *Lolita* and then to meet with Vladimir Nabokov in New York to discuss her impressions of the book. Winters was actively campaigning for Senator Jack Kennedy, who was running for President, but she found the time to read the book, which greatly impressed her. JFK saw her reading it and as a joke got his press secretary, Pierre Salinger, to tell her to get a brown paper cover if she had to read the book in public.

Winters met with Nabokov and discussed the character of Charlotte Haze at great length. Nabokov arranged for his wife, Vera, to meet Winters, and the three had dinner at the Sherry Netherland Hotel. When Winters returned to New York after the campaign was over, the script for *Lolita* was waiting for her. Winters wanted the part but fought with her agent over signing the contract. Even though it was still before election day, she insisted that shooting be set back until Kennedy was inaugurated so she could attend the inaugural ball. After much bickering, Winters agreed to leave for England after the election but before the inauguration, but only after Kubrick promised she could return to Washington to attend the inaugural ball.

Winters left for England after Kennedy won the election, defeating Richard Nixon by a narrow margin. Her contract demands included five round-trip air tickets so she could fly over with her mother, her daughter, and two other adults in her entourage. They all stayed on the top floor of the Dorchester Hotel, which contained the Oliver Messel Suite, where Elizabeth Taylor and her retinue stayed while Liz starred in the notorious and ill-fated *Cleopatra*. Other residents of the hotel included Jack Palance and his family and Kubrick's former star and boss, Kirk Douglas.

Kubrick gave the actors a long time to develop their roles. There was a lengthy rehearsal period before principal photography began. During shooting, time was put aside to rehearse each scene before it was shot.

In the initial rehearsal period Kubrick learned that Sue Lyon had memorized her lines so well that she had a tendency to rush through them. Kubrick then suggested that all of the actors pretend to forget the lines they had memorized and express the character in their own words, while being aware of the aim and content. This technique had a positive impact on Lyon's performance, corrected her pace, and allowed the character of Lolita to come to life.

The actors were encouraged to improvise during the rehearsal period, but Kubrick asked the cast to incorporate what occurred during run-throughs into a finished script performed in front of the camera without deviation. The exception was Peter Sellers. Kubrick sanctioned Sellers to experiment in front of the camera and stretch the boundaries of the multifaceted character of Clare Quilty.

Kubrick asked the actors not to reveal that there were departures from the words written by Nabokov. The cast had known that Kubrick was rewriting Nabokov's script. The director was concerned that during production Nabokov would learn that his words had been altered. He was especially concerned that Shelley Winters would leak the news, as she was always courting the local press.

At the first rehearsal for *Lolita,* Winters reminded Kubrick, Sellers, and the teenage Sue Lyon that they promised that she could go back to Washington for Kennedy's inaugural. Kubrick reiterated his promise. Shelley ordered a dress from the Queen's couturier.

Winters often arrived late to the *Lolita* set because she was off with Elizabeth Taylor helping her spend her £2,000 *Cleopatra* per diem. Kubrick and James Mason became impatient with her tardiness, and the director ordered a car to get Winters to the set on time and put in a call to Taylor's producer to tell him his actress had to study lines for Charlotte Haze by herself every morning.

Cinematographer Oswald Morris told Bob Baker and Markku Salmi of *Film Dope* magazine that Kubrick was selective in the amount of attention he thought each actor required, saying, "Sue Lyon he directed very carefully, but James had got it all worked out already."

Shelley Winters had the highest regard for her experience with Kubrick. "I was enchanted with Charlotte and very proud of her. Kubrick had the insight to find the areas of me that were pseudointellectual and pretentious. We all have those things in us," she wrote in the second volume of her autobiography.

Winters found it stressful working with Peter Sellers and James Mason. She told Kubrick that it was difficult connecting with both men. "Whenever I complained to Kubrick about trying to connect with my two leading men, he would agree with me," Winters said in her autobiography. "But he didn't change their performances, and this very frustration that I had in real life was what was so sad and funny about Charlotte. I never felt anyone was listening to me when I talked, except for the sound man. Again, I didn't understand the lonely quality it gave me until I saw the film."

Shelley Winters experienced particular trouble during the wedding night sequence between Humbert and Charlotte Haze. She wore a silk robe for the scene. Kubrick directed her to sit on the bed with her back to camera. He had worked it out so only her bare back would show—and that just for a second, but Winters (who freely discusses her prolific sex life in her books) could not get herself comfortable to perform the scene. In her nervousness she flubbed lines and broke Mason's glasses as she continued to clutch the robe tightly to her body.

When word of the scene got to the *Cleopatra* crew, they began to come over to watch. During lunch, Winters was given some gin to loosen her up and Kubrick cleared the set. In the afternoon, only the necessary

Lolita crew remained. Winters still couldn't play the scene. Mason said to her, "I can't believe you can't do such a simple thing! Drop the robe in the back, cover your bosom, get under the cover, and snuggle up against me," Winters recalled in her autobiography. At one point Winters was squirming with embarrassment behind Mason with just her panties on. Mason turned to Winters and said, "Would it make you more comfortable if I tell you that a long time ago my name was Moskowitz, and not Mason?" "No," Winters returned. "The only thing that would make me feel more comfortable is if you lie absolutely still when I put my naked bosom up against your back." The witty Mason replied, "That would be very ungallant," Winters recalled in her autobiography.

The sequence helped to improve the working relationship between Mason and Winters, but Kubrick was never able to get the scene the way he wanted. Ultimately Winters had to get in the bed with her robe on.

For the opening scene when Humbert comes to shoot Quilty at his home, Kubrick and art director William Andrews came up with a design that looked like the interior of a Victorian mansion, complete with a grand staircase and chandeliers. Kubrick asked James Mason if he could think of any items to introduce on the set to suggest Quilty's bizarre lifestyle. Mason suggested a Ping-Pong table, which could be put under the chandelier. Kubrick incorporated the idea. As the scene developed, Humbert and Quilty began to play the game while Humbert contemplated murdering him. Sellers improvised, calling the game while bombarding Mason with hysterical ad-libbed lines.

For a scene in which Humbert and Charlotte Haze honeymoon at a lakeside resort, Kubrick had the art department create the setting in the studio. He became so concerned with shooting such an important exterior sequence in the studio that he began to refashion the script so he could stage the entire event involving Humbert's homicidal feelings toward Charlotte in their house.

To create the new sequence Kubrick consulted James Mason closely and began to piece the story elements together to bring the scene indoors.

Kubrick's patience with actors continued to hold him in good stead. During the filming of the scene where Charlotte Haze dances the cha-cha, Shelley Winters had difficulty finding the rhythm of the music. A dance scene without dialogue can be performed to playback so the actors can actually hear the music, but this one had dialogue. Kubrick did not want to loop the scene, so he asked the actors to dance without the music. Winters felt she couldn't work this way, so after a director-actor conference it was decided that a drummer would be brought in to give the actress the beat. Harris and Kubrick felt that the drumbeat wouldn't interfere with the production recording of the dialogue because in the finished scene there would be a cha-cha record playing and the drummer's guiding beat would blend in with the music. A top drummer from London was brought in, but the problems were still not resolved. Winters insisted that the drummer be positioned out of her sightline and began to complain that the beat he was playing wasn't right. Inscrutable in the face of temperamental and emotional outbursts, the logical and steadfast Kubrick refused to react and pressed on until he got what he wanted.

Winters tried Kubrick's patience. "Shelley Winters was very difficult," Oswald Morris told *Film Dope* magazine, "wanting to do everything her own way. She was very nearly fired off the film. At one point Kubrick said to me, 'I think the lady's gonna have to go'—which would have been very serious halfway through production. But he'd have got rid of her, he really didn't care about the consequences."

The set for the high school dance scene, which took place in a gym, was built on the stage by art director William Andrews and his crew. The scene took many days to shoot. The inauguration of John F. Kennedy was a few days off and a blizzard forming over the ocean threatened London. The day before the inauguration, Shelley Winters brought her packed suitcase to the studio, ready to leave for Washington, D.C. At the end of the shooting day, Kubrick, Peter Sellers, and James B. Harris asked her to come to the back of the American high school gym set for a talk. "Peter, you explain to her," Kubrick said to Sellers. "Stanley, you're the director," Sellers returned. Winters began to worry whether she was being fired. Finally, rather nervously, Kubrick said, "I know we promised you that you could go to Kennedy's inaugural, but there is a blizzard over the Atlantic now, and it will invalidate our insurance, you can't fly, understand!" Winters broke down in tears, weeping. Sellers tried to console her by saying, "They've promised to get President Kennedy to say something super personal to you on British television," Winters recalled in her autobiography. Winters returned to the Dorchester in tears. When she got there, she received a cable telling her she was to be the mistress of ceremonies of a White House press photographers' ball at which she would be the only woman in the room. The news consoled Winters, who went on to finish her work in *Lolita*.

Kubrick got high marks from all of the actors on *Lolita*. Sue Lyon said, "Mr. Kubrick never humiliates or bullies any actor. *Lolita* could have been an embarrassing film for everyone in it, but he saw that it wasn't."

The idea for the image that would open *Lolita* came after the principal photography was completed. The titles were to play over a tight shot of Lolita's foot as Humbert painted her toenails. The director of photography, Oswald Morris, had completed his work on the film and was on another project. The shot was a simple one, but Kubrick approached it with the same meticulous care he gave to every cinematic detail. He had remembered a 1955 film, *The Dam Busters,* which had been photographed by Gilbert Taylor, a British cameraman who began as a camera assistant in 1929 and had been a lighting cameraman on films since the late forties. Taylor was available and delicately lit the elegant shot. The long take dwelled obsessively on Lolita's foot with the zeal of a fetishist and the lightheartedness of a satirist.

For Oswald Morris the experience of working with Stanley Kubrick was not a pleasant one, prompting him to say that he would never want to work with the director again. Morris was forty-five years old when he shot *Lolita.* He had entered the British film industry when he was sixteen and worked his way up from apprentice to clapper boy to assistant cameraman to director of photography. Before working with Kubrick he had photographed many films, including *Moulin Rouge, Indiscretion of an American Wife, Beat the Devil, Moby Dick, Heaven Knows, Mr. Allison, A Farewell to Arms, Our Man in Havana, The Entertainer,* and *The Guns of Navarone.* Despite this tremendous experience and accomplishment, Kubrick continued to dominate the way his films were lit and photographed. "He'd say, 'Now I want this scene lit as though there's just one light bulb in the middle of the set . . .'" Morris told *Film Dope.* "Fifteen minutes later he'd come back and say, 'What are all those lights? I told you just one light-bulb.' I said, 'It's basically and faithfully lit as if with one light-bulb.' I defied him, you see. . . . So we used to fight . . . it all got a bit boring, inquest after inquest about the lighting."

The relationship on the *Lolita* set between Oswald Morris and Kubrick may have been prickly, but Morris's delicate chiaroscuro and Kubrick's mastery of the long take give the film a veneer that is appropriate for Nabokov's delicious prose.

Kubrick contacted Bob Gaffney, the cameraman he had met in New York on the set of Alexander Singer and James B. Harris's short film. He asked Gaffney to work on the second unit for *Lolita.* Dennis Stock, a still photographer who had taken many well-known pictures of James Dean, was hired and credited for second-unit work with the uncredited Gaffney. "Dennis and I and one other guy went on the road with two station wagons," remembers Bob Gaffney. The second unit was in charge of photographing all the background plates to be used for the scenes of

Humbert and Lolita driving through the United States. The scenes with Sue Lyon and James Mason would be filmed in a mock car in England as the second-unit traveling footage was projected behind them. They also filmed exterior shots of the station wagon driving on the road. "We had a dummy done up as Lolita and the other guy played Humbert and was the grip. The station wagon had a hole in the roof and was all sealed in with a camera mount in the front. I'd pop up, stand on the seat, and do the photography. We were shooting plates, backgrounds and car-bys going through different places.

"We went South and wound up at Gettysburg in the fog, and we drove through the battlefield with all these statues and monuments that became the opening scene in *Lolita*. Then all of a sudden we get a telegram from Stanley: 'Stop.' So we stopped, and then months went by and Stanley called me and said, 'I'm in New York, do you want to go out and do some more second unit?' He didn't want anybody directing the second unit, so he and I and Christiane took the two station wagons and went off on the road with another guy, who would go in and make the deals we needed to take a picture of a motel or this or that.

"We spent two or three weeks on the road. We drove up through Rhode Island and then over through Albany and then clear across back over to Rhode Island to Newport. We were driving around all over the place. I remember coming down Route 128. I'm standing on the top of the station wagon, Stanley is driving. We had his favorite Eyemo, which was a Royal Navy Eyemo and an Arriflex. We were driving into a terrific rainstorm. I could see it coming toward us, this big dramatic sky. It was fantastic, and we drive right into the storm and I can't get the camera down fast enough. It was one of those torrential summer downpours. I got the camera down, but I couldn't get the top in. I put up a plastic garbage bag and I started taping it on the inside and we're driving and driving. This big bubble started as the water filled up the garbage bag. Then it just burst and sprayed all over both of us. We were laughing—so we drove off the highway and Stanley drives through the side streets in this little town and drives right into somebody's garage. This woman comes out screaming, 'Help, I'm going to call the police!' We did everything as quick as we could and we just backed out of the driveway and left."

Principal photography had been completed in England, so Kubrick was interested in getting exterior material to bring reality to the studio work. There was a scene involving a taxi picking up Humbert at a train station, and the taxi had been painted to Kubrick's specifications and shot on the stage. When Kubrick and Gaffney were in Rhode Island they found a train station that the director liked. They got the train schedule and knew when the trains arrived. A cab was found, so they could get a shot of a diesel engine train coming into the station. Unfortunately the cab was the wrong color and Kubrick didn't want to pay to have the cab painted.

"So we got out the *American Cinematographer Handbook*," Gaffney recalled, "and they had a color photo of yellow, red, blue, green dinner plates and showed what would happen if you took a black and white photo with a red filter, a yellow filter. We matched the car by picking the right filter out of that book, which told us which filter would turn the red to the appropriate gray. We got the cab and Stanley said, 'You drive here.' So Stanley was setting up the shots the way he wanted them and we used to shoot early in the morning and late in the afternoons so we would get nice soft light. Listen, we had the cheapest crew in the world."

Gaffney and Kubrick shared a love of literature. Gaffney was constantly exploring the work of new and innovative writers. He read *The Magic Christian*, by Terry Southern, and told Kubrick to read the book. Always searching for information and material, Kubrick read the book and began to discover the outrageous and irreverent writer he would work with in the future.

In 1961 Anthony Harvey, a graduate of the Royal Academy of Dramatic Art who had appeared in the film *Caesar and Cleopatra*, was working as a film editor for the Boulting brothers on films such as *Private's Progress* and *I'm All Right, Jack*, and *The Spy Who Came in From the Cold* for director Martin Ritt.

Harvey, who later became the director of *The Lion in Winter, They Might Be Giants*, and *Dutchman*, had just finished cutting *The L-Shaped Room* for director Bryan Forbes when he decided to write a letter to Stanley Kubrick, who was now working in Harvey's native London. In hopes of getting the assignment of editing *Lolita*, Harvey asked if he could meet with Kubrick.

"I really loved *Paths of Glory*," Harvey recalls. "I thought it was extraordinary. I remember sitting with sweat on my hands, I was knocked out by it. I wrote to him and had five or six interviews with him because mostly he was very careful to find out if I was available."

"He gave me the MI-5 treatment," Harvey told film director and historian John Andrew Gallagher. " 'What kind of hours do you work? What time do you go to bed? Are you married? Do you go on holidays?' He wanted somebody who was going to be there seven days a week, twenty-two hours a day.

"Anyway, after about six interviews, he said, 'I'd like you to edit it,' so that was thrilling." Harvey set up an editing room at Elstree Studios and prepared to edit *Lolita*.

Kubrick's directorial style for *Lolita* was to capture the performances and story in long takes. "He conceived the film in long, long takes," Anthony Harvey remembers. "He did long takes, which is extraordinary for the actors to build an emotion. If you keep saying, 'Cut,' it's hopeless. He sometimes took ten-minute takes." The critical lesson of when not to cut served Harvey well when he became a film director. "I've always done long takes myself. I was influenced by Stanley," Harvey said.

Anthony Harvey and Kubrick worked very closely during the editing of *Lolita*. They began to develop a style of editing a scene by fading to black with a long pause in black before fading in the next scene. This created a chapter-like structure while remaining cinematic in technique. Fading scenes out, then fading the next scene in was nothing new, but Kubrick and Harvey began to push the limits—giving the film its own style. "These things come out, not of the script, but these things always come out of being on a Moviola."

Kubrick did not shoot a lot of conventional screen coverage, but he ran a high take ratio on long takes until he got the performance he was looking for, rarely shooting reaction shots. "His great thing was—don't cut to a reaction if the actor is giving a brilliant performance, you imagine the reaction for yourself," Anthony Harvey explains.

"He is the most extraordinary fellow I've ever worked with. I never met anybody who was so inquisitive about life, about every single book, words, detail—enormous, complete, and utter concentration. I loved working with him. He had a very black, funny kind of sense of humor, and we got on terribly well. I used to drive back from the studio with him and we'd discuss all the way home. Then he'd say stay for dinner. I spent a holiday in Paris with Stanley and Christiane. I was very fond of him."

The final cut of *Lolita* remained close to the shooting script, which was based on Nabokov's screenplay adaptation of his novel. Kubrick's *Lolita* follows the spirit of Nabokov but is fashioned into a new screen story.

Nelson Riddle, the orchestrator, composer, and conductor who had done the arrangements for many classic Frank Sinatra recordings, was selected to score *Lolita*. Riddle, best known for his luscious and romantic orchestral arrangements, was a canny choice to give emotional credibility and an ironic counterpoint to the film's forbidden love affair.

For the main theme, James B. Harris went to his brother, a composer who specialized in song themes and had a studio on Fifty-seventh Street in Manhattan. The theme used for *Lolita* was not written for the film, but when James B. Harris brought it to Kubrick, he immediately fell in love with it.

Kubrick had earlier asked Bernard Herrmann, who had scored *Citizen Kane*, *Vertigo*, and *Psycho* and was considered to be Hollywood's most psychologically intense composer, to write the music for *Lolita*, but Herrmann turned the director down when he learned he would be required to use Bob Harris's theme.

Nelson Riddle was flown to London to score the film along with his orchestrator, Gil Grau. Harris and Kubrick were very concerned with keeping any hint of depravity out of the film. There was enough to deal with inherent in the premise of the story to shake up a country still governed by moral conservatism. It was at the dawn of a decade that would see a sexual revolution. *Lolita* helped open the door, but first it had to get through an old system that was still in power.

During the recording of a love theme composed by Riddle, Harris and Kubrick were concerned to hear that the piece had been written in a minor key. The musicians were asked to stop playing as Harris and Kubrick talked to Riddle. They wanted a straightforward romantic sound and not any form of dissonance, which might disparage Humbert in the audience's eyes.

When *Lolita* was complete, the final process of getting the MPAA Code Seal was at hand. The film was brought from England to the United States. Film editor Anthony Harvey and his assistant came to the States and stayed in a hotel to be available if needed. The approval could be granted only to a completed film that fell within the requirements of the Code. Harris and Kubrick had gotten advice early on in the process from Martin Quigley, head of Quigley Publications, who had been involved in the earlier days of the Code. Quigley was able to give them guidelines about the MPAA's areas of concern. So the film that Harris-Kubrick had been producing avoided some of the more obvious pitfalls of the system. They knew they wouldn't be able to explore the deeper levels of sexuality in the book and were cognizant of the importance of not making Humbert appear depraved in any manner. The minefield of sexual metaphor had to be approached with subtlety and sophistication. Above all, Lolita could not be perceived to be as young as she was in Nabokov's book—this was forbidden by the MPAA.

The process of getting *Lolita* through the quagmire of censorship began in September 1958 while Harris and Kubrick were considering purchasing the forbidden novel. In his notes Geoffrey Shurlock stated that he thought the subject matter would probably fall into the area of sex perversion, which was prohibited by the Code. Harris and Kubrick suggested that they would imply that Humbert was married to Lolita in a state like Kentucky or Tennessee where the union would be legal. Shurlock agreed that a legal marriage would remove the subject from the area of perversion but maintained that if the girl still looked like a child the film could nevertheless be offensive and not receive a Code Seal. Kubrick and Harris promised Shurlock the film would not be offensive and that they would use humor to make the relationship palatable. Harris-Kubrick wanted to avoid the avalanche of problems that had faced Otto Preminger's *The Man with the Golden Arm,* which had its Code Seal withheld, and Elia Kazan's 1956 production of *Baby Doll,* which was condemned by the Legion of Decency.

In March 1959, when Warner Bros. was interested in the film, Shurlock had a meeting with Warner executives to discuss the possibility of raising Lolita's age to fifteen and to make the story about a middle-aged man married to a young wife who ruins his life. Shurlock counseled Warner's to seriously consider the adverse reaction to the project. He told the executives he thought *Lolita* was a problem no matter how it was rewritten.

In June 1959 Shurlock met with Columbia executives and filled them in on what he had told Warner Bros. They discussed Lolita's age and this time Shurlock told them the Code could not approve the story if she was fifteen years old.

On February 9, 1960, Kubrick wrote a letter to Shurlock from an office at Universal International Pictures to apologize for an item he had spotted concerning *Lolita.* An A.P. wire story by reporter Bob Thomas quoted Kubrick as saying he felt that the MPAA didn't make much of a difference anymore. Kubrick assured Shurlock that he had been misquoted and he did not believe that to be true. Shurlock, ever the diplomat, wrote back to Kubrick, telling him he had not seen the misquote and fully accepted Kubrick's apology, explaining that he had often been misquoted himself. Shurlock told Kubrick that he was gracious and said he was eagerly looking forward to seeing Kubrick's production of *Spartacus.*

In December 1960, Kubrick received a letter from the MPAA telling him that examiners found the screenplay to *Lolita* to be unacceptable. "Whatever opinion one may have of the morality of the book, it was superbly written," the examiner stated. "This script, in my opinion, has turned an important literary achievement into the worst sort of botched-up pastiche that could be imagined." A long list of complaints concerning language and innuendo were included in the lengthy report.

On December 14, John Trevelyan of the British Board of Film Censors wrote to Geoffrey Shurlock concerned about whether the MPAA would give *Lolita* a Code Seal. Trevelyan had a discussion with Kubrick, who was exploring the position of the British censors toward his project. Trevelyan told Shurlock that if the British Board of Film Censors had to refuse *Lolita* a certificate, many who had not read the novel would be on their side. "Of course, the intellectuals would tear us apart," Trevelyan told his American counterpart. On January 10, 1961, Shurlock wrote to Trevelyan saying he had not yet seen the script to *Lolita* and it was his opinion that Kubrick knew the project would be unacceptable for a Code Seal.

Three days later, on January 13, James B. Harris wrote to Martin Quigley of Quigley Publishing at Rockefeller Center in New York. Harris was communicating from the Harris-Kubrick offices at Elstree Studios. "There is not much to say about the two enclosed scripts other than they are completely revised in accordance with all our discussions," Harris wrote. "Please notice that all descriptions have been edited very carefully so as to avoid confusion. Both Stanley and I will anxiously await word from you on the reaction to the script in California."

Quigley began to communicate with Shurlock on behalf of Harris-Kubrick. Quigley acted as an intermediary, agreeing to Code objections and tutoring Harris and Kubrick in problem resolution. Kubrick continued to press ahead with shooting the film. On January 23, 1961, Quigley advised Shurlock that *Lolita* was "only forty percent photographed, so there may well be time for many additional changes even this side of what [may] be necessary to be done on the rough cut," thus keeping the negotiating system alive.

On January 30, Harris wrote to Quigley to tell him that he and Kubrick were encouraged by the MPAA's reaction to the script and assured Quigley they never intended to commercialize or sensationalize Nabokov's novel. Harris also guaranteed Quigley that they had made every effort to dispense with smuttiness and gratuitous material and would continue to follow Quigley and Shurlock's suggestions. Harris included a point-by-point document from Shurlock that they had addressed. Harris assured Quigley that "in the widest stretch of the imagination," the rushes did not portray Lolita as under the age of fifteen. Harris gave Quigley "my sincere thanks for your efforts and concern and also our assurance that you will be gratified when you see the finished product."

On February 6, 1961, Quigley wrote to Shurlock pledging that there was still time to discuss problems concerning *Lolita* with Harris and Kubrick. Two days later Shurlock wrote back to Quigley saying that he urged Harris to consider making protection shots for a few items that the MPAA still did not agree on, suggesting that Kubrick shoot the scenes in alternate ways that would ensure that the Code was not violated. Shurlock was most concerned with a scene between Lolita and Humbert where she discusses a game she played with a boy. "The succeeding dialogue seems to us to be an overly emphasized discussion of fornication," Shurlock wrote. "The whispering in Humbert's ear will be interpreted as obscene, we believe, under the circumstances."

Quigley continued to work back and forth between Shurlock and Harris-Kubrick. On May 25, 1961, he wrote to Harris, telling them that *Lolita* had received Code Seal number 20000. "Let us assume that this good, fat number bespeaks a good omen," Quigley wrote to Harris. The number was given as a convenience for the producer to prepare the main title. The Code Seal could not appear on the film until the finished film was reviewed and received the official Code Seal certificate.

In England, Christian Action leader Canon John Collins asked the British Board of Censors to refuse a certificate to *Lolita*.

On August 29, 1961, Geoffrey Shurlock wrote to James B. Harris to inform him that *Lolita* was close to being approved with the exception of four items in question. Shurlock suggested that the seduction scene between Humbert and Lolita should fade out earlier, possibly when Lolita starts to whisper in his ear. Shurlock also objected to Humbert's reply to a line from Charlotte about a limp noodle, Humbert's grunting in the bathroom, and Charlotte's line "Where can you get more peace." Shurlock told Harris he wanted the items corrected before a certificate would be granted to *Lolita*.

Upon receiving the letter, Harris wrote back to Shurlock, "We have conferred with Stanley Kubrick, now in London, by telephone. The four points cited in your letter were discussed. It was agreed that revisions in the picture intended to satisfy the points you have questioned insofar as technical matters permit will immediately be taken in hand." Harris advised Shurlock to put the Code Seal certificate in issue of A.A. Productions, Ltd., in England. Harris was on his way to New York and asked Shurlock to call him in care of their attorney, Louis C. Blau.

On August 31, Harris wrote Shurlock again, telling him that he and Kubrick agreed to eliminate the off-screen vocal noises of Humbert when Charlotte is outside the bathroom door and to fade out after Lolita has moved to the side and is about to say, "This is how we start," thus eliminating the line.

Michael Linden, associate director of the Advertising Code Administration, wrote to Sid Glasser of MGM that the Legion of Decency and Seven Arts agreed to place captions on the advertising for *Lolita* stating, "This movie has been approved by MPAA." It was suggested that it should be changed to PCA, the Production Code Administration.

In September 1961 Columbia Pictures expressed interest in distributing *Lolita*. In England the British Board of Film Censors gave *Lolita* their X certificate, which meant the film could be seen only by adults. Canon John Collins, chairman of the Christian Action group, campaigned to have the film banned entirely, proclaiming, "The showing of *Lolita* might lead to rape or even murder." The X rating stated, "This is to Certify that 'Lolita' has been Passed for Exhibition when no child under 16 is present."

The process in England was a matter of getting the film approved by John Trevelyan, who was in charge of the industry-financed British Board of Film Censors. During the screenwriting process Kubrick had conferred with Trevelyan and, as with Shurlock, managed to solve many of the problems before shooting began. Trevelyan's principal problem with the screenplay was a proposed sequence that had Humbert's narration about his attraction to nymphets illustrated with a montage of young schoolgirls, store clerks, and usherettes. Trevelyan counseled Harris-Kubrick against the scene, and it was deleted from the script.

Ultimately *Lolita* was distributed by MGM. Harris-Kubrick created two production companies to make the film: Anya Productions, named after Kubrick's middle daughter, his first with Christiane, and Transworld Pictures. Both companies were registered in Switzerland.

The meetings with Quigley were crucial to Harris and Kubrick, but at times their dark sense of humor and an occasional tendency to lapse into silliness made it difficult for them to talk seriously about the absurdity of the strict guidelines of the Code. It was in their best interests to play it straight, so when giddiness infected them, they did their best to grin and bear it.

The casting of Sue Lyon was key in getting the film approved. She was selected because she didn't look like a twelve- or fourteen-year-old who was made into a sex object to legitimize Humbert's obsession with her.

During production of the film, Eliot Hyman of Associated Artists formed a new company, Seven Arts, with Ray Stark, who had engineered the Bryna–Kirk Douglas deal with Harris-Kubrick.

Eliot Hyman, James B. Harris, and Stanley Kubrick were very anxious to get the Condemned rating given by the Legion of Decency removed from *Lolita* so that distribution deals could be made. They took the film to Monsignor Little of the Legion, where *Lolita* was screened for an audience of clergy, nuns, and priests. After the film was over, they filled out preview cards with their reactions. Several days later Harris met with Monsignor Little, who showed him the cards. There were some at the screening who liked the film, but the Monsignor told the producer he had decided to condemn the film, as he had another recent film, Fellini's *La Dolce Vita.* The C rating meant that *Lolita* would go on a list of films that the Church had condemned—the list would be distributed through parish newspapers like *The Tablet* in Queens, New York. The message to Catholics everywhere was—do not see this film—anyone going to see *Lolita* would be committing a sin.

Eliot Hyman began to talk to Harris and Kubrick about their contractual right to improve any sale or distribution deal made by Seven Arts within sixty days. He was trying to get them to loosen their control in this area so he could sell the film, which was now in trouble with the Catholic Church. Harris and Kubrick wouldn't budge on their control.

Harris next received a call from Ray Stark as a representative of Seven Arts, who summoned the producer to his New York apartment to tell him, "You're killing Eliot, you making a sick man out of him," Harris recalls. "You're standing in the way of the picture." Harris was beginning to suspect that Seven Arts wanted to use the completed *Lolita* as part of a development deal at a studio. " 'Every time you get together with Eliot you irritate him and you're either going to have to buy us out or we're going to have to buy you out, because we can't continue like this,' " Harris recalls Ray Stark saying. "So I said, 'Well, Ray, how can I buy you out, the picture costs a million, eight. You're not going to just sell it for your money back, you're going to want a profit and where am I going to get that kind of money to buy you out?' So he said, 'Well, then we're going to have to buy you out.' " Harris-Kubrick was able to maintain control over the final cut of the film, get out of the deal, get up-front money, and manage to even the score for the *Paths of Glory* deal engineered as Stark's swan song as an agent. The deal with Stark was predicated on one price if the C remained on *Lolita* and a higher price if Harris-Kubrick was able to get the Condemned rating removed. So they proceeded to mediate with the Legion of Decency to change the rating. At one point Eliot Hyman even tried to offer the Church a sizable contribution, but Monsignor Little was not susceptible to bribery—he was motivated by his calling to protect the morals of Catholics across the country.

The Monsignor was very direct in expressing what he found offensive in *Lolita*. He told Harris that he was aware of all the sexual innuendos in the film, and he challenged many of them—for example, the scene between a hotel manager, Peter Sellers, and the Vivian Darkbloom character. He told the producer the tone between the men blatantly portrayed a homosexual advance, citing lines about getting rid of excess energy and references to thigh locks during judo.

Harris didn't try to convince the savvy religious leader that these sexual messages did not exist, but he appealed to him nevertheless, arguing that the Legion of Decency was being particularly tough on the film because the nature of Nabokov's book left them predisposed to thinking the movie was sinful.

After a long series of negotiations, getting the Code Seal was a matter of a few cuts. A shot of Humbert looking at a picture of Lolita on his desk and a close-up of the picture were deleted because it was perceived that his repeated viewing of the picture was a sexual stimulant and emphasized his obsessive feelings for the girl. Another provocative scene involved revision. Lolita and Humbert are on a cot, and she whispers in his ear and says, "You mean you didn't do that when you were a kid?" and she begins to bend over to him implying they're about to make love. The scene then faded to black. In order to retain the scene, the fade is anticipated earlier. When Charlotte Haze said, "Oh, Humbert, when I get near you, I'm as limp as a noodle," Harris and Kubrick originally wanted Humbert to reply, "The same thing happens to me," but it was changed to "I know the feeling."

Monsignor Little compelled the producers to agree to two captions for the ads: "For persons over eighteen only" and "This movie has been approved by the MPAA." Kubrick and the media made much of the fact that the now sixteen-year-old Sue Lyon appeared in *Lolita* but was not old enough to go see it. Lyon claims to have first seen the film at the London premiere because in England you could see the film if you were sixteen.

Lolita officially received Code Seal Certificate No. 20000 on August 31, 1961, signed by Geoffrey M. Shurlock, President of the Motion Picture Association of America. The film had finally received a Code Seal, and a deal was made with MGM to release *Lolita*. The studio capitalized on the Harris-Kubrick struggle to get the film through the censors with the tag line "How did they ever make a movie of *Lolita*?"

Various points of view have been presented about whether Vladimir Nabokov was happy with the film. Shortly after screening the film, Nabokov told James B. Harris that he wished a lot of things in the movie were in his book, leaving the producer to feel that the author had liked the results. Nabokov also told James Mason at a dinner party given for the film by Kubrick at the Four Seasons restaurant in New York that he admired the film and congratulated Kubrick on adding a number of touches he would not have thought of.

A month after the film opened, Vera Nabokov wrote to a cousin, saying, "Vladimir had been worrying about the picture but already after the preview . . . he felt completely reassured. The picture might have been somewhat different had he made it himself but it certainly was excellent anyway and contained nothing whatsoever that he could find offensive, false or in bad taste. He . . . even found some of the deviations from his script were very fortunate."

Nabokov was interested in publishing his script when the film came out, but he agreed not to come out with his screen interpretation of the book for a year after the film was released. Kubrick was very sensitive about having any competition or negative reaction to his movie from the author. Nabokov waited ten years to publish his screenplay. In the foreword written in 1973 to the published script of *Lolita,* Nabokov talked about his initial reaction to the Harris-Kubrick production. Nabokov saw the film on June 13, 1962, at the Loew's State in New York City. In the foreword to the published screenplay of *Lolita,* Nabokov said he thought Kubrick to be "a great director," and *Lolita* "a first-rate film with magnificent actors," but felt that "only ragged odds and ends" of his script had been used. He called the film as unfaithful as "An American poet's translation from Rimbaud to Pasternak." He described his first reaction as a "mixture of aggravation, regret and reluctant pleasure."

Nabokov was delighted by the Kubrick and Sellers inventions of the Ping-Pong scene and Mason drinking Scotch in the bathtub after Charlotte's death. He found the collapsing cot and the frills of Sue Lyon's nightgown painful. Overall, he found most of the sequences to be an improvement over his own. The most interesting contrast between Nabokov's script and Kubrick's movie was that the author tried hard to make his script cinematic writing in filmic devices and structure. Kubrick's film worked hard to tell Nabokov's story and was less adventurous in cinematic technique. At Oscar time *Lolita* received only one nomination, and that was for the screenplay. Nabokov was given a solo credit by Harris and Kubrick, so the screenplay nomination was in the writer's name.

Lolita was Stanley Kubrick's first foray into black comedy. His dark sensibilities and wicked humor embellish the stylish film with a veneer of cynicism. Kubrick employed long takes and a complex mise-en-scène.

The literary nature of the material is cinematically translated by a clever narration and structured by languorous dissolves and slow fades to black. Between many scenes Kubrick holds in black—long past the duration commonly held—which has the effect of completing a chapter of the book. This cinematic transition links *Lolita* to its literary source while Kubrick's additions and revisions to Nabokov's novel and script make the film play on the screen. Nabokov's elegant prose delved into the dark hollows of Humbert's perversity. The censor's glare prevented a true adaptation of *Lolita,* so Kubrick circumvented the problem with comic inventions utilizing the multi-personality skills of Peter Sellers to maintain the tone of the book while delighting and entertaining the audience.

Although the film was produced primarily in England using British actors, Kubrick brought a quintessential American quality to *Lolita.* The road sequences shot all over America by Bob Gaffney, Dennis Stock, and Stanley Kubrick himself give the film the resonance of a Jack Kerouac novel, a Robert Frank photograph, and an Allen Ginsberg poem. *Lolita* is an American road movie, the road leading to the underbelly of obsession.

After completing work on *Lolita* in London, Kubrick returned to New York, leaving his editor, Anthony Harvey, to take care of the original negative and to oversee the quality of print production. Harvey quickly became a very trusted member of Kubrick's English production team.

In 1974, McGraw-Hill published Nabokov's original screenplay for *Lolita.* It was dedicated to his wife, Vera. Nabokov explained to the reader that this was not the script by Stanley Kubrick, saying, "This is the purely Nabokov version of the screenplay and not the same version which was produced as the motion picture *Lolita,* distributed by Metro-Goldwyn-Mayer, Inc." The script is dated summer 1960 and was revised in December 1973, when Nabokov restored a few of the scenes from his original four-hundred-page version.

In retrospect, Kubrick felt that the censors had taken their toll on his *Lolita.* "I wasn't able to give any weight at all to the erotic aspect of Humbert's relationship with Lolita in the film and because I could only hint at the true nature of his attraction to Lolita, it was assumed too quickly by filmgoers that Humbert was in love with her," he told Gene D. Phillips. "In the novel this comes as a discovery at the end, when Lolita is no longer a nymphet but a pregnant housewife; and it's this encounter, and the sudden realization of his love for her, that is one of the most poignant elements of the story."

Film critic Pauline Kael liked *Lolita,* saying in her review: "The surprise of *Lolita* is how enjoyable it is; it's the first new American comedy since those great days in the forties when Preston Sturges created comedy with verbal slapstick. *Lolita* is black slapstick and at times it's so far out that you gasp as you laugh."

Kubrick shot *Lolita* in eighty-eight days at a reported cost of between $1,900,000 and $2,250,000, and it grossed an estimated $4,500,000 in its opening showcase run. Business began to drop off as the film moved to the outskirts and local neighborhoods. Harris-Kubrick had Sue Lyon under contract, so they would receive a percentage of salary from her next two films, *Night of the Iguana* and *Seven Women.*

In France, Jean-Luc Godard, who was busy changing the face of the cinema with his films *Breathless, A Woman Is a Woman,* and *My Life to Live,* was keeping an eye on Stanley Kubrick and keeping him on a short leash in his cranky but passionate writings on film. "Stanley Kubrick began flashing by making glacial copies of Ophuls' tracking shots and Aldrich's violence," Godard wrote, "then became a recruit to intellectual commerce by following the international paths of glory of another K, an older Stanley who also saw himself as Livingston, but whose weighty sincerity turned up trumps at Nuremberg, whereas Stanley Junior's cunning look-at-me tactics foundered in the cardboard heroics of Spartacus without ever attaining the required heroism. So *Lolita* led one to expect the worst. Surprise: it is a simple, lucid film, precisely written, which reveals America and American sex better than either Melville or Reichenbach, and proves that Kubrick need not abandon the cinema provided [it is] the film's characters who exist instead of ideas which exist only in the bottom drawers of old scriptwriters who believe that the cinema is the seventh art."

Kubrick, as always, was protective of his films. He carefully watched the reviews and articles written on *Lolita*. He was pleased with the reviews that were generally favorable, but he wrote a sharp letter to the *Observer* in England, which they ran on June 24, 1962. From New York Kubrick complained about a cynical piece written by Michael Davie about *Lolita*. Kubrick was angry that the negative and nasty piece was published four months before the film premiered in England. The director felt this violated his sense of professional ethics. Always prepared, Kubrick detailed his arguments to the piece and supplied a list of facts and provided a barrage of complimentary reviews received by *Lolita* to defend his production.

The *New York Herald Tribune* sent out its man-on-the-street photographer to get a wide response of what the average answer was to the question, "What did you think of *Lolita*?" The article was reminiscent of the work done by the young Kubrick in his early *Look* magazine days.

The responses had the kind of worked-over quality that Kubrick learned from his *Look* days, getting people to say what you want them to say. The man on the street seemed to like *Lolita*. The overloaded talk of controversy, sex, perversion, and censorship had little effect on New York audiences, who seemed to enjoy the film. Miss Barbara Levine of Merrick, Long Island, said, "I liked the picture better than the book. I had heard the picture was pretty sexy, but I didn't think it was." Thomas Incantalupo of Astoria, Queens, called *Lolita*, "a wonderful picture and a nice story. There was nothing dirty in it. It was dramatic all the way through," and Mrs. Alice Romanouski of Niagara, New York, said, "It was a very fine picture. It was done with great finesse. I would even recommend it for teenagers."

Stanley and Christiane Kubrick maintained New York addresses at 239 Central Park West and at 145 East Eighty-fourth Street. Christiane continued to study painting, enrolling at the famed Art Students League of New York on Fifty-seventh Street (where Kubrick had taken a children's class in 1943 when he was fourteen), taking a course in life drawing and painting with Harry Sternberg from February through the end of September 1962. Christiane, like Stanley Kubrick, was an independent artist who demanded the solace to think, study, and practice her craft.

"She was one of the most beautiful women I have ever seen. She was gorgeous and very much a lady," recalled painter and teacher Harry Sternberg at age ninety-one, who taught at the League for thirty-four years and now lives in California. "She was a very handsome woman, very genteel. She attended the League regularly. We did have some lunches together. She was a very discreet woman. You were friends with her, but that's as near as you got. She didn't radiate sexual attraction. She was very cool and yet very warm and friendly at the same time as long as you kept your distance. There was a lot of playing around done in those days at the school, and she participated in none of this—she kept to herself pretty much. She had rather pretty kids and was a real mother. She was altogether quite a wonderful gal. I was very impressed with her."

Sternberg's class was Life Painting and Drawing. Christiane Kubrick attended every day. The class was a three-hour session from 1:00 P.M. to 4:00 P.M. Three days were devoted to workshop, where the students painted in oils. On two days out of the week Sternberg came in to evaluate and criticize the students' work. This combination of workshop and studio work was the League's philosophy. Sternberg, a working painter who exhibited frequently, was interested in social realism and representation and encouraged his students to paint out of their experience. He was a progressive man who had been involved with Artists Equity and the Artists Union, and many students were attracted to his liberal nature. The students in Sternberg's class worked in oil on canvas. "I didn't like watercolor and I didn't allow it much in the class any more than I allowed charcoal for drawing, I wanted everything to be very direct and harsh. They had to draw with pen and ink that they couldn't erase and couldn't horse around with. They had to work. If I came in Tuesday and they didn't have a body of work to show me that they had done on Monday, I wouldn't even talk to them.

"She spoke beautifully and was an educated gal. She was very happy doing very pleasant pictures. Her English was impeccable, there wasn't a vestige of a German accent. She never talked about her German background, never. I never really talked to her about it because with Stanley being Jewish and she being German it was ticklish at this point, so I left it alone."

In retrospect, Kubrick looked back on *Lolita* as a film that wasn't completely successful artistically. "Had I realized how severe the limitations were going to be, I probably wouldn't have made the film," he told *Newsweek* in 1972 in referring to the censorship restrictions. With further reflection, in 1987 he told *Der Spiegel*, "If it had been written by a lesser author, it might have been a better film," feeling he didn't find a cinematic translation of Nabokov's literary voice.

Jane de Rochemont, the widow of Dick de Rochemont, Kubrick's early benefactor who had hired him to work on the Lincoln show done for *Omnibus*, remembers her husband being one of the first people to tell him about Nabokov's *Lolita*. "Stanley never gave Dick credit, but he did tell him about *Lolita*," Jane de Rochemont recalls. "Dick was a little bit hurt by the fact that Stanley did it and didn't call him back or didn't do anything much about it."

Years after *Lolita* was released, James Mason ran into Vladimir Nabokov in Switzerland, where they both had lived. The writer told Mason that he would like to see the film made again because Sue Lyon had been too old for the part. This left Mason wondering if Nabokov actually thought a twelve-year-old girl should have played Lolita.

In 1971 *Lolita* was adapted into a musical *Lolita My Love*. The show had a book by Alan Jay Lerner and music by John Barry. The production opened on the road in Philadelphia with John Neville as Humbert, Dorothy Loudon as Charlotte, and Leonard Frey as Quilty, closed for revision and reopened for five days. Lerner had originally wanted Richard Burton to play Humbert. The show never made it to Broadway.

In 1981 Edward Albee adapted *Lolita* into a play. The production had a very short run on Broadway with Shirley Stoler as Charlotte, Donald Sutherland as Humbert, Clive Revill as Quilty, and Carroll Baker's daughter, Blanche, as Lolita.

In 1995, director Adrian Lyne announced a remake of *Lolita* with a screenplay by James Dearden, who wrote *Fatal Attraction* for Lyne, Jeremy Irons as Humbert, Melanie Griffith as Charlotte, and introducing Dominique Swain as Lolita. The film rights had reverted back to the Nabokov estate and were sold to Carolco Pictures International for $1 million. The deal was engineered by Swifty Lazar, who had negotiated the original sale to Harris-Kubrick. Dmitri Nabokov, Vladimir's son, had consultation rights, watching over his father's creation after his death.

In his autobiography, *Before I Forget,* James Mason commented prophetically on the future of *Lolita*: "If one of the new young directors attempts another version I assume that the sex act will be prominently featured; but from no matter what viewpoint, I am sure that we have not seen the last of her." Mason was right.

CHAPTER 12

"Do You Think This Is Funny?"

The deal with Ray Stark and Seven Arts for *Lolita* involved a follow-up film from Harris-Kubrick. Kubrick had remained in England to deal with postproduction work and to prepare the foreign versions of *Lolita* for distribution while Harris was dealing with the censorship machinations.

Since 1958 Kubrick had been intrigued by the subject of thermonuclear war, and lately he was becoming preoccupied with it. Kubrick had reached the obsessive state that slowly overtakes him and culminates in a film project. The idea of an impending nuclear holocaust often crept into his already dark and pessimistic vision of the world. Kubrick had read intensively on the subject. Having come of age in the post–World War II era and during the advent of the Cold War, Stanley Kubrick was constantly reminded of the nuclear threat. Living in New York City, he was perpetually in fear of being in the eye of a major nuclear target. When he lived on East Tenth Street he told David Vaughan he was considering moving to Australia—a country well out of central nuclear bomb target range.

While still in London, Kubrick asked Alastair Buchan, the head of the Institute for Strategic Studies, a nongovernmental research group, to recommend a serious course of books for him to study about nuclear weapons. Buchan told Kubrick that a film about the global nuclear situation was "unwise because he would not be able to describe precisely what precautions the United States or other nuclear powers take to guard against the danger of accident or false command." Buchan was concerned that this would "mislead anxious people." In a list of books he thought Kubrick should read, Buchan recommended the novel *Red Alert,* by Peter George, who had been a Royal Air Force navigator and a British intelligence agent.

Kubrick read the novel and saw in it the potential for his movie about nuclear global conflict. When he inquired into the screen rights to *Red Alert,* Kubrick was told by literary agent Scott Meredith, who handled the book, that the motion picture rights had been sold outright in June 1959 for $1,000. The book then went through a series of sales as it went from one owner to another, but no one was able to acquire the financing necessary to make the film. In the early sixties the current owner asked Meredith to represent him. Meredith then sold the motion picture rights for *Red Alert* to Stanley Kubrick's Polaris Productions for $3,500. Kubrick began to work with Peter George on the screenplay of the serious drama.

One night Harris and Kubrick were working on the script, and they began to depart from *Red Alert*'s serious premise. "We started to get silly," Harris remembers, "kidding around. 'What would happen in the War Room if everybody's hungry and they want the guy from the deli to come in and a waiter with an apron around him takes the sandwich order?' We started to giggle about it and say, 'Do you think this could be a comedy or a satire? Do you think this is funny?' "

After the silliness left them, they both agreed that the script was a good dramatic story and that they would stay with the original idea. Harris then took the script to Eliot Hyman at Seven Arts and convinced him to accept it as their second picture commitment.

The idea of turning *Red Alert* into a satire didn't leave Kubrick. A month before *Lolita* opened in New York on December 31, 1962, Kubrick told A. H. Weiler of the *New York Times* that he and James B. Harris were doing a film called *Dr. Strangelove or: How I Learned to Stop Worrying and Love the Bomb* with Seven Arts, which had produced *Lolita.* Kubrick announced that Peter Sellers would be in the new film, which he described as the story of "an American college professor who rises to power in sex and politics by becoming a nuclear Wise Man." He told Weiler that it would be a satiric approach and that he was working with British writer Peter George. Kubrick said he would shoot the film on location, "here in the East and elsewhere this September." There was no distributor at this time.

James B. Harris began to feel that he wanted to pursue a directorial career of his own, and he decided not to produce the film. Satisfaction of the deal with Seven Arts signaled the end of Harris-Kubrick. Together they had made *The Killing*, *Paths of Glory*, and *Lolita*. Stanley Kubrick and James B. Harris had set out as partners with equal say and remained so throughout almost ten years. Both came to the realization it was time to move on. For James B. Harris it was time to direct. For Stanley Kubrick, it was an ongoing quest for even greater control, being his own producer, and the fulfillment of a series of obsessions, themes, and subjects. First up—nuclear war.

As Kubrick continued to develop *Red Alert* with Peter George, Harris headed back to the West Coast to open his own office and to pursue directorial projects. Several weeks passed, then Harris received a call from Kubrick telling him he was considering turning *Red Alert* into a comedy, a satire about total nuclear destruction. Trying to protect his friend, Harris attempted to warn Kubrick of the problems of sustaining a comedy about nuclear war for a feature-length film. "The only way this thing really works for me is as a satire. It's the same point, but it's just a better way of making the point," Harris remembers Kubrick telling him. Kubrick went on to tell Harris about Terry Southern, a writer he was beginning to work with. "I said, 'Okay, anything I can do for you, Stanley, let me know,' and I hung up," Harris remembers. "I said to myself, 'I leave him alone for ten minutes and he's going to blow his whole career.' I was actually convinced he was out of control to do this as a comedy—as it turns out, it's my favorite Kubrick picture."

Over the years Harris and Kubrick have talked about working together again. One project that held a mutual attraction was *The Passion Flower Hotel*, about a group of young women from an all-girls school who decide to sell their services to an all-boys school down the road. The film was never made, and the property eventually became a musical. Harris and Kubrick have remained friends and have continued to communicate over the years. They have never made another film together. Harris has directed *The Bedford Incident*, *Some Call It Loving*, *Fast Walking*, *Cop*, and *Boiling Point*, and he continues to get moral and critical support from Kubrick on his solo career as a director.

Kubrick was taking a bold and dangerous leap in his decision to make *Red Alert* into a comedy. American film audiences were accepting of a witty social satirist like writer-director Preston Sturges in the forties, but there were still subjects that were considered taboo. The forties and fifties had been a time of great fear surrounding the use of the atomic bomb. In the early sixties, the Cold War and hostilities between the Soviet Union and the United States put the subject of nuclear annihila-

tion into the dark recesses of everyone's mind. Although the sixties became a decade of change in the American film lexicon, in 1963 the
studios were not ready to break with convention. The majority of films
were fashioned as entertainment. A comedy about nuclear war was
hardly socially acceptable.

"My idea of doing it as a nightmare comedy came in the early weeks
of working on the screenplay," Kubrick told Gene D. Phillips. "I found
that in trying to put meat on the bones and to imagine the scenes fully,
one had to keep leaving things out of it which were either absurd or
paradoxical in order to keep it from being funny; and these things seem
to be close to the heart of the scenes in question."

"I started work on the screenplay with every intention of making the
film a serious treatment of the problem of accidental nuclear war,"
Kubrick told Joseph Gelmis. "As I kept trying to imagine the way in
which things would really happen, ideas kept coming to me which I
would discard because they were so ludicrous. I kept saying to myself: 'I
can't do this. People will laugh.' But after a month or so I began to
realize that all the things I was throwing out were the things which were
most truthful. After all, what could be more absurd than the very idea of
two mega-powers willing to wipe out all human life because of an accident, spiced up by political difference that will seem as meaningless to
people a hundred years from now as the theological conflicts of the
Middle Ages appear to us today.

"So it occurred to me that I was approaching the project in the wrong
way. The only way to tell the story was as a black comedy or, better, a
nightmare comedy, where the things you laugh at most are really the
heart of the paradoxical postures that make a nuclear war possible. Most
of the humor in *Strangelove* arises from the depiction of everyday human behavior in a nightmarish situation, like the Russian Premier on the
hot line who forgets the telephone number of his general staff headquarters and suggests the American President try Omsk information, or the
reluctance of a U.S. officer to let a British officer smash open a Coca-
Cola machine for change to phone the President about a crisis on the
SAC base because of his conditioning about the sanctity of private property."

To subvert the serious material in *Red Alert,* Kubrick needed a devi-
ously subversive mind, an anarchist who could find satire and humor in
the deadliest of subjects—he needed the comic gifts of Terry Southern,
the author of *Candy* and *Flash and Filigree.* Southern was a writer
steeped in black humor. Southern was a hard-drinking, drug-experi-
menting hipster. He was also shy and reluctant to talk about himself, and

he worked well as a collaborator, bringing his distinctive voice to many literary, film, and television projects, including *Easy Rider, The Loved One,* and *Saturday Night Live.* Kubrick had heard about Terry Southern from two sources. Peter Sellers had sent copies of Southern's *The Magic Christian* to his friends as gifts. Bob Gaffney had been reading Southern and told Kubrick about the wildly imaginative writer.

Even though Kubrick was treating the theme of world nuclear destruction as a satiric comedy, his research into the subject was exhaustive. After the film was released, Ken Adam, who designed the film, told Elaine Dundy, writing for *Glamour* magazine, "Stanley's so steeped in his material that when we first met to discuss it, his conversation was full of fail-safe points, megadeaths, gyro-headings, strobe markings, and CRM-114s. I didn't know what he was talking about."

Kubrick studied forty-six research books, among them *The Effects of Nuclear Weapons, Soviet Military Strategy, Man's Means to His End, The Causes of World War III,* and *Nuclear Tactics.* He devoured the work of leading nuclear strategists Herman Kahn, Thomas Schelling, and Edward Teller—the man known as the "father of the bomb." Continuing his reading, Kubrick went through everything on the subject by Bertrand Russell, Erich Fromm, Bruno Bettelheim, Albert Einstein, and Leopold Infeld. Other sources included the Blue Books of the Air Force, the Army, and the Navy, as well as such journals as *Missiles and Rockets, Bulletin of the Atomic Scientists,* and *War/Peace Report.* In addition to rows of books on nuclear warfare that Kubrick had in his office, he also kept a baseball bat, ball, and mitt handy at all times, a sign that he was ready for another of the backlot ball games he enjoyed during the arduous production of *Spartacus.*

Production designer Richard Sylbert was sitting in his office with director John Frankenheimer preparing *The Manchurian Candidate* when the phone rang. It was Stanley Kubrick. The last time they had spoken was in 1952 when they met on the television set of *Patterns* and Kubrick made the pronouncement he wanted Sylbert to design his films. Sylbert was becoming one of the hottest and most respected production designers in the business. He had recently designed *Splendor in the Grass* for Elia Kazan. " 'I've got a terrific script, Terry Southern wrote it. I'm sending it to you. When you come back to New York from *The Manchurian Candidate,* we'll make this movie,' " Sylbert remembers Kubrick telling him. "*Dr. Strangelove*—I read it, it was terrific. So for thirty days we sat in coffee shops trying to figure out how to make this damn movie in New York. We don't even have a stage big enough. We have no studio big enough to throw a rear screen projection on. We've got one little guy who has a projection room. Kubrick wanted a 150-foot beaded front projection screen. We get no cooperation from NASA, and by the end of these coffee shop meetings, I said to him, 'We can't make this picture in New York, you can't even make it in America, let alone New York,' and he said, 'Yes, you're right,' and he left for England and he never came back. He developed the first important visual effects crew in the world and he had no trouble with the bombers in England because they weren't NASA. He built everything."

The exhaustive talks with Sylbert and the economic factors that informed Kubrick's decision to make *Lolita* in England convinced him he had to return to Great Britain to produce *Dr. Strangelove.*

Before shooting began, Kubrick was concerned with potential problems he might have with the Motion Picture Association of America. It had been a monumental task to get *Lolita* the Code Seal necessary for a film to be distributed. On January 11, 1963, Kubrick sent a copy of the *Dr. Strangelove* script to the MPAA president, Geoffrey Shurlock, telling him he was going to start shooting on January 28. Kubrick quipped that he hoped the *Dr. Strangelove* script would be easier to deal with than *Lolita* and said he looked forward to hearing from Shurlock.

Shurlock read the script and wrote back to Kubrick on January 21. He expressed concerns about a satire involving the President of the United States and the Armed Forces, uncertain how the public would receive the film. Shurlock told Kubrick he wanted to get counsel from his board of directors on the abundance of profanity in the script written by Kubrick, Peter George, and Terry Southern. Shurlock didn't like the use of the words "hell" and "damn" throughout the script and told the director that the phrase "rotten sons of bitches" used in the screenplay was unacceptable and could not be approved. Shurlock also included a list of items he felt could be troublesome, warning Kubrick not to have an "extreme type" of bikini worn by Miss Scott, "Buck" Turgidson's secretary, and to delete the reference to prophylactics, which he found "distasteful," in a scene taking place in the mission aircraft. Shurlock was most emphatic in his concern for the conclusion of the film, which called for a pie-throwing sequence involving the President. Speaking as a moral voice for the film industry, Shurlock advised Kubrick to consider omitting the President from the pie-tossing event.

On February 11, Kubrick addressed Shurlock's concerns in writing. He argued that because the film took place in the indefinite future, it avoided ethical problems as they related to the current administration. He explained to Shurlock that there was nothing in the film which hadn't been represented in statements by government officials. By way of example, Kubrick included a statement given at the United Nations by President John F. Kennedy: "Every man, woman, and child lives under a nuclear sword of Damocles, hanging by the slenderest of threads, capable of being cut at any moment by accident, miscalculation, or madness." Kubrick told Shurlock he was trying to delete as many "hells" and "damns" as possible but explained that in some instances they were irreplaceable. He assured the MPAA president that the bikini in *Dr. Strangelove* would not be of the most extreme type and the reference to "prophylactics" represented a vivid moment of reality the audience would deeply identify with.

In reference to scene 74, Kubrick was at a complete loss as to why the pie-throwing sequence should be a cause for concern from the standpoint of industry policy. He closed by assuring Shurlock he would find all points acceptable in the completed film.

On February 20, Shurlock wrote Kubrick, telling him, "You have already more than proved your ability to handle the most difficult kind of subject matter and if you are convinced that what you intend to put on the screen will be without offense, that ought to be enough for us."

Kubrick and Terry Southern worked closely to transform *Red Alert* into an outrageous black comedy. Kubrick would pose questions and situations to the madly ingenious writer, who would develop outrageous dialogue and pose even more bizarre situations as the screenplay took shape.

To create the dialogue for Buck Turgidson when he tells the President that they may lose only ten to twenty million Americans but can win the war, Kubrick drew on the philosophy he had read about in military journals. As ludicrous as Turgidson's babble about winning a nuclear war was, Kubrick found it really was a summary of the military mind-set about nuclear confrontation.

Kubrick was living in Knightsbridge, London, while working on *Dr. Strangelove*. Terry Southern would arrive at 5:00 A.M. and work in the backseat of an old Bentley while Kubrick's driver made the trip to Shepperton Studios. In the car Southern and Kubrick worked on two tabletops in front of them, with the driver's partition closed, to give them a private moving office. As in any great collaboration, only the participants know what they really contributed, but Kubrick's inbred, devilishly dark sense of humor—endemic to the streets of the Bronx and New York City—and his deep cynicism merged with Southern's as Southern pushed the limits of the envelope of civility with his manic comedic mind to concoct a raucous satire on the political and military-industrial complex.

For the production design of *Dr. Strangelove* Kubrick hired Ken Adam, who was born in Berlin and educated in England, where he worked as an architect. During World War II Adam was an RAF pilot, and after the war he began his illustrious career as a designer in film. Adam had received an Academy Award nomination in 1955 for his work on *Around the World in 80 Days,* along with the father of production design, William Cameron Menzies. He had worked for directors John Ford, Jacques Tourneur, and Robert Aldrich, and he designed the first James Bond film, *Dr. No.* Kubrick had seen *Dr. No.* He was very impressed with the look of the film and set up a meeting with Adam to discuss his doomsday satire.

In the early days of film and during much of the studio system through the fifties, production designers and art directors were accustomed to designing interiors without ceilings so the director of photography could light from above and around the set. There had been ceilings on sets before *Dr. Strangelove,* but only rarely were they put to dramatic use—as by Orson Welles on many of his films—most notably *Citizen Kane.* A ceiling on a studio set allowed the use of low camera angles and required source lighting. Kubrick told Ken Adam early on that he wanted ceilings on all of the sets for *Dr. Strangelove.* "Stanley said to me, 'Nail the bloody ceilings down,'" Adam recalls. "'I don't want the cameraman to light from the top, I want to use source lighting.'" This concept fired Adam's imagination in creating dramatic architectural structures for the basis of the design.

To design the all-important War Room set, Adam began to do conceptual drawings to develop his ideas. His original notion was an amphitheater with a second level that had a glassed-in control room. Kubrick was very enthusiastic when he saw the drawings, telling Adam, "Gee, Ken, it's great, great!" Thinking this constituted approval, Adam went forward and assigned his staff to create the necessary working drawings and models to design and build the set. After three or four weeks of mulling over the idea, Kubrick came into the design department, which by that time was far advanced on the amphitheater concept, and said, "You know, Ken, that second level up there, I need at least sixty or seventy extras and they have to be sitting around all the time. What are they going to do? It could be costly. Come up with something else."

"It threw me completely," Ken Adam recalled. "Then once I started calming down, my mind started ticking again, thank God. Stanley used to come and was practically standing behind me when I was drawing. Then this triangular concept evolved and he liked it. I had the answer when he said, 'Yes, it's all very well with the triangle, what material do you think you're going to do it in?' and I said, 'Concrete, like a bomb shelter.' "

The two men created a unique collaboration. Adam was an instinctual and imaginative designer with strong architectural training and a penchant for heightened reality. Kubrick was a director who questioned everything and demanded a rationale for every detail in his movie. Adam intuitively felt that the table that the President and his men sat around should be large and round. When Kubrick saw the design for the table he asked Adam if it could be covered with green baize even though the film was being shot in stark black and white. "Sure," Adam said and Kubrick replied, "It should be like a poker table—the President, the Russian Ambassador, and the generals playing a game of poker for the fate of the world."

Kubrick and Adam were trying to figure out what to put on the low side of the triangular set when Kubrick said, "What if we have a big buffet where everybody could help themselves to sandwiches, cups of coffee, or drinks?"—an idea that may have been inspired by his late-night giddiness with James B. Harris when *Red Alert* was still a serious nuclear drama.

When the art department finished building the War Room set on the stage at Shepperton Studios, it was 130 feet long, 100 feet wide, and 35 feet high. The round table where the President and his men decided the fate of the world took up 380 square feet.

For *Dr. Strangelove* Kubrick hired Gilbert Taylor, the cameraman he had called in to shoot Humbert painting Lolita's toenails, for the opening credit sequence. Kubrick was well in control of his lighting concept and operated the camera himself for the hand-held shots during the attack on Burpelson Air Base and inside the fateful bomber.

"Stanley is a brilliant cameraman, and he wanted only source lighting," Adam explained, referring to light that is justified by an identifiable source, like a window or an interior light fixture. "I had designed a suspended circular light fitting and he used to sit in my office and we used to experiment with varying types of photofloods," Adam recalled, citing the use of a high-intensity incandescent lighting instrument. "I sat in a chair and we put up a photoflood at a certain distance to see how much light would fall on my face. The lighting of all the personnel around the table was done through that circular light. It was not something that just came about, it was very much researched."

To cast the film, Kubrick once again approached Peter Sellers because of his ability to play multiple characters. In *Lolita* Sellers played one character in several guises. For *Dr. Strangelove,* Kubrick wanted Sellers to play what he called "the lead and the lead and the lead." At first Sellers was reluctant to take the multiple roles. He felt that it was a gimmick and that audiences would compare him to Alec Guinness, who played multiple characters in *Kind Hearts and Coronets*. Kubrick convinced Sellers that he couldn't find a better actor to play the parts of President Merkin Muffley, Group Captain Lionel Mandrake of the RAF (for which he donned a prosthetic nose), and Dr. Strangelove himself, so he wanted Sellers to play all three roles.

Sellers was paid in the range of $1 million to play the three roles in *Dr. Strangelove*, prompting Kubrick to jest, "We got three for the price of six." Sellers was in the process of getting a divorce and was not able to leave England. Kubrick told the press this was the reason he produced the film in England, but it was only one factor. Economics played a big part. Kubrick was able to make *Lolita* for a low budget, and he enjoyed working with British technicians and performers. He and Christiane felt a growing tension in New York City and were looking for a gentler place to raise their family.

In 1963, James Earl Jones was a theater actor playing a variety of roles. Kubrick came to New York's Central Park to see George C. Scott, who was playing Shylock in Shakespeare's *The Merchant of Venice*. Jones was also in the production, playing the Prince of Morocco, which prompted Kubrick to say, "I'll take the black one, too," Jones recalled in his autobiography. Thus the actor got his first role in a motion picture, as Lieutenant Lothar Zogg. Scott was given the role of General "Buck" Turgidson.

At one point Kubrick even had Sellers play Major T. J. "King" Kong, the officer in charge of the B-52 that has the mission of dropping the bomb. Sellers struggled with the role for a week but just couldn't get the Texas accent. The part required a lot of physicality, with Kong running around the aircraft. Finally, Sellers cracked his ankle and was not able to continue with his fourth role in *Dr. Strangelove*. Kubrick felt that subconsciously Sellers may have brought the injury on himself. Sellers continued to be very concerned about exploring the part of his talent that allowed him to create multiple characters. Kubrick was pleased with the energy and invention that Sellers delivered to the three parts he played, and he decided to cast another actor as Major Kong.

One night while production designer Ken Adam was driving Kubrick home from Shepperton Studios, he got an idea about the perfect person to play Kong. Kubrick turned to Adam, a skilled driver and lover of sports cars, and said, "I know this cowboy back home and I'll give him a call tonight," Adam recalled. "I had already built the bomb bay, which was a gigantic set but we didn't require a practical bomb door because it was a completely different sequence. Stanley came up with the idea of this cowboy riding down on the nuclear weapon like a bronco."

"I got a call from London, where they were shooting, at my farm near Fresno on a Friday asking if I was available. I was. I was generally available in those days," Slim Pickens told the *New York Times*. "I drove down to the courthouse and got me a passport—I'd never had one before—and I was on my way to England that Monday. Kubrick wouldn't show me anything that he had shot. He just said, 'Play it straight as you can, it'll be fine.' I guess it was."

Slim Pickens was born Louis Bert Lindley, Jr., in Kingsberg, California. He adopted the name Slim Pickens when he began a career as a clown at the nearby Pines Rodeo in the thirties. He became a successful bronco and bull rider, a skill that would come in handy for the climax in *Dr. Strangelove*, when Kong rides the nuclear bomb to its fatal target. Pickens had appeared in many Hollywood westerns and worked with Marlon Brando in *One-Eyed Jacks* after Kubrick left that project as director.

When Pickens arrived in England, the local actors guild decided not to give him a work permit. The Westerner was not let off the plane until negotiations cleared him. Pickens walked on the stage at Shepperton wearing a ten-gallon hat, sheepherder jacket, frontier pants, and high-heeled alligator cowboy boots.

When Kubrick decided that his cowboy Kong would ride the bomb down to its target like a bucking bronco, Ken Adam had to redesign the set to have the bomb bay doors open and find a way that the visual effect could be accomplished. "I was desperate, because we were going to shoot initially within forty-eight hours," Adam recalled. "There was no way I could have made those bomb doors practical." Wally Veevers, a British special effects master who learned his craft working with the Korda brothers on *Things to Come* and worked for years at Shepperton, was doing effects on *Dr. Strangelove*. Adam had introduced Kubrick to Veevers.

"I saw Wally and he said, 'Give me overnight to think about it and tomorrow morning I'll tell you what we'll do,' " Adam recalled, "And he came up with a very simple idea of taking an eight-by-ten still photograph of the interior of the bomb bay and cutting the opening of the bomb door out of the still—that's how it was shot. We strung up the full-sized missile on the large stage at Shepperton with Slim Pickens on top of it, and then we craned back."

In the original script Lieutenant Zogg was the only one of the team who questioned the patriotic nature of the mission, but many of the lines defining this part of his character were cut before they could be shot. Jones was upset about losing this element of his characterization and felt he was unable to get a satisfactory answer from Kubrick as to why he was dropping the lines.

This was Sterling Hayden's second role in a Kubrick film. His appearance in *The Killing* had helped to get the production going. Now the part of General Jack D. Ripper was an enormous emotional challenge. "My first day was torture," said Hayden. "I was nervous, scared, did forty-eight takes. I expected Kubrick to explode, but instead he was gentle, calmed me, convinced me that the fear in my eyes would help the character."

George C. Scott had appeared in *The Hanging Tree, Anatomy of a Murder, The Hustler,* and *The List of Adrian Messenger,* but working with directors Delmar Daves, Otto Preminger, Robert Rossen, and John Huston didn't prepare him for the relentless perfectionism of Stanley Kubrick. "Stanley is very meticulous and hates everything that he writes or has anything to do with," Scott said. "He's an incredibly, depressingly serious man, with this wild sense of humor. But paranoid. Every morning we would all meet and practically rewrite the day's work. He's a perfectionist, and he's always unhappy with anything that's set.

"He is certainly in command," Scott said about his director, "and he's so self-effacing and apologetic it's impossible to be offended by him."

Not one to pass up any opportunity to strengthen his domination over his work, Kubrick often set up a chessboard during breaks in shooting and played willing cast and crew members. During *Dr. Strangelove* he played many rounds with George C. Scott, a good player who rarely won a match. Kubrick viewed his victories as an advantage in directing the actor. "This gave me a certain edge with him on everything else. If you fancy yourself a good chess player, you have an inordinate respect for people who can beat you," Kubrick said to Michel Ciment.

As much as Kubrick enjoyed working in England, he did voice a complaint about the British system to Jack Piler of *Variety* during the shooting of *Dr. Strangelove.* "The only thing that does bother me in Britain is the difficulty over arranging overtime in a hurry and the tea breaks. Tea costs a producer a half hour a day every shooting day—fifteen minutes every morning and afternoon. And to get the crew to stay on for some overtime which might be absolutely essential to the schedule of the production, you have to go through such a rigmarole it is not worth the trouble."

Kubrick continued to have the highest regard for Peter Sellers. "He's the hardest worker I know," Kubrick commented. "I'd come into the studio at seven o'clock in the morning and there would be Peter Sellers. Waiting, ready. Full of ideas.

"When you are as inspired and professionally accomplished as Peter, the only limit to the importance of your work is your willingness to take chances," Kubrick explained. "I believe Peter will take the most incredible chances with a characterization, and he is receptive to comic ideas most of his contemporaries would think unfunny and meaningless. This has, in my view, made his best work absolutely unique and important."

At first Sellers approached playing President Merkin Muffley with limp-wristed gestures, as a passive man who continually used a nose-inhaler. After shooting several scenes with this characterization, Kubrick told Sellers he wanted the President to display reasonable sanity amid chaos. Kubrick reshot the scenes, with Sellers now playing the President as a liberal humanist, loosely modeled on Adlai Stevenson.

Sellers did expand on some of the scenes with improvisation. In the sequence where the President talks on the phone to the Russian Premier, Sellers added, "Well, how do you think *I* feel, Dimitri?" Sellers played Mandrake mostly as written, though improvising the line, "My string's gone, I'm afraid," (referring to his bad leg) to General Jack D. Ripper who was played deliciously mad by Sterling Hayden.

"During shooting many substantial changes were made in the script, sometimes together with the cast during improvisations," Kubrick told Gene Phillips.

Many thought that the reason Sellers played Dr. Strangelove in a wheelchair was because of his injured ankle. Both Kubrick and Sellers believed that politically powerful figures are impotent in some way, and they found the wheelchair to be an effective prop for the demented doctor. Much talk over the years surrounded the similarities between Dr. Strangelove and Dr. Henry Kissinger. Kissinger had been a Harvard professor and the author of a book on nuclear warfare, but neither Kubrick nor Peter Sellers had seen the man who was later to become President Nixon's secretary of state. "Strangelove's accent was probably inspired by the physicist Edward Teller, who became known as the father of the H-bomb," Kubrick told Alexander Walker, "though Teller's origins are Hungarian and his accent isn't really that close to what Peter did."

The sets for the film were built and photographed at Shepperton Studios. For a full shot of the base, Ken Adam scouted London Airport and found a section that could double as a SAC base. The computer room was shot at an IBM facility in London. The exterior scenes of the base for the sequences where the American troops fight against each other were created outside on the backlot of Shepperton. Military vehicles were rented from companies that specialized in military surplus.

Kubrick continued to impress the British film crew working with him. Victor Lyndon, the associate producer, found working with Kubrick a military-like challenge. "My mind is working at twice the speed it generally does," Lyndon told novelist Elaine Dundy, who was on the Shepperton stage doing an article for *Glamour* magazine. "It's no good just saying to Kubrick such and such will or won't work. You've got to prove it to him to his satisfaction and that means you've got to have all your arguments lined up very logically and precisely. Not that he doesn't leave you alone to get on with it—he delegates power but only on the non-creative side of the film and even then he checks and double checks. The creative side is entirely in his hands. He even designs his own posters. A stimulating man to work with. The mind of a crack chess player—which he is."

Ken Adam told Elaine Dundy about Kubrick's intense concentration on the set. "He's a funny combination of coldness and hypersensitivity. He walked through my wife on the set the other day as if totally unaware of her existence and then rang her that evening to apologize. When he's working he just doesn't take in anything else."

Kubrick had the telephone number changed when Terry Southern began getting too many calls. Southern found working with Kubrick to be stimulating and was amazed at how the director could be so focused on his work that he ignored everything else. "He'll pour himself a drink and then begin talking about something and just forget to drink it," Southern told Elaine Dundy. "The other night I started to get myself a drink—he forgets to offer you one too—and there was no glass. So I asked him about a glass and he said, 'Well, drink out of the bottle then.' But that was all right. Inessentials don't bother him. No, he's something else; probably a genius."

Kubrick wanted the military technology of the film to be totally realistic. Because of the black comedy approach, cooperation from the United States military was out of the question. Kubrick and Adam found other ways of researching what the U.S. military considered to be classified information about the aircraft used in nuclear combat. "It was so amazing that through a technical flight magazine like *Janes* we could get all the information we wanted," explained Adam. "So we had all of it at our fingertips and then copied the B-52. The only thing we were not sure about was that little box, the CRM, the fail-safe device. I came up with an idea, and during the shooting we invited some Air Force personnel to visit the set. They went white when they saw that CRM, so it must have been pretty close. I got a memo from Stanley that said, 'You better find out where you got your research from because we could be investigated.' Basically, it was all from technical data in magazines."

Kubrick was fascinated with the switches inside the B-52 and the Air Force jargon used by the flight crew. Peter Murton, the art director, was able to find pebbled metal instrument panels, which he rigged with toggle switches.

Models of the B-52 were created in many different scales, sized for the exterior shots of the plane flying. The footage for the background of the flying scenes was shot from a Mitchell aircraft in a region of Norway by John Crewdson, who was credited in the film as aviation adviser.

To create the wall maps in the War Room used to track the plane carrying the bomb, Adam and the art department drew maps the size of a drawing board and then had them photographed and enlarged on photographic paper. Kubrick and Adam decided to animate the moving symbols that tracked the flight pattern mechanically, after determining it would have taken too many 16mm projectors and would have been too time-consuming to do it photographically with rear or front screen projection. Light bulbs were placed behind each symbol, and each one was covered with Plexiglas. The photographic material of the map was stretched over the Plexiglas. They later learned that the heat of the bulbs eventually blistered the photographic emulsion and lifted it off the plywood-and-Plexiglas frames. The problem was solved by installing an air conditioning system behind the large screens to keep them cool.

The black shiny floor that Adam wanted for the War Room also caused headaches. Eight-by-four sheets coated with a black shiny surface were laid down on the floor of the enormous War Room set. The subfloor on the Shepperton soundstage was old and uneven. The result was too irregular, so the subfloor had to be built up for it to work.

When the floor was completed, it was kept highly polished. So as not to scratch the shiny surface, the actors were allowed to wear shoes only when they were actually making a take. They were given cloth flopabouts to wear between takes.

For the design of the missiles carrying the bomb, Adam had to rely on his creative imagination. "I had no idea of what a missile would look like. In 1962 nobody certainly had seen a nuclear bomb, so it was a question of making it very small or making it very large. So I came up with this strange design and then Stanley came up with the idea of the graffiti." Kubrick had the bombs painted three times, trying to find out what they should look like.

Again Peter Sellers used his genius of improvisation in all three of his roles—especially in the creation of the mad Dr. Strangelove himself. As in *Lolita*, Kubrick allowed Sellers first to explore in an unbridled fashion, and then the director selected moments and lines from his improvisations to rewrite the scene, sharpening the inspirational effect. During one of his hysterical tirades for the conclusion of the film, Sellers as the maniacal doctor who has little control over his body threw his arm into a Nazi salute and screamed, "Heil Hitler." Kubrick encouraged Sellers to work the moment in as they refined the scene over a series of takes.

During production of *Dr. Strangelove*, Stanley Kubrick learned that a film was being made of the best-selling book *Fail-Safe*, written by Eugene Burdick and Harvey Wheeler. Harvey Wheeler was a professor who had written the short story "Abraham '59," which was published in 1959 in *Dissent* magazine. This gave him the basic plot. Eugene Burdick, who wrote *The Ugly American*, collaborated with Wheeler to write the novel *Fail-Safe*. Like *Red Alert*, *Fail-Safe* was a dramatic novel that also dealt with the accidental launching of a nuclear weapon. Max Youngstein, who had bullied Harris-Kubrick on *The Killing*, was now the head of Entertainment Corporation of America, a new company that had purchased the rights to *Fail-Safe* and was bursting to get its movie made and out in six weeks to beat *Dr. Strangelove* to the nation's movie screens. Youngstein was rumored to have paid as much as $500,000 to acquire the screen rights to *Fail-Safe*.

When Kubrick learned of the Youngstein plan he announced he would file a lawsuit in retaliation. A plagiarism suit was launched against Youngstein's ECA, Burdick, Wheeler, their publisher McGraw-Hill, and Curtis Publishing, which serialized *Fail-Safe*. The objective of the suit was to stop production of *Fail-Safe*, which Kubrick alleged was "copied largely from plaintiff Peter George's book."

It was February 1963. In addition to the suit, Kubrick was pushing to get *Dr. Strangelove* out by July to beat his competition. Kubrick revealed that he was planning an intensive TV campaign of one-minute spots, as well as longer ones.

Kubrick told *Variety* that *Red Alert*, originally published under the title *Two Hours to Doom*, was written well before *Fail-Safe* and Peter George had been acclaimed for his accuracy in the subject by such experts in the field of nuclear warfare as Thomas C. Schelling, of Harvard's Center of International Affairs, and Herman Kahn, the foremost strategist in the United States. *Fail-Safe* was to be ECA's first production.

Two Hours to Doom was published in 1958 under the pseudonym Peter Bryant. The book was published in the United States as an ACE paperback with the title *Red Alert* and sold upwards of 250,000 copies. Kubrick's legal action was filed in New York Federal Court.

Wheeler discussed with his lawyer filing a countersuit, claiming he had the plot in his mind for years and that "Abraham '59," on which the plot of *Fail-Safe* was largely based, was originally called "Abraham '57," but the story took two years to sell.

Youngstein was still planning to go ahead with his production, and he was assured by McGraw-Hill, the publishers of *Fail-Safe*, that there was nothing to worry about. Youngstein announced, "We'll start on April 15."

There were similarities. Each book had the United States offering military secrets to the Soviets to help them destroy American bombers, each implied that the loser had a device that would blow up what was left of the winner. Both stories had War Rooms, military gadgetry, and officers and diplomats with stiff upper lips. *Red Alert* gave the message that the balance of terror is the only thing that will keep world peace. *Fail-Safe* took a more moral approach and stated that war by mechanical accident was possible.

Ultimately Kubrick prevailed. Columbia Pictures, which was committed to *Dr. Strangelove*, took over distribution of *Fail-Safe*, which was directed by Sidney Lumet, and promised to release it after *Dr. Strangelove* ran its course in the theaters. *Dr. Strangelove* opened in December 1963 and *Fail-Safe* opened in October 1964.

Anthony Harvey was back as film editor on *Dr. Strangelove*. He had proved his editing skill, patience, and loyalty on *Lolita*. Harvey put together the traditional first cut, the editor's version of the film, created while the director is shooting, and he finished shortly after principal photography was completed. Harvey cut in an editing room at Shepperton Studios. The editor's first cut contained all the scenes the director had shot and developed in place. Then Kubrick and Harvey worked together to create the director's cut, which was Kubrick's vision of the film. "I would sit with him on the studio floor for quite a lot of the time and we'd talk, but not much, because his concentration was getting the film shot. Then I just put together a first cut and Stanley would come in and see it and we'd start with the first reel to the last in minute detail," Harvey explained.

The editing crew was small, consisting of Harvey and a first and second assistant. The postproduction sound was handled by Winston Ryder, the brilliant sound editor who worked with David Lean on *Lawrence of Arabia*.

"*Strangelove* certainly bore very little resemblance to the original script," Harvey explained. "We were very depressed. I remember I took the whole film apart. Stanley and I put cards up on a big corkboard and rearranged them in many different ways until it looked like a more interesting way to cut it. We recut the whole film, the juxtaposition of placing one scene to another was totally different. When you've got the film on the Moviola, one so often does rearrange things—it was major in this case."

The comedy of *Dr. Strangelove* was breaking new ground in its dark approach to satire. The deadpan seriousness of the approach made the film even funnier, allowing audiences to laugh at the unthinkable act of nuclear annihilation. "The Boulting brothers, who I started with, always said, 'If you start laughing on the floor or the unit thinks it's funny at rushes—God help you,'" Harvey explained. "Comedy is very serious. When an actor thinks he's being funny and playing to the crew, it's death. When it comes on film, it'll never work. Stanley had that theory every time."

During the editing of *Dr. Strangelove* the kind of disaster most feared by a meticulous and compulsive director like Stanley Kubrick finally struck. When Anthony Harvey had completed the intricate cutting for the bomb-run sequence, the scene was sent to the laboratory to have a print made of the original cut, so it could be given to Winston Ryder to begin the process of designing, recording, and editing the sound effects. This was the only record of the cut scene. When Ryder was called, he said that he had never received the print of the scene. The cut sequence had vanished. So Harvey had to re-create his cut from memory. The dailies for the sequence had to be reprinted, and Harvey painstakingly reconstructed the sequence a shot at a time, relying on his memorization of the material and how it had been cut.

Kubrick had studied advertising and publicity campaigns carefully, and he knew the figure breakdowns. He began to haunt the Columbia publicity offices at 711 Fifth Avenue in New York. Knowing that he had a breakthrough film in *Dr. Strangelove,* he spent six weeks with the advertising executives, insisting that the film receive the same treatment and budget as the *The Guns of Navarone,* a major 1961 Columbia release.

John Lee, a twenty-two-year-old junior publicist who had been educated at Cambridge, was in training at the Columbia advertising department while Kubrick was launching a personal ad campaign for his film. Kubrick took a liking to the young man and spent hours sitting on Lee's desk talking to him about *Dr. Strangelove* and old movies. Lee found Kubrick to be "short, dark, pudgy and intense," an ambitious, hardworking man who knew that *Dr. Strangelove* was his opportunity to break into big-time international filmmaking.

Kubrick brought the film in at a cost between $1.7 million and $2 million. The first critics' screening for *Dr. Strangelove* was set for November 22, 1963. Film editor Anthony Harvey was there to oversee the film's critical debut when the news came in from Dallas that President John F. Kennedy had been struck by an assassin's bullet and had been pronounced dead. The film, which certainly would have gotten a private chuckle from the thirty-fifth president, was not shown that day. The screening was canceled and everyone went home to grieve.

Out of respect for the president, Kubrick changed Kong's line in the scene where he explains the mission survival kit to his men. It was originally shot as "A fella could have a pretty good weekend in Dallas" but became "A fella could have a pretty good weekend in Vegas." Ironically, the pie-throwing sequence had a line where Buck Turgidson said, "Gentlemen, our beloved President has been struck down in his prime."

Shortly before *Dr. Strangelove* opened in New York, Kubrick told Eugene Archer that he didn't agree with Columbia executives who thought the Kennedy assassination would have an effect on the film. "There is absolutely no relationship between our President, the one played by Peter Sellers, and any real person. It is clear that no one can see *Strangelove* and take it just as a joke," Kubrick told Archer. "It's interesting to think about ways of influencing people in a medium such as mine. People react, as a rule, when they are directly confronted with events. Here, any direct contact with the bomb would leave very few people to do any reacting. Laughter can only make people a little more thoughtful."

Dr. Strangelove was originally scheduled to open in London on December 12, 1963. On November 28, 1963, after a period of mourning for the fallen president, Reuters reported that Columbia Pictures would cancel the London world premiere of *Dr. Strangelove* out of respect for President Kennedy. The report went on to state: "Columbia said Stanley Kubrick, producer-director, and the corporation directors decided that it would be inappropriate to release a political comedy at the present time." The London premiere was rescheduled for 1964.

When *Dr. Strangelove* was screened for executives at Columbia Pictures, the reaction was far from enthusiastic. Vice president in charge of production Mike Frankovich, the adopted son of comedian Joe E. Brown, and his wife, actress Binnie Barnes, were distressed when the lights came up in the studio screening room after they had just watched a comedy about the total destruction of the earth. Frankovich found the film unshowable, a disgrace to Columbia Pictures.

It certainly didn't help that at the time the film contained a sequence inspired by the great screen comedians. Throughout the film the War Room sported a buffet table filled with fine food. Also on that table was a series of creamy custard pies. The Russian Ambassador grabs a pie and throws it. The pie misses its target and hits the President squarely in the face. In the great tradition of pie-throwing sequences, pandemonium breaks out and the custard flies across the War Room, leaving everybody covered in cream. As the sequence ends, the President of the United States and the Ambassador of the USSR sit on the floor, covered in custard playing "pattycake, pattycake" and singing "For he's a jolly good fellow" in praise of Dr. Strangelove himself.

The sequence took nearly two weeks to shoot. Two thousand shaving cream pies were ordered each day. At the end of the first day of pie-throwing mayhem Kubrick realized that he needed an additional shot of the War Room and the men before the pie-throwing sequence. Bridget Sellers, who was in charge of the wardrobe, brought the soiled costumes to a dry cleaner in Kingston-on-Thames while the crew cleaned up the set. The owner of the dry cleaners stared in disbelief when she saw the bundle of lathered clothing. She was convinced that she was the victim of a *Candid Camera* stunt. Eventually Bridget persuaded her it was for real and got the costumes ready for the pre-pie shot.

Peter Bull, who played the Russian Ambassador, was in the thick of the flying cream bombs, and in an article he wrote for the *New York Times* in 1966 he fondly remembered working on the legendary, largely unseen, sequence. "The early days of the sequence were really quite droll," he wrote, "and there was a great deal of experimental throwing and receiving of the pies, to see which way the cookie would in fact crumble. The prop men had a ball as they were always safely on the camera side of the action and in charge of the missiles. They got rather too accurate by the end and after a time the discomfort endured by the actors was considerable. Though no serious hurt was registered, there was always the sudden misery of smarting eyes or the shock when a bit of vintage crust caught one's talking tube and/or the schnozzola.

"After a few days the beautiful floor was like something caught up in the Blitz and there was no question of redonning the cloth shoes, provided in earlier and cleaner days. If we had worn them, we would have slithered endlessly across the studio. On some days, the actors weren't allowed to go to the studio restaurant as they left a ghastly trail everywhere they walked. All the corridors, lavatories and dressing rooms looked quite extraordinary as if some creature from Outer Space, constructed rather loosely from a lot of vegetables, had been cruising round. There was a curious feeling of degradation about walking round caked in the stuff, which I, for one, found profoundly depressing.

"Finally the last pie was thrown and I left almost immediately for the isles of Greece where they were merely throwing pots out of windows as part of the Easter ritual." The War Room sequences had taken five weeks to film.

Kubrick eventually decided to take out the pie-throwing sequence, telling Gene Phillips, "It was too farcical and not consistent with the satiric tone of the rest of the film."

Kubrick decided to score the climax of the film depicting the end of the world with the original World War II recording of "We'll Meet Again," sung by Vera Lynn. The film gave Lynn good publicity and brought her back to popularity. The song was created as a morale booster. During the production of the film, Kubrick told Lyn Tornabene, who was visiting Shepperton Studios to interview him for a *Cosmopolitan* magazine article, that he was considering running the lyrics of the song over the mushroom cloud footage of the bomb detonating at the end of the film, which signals world destruction. He told Tornabene there would be a bouncing ball and an invitation for the audience to join in on the song. This idea was discarded.

Kubrick tried to control Columbia's preview screening of *Dr. Strangelove.* For one of the Columbia private screenings, he placed many of his friends in the audience in hopes of manipulating the reaction to the film in his favor. Bob Gaffney, who had worked on the second unit of *Lolita* with Kubrick, was there, and he immediately realized that it wouldn't be so simple. As Gaffney looked around, he saw a majority of women with beehive hairdos, and they looked unprepared for the upheaval of *Dr. Strangelove.* "I said, they won't know what this is all about, and sure enough, the reaction was like, 'What? What is this?' "

Dr. Strangelove received the Code Seal Certificate from the MPAA on January 2, 1964, with little or no trouble.

Kubrick, Southern, and Adam's conception of the War Room not only made audiences laugh, it created an image of a political reality that even captured the imagination of an actual president of the United States. When Ronald Wilson Reagan first took office in 1981 and was touring his new home and base of power at the White House, one of the first facilities he asked to see was the War Room. When Ken Adam was told this, he replied, "You must be joking."

The powerful *New York Times* film reviewer Bosley Crowther was appalled at Kubrick's doomsday comedy. Philosopher Lewis Mumford wrote back to the *Times*, saying, "This film is the first break in the cata- tonic Cold War trance that has so long held our country in its rigid grip." Elvis Presley was a fan of *Dr. Strangelove* and screened a print of the film at Graceland. Steven Spielberg stood in line in San Jose, California, on the opening weekend of the film. As he was waiting to get in, his sister and father ran up to him with a Selective Service envelope telling him he was now 1-A and eligible for the draft. "I was so consumed with the possibility of going to Vietnam that I had to see it a second time to really appreciate it, and that's when I realized what a piece of classic, bizarre theater it was," Spielberg recalled. Oliver Stone saw *Dr. Strangelove* with his father, Louis Stone. "I was eighteen years old, and it seemed so silly and ridiculous; and yet there was something undeni- ably powerful about it. It was probably my first experience, having grown up on Danny Kaye movies, of seeing a serious subject treated that way," Stone recalled. "It was one of the first films that I saw as a young man that pointed to the government as indifferent to the needs of people, government as an enemy to the people. I suppose many of our fears of big government are rooted in that theme, in Kubrick's paranoia."

Film critic Judith Crist put it on her top ten list of the year. The film won the best film award from the Society of Film and Television Arts.

Kubrick was nominated as best director by the Directors Guild of America and won the best director of the year award from the New York Film Critics. *Dr. Strangelove* also won the Hugo Award for best science fiction film of the year.

Kubrick, George, and Southern were nominated for an Academy Award for best screenplay. *Dr. Strangelove* also was nominated for best picture, Peter Sellers for best actor, and Kubrick for best director. The film won the Writers Guild Award for best screenplay of 1964.

Dr. Strangelove received international acclaim. "I find his films quite long and boring, but I quite liked *Dr. Strangelove*," said director Ken Russell. The film did very well in Europe, getting good reviews and mounting strong box office receipts in Scandinavia, Italy, and France. Communist newspapers in Rome and Paris liked the film and applauded its lampooning of the nuclear insanity in America.

The film started a dialogue about the possibilities of accidental nuclear war and the morality of turning such a serious subject into a comedy. The newspapers and media in the United States and England were filled with discussion, opinion, and condemnation of Kubrick, and many began defending the film's audacity and style.

In August 1964 Kubrick became incensed when MGM and Filmways ran an ad for *The Loved One,* a new film written by Terry Southern. The ad read: "What happens when the director of *Tom Jones* [referring to Tony Richardson] meets the writer of *Dr. Strangelove?*" Kubrick instructed his lawyer to contact MGM and Filmways threatening legal action if they didn't withdraw the ad. In a formal statement, Kubrick explained his actions, saying, "I have been strongly urged by my attorneys to publicly place Mr. Southern's contribution in its proper perspective and to take legal action to restrain MGM and Filmways from repeating the advertisement." Kubrick went on to explain that the screenplay for *Dr. Strangelove* was primarily written by him and Peter George. He claimed that Southern came on the project for a brief period after the basic work on the script had been completed. Kubrick said that Southern was brought on "to see if some more decoration might be added to the icing on the cake." Kubrick stated that they were eight months into the process when Southern came on and was employed from November 16 to December 28, 1962. He stated that during shooting substantial changes were made in the script by himself and Peter George, and also by the cast in improvisations. Kubrick said that Southern visited the set but never in a professional capacity and took no part in the activities of changing the script during the shooting process. Kubrick closed by saying, "I'm glad he worked on the script, and that his screenplay credit in third place is completely fitting and proportionate to his contribution."

The area of contribution to a screenplay was always a sore subject for Kubrick, and as with the family of Jim Thompson, there is a sense that he rarely gives writers their proper credit. Kubrick fought hard to protect his ideas and to preserve his status as an auteur.

The assault on Terry Southern must have been painful, but he remained loyal to the film throughout the years. *Dr. Strangelove* wouldn't have been the same without the moral larceny that Southern committed. Southern often talked warmly about working on the legendary film to his screenwriting students. On October 31, 1995, on his way to teach a class on screenwriting at Columbia University, Terry Southern collapsed and later died of respiratory failure. He was seventy-one.

Kubrick stayed on top of technological developments in filmmaking and continued to integrate them into his mastery of the medium. Always working independently of the conventional system, he incorporated techniques that he felt would take him deeper into his own process. Photography was at the root of Kubrick's approach. Experienced Hollywood cameramen understood how light would be read on the film's emulsion. If necessary, tests could be made to determine the final lighting for a complicated scene. The Polaroid camera allowed the photographer to see an on-the-spot print, and Kubrick began to use the instant photographic technique on his film sets. He would take a black-and-white Polaroid of a lighting setup and use the instant photograph to judge and refine the lighting. Polaroid film read the light differently than 35mm motion picture film did, but he quickly learned how to judge the differences so he could apply it to fine-tuning the lighting on the set. This use of Polaroid on film sets ultimately became an industry standard, but Kubrick began using it early on, guided only by his artistic and technical prescience.

Christiane Kubrick continued to paint and study her craft as an artist. In September 1964 she returned to the Art Students League, taking a sculpture class with Jose de Creeft and, in October, a life drawing and painting class with Vaclav Vytlacil.

In 1964 the United Nations announced that it was going to do a six-drama film series, to be financed by Xerox. The filmmakers to be involved were Peter Glenville, Joseph Mankiewicz, Otto Preminger, Robert Rossen, Fred Zinnemann, and Stanley Kubrick. Peter Hollander, Kubrick's old Moviola buddy from Titra Films in the days when he was finishing *Killer's Kiss,* was now at the executive level at the film department of the United Nations. "I always wanted to get Stanley to do something for the United Nations," Hollander said. The film was never made.

In the early nineties, after a long search for the original negative to *Dr. Strangelove,* Kubrick decided to personally restore the film by photographing each frame of a vault print he owned with his Nikon camera. "We discovered that the studio had lost the picture negative of *Dr. Strangelove,*" Kubrick told Tim Cahill of *Rolling Stone* magazine. "And they also lost the magnetic master soundtrack. All the printing negatives were badly ripped dupes. The search went on for a year and a half. Finally, I had to reconstruct the picture from not-too-good fine grain positives, both of which were damaged already. If those fine grains were ever torn, you could never make any more negatives." The print was rereleased in 1994 for the film's thirtieth anniversary and shown at Film Forum in New York. *Dr. Strangelove* was originally projected in the 1.85:1 ratio. Kubrick's new print restored his original intention to shoot the film in 1.66:1. The new ratio revealed the full scope of Ken Adam's brilliant sets and Kubrick's mise-en-scène.

Dr. Strangelove continues to stimulate our imagination. In 1995 *Movieline* magazine called it one of the hundred greatest movies of all time (along with two other Kubrick movies, *Paths of Glory* and *2001*). On the November 10, 1995, edition of ABC's *Nightline,* Forrest Sawyer hosted a program on the dismantling of the nuclear arsenals of the United States and the former Soviet Union. The *Nightline* producers decided to call the show *Dr. Strangelove Revisited,* and they showed a clip of Slim Pickens riding the bomb to total destruction. On November 14, Russell Baker wrote an Observer piece for the *New York Times* about the current sad state of memorable movie lines. *"Dr. Strangelove or: How I Learned to Stop Worrying and Love the Bomb* had entire scenes like Keenan Wynn's defense of the Coca-Cola machine, which I have heard recited by great-line collectors with Wynn's and Peter Sellers' voices captured flawlessly," Baker wrote.

With the completion of *Dr. Strangelove,* Stanley Kubrick had achieved the status of international film director/producer. He had vision and control over the financial, artistic, and technical confines of the filmmaking process.

It was time to take the next step.

PART FIVE

1964–1987
Isolation
Solitude
Hermitage

CHAPTER 13

The Ultimate Trip

Among the younger generation Kubrick strikes me as a giant.
——Orson Welles

He's made a transplant. He never had a home here. They would have
gotten to him. He's got Welles as an example—they killed him.
——Faith Hubley

A n exalted trumpet projects three pristine notes—C, G, C—each
reaching higher than the last, exploding into a two-stage chord.
Resounding strikes of tympani drums herald the coming of a now even
more determined trumpeter restating the triumphant calling. A third
and then a final harmonic triad erupts with a surge of exploding bursts of
sonic energy, culminating in a chord that reaches above us to a higher
power. As it speeds to its destiny, the thunderous majesty of a pipe
organ's splendor shakes with its glory.

Richard Strauss composed *Thus Spake Zarathustra* in 1896, four years
before the dawning of a new century that would embrace mankind's
journey beyond the stars. Strauss never could have imagined that this
musical motif, intended for his tone poem, would become one of the
most celebrated, parodied, and recognizable motion picture signatures in
film history.

By merging the visionary music of the nineteenth century and the
imagined reality of the twenty-first century with the seeds of an embry-
onic special effects film technology in *2001: A Space Odyssey*, director

Stanley Kubrick, with cinematic prescience, reinvented our perception of feature film storytelling and the moviegoing experience.

The story line of *2001: A Space Odyssey* is an armature for a complex cinematic experience told in images, sounds, and music. The narrative plot concerns a journey that spans more than three million years. The film begins in the Earth's prehistoric period with a segment identified as "The Dawn of Man." A clan of apes engages in a territorial struggle over domination of a water hole that divides them from an enemy ape tribe. They discover an enigmatic black monolith, which inspires the ape leader to learn that his bone club is both a weapon and a tool. At the dawn of the twenty-first century, space scientist Dr. Heywood Floyd is dispatched to investigate a similar monolith discovered below the surface of the moon. The spaceship *Discovery* is sent on a nine-month mission to Jupiter. The crew consists of astronauts Dave Bowman and Frank Poole, three colleagues who are in a state of hibernation for the duration of the trip, and HAL 9000, the ship's on-board computer. During the voyage HAL deliberately terminates the lives of Poole and the hibernating crew members, forcing Bowman to disconnect the computer and continue alone to Jupiter. In deep space Bowman witnesses a floating monolith and is drawn into a star gate, which leads to a Victorian room where he sees himself age, die, and be reborn into a star child by the power of another monolith.

In 1957, Alexander Walker interviewed Kubrick at the director's New York apartment in connection with the release of *Paths of Glory*. As Walker was leaving after a stimulating conversation, Kubrick was receiving a delivery of films to screen. Walker glanced at the titles and noted they were a group of Japanese-made science fiction films. Turning back to Kubrick, Walker inquired, "Are you making a film about outer space?" Kubrick glared at Walker and said, "Please! Be careful what you write."

In February 1964, Stanley Kubrick had lunch at Trader Vic's with Roger Caras, who worked for Columbia Pictures. Kubrick told Caras he was going to do a movie about extraterrestrials. Caras asked who was writing the screenplay. Kubrick explained he was in the process of reading every major science fiction writer in search of a collaborator. "Why waste your time?" Caras asked Kubrick. "Why not just start with the best—Arthur C. Clarke?" Caras had first met Clarke in 1959 during a weekend with Jacques Cousteau, and he recommended him as a collaborator. "But I understand he's a recluse, a nut who lives in a tree in India someplace," Kubrick replied. Caras told him that Clarke lived peacefully in Ceylon and agreed to contact him for Kubrick.

Caras cabled Clarke, saying: STANLEY KUBRICK—"DR STRANGELOVE,"

"PATHS OF GLORY," ET CETERA, INTERESTED IN DOING FILM ON ET'S. INTER-
ESTED IN YOU. ARE YOU INTERESTED? THOUGHT YOU WERE RECLUSE."
Clarke immediately replied: "FRIGHTFULLY INTERESTED IN WORKING WITH
ENFANT TERRIBLE STOP CONTACT MY AGENT STOP WHAT MAKES KUBRICK
THINK I'M A RECLUSE.

Arthur Clarke's agent, Scott Meredith, who had sold Kubrick the
screen rights to *Red Alert,* contacted him and suggested he select some
of Clarke's stories to adapt into a screenplay.

The epic journey that brought *2001* to the screen began in Stanley
Kubrick's large Manhattan penthouse apartment in March 1964, the
year that *Dr. Strangelove* was released. He had arrived at a decision on
his next project, his eighth feature film. As Kubrick walked through his
apartment to his office, he took a quantum leap in his career as a film
director. Stanley Kubrick was about to change the way he conceived and
made movies by fusing his life and art to gain absolute creative control.
This had been Kubrick's artistic fate since 1953, when at age twenty-five
he independently produced, directed, photographed, and edited his first
feature film, *Fear and Desire.*

Kubrick's apartment embodied his passions and obsessions. He co-
cooned himself in surroundings that contained only what mattered to
him. Cameras and books were everywhere. The decor included a collection of tape recorders, hi-fi sets, and a shortwave radio he used to
monitor broadcasts from Moscow to learn the Russian perspective on
Vietnam. The effects of his three young daughters, Katharina, Anya, and
Vivian, were evident throughout the apartment.

Every day now boxloads of science fiction and fact books were being
delivered to the apartment. Kubrick was immersing himself in a subject
he would soon know better than most experts. His capacity to grasp and
disseminate information stunned many who worked with him. Like a
human computer, Kubrick filed everything into the synapses of his brain.

Stanley Kubrick was not a prototypical Hollywood film director. In the
past, directors D. W. Griffith, Josef von Sternberg, and Eric von
Stroheim invented the uniform of the director: imposing hats, chapped
pants, monocles, riding boots, and walking sticks. John Huston and Orson Welles smoked big cigars and were surrounded by opulence. In contrast, the Bronx-born director from an American Jewish family usually
wore an ill-fitting, lived-in sport jacket and slacks with no tie.

By 1964 Stanley Kubrick's appearance was beginning to transform.
With each year his eyes became more intense and deeply lined, and his
eyebrows formed ever higher arches. His hair, once kept barber-
trimmed, was growing longer. The clean definition of the former taper

haircut had shaggy wisps tumbling over his ears and back collar. The top was no longer parted neatly to the side; it was uncombed and beginning to thin. As this new project germinated he grew a beard. It was full and unmanicured, giving Kubrick the aura of a Talmudic scholar. The glen plaid business suits and white shirts he had worn at age nineteen at the urging of the senior photographic staff of *Look* were long gone.

Of her husband's lack of concern with his wardrobe, Christiane Kubrick said, "Stanley dresses like a balloon peddler." "Stanley would be perfectly happy with eight tape recorders and one pair of pants."

In a *New Yorker* profile, writer-physicist Jeremy Bernstein described Kubrick as having the bohemian look of a riverboat gambler or a Rumanian poet. Bernstein noted that Kubrick "had the vaguely distracted look of a man who is simultaneously thinking about a hard problem and trying to make everyday conversation."

Kubrick turned to his typewriter and began to compose a first correspondence to Arthur C. Clarke with deliberate speed. In the letter he asked the noted science fiction–science fact writer to be his collaborator on a new venture. All Kubrick revealed about the proposed film was his desire to make "a really good sci-fi movie," and he expressed his attraction to the genre as "the reasons for believing in the existence of intelligent extraterrestrial life and the impact such a discovery would have on earth in the near future." Kubrick closed by suggesting that they discuss this notion further. The project had no title. No original script had been written, no novel had been optioned for screen adaptation. Kubrick had an amoeba of an idea that would multiply from a single point of stimulation. An airmail stamp was affixed to the letter, which made the long journey to Clarke's home in Ceylon.

Later Kubrick explained his interest in extraterrestrial life to William Kloman in the *New York Times*, "Most astronomers and other scientists interested in the whole question are strongly convinced that the universe is crawling with life; much of it, since the numbers are so staggering, equal to us in intelligence, or superior, simply because human intelligence has existed for so relatively short a period."

When the letter from the States arrived, Arthur Clarke was in his study preparing the manuscript for the Time/Life Science Library book *Man and Space*. He had never met Stanley Kubrick, but he had seen *Lolita*, which he enjoyed immensely. Clarke was beginning to hear a positive buzz about the director's latest release, *Dr. Strangelove*, and was anxious to see it.

Arthur C. Clarke was forty-seven years old, born in Minehead, in Sommerset, England. As a child he was enthralled with paleontology, the science of life in the geological past. He collected fossils, built telescopes, and spent many nights mapping the moon.

As a teenager, Clarke built a photophone transmitter from a bicycle lamp, an invention that sent his voice out on a light beam, and he experimented with the audio modulation of sunlight through mechanics, predating the development of such a device for space communications. As a kid, his nickname was "Scientific Sid." Clarke devoured the futuristic visions of fictional science speculation in the pages of *Amazing and Astounding Stories* magazine. This exposure merged with a solid grounding in science fact and eventually produced a writer whose command of science kindled his fanciful imagination.

By 1964 Clarke was as distinguished in his field as Robert Heinlein and Isaac Asimov. Clarke's novel *Childhood's End* was a classic in the genre. His intelligent writing style, both pragmatic and philosophical, inspired a generation with his visions of our future in the universe. Accomplishments in speculative fiction and a prolific trail of probing books on scientific thought made Arthur C. Clarke the ideal choice for Kubrick's sci-fi movie.

Clarke reread Kubrick's letter. He was perplexed by the lack of information concerning the proposal, but Kubrick's childlike fascination for the subject of extraterrestrials tweaked Clarke's curiosity.

Although there were science fiction films he admired, Clarke was wary of Hollywood producers more partial to exploitation than honor to the genre. None of his work had been adapted to the screen. He had never written a screenplay and had little regard for what he considered a subliterary form. Arthur C. Clarke was a quiet, cautious man, proud of his status in literature and protective of his work.

After careful consideration, Clarke decided to pursue Kubrick's offer to further discuss the project, and he wrote a letter expressing interest. He was unclear whether Kubrick wanted him to collaborate on an original screenplay or to adapt one of his published works. To be prepared, Clarke prudently went through his extensive files of short stories. He felt that a well-developed short story was good material for a feature-length film, since novels often lost too much of their content and texture when adapted to the format.

After a thorough search Clarke chose to offer "The Sentinel" to Kubrick for possible screen adaptation. The intriguing story had been written during the 1948 Christmas holiday for a BBC contest. It was not a prizewinner, but Scott Meredith sold the story to the magazine *Ten Story Fantasy*, which published it in 1951 under the original title, "Sentinel of Eternity." "Unlike most of my short stories," Clarke recalled, "this one was aimed at a specific target—which it missed completely. The BBC had just announced a short story competition; I submitted 'The Sentinel' hot from the typewriter and got it back a month later. Somehow, I've never had much luck with such contests." Clarke anticipated that Kubrick would be absorbed by evocative presentation of the extraterrestrial theme in "The Sentinel."

"The Sentinel" was a nine-page story that suggested that extraterrestrial visitors explored the earth before man and arrived at the conclusion that the planet would one day be inhabited by intelligent beings. The callers left a physical marker described by Clarke as "a glittering, roughly pyramidal structure, twice as high as a man . . . set in a rock . . . like a gigantic many faceted jewel." "The Sentinel" was rich in speculative and intellectual substance and provocative imagery for the film medium.

Clarke rarely left his treasured Ceylon, but he was scheduled to fly to America in the next month for editorial meetings and production work on *Man and Space* at the Time/Life offices in New York City. After exchanging letters, Clarke and Kubrick set a date to meet and discuss the director's project. Clarke arrived in New York and immediately checked into the Hotel Chelsea in downtown Manhattan.

The encounter between Stanley Kubrick and Arthur C. Clarke was planned for April 23, opening day of the 1964 New York World's Fair. This coincidence provided a conducive backdrop for Kubrick's sci-fi movie. The World's Fair projected a vision of the future. Film played a significant role in visualizing and communicating the dreams of a better life to come, aided by an emerging computer and space technology that would forever change our daily existence. Wide-screen formats, multi-screen, and multimedia productions using such experimental techniques as 360-degree projection forecasted a new kind of cinema being born in the sixties.

For a meeting place, Kubrick had selected Trader Vic's, the popular watering hole located inside the Plaza Hotel where he had first discussed Clarke with Roger Caras. As Arthur Clarke took the short walk from his office on the thirty-second floor in the Time/Life building to the Plaza after a day of production meetings on his manuscript, he felt an arrow of anxiety shoot through his nervous system. What did Stanley Kubrick really want? Was he endangering his hallowed place in the science fiction community by philandering in the movies? As he walked into the Plaza and through the hotel to Trader Vic's, Clarke hoped that Kubrick wouldn't be a typical Hollywood type. The archetypical image of the deeply tanned, fast-talking, cigar-smoking, "let's do lunch" Hollywood producer dominated Clarke's image of movie people. Clarke was early.

He approached the bar and ordered a drink. Kubrick was punctual and immediately walked up to Clarke. Before contacting him, Kubrick had read everything Clarke had published. The back cover author's picture made the writer instantly identifiable.

Clarke was relieved. Stanley Kubrick looked like an average New Yorker, nothing like a Hollywooden producer, although Clarke was a little suspicious of Kubrick's high energy, since it was now after 7:00 P.M. Clarke observed that Kubrick had a night person's pallor, in stark contrast to his own diurnal characteristics. Clarke lived by the self-subscribed motto "No sane person is awake after 10:00 P.M. and no law-abiding one after midnight."

Trader Vic's was a likely place for a movie confab, but Stanley Kubrick did not anticipate making the kind of motion picture usually discussed over cocktails. The conversation was lively and stimulating. Kubrick's charm made Clarke feel at ease. Kubrick didn't make a pitch. He never said the words "deal" or "baby." In fact, the subject of his film project was not part of the discussion. The evening ended cordially, with a date agreed upon to reconvene. Clarke emerged from the meeting impressed with Kubrick's pure intelligence and his ability to comprehend new ideas and concepts instantaneously.

Kubrick contacted Clarke again and asked him to set aside a full day for the second meeting. For hours Kubrick led them in spirited dialogues investigating a wide spectrum of topics: science fiction, *Dr. Strangelove,* flying saucers, the U.S. and Russian space programs, Senator Barry Goldwater. Each exchange was intense, full of data, multiple viewpoints, and attention to detail. Clarke enjoyed the intellectual stimulation, but as the day wore on he couldn't get his mind off the tantalizing Kubrick sci-fi project.

Finally, near the end of the day, Kubrick officially asked Clarke if he would agree to collaborate on a science fiction film. Kubrick felt that no matter how unsound the idea of the possibility of extraterrestrial life was it could be transferred to film. He told Jeremy Bernstein, "One of the English science-fiction writers once said, 'Sometimes I think we're alone, and sometimes I think we're not. In either case, the idea is quite staggering.' I must say I agree with him."

Kubrick explained to Clarke that together the two men would fashion the screen story, using "The Sentinel" as a starting point. Clarke, captivated by Kubrick's charismatic allure, said yes, but he was unaware of the significance of this gentlemen's agreement. To Kubrick this was the beginning of a formidable process, one he embraced and thrived on. Writing a screenplay for Stanley Kubrick and being a part of his pains-

taking production methods would be a task of mental and physical en-
durance beyond Clarke's immediate comprehension. A handshake
signaled that it had already begun.

"Even from the beginning, he had a very clear idea of his ultimate
goal. He wanted to make a movie about man's relation to the universe—
something which had never been attempted, much less achieved, in the
history of motion pictures. Stanley was determined to create a work of
art which would arouse the emotions of wonder, awe—even, if appropriate, terror," Clarke remembered.

For the next month Clarke continued to work on *Man and Space,*
while devoting as much as five hours a day to a regular schedule of
meetings with Kubrick. During the spring of 1964, Clarke and Kubrick
discussed the project for as many as ten hours a day. The talks were held
at Kubrick's apartment and various restaurants, including that familiar
New York haunt—the Automat. They visited the Guggenheim Museum,
Central Park, and the World's Fair, which was being held in Flushing
Meadows Park in Queens, also the site of the 1939 event. They continued to walk and talk about space, extraterrestrials, and movies. Working
with Kubrick was both exhilarating and exhausting for Clarke. Kubrick's
mental computer accessed perpetual information banks, and obsession
gave him stamina. His endless questions and mania for details within
details tapped Clarke's own enormous knowledge. Although Kubrick was
attracted to the concept of a marker left on earth by an alien culture, his
ideas for the film went well beyond the confines of "The Sentinel." To
Clarke, Kubrick seemed driven to the brink of neurosis, fed by an un-
quenchable thirst for total perfection.

The first approach to developing the film involved a series of sequences depicting interplanetary discovery and exploration of the moon.
Kubrick and Clarke's mock working title for this concept was "How the
Solar System Was Won," a spoof of the MGM Cinerama western epic
How the West Was Won. These scenes were developed in a semi-docu-
mentary structure to portray the pioneering days of the new frontier in
space. These events were to climax with what eventually became the
spiritual mystery of *2001*—the sighting of an extraterrestrial artifact—
but this approach was quickly dropped as Kubrick began to investigate
other possibilities. On the evening of May 17, 1964, after one of their
marathon meetings, Clarke reports that he and Kubrick walked out onto
the director's veranda to refresh themselves. At 9:00 P.M. they jointly
witnessed what they perceived as a UFO glittering in the smog-filled
heavens above. Kubrick pressed Clarke for an explanation, but Clarke
drew a blank. Kubrick's paranoia overwhelmed him. He feared that the

discovery of extraterrestrial life would destroy the film plans as they slowly formed. They phoned the Pentagon and filled out a standard government UFO-sighting form. Clarke discussed this occurrence with friends at the Hayden Planetarium, who employed their computers to solve the interstellar mystery. The director and his scenarist had witnessed an *Echo I* transit and not a sign of extraterrestrial life. Clarke relates, "I can still remember, rather sheepishly, my feelings of awe and excitement and also the thought that flashed through my mind: 'This is altogether too much of a coincidence. *They* are out to stop us from making this movie.' " Kubrick's anxiety recurred when the *Mariner 4* space probe approached Mars. He felt compelled to develop alternate story lines in case life was discovered on the Red Planet. Kubrick even tried to insure the film against the possibility of being upstaged by the reality of the space race. He asked the famed Lloyd's of London to draw up a policy that would compensate him if extraterrestrial life was discovered, but the cost, like the claim, was astronomical. Clarke has said that there would never have been a *2001: A Space Odyssey* if they truly had seen their hypothesized visions in the skies that spring evening.

Kubrick discarded ideas at breakneck speed. To replenish fuel for thought, Clarke returned to his files and presented Kubrick with additional short stories to help propel the space epic.

On May 20, 1964, Arthur C. Clarke signed a contract to formalize work on Kubrick's project. The agreement included the sale of "The Sentinel" and other Clarke stories: "Breaking Strain," "Out of the Cradle," "Endless Orbiting . . . ," "Who's There," "Into the Comet," and "Before Eden." Kubrick's lawyer, Louis Blau, and Scott Meredith worked out the deal. Clarke received a $10,000 option for the stories. By May 28, it had been decided that Clarke would write a treatment based on "The Sentinel" for $30,000, $15,000 to be paid when principal photography began and the remaining $15,000 when the film was complete. Kubrick also was to receive a percentage of all sequel novels and film rights related to *2001*.

Moving toward production, Kubrick drew up a working schedule with 12 weeks allocated to complete the script, to be followed by 2 weeks of consultation, 4 weeks of script revisions, 4 weeks to finance the film, 4 weeks to prepare the visuals, 20 weeks of shooting, 20 weeks of editing, and 12 weeks to prepare before release. This enormous schedule actually more than doubled before Kubrick wrapped the film.

For phase one, the completion of a shooting script, Kubrick rejected the notion of writing a conventional screenplay, calling the form "the most uncommunicative form of writing ever devised." He instinctively knew that the project would crystallize in the filmmaking process, but a words-on-paper draft became imperative when MGM expressed interest in distributing Kubrick's secretive project.

Kubrick's method of compromise with the conventions of the film industry was to devise an unconventional way of generating a screen story. He proposed to Clarke that they first collaborate on writing a full-length novel with attention to filmic possibilities. Kubrick's strategy was to develop a shooting script from the novel.

Kubrick placed Clarke in his Central Park West office with an electric typewriter and plenty of blank paper, but after one day under the director's scrutiny, Clarke quietly withdrew to the more suitable literary atmosphere at the Chelsea Hotel, where he was stimulated to create in the company of Arthur Miller, Allen Ginsberg, and William Burroughs (all of whom resided at the Chelsea in the flesh) and Dylan Thomas and Brendan Behan (who presided in spirit). In addition to being the hotel of choice for many of Andy Warhol's superstars, the Chelsea also became the place where *Naked Lunch* and *2001* were written.

Kubrick and Clarke were at opposite ends of the spectrum when it came to working and resting patterns. "Arthur and Stanley were very interesting foils," Roger Caras told Neil McAleer, Arthur C. Clarke's authorized biographer. "There was some slight conflict in that Arthur goes to bed very early. Arthur gets very tired, and typically nine to nine-thirty is his bedtime. Stanley goes to bed about three in the morning and sleeps till about three in the afternoon. That presented problems sometimes. But when their times meshed, they were terrific foils." Caras called the meeting of the two minds "a good cerebral marriage."

In January 1965 Harry Lange and Frederick Ordway were in town for the American Institute of Aeronautics and Astronautics convention at the New York Hilton. The two men had a space consultancy company and were meeting with publishers to discuss a book on extraterrestrials.

Harry Lange designed pilot training manuals for the United States Army and later designed advanced space vehicles for NASA. In 1964 he and Frederick Ordway began to develop space projects on their own.

Ordway, who also worked for NASA and at the Army Ballistic Missile Agency at Huntsville, Alabama, arranged to meet with Clarke while they were in town.

Clarke, Lange, and Ordway met for lunch at the Harvard Club. During the meal and chat, Clarke told the men that he was working with Stanley Kubrick on a film project. Ordway told Clarke about a project they were putting together for Prentice-Hall called *Intelligence in the Universe.* Clarke was very impressed with the visualization that Lange had created for the project. Lange and Ordway excused themselves, having to leave for another engagement. Outside, a snowstorm had begun and the two men waited for a cab. While they waited and unbeknownst to them, Clarke pushed through the snowstorm to the nearest pay phone to call Kubrick about Lange and Ordway. Kubrick hung up and immediately called the Harvard Club, asking the management to page the snowbound duo still outside waiting for a cab. Ordway was paged and brought back inside to the phone, on which a voice said, "Mr. Ordway, my name is Stanley Kubrick."

Lange and Ordway spent the next day in discussion with Kubrick and signed six-month contracts to work on the film project. Ordway was brought on as the principal technical adviser, and Lange was to create spacecraft designs. They would work out of the Polaris production office and be responsible for briefing Kubrick on current space exploration research. Polaris was the latest in a series of production companies that Kubrick had created for his projects. The decor of the office was sedate, furnishings were minimal. Kubrick spent hours of his tightly booked schedule interviewing for his technical crew and probing the best minds in science and aerospace technology.

During the writing of the novel, Kubrick and Clarke continued daily penthouse meetings to engage in constant discourse and revision. Kubrick's work method was torturously slow for Clarke. Wastebaskets overflowed with sheets of paper. In search of Kubrick's grail, a stream of words formed ideas that constantly expanded the scope of the story in time and space.

Arthur Clarke suggested that he and Kubrick talk to the young scientist Carl Sagan, who was an astrophysicist at the Smithsonian Astrophysical Observatory in Cambridge, Massachusetts, and later became the renowned author and host of *Cosmos*. The under-thirty Sagan was invited to the Kubrick penthouse for dinner and talk. The before-, during-, and after-dinner conversation centered on what extraterrestrial creatures would look like. On whether the creature should have a human appearance, Kubrick was pro and Clarke was con. "I said it would be a disaster to portray the extraterrestrials. What ought to be done is to suggest them," Carl Sagan told Neil McAleer. "I argued that the number of individually unlikely events in the evolutionary history of man was so great that nothing like us is ever likely to evolve again anywhere else in the universe. I suggested that any explicit representation of an advanced extraterrestrial being was bound to have at least an element of falseness about it and that the best solution would be to suggest rather than explicitly to display the extraterrestrials."

Kubrick and Clarke began to gather influences, reading Louis Leakey's *Adam's Ancestors* and Robert Ardrey's *African Genesis,* a book that would later have a key impact on Sam Peckinpah and his controversial film *Straw Dogs.* They began to study Joseph Campbell's *The Hero with a Thousand Faces* for the inspiration of myth, a book that would later influence the *Star Wars* trilogy. Clarke paid a visit to Dr. Harry Shapiro, director of anthropology at the American Museum of Natural History in New York.

Frederick Ordway wooed aerospace and technology corporations to become involved in Kubrick's space film, gaining the interest of NASA, IBM, Honeywell, Boeing, Bell Telephone, RCA, General Dynamics, Chrysler, and General Electric. Kubrick enticed the companies into contributing ideas and designs to the film in return for having their corporate logos displayed well before the idea of product placement became a mainstay of the film industry.

The Polaris production office began to get crowded. Kubrick's assistant Ray Lovejoy, who had worked as assistant editor on *Dr. Strangelove,* came over from England, as did Victor Lyndon, the executive producer of the project. Richard McKenna and Roy Carnon were also there, doing color preproduction art work.

Christiane Kubrick had talked to painting teacher Harry Sternberg about her film director husband over several pleasant lunches. "I looked forward to the time I would meet him, and Stanley came up to my studio on East Fourteenth street," Sternberg recalled. "He was one of the most overactive, dynamic, excited, filled-with-energy guys I ever met. He came tearing in and we had a few words, then the rest of the time he was mostly on the phone. Every time we'd start a sentence the damn phone would ring. I was very excited about meeting him, but he was either on the damn telephone or people were calling him so steadily that I had very little conversation with him. He and his wife were two such different human beings. When I met both of them it was fantastic to me that they could be a pair, and they seemed to be a very happy pair. They were utterly different—he was just as frenetic as she was calm—it seemed to work." Later Sternberg had a second encounter with Kubrick when he came to see an exhibit of the painter's work. "The director of the gallery and I were just talking, and all of a sudden Stanley took his camera and said, 'Let me take a shot of this.' He sent me a copy, it was a nice big color print—it's a great portrait of me."

Although Kubrick attempted to keep his project in a state of secrecy more common to one conducted by NASA than by a film studio, his venture attracted curiosity that buzzed through New York City. The knowledge may have helped to corral artistic and scientific minds and bring them to Kubrick's door, but it also presented potential dangers. Once a deranged man came to the office insisting that Kubrick hire him. The man was politely but swiftly ushered out. Unwilling to take no for an answer, he began to keep daily vigil on a park bench opposite the office building to make his persistence for a staff position known. Periodically he appeared inside the office trying to take his rightful place on the production. With a heightened sense of personal security, Kubrick began carrying a large hunting knife stuffed in his briefcase along with the reams of lists, charts, and technical data.

Arthur C. Clarke also had a brush with a threatening alien force of a different sort. On May 1, a fire started on the third floor of the Chelsea Hotel. As firemen fought the blaze, Clarke joined the other residents in the lobby, all the while imagining with horror the flames rising seven more floors to turn the only copy of the manuscript into a pile of worthless ashes—what would he tell Stanley Kubrick then!

July 1 was Clarke's last day at Time/Life—*Man and Space* was now complete. His original agenda had him returning to Ceylon immediately, but home was far from sight with so much yet to accomplish on the Kubrick project. By the end of the first week of July, Clarke had finished the first five chapters of the novel, averaging one to two thousand words a day. He typed on an old gray Smith-Corona typewriter, working in Suite 1008 in the Chelsea Hotel nourishing himself with tea, crackers, and liver paté. At the end of the month the writer took a momentary break from the manuscript to buy a birthday card for Stanley Kubrick's thirty-sixth birthday on July 26. While strolling through Greenwich Village he found a fitting message for the director of *Dr. Strangelove* in a card that pictured the Earth about to explode. The inscription read: "How can you have a happy birthday when the whole world may blow up any minute?"

By the end of August, three of the novel's main characters emerged. Two were astronauts and one was a computer. Kubrick decided that the computer, which continued to take on more weight and purpose in his story, would be a female named Athena after the Greek goddess of warfare and wisdom. Ultimately, the computer changed gender and became filmdom's most famous mainframe—HAL.

After *2001* was released clever members of the audience came to the conclusion that the name HAL was conceived because the letters that follow *H*, *A*, and *L* in the alphabet were *I*, *B*, and *M*, producing a reference to IBM—the company at the time synonymous with computers. "It was an amazing coincidence," Kubrick told Alexander Walker. "Arthur

C. Clarke and I called the computer HAL, which is an acronym based on the words, 'heuristic' and 'algorithmic,' the two forms of learning which HAL mastered. Several years later, a code-breaker friend pointed out that the letters of HAL's name were each one letter ahead of IBM and congratulated us on the hidden joke." "I remember there was one kid who wrote to Stanley and told him how he understood that HAL was IBM," Bob Gaffney remembered. "People would read anything into it. Those kids on acid trips were just looking for the meaning of life."

While Clarke continued to flesh out the story, Kubrick began to amass a multitude of questions about the portrayal of the astronauts concerning every aspect of their job and life in space. All of these inquiries were researched and clarified by Kubrick staffers.

One of the areas of Kubrick's research was in stories in which people were out of touch for a long time. He was trying to understand what the astronauts would be feeling when isolated from their natural environment and others. One story Kubrick came upon was a book on Ernest Shackleton, an Irish explorer who crossed the Arctic with a team of people. After absorbing the story, he gave the book to his friend and colleague Bob Gaffney and encouraged him to make a film out of it.

Clarke was increasingly fearful that he would never come up with a suitable plot for the film. Nightmares interrupted his fitful sleep. He has described one that envisioned the writer on the set—the shooting had begun—and actors were standing around with nothing to say, while Kubrick continued to question and probe the writer, who still hadn't found the story line the director was searching for. In Clarke's waking hours, long walks with Kubrick ended at the East River with few answers and many new prospects to consider.

As December 25 approached, Arthur C. Clarke slowly typed the final pages of the novel, which he presented to Kubrick for Christmas.

Throughout the writing process Clarke and Kubrick put in an average of four hours a day, six days a week, or approximately twenty-four hundred hours of writing for two hours and forty minutes of film, a staggering 900:1 ratio.

Kubrick was ecstatic about the manuscript, telling Clarke, "We've extended the range of science fiction." The story went up to the point where Dave Bowman entered the Star Gate but ended without a firm conclusion. Clarke thought the screenplay would easily emerge from this blueprint, but for Kubrick the project was still in gestation.

Kubrick used the manuscript of the novel to sell the idea to MGM and Cinerama with a projected budget of $6 million. "I took the treatment that they had " Kubrick's lawyer, Louis Blau, told Neil McAleer "and presented it to MGM to read. They had a two-or-three-day dead-line during which they had to come back to me, and that's how I made the deal. Stanley never uses a traditional screenplay like some directors who want to know all the stage details. Instead he keeps working up to and through his shooting to make sure it's better all the time."

MGM issued a press release on Tuesday, February 23, 1965, from its offices at 1540 Broadway in New York City, announcing the intention to join with Kubrick to film *Journey Beyond the Stars,* a working title used to sell the idea, as Kubrick continued to search for the right words to define his vision. The release stated the project had just been announced by MGM president Robert H. O'Brien and was to be made in color and in Cinerama. The interiors were to be filmed at the MGM studios in London. Included in the release was Kubrick's description of the project: "*Journey Beyond the Stars* is an epic story of adventure and exploration, encompassing the Earth, the planets of our Solar System, and a journey light-years to another part of the Galaxy. It is a scientifically-based yet dramatic attempt to explore the infinite possibilities that space travel now opens to mankind. The great biologist J.B.S. Haldane said: 'The Universe is not only stranger than we imagine; it is stranger than we *can* imagine.' When you consider that in our Galaxy there are a hundred *billion* stars, of which our Sun is a perfectly average specimen, and that present estimates put the number of Galaxies in the visible Universe at a hundred *million,* Haldane's statement seems rather conservative."

With this official MGM commitment and announcement, the deal was sealed—the odyssey would begin.

Robert O'Brien authorized $6 million for Kubrick's space movie, planning its release by the end of 1966 or in the spring of 1967. He encountered stockholder and executive criticism for his decision, but he put his money and his faith behind Stanley Kubrick.

Armed with a first draft, Clarke began the enormous task of revising and expanding the novel that would serve as the narrative path for the film. Entire sections of the novel previously approved by Kubrick were discarded. Nothing remained final; ideas were shifted as Kubrick moved closer to the rigors of the production.

In April 1965, Tony Masters came to New York from England and was hired as a production designer. Masters was a major in the Royal Artillery during World War II and had worked in films since 1946. In 1962 he worked in the art department for David Lean's *Lawrence of Arabia.*

As Clarke hunkered down in front of the typewriter to put closure on the novel, the 1965 spring season bloomed in New York. Kubrick began to interview technicians, department heads, and actors and tackled the onslaught of details and decisions that confronted preproduction at the offices of Polaris Productions. Clarke called Roger Caras, who was surprised the writer was in New York. "I said, 'Hey, Arthur, when did you get in town?' " Caras recalled to Neil McAleer. "And he told me that he had been in the city for nearly six months, working on the new project. I spoke to Arthur for a few minutes, and then Stanley came on the phone. 'Do you want to come to England with us and make a movie?' he asked. It was a Sunday night, about eleven-thirty, which is late for Arthur. I called over to my wife and said, 'Jill, do you want to move to England?' And she said, 'Sure.' So the next day I resigned from Columbia Pictures after ten years and prepared to move to England with Arthur and Stanley and the rest of the team. I had become the director of publicity for *2001: A Space Odyssey.*"

Roger Caras was given the arduous mandate to locate every science fiction book ever written and compile a personal archive of articles detailing space travel and related sciences. A staff archivist searched out and procured prints of every science fiction film. Clarke and Kubrick screened George Pal's *Destination Moon* (based on the novel by Robert Heinlein), *The Day the Earth Stood Still*, *The Thing*, and *Forbidden Planet*. After seeing William Cameron Menzies' landmark film *Things to Come*, which Clarke admired, Kubrick turned to the writer and said, "What are you trying to do to me? I'll never see another movie you recommend." Kubrick was highly critical of all the films they viewed, but he insisted on seeing every one in its entirety in his search for ideas and techniques that could be valuable. Even a grade Z Russian sci-fi film, *Astronauts on Venus*, was viewed by Kubrick, Christiane, and Jeremy Bernstein on a Saturday afternoon at a neighborhood movie house in North London. Though the film was dubbed and filled with crude effects, Kubrick hedged his bets and insisted on staying to the bitter end.

At the end of April 1965 it was time for Kubrick to put his project into production. The first step was to drop the working title, *Journey Beyond the Stars*—more suitable to a Roger Corman American International B picture than the iconoclastic cinematic experience that Kubrick planned to deliver. From the outset Kubrick was inspired by Homer's masterwork, the *Odyssey*. Like Odysseus, the astronauts would embark on a voyage in Kubrick's film. The audience would also take this trip through the galaxies less than half a century away. Stanley Kubrick formally announced to the world press that his film *2001: A Space Odyssey* was to be produced in England.

Always cautious on details, Kubrick asked Frederick Ordway how to pronounce his new title. "Stanley asked me if we should say 'two thousand and one' or 'twenty oh one' like we say 'nineteen oh one'," Ordway told Neil McAleer. "And we decided that 'two thousand and one' sounded better. We often wondered among ourselves whether the fact that the film was called 'two thousand *and* one' would have an influence on the English language when we got into the twenty-first century."

Clarke returned to Ceylon to continue rewriting the novel through the spring of 1965. Instead of a few months, he had been gone for a full year. As Clarke headed for home, Kubrick moved his production unit to MGM Studios at Boreham Wood, fifteen miles north of London. Twenty truckloads of data and drawings were shipped from New York to England on the S.S. *France.* Nine stages were booked for Kubrick's project. MGM was doing ten to twelve productions a year at the facility. This commitment would mean they could support only half that during Kubrick's stint at Boreham Wood. Robert O'Brien promised that operating costs would not be charged to the budget of Kubrick's production, a common practice, which ate into a film's creative life. MGM's British studios were already considered a liability to the parent company, and this only increased the pressure on O'Brien. The MGM president was counseled against the risk by both friends and enemies. But Stanley Kubrick could be very persuasive, and he convinced Robert O'Brien that the gamble was worth it.

Stanley and Christiane Kubrick and their family moved into a large apartment in London's Dorchester Hotel. England had become the Bronx director's location of choice for film production. His one encounter with the Hollywood studio system on *Spartacus* proved disastrous for preserving the creative freedom and control essential to his obsessive work methods. He had quickly learned that he could only be a hired hand in Hollywood. To be the sole authority, he had to settle elsewhere. As with *Lolita* and *Dr. Strangelove,* Kubrick decided to produce *2001* in England.

Although he was a true New Yorker who thrived on the manic energy of the city, Kubrick found himself rapidly adapting to the civility and less frenetic pace of Great Britain. About their life in New York City, Christiane Kubrick told Ann Morrow of the *Times* of London, "We lived on Central Park West at 84th Street. I began to get used to seeing the streets white with smashed Coke bottles, to seeing police taking the children to school. In the shops, roughs would just slouch and sprawl across the doorways so you'd have to step over them as if it was quite normal. The women were harsh, too. You just got elbowed out of the way by them. The terrible danger was going home and taking it out on somebody weaker like a child. Just like the animal kingdom. New York did something to me. Before we went there we thought that Americans who complained about the schools and the atmosphere were just right-wing creeps, but of course they had a point." For Stanley Kubrick, what began as a utilitarian business decision became a lifestyle choice.

Stanley Kubrick's parents, Jacques and Gertrude, had moved from the East to the West Coast. Jacques applied for and received a medical license in California, listing his specialty as radiology. Dr. Kubrick was also a member of the American College of Gastroenterology.

For *2001* Kubrick struck a deal with MGM to lease its studios at Boreham Wood. In addition to the excellent production facilities there, Kubrick chose the site for the surrounding region, which was dotted with electronics companies and firms that manufactured precision instruments—high technology would be the lifeblood of *2001*.

The exterior architecture of the Boreham Wood studios fit in perfectly with the neighboring factories nestled around it. The main building was painted white and looked like a nondescript factory. It was two stories with a small tower that had a clock with no numbers and the simple inscription "MGM Studios." Close-cropped grass and a few shrubs were all that landscaped it. The studio was not adorned with the show-biz glitz associated with Hollywood movie mills. The businesslike studio sported ten large sound stages clustered with carpenter shops, paint shops, craft shops, and offices. Behind the buildings was a huge backlot filled with bits and pieces of other productions—the facade of a French provincial village, the hulk of a World War II bomber, and other remains. The vast complex was laid out in a bungalowlike formation so Kubrick, like a New Age Mayer, Zukor, or Zanuck, could oversee his own mini film factory.

Kubrick asked production designer Ken Adam to join the production, but Adam, who had designed *Dr. Strangelove,* knew that Kubrick had been researching the project for a very long time, and he felt that he would be able to design the film only if he knew as much about the subject as Kubrick. So he politely declined, explaining that he felt at a disadvantage, not being up to speed on the complex technologies involved in *2001*.

The offices for the *2001* team were located at the front of the complex. A special section was designated "Santa's Workshop" by Kubrick—these were the quarters for the commune of young model builders who worked on miniature spacecrafts and planets under the experienced eye of special effects supervisor Wally Veevers. The production employed 103 modelmakers from varied backgrounds. Kubrick hired boat builders, architecture students, fine artists, sculptors, lithographers, metalworkers, and ivory carvers who had just stepped off a whaling boat. Orthodoxy was checked at the front door of this creative den of long-haired and unbuttoned-down elves. Everyone was hired on short-term freelance contracts, and turnover was high. Art director John Hoesli worked with more than thirty draftsmen to produce the plans for Harry Lange's spacecrafts. Anthony Pratt, a young designer who went on to work with John Boorman on *Zardoz, Excalibur,* and *Hope and Glory,* was brought on to help create the concept for the space pods.

Kubrick began to assemble a special effects team for the film. Of the plethora of films that he screened none met his standard for visual effects. His project called for a different approach. Ideas that were already conceived for the sequences in space demanded a special effects technology far more advanced than the status quo of the traditional Hollywood studio film.

To find special effects techniques that met Kubrick's criteria, the director issued a decree to see and read *everything* available on space. Kubrick's personal staff left no stone unturned. They were driven beyond the racks of familiar films. *Everything* meant films from all over the continents, television programs, short subjects, documentaries, films made for the World's Fair, and experimental films. When they searched beyond the full-length feature film, the staff uncovered *Universe,* a short film produced by the National Film Board of Canada in 1960. As the film unspooled, Kubrick watched the screen with rapt attention while a panorama of the galaxies swirled by, achieving the standard of dynamic visionary realism that he was looking for. These images were not flawed by the shoddy matte work, obvious animation, and poor miniatures typically found in science fiction films. *Universe* proved that the camera could be a telescope to the heavens. As the credits rolled, Kubrick studied the names of the magicians who created the images: Colin Low, Sidney Goldsmith, and Wally Gentleman. Staff members set about locating this visual effects crew and researching how they had achieved their miracles.

Universe was produced by the Canadian Film Board Unit B. Colin Low and Roman Kroitor had long been fascinated with cosmology. The project had its genesis five years before *Sputnik,* as a proposed classroom film. Interest in the project grew, and it attracted others who wanted to make a film that would allow the viewer to experience the wonders of the universe. *Universe* took four years to complete and cost more than $60,000.

After witnessing the awesome achievements of *Universe,* Kubrick was convinced that he had found his special effects team. He was unable to secure the entire *Universe* team but did hire Wally Gentleman, who put in several weeks of preliminary work before resigning in ill health. In the early eighties, Gentleman went on to tackle another unwieldy project, Francis Ford Coppola's *One from the Heart.*

Ultimately Kubrick selected four men to head his special effects team: Wally Veevers, Douglas Trumbull, Con Pederson, and Tom Howard.

Kubrick knew that the spacecraft in the film would have to be created in miniature. Wally Veevers, special effects supervisor on *Dr. Strangelove,* was hired for his expertise in the precise and tedious art of model building. Kubrick wanted the ships to move with swanlike grace through a sky filled with stars and planets. This would require painstaking attention to detail and a craftsman who understood every aspect of this demanding art. Kubrick was in good hands with the selection of Veevers, who had been chosen by the Korda brothers as an apprentice for the special effects staff of William Cameron Menzies' *Things to Come.*

Tom Howard was tapped for his long experience in the field of optical effects. Howard worked on *The Thief of Bagdad* and won Oscars for David Lean's *Blithe Spirit* and for the George Pal production of *Tom Thumb.*

The youngest member of the special effects team was a twenty-three-year-old American, Douglas Trumbull. Born in Los Angeles, Trumbull wanted to become an architect until he was hired by the Graphic Films Corporation in Hollywood after they examined his portfolio of space illustrations. As the head of the Graphic Films background department, Trumbull worked on *Lifeline in Space* for the USAF and *Space in Perspective* for NASA. Kubrick discovered Trumbull's name in the credits of *To the Moon and Beyond,* a Cinerama 360 film produced for the 1964 World's Fair. Kubrick commissioned background drawings from Graphic Films rendered by Trumbull. Impressed with Trumbull's talent, he quickly assigned him some of the film's greatest challenges, including the Star Gate sequence that concludes *2001.*

Kubrick was looking for a director of photography with exceptional abilities. He required a cameraman who not only was a master of conventional cinematography but could comfortably work on the wide screen canvas and deal with the optical and mechanical processes that dominated the long shooting schedule.

After many interviews and careful study, Stanley Kubrick chose fifty-five-year-old Geoffrey Unsworth. An amiable English gentleman, Unsworth had worked on *The Four Feathers, The Thief of Bagdad, The Life and Death of Colonel Blimp, The World of Suzie Wong, Becket,* and *Half a Sixpence. 2001: A Space Odyssey* would become a landmark in his sterling career.

In a world not yet linked by computer modems and fax machines, Kubrick talked to designers and technicians in person, on the phone, through the mails, and by telegram. The staff for the film grew to near-unprecedented numbers. A total of 106 staff members were assembled, including 35 designers, who represented a vast range of disciplines and artistic styles, and 25 special effects technicians.

In September 1965 Kubrick decided that the *Discovery* mission should go not to Jupiter but to Saturn. The visual possibilities of Saturn's rings lured Kubrick, but the special effects staff was thrown into a state of panic because they had spent three months planning and preparing for the trip to Jupiter. Ultimately Kubrick would change his mind again and head the *Discovery* back to Jupiter.

When Kubrick learned of the U.S. *Orion* project, he ordered the *Discovery* to be redesigned, only to later cancel the redesign when he decided that a bomb-carrying craft was too much like the B-52 in *Dr. Strangelove.*

On October 3, Clarke told Kubrick on the phone that the story should end with Bowman regressing to infancy. "We'll see him at the end as a baby in orbit." Clarke and Kubrick continued to justify all of their ideas. "It's the image of himself at this stage of his development. And perhaps the Cosmic Consciousness has a sense of humor," Clarke said to Kubrick.

Clarke came up with the idea, which he introduced in the published novel, that the Star Child detonated nuclear weapons on earth. The idea was in the shooting script, but eventually Kubrick felt he had done that particular idea already for the ending of *Dr. Strangelove.*

"The ending was altered shortly before shooting it," Kubrick said to Jerome Agel. "In the original there was no transformation of Bowman. He just wandered around the room and finally saw the artifact. But this didn't seem like it was satisfying enough or interesting enough, and we constantly searched for ideas until we finally came up with the ending as you see it."

2001 demanded a subtle naturalistic acting style devoid of overt dramatic interpretation. There was little dialogue in the film—action and gesture defined the characters. These astronauts were not the heroic, boyish, archetypical portraits of *The Right Stuff.* Dave Bowman and Frank Poole were poised and conditioned for a long stint in space. The astronauts had to look and act like the men of NASA, outwardly pleasant but cool and emotionally enclosed. Kubrick did not want the roles of

Bowman and Poole to be a showcase for superstars. The characters were to be integrated into the visual fabric of the film.

Twenty-nine-year-old Gary Lockwood was cast as Poole. The California native began in the business as a stuntman and as stand-in for actor Anthony Perkins. In 1960 a role in *Tall Story* launched his acting career. He had been in only a handful of films: *Wild in the Country, Splendor in the Grass, The Magic Sword, It Happened at the World's Fair,* and *A Firecreek.* A role in *2001* offered international exposure to the former college football star.

If *2001* had been a Hollywood production, a star with the box office draw of Paul Newman or Steve McQueen would have played Dave Bowman. In today's market first look would go to Tom Cruise or Brad Pitt, but Kubrick wanted a verisimilitude that would have been shattered by star recognition. In thirty-year-old Keir Dullea he found the boyish appeal of an American astronaut. Dullea was handsome and generated the requisite qualities of bravery, strength, reason, intelligence, and calm with a disquieting James Dean–like undercurrent. His portrayals of emotionally disturbed youths in *The Hoodlum Priest* and *David and Lisa* revealed to Kubrick that he could communicate the emotional fervor engendered by the stresses of Bowman's fateful mission. With little or no dialogue, Dullea had to portray the metaphysical transformation that was the destiny of Dave Bowman.

At the time he was cast by Kubrick, Keir Dullea was working with Otto Preminger on *Bunny Lake Is Missing.* On a day off in New York, Dullea went to a fair near the Chelsea section where he encountered a palmist who read fortunes. As a lark Dullea went in. "This man looked at my palm for a while and he started questioning me," Dullea remembers. "He said, 'Are you an engineer?' I said, 'No.' 'Do you have anything to do with mechanics or science?' He used the word 'rocketship.' A day or two later I got a call from my agent saying that I had a firm offer to play the lead in Stanley Kubrick's next film, and I just about fell over because I was a real Kubrick fan."

Kubrick made his decision to cast Keir Dullea as astronaut Dave Bowman after screening the actor's work in *David and Lisa* and *The Thin Red Line,* a film based on James Jones's sequel to *From Here to Eternity.* Otto Preminger sent dailies from *Bunny Lake Is Missing,* which was still shooting, so Kubrick could see Dullea's most recent work.

Dullea had first heard about Stanley Kubrick in 1957 when he was studying acting in New York City. On a day off he wandered to a local Loew's movie theater and decided to see *Paths of Glory* because he saw Kirk Douglas's name on the marquee. "I remember absolutely being blown away by that film," Dullea recalls. "The opening looked like a monochromatic painting painted in mud."

When he was in junior high school Dullea went through an intensive period of reading a lot of science fiction. He subscribed to *Astounding Science Fiction* and *Galaxy* magazines. His mother would buy him the annual collections of the best science fiction stories in the early fifties. "When I read the screenplay I said, 'My God, there's something familiar about this!'" Dullea remembered. "It turned out I was recalling correctly that I had read a story by Arthur C. Clarke called 'The Sentinel' as a young teenager and it stuck in my mind. It was an outstanding enough story. I don't remember most of the science fiction stories I read at that time. I remembered 'The Sentinel.'"

Dullea was given a full script, which was quite lengthy and was much wordier than the finished film. The sequence where HAL reads Bowman's and Poole's lips as they discuss the computer's erratic behavior originally contained more dialogue.

Keir Dullea was cast sight unseen. He arrived on the *Queen Mary* at the very end of December 1965 and was given a rented cottage in Hampstead in North London. A car was dispatched to pick up Dullea and bring him to his cottage. He had been there no more than half an hour and was in the midst of unpacking when the phone rang. Dullea listened to a quiet American voice asking if he was Keir Dullea. When he replied yes, the man said, "Oh, hi, this is Stanley."

Arthur Clarke continued working on the script until Christmas and on December 26, 1965, gave Stanley Kubrick the completed draft. Kubrick phoned Clarke to tell him he didn't like the dialogue—he found the script too wordy. Kubrick wanted *2001* to be a film that relied on pictures and sound more than words. Ultimately there would only be 46 minutes of dialogue out of the 139-minute running time. Kubrick later said to the *New York Times*, "There are certain areas of feeling and reality that are notably inaccessible to words. Nonverbal forms of expression such as music and painting can get at these areas, but words are a terrible straitjacket. It's interesting how many prisoners of that straitjacket resent its being loosened." "I don't like to talk about *2001* much," Kubrick later told Jerome Agel, "because it's essentially a nonverbal experience. It attempts to communicate more to the subconscious and to the feelings than it does to the intellect. I think clearly that there's a basic problem with people who are not paying attention with their eyes. They're listening. And they don't get much from listening to this film. Those who won't believe their eyes won't be able to appreciate this film."

Dullea and Lockwood were given extensive research on the background of astronauts in the year 2001. Kubrick's astronauts were nurtured from grammar school and were developed in their intelligence and psychological profiles. Bowman and Poole had double doctorates and were stress-resistant so they could spend long periods of time in the solitude of space travel. "We had our histories, we knew who we were," Dullea explained. "We knew what our relationships were with each other. We knew the events at least subjectively, from the astronaut's point of view, from the character's point of view. There was a lot that was going on that we weren't supposed to know. We didn't understand why HAL went haywire and the hidden mission that wasn't going to be revealed to us until later."

In addition to Lockwood and Dullea, two other actors received star billing in the credits. The urbane William Sylvester was cast as Dr. Heywood Floyd, chairman of the U.S. Council of Astronauts, and Daniel Richter was given the unusual role of Moon-Watcher, the ape at the center of the Dawn of Man sequence.

To play the voice of HAL on the set, Kubrick originally hired the British actor Nigel Davenport, who had appeared in *Look Back in Anger, Peeping Tom,* and *A Man for All Seasons.* Davenport was to play the voice of HAL off camera so that Dullea and Lockwood could react to him. Later, Davenport was to go into the studio and re-record all of HAL's dialogue. Kubrick quickly learned that he didn't want HAL to have a British accent. Davenport was relieved of his duties and Kubrick decided to search for someone with a standard American speech pattern.

While he was looking for an actor to play the voice of HAL in post-production he gave the on-set position of reading HAL's lines to his assistant director, Derek Cracknell, who fed lines like "I'm afraid, Dave, my mind is going" in his proud Cockney accent.

Actor Martin Balsam, best known at the time for his roles as the jury foreman in *Twelve Angry Men* and as the ill-fated insurance detective in Alfred Hitchcock's *Psycho,* was also chosen to be the voice of the all-knowing, all-seeing computer HAL. Kubrick recorded Balsam's voice for the role, but found his vocal quality too American and overly emotional and so dropped Balsam from the cast.

At one point during the selection process for HAL's voice, Kubrick kidded, "Maybe it ought to sound like Jackie Mason."

Canadian actor Douglas Rain was initially hired to narrate the earliest version of the shooting script. Clarke had been asked by Kubrick to write narration for the Dawn of Man sequence that opened the film. Rain had narrated the commentary for *Universe.* The narration for *2001* was even-

Stanley Kubrick's father, Dr. Jacques
Leonard Kubrick, as he appeared in the
1927 yearbook, *The Fleur-O-Scope,* upon
graduation from New York Homeopathic
Medical College and Flower Hospital.
(COURTESY MEDICAL SCIENCES LIBRARY
OF NEW YORK MEDICAL COLLEGE)

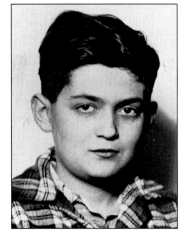

Young Stanley Kubrick
prior to entering
William Howard Taft High School.

2160 Clinton Avenue,
Bronx, New York,
circa 1971. Family
residence at the time
of Stanley Kubrick's
birth on July 26, 1928.
(COURTESY OF THE
BRONX COUNTY
HISTORICAL SOCIETY
COLLECTION, BRONX,
NEW YORK)

The newly built William Howard Taft High School, Bronx, New York, circa 1945. Kubrick's alma mater. (COURTESY WILLIAM HOWARD TAFT HIGH SCHOOL)

Kubrick's Taft art teacher, Herman Getter, circa 1946. (COURTESY WILLIAM HOWARD TAFT HIGH SCHOOL)

STAN KUBRICK - PHOTO
1414 SHAKESPEARE AVE., N.Y.C.

Taft High School cheerleaders of June 1945 as photographed by Stanley Kubrick. Back row, third from left is Eydie Gorme, also singer in the Swing Band. Back row, extreme right is Claire Abriss. Kubrick distributed photos to the squad with personal imprint on the back. (COURTESY CLAIRE ABRISS)

Stanley Kubrick's photographs of Taft English teacher Aaron Traister performing Shakespeare, as they appeared in *Look* magazine, April 2, 1946. (COURTESY DANIEL TRAISTER AND JANE TRAISTER NOBLE)

Stanley Kubrick's high school graduation picture, January 1946. (COURTESY TAFT HIGH SCHOOL)

Toba Metz's high school graduation picture, January 1948. (COURTESY TAFT HIGH SCHOOL)

Exterior of Park Plaza movie theater, circa 1951, where Kubrick photographed Bernard Cooperman for "A Short Short in a Movie Balcony," which appeared in *Look* magazine, April 16, 1946. (COURTESY OF THE BRONX COUNTY HISTORICAL SOCIETY COLLECTION, BRONX, NEW YORK)

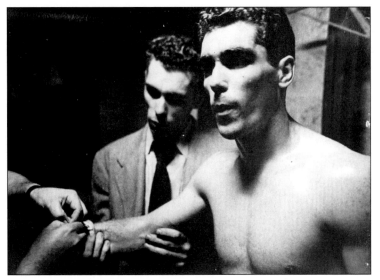

Photographs taken by Kubrick for "Prizefighter," which appeared in *Look* magazine, January 18, 1949. ABOVE: Twin brothers Vincent (*left*) and Walter Cartier as Walter prepares for a middleweight fight. (COURTESY VINCENT CARTIER)

Middleweight boxer Walter Cartier and manager Bobby Gleason before bout.

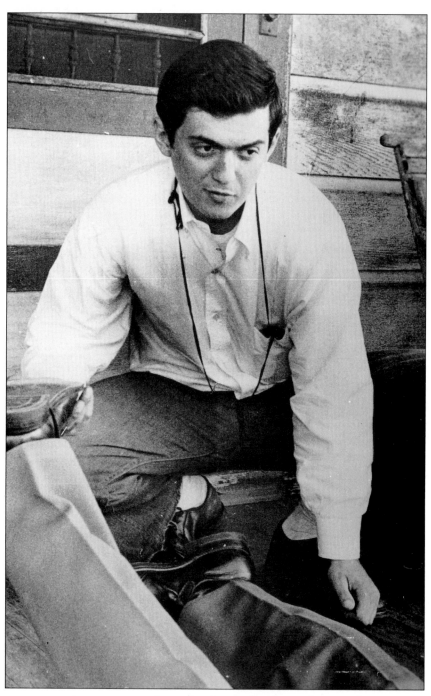

A twentysomething Stanley Kubrick on the set of
Fear and Desire. (PHOTOFEST)

Ruth Sobotka,
August 1963.
Photograph by
Roy Schatt.
(Courtesy
David Vaughan)

Snapshot of Ruth Sobotka and Stanley Kubrick at
Hollywood Airport during the production of *The Killing*.
(Courtesy David Vaughan)

Kubrick, on location for *Paths of Glory*, with Arriflex at his side. (PHOTOFEST)

A common sight on a Kubrick set: the director lines up a shot. (ARCHIVE PHOTOS)

Stanley Kubrick, Tony Curtis, and Laurence Olivier
on the set of *Spartacus*. (PHOTOFEST)

Kubrick listens to
Kirk Douglas at
gladiator school
during the
production
of *Spartacus*.
(ARCHIVE PHOTOS)

An enthusiastic Kubrick on set of the diabolical
Dr. Strangelove. (ARCHIVE PHOTOS)

An undistracted Kubrick on the set of *Dr. Strangelove* as
Tracy Reed flaunts her bikini while George C. Scott
looks on. (PHOTOFEST)

Kubrick looking through a lens darkly at Sterling Hayden
and Peter Sellers. (PHOTOFEST)

George C. Scott
sits in the director's
chair, playing white,
while Kubrick hovers
over the chessboard.
(PHOTOFEST)

A portrait in
contemplation—
Stanley Kubrick on set.
(PHOTOFEST)

Kubrick, Keir Dullea, Gary Lockwood, and crew inside the
30-ton centrifuge for *2001*. (PHOTOFEST)

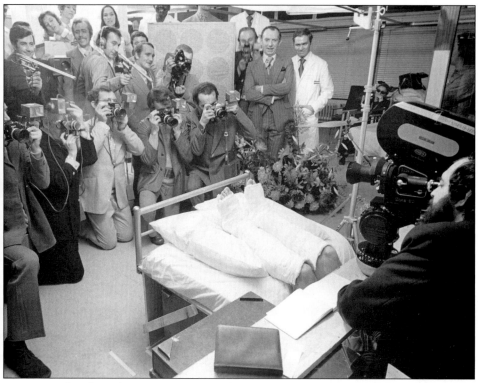

Kubrick at the eyepiece for a shot from Alex's POV of a photo op
in the last sequence of *A Clockwork Orange*. (PHOTOFEST)

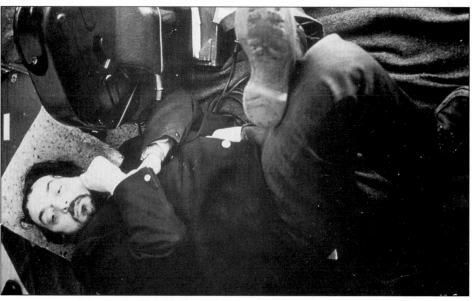

A favorite Kubrick uncompromising position—on the floor
of a film set. (ARCHIVE PHOTOS)

General Kubrick
and his troops on
Barry Lyndon.
(PHOTOFEST)

Kubrick filming a hand-held shot
on *The Shining*. (ARCHIVE PHOTOS)

Kubrick on *The Shining*—"The crown of his head almost bald, now
framed by a mane of wispy hair . . . his glasses, aviator-style, were
well crafted in high-quality ocular material . . . often held in his
hand as he peered through the lens looking for focus,
composition, and design." (ARCHIVE PHOTOS)

The late John Alcott and Kubrick on *The Shining*.
Alcott's work as a cinematographer on *A Clockwork Orange,
Barry Lyndon*, and *The Shining* illuminated Kubrick's
cinematic vision. (ARCHIVE PHOTOS)

Lining up a shot at the
Overlook Hotel's Gold Room
Ballroom bar for *The Shining*.
(ARCHIVE PHOTOS)

A relentless perfectionist,
Kubrick checks 35mm strips
of film for *The Shining*.
(PHOTOFEST)

"Stanley is very monastic. He's a great beard scratcher.
He thinks, he rubs his beard." (PHOTOFEST)

tually dropped and Rain was cast in the celebrated role of HAL's human voice. Rain, a Shakespearean-trained actor, found Kubrick courteous but withholding. In the nine and a half hours Rain spent in a studio recording the voice-over for HAL, Kubrick never showed the actor a screenplay or a single frame of the film. Reading from a script composed entirely of HAL's lines, Rain performed under Kubrick's critical ear. Kubrick was pleased with the patronizing, asexual quality he elicited from the actor. About Rain's off-screen performance Kubrick later joked, "Maybe next time I'll show Rain in the flesh, but it would be a nonspeaking part, which would perfectly complete the circle."

Kubrick's directorial demeanor was always calm and convivial with actors on the set. He never became angry or raised his voice. Still, his polite but persistent manner fatigued many of his cast members. He would call for take after take, as many as fifty, saying little more than, "That was good, let's try another." Like a chess master who never signals a break in the game, Kubrick rarely showed his excitement for a particularly good take and steadfastly called for another. During a halt in the shooting he would engage his actors in intense discussions about their characters. He encouraged them to perform every gesture and line in ways they had never done before. Each take was ground zero and it took an actor with confidence to press on.

Kubrick was monomaniacal in pursuing an accurate depiction of the universe in the year 2001. He asked leading aeronautical companies, government agencies, and a wide range of industries in both the United States and Europe to share their prognostications about the future. The long list of contributors began with the Aerospace Medical Division of Wright Patterson Air Force Base and moved through the alphabet to the Whirlpool Corporation.

The enormous range of subjects covered designs for vehicle-monitoring instrumentation, space suit designs, information on nuclear rocket propulsion, biological and medical instrumentation for the centrifuge and planetary probing, maps of the moon, data and photography of space food and preparation devices, telecommunications, computer design, monitoring devices for the hibernation sequences, interior designs of the space pods, spacecraft kitchen designs and menus for long space voyages, space station technology, astronaut training, maintenance and repair of space vehicles, and the Soviet and U.S. space programs.

Films, maps, models, and photographic materials streamed into the production offices. Many other companies and governmental agencies were consulted, often on similar aspects of the film, to satisfy Kubrick's gluttonous data bank. Associates were constantly attending meetings and collecting information destined for ultimate approval or disapproval by the central authority of Stanley Kubrick.

Extensive interviews with leading minds in the areas of space, science, and religion were conducted for a dual purpose. These experts were selected to answer specific questions to solve problems constantly developing in the story line. They also were part of a planned ten-minute black-and-white prologue that would open 2001. The talking heads mini documentary would present discussions with the interview subjects as they were queried on the probability of extraterrestrial life. The opening was conceived to establish a realistic prelude to the speculative visual film poem that would follow.

Roger Caras, Frederick Ordway, and others had made a trip to the Grumman Corporation in Bethpage, New York, to take a look at the legs of the lunar module they were building so the lunar craft in 2001 would be authentic.

Production designer Tony Masters supervised the construction of the sets while Harry Lange translated his conceptual drawings into models using the components from plastic kit models for the fine detailing.

Harry Lange designed the helmets to be worn by the astronauts in the film, and a London company was contracted to mold and produce them. The British Hawker Siddley Aircraft Company was hired to produce the pod interiors and the instrument panels.

At one point a private contractor was asked to mold a large block of Lucite. Kubrick was interested in experimenting with projecting images on the surface. The block was cast and received a lot of newspaper coverage about its being the largest casting of plastic ever attempted. The optics weren't up to Kubrick's standards, though, and he scrapped the idea.

Animating the spacecraft models was a meticulous challenge. In order to get the proper depth of field to create the illusion of large-scale spacecraft, the lens aperture had to be fully stopped down. To get movable parts of the miniatures to move smoothly, the motors driving the mechanisms were geared down so the motion created frame by frame was undetectable. Kubrick talked to Herb Lightman of *American Cinematographer* magazine about the painstaking operation. "It was like watching the hour hand of a clock. We shot most of these scenes using slow exposures of four seconds per frame, and if you were standing on the stage you would not see anything moving. Even the giant space station that rotated at a good rate on the screen seemed to be standing still during the actual photography of its scenes. For some shots, such as those in which doors opened and closed on the spaceships, a door would move only about four inches during the course of the scene, but it would take five hours to shoot that movement. You could never see unsteady movement, if there was unsteadiness, until you saw the scene on the screen—and even then the engineers could never be sure exactly where the unsteadiness had occurred. They could only guess by looking at the scene. This type of thing involved endless trial and error, but the final results are a tribute to MGM's great precision machine shop in England." The process employed animation, motion control, and a long list of painstakingly detailed steps. The unit producing the flying footage was dubbed "The Sausage Factory."

Kubrick's favorite room was the "Mission Control" of his production. Like NASA, this room was carefully monitored around the clock. This is where the progress of 2001 was charted in every detail imaginable. The walls were filled with flowcharts, diagrams, storyboards, and log sheets. A state-of-the-art organizational system was purchased from a European firm. It allowed Kubrick to rearrange scheduling, equipment, staff, the script, data, and shooting days to suit the growing artistic demands of the film. Punch cards and every filing system then available was used to track the twenty-four-hour-a-day production schedule.

Keeping track of each shot was a major effort. According to special effects supervisor Douglas Trumbull, the production used an offbeat language system to solve the problem. "With a half-dozen cameras shooting simultaneously, some on twenty-four-hour shifts, and different aspects of many sequences being executed at once, the problem of keeping apprised of each shot's progress was difficult at best. For the purpose of being able to discuss a shot without referring to a storyboard picture, each scene had a name as well as a number. For example, all scenes in the Jupiter sequence were named after football plays—'deep pass,' 'kick-off,' 'punt return,' etc. Each of these terms called to mind a certain scene, which related in some way to the name."

Kubrick explained the production's need for such a complex tracking system to Herb Lightman. "It was a novel thing for me to have such a complicated information-handling operation going, but it was absolutely essential for keeping track of the thousands of technical details involved. We figured that there would be 205 effects scenes in the picture and that each of these would require an average of ten major steps to complete. I define a 'major step' as one in which the scene is handled by another technician or department. We found that it was so complicated to keep track of all of these scenes and the separate steps involved in each that we wound up with a three-man sort of 'operation room' in which every wall was covered with swing-out charts including a shot history for each scene. Every separate element and step was recorded on this history—information as to shooting dates, exposure, mechanical processes, special requirements, and the technicians and departments involved. Figuring ten steps for two hundred scenes equals two thousand steps—but when you realize that most of these steps had to be done over eight or nine times to make sure they were perfect, the true total is more like sixteen thousand separate steps. It took an incredible number of diagrams, flow charts and other data to keep everything organized and to be able to retrieve information that somebody might need about something someone else had done seven months earlier. We had to be able to tell which stage each scene was at any given moment—and the system worked."

Kubrick told Jeremy Bernstein that chess sharpened his retentive memory and gift for organization. "With such a big staff, the problem is for people to figure out what they should come to see you about and what they should *not* come to see you about. You invariably find your time taken up with questions that aren't important and could have easily been disposed of without your opinion. To offset this, decisions are sometimes taken without your approval and that can wind up in frustrating dead ends."

The redundancy required to achieve the technical perfection Kubrick strived for caused him to come up with an original term to describe the process. "We coined a new phrase and began to call these 'redon'ts.' This refers to a redo in which you don't make the same mistake you made before."

Stanley Kubrick's intensity remained constant. As he watched and supervised every minute detail, he rarely blinked, his eyes trained like a laser. A heady thinker and a heavy smoker, Kubrick always had a cigarette in his hand.

Kubrick's personal office mirrored the pragmatic clutter of his New York apartment. An arsenal of tape recorders facilitated the mammoth shooting script process. Kubrick dictated the first draft of the film's sparse dialogue and other material into one of the machines. Secretaries transcribed the tapes, which produced draft after draft in screenplay form. The office warehoused an enormous record collection of every recorded modern musical composition available. As Kubrick cogitated he spent hours listening to musique concrète, electronic music, and Carl Orff, searching for inspiration and the key to the right musical direction for his space opera.

"Stan and I used *Carmina Burana* a lot for atmosphere during writing," Clarke told a friend. Kubrick had even tried to hire Carl Orff, the composer of the piece, which has since appeared in many films, including *The Omen,* but Orff told him he was too old to tackle such a major project.

Kubrick kept track of production details in a series of small black notebooks. He ordered a sample sheet of every type of notebook paper manufactured by a prominent paper company to find exactly the right paper for his note keeping.

On Jeremy Bernstein's visit to Boreham Wood to observe Kubrick at work on *2001,* the director sat behind his desk at command central signing letters and making countless phone calls while approving and rejecting choices of costumes, props, and spacecraft and slavishly examining endless production details. Bernstein witnessed Kubrick nixing a design proposal for the ID shoulder patches to be worn on the astronaut uniforms. Kubrick suggested to the art department representative that the next version follow the lettering used on the official NASA patch. Constantly moving from one detail to a slew of others, Kubrick quipped to Bernstein, "At this stage of the game, I feel like the counterman at Katz's Delicatessen on Houston Street at lunch hour. You've hardly finished saying, 'Half a pound of corned beef,' when he says, 'What else?' and before you can say, 'A sliced rye,' he's saying 'What else?' again."

Kubrick asked a large field of designers to submit their costume ideas on dress in the year 2001. Some reached back to the Edwardian era, others had futuristic ideas. Before settling on costume designer Hardy Amies, Kubrick talked to Jeremy Bernstein about the challenge presented by the costumes. "The problem is to find something that looks different and that might reflect new developments in fabrics but that isn't so far out as to be distracting. Certainly buttons will be gone. Even now, there are fabrics that stick shut by themselves."

In August, Clarke rejoined Kubrick at Boreham Wood studios as the production staff scrambled to prepare for the first day of shooting—a date the director hoped would materialize before the year was over. In addition to his writing chores, Clarke became the production's in-house science consultant and coordinated the mass of technical data that engulfed the office. Clarke stayed with his brother, Fred, and his wife, Sylvia, at 88 Nightingale Road in London.

Kubrick was revising the novel with Clarke and simultaneously preparing his shooting script, a necessary blueprint to exactingly plan the principal photography.

At the end of August Clarke decided that the novel should end with Bowman standing beside an alien ship. Kubrick was not satisfied with this conclusion, and the search went on.

A select cadre of designers and futurists spent all their hours working on a single project—the visualization of the marker left on earth by the extraterrestrials envisioned by Clarke in "The Sentinel." Sheaves of concept sketches were scrutinized, debated, and rejected by Kubrick, who always managed to spin a detail from an idea off into the next conceptualization.

Kubrick explored every geometric shape for the marker and demanded an intellectual rationale for every configuration. He was looking for a primal design that could communicate with the audience in a single image. A mysterious transparent cube was strongly considered. At one point it was a pyramid, a concept linked to the engineering marvels of Ancient Egypt. The bold simplicity of the pyramid transfigured into the magical complexity of the tetrahedron, a solid object consisting of a three-sided pyramid and a triangular base. Although the marker appeared to be solidly planted on the Earth's surface, Kubrick needed to know that the object could have been transported to Earth via space travel. A fifteen-foot-high model of a tetrahedron attracted Kubrick because its vast surface was ideal for a sun-powered device. A solar-powered tetrahedron had the right scientific and mythic qualities, but ultimately it received a directorial veto.

Kubrick's definitive choice was a singular, black, rectangular block known as a monolith. To Kubrick, the monolith contained the Jungian power of a primordial force. The visual impact of the solid black object with its perfectly smooth surface became 2001's stark poetic central image. The monolith confirmed Kubrick's belief that "the truth of a thing is in the feel of it, not in the think of it." Later Clarke said, "I like to think of the monolith as a sort of cosmic Swiss Army knife—it does whatever it wants to do."

In November Clarke paid a visit to the set that was being designed for the Earth orbit ship, Orion III. As he reviewed the set with Kubrick and the design staff, Clarke made a joke about the cockpit looking like a Chinese restaurant. The set didn't look the same again for Kubrick, who instantly called for revisions on the design, prompting Clarke to note, "Must keep away from the art department for a few days."

December was a frantic time to inaugurate the production process of 2001. The first day of shooting was scheduled for Wednesday, December 29, 1965. Kubrick chose to begin filming with the discovery of the monolith on the moon sequence. The art department put all its energies into building what the shooting schedule called the TMA-1 excavation site set on Stage H at London's Shepperton Studios, the second-largest stage in Europe. The set construction crew created a 60-by-120-by-60-foot pit for the excavation site of the monolith. The lunar terrain and background set would be constructed and photographed at a later date. The negative for the excavation-pit shot was given a sync mark and held in a film vault. In postproduction the two negatives were printed together to complete the illusion.

Kubrick was under a tremendous time constraint. Another production was scheduled at Stage H in the first week of 1966. This allowed Kubrick only one week to shoot the crucial confrontation between modern man and a communication marker from a higher intelligence. The set had to be completed for the December 29 shoot and taken down exactly a week later. A typically unrelenting Kubrick worked with the crew straight through the holidays.

On Wednesday, December 29, 1965, William Sylvester and the five other actors playing the exploration team began makeup at 7:30 A.M. for a 9:00 call. *2001: A Space Odyssey* began shooting.

Kubrick managed to shoot the entire TMA-1 sequence in less than the one-week deadline. The most difficult challenge facing Geoffrey Unsworth and his camera crew involved lighting the black slab to create the magical visual effect necessary to unlock its bold power. At one point during the shooting Arthur Clarke showed Kubrick a section of the monolith that had been smeared by handling. The monolith was made of wood. A special blend of black paint and pencil graphite had been applied to give it a unique luster. Kubrick began to come up with procedures to prevent the smearing from happening again. Prop personnel took great pains to see that the monolith remained sleek, smooth, and free of dirt, dust, and human fingerprints. When shooting was completed on the sequence, the prop department carefully wrapped the monolith in soft cotton wool and stored it until its next appearance. A miniature monolith was created for a scene in which it floated over Jupiter.

For a hand-held shot that followed Dr. Floyd and the team as they walked down a ramp into the excavation toward the monolith, Kubrick manned the camera himself. A dolly shot was not possible because the grated metal ramp would not allow wheels to roll over it smoothly and the invention of the Steadicam was still nowhere in sight. Kubrick hand-held the 65mm Mitchell by having grips and assistants help him to support the weight of the heavy camera.

The new year of 1966 arrived. On January 8 the production moved from the spacious Shepperton complex back to the smaller Boreham Wood studios in North London where the art department was putting the finishing touches on the interior set for the *Orion* spacecraft. Kubrick began filming the sequences that transport Dr. Floyd and his mission contingent to the space station.

As shooting progressed, long talks and even longer hours at the type-writer brought fatigue and a numbing tension headache to Clarke, who finished the revised first draft of the novel on January 17. Two days later Kubrick phoned proclaiming that the story was now firm. Clarke then began the arduous wrangle of getting Kubrick to okay the "final" version so the novel could be sent out to publishers.

For the sequence when Bowman forces his way back into the *Discovery* through the air lock after being shut out by HAL, Keir Dullea did the feat himself without a stuntman or a net. "I adored Stanley and would have done anything for him. I suspended the kind of caution I normally would show on film in terms of doing stunts." Several shots in the film required Dullea and Lockwood to be suspended by wires. For the blast through the air lock, Dullea was positioned on the top of the set on a wire that came through the crotch of his astronaut costume. The set was several stories high. When the door opened, Dullea was dropped from the top of the set and traveled down the wire to the bottom of the set without a net. The camera was put on a 180-degree angle to the vertical set to give the illusion that Bowman was flying into the camera. Dullea began the trip on a scaffold outside the set next to a technician with a pulley arrangement. The technician had a knotted rope. When he let the rope go through his gloved hands, Dullea flew to the bottom of the set. When the knot hit, the man jumped off the scaffold so Dullea bounced back and forth several times to create the impression that Bowman was being pushed back and forth by the intense pressure of the air lock.

Kubrick hand-held a camera for the shot following Dave Bowman when he got out of the air lock and walked through the ship and up the ladder to HAL's mainframe. Again assistants and grips supported the weight of the heavy camera so Kubrick was able to operate the hand-held equipment and get the shot.

The senior NASA administrator for the *Apollo* project, George Mueller, and astronaut chief Deke Slayton came to visit the *2001* set. Mueller looked around and dubbed Kubrick's space project "NASA East." "You must have been conned by a used-capsule salesman," the laconic Slayton joked to Kubrick.

Shooting on the *Discovery* sequences went on very slowly. Kubrick and Geoffrey Unsworth would take Polaroid after Polaroid of each camera setup, mounting them on a board to analyze the lighting, composition, and every photographic detail. Often it would take most of the day to set up before the actors were finally called to start making takes.

Although Kubrick kept the particulars of his film as covert as a CIA mission, he was a pragmatic businessman. On January 18, he greeted celebrated photographer Lord Snowdon, husband of Princess Margaret, who arrived at Boreham Wood to shoot a photo-essay on the director and *2001* for the immensely popular *Life* magazine. Kubrick was aware that the right publicity would stimulate excitement for the film.

Kubrick remained fascinated with new technology. "Somebody would come on the set with a new computerized toy or whatever and everything would stop," Keir Dullea recalled. "He had the curiosity of a kid in that sense."

Kubrick tried to hire the effects team from the 1966 British television series *The Thunderbirds,* but the producers, Sylvia and Gerry Anderson, caught on to him when he called asking to take Sylvia to lunch. Later, members of the *2001* production team were able to convince a couple of the effects people from *The Thunderbirds* to defect.

On April 19, 1966, Arthur Clarke returned to the studio. Kubrick worked the crew for long and hard hours. Production designer Tony Masters's wife, Heather, recalls rarely seeing her husband before ten o'clock at night. When Masters was home he spent a good deal of the time on the phone to Kubrick. This pattern continued for two years as the project wore on. Kubrick was patient but demanding when a sound recordist apologized for not having his work completed. Kubrick called a halt to the shooting until the man was finished and told him in a quiet but firm voice, "The next time I have a five-hour camera rehearsal, perhaps you might think of getting your sound problems solved in the same period of time." Some respected his demanding perfectionism, others broke down from the strain. One of the freelancers working on models of the lunar surface kept making revision after revision but never receiving Kubrick's approval. The young man was last seen being carted off the Boreham Wood grounds in tears. Kubrick kept a psychological edge over his team by creating a competitive atmosphere. At times he would give two separate crews the same objective so they would work hard to compete with each other. Harry Lange said of Kubrick, "You just get carried along by his incredible enthusiasm. He has a great capacity for making you believe in what he's doing. You learn a hell of a lot from him. A lot of people owe their entire careers to Stanley." "Stanley *inspires* people," art director John Hoesli said. "I can't really tell you how, but he has this knack of making people do that little bit more. Even the office boy!" The office boy Tony Frewin later became Kubrick's personal assistant and has been with the director since 1965. Brian Johnson, a member of the special effects team, noticed that Kubrick seemed to ignore a person if he or she talked about anything but the movie at hand. One day Johnson mentioned in passing that he was interested in aviation. Kubrick just ignored him and walked off. But Johnson found a pile of aviation magazines on his desk with a note from Kubrick, saying, "You might find these useful."

Kubrick had the reputation of being cool and unemotional toward many he worked with. At one point Tony Masters's son came down with a serious case of the croup and Kubrick ordered an inhaler flown in from the United States. The logical computerlike mind of Stanley Kubrick employed reason to solve every problem in front of him. His emotional life was more difficult to interpret. He worked hard, shoulder to shoulder with his crew, moving a piece of equipment when necessary and lying on the floor to get a low-angle shot. His emotions went into the synapses of his brain and were translated into visions. "Stanley's a genius," Roger Caras told Piers Bizony. "I've known maybe five or six in my life and I include Arthur [Clarke] in this—well, they have a monster inside of them that's eating them alive, and that's their frontal lobes. They must feed this thing constantly, and they can't tolerate boredom. That's what drives them on to yet greater depths of understanding, of digging. Stanley's basically secretive, a very private person. He's tolerant and unassuming. He doesn't lord it over others, but understanding something twenty minutes before anybody else in the room does, and having an incredible memory that probes to unbelievable depths when he is interested in something—that tends to make Stanley seem quiet and reserved unless you know him well. But he has a really wonderful sense of humor when he's relaxed with some—and, of course, he has this absolutely insatiable curiosity."

Kubrick asked his friend Bob Gaffney, who had done the second-unit work on *Lolita,* to do the same for *2001.* While Gaffney was on the set he witnessed Kubrick's skill with the motion picture camera. "He operated the camera very well," Gaffney recalls. "I was over in Turkey and Stanley had called and said, 'Would you drop by London on the way home? I want to talk to you.' So I went to London and he was doing *2001.* He had an idea for the end sequence but he wasn't explicit. He just took out a book and said, 'I want scenes in Monument Valley that are shot in very low light, flying over the monument and the terrain as low as you could go.' But he didn't say why.

"That afternoon we were out on the backlot. Arthur C. Clarke and I were standing there talking. They were shooting the bone going up in the air and the operator couldn't get it. It's a very difficult shot. They were shooting high speed. When you throw something up, you don't know how high it's going to go, because the guy was throwing the bone differently every time. They threw it to go end over end. So you'd follow it up and then follow it down. The operator missed it three or four times. Stanley got behind the camera and did it the first time, and that's the shot that's in the picture. Stanley operated the camera."

The scene of Moon-Watcher discovering the bone/weapon was the only one in 2001 that Kubrick directed on location, although he didn't have to travel far. A platform was set up in a field just a few yards from the studio. As Dan Richter in his Moon-Watcher ape suit smashed wart-hog skulls and bones, Kubrick positioned the camera from a low angle shooting up to the sky. Cars and buses passed as they continued to shoot. They were out of camera range, but an occasional plane flying by disturbed the prehistoric period of the scene and Kubrick had to wait as the twentieth century slowly passed by.

The ape's bone/tool weapon and the astronauts' computer held significance for Kubrick, who told William Kloman of the *New York Times*, "It's simply an observable fact that all of man's technology grew out of his discovery of the tool/weapon. There's no doubt that there is a deep emotional relationship between man and his machine-weapons, which are his children. The machine is beginning to assert itself in a very profound way, even attracting affection and obsession."

The shot of the bone flying in the air would be used as a transition to cut to a shot of a spacecraft in flight, which Arthur C. Clarke called, "The longest flash-forward in the history of movies—three million years."

Originally Kubrick wanted to shoot 2001 in the wide-screen format of 1:85. In one of their countless technical discussions, Bob Gaffney talked to Kubrick about other possibilities. "I said, 'You've got to make it visceral. If you are going to put people in space there's nothing bigger than 70mm wide screen to do that and Cinerama is even better because it would be curved,' and he agreed. He did it. It cost MGM some money, too." Gaffney had worked in the Cinerama format for several years. He was also quite an authority on 70mm production and had done several short films in Todd-AO.

"I spent hours on the phone with him," Gaffney recalls. "Not soliciting him. I planted the idea and then he'd quiz me for days. Stanley is a man with an open mind. Now, that makes life difficult for people, but he does not have a closed mind to *anything*. He will listen, evaluate it, and see whether it works for him. It's tough on people around him because it's like going to the vacuum cleaners. He sucks your brain. If you make a mistake he catches you. I used to get strange phone calls. 'Now if you would put a 750 one foot away from you and you put another 750 in the same spot would you have twice the amount of light?' He wanted to see if I knew the answer, he already knew the answer. Sometimes he didn't know the answer and if you just said something casually he'd say, 'What!' He once asked me, 'How can you tell the distance between here and there?' I said, 'It's triangulation. You've got a point here and a point there. You measure the angles of the triangle.' 'Well, how do you do that?' 'Well, you have to know the sine, the cosine, and the tangent.' He never studied that in school. 'Memo to Margaret, get me this book and that book.' Then he would just sit and read about it."

Gaffney photographed the terrain footage for the Star Gate sequence with the minimal information Kubrick gave to him about flying low and shooting it in low light.

When 2001 opened, many thought Kubrick had used solarization—the technique that still photographer Richard Avedon had used for his famous photographs of the Beatles in the glories of psychedelic color. But Bob Gaffney's aerial photography was not treated with solarization. Several years after the film came out, Gaffney saw a demonstration that was shown to Kubrick by the Film Effects of Hollywood company. The demo was a scene of an ocean wave rolling in. As the wave broke, the white water exploded in color. Kubrick was told that this effect was the result of mixing the records of the black-and-white separation masters used to make a color print. By printing the yellow record on the cyan master and printing the cyan on the magenta, the mixing of master and record produced spectacular color effects. Kubrick realized through careful experimentation and exacting tests that the color could be controlled to alter the American terrain to look like alien vistas.

The majority of the footage for the sequence was filmed over Page, Arizona. One or two scenes were shot over Monument Valley, where Gaffney almost met with disaster. "I almost got killed," Gaffney recalled. "The erosion there happens from high wind. I was in a Cessna 210 with the camera out under the wing to get away from the motor. We would go in the early morning and late at night. The first night we were there, our airstrip was the Texaco station across the street from the motel and there were goats and mules walking all over. I looked at the little wind sock there and it was deader than a doornail. We took off and just got above the top of the mesa and got hit by a hundred-mile-an-hour wind, which threw the plane. The pilot was screaming at me, 'I knew you were going to get me killed one of these days, you stupid son of a bitch!' I said, 'Push the stick down or I will!' I shoved the stick down and we made a dive to get back to where the air was calm. We leveled off and turned around to where we had just taken off. The sun was setting right in back of the runway with all the dust we just made taking off. There was no wind there. It was just hanging in the air and we could not see the dirt strip, we could not see anything. I said, 'You fly, I'll be the radar, two degrees left, right, let the prop down, chop the power down, *boom* I put him on the ground."

Kubrick had artistic dominance over *2001*, but he still had to answer to MGM, the film's principal benefactor and distributor. The company had been drifting into debt throughout the production. Kubrick decided the best way to appease the tremendous anxiety of the studio heads was to present a short demonstration reel of footage that had been photographed over the first month of production. The presentation included interior shots of the space station and the moon shuttle craft *Orion*. Most of the material was photographed without sound, so Kubrick added pieces of recorded music he had been listening to throughout preproduction. Kubrick scored scenes of the astronauts in weightlessness with Mendelssohn's *A Midsummer Night's Dream*. For the lunar material and tests of the film's spiritual climax—the experimental Star Gate sequence—Kubrick put Vaughan Williams's *Antarctica Suite* on the soundtrack. MGM was impressed with the presentation but nervously waited to see how these startling, realistic space images would come together and fare at the box office. Robert O'Brien, the president of MGM, and his top executive brass were impressed with what they saw and held their breath as they waited for the film to be completed. The relationship between classical music and futuristic images had begun to coalesce in Kubrick's vision.

A tireless Stanley Kubrick demanded a protracted shooting schedule with twelve-hour days. He arrived on the set at 8:15 each morning and worked until 8:30 in the evening for months on end.

The most challenging and impressive set of the film was the centrifuge, the hub of the spaceship *Discovery*, which carried the astronauts. A large studio stage resembling an airplane hangar was selected for the site. After approving the final design, based on plans from the United States and Russian space programs, Kubrick unequivocally demanded a technology beyond conventional film production design. He commissioned the Vickers Engineering Group to construct a working centrifuge in actual scale large enough for the astronauts to live in and function.

The six-month project cost the production $750,000. The centrifuge was thirty-eight feet in diameter and constructed of steel girders. It weighed thirty tons and was able to rotate at a maximum speed of three miles per hour. Viewed from the outside, it closely resembled an amusement park Ferris wheel. All 360 degrees of the eight-foot-wide interior were designed and decorated down to the most minute detail by the art department crew to depict a projection of spacecraft to come. This presented the challenge of securing the interior furnishings, which would be rotating in a constant circular movement. Up to two dozen separate film projectors were installed inside the centrifuge. Everything inside the centrifuge was physically bolted to the floor, including a computer console, an electronically operated medical dispensary, a shower, a sunroom, a recreation room complete with a Ping-Pong table and electronic piano, and five plastic-domed sleeping compartments for the *Discovery* members in hibernation. Cables and lights hung from every inch of the steel-girded structure. Kubrick quipped about the centrifuge to Jeremy Bernstein, "Maybe the company can get back some of its investment selling guided tours of the centrifuge. They might even feature a ride on it."

When the actors were inside the centrifuge a trapdoor closed, sealing them in. Kubrick ordered a fire department rescue team on call. There were fire drills to practice how to extract the actors from the centrifuge if there were to be a fire inside. "There was a lot of electricity and flammable set elements like wood and plastic," Roger Caras told Neil McAleer. "Had there been a fire inside that machine, it could have been a flash fire like the one in *Apollo 11* that killed the three astronauts. There were special bolts, strategically placed, which could be hit with sledgehammers and cause the actors to drop out. The actors were always on the bottom of the centrifuge, you see. The camera moved and the machine moved, but the actors were always at the bottom, only about four or five feet above the soundstage." A large air conditioning system helped to take out the hot air caused by the enormous wattage of lights and pumped in fresh air.

Kubrick told Herb Lightman how he employed the camera inside the centrifuge. "There were basically two types of camera setups used inside the centrifuge. In the first type, the camera was mounted stationary to the set, so that when the set rotated in a 360-degree arc, the camera went right along with it. However, in terms of visual orientation, the camera didn't 'know' it was moving. In other words, on the screen it appears that the camera is standing still, while the actor walks away from it, up the wall, around the top, and down the other side. In the second type of shot, the camera, mounted on a miniature dolly, stayed with the actor at the bottom while the whole set moved past him. This was not as simple as it sounds because due to the fact that the camera had to maintain some distance from the actor, it was necessary to position it about twenty feet up the wall—and have it stay in that position as the set rotated. This was accomplished by means of a steel cable from the outside which connected with the camera through a slot in the center of the floor and ran around the entire centrifuge. The shot was concealed by rubber mats that fell back into place as soon as the cable passed them."

At one stage during the shooting inside the centrifuge, as the camera was traveling around the walls of the set, something caused it to tear lose of its track and sent it crashing more than thirty feet down to the floor. The actors luckily were out of the way. The weight of the camera could have killed them. "During the shooting of 2001 Stanley was the only one on the set to wear his safety helmet at all times," Keir Dullea said to Newsweek.

In order to create the correct exposure and light balance on this unusual set, Kubrick and Geoffrey Unsworth took black-and-white Polaroid shots to check the intricate lighting scheme. During the course of production Unsworth shot more than ten thousand Polaroids, which saved time and gave him an instant look at the lighting.

The centrifuge set presented the kind of dangers more common to skyscraper construction workers than a movie crew. All production personnel were outfitted with steel helmets to protect them from flying debris caused by the rotating set. Unsworth's camera crew had to secure lighting equipment to the steel framework. The helmets came in handy when an occasional lamp exploded, scattering shards of glass, or when screwdrivers and other tools came flying down. In addition to the helmets, soft-soled tennis shoes were standard issue so that crew members could walk about the set quietly and easily. To reach various areas on the centrifuge, crew personnel climbed up the outer steel foundation or made their way to the top of the cylindrical workspace by holding on to pieces of bolted-down furniture until they reached their destination. Once they arrived, they would cling dearly for safety. Sixteen-millimeter projectors were mounted outside the centrifuge structure to allow Kubrick to create the front projection effects being developed by special effects supervisor Tom Howard. A closed-circuit television system was installed inside the centrifuge, which enabled Kubrick to direct the scenes from a staging area outside the set.

Early in the Discovery section of the film, astronaut Frank Poole jogs and shadowboxes around the perimeter of the ship. The austere simplicity of this scene dazzled viewers, who were immediately transported into the zero gravity of space. The centrifuge was necessary to create this mesmerizing sequence. In the dailies screening of the sequence, Kubrick ran a Chopin waltz, a choice he felt an intelligent man in 2001 would select. Kubrick's voice could be heard on the soundtrack rising over the

Chopin, talking Lockwood through the technically difficult sequence. "Gain a little on the camera, Gary! . . . Now a flurry of lefts and rights! . . . A little more vicious!" After screening the material, Kubrick remarked, "It's nice to get two minutes of usable film after two days of shooting."

During the filming Kubrick was positioned at an electronic console outside the centrifuge. Six microphones and a speaker system were installed inside and outside the set, which along with the closed-circuit television system allowed the director to observe on three monitors and communicate with his cast and crew. A large and clumsy videotape recorder was on hand so Kubrick could see a take after it was filmed.

Video-assist, a technique that allows a director to see a take immediately, is now a standard part of contemporary film production, but no such off-the-shelf technology existed in 1966. Kubrick's cutting-edge use of video in feature film production would come of age in the 1980s when Francis Coppola directed *One from the Heart* inside an electronically outfitted van parked on the set—a method he dubbed Electronic Cinema.

There were shots for which Kubrick did not have room to have a camera operator inside the centrifuge. On those shots, Dullea or Lockwood would first go and start the camera themselves and then return to their marks to play the scene while Kubrick watched outside the centrifuge on a television monitor. For other scenes the camera would be mounted on a dolly to follow the astronauts as they walked through the ship. In addition to the centrifuge, other pieces of sets were used for the other parts of the interior of the massive spacecraft. Several of these units also rotated and had two halves to create effects like the scene where a flight attendant walks up a wall and into a hatch in the ceiling.

For the shot where Poole is sitting in front of HAL eating dinner and Dave comes down a ladder on the other side of the craft and walks up to him, Gary Lockwood was actually strapped into his seat upside down. The food was secured to the table and to Lockwood's fork. Keir Dullea walked in place as the centrifuge was revolved toward him, giving the illusion that he was walking to Lockwood.

During the process of shooting, the script grew in length as improvisations contributed to a scene. "When we were filming a scene but we knew another scene was coming up in a week and a half in the schedule, we would go to Stanley's trailer on the set and he'd turn on the tape recorder. We would improvise using the lines and then we'd get a new script the next day," Keir Dullea recalled.

"There was a lot of free time for us, a lot of waiting. All films are hurry up and wait, but I never waited so long in between setups in my life. The longest waits for setups were in that film. So we had the time. He would have his secretary put whatever we would record on paper and we'd improvise on that the next day. So we improvised on an improvisation on top of an improvisation onto another improvisation until it just got honed down to the bare bones," Dullea said.

For the shot where Bowman and Poole walk around a hub that leads to a open hatchway connecting to another part of the ship, the camera was bolted to the foreground half of the cylinder of the centrifuge while the background cylinder rotated. Lockwood and Dullea walked into the shot and stepped over the section where the camera is, onto the other half of the cylinder, which was rotating. As soon as they walked onto the second section, it stopped rotating and the camera section began to rotate, giving the impression that the men are walking up the walls and into the hatch above them.

Shooting inside the centrifuge was slow. Changing the lighting patterns for a new camera setup required careful logistical planning as the crew climbed the curved sides of the set until they were able to reposition a light or hang a new lamp.

The astronauts wore Velcroed shoes, which allowed them to walk in the weightless state of the ship. When Kubrick saw the finished design of the shoes, he disapproved of the shape. Shooting was halted for the day while the shoes were redesigned.

Kubrick worked privately with the actors, taking individuals aside as he had in the past with Marie Windsor on *The Killing*. "He's a very quiet man and your dealings with him were intimate in that sense," Keir Dullea recalled. "He was very easy to work with. Good directors are wonderful con men. You can con an actor and make him think he's doing something because the actor thinks it's a great idea and actually it's something that the director's done. I think that's great and Kubrick certainly had that. The best directors I've worked with all have that facility. He had a quiet power. He was such a stickler for detail, but there was nothing tyrannical about him. He didn't create dramas on the set. He really is an extremely private person."

During the arduous production of the film, Stanley and Christiane Kubrick hosted a weekly series of elegant dinners for the cast, crew, and invited guests. The Kubricks entertained scientists, philosophers, and writers. "Stanley is a true Renaissance man," remembered Keir Dullea, who attended many of the lively parties, which were filled with stimulating talk. "I mean, he will have an art historian and absolutely match that art historian discussing the Renaissance or Cubism. I observed that he was able to do that in all kinds of different areas. He was always a man with insatiable curiosity. He would question you about a lot about things. He *knew* in depth about so many things having nothing to do with film-making."

Originally, Kubrick had planned 130 shooting days for the principal scenes of the movie (the special effects shots had a separate lengthy schedule), but the unexpectedly snail-paced work on the *Discovery* interiors added a week to the already prolonged calendar. The uncompromising Kubrick took the slow shooting pace in stride. When a new setup was called for, he used the time to his benefit. Crew members would wheel a blue trailer once used as Deborah Kerr's dressing room onto the stage floor. The trailer was a fully equipped portable office. As Jeremy Bernstein watched the difficulties involved in shooting inside the centrifuge, Kubrick turned to the writer and remarked, "I take advantage of every delay and breakdown to go off by myself and think. Something like playing chess when your opponent takes a long time over his next move."

Chess would make another appearance in a Kubrick film. Poole plays a game of computer chess with HAL and is defeated by the programmed chess master. Kubrick had asked Parker Brothers, the distributors of Monopoly, to design a computer game for HAL to play with Bowman and Poole. Parker designed the game and manufactured a board game version they were planning to market. The game did not get into *2001* and Parker never distributed it. Keir Dullea received a copy of the board game as a memento of his cinematic journey in space.

HAL, the on-board computer, was a major character in the *Discovery* scenes. Dullea and Lockwood peered into HAL's red, camera lens–like eye and carried on conversations as if he were a full-bodied, living being. As the camera rolled, HAL's responses at times came from the voice of Stanley Kubrick at his electronic outpost via the microphone and speaker hookup. The actors responded to HAL's lines, delivered in the director's irrepressible Bronx accent, which later would be rewritten and dubbed by Douglas Rain. Kubrick fed the actors the more mundane lines, like "Good morning, what do you want for breakfast?" The exchange produced an engaging and electrifying relationship between man and machine. This intimate psychological interaction renders HAL's death scene one of the most unusually poignant in contemporary film.

In the sequence where Bowman shuts down HAL, Keir Dullea was suspended by wires and in close-ups slowed down his body movements to heighten the impression that he was floating through the mainframe. Assistant director Derek Cracknell read HAL's lines in his accent, begging Dave to stop, and then did a Cockney rendition of "Daisy, Daisy" so Dullea could react while he shut HAL down. "It was a little like George shooting Lenny in *Of Mice and Men*," Dullea said of the poignant scene.

The room housing HAL's mainframe was called "The Brain Room" by the production. It was three stories high, constructed vertically but filmed from the side so that it appeared horizontal on the screen. Working on the set was dangerous. At one point during construction a worker fell from the top and seriously injured his back.

The days in the centrifuge and *Discovery* sets continued to drag on. The cast and crew put in ten- to twelve-hour days. British crews at the time were not used to working this kind of overtime. Kubrick's English crew remained motivated and willing to press on for this unique project. On occasion some of the crew did become exasperated at their director's insistence on perfection. Keir Dullea recalls overhearing one crew member complaining to another and concluding: "But you know what gets you, the bloody bastard's always right!"

For the sequences of Bowman and Poole floating in space, stuntmen were suspended by a harness on wires and equipped with a radio set to communicate with Kubrick and the crew, as well as oxygen bottles to help them deal with the height.

Scouting teams were sent to many parts of the world to find background locations for the Dawn of Man and Star Gate sequences, but Stanley Kubrick never left the confines of the studio. This was not because of time constraints. Kubrick was an authority on aviation, and in fact had a pilot's license, but he would no longer set foot inside of an airplane. He had put in 150 hours of flying time, mostly around Teterboro Airport in New Jersey. After practicing landings and takeoffs, flying solo to Albany, and taking his friends up for rides, he stopped getting into the cockpit.

The fact that Kubrick doesn't fly has typically been attributed to a fear of flying, and to his sense of logic and odds that it was a risk not worth taking, but he had flown from coast to coast and actually piloted himself. The fear that has kept him from flying for almost thirty years has its roots in one particular incident.

On a particular day when he was a pilot flying out of Teterboro Airport, he taxied out on the runway. As he was checking the switches, one got stuck in the middle. The plane bolted and took off with one side of the engine not firing. After a struggle Kubrick was able to land the plane, but the incident, which showed him how thin the line between life and death could be, ended his aviator's career.

What could be interpreted as an irrational fear of flying was a pragmatic issue to the ever-rational Kubrick. He constantly read aviation magazines and spent hours monitoring transmissions of the London airport air traffic control towers with his shortwave radio. The margin of flight error was too great for him. Kubrick made his decisions based on collected data and sound logic, and he could not risk his personal safety on such records—so he restricted his flights to the travel on celluloid in *2001*. He ordered his circumstances so he didn't have to fly, and he created his life in England so he could avoid risks.

As location scouting continued, Kubrick told Jeremy Bernstein about locations he was considering for the Dawn of Man segment. "We're looking for a cool desert where we can shoot some sequences during the late spring. We've got our eye on a location in Spain but it might be pretty hot to work in comfortably, and we might have trouble controlling the lighting. If we don't go to Spain, we'll have to build an entirely new set right here. More work for [production designer] Tony Masters and his artists."

Production designer Ernie Archer was put in charge of designing the landscapes that would match the photographic transparencies projected for the Dawn of Man settings.

In June, Clarke flew to Hollywood to calm the jittery MGM executives about the status of their sci-fi movie. Back at Boreham Wood, Clarke attempted to convince Kubrick that the novel's manuscript was ready for publication. Kubrick still was unwilling to declare the novel finalized. He wanted to continue tinkering with the novel, but the pressures of moviemaking precluded it. Clarke firmly stated that he was the writer and should have the clout to pronounce the novel complete. Clarke was frustrated that he had lost $15,000 in commissions while working on the lengthy revisions for *2001*. He was in debt and had to borrow money. Kubrick offered a compromise, predictably on his own terms. Within the next few weeks the director would make notes of changes on Clarke's final version.

On June 18, Clarke received a nine-page memo, composed of thirty-seven paragraphs, that blanketed the manuscript with calculated minutiae. Using bits of snatched time throughout the maddening days of production, Kubrick questioned even the smallest items. Some snippets from the memo included: "Can you use the word *veldt* in a drought-stricken area?" "Do leopards growl?" "I don't think the verb 'twittering' seems right. We must decide how these fellows talk."

Feeling confident that he now had the final corrections in hand, Clarke instructed his agent, Scott Meredith, to proceed with a publishing deal. Meredith obtained a commitment from Delacorte Press, and

Clarke signed the contract. The deal was for Dell to publish the book as a Delacorte hardcover and a Dell paperback. Meredith obtained a $65,000 advance from Helen Myer of Dell. The total deal, which represented $160,000, had been signed by Clarke on April 28, 1967, and was predicated on publishing the book before the film's release—but Kubrick wouldn't sign the contract. All of the delays had lowered the price. Clarke spent a month rewriting the novel to accommodate the changes outlined in Kubrick's memo. He would address the criticisms and rewrite the section, Kubrick would immediately praise the new version, then within a few days point out flaws, errors, and imperfections until the new prose crumbled into worthless fragments. Kubrick's penchant for perfection and recalcitrant tactics shattered Clarke's hopes for closure and Kubrick's signature on the contract's dotted line.

Clarke tried desperately to keep up with the rapidly accumulating revisions that Kubrick demanded after reading the new material written in response to the memo. Kubrick unremittingly refused to sign the contract to publish the book. Unfortunately, Delacorte had proceeded to copyedit Clarke's manuscript and set the book in type. Clarke and Meredith had the distasteful responsibility of informing Delacorte that the book couldn't be published without Kubrick's modifications. By mid 1967 Dell had spent $10,000 on the project, Clarke was now $50,000 in debt, and Kubrick would not sign the contract. Delacorte was forced to break up the set type and the printing plates as Clarke resigned himself to more revisions and the realization that the book would not be released until Kubrick had completed his film. At this point that date was unknown. Kubrick tried to reassure Clarke by saying, "Don't worry, everything will work out in the end."

At the beginning of the summer of 1967 David Vaughan, the choreographer of *Killer's Kiss* and friend of Ruth Sobotka, was working as an actor in the theater and preparing to spend the season in Seattle. Before he left, Sobotka, who had been divorced from Stanley Kubrick since 1961, told Vaughan she was not feeling well. "Not long after I got out to Seattle somebody called me and said that Ruth had died suddenly. I never really knew what it was that she died of. It was some strange infection that she had and the doctor was away on the weekend when she needed treatment—it was all terrible. She had a terribly high fever and they feared damage to the brain if she did survive. I felt that one thing she died of was of not wanting to live anymore. She didn't want to live to become like her mother. She had quit the ballet company and started to pursue a career as an actress. She was a physically strong person and incredibly attractive, but at the time she was having a really awful relationship with a terrible man. It was tragic and unnecessary."

After her marriage to Stanley Kubrick, Ruth Sobotka had other love affairs, which ended unhappily. She died on June 17, 1967, in New York. Sobotka was forty-two years old. Her obituary, which ran in *Variety* on June 21, 1967, stated that she "died of a cause not immediately determined." The obit went on to detail that she had designed costumes for both the ballet and the theater and after her divorce from Stanley Kubrick had concentrated on acting for Off-Broadway shows and television. She was survived by both of her parents.

In the autumn of 1967 Kubrick began to work on the fifteen-minute Dawn of Man segment, which opens *2001*. The scenes, which depicted Earth before man, presented apes to illustrate the beginning of man's conflicts over territory, food, and power. After studying stills and footage of Africa and other remote sites, Kubrick made the bold decision to shoot the sequence exclusively at Elstree Studios. He reasoned that unpredictable weather conditions would make it difficult to shoot in the isolated and distant locations that best represented the untouched beauty of the earth before man. Above all, Kubrick wanted control. Ultimately his decision not to fly and the obsession for control led to the sequence being shot on a sound stage in England.

First, teams of cinematographers and still photographers were dispatched to designated locations to shoot background landscape materials. The cameramen shot thousands of feet of film and transparencies based on Kubrick's explicit instructions. Production designer Ernie Archer and photographer Robert Watts went to South-West Africa to shoot large-format ten-by-eight Ektachrome high-definition transparencies of the sky and landscape terrains. On one of their trips they were driving on a narrow road in the Namibian desert and ran head on into a truck traveling in the opposite direction.

Second-unit background footage had become a standard method for Hollywood to bring exotic locations to their films. Stars would perform in front of a rear projection screen in the studio while the previously photographed scene was back-projected, creating the illusion that the actors were in an exterior locale.

Kubrick had always disliked the results of rear screen projection, or what Hollywood called the process shot, which produced a slightly out-of-focus, grainy image that rarely looked like a true exterior location. Alfred Hitchcock, another director with an obsession for control on the set, used the technique extensively. The plausibility of the exotic locations in films like *To Catch a Thief* and the color remake of *The Man Who Knew Too Much* were marred by an overuse of process shots.

Experiments in front screen projection had been conducted since the early forties. The technique had been used occasionally for a random shot but had not been used for a segment of this magnitude. Sherman Fairchild, who developed and built the first automatic camera for the U.S. Army Signal Corps, collaborated with Hollywood technician William Hansard to develop the Fairchild-Hansard technique of front projection. In the mid-sixties science fiction writer Murray Leinster had written about the process.

Special effects supervisor Tom Howard researched all the equipment and techniques available at the time for front screen projection and advised Kubrick to adopt the process. To maintain a believable image, Howard felt that the front screen method was essential to project the giant backgrounds and actual components of large sets that many sequences required. After a careful inventory of existing equipment, Howard and Kubrick designed and patented a vast array of new front screen projection apparatus.

The basic setup for front screen projection in the Dawn of Man segment shot at the MGM Elstree Studios involved a large reflective screen on which the background images photographed in Africa were projected. The screen was composed of millions of tiny glass beads from material devised for the 3M Company's development of reflective road signs. In front of the screen, the art department created the prehistoric environment to perfectly match the projected backgrounds. Shooting through a two-way mirror positioned on a forty-five-degree angle eliminated the shadows caused by the actors. The result produced an anthropologically correct rendering of prehistoric Earth in the controlled environment of the studio. Kubrick used a pair of binoculars to make sure the focus on the projection screen stayed crisp and sharp.

Ernie Archer created the foreground terrain areas in the studio, which he matched to the projected material shot in Africa and other areas. Settings were created on a rotating platform so that different scenery could be brought in front of the projection screen.

Front projection became the technique of choice for Kubrick throughout *2001*. One of the most spectacular uses of the technique was an exterior shot of a massive space station as Dr. Floyd's ship approaches. As the camera slowly tracks forward into the space station, we begin to see several control rooms that are manned by busy crews. To execute this illusion, Kubrick had a model built to scale, with blank sections reserved for the control rooms. After the control room scenes were filmed on full-sized sets, they were projected and rephotographed within the context of the full space station set. The completed illusion gave the impression that we were seeing the hub of a functional space station. The small human figures were a key ingredient that gave the already detailed model complete believability.

The apes were played by dancers and mimes in makeup designed by Stuart Freeborn. Actor Daniel Richter played Moon-Watcher, the leader of the tribe, who makes the fateful discovery of the bone weapon/tool. The sequence contained the last live action scenes to be filmed on *2001*.

Geoffrey Unsworth left the *2001* set at the end of June 1966 when Stanley Kubrick was readying the shoot of the Dawn of Man sequence, moving on to another assignment. Unsworth had been behind the camera on *2001* since Christmas 1965. His assistant John Alcott stayed behind to oversee the front projection system and was next in line to work with Kubrick on future projects.

The bold opening of *2001* was Kubrick's way of linking the past with the future. "Somebody said that man is the missing link between primitive apes and civilized human beings," he told Gene D. Phillips. "You might say that the idea is inherent in the story of *2001* too. We are semicivilized, capable of cooperation and affection but needing some sort of transfiguration into a higher form of life. Since the means to obliterate life on earth exists, it will take more than just careful planning and reasonable cooperation to avoid some eventual catastrophe. The problem exists as long as the potential exists, and the problem is essentially a moral and spiritual one."

The interior of the *Discovery* required many animated graphic images on screens and control panels throughout the ship. The red lens-like central computer eye of HAL was surrounded by graphic readouts of information that were constantly changing. Other monitors displayed ship functions, mission control, a birthday message from astronaut Poole's parents on earth, and a tabletop news pad that transmitted a videotaped BBC television segment on the flight. In the late seventies, special effects wizards at George Lucas's Industrial Light and Magic perfected the computer, digital, and video technology to program graphics at their fingertips. This was not yet available to Stanley Kubrick. All of the graphic images were designed by the art department using data furnished by futurists from the array of consulting companies and filmed by the camera crew with 16mm equipment. When the master scenes were shot on board the *Discovery* set in Super Panavision, the graphics were rear-projected using screens built into the set.

Kubrick had been calling Harry Lange a technical adviser to appease the film unions. Although he had no training as a film designer, Lange made an enormous contribution to the art direction of *2001*. Eventually the film industry began to accept Lange, and Kubrick was able to give him a production designer credit.

The Star Gate segment, which concludes the film, earned *2001* its reputation with the children of the Age of Aquarius as the penultimate sixties film. The plot required Bowman, now the sole survivor of the tragic Jupiter mission, to journey on a solo flight that would end in his spectacular rebirth. Kubrick wanted the visualization of the journey to be what the *2001* print ads proclaimed—The Ultimate Trip. The Star Gate unified vivid high-speed space travel with bursts of psychedelic colors. This conglomeration of cinematic chemistry was unprecedented in commercial filmmaking and only hinted at in experimental films.

Kubrick gave this heady assignment to Douglas Trumbull, who envisioned a magic image machine that would produce his filmic light show. After many months of experimentation, Trumbull invented the Slitscan machine. The device used a streak photography process in which the shutter of the camera was held open for a long period of time while images were being recorded directly on the celluloid surface rather than one frame at a time. The art department prepared a flow of abstract creations utilizing op art paintings, architectural drawings, printed circuits, and electron-microscope photographs of crystal and molecular structures that were processed through the Slitscan machine, forming a corridor of two infinite planes of illumination. This liquid-light tunnel charted the course for Bowman, who shook, squinted, and stared as the constantly changing colors lit his face with terror and wonder.

"I'd met the experimental filmmaker John Whitney, so I had some idea about his technique of making many exposures onto a single frame of film, automatically," Douglas Trumbull told *Sight and Sound* magazine. "John was working on a device for moving a slit across a film frame, and moving artwork behind the slit, to create patterns and textures and things. I never actually saw this thing, I just had a picture in my mind. But it occurred to me that if you could do that flat, you could do it three-dimensionally as well. After an experiment, I walked across the studio to Kubrick's office and said, 'I'm going to need to build a machine as big as a house, with tracks and motors, and big pieces of glass to scale this whole thing up.' He said, 'I think you're right. Do it, get it, whatever you need.' The pieces of artwork were on Kodalith transparencies about four or five feet tall by 10 or 12 feet long; hundreds of patterns from Op Art books, strange grids out of *Scientific American* magazine, electron microscope photographs blown up high-contrast and reversed; lots of things I drew. Very strange patterns, plus colored gels, mounted together on a huge light table. The camera was mounted on a track, moving in one direction, while the artwork was moving behind the slit in another. There's the sense of plunging into a space that has infinite depth. There was no name for this procedure, because it had never been done before. I called it Slitscan. I don't know what Whitney called it.

"When Keir Dullea has his helmet on you're seeing the reflections of off-screen 16mm films as well as all the lights and instrumentation and the HAL readouts inside the pod. In the sequence when he's being locked outside, and doesn't have his helmet on, some films are being projected onto his face. It makes no sense, but it looks great."

Trumbull also created the mountainous graphic material to project onto rear screens installed in many of the sets. Some of the sets had up to eight screens showing computer readouts and other mission information.

For the shots of Bowman inside the pod as he went through the Star Gate, Kubrick shot Keir Dullea reacting to the trip as the light show played on his face. There was no dialogue in the sequence, so Kubrick went back to the technique of playing music to get the actor in the proper mood, as he had done for Woody Strode and Kirk Douglas in *Spartacus*. Kubrick chose a movement from Vaughan Williams' *Antarctica Suite*. Keir Dullea described the music as having "the most beautiful but most haunting mysterioso quality to it," helping him to project what Bowman would have been thinking during the life-altering journey. "They had some lights shining on my face. In the control panel of the pod in addition to having multicolored buttons that lit up and that kept blinking on and off, there was a monitor that was supposed to be a computer screen where you could see a kind of digital representation. So that was playing on my face. I was just looking into the camera and I could see the studio. That's why he played this music—I had nothing to work with."

To create the intense pressure that was on Bowman and the pod as it moved through the Star Gate, Dullea put his body through an intense isometric exercise that made him shake violently.

To photograph the extreme close-ups of Bowman's eye as it goes through a series of color changes, Kubrick asked Dullea to sit for the shots as the camera filled the screen with his blinking eye. "That was a little scary," Dullea recalls, "because I didn't know if I was going to get blinded or not. They used an arc light and it was close to me. I mean nobody ever gets that close to an arc. There are things that I would never do for anybody else that I would do for Stanley." Later, during the arduous postproduction process, Kubrick would alter the color of Dullea's eye as part of the color-flashing journey of the Star Gate.

Dullea's makeup for the oldest depiction of Bowman as he metamorphosed took twelve hours to apply. To speed up the laborious process, Kubrick instructed the makeup team to cast a mold of Dullea's face. The bust-size model was then used to build the latex pieces so they could be readied for application.

In the original script, after Bowman traveled through the Star Gate he landed in a hotel room that was created by the extraterrestrials so he would feel comfortable. Bowman sees a telephone book next to a telephone on a desk. When he walks over to look at it, he sees that the printing is blurred and isn't real. Kubrick decided against this approach and had production designer Tony Masters come up with an elaborate futuristic take on the Victorian-style room.

Kubrick never talked to his actors about the meaning of the film. "Never! He *never* talked about the philosophy of the film to us," Keir Dullea stated. "I think that may have been intentional with Gary and me because the characters we were playing would have no concept of all of that because their experience was totally subjective, *totally subjective.* I knew it was going to be a special film because I was in a Stanley Kubrick film. I knew I wasn't just going to be in another science fiction film."

In December 1967 Kubrick turned his attention to the scoring of the film. He phoned Alex North, who had received an Academy Award nomination for his heroic orchestral score to *Spartacus.* North was living in the Chelsea Hotel, where Arthur Clarke had written the *2001* story. Kubrick told North that he was the film composer he most respected and that he wanted him to write the music for *2001.* Describing the nonnarrative structure, he told North that the film had about twenty-five minutes of dialogue and no sound effects. North saw this as a unique opportunity to compose a creative film score that would complement the film.

Kubrick indicated that North would not be able to see the completed film while he composed the score because the massive special effects work would not be complete until the end of postproduction. He requested that North compose a waltz to accompany scenes of the spacecraft in flight. Instead of screening material, he would have to compose and record a score for the film based primarily on lengthy conversations with Kubrick.

In early December, Alex North flew to London to discuss the music for *2001* with Stanley Kubrick. The director played the temporary music track he had been using during production and told North he wanted to retain some of the pieces in the finished film. North couldn't accept the idea of having his original score interpolated with the music of other composers. He felt that he could compose original music that captured the essence of what Kubrick wanted.

Alex North returned to London on December 24, 1967, to prepare for the recording of the score on January 1, 1968. Kubrick provided North with a luxury apartment on the Chelsea Embankment and furnished him with a record player, a tape recorder, and records. North worked day and night to meet the date, but the stress created muscle spasms that gave him severe back pain, and he was brought to the recording studio in an ambulance. In North's stead, the orchestra was conducted by Henry Brandt, while North stayed in the control room. Kubrick was in and out of the session to give North suggestions. The composer felt the opening he wrote to replace *Thus Spake Zarathustra* probably wouldn't satisfy Kubrick, but he tried to capture the dramatic nature of the piece.

North composed and recorded more than forty minutes of music in the two-week period. As he waited to see the balance of the film and to spot the music, he rewrote some of his score. Over the phone Kubrick perfunctorily suggested changes for a subsequent recording. North waited for eleven days to see more of the film in order to prepare for another recording session in early February, but instead Kubrick called and said he didn't need any more music and would use breathing sound effects for the remainder of the film. North found this strange but told Kubrick that he could do whatever was necessary back at the MGM Studios in Los Angeles. North hoped to be called at a later date to write more music for the film. He returned home and waited to hear from the director.

After principal photography was completed, the majority of 1967 was dedicated to the mammoth special effects work to be done on the film. In all, eighteen months were given to completing the 205 special effects shots in *2001*, almost half the number of shots in the entire film. Of the $10,500,000 total budget, $6,500,000 was absorbed by special effects work, an unparalleled sum for the time. Months of color experimentation in the film lab transformed second-unit footage of aerial views of the Hebrides in Scotland and Monument Valley in Arizona into the panorama of other worlds experienced by Bowman after he exits the Star Gate. To ensure a consistent photographic result, Kubrick insisted that the unexposed film be held in a vault so that each negative for a particular shot could be developed in the same chemical bath. This meant that Kubrick had to wait up to a year with Zen-like discipline to see if a composite shot had worked. More than 16,000 separate shots were involved to create the 205 special effects shots. The Star Child that appears at the close of *2001* was created by sculptor Liz Moore, and the sequence took eight hours to film.

For the arduous job of editing *2001* Kubrick promoted Ray Lovejoy, Anthony Harvey's assistant editor on *Dr. Strangelove.* Kubrick sensed that it was time for Harvey to move on to directing. During a rest-room stop one day Kubrick turned to Harvey and said, "You know, Tony, you've become quite impossible. You've become the Peter Sellers of the cutting room. You better get out and direct before you drive me mad." Later he gave Harvey a script and suggested that the editor consider directing it. Nothing came of that project, but Harvey was getting ready to move on.

After a much-deserved rest on a banana boat to the Caribbean, far from the rigors of editing *Dr. Strangelove,* Harvey returned two months later to New York to discuss Kubrick's new science fiction project. While in the city Harvey went to see the LeRoi Jones play *Dutchman* at the Cherry Lane Theater, which led to his optioning the piece and directing his first film.

As the labs worked overtime to develop the shots, the rigorous editing process of *2001* began. Chief film editor Ray Lovejoy and his crew continued to catalog and file the voluminous footage amassed during production. Kubrick presided over the editing room. Lovejoy and his team operated a series of flatbed editing tables as Kubrick selected each shot and determined exactly when it would begin and end, a method counter to the more typical Hollywood procedure in which the film editor completes a first cut during shooting before collaborating with the director. The pacing of the film was dictated by the lyricism of the images rather than the imposed dramatic tempo often used in commercial films. Several scenes that served as transitional devices were removed.

Kubrick had filmed scenes of family and social life on the moon base that were shown to Dr. Floyd during his visit. One of the scenes took place in a blue room that had a circular pool and an AstroTurf-like rug. As Dr. Floyd took his tour he saw a group of young girls, daughters of the base workers, painting on easels. Anya and Katharina Kubrick played two of the girls, emulating their mother, Christiane. The scene was eliminated during the editing process but six-year-old Vivian Kubrick played Dr. Floyd's daughter, making an appearance on a video phone. Vivian was the only Kubrick daughter to make the finished film.

Kubrick made numerous substantive excisions after a contractually bound screening for MGM executives in Culver City, California. The prologue of experts discussing the possible existence of extraterrestrials was cut from the work print. In an attempt to give even more power to the visuals, a voice-over narration that helped explain many of the film's scientific and philosophical principles was also removed. *2001: A Space Odyssey* was a new kind of nonnarrative feature film.

After listening to Alex North's recorded score, Kubrick decided to abandon it completely. Screening dailies with classical music throughout the production of the film influenced Kubrick to score *2001* with a series of previously existing recorded compositions, ranging from a nineteenth-century waltz to twentieth-century avant-garde atonal works. Johann Strauss's "Blue Danube" was chosen to express the poetic grace of space flight. By selecting *Thus Spake Zarathustra*, Kubrick echoed Friedrich Nietzsche's masterwork to enrich the philosophical tenor of the film. Richard Strauss's majestic, heroic theme resonates Nietzsche's tale of prophecy.

Kubrick brought the music of Khachaturian, Ligeti, and the Strausses to the ears of a new generation and redefined the concept of film scoring in the process. The use of preexisting music in *2001* influenced films as diverse as *Easy Rider*, *Apocalypse Now*, and *The Four Seasons*.

For all his hard work in completing a full score, including an original waltz, Alex North was never told by Stanley Kubrick that his score had been scrapped. After leaving London in February, North never heard from Kubrick again about his music for *2001*. The composer was reduced to learning the sad fact when he saw a screening of the completed film shortly before release. Friends say he was crushed by the event, although his public accounts of the experience express no bitterness.

After *2001* was released, Alex North told Irwin Bazelon for his book *Knowing the Score: Notes on Film Music* that another composer was originally hired to do the score on *2001*. The undisclosed composer took Gustav Mahler's Third Symphony, which Kubrick was planning to use in the film, and recorded a section of it. "Then Stanley called me in New York at the Chelsea Hotel and asked me to come over and write a new score," North told Bazelon. "And I did half the score. I was very, very frustrated by it all. I really knocked myself out. It was the greatest opportunity to write a score for a film where there are no sound effects, or hardly any sound effects.

"I wrote fifty minutes of music in three weeks. I was taken to the recording in an ambulance, because my whole body was tied up in knots from having to work day and night, but I'm glad I did it, because I have the score, and I did some very fresh things as far as I myself am concerned. In many cases, a director who used a 'temp' track and takes it out for preview gets so latched onto this temporary music that he can't adjust to a new score."

Unreleased for twenty-five years, Alex North's original score was given a new recording by film composer Jerry Goldsmith. In 1993 Varèse Sarabande released the world premiere recording conducted by Goldsmith and played by the National Philharmonic Orchestra in posthumous tribute to North.

Goldsmith was a longtime admirer of North's work and a detractor of the music that Kubrick used in *2001*. "I remember seeing Stanley Kubrick's *2001: A Space Odyssey* and cringing at what I consider to be an abominable misuse of music," Goldsmith told Tony Thomas. "I had heard the music Alex North had written for the film, and which had been dropped by Kubrick, and I thought what Kubrick used in its place was idiotic. I am aware of the success of the film but what North had written would have given the picture a far greater quality. The use of the 'Blue Danube' waltz was amusing for a moment but quickly became distracting because it is so familiar and unrelated to the visual. North's waltz would have provided a marvelous effect. He treated it in an original and provocative way. It is a mistake to force music into a film, and for me *2001* was ruined by Kubrick's choice of music. His selections had no relationship, and the pieces could not comment on the film because they were not a part of it. So I come back to my theory that a score is a fabric which must be tailored to the film."

In February 1968 Stanley Kubrick—chess and poker player and lifelong stock market speculator—took a gamble on his talent. Feeling confident that *2001* was going to do well at the box office, Kubrick purchased five hundred shares of MGM stock—an investment of $20,500.

In March 1968 Stanley Kubrick saw the first composite print of *2001*, four years after his Trader Vic's rendezvous with Arthur C. Clarke. Kubrick braced himself for industry and public reaction. Nothing could really have prepared him for the phenomenon of *2001: A Space Odyssey*.

In the spring, Kubrick finally granted Clarke permission to publish the novel simultaneously with the film's national release. Scott Meredith went back to Helen Myer at Dell, but she was not interested in publishing the novel after the July 1966 debacle. Scott Meredith sold the book to Sidney Kramer of New American Library for an amount in the neighborhood of $130,000.

MGM was very concerned about the future of the film. A preview of *2001* was arranged, and Meredith brought Kramer to see it. During the intermission Kramer didn't quite know what to make of the film, and by the end he asked Meredith what he should do. Meredith told Kramer the book and the movie would become classics. Kramer agreed to the sale, saying, "Okay, I'll buy it, purely on your recommendation, because I'll tell you the truth, I don't know what the hell this picture is all about!" The agreement was less than the original Dell deal, but more than the second Dell deal, which fell through when Kubrick refused to sign the contract.

The novel *2001: A Space Odyssey* was published in July 1968. Arthur Clarke dedicated the book "To Stanley." The book is not a novelization of the movie. The movie is not a direct adaptation of the novel. Kubrick used the novel-in-progress to generate the screenplay, but his images use Clarke's words in abstract and symbolic relationships. The film is primarily a visual experience; the novel fills in many details with its strong narrative structure. The novel functions as the film's reader's guide by deciphering its abstract and symbolic nature. For many it is the key to understanding the meaning of the monolith and Bowman's trip into the Star Gate. The film and the novel complement each other, and devotees repeatedly viewed the film with new information gleaned from the novel. Arthur C. Clarke was fond of saying, "I always used to tell people, 'Read the book, see the film, and repeat the dose as often as necessary.'" Since the novel of *2001* was first published in 1968, it has been through more than fifty printings and sold more than 4 million copies. Clarke and Kubrick continue to share the 60/40 deal.

On April 3, 1968, while America was exploding in a counterculture of rock music, psychedelic drugs, and Vietnam War protests, New Yorkers were the first of the general public to see Stanley Kubrick's long-awaited film, *2001: A Space Odyssey.*

On April 5, in New York City, Kubrick cut 17 minutes out of the original 156-minute version that had been screened for film critics. Kubrick had crossed the Atlantic on the *Queen Elizabeth,* where he had a specially converted editing-room suite on board. He continued to refine the cut of his film as the ship headed to the New York premiere. Even as they docked, he saw areas that needed to be tightened up a bit. During the press screening Kubrick walked up and down the aisle, watching the audience to determine their reactions and where the film might be dragging. He felt he hadn't had enough time to get the film to its proper length, and the audience reaction helped him to see where he should trim the current 156-minute version. "Stanley sat up all night doing the trimming in the basement of the MGM Building on Sixth Avenue," Roger Caras recalled. "It took thirty individual cuts to make up the seventeen minutes, and they came from several different scenes, including the Dawn of Man, *Orion III* spaceship to orbit, *Space Station V,* exercising in the centrifuge of *Discovery,* and Poole's space pod exiting from *Discovery.* There was a whole sequence in the space station that was cut. A village square inside the station, with shops and a playground with children running around—that came out. And Gary Lockwood's 'breathing' sequence outside the spaceship, before he was killed by HAL, was greatly shortened." A segment showing HAL powering down Poole's radio before the computer terminated him was deleted, as was a segment of Dave Bowman looking in the storage corridor for a spare antenna. Kubrick also added a one-second flashback of the monolith to the scene of Moon-Watcher discovering the bone tool/weapon to connect the power of the slab to the *Discovery.*

The film opened in Hollywood the day after the New York premiere. In press interviews Kubrick tried to make it clear that *2001* was no ordinary sci-fi flick. He told Henry T. Simon of *Newsweek,* "I don't regard *2001* simply as science fiction. Science fiction is a legitimate field, of course. But there has been bad execution of the visual effects and too much emphasis on monsters. *2001* is not fantasy, though a portion of it is speculative." Arthur Clarke told Simon, "There is nothing we wanted to do we couldn't do or wouldn't do. Stanley would say, 'If you can describe it, I can film it.' "

2001 premiered in Washington, D.C., in New York, and in Los Angeles in the first week of April 1968. The press got their first look at Kubrick's top-secret project.

Keir Dullea saw the completed *2001* at the film's world premiere in Washington, D.C., where he lodged at the infamous Watergate when it was still only a hotel. "I was blown away from the beginning with the Dawn of Man. I just couldn't believe it, it just took my breath away," he recalled. "I knew I was in a great film before I even saw myself, just based on the Dawn of Man sequence. It was the first of the big science fiction films."

As the reviews came in, it was apparent that most establishment critics were not prepared to deal with a new kind of American film. Writing for *The New Republic,* Stanley Kauffmann called *2001* "a film that is so dull, it even dulls our interest in the technical ingenuity for the sake of which Kubrick has allowed it to become dull. He is so infatuated with technology—of film and of the future—that it has numbed his formerly keen feeling for attention-span." In *Vogue* magazine, Arthur Schlesinger, Jr., said, "It is morally pretentious, intellectually obscure and inordinately long. The concluding statement is too private, too profound, or perhaps too shallow for immediate comprehension." Peter Davis Dibble in *Women's Wear Daily* sniped, "*2001* is not the worst film I've ever seen. It's simply the dullest." And Renata Adler, writing in the powerful *New York Times,* contended, "The movie is so completely absorbed in its own problems, its use of color and space, its fanatical devotion to science-fiction detail, that it is somewhere between hypnotic and immensely boring."

Pauline Kael took a nasty swipe at Kubrick and *2001,* writing, "It's fun to think about Kubrick really doing every dumb thing he wanted to do, building enormous science-fiction sets and equipment, never even bothering to figure out what he was going to do with them. In some ways it's the biggest amateur movie of them all, complete even to the amateur-movie obligatory scene—the director's little daughter (in curls) telling daddy what kind of present she wants. It's a monumentally unimaginative movie." Kubrick was particularly angered by Kael's review.

The reviews did not deter audiences. The under-thirty crowds patiently and reverently waited on lines around the Capitol Theater as if it were a church. With little advance sale, the film broke the opening-day record. *2001* had a spiritual and religious power to the children of McLuhan, who stared at the screen and remained staring as the curtain closed after witnessing Bowman's spectacular rebirth. At one screening a young man ran down the aisle during the Star Gate sequence and crashed through the screen screaming, "I see God!" The smell of burning marijuana permeated theaters packed with young people, their pupils dilated, their minds stimulated with the power of pure film. "I was present at an MGM meeting when a verbal report was presented by someone whose job it was to stand in the lobby and note what people were saying about the film," Kubrick told *Rolling Stone.* "When they asked him what types had seen the film, he told them, 'Mostly Negroes and people with beads.'" This greatly puzzled the sales department. Kubrick was pleased with the interest in his visual film experience. "If *2001* has stirred your emotions, your subconscious, your mythological leanings, then it has succeeded," he said.

As the press argued over the meaning of *2001* in print and on radio and television broadcasts, it was cheered by a burgeoning underground press. Baby boomers claimed *2001* as their own, certifying it a box office hit. Flabbergasted MGM executives who couldn't make heads or tails of the film began to see the light as they tallied the box office receipts.

Although the under-thirty audiences were hailing the film for the psychedelic nature of the Star Gate sequence, Kubrick's intent was not drug-related. "I have to say that it was never meant to represent an acid trip," Kubrick told *Rolling Stone*. "On the other hand a connection does exist. An acid trip is probably similar to the kind of mind-boggling experience that might occur at the moment of encountering extraterrestrial intelligence. I've been put off experimenting with LSD because I don't like what seems to happen to people who try it. They seem to develop what I can only describe as an illusion of understanding and oneness with the universe. This is a phenomenon which they can't articulate in any logical way, but which they express emotionally. They seem very happy, very content and very pleased with the state of mind, but at the same time they seem to be totally unaware of the fact that it deprives them of any kind of self-criticism which is, of course, absolutely essential for an artist to have. It's very dangerous to be zonked out by everything that you see and think of, and to believe all of your ideas are of cosmic proportions. I should think that if one had no interest in being an artist, this illusion of understanding would be delightful but for myself I think it is a pleasure which I'll forgo for as long as I'm interested in making films."

The release of *2001* became a sixties happening. At cocktail parties and sit-ins the air was filled with discussions as audiences struggled to comprehend the meaning of the monolith and the symbolic, abstract nature of the film. In newspapers throughout the country, heated arguments burned in letters columns. Many praised Kubrick's brave new film, others sent him their ticket stubs demanding a refund. One fourteen-year-old wrote Kubrick asking for guidance in becoming a filmmaker, another teenager asked for a letter of recommendation to join the cameraman's union, another described his own space epic and asked if the director could put off his next project to film a Star Child sequence using the young man's likeness.

Kubrick was repeatedly asked about the meaning of his film, which he had created primarily as a visual experience. "On the deepest psychological level, the film's plot symbolized the search for God, and it finally postulates what is little less than a scientific definition of God," he told *Rolling Stone*. "The film revolves around this metaphysical conception, and the realistic hardware and the documentary feelings about everything were necessary in order to undermine your built-in resistance to the poetical concept."

Alexei Leonov, the Russian cosmonaut who was the first man to walk in space, saw the film and commented, "Now I feel I've been in space twice." Neil Armstrong saw the movie before his historic walk on the moon and said, "It was a particularly fine production with exceptionally accurate portrayals of spaceflight conditions and visual effects." *Apollo 8* astronauts Frank Borman, James Lovell, and William Anders saw the film before their mission in December 1968, prompting Anders to joke, "I remember thinking at the time I saw the picture that it might be worth a chuckle to mention finding a monolith during our *Apollo* flight."

Harry Sternberg, Christiane Kubrick's painting teacher, who was a proud owner of an original Stanley Kubrick photographic portrait, went to see the film that the director had been so excited about when he visited with him. "The inventiveness of this man's thinking was absolutely fantastic. Powerful, powerful, and very convincing, a passionate, passionate film. He threw everything he had into making that film. After I saw *2001* I was very proud to have shaken hands with him."

As the film made its way into wider release, it baffled Saturday night suburban audiences. Novelist John Updike chronicled this culture clash as Rabbit Angstrom sat nonplussed among a confounded audience in *Rabbit Redux*.

World reaction was positive and embracing. Italian directors Franco Zeffirelli and Federico Fellini telegrammed their American colleague, applauding his accomplishment. Favorable reaction came also from France, Japan, and the Soviet Union. By communicating in image and sound and not language, *2001* was universal in its appeal.

Fellini and Kubrick began to correspond and share their admiration for each other's films. Later Fellini told Charlotte Chandler that Kubrick was "capable of making me believe what I see, no matter how fantastic it is. . . . Kubrick, I think, is a great director who is a visionary and very honest. What I admire especially in Kubrick is his ability to make pictures in any time." Fellini the maestro of dreams found the death of HAL to be sad. In the 1992 *Sight and Sound* magazine International Director's Poll, Fellini listed *2001* as one of his top ten favorite films.

Fellow Italian film director Michelangelo Antonioni told Charles Thomas Samuels, "So you see I'm an admirer of technology. From an outsider's view the insides of a computer are marvelous—not just its functioning but the way it is made, which is beautiful in itself. If we pull a man apart, he is revolting; do the same thing to a computer and it remains beautiful. In *2001*, you know, the best things in the film are the machines, which are more splendid than the idiotic humans."

Director John Boorman said, "As the western declined in the sixties, the mythic stories passed on to the spy film, and when that strain was exhausted the mantle was picked up by science fiction, notably by Stanley Kubrick with *2001*. Myth in all its mysterious, irrational glory was back on the screen."

IBM, the company that personified computers, was not happy with a film that featured a computer that murdered people. Kubrick had removed prominent IBM logos from pieces of equipment on the set, but some still remained on the instrument panels of the *Discovery*. Management frowned upon mention of the film and counseled their employees against seeing *2001*.

2001 was largely ignored by the Academy of Motion Picture Arts and Sciences, which did not nominate it for best picture. It was nominated for best director, original screenplay by Kubrick and Arthur C. Clarke, art direction by Tony Masters, Harry Lange, and Ernie Archer, and special visual effects, but the film's only Oscar was awarded for special visual effects. Kubrick had submitted only his name to the Academy for the special visual effects category. He won the award personally. The names of the special effects team headed by Wally Veevers, Tom Howard, Douglas Trumbull, and Con Pederson were not part of the award.

Arthur Clarke was at the ceremonies and watched as Mel Brooks accepted the Oscar for best screenplay for *The Producers.* "I tore up one of the best speeches of thanks never delivered. When I ran into Mel Brooks years later, I snarled: 'Mel—you stole my Oscar.' " Brooks replied, "You're a genius," which soothed Clarke's legendary ego. Clarke was especially angered that the Academy gave an honorary statue to *Planet of the Apes* for outstanding makeup achievement, chiding, "*2001* did not win the Academy Award for makeup because the judges may not have realized the apes were actors."

2001 was shown at the 1969 Moscow Film Festival. Motion Picture Association of America president, the ever-articulate Jack Valenti, managed to get permission for MGM head Edgar Bronfman to fly to Russia with his own plane providing that Bronfman stop in Copenhagen. From there, two Soviet pilots would fly the plane to Moscow. When he arrived, Bronfman boasted that it wasn't Valenti who got the permission but Bronfman himself, who sent a cable to Kosygin. "I'll be watching," Stanley Kubrick reported to Joyce Haber in the *Los Angeles Times.* "Bronfman had better not charge that flight to the movie's budget."

On July 20, 1969, Keir Dullea was working on a film being shot in the Bahamas when he got a call from his agent telling him that CBS News wanted him for a human-interest story in their coverage of the first moon walk. The spacecraft had landed, and it would be another six hours before Neil Armstrong took his historic steps. CBS sent a Lear jet and flew Dullea to their New York studio where Harry Reasoner was waiting. The network also brought in Buster Crabbe, who had played Flash Gordon in the motion picture serial. The idea was to talk to one of the first and one of the most recent actors to portray an astronaut about the first man to walk on the moon. Mission Control had a change of plans, cut four hours off the wait, and gave Neil Armstrong the go-ahead to make his walk. "I had barely done the interview and suddenly word came, 'Hey, he's coming out,'" Keir Dullea recalls. "So I went right into the CBS News control room. I didn't know he was there, but sitting next to me was Arthur C. Clarke, and we both together watched the first man walk on the moon. I remember looking over and he had tears in his eyes."

Kubrick's collaboration with Arthur C. Clarke had produced one of his most important films. Clarke had a tremendous impact on the project. "Arthur's ability to impart poignancy to a dying ocean or an intelligent vapor is unique," Kubrick said. "He has the kind of mind of which the world can never have enough, an array of imagination, intelligence, knowledge, and a quirkish curiosity that often uncovers more than the first three qualities." Roger Caras commented on the collaboration of Clarke and Kubrick, telling Piers Bizony, "Arthur has a tremendous ego, and quite rightly, because of his many accomplishments. In fact that was one of his nicknames some while back, I believe: 'Ego.' But he loves taking pride in what he's done, and I think that's a wonderful thing. Now, I've never seen Arthur take a back seat to anybody in his entire life, except for Stanley. . . . But I believe Stanley was also very impressed by Arthur. When those two were together, bouncing ideas off each other, it was like watching two intellectual duelists."

In the first thirty days of release, box office growth was slow. Advance bookings were minimal. Richard McKenna had been hired to design a series of space illustrations, and one of the space station was used for the ad campaign. MGM had marketed the film as a big family entertainment film, and that was not 2001's main audience. There was a lot of corporate pressure on Robert O'Brien to pull 2001 from its Cinerama showcases in favor of another MGM movie, Ice Station Zebra. By the end of 1969 MGM was $80 million in debt. In 1970 the home of Leo the Lion was taken over by Las Vegas corporate raider Kirk Kerkorian.

2001 ultimately became one of the five most successful MGM films, joining Gone With the Wind, The Wizard of Oz, Dr. Zhivago, and Lawrence of Arabia. In its original run some theaters screened the film continually for two years. 2001 became one of MGM's crowning achievements. By 1972, 2001 had still been in release since its opening in 1968. MGM formed a repertory package called "The Fabulous Three," teaming the film with Dr. Zhivago and Gone With the Wind.

In the seventies, 2001: A Space Odyssey was re-released five times, including a successful run at New York's premier motion picture theater, the Ziegfeld. Kubrick asked Bob Gaffney, who had photographed the graphically altered aerial material for the Star Gate sequence, to be the director's representative, talking with the press and making sure the technical standards of the presentation met with Kubrick's approval. By 1973, domestic rentals totaled $20,347,000, and the foreign box office had reached $7,500,000 by July 1974. The American gross of the film had surpassed $25,000,000. Worldwide, *2001* has made up to $40,000,000.

In April of 1973, the Sherwood Oaks Experimental College ran a course studying the films of Stanley Kubrick. California resident, physician, and father of the director Jack L. Kubrick audited the class. In the family tradition, no doubt, the senior Kubrick kept his son apprised of any information concerning his work.

2001 influenced a generation of filmmakers. James Cameron, director of *Aliens, The Abyss,* and *Terminator 2: Judgment Day* told screenwriting Zen master Syd Field about the film's profound effect on him at age fifteen. "As soon as I saw that, I knew I wanted to be a filmmaker. It hit me on a lot of different levels. I just couldn't figure out how he did all that stuff, and I just had to learn." Kubrick's editor on *2001*, Ray Lovejoy, later worked with Cameron on *Aliens* and said, "*2001* is the reason Jim went into film. I've met a lot of American technicians who've said exactly that—that the film inspired them to follow the careers they did in the film industry." Dan Bronson, an executive story editor at Paramount, said, "I discovered that there is another kind of language—a language every bit as exciting as the words that F. Scott Fitzgerald put together. I made this discovery while I was watching Kubrick's *2001*, in particular a scene I'm sure you must remember. The apes touch the monolith and they begin to evolve, they begin to learn to use primitive tools. There's one magnificent scene, after the ape has ironically taken his first step toward civilization and learned to kill with a tool. He picks up that thigh bone and he crashes it down, again and again, on that pile of bone, and they shatter and fragment and fly all around. And finally, in a sense of elation and triumph, he throws it up end over end and, cut to, as the bone comes down, a nuclear satellite circling the Earth. My God, hundreds of thousands of years of evolution in a split second on a screen. That's when I thought, 'Yes I want to know about that, too.' " When asked about the film, John Lennon replied, "*2001*, I see it every week."

2001 has been revered, quoted, and parodied since its initial release. In *Minnie and Moskowitz* John Cassavetes had his title characters cruise down Hollywood Boulevard in a truck to the strains of the "Blue Danube" waltz. In a 1969 piece on director Don Siegel, painter and film critic Manny Farber saw the opening sequence of Siegel's *Coogan's Bluff*, starring Clint Eastwood, as a "slambang parody of Kubrick's *2001* start: space-devouring images, a sheriff's jeep whipping across the desert floor, and a ravaged-faced Indian hopping around in the hills, setting up his arsenal to destroy the world as the jeep approaches." Also in 1969 David Bowie, stimulated by a visit to the cinema to see *2001*, wrote and performed *Space Oddity*, a song about an astronaut who drifted into space. Commercials, ad campaigns, and music videos have utilized the music and the monolith in endless popular culture tributes to the film.

  2001 was a groundbreaking, influential film, but it did owe a debt to the experimental films of Jordan Belson and the Whitney brothers. In 1970 Gene Youngblood, in his book *Expanded Cinema* and in the pages of *Film Culture* magazine, pointed out that Jordan Belson's film *Allures* was "strongly reminiscent of Kubrick's *2001*—except that it was made seven years earlier." In talking about Belson's film *Re-Entry*, Youngblood said, "This becomes a dizzying geometrical corridor of eerie lights almost exactly like the slit-scan Star Gate Corridor of Kubrick's space odyssey—except that *Re-Entry* was made four years early." Youngblood went on to say, "If one were to isolate a single quality that distinguishes Belson's films from other 'space' movies, it would be that his work is always helio-centric, whereas most others, even *2001*, are geocentric."

  In the final decade of the twentieth century, the legacy of *2001: A Space Odyssey* endures. Ray Bradbury illuminates our immutable fasci-nation: "Why do we go back to see *2001* over and over and over? Surely not for its one-track acting and baffling finale. We return to it because the very possibility of its interpretations frees us to carom off into the greatest of all architecture: the universe itself."

  Spawning a new era in the genre of science fiction, *2001* is the proto-type for the special effects technology of *Star Wars*, *Close Encounters of the Third Kind*, *Blade Runner*, and *Terminator 2*. Kubrick's visual story-telling structure expanded the American film lexicon. His epic fable in-variably emerges on international ten best lists along with ageless classics *Citizen Kane*, *Rules of the Game*, *Modern Times*, and *The Seven Samu-rai*.

  Kubrick continued to identify and be compared with America's origi-nal enfant terrible, Orson Welles. One night Bob Gaffney stopped at Kubrick's office on his way to a recording session for a television com-mercial with Orson Welles. Kubrick knew Gaffney was going to see Welles, and he wanted to send the masterful director a message. "Stan-ley was furiously digging through his files and he brought down a review of *Citizen Kane* by Bosley Crowther where he panned the film," Gaffney remembers. "Stanley said, 'Show this to Orson.' Each generation has its own visual language," Gaffney explained about his link to two men who made indelible marks on the history of film.

The making of *2001* had a lasting impact on Stanley Kubrick. England was now his home. The country afforded Kubrick the autonomy he had been striving for since the beginning of his career. He settled with his family on a rambling estate in Hertfordshire in the English countryside. This refuge was situated on the outskirts of London near a rest home for horses and within driving distance of many major production facilities with access to the finest film craftspeople and services. The Kubricks moved their belongings from New York in ninety numbered dark-green summer camp trunks, "the only sensible way of moving," Kubrick remarked to Jeremy Bernstein. The house had many rooms, including a billiard room with a big snooker table. Christiane Kubrick created a painting studio out of one of the rooms. One room became Kubrick's office, filled with his ever-present cameras, tape recorders, and black notebooks. Two suits of armor stood in one of the lower halls.

Kubrick began to create an all-encompassing world for himself much as Hugh Hefner did in his Chicago Playboy Mansion. Hefner was a hedonist—Kubrick was a control freak fixated on producing movies under conditions he dictated. He created an environment where everything served that singular purpose.

Isolation from the international film community and his roots in the United States began to affect Kubrick's already strident self-discipline. He became more and more protective of his personal safety. His refusal to fly continued. Reports stated that his driver was instructed to operate the car at no faster speed than 35 mph. His highly logical mind and an existential cognizance of death that permeated many of his films pushed him into a deeper introversion. Kubrick established a modus operandi in which the cinematic worlds he discovered would be mounted on the bare stage of a sound studio. He never had to leave his base of operations. Second units could travel to desired locations, but the communications era still in its infancy would allow him to correspond with anyone in the world from his own home, on his own terms.

With *2001* a distinctly new pattern of cultivating screen material emerged for Kubrick. He departed from conventional narrative storytelling devices and production methods. He would explore all vistas before committing to his next project. In order to produce a film he would have to reach an intense obsessional state that drove him to make a film no matter how long it took.

2001: A Space Odyssey positioned Stanley Kubrick as a pure artist ranked among the masters of cinema. The quantum leap was complete. Arthur Clarke returned to Ceylon, the crew went on to their next projects. Stanley Kubrick sat in his office pondering his next project, waiting for an idea to reach the obsessional level. This time he was in not the cacophony of New York City but the solitude of bucolic England. A small staff began to research areas of interest for another project. The industry press and the public tried, to no avail, to learn what direction Kubrick was headed in. His office maintained the secrecy of a major intelligence agency but on September 23, 1968, an item in *L'Express* gave a portent of things to come: "This week, several hundred books on Napoleon were shipped from Paris to the London office of Stanley Kubrick."

Stanley Kubrick just couldn't stop thinking about Napoleon Bonaparte.

CHAPTER 14

"He Is Napoleon Really, Isn't He?"

It would have been the epic to end all epics.
—Bob Gaffney

I found him a likeable man. He's also very distant. There was always going to be this Napoleon film. I always thought he would have played the part very well himself.
—Jonathan Cecil

When *2001* opened, Kubrick, Christiane, and their three daughters were living in a Gatsby-like mansion out on Long Island, New York. Bob Gaffney got an unexpected phone call from Kubrick requesting to see him. Gaffney loaded up his family, drove out to Long Island, and sat down with Kubrick. "Stanley said, 'I'm going to start a project and my next project is on the life of Napoleon,'" Gaffney recalls. "I want you to come to England with me," Kubrick continued. "People don't understand the problems of what a director has to go through. You're the only person I can think of who understands what's going on." "Okay, I'll do it," Gaffney told Kubrick. Bob Gaffney had just begun a thriving business, but for Stanley Kubrick he shut it down and moved his family to England.

Napoleon Bonaparte was born in 1769 on the island of Corsica. As a boy he attended the royal military school in France and quickly rose through the ranks. By twenty-six he was second in command in the Army of the Interior. On March 9, 1796, he married Josephine de Beauharnais and continued to lead his army to victories in Italy and Egypt. He ruled France as a dictator and fought wars in Austria. In 1802 he was given the title of First Consul for life but continued to quest power until he was voted Emperor by the French Senate in May 1804. He dominated Europe in a series of epic battles until he overreached his power by trying to conquer Russia, where he was defeated. Napoleon was exiled to the island of Elba. After escaping he tried to regain his power and lost to British and allied troops at the battle of Waterloo. He died of cancer on May 5, 1821, again in exile.

"He fascinates me. His life has been described as an epic poem of action," Kubrick said of Napoleon to Joseph Gelmis for his book, *The Film Director as Superstar*. "His sex life was worthy of Arthur Schnitzler. He was one of those rare men who move history and mold the destiny of their own times and of generations to come—in a very concrete sense, our own world is the result of Napoleon, just as the political and geographic map of postwar Europe is the result of World War II. And, of course, there has never been a good or accurate movie about him. Also, I find that all the issues with which it concerns itself are oddly contemporary—the responsibilities and abuses of power, the dynamics of social revolution, the relationship of the individual to the state, war, militarism, etc., so this will not be just a dusty historic pageant but a film about the basic questions of our own times, as well as Napoleon's. But even apart from those aspects of the story, the sheer drama and force of Napoleon's life is a fantastic subject for a film biography. Forgetting everything else and just taking Napoleon's romantic involvement with Josephine, for example, here you have one of the great obsessional passions of all time."

Napoleon was an ideal subject for Kubrick: it embraced the director's passion for control, power, obsession, strategy and the military. Napoleon's psychological intensity and depth, his logistical genius and craving for power could be dissected in explicit detail. Kubrick lusted after the big subject; war, sex, the meaning of existence, and the evil nature of man—here it was rolled up in one man.

Kubrick's research on Napoleon Bonaparte was extensive. He had read several hundred books on the subject, including nineteenth-century English and French accounts and modern biographies. "I've ransacked all these books for research material and broken it down into categories on everything from his food tastes to the weather on the day of a specific battle, and cross-indexed all the data in a comprehensive research file," Kubrick told Joseph Gelmis.

"I've tried to see every film that was ever made on the subject, and I've got to say that I don't find any of them particularly impressive. I recently saw Abel Gance's movie, which has built up a reputation among film buffs over the years, and I found it really terrible. Technically he was ahead of his time and he introduced inventive new film techniques—in fact Eisenstein credited him with stimulating his initial interest in montage—but as far as story and performance go, it's a very crude picture."

Kubrick did find the Russian *War and Peace* to be better than most films on the subject. "It was a cut above the others, and did have some very good scenes, but I can't say I was overly impressed. There's one [scene] in particular I admired, where the Tsar entered a ballroom and everyone scurried in his wake to see what he was doing and then rushed out of his way when he returned. That seemed to me to capture the reality of such a situation. Of course, Tolstoy's view of Napoleon is so far removed from that of any objective historian's that I really can't fault the director for the way he was portrayed. It was a disappointing film, and doubly so because it had the potential to be otherwise."

Kubrick also created a consulting arrangement with Professor Felix Markham of Oxford University, who had studied Napoleon for thirty-five years and was considered one of the world's leading Napoleonic experts. Markham's monumental task was to answer any question that Kubrick had about the life and times of Napoleon. Kubrick's demand to understand every detail within details was a challenge even to the wealth of knowledge of the noted scholar.

Kubrick set up headquarters for his Napoleonic campaign at his home in Abbot's Mead. The Gaffney family lived in a cottage on the estate of romance novel queen Barbara Cartland. Bob Gaffney would arrive at the Kubrick household every morning, wake up everyone, and then cook breakfast for the three Kubrick girls, Katharina, Anya, and Vivian before they went off to school.

England had created a powerful anti-smoking campaign aimed at children, which was conducted on television and presented in the schools. As Gaffney continued to research Napoleon and helped plot Kubrick's own campaign against the general, he smoked American cigarettes, which cost up to $5 a pack in England. Little Vivian Kubrick, fresh from international stardom in her role as Dr. Floyd's daughter, would sneak in while Gaffney was working, steal his cigarettes, and then throw them away, a testament to the effectiveness of England's early crusade against smoking.

Bob Gaffney remembered many memorable Ping-Pong games on the lawn at Kubrick's home. "He and I were playing one day and we got bored so we were hitting the ball up in the air and running way back and swatting it. He stepped into a hole and I heard a crack. Stanley broke his ankle, he was in bed for months. I still have a vision of him sitting in his bedroom with a ruler down inside the cast, scratching it. It was a bad break."

Kubrick applied his legendary attention to detail to the world of Napoleon Bonaparte. On a visit to Abbot's Mead, Keir Dullea watched as the director studied a grid he placed over the copy of a nineteenth-century painting of a Napoleonic battle. The enlargement was wall-size and divided into one-inch squares. Kubrick patiently counted the number of soldiers in each square to determine the size of Napoleon's army.

Kubrick and Gaffney organized scouting crews all over Eastern Europe, France, Italy, Rumania, Yugoslavia, Czechoslovakia, and Hungary, while Kubrick worked on a screenplay based on a compilation of historic research on Napoleon.

"I went to the Rumanian Government and told them I wanted thirty-five thousand troops in the field," Bob Gaffney recalled. "We had shots dreamed up where we were going to just fly endlessly over the heads of a marching army with a cavalry of five thousand horses and fifteen to twenty thousand troops in a helicopter. I would have to sit down and figure out the spacing in the march with the length of the horses and then say, 'Stanley, it will be ten miles long. If I fly at 120 miles an hour it's going to take . . .' We had all of that figured out. I had to get bids. I had specifications right down to two hundred thousand gallons of Technicolor blood. Stanley said, " 'Wait a minute, let's type it in the typewriter sideways on the long-carriage typewriter, they'll think we have a computer.' This was before personal computers, we were working with pencil and paper. So we did that and they thought we had a computer. There was one typo in the electrical requirement. It was one digit off and it was enough power to run Paris, Rome, and three or four other cities."

"We're now in the process of deciding the best places to shoot, and where it would be most feasible to obtain the troops we need for battle scenes," Kubrick told Joseph Gelmis. "We intend to use a maximum of forty thousand infantry and ten thousand cavalry for the big battles, which means that we have to find a country which will hire out its own armed forces to us—you can just imagine the cost of fifty thousand extras over an extended period of time. Once we find a receptive environment, there are still great logistic problems—for example, a battle site would have to be contiguous to a city or town or barracks area where the troops we'd use are already bivouacked. Let's say we're working with forty thousand infantry—if we could get forty men into a truck, it would still require a thousand trucks to move them around. So in addition to finding the proper terrain, it has to be within marching distance of military barracks."

Kubrick asked Gaffney to arrange to fly in massive amounts of flu vaccine because he was concerned that a flu epidemic could bring down his entire crew and military cast and cost the production millions.

Kubrick felt it was necessary to stage the Napoleonic battles in "a vast tableau where the formations moved in an almost choreographic fashion." He told Gelmis, "I want to capture this reality on film, and to do so it's necessary to recreate all the conditions of the battle with painstaking accuracy.

"There are a number of ways this can be done and it's quite important to the accuracy of the film, since terrain is the decisive factor in the flow and outcome of a Napoleonic battle. We've researched all the battle sites exhaustively from paintings and sketches, and we're now in a position to approximate the terrain. And from a purely schematic point of view, Napoleonic battles are so beautiful that it's worth making every effort to explain the configuration of forces to the audience. And it's not really as difficult as it at first appears.

"Let's say you want to explain that at the battle of Austerlitz the Austro-Russian forces attempted to cut Napoleon off from Vienna, and then extended the idea to a double envelopment and Napoleon countered by striking at their center and cutting their forces in half—well, this is not difficult to show by photography, maps and narration. I think it's extremely important to communicate the essence of these battles to the viewer, because they all have an aesthetic brilliance that doesn't require a military mind to appreciate. There's an aesthetic involved: it's almost like a great piece of music, or the purity of a mathematical formula. It's this quality I want to bring across, as well as the sordid reality of battle. You know, there's a weird disparity between the sheer visual and organizational beauty of the historical battles sufficiently far in the past, and their human consequences. It's rather like watching two golden eagles soaring through the sky from a distance; they may be tearing a dove to pieces, but if you are far enough away the scene is still beautiful.

"It's obviously a huge story to film, since we're not just taking one segment of Napoleon's life, military or personal, but are attempting to encompass all the major events of his career. I haven't set down any rigid guidelines on length; I believe that if you have a truly interesting film it doesn't matter how long it is—providing of course, that you don't run on to such extremes that you numb the attention span of your audience. The longest film that has given consistent enjoyment to generations of viewers is *Gone With the Wind,* which would indicate that if a film is sufficiently interesting people will watch it for three hours and forty minutes. But in actual fact, the Napoleon film will probably be shorter."

Kubrick was considering the use of a narrator and animation or charts to illustrate and explain the Napoleonic battles and campaigns. Production for the exterior location work was planned for the winter of 1969. Kubrick estimated he would complete the location filming in two to three months and another three to four months for the studio work. The actual Napoleonic battlefields had been taken over by industrial and urban development, so Kubrick was deciding the best places to shoot the film.

"We were always trying to figure out how we were going to do that many costumes," Bob Gaffney remembered. "Stanley and I had figured out that there would be four thousand costumes—medium-background costumes, and full-background costumes, then way-in-the-distance costumes. Then at one point I met some people who were taking a Du Pont fabric and making throwaway dresses and bathing suits. The fabric was indestructible and mostly used in hospitals. It was strong enough to lift people up on. You could print a pattern on it. We had drawings called Rousellot plates of every uniform of the Napoleonic wars, Russians, Prussians, Hessians, French, French Corsicans, I mean, it went on and on and then different military periods, this was a long period. I brought these people a picture and said, 'Can you blow that picture up and print it on a jumpsuit and make a little hat to go on the top?' and they said, 'Sure.' 'How much?' 'Two dollars and fifty cents.' I said, 'I'll find out whether the Rumanians have printing presses.' The Rumanians came back to me and said, 'Mr. Gaffney, we can meet the price on the foreground costumes and the medium-background costumes, no problem,' but they came up with some bizarre figure—it was like twenty million dollars. I said, 'No, no, no, no, no, no.' 'Well,' they said, 'how much were you going to pay?' I said, 'Two dollars and fifty cents.' They scratched their heads and went off into another room.

"I went scouting around Rumania with a director-friend who was a

Jew who escaped from Rumania. He said, 'We would have to draft people into the army to do the picture, but we're willing to do it.'"

"We're also in the process of creating prototypes of vehicles, weapons, and costumes of the period which will subsequently be mass-produced, all copied from paintings, and written descriptions of the time and accurate in every detail," Kubrick explained to Joseph Gelmis. "We already have twenty people working full time on the preparatory stage of the film."

Bob Gaffney had been a consultant to the IMAX company and showed Kubrick examples of the wide screen process. Gaffney felt that the film could have employed IMAX background scenes of France taken from eight-by-ten photographs and projected onto reflective screens as Kubrick had done for the Dawn of Man sequence in 2001.

"We even had it in our budget to blow up a building to be filmed for front projection," Gaffney remembers. "I had a bid from Krupps to fly into Rumania and blow up the building. You weren't worried about airplanes coming overhead, they had like three airplanes. We had Cyrus Eaton on the completion bond. He had some financial dealings with the Rumanians."

While Gaffney was in Rumania trying to make preproduction deals, he learned there were several projects in the works about Napoleon. The most notable was *Waterloo*, directed by Ukrainian-born Sergei Bondarchuk and starring Rod Steiger as Napoleon. *Waterloo* was made and opened to a poor critical and box office reception, but during the making of the film, forces working with the production tried to deter the potential of competition from Stanley Kubrick. Bob Gaffney received threats and was told by the Rumanians that they were warned, "If you work with these people we're going to kill you."

In doing their massive research on Napoleon, Kubrick and Gaffney kept coming up with many entries from Napoleon's generals constantly referring to their leader's forgetting ice nails for the horses' hoofs. Understanding every detail was required for a Kubrick project. Gaffney remembered the book about Ernest Shackleton that Kubrick had given him during the making of 2001 when he was researching stories of isolation. The explorer's team had their sailboat stuck in ice for an entire winter. When spring came, it broke up the boat, forcing them to walk across the ice dragging their lifeboats. They then had to row across the most treacherous stretch of ocean to get to the last outpost—a little Norwegian whaling colony. The trek took two years and all survived. In researching the book, Gaffney learned that after Shackleton, Robert Falcon Scott failed to make the trip and perished, but he had used Shetland ponies rather than dogs to walk in the snow. Gaffney began to research what kind of horses the Russians used to defeat Napoleon and found out they were ponies whose feet were perfect for the snow. He began to survey country people in England and found that there is no protection for a horse in the winter snow, concluding that Napoleon used the wrong horses, which led to his downfall. Eventually Kubrick and Gaffney determined that because Napoleon was from Corsica he was unable to comprehend ice. They found a story concerning Napoleon when he was a young man in a French military school. It was his first winter in France. He woke up one morning and picked up a pitcher to wash his face and nothing came out. He looked inside and said, "Somebody has put glass in my pitcher." Water—frozen or moving—became a metaphor that Kubrick was interested in for his epic tale.

Gaffney discovered .09 and .07 lenses during his technical research for *Napoleon* and laughs now when he remembers saying to Kubrick at the time: "Stanley, you don't realize that with the speed of the new film and the speed of these lenses you could shoot *Napoleon* with candlelight." The information apparently went into the Kubrick mental data computer, to be retrieved for *Barry Lyndon*.

Kubrick developed an inherent distrust for doctors he didn't know. Once when he needed oral surgery, Bob Gaffney had to find a way to get the director to a dentist. Kubrick did not want to go to the local English dentists because he didn't know them, and he didn't want to fly to New York, so Gaffney, through connections he had in an embassy compound, got permission to use the naval dentist chair. Then he called Kubrick's personal dentist from the Grand Concourse in the Bronx and flew him into London, where he performed the dental procedure in the embassy's naval dentist chair—the only facility in which the New York–licensed dentist could legally practice.

Living in England brought peace to the Kubrick family. Stanley and Christiane found it a good place to raise the three girls, but Kubrick was still the kid from the Bronx. He threw a Fourth of July party at the estate and ironically had members of his British staff set off the fireworks from his lawn.

Kubrick needed an actor of remarkable talent to portray the French emperor. Marlon Brando had played him in the 1954 film *Desiree,* but after the debacle of *One-Eyed Jacks* it was inevitable that they would never work together. Kubrick set his sights on a young actor who was on his way to becoming a major star and an explosive talent that rivaled Brando's.

Jack Nicholson's first film performance was in *The Cry Baby Killer* in 1958, and throughout the sixties he worked in low budget B-movies like *Studs Lonigan, Little Shop of Horrors, The Shooting, Ride in the Whirlwind,* and *Hell's Angels on Wheels.* Nicholson broke through with a career-defining performance in *Easy Rider* and dominated the seventies with roles in *Five Easy Pieces, Carnal Knowledge, The Last Detail,* and *Chinatown.*

Kubrick had talked about working with Nicholson since the release of *Easy Rider* in 1969. He began to entice Nicholson with the notion of playing Napoleon and eventually got the actor to become equally obsessed with the emperor.

In the 1975 book *Jack Nicholson Face to Face,* Christopher Fryer and Robert David Crane interviewed the actor about *Napoleon.* When Nicholson was asked if Kubrick had approached him about playing the emperor, he said, "We had some talks about it. I was very excited about it, and still would be, but at this point I've been involved with him and it for so long that it's moved in the realm of semi-day-dream. I don't think it's ever going to come together, knowing how directors are, whims and fancies and all. It would be good. I have a counter-plan if he doesn't use me. I'll just make a better movie. I said that kiddingly of course. He's gotten me interested in the character. I've done research on it, and all that kind of stuff, and I'd like to use that material sometime."

United Artists was interested in Kubrick's *Napoleon,* but after being taken over by the Transamerica Corporation in 1967, they were beginning to mount up losses of $45 million with the failure of the films *The Sailor from Gibraltar, Mademoiselle, Charge of the Light Brigade,* and others. The dismal financial situation forced the studio to turn Kubrick down.

The economics of the time conspired against an epic project like *Napoleon.* Because of inflation Kubrick estimated that an American studio financing the film would have to borrow funds at nearly 20 percent interest. The script was massive, the breadth was epic, possibly a three-hour movie.

When it was apparent that *Napoleon* was not going to be made at this time, Bob Gaffney and his family left England. Kubrick was beginning to look into other possibilities for projects. One of the projects in which he was interested was an adaptation of Arthur Schnitzler's *Traumnovelle.*

Kubrick asked Terry Southern if he could read the galleys to his new book *Blue Movie,* about the making of a big-budget Hollywood porno movie. While he was reading the book, Christiane picked it up and, after perusing the pages, said to her husband, "Stanley, if you do this I'll never speak to you again."

Andros Epaminondas was an office boy for Kubrick and Gaffney while they were preparing the *Napoleon* project. Now that Gaffney was leaving, Andros, who was born in Cyprus, began to run the office. Gaffney was impressed with Epaminondas's negotiating skills and knew he was leaving Kubrick in good hands.

Before he left England, Gaffney, an avid reader, said to Kubrick, "I read a book just recently that was really great fun, *The Wanting Seed* by Anthony Burgess." The book was a futuristic tale with elements of science fiction. After working for years on *2001*, Kubrick wasn't interested in reinvestigating sci-fi, but he began to read through the canon of Anthony Burgess. It would be just a matter of time before he came upon *A Clockwork Orange*.

Napoleon would continue to haunt Stanley Kubrick. When he was making his next film, *A Clockwork Orange*, Kubrick tried to interest Anthony Burgess in writing a novel on Napoleon to use for adaptation into a film. For quite some time Burgess was contemplating writing a Regency novel that would parody the style of a Jane Austen novel following the structure of a Mozart symphony. Burgess planned the work in a series of movements—an allegro, andante, a minuet and trio and a presto finale. The plot was to be dictated by symphonic form, not psychological probability. The project presented an enormous challenge, and Burgess finally decided to put it away. "I mentioned this to Kubrick in a discussion of narrative techniques, and he suggested I should have already had narrative associations and, for plot, the filling out of the theme which had inspired the symphony," Burgess wrote in part two of his autobiography, *"You've Had Your Time": The Second Part of the Confessions*. "He meant Beethoven's Symphony number 3 in E flat, the 'Eroica,' which began by being about Napoleon and ended by being about any great military hero. Where were these narrative associations? The first movement was clearly about struggle and victory, the second about a great public funeral, and in the third and fourth the hero was raised to the level of myth—a specific myth, that of Prometheus, which Beethoven spelt out by drawing on his own Prometheus ballet music. Kubrick was not presenting this idea in a generous void. He wanted to make a film on *Napoleon*, using techniques denied to Abel Gance, and he wished Napoleon's career to be contained in a film of moderate length. He needed a script, but the script must be preceded by a novel. The musicalization of Napoleon's life from the first Italian campaigns to the exile on St. Helena, would be an act of compression, and it would suggest compressive techniques in the film. Thus, if the battle of Waterloo came with Beethoven's scherzo, then the cinematic narrative would be justified in speeding up the action to an almost comic degree. Exile and death on St. Helena would have to follow Beethoven's technique of theme and variations—perhaps recapitulated film styles from Eisenstein on—and Napoleon's death would have to be followed by his mythic resurrection, since Beethoven says so. The financing of such a film—with helicopter shots of the major battles, all reproduced in pedantic detail—would run into more millions than *A Clockwork Orange* had cost, but the film had to be made some day and Kubrick was clearly the man to make it. Meanwhile, the writing of a novel called *Napoleon Symphony* (the only possible title) would cost only time."

In August 1972, from his apartment in Rome, Burgess told Sheila Weller of the *Village Voice* about his new project. "It's a novel about the life of Napoleon. I'm writing it in the shape of a Beethoven symphony. Kubrick is going to make it into a movie."

"Kubrick wanted to make a film about Napoleon," Burgess told Weller. "This was going to be his next project after *2001* but he'd had great difficulty writing the script. He knew I'd been intending to write a novel in the shape of a symphony. I'd had a very simple idea: to take a Jane Austen situation and write it in the form of a Mozart symphony: where the themes turn upside down and you get a development or fantasy section. I was going to combine Jane Austen and the Marquis de Sade. It would have been rather amusing. . . . But Kubrick got on the phone and said, 'Annnthony, if you're gonna write a symphony why don't you write about Napoleon, cause yunno, you've already got a symphony to work with: Beethoven's Eroica, which was of course, dedicated to Napoleon.' So he suggested that instead of that I just write the novel that I wanted to write, and that we would use my novel as the basis for a film. But I shall push on with it, anyway. It's entirely up to Kubrick whether or not it *will* be made into a film. But I mean he asked me to do it, and if he changes his mind and asks me to do it some other way, well I don't mind that." Burgess did write the novel *Napoleon Symphony: A Novel in Four Movements*, and it was published by Knopf in 1974.

When *A Clockwork Orange* was released, Kubrick told Joseph Gelmis, writing in *Newsday*, "As rare as great stories are, there seem to be fewer of them about women than about men. I suppose that when I finally make *Napoleon* I'll have Josephine and the other women in his life." Gelmis asked Kubrick if the women would be tools of Napoleon. "Only to the extent that women are tools of men," Kubrick replied. "But certainly treated as major characters, rather than as victims, as in *Clockwork*. It isn't exactly an unreal representation of the role of women in society."

After *A Clockwork Orange* Kubrick was telling journalists that *Napoleon* would be his next film. "I plan to do *Napoleon* next," he told Penelope Houston for *Saturday Review*. "It will be a big film but certainly not on the scale that big films had grown to just before the lights went out in Hollywood. Most of the palatial interiors can be shot in real locations in France where the furniture and set dressing are already there, and one has only to move in with a small documentary-size crew, actors, wardrobe, and some hand props. The large crowd and battle scenes would be done in Yugoslavia, Hungary, or Rumania where undertakings of this sort can be accomplished by using regular army formations."

Kubrick would return to the *Napoleon* project several times in his career. After *A Clockwork Orange* he seriously considered it, and during the making of *Barry Lyndon* there were rumors he was shooting the battle scenes for *Napoleon* while he was working on the landmark period film.

In 1983 Jack Nicholson continued to talk about the project. When asked by *Variety* whom he would like to direct him in the film Nicholson replied, "Stanley Kubrick—I feel obligated to give it to him first. After all, he got me 'Napoleonized' in the first place!"

As recently as 1986 Jack Nicholson was still fascinated with the idea of playing Napoleon. The actor had paid $250,000 for the rights to a book called *The Murder of Napoleon*, which he contemplated either acting in, producing, or directing. Nicholson was talking to screenwriter Robert Towne to write the script for him. "I've invested a lot in the subject," he told Ron Rosenbaum for the *New York Times Magazine*. "I sort of look at it like Shaw, Nietzsche, those kind of thinkers did, who consider Napoleon *the* man. When I'm thinking about him, I got a feeling of autobiography about it—again, in terms of poetics—in the sense that he was a man who conquered the world *twice*. And because he's a symbol for the Devil. That's the way they described him in England. But he was ultimately the man who overthrew feudalism, after all. . . . Up until that time, it was all about family. And now, after him, you could just be who you are."

In 1994 Ray Connolly, a journalist and screenwriter, wrote the novel *Shadows on a Wall*. The book was about the most expensive movie ever made by an unrestrained director with sweeping vision and an endless appetite for more footage. The movie was an epic filmed on location with a super-size cast and battalion-size production cost.

The movie in the book was based on the life of Napoleon Bonaparte.

The Stanley Kubrick film on the life of Napoleon still remains only in the recesses of Kubrick's internal archive.

CHAPTER 15

Ultra-Violence

He is everything. I loved him. I hated him. I went through every emotion with him. But the thing that I really remember, is that when I would do something, he would ram his handkerchief into his mouth, he was laughing so much. And there is nothing more adrenaline giving to an actor than seeing his director stuff his mouth with his handkerchief.

—Malcolm McDowell

A Clockwork Orange is my current favorite. I was very predisposed against the film. After seeing it, I realized it is the only movie about what the modern world really means.

—Luis Buñuel

I hate reading, I can't stand it. I only ever read two books. One about the Kray brothers. And *A Clockwork Orange*.

—Paul Cook, drummer of the
Sex Pistols

Stanley, Christiane, Katharina, Anya, and Vivian Kubrick were now settled in England. For Stanley Kubrick the English countryside was a place with few distractions and convenient access to the tools of his trade. For Christiane Kubrick, her family was away from the mounting violence in America. As they were leaving the United States, the country was torn by the war in Vietnam, racial tension, unrest on the nation's campuses, and the assassinations of Robert Kennedy and Martin

Luther King. While traveling across to England to relocate their family, Stanley and Christiane Kubrick knew they were headed in the right direction when they heard their first BBC radio program, *Gardener's Question Time*, on the ship radio. "It was all about putting mulch around your roots and using John Innes No. 2 compost—and the world was going mad all around," Christiane Kubrick told Valerie Jenkins of the *Evening Standard* in England. "We thought—this is the place to live." The population of Hertfordshire, an area known as the stockbroker belt, gave the Kubricks the privacy they required and gave Stanley Kubrick, a longtime private investor, an environment in which he could flourish. "Stanley is such a city-boy: all this is brand new to him," Christiane Kubrick told Valerie Jenkins. "I suppose we're typical of people who have lived in New York, starved of everything that moves without a car. So we love being among all these moving, growing things." Christiane loved the old Victorian house, for most of her life she never lived anywhere much more than a year—now in Hertfordshire she felt settled. When they first stayed in London during the making of *Lolita* and *Dr. Strangelove*, the Kubricks lived in St. John's Wood, which embraced an abundance of artistic heritage. Then they lived in Kensington while traveling between New York and London, then Elstree before finding a place in the English countryside. The surrounding area was dotted with country houses encircled with landscaped parks, animals, and nurtured gardens.

In 1959, at age forty-two, Anthony Burgess was diagnosed with a brain tumor and told he had one year to live. Burgess, who had begun writing only three years before, at age thirty-nine, outlived his diagnosis by almost a quarter of a century and produced more than fifty works. But in the year 1959, in order to leave his family a legacy, he sat at the typewriter and wrote five books, then survived to see them published. With Burgess's bills mounting, he searched for ideas to generate income. First he tried to write two novels at once: *I Trust and Love You*, based on the fourth book of the *Aeneid*, and a second, *Sealed with a Loving Kiss*, a retelling of John Ford's *'Tis Pity She's a Whore*. "In despair I typed a new title—*A Clockwork Orange*—and wondered what story might match it," Burgess wrote in the second volume of his autobiography. "I had always liked the Cockney expression (as queer as a clockwork orange) and felt there might be a meaning in it deeper than a bizarre metaphor of, not necessarily sexual, queerness. Then a story began to coalesce."

Burgess had witnessed English marauding gangs of young men, the Teddy Boys, the Mods and Rockers. His first thought was to base a story in the 1590s centering in on young thugs who beat up women who sold

butter and eggs at high prices, but he abandoned that concept and decided to look into the future. It was the beginning of a new decade, the
sixties, so Burgess set his story in the near future of 1970. He projected
that gang violence would have gotten so severe that the government
would use Pavlovian techniques of behavior modification to fight the
scourge. Burgess conceived of his idea with a theological foundation:
Was the notion of tampering with the right of free choice to choose evil
over good a greater evil than the evil itself? The story would be told in
the voice of a thug speaking in his unique futuristic version of English.

"It was the most painful thing I've ever written, that damn book,"
Anthony Burgess told Sheila Weller of the *Village Voice* about the writing of his novella, *A Clockwork Orange*. "I was trying to exorcise the
memory of what happened to my first wife, who was savagely attacked in
London during the Second World War by four American deserters. She
was pregnant at the time and lost our child. This led to a dreadful de-
pression, and her suicide attempt. After that, I had to learn to start
loving again. Writing that book—getting it all out—was a way of doing it.
I was very drunk when I wrote it. It was the only way I could cope with
the violence. I can't stand violence. I . . . I *loathe* it! And one feels so
responsible putting an act of violence down on paper. If one can put an
act of violence down on paper, you've created the act! You might as well
have *done* it! I detest that damn book now."

To create the special language for the futuristic thugs, Burgess decided against using contemporary slang, which could quickly fall out of
fashion, and set out to create a slang of the future seventies. Halfway
through the book Burgess put the manuscript aside, feeling that the
arbitrary slang he was creating wasn't working, and he moved on to other
projects.

Eventually Burgess arrived at a linguistic solution and created a language he called Nadsat, the Russian suffix for teen. Borrowing about two
hundred words from a Russian volume on brainwashing, Burgess created
a mix of Russian, demotic English, rhyming slang, and gypsy bolo to
form Nadsat.

A Clockwork Orange was published in England in May 1962 and British reviewers were brutal. The author was accused of destroying the
English language rather than being praised for his linguistic ingenuity.
Burgess was invited to be interviewed by the BBC, which dramatized a
good portion of the first chapter of the novella. Even though as many as
nine million people watched his appearance on the BBC *Tonight* program, the book sold poorly, less than any of Burgess's previous works.

Discussion rarely touched on the themes of the book. The British were perturbed by Burgess's experiment with language.

Burgess had designed the book in three sections of seven chapters each, the total of twenty-one representing the symbol of human maturity—twenty-one years of age.

When *A Clockwork Orange* was purchased in the United States, Eric Swenson, a vice president of W.W. Norton, decided to drop the seventh chapter of the final section because he felt Burgess had softened his story in this concluding chapter. Against Burgess's better judgment, Norton also added a Nadsat glossary as a reader's guide.

The book was a success in America. "It was gratifying to be understood in America, humiliating to be misread in my own country," Burgess wrote in his autobiography. "American critics forced me to take my own work seriously and to ponder whether the implied moral of the novel was sound.

"I saw that the book might be dangerous because it presented good, or at least harmlessness, as remote and abstract, something for the adult future of my hero, while depicting violence in joyful dithyrambs. But violence had to be shown," Burgess wrote in his autobiography, addressing the brutality exhibited by the main character, Alex, and his droogs. "If I had begun my story with Alex in the dock, condemned for crimes generalized into judicial rhetoric, even the gentlest spinster reader would rightly have complained about evasion. Fiction deals with the concrete and the particular, even in Henry James, and the sin of showing juvenile brutality was, for me, behovely. But I was sickened by my own excitement at setting it down, and I saw that Auden was right in saying that the novelist must be filthy with the filthy."

When Anthony Burgess first heard that Stanley Kubrick had purchased the rights to *A Clockwork Orange* and was going to make a film of it, he didn't completely believe the news. From a business standpoint Burgess was disinterested. He had sold the rights to *A Clockwork Orange* many years earlier to Si Litvinoff, a New York lawyer, and Max Raab, a clothing-chain executive from Philadelphia—the transaction amounted to only a few hundred dollars. There wouldn't be any money involved for Burgess because he no longer had any connection to the screen rights.

Kubrick wasn't the first to be interested in *A Clockwork Orange* film adaptation. In the mid-sixties the Rolling Stones were planning a film version, with Mick Jagger as Alex and the Stones as the droogs. In 1968 Ken Russell considered directing a film interpretation of the Burgess novel before he turned to Aldous Huxley's *The Devils.* As interesting and commercial as these prospects were, the projects didn't get off the ground and Litvinoff and Rabb held on to their ownership of the motion picture rights to A *Clockwork Orange* until they were approached by Warner Brothers and Stanley Kubrick.

Kubrick first learned about A *Clockwork Orange* while he was making *2001,* when a visiting Terry Southern gave him a copy. The volume rested on his crowded and well-organized bookshelf for two and a half years while Kubrick was immersed in space travel and extraterrestrial life.

When he got around to reading A *Clockwork Orange,* Kubrick was immediately attracted to the book. "One could almost say that it's the kind of book that you have to look hard to find a reason not to do," Kubrick told Andrew Bailey of *Rolling Stone* magazine. "It has everything: great ideas, a great plot, external action, interesting side characters and one of the most unique leading characters I've ever encountered in fiction—Alex. The only character comparable to Alex is Richard III and I think they both work on your imagination in much the same way. They both take the audience into their confidence, they are both completely honest, witty, intelligent and unhypocritical."

"The book had an immediate impact," Kubrick told Bernard Weinraub of the *New York Times.* "I was excited by everything about it, the plot, the ideas, the characters and, of course, the language. Added to which, the story was of manageable size in terms of adapting it for film."

"The story has two levels," Kubrick told Joseph Gelmis. "There are the sociological implications of whether it's a worse immorality to deprive a man of his freedom, by imprisoning him, or his free will, by turning him into a clockwork orange, a robot being. And the power of the story is in the character of Alex who wins you over somehow, like Richard III despite his wickedness, because of his intelligence and wit and total honesty. He represents the id, the savage repressed side of our nature which guiltlessly enjoys the same pleasures of rape."

"I'd say that my intention with A *Clockwork Orange* was to be faithful to the novel and to try to see the violence from Alex's point of view, to show that it was great fun for him, the happiest part of his life, that it was like some great action ballet," Kubrick told Andrew Bailey. "It was necessary to find a way of stylizing the violence, just as Burgess does by his writing style. The ironic counterpoint of the music was certainly one of the ways of achieving this. All the scenes of violence are very different without the music."

"My problem, of course, was a way of presenting it in the film without benefit of the writing style," Kubrick told Penelope Houston. "The first

section of the film that incorporates most of the violent action is principally organized around the Overture to Rossini's *Thieving Magpie,* and
in a very broad sense, you could say that the violence is turned into
dance, although, of course, it is in no way any kind of formal dance. But
in cinematic terms, I should say that movement and music must inevitably be related to dance, just as the rotating space station and the docking
Orion spaceship in *2001* moved to the "Blue Danube." From the rape
on the stage of the derelict casino, to the super-frenzied fight, through
the Christ figure's cut, to Beethoven's Ninth, the slow-motion fight on
the water's edge and the encounter with the cat lady where the giant
white phallus is pitted against the bust of Beethoven, movement, cutting,
and music are the principal considerations—dance?"

"Although a certain amount of hypocrisy exists about it, everyone is
fascinated by violence," Kubrick told Paul D. Zimmerman for *Newsweek*
magazine. "After all, man is the most remorseless killer who ever stalked
the earth. Our interest in violence in part reflects the fact that on the
subconscious level we are very little different from our primitive ancestors."

Warner Bros. paid Si Litvinoff and Max Raab $200,000 for the rights
to *A Clockwork Orange.* The Warner deal gave Litvinoff and Rabb a 5
percent profit clause—a potential windfall of around $1.2 million for
holding on to a property they got dirt cheap.

Burgess clearly knew that Stanley Kubrick was turning his novel into a
film when the director began sending the writer a series of urgent cables
asking to meet in London over the script. Burgess's worst fears came to
fruition—the film would feature frontal nudity and rape.

"The film and the book are about the danger of reclaiming sinners
through sapping their capacity to choose between good and evil. Most of
all, I wanted to show in my story that God made man free to choose
either good or evil and that this is an astounding gift," Burgess said to
the *London Evening News.*

Kubrick saw the story of *A Clockwork Orange* as a layered study of
man's natural state of behavior untempered by society's rules. "Really
Clockwork Orange operates on two levels," he told Andrew Bailey. "One
is the sociological argument—the question of the evil committed by the
government in trying to change Alex's nature. It's an interesting level, it
serves to provide the structure of the plot, but I don't think that it's
actually from this aspect that the story derives its uniqueness or its
power. More importantly, Alex represents natural man in the state in
which he is born, unlimited, unrepressed. When Alex is given the
Ludovico treatment, you can say this symbolizes the neurosis created by

the conflict between the strictures imposed by society and our own natures. This is why we feel exhilarated when Alex is 'cured' in the final
scene. If you accept the idea that one views a film in a state of 'daydream,' then this symbolic dreamlike content becomes a powerful factor
in influencing your feelings about the film. Since your dreams can take
you into areas which can never be part of your conscious mind, I think a
work of art can 'operate' on you in much the same way as a dream does."

Kubrick's first-draft screenplay adaptation of Anthony Burgess's *A
Clockwork Orange* is dated May 15, 1970. For the first time, Kubrick
struck out alone to write a screenplay. He began to experiment with the
classic screenplay format, which structured scenes by presenting the dialogue in a centered column and the description straight across the page.
For his screen adaptation of *A Clockwork Orange*, Kubrick did the opposite, centering the description so it read like a poem and running the
dialogue from the left margin so the imagery captured the reader's eye.

For the crucial role of Alex, Kubrick was interested in Malcolm Mc-
Dowell, a twenty-seven-year-old British actor born in Leeds who had
made a tremendous impact in Lindsay Anderson's *If. . . .* The actor
had also appeared in Joseph Losey's *Figures in a Landscape* and the film
Long Ago Tomorrow.

When Kubrick first read *A Clockwork Orange* he had Malcolm Mc-
Dowell in mind by the time he'd finished the fourth chapter. "One
doesn't find actors of his genius in all shapes, sizes and ages," Kubrick
told Penelope Houston.

"Stanley gave me a copy of the book," McDowell told Kitty Bowe
Hearty for *Premiere* magazine. "I called him and said, and I must have
been absolutely nuts, but I said, 'Are you offering me this?' And there
was a long pause and he said, 'Yes.' Having got that out of the way, I
said, 'Well, look, I'd like to meet with you further and talk about it.
Would you like to come to my house.' Another long pause: 'Where is it?'
And he came. In sort of a convoy. I didn't realize that it was such a big
deal for Stanley Kubrick to leave his home. He 'doesn't travel well' as
they say."

"I was totally seduced by him," McDowell told Kitty Bowe Hearty
about playing Alex. "I thought he was a hoot. I honestly thought I was
making a black comedy and played it for the humor. I learned early on
in life that you must not worry about being disliked. It's great fun—
suicidal parts."

"Alex is free at the end; and that's hopeful," McDowell told journalist
Tom Burke. "Maybe in his freedom he'll be able to find someone to help

him without brainwashing. If his 'Ludwig van' can speak to him, perhaps others can."

Kubrick has said that Burgess's ideas were so clearly presented in the form of the novella that he didn't have to involve him in the screenwriting process and only called on occasion to say hello. During the four months it took Kubrick to write his screenplay adaptation of *A Clockwork Orange,* he was aware only of the American version of the book. When he later learned of the missing chapter in which Alex grew out of his violent nature, Kubrick told Andrew Bailey of *Rolling Stone* that he found it to be "completely out of tone with the rest of the book."

Kubrick's preparation for the film involved an immersion into the world of developmental psychology. To understand the Ludovico treatment described in Burgess's book, Kubrick did intensive research into psychological conditioning. His reading led him to the classic Pavlov experiments, conditioned-reflex training employed by the Russians during World War II, and the work of B. F. Skinner. "I like to believe that Skinner is wrong," Kubrick told *Rolling Stone,* "and that what is sinister is that this philosophy may serve as the intellectual basis for some sort of scientifically oriented repressive government.

"Another area where Skinner should be attacked is in his attempt to formulate a total philosophy of the human personality solely in terms of conditioning. This is a dreary conception. I like to believe that there are certain aspects of the human personality which are essentially unique and mysterious."

Even though his last film had had a murderous computer, Kubrick was utilizing computers in the process of making a film. He called the computer "one of man's most beautiful inventions" in *Rolling Stone* magazine and began to experiment with the structure of a film by rearranging the scenes digitally rather than rearranging cards on a corkboard.

Kubrick's home, thirty minutes outside of London in Abbot's Mead, was a command center, a compound, a bunker for the director. The area was home to the Elstree, MGM Studios, and EMI Studios. The sprawling estate surrounded by a brick wall encased the living quarters for Stanley, Christiane, Katharina, Anya, and Vivian Kubrick, seven cats, three golden, floppy retrievers, the director's offices, and the editing facility where *A Clockwork Orange* was edited. "It's very pleasant, very peaceful, very civilized here. London is in the best sense, the way New York must have been in about 1910," Kubrick told Bernard Weinraub for the

New York Times. "I have to live where I make my films, and as it has worked out, I have spent most of my time during the last ten years in London." As Weinraub talked with Kubrick at a restaurant near the director's home, he observed that the director spoke gently and unaffectedly, with a New York accent, but at times he seemed tense and distracted. At their luncheon interlude, Kubrick ate his meal in fifteen minutes wearing a heavy windbreaker, then remembered to remove his coat.

Kubrick continued to work on his films without respite. With *2001* they were beginning to take longer to conceive, research, produce, and promote. The historical American and British director's vacation or holiday after completing principal photography was not the Kubrick way. Stanley Kubrick hadn't taken a vacation until *Lolita* was completely finished. He and his wife took a five-day "holiday" to see the World War II D day bunkers in Normandy, and surely the information was filed away for a future film. "Telling me to take a vacation from filmmaking is like telling a child to take a vacation from playing," Kubrick told Paul D. Zimmerman. Another rare vacation, to a Black Sea resort, gave Christiane Kubrick insight into her husband's heritage. As they watched a play, five hundred extras streamed into an arena, each one with a fierce black beard, looking like a twin of Stanley Kubrick. Christiane saw the link between her husband and his Eastern European ancestry.

At one end of a room in Kubrick's office and communication center were two large speaker cabinets. Carefully catalogued record albums were kept in industrial-shelving units. Music ran the gamut from the standard classical repertoire to international free-form jazz. A file cabinet with as many as two hundred small drawers was carefully and explicitly identified.

The label "recluse" was beginning to stick to Stanley Kubrick. He was not a member of any identifiable social or artistic scene in Hollywood, New York, or London. Nevertheless, he was very much in touch with the outside world—but the outside world came to him. The phone became a principal communication tool. The *New York Times* was flown to him every day. Shortwave radio kept him in touch with America and other parts of the globe. Close friends, relatives, and colleagues came to Kubrick's turf. He conducted his personal life and his professional life with purposeful exclusivity.

On the Kubrick estate grounds under a marquee a Ping-Pong table was set up where the director played matches with friends and visitors. Kubrick especially liked to encounter actors over the Ping-Pong table or chessboard to establish a superiority he could use behind the camera.

Kubrick's relationship with director of photography Geoffrey Unsworth on *2001* had been a positive one, with spectacular results. In the past, Kubrick's experience as cinematographer of three of his own short films and two features had affected his relationships with directors of photography. Kubrick's knowledge of cameras, lenses, and lighting made him an awesome force for even the most experienced cinematographer. His contribution to the photography of his films was hands-on. Other directors would tell their DP what they wanted for the look and feel of a scene and then let the cinematographer light and shoot it. Stanley Kubrick called the shot, the lens, and the method. Kubrick often operated the camera and consistently shot all of the hand-held sequences. To work with him took a strong ego, a firm and complete knowledge of the craft, the ability to collaborate, and a willingness to defer to Kubrick's photographic wishes. Long, grueling hours, days and months of dedication were a must.

John Alcott was a handsome, aristocratic-looking man, born in London in 1931. Alcott started as focus puller on British film productions such as *The Singer Not the Song, Whistle Down the Wind, The Main Attraction,* and *Tamahine,* and he worked with Geoffrey Unsworth on *2001.* When Unsworth had to leave the endless shooting schedule for another assignment, Alcott took over and shot additional photography for the production. His work on Kubrick's landmark film had impressed the director, who was now looking for a lighting cameraman for *A Clockwork Orange.* "*A Clockwork Orange* employed a darker more obviously dramatic type of photography," Alcott told *American Cinematographer* magazine. "Although the period was never actually pinpointed in the picture, that period called for a really cold, stark style of photography."

Kubrick constantly kept abreast of technical innovations that he could implement in his filmmaking. Often he would come up with an aesthetic or conceptual idea and then find the technical resources to achieve something that reached beyond off-the-shelf technology.

For *A Clockwork Orange* Kubrick had envisioned shots where he would utilize a zoom lens to go from very near to very far in one continuous zoom out. "Stanley just calls from his office in London and contacts people from all over the world as he needs information," explained Ed Di Giulio, president of Cinema Products Corporation in Los Angeles. The noted cinematographer Haskell Wexler had told Kubrick that Di Giulio was very responsive to the demanding needs of filmmakers. "Stanley started chatting with me about getting a 20:1 zoom lens and I said, 'We could do it.'" Di Giulio explained to Kubrick that he could take an Angenieux 16mm 20:1 zoom lens and put a two times extender behind it so that it would cover the 35mm format. "But of course you lose two stops of light in the process because of the two times extender so that makes it pretty slow," Di Giulio explained on the long distance call to Kubrick in England. "And he says, 'Well, do you have to do that?' This is the consummate and classic Stanley Kubrick because we hang up and the next day I get a telex that's a yard long in which he goes on to explain to me that the 35mm format he's shooting in is 1:85. Then he recites Pythagorean theorem to show me how x squared plus y squared equals the diagonal root of the sum of the squares. And to point out that going up from a 16mm format I didn't need a 2 to 1 extender, that I could do it with a 1.61. Therefore I wouldn't have to lose as much light. I didn't have to lose two stops maybe a stop or stop and a half. So here he is lecturing me and I'm saying, 'Why this smart ass, another one of these wild ass directors.' So I called my old buddy Bern Levy who was working for Angenieux at the time and I said, 'Bern, I've got this wacko director who wants to do this.' Bern said, 'Well, you know, Ed, as a matter of fact we do have a 1.6 extender.' And I said, 'Oh, shit.' This extender existed for some other application but the bottom line is I was able to take a 16mm zoom lens, put this extender on it and give Stanley the exact lens he wanted. So he went and used it." Di Giulio also purchased a standard Mitchell BNC for Kubrick, which Cinema Products overhauled for the *Clockwork Orange* production. They also supplied a joystick control that allowed for smooth automatic operation of the zoom lens.

A *Clockwork Orange* was shot on location for $2 million during the winter of 1970–71. Kubrick wanted to create the near-future by utilizing the modern architecture of contemporary England. An old factory was converted into production headquarters and an ad hoc studio. The only studio work in the film was the creation of the Korova Milkbar, the prison reception area, a mirrored bathroom, and the mirrored hall at the writer's house. These sets were designed solely because they couldn't be found on location.

Kubrick began the design process by purchasing ten years of back issues of several architectural magazines. Kubrick and production designer John Barry spent two weeks going through the magazines, taking out pages and carefully filing and cross-referencing pictures they found interesting. The material was put into a special display file called Definitiv—made by a German company. When the file was hanging in the innovative system, various signals using colors and alphabetical and numerical symbols allowed Kubrick and Barry to cross-reference the material in limitless ways.

Kubrick found this to be a more efficient method than the typical location scouting—sending scouts out to take photos of places they had found. The majority of the locations used in the film were identified and found by first spotting them in the magazines.

The block that is home to Alex's flat was shot at Thamesmead, an architecturally bold project in London. The auditorium used to display Alex's cure during a press conference was a library in South Norwood. The writer's house was shot at two separate locations. The exterior was a house at Oxfordshire and the interior a home in Radlett. Brunel University was used for locations. The record boutique was filmed at the Chelsea Drugstore. The deserted theater where a woman is raped and Alex and the droogs fight another gang was filmed on the derelict stage of the old casino at Tagg's Island where Charlie Chaplin had performed with Fred Karno.

Kubrick again hired Liz Moore, who had sculpted the Star Child for *2001,* to create the tables in the Korova Milkbar, which were in the shape of naked women. The talented artist was later killed in a car crash while working on location for Richard Attenborough's production of *A Bridge Too Far.*

Sexually oriented paintings are featured in several scenes, but for the home of the writer and his wife, who are brutally assaulted by Alex and the droogs, Kubrick needed a canvas that reflected the humanity and sophistication of the couple's home. For this set Kubrick selected *Seedboxes,* a large 60 inch-by-120-inch painting by Christiane Kubrick. The sunny picture is drenched in ochre light, featuring rows of aquamarine seedboxes holding sprouting plants and flowerpots with white and cranberry flowers blooming. In the background, surrounded by trees, is a large white tent, inside which two figures (one presumably could be Stanley Kubrick) are playing Ping-Pong. In the scene the painting is an ironic contrast to the violence inflicted on the writer and his wife.

"I couldn't watch the action in that scene for worrying that the picture might get kicked," Christiane Kubrick told Valerie Jenkins of the *Evening Standard.* When filming was complete, *Seedboxes* was given its own wall in the Kubricks' dining room. Their large home became a museum to Christiane Kubrick's prolific work. Finding space to hang the ongoing one-woman show was a challenge even for an estate with so many rooms.

Stanley Kubrick also had his handiwork hanging. He became enthralled with created signs detailing specific information to impart to staff and visitors. The many announcements included, "Guard dog inside. Do not enter unaccompanied." "Keep this gate closed at all times." "Caution—children and dog." and "Cat in heat." His most copious message may have been: "We have a serious problem with the dog, who runs away if the front door is left open. Please always make sure that you close the door when you leave. The dog has nearly been run over on a number of occasions."

New technology was making it easier for Kubrick to shoot on location while still maintaining his strict technical standards. The record boutique was shot with a 9.8mm lens, giving him a ninety-degree viewing angle. The f0.95 lens made it possible for Kubrick and Alcott to shoot in a room with natural light until late in the afternoon with 200 percent less light than the earlier standard f2.0 lenses.

Sound was once a location problem and required that filmmakers re-record all of the production track during the postproduction process. There was no post-synchronization dialogue on *A Clockwork Orange*. All of the dialogue was recorded on location. Kubrick utilized miniature microphones and FM transmitters that were hidden and thus eliminated microphone booms. The scene where Alex is recognized by the tramp he had beaten earlier in the story was shot under the Albert Bridge—a location so noisy that Kubrick and the crew had to shout in order to hear themselves. The state-of-the art audio used on the film enabled them to record Alex and the tramp so well that a lot of the background traffic had to be added on an effects track during the re-recording mix. Kubrick hid a Sennhesier microphone, no larger than a paper clip, in the actors' lapels. This new technology allowed Kubrick to personally shoot hand-held with an Arriflex as close as six feet from the actors without utilizing a heavy blimp encasing, which weighed the camera down and made smooth hand-holding difficult. Kubrick liked using the Arriflex, which weighed only 37 pounds as opposed to the Mitchell, which for years had been an industry standard and weighed close to 125 pounds.

To light the film, Kubrick used primarily the practical lamps seen on the set as a light source. By selecting lamps that had both the right aesthetic, futuristic look and the ability to house a photoflood or small quartz light, Kubrick and Alcott were able to shoot without cumbersome additional studio lamps. He also used very lightweight Lowell 1,000-watt quartz lights bounced off the ceiling and reflective umbrellas. This technique allowed him to shoot 360-degree pans without concern for hiding the lights and made shooting efficient, shaving time off the schedule.

The shooting of *A Clockwork Orange* was a physical ordeal for Malcolm McDowell. The actor was terrified of snakes and Alex had a pet snake he kept in a drawer in his room. After Alex has completed the Ludovico treatment he appears before a group in an auditorium to show how he has been "cured" by the state. On stage a man comes out and provokes Alex by throwing him on the floor and stomping on him. During the shooting McDowell's ribs were broken when the actor playing the provocateur stomped too hard. Later in the film Alex again meets up with two of his former droogs, now policemen. In a very long take, with no cutaways, they hold Alex in a trough filled with dirty water. McDowell actually performed the stunt immersing his head in beef broth, and nearly suffocated while holding his breath for the long take. The most difficult scenes to shoot were the Ludovico treatment sequences. McDowell's eyes were held open with clamps as Alex watched the violent films used to purge him.

"We used a piece of standard surgical equipment called a lidlock," Kubrick told Andrew Bailey of *Rolling Stone* magazine. "It took courage and a local anaesthetic for him to wear them. I can assure you he didn't like it at all and we never really got it finished the first time. He had to go back and face it again at the end. He had to do it. The scene wouldn't have been credible otherwise. One of the worst fantasies you can imagine is being in a straitjacket, strapped to a chair, and unable to even blink your eyes."

Kubrick spent considerable time working on key scenes. "Chess masters will sometimes spend half of the entire time allotted them on a single move because they know, if it isn't right, their whole game falls apart," Kubrick told Paul D. Zimmerman for *Newsweek* magazine. "In much the same way, you have to devote what appears to be dangerous amounts of time on certain crucial aspects of your film. The rape scene in *A Clockwork Orange* in which Alex does 'Singin' in the Rain' was one of those moments. It took three days to work it out." Kubrick called those moments the "CRM"—the "critical rehearsal moment," a point in time when the director and actors come together to create a defining scene in a film.

During the shooting, Malcolm McDowell was invited to Kensington Palace for a lunch hosted by Princess Margaret. When McDowell asked Kubrick if he could be released, Kubrick replied, "Aw Malc, I don't wanta shut down the whole unit a day just for *her!*" the actor told Tom Burke.

After working with Kubrick on *Paths of Glory* and *Spartacus* and having seen *A Clockwork Orange,* Kirk Douglas ran into Malcolm McDowell and asked him how he liked working with the director. "I scratched the cornea of my left eye," McDowell told Douglas. "It hurt, I couldn't see. Kubrick said, 'Let's go on with the scene. I'll favor your other eye.' "

McDowell developed a love-hate relationship with his director. Kubrick wrote McDowell after the film was released, expressing regrets about their differences during the shooting. "I've discovered something: that I'm really very fond of Stanley, in a love-hate way," McDowell told writer Tom Burke. "There's only one of him, there's no technician like him. He's a genius, but his humor's black as charcoal. I wonder about his . . . *humanity.*"

For the role of a policeman who interrogates Alex, Kubrick selected Steven Berkoff, a theater actor and director. When Kubrick cast Berkoff, he had already directed acclaimed theater productions of Kafka's *Metamorphosis* and *The Trial* and Shakespeare's *Macbeth.* Steven Berkoff's career continued with striking performances in *Beverly Hills Cop, Rambo: First Blood Part II, Absolute Beginners, The Krays,* and Kubrick's *Barry Lyndon,* as well as many theater productions, such as his 1995 production of *Salome.*

The scene was shot in an old building, part of the Brunel University complex. "Stanley Kubrick was incredibly gentle and highly informative about what he wanted," Berkoff recalled. "He was a wise person and had a professional manner, very sensitive to the actors. If you were giving him what he wanted then you had no problems at all."

During the scene Berkoff gives a powerful performance as a tough cop who squeezes Alex's face right where he had been hit with a bottle by one of the droogs. Alex is brought to the floor in pain and for the remainder of the scene the interrogators are shown from Alex's point of view. Kubrick gave Berkoff the chance to look through the camera for the unique, low, wide-angle lens shot. "He offered me the opportunity to look through the lens, to see exactly how I was being framed," Steven Berkoff related. "He thought it looked interesting because it was an acutely wide-angle lens. It was a very interesting shot, indeed. He was showing me one effect and we got on very well. Stanley was very patient with the actors. I noticed that he never got or appeared to be upset or disturbed by what they did or didn't do. I remember one actor who I was doing the scene with who was learning his lines on that day on the theory that he didn't want to learn before he knew exactly where he was going. Stanley said, 'You should always learn your lines beforehand because then you have them inside you. No matter how we do them or change or adapt, at least you've got a basis there.' He very mildly chastised the actor. I thought the actor was pretty dumb not to learn his lines, especially when you're working for the master. I did learn my lines. I mean I learned them backwards, forwards, inside out, and upside down, so that I would never be guilty of fluffing a take."

As a theater actor, Berkoff appreciated Kubrick's emphasis on discipline and repetition to fine-tune the performances. "He did a lot of takes, he wanted to have as much as possible. Stanley was of the opinion that the actor, like a rehearsal in a theater, could rehearse over and over again. So I suppose he felt it might improve if we rehearsed, if we did a lot of takes. I remember doing quite a lot of takes, not too much but substantial.

"He would give you very general notes in front of the other actors. But if it was something more specific, he'd take you aside and never humiliate you or indicate you were wrong in front of others."

Stanley Kubrick went to see the London production of *The Contractor*, a play by David Storey directed by Lindsay Anderson. Actor Philip Stone played a strange, silent leader of a group of workers erecting a large tent. The production had been running for several months—ultimately it ran for a year. Kubrick came to the theater twice to see the play, and Philip Stone's performance made an impression. "Suddenly Stanley asked me to meet him on location. The filming of *A Clockwork Orange* had already begun," Philip Stone recalled. "We met. He said, 'That's quite a performance you give in the play; would you like to be in this movie?' I said, 'Well, I think we could do some good work together.' He said, 'Yeah, yeah, we could. Okay, you play Dad.' I didn't know I was going to take part in film history.

"Dad seemed to be a sad, downbeat character. I have a sadness side to my personality and it wasn't particularly difficult, so long as you were true. Stanley doesn't take 'crap.' He's endlessly, painstakingly careful of everything before you go for a take—lights and particularly the sound. Small microphones were stuck all over the set. Stanley likes the authentic immediate sound. With that preparation it gives you confidence—just to let go and be true.

"At the time I was filming *A Clockwork Orange* for about two or three weeks, I was also working every night on stage in *The Contractor*. Long days. I was up at five-thirty and back to bed at midnight. I was very mentally turned on, working all day and part of the night. I had to finish at six o'clock in the evening. A car took me from location back to London. I ate a ham sandwich in the car for sustenance and then on to the stage, tent erecting. It was bloody hard, I couldn't do it now."

Kubrick cut the film with his editor, Bill Butler, in editing rooms located on the premises of his estate. "The basic equipment I use is two Steenbeck editing tables and a Moviola," Kubrick told Alexander Walker. "I use the two Steenbecks for selection, and by having two of them, I can continuously look at the film without waiting for the last roll to be taken off and replaced by another. I don't feel too guilty about having the two Steenbecks, because their combined rental cost is only a small fraction of the daily interest charges which exist on the production loan of even a small film during the editing phase of a production. I find the Steenbeck marvelous for selection. It allows the fast forward and reverse and runs very quietly at normal speed. But for the actual cutting of the film and the handling of small bits of film, the Moviola is far superior, for all of its noisy, clattery, old-fashioned self. When I am editing, I work seven days a week. In the beginning I work ten hours a day and then as we get closer to the deadlines I usually push that up to fourteen or sixteen hours a day."

The music for A *Clockwork Orange* was a crucial element at the center of Burgess's story. Alex had a supreme love for the music of Ludwig van Beethoven. The Ninth Symphony was an integral component of the plot. Kubrick instinctively knew that he wanted classical music throughout the film for point and counterpoint with the story. All the elements in the film had a futuristic treatment. In order to bring a futuristic quality to eighteenth-century motifs, Kubrick looked to the cutting edge in music—electronics.

The year 1968 saw the release of one of the best-selling classical albums of all time—*Switched-on Bach*—a record of synthesizer performances created by Walter Carlos. Carlos composed *Trio for Clarinet, Accordion, and Piano* when he was ten years old and had constructed a small computer by the time he was fourteen. This love of music and technology melded when Walter was seventeen, and he assembled an electronic music studio. In 1966, after studying music and physics at Brown University and working at the Columbia-Princeton electronic music center, Carlos collaborated with engineer Robert Moog. The result was a prototype of a synthesizer used to perform realizations of Bach and other classical composers—the Moog synthesizer.

Carlos and his partner, Rachel Elkind, met with producer Mike Frankovitch about doing a score for the 1969 film *Marooned*. Ultimately the producers decided against music for the film, and Rachel was interested in pursuing Stanley Kubrick, who they had heard was doing a new film. Rachel told literary agent Lucy Kroll that she and Walter were interested in contacting Stanley Kubrick. Kroll put them in touch with Louis Blau, Kubrick's longtime colleague and lawyer. Kubrick was sent copies of the first two albums of synthesizer music created by Carlos and Elkind, and he requested to meet with them.

Carlos and Elkind began to create test pieces, which Kubrick would cut into the work print of the film. As the film was edited they began to create custom pieces to suit the nature of A *Clockwork Orange*.

Kubrick asked Carlos and Elkind to come to England to see a cut of A

Clockwork Orange. The film was almost complete, but some of the intercuts of Alex's fantasies had not been put in yet. There were a couple of missing scenes, and the cut still had sequences to be trimmed. During the screening Carlos and Elkind noticed that many of the test pieces they had sent were in the film. One of the pieces, "Timesteps," one of Carlos's original compositions, had been composed years before Kubrick approached making a film out of *A Clockwork Orange.* Walter had read the book and was inspired to create "Timesteps"—a piece filled with a montage of atmospheric electronic sounds and passages that weave a narrative sound poem. "Stanley was fascinated by the sounds," Carlos, now known as Wendy, recalled. "I remember Stanley asking me, 'Why don't you come over to the piano and show me exactly what these notes are?' The section that ends the first large chunk of 'Timesteps' ends with a little melody and I had to pick it out on the piano and show him. He had this large upright piano that looked like it had been gotten from some Salvation Army rescue store. Stanley was teaching his children about music, they were taking piano lessons.

"Stanley was always open with us. He would always answer any questions I had, and I had tons of questions about *2001,* since that was a film that had bowled me over. He answered everything, so when he asked me questions, it very nice to have that kind of communication."

Originally the orgy sequence had a conventional orchestra recording of the *William Tell* Overture. "I quipped that it would be much funnier if I did a speeded-up synthesized version," Wendy Carlos recalled. "It was funny enough, but it wasn't as funny as it could be." "Oh, what do you mean by that? Could you show me?" Kubrick replied. As soon as he heard Carlos's synthesized realization of the Rossini classic, Kubrick had it cut right into the film.

Kubrick was filled with queries about the synthesizer and music. "He's very collaborative, he's a very open person," Wendy Carlos said. "It's very easy to talk with him. He's extremely bright. Rachel and I had sparks going with him when we were there. I mean we almost couldn't get back to the hotel room to sleep. You'd be so wound up, you couldn't let go. Then he'd have his driver coming to pick you up at the crack of dawn for the next thing. I don't know where the man gets his energy from, but he's fascinated by everything."

Elkind, Carlos, and Kubrick would sit at the Steenbeck flatbed editing table in Kubrick's compound with a library of records. They listened to myriad pieces of music against the cut of the film. "He'd try things," Carlos recalled. "It was literally needle dropping. Of course, in those days it was all LPs. *Rip, rip,* the needle would go down. 'Let's hear this, let's back that up.' Stanley would have his Steenbeck there and we'd wind back and check something else out. This cue would come in. 'Well, does that really work? Let's try it a little earlier.' Stanley did it from some of the records we had cut, and in the end we had to take the tapes we had sent him and send them off to a place to cut acetates so he could have thirty-three and a third LPs that he could spot. It was much more convenient for him than having music on quarter-inch tape that would have to be transferred to mag stripe and be plopped into the Steenbeck in order to get an idea if it would work or not. That step could be coming, but the first step was, let's just play it off of the acetate, which doesn't have to sound great, just to have an idea if we're in the right ballpark. That was Rachel's idea, she was responsible for an awful lot of the energy, creativity, and the asides that are easily taken for granted but make a project happen and make interactions productive.

"There were times that Stanley would get frozen in on things even though I was convinced we had much better ideas. Nope, that was the way he wanted it and, of course, that's his prerogative, being the director. That goes on in all joint creative ventures, film being the best example. I worked with Rachel for many years, and you don't know where the idea for the music comes from, you just know they do come—that's the only thing that's important."

In addition to the synthesizer realizations created by Carlos and Elkind, Kubrick was using previously recorded classical performances, many from the Deutsche Gramophon collection, as he had on 2001. Christiane Kubrick's brother, Jan Harlan, who was assistant to the producer, was essential in providing service in music and cultural areas. "Jan studied music," Wendy Carlos explained. "He and his wife are very cultured in that marvelous European way. When Stanley would say, 'Is there a piece of music that sounds a little like . . .', Jan would say, 'Oh, yes, Stanley, of course, there's so and so by so and so,' and he'd have them right on the tips of his fingers. When I did the Beethoven realizations and I needed a full score, Jan had it. He had these beautiful German editions that were wonderful."

When Carlos and Elkind returned to New York from London, they reentered their studio with a tremendous stack of notes. They blocked their schedule for the next month and beyond to create the music for A Clockwork Orange. "We made sure that everything was aligned and working in the studio, got in a few people to help and just started doing research, running to the library to get scores and sending music to Kubrick," Wendy Carlos remembered. "Advent came out with one of the very first Dolby cassette tape machines. We got one and Stanley got

one. That became the way we sent music back and forth. It was perfect.
He could send us things that he had heard. 'Could you listen to a little of
this? Can you try something in this?' So he'd send us a cassette. Those
were the days before Fed Ex. So we would go down to the airport and
have air courier–type packages sent back and forth. When we were done
with certain mixes of the sound, we'd take the one-inch, eight-track tape
and cart it down to the airport at the end of the evening. It was summer.
You'd be in a steamy-hot traffic jam. We'd make it to the airport, get to
the courier service place at Kennedy, drop it off, get our receipt, drive
back, grab something to eat on the way home, and then make the call to
Stanley's phone-answering machine: 'We got it on the plane, you'll be
getting it tomorrow morning. You'll see track one is this track, track two
is this, track three is a version of it we tried this way, track four is a
different version, track five is the way you had first suggested it but we
didn't think it worked, track six is a variation of that, which maybe does
the best compromise of all.' By mid-afternoon the plane courier had
dropped the thing off at his place. Then he would take it to the studio,
which he had booked solid, and he'd see if he could use any of it. So we
worked over the long distance in a way that would be considered clumsy,
because it can be done so much more easily now.

"The problem was that Stanley always works in London. He doesn't
travel, and at the time for both *A Clockwork Orange* and *The Shining*
our equipment was totally unportable. We talked about it. We could rent
a flat in London and we could get some of the stuff shipped, some of it
would die, some would have to be repaired. In the fifties when the
Barrons did the score of *Forbidden Planet* they worked right here on
Eighth Street in New York while the film was being done at MGM and
they sent stuff back and forth."

Elkind and Carlos tried to convince Kubrick to use an alternate to his
choice of Henry Purcell's "Music for the Funeral of Queen Mary" for
the title and other cues in the film, but he wouldn't budge from his
decision, however, he didn't care for the performance that he was using
from a previously recorded LP. He turned to Carlos and Elkind and
said, "See if you can make a version of this that would be better for the
film," and they came up with the eerie and haunting performance that
has become identified with Alex and his droogs. "The right term is
'transmogrified,' " Wendy Carlos explained. "The Purcell is transmogrified into something more spacy, electronic, weird, and it worked. Stanley
liked it very much and he never looked back."

Kubrick used diplomacy to deal with the profusion of musical ideas
that Carlos and Elkind offered. "When Stanley didn't want something

for the film," recalled Wendy, "he'd always say, 'Well, looks like there's another good cue for the record,' meaning—at least you could get mileage out of it that way. It was a way of using his sense of humor to get over something that wasn't going to be well-received news. You don't want to be the messenger of death, as it were."

Carlos and Elkind's music was recorded in stereo, but Kubrick disliked stereo recording for film, so the tracks on the soundtrack to *A Clockwork Orange* were re-recorded in mono. *A Clockwork Orange* became the first feature film to use Dolby noise reduction on all aspects of the re-recording mixing process, but Kubrick was not yet ready to use Dolby during the production sound process.

Kubrick wanted his name above the title of his new film. David Lean's name preceded the title of his recent films with the words "David Lean's Film of." The placement gave the director of *Lawrence of Arabia* and *Doctor Zhivago* a superstar status. Kubrick insisted on billing the film *Stanley Kubrick's A Clockwork Orange.* The presentation and intention implied ownership. Anthony Burgess was the author and creator of the text, but the film was Stanley Kubrick's. Kubrick's phraseology gave the clear message that he was a superstar director. (In fact, he was chosen to be interviewed for the book *The Film Director as Superstar.*) Kubrick wanted everyone to know that he was the sole creator of the film. He was author of the screenplay, produced and directed and maintained total artistic control. Kubrick also had the majority control over the business aspects.

In the fall of 1971, Warner Bros. brought Anthony Burgess, his wife, Liana, and his seven-year-old son from their home in Italy to London, where they stayed in a lavish suite at the Claridge Hotel and were to see a private showing of the film.

Burgess was an admirer of Stanley Kubrick's films, especially *Paths of Glory* and *Dr. Strangelove. Lolita* gave him some concern because he perceived that it bore similarities to the way Kubrick approached *A Clockwork Orange.* Burgess felt that Kubrick was unable to find a cinematic style for Nabokov's literary dance. Burgess felt that both he and Nabokov focused on the use of language rather than on sex or violence but that Kubrick did not. "The writer's aim in both books had been to put language, not sex or violence into the foreground. A film, on the other hand, was not made of words," Burgess wrote in his autobiography. "I feared that the cutting to the narrative bone which harmed the filmed *Lolita* would turn the filmed *A Clockwork Orange* into a complimentary pornograph. What I hoped for, having seen *2001: A Space Odyssey,* was an expert attempt at visual futurism. *A Clockwork Orange,* the book, had been set in a vague future which was already probably past; Kubrick had the opportunity to create a fantastic new future which, being realized in decor, could influence the present."

Arthur C. Clarke, Kubrick's collaborator on *2001*, saw *A Clockwork Orange* as a work in progress. Clarke phoned fellow author Anthony Burgess to tell him the film was visually exciting.

Burgess and his wife went to a Soho screening room to see *A Clockwork Orange*. Kubrick stood in the back of the theater during the screening. Ten minutes into the screening, Deborah Rogers, a guest of Burgess's, told Anthony she couldn't stand any more and wanted to leave. A minute later, Liana turned to her husband and also announced she was leaving. Burgess quickly appealed to the women to avoid being discourteous to the ever-polite Stanley Kubrick. They stayed until the film's end.

Despite his fears, Burgess thought the film was a brilliant response to his wordplay. He especially liked the cinematic treatment utilizing slow motion for Alex's attempted suicide and the high-speed treatment of Alex's orgy.

Leo Greenfield, the head of distribution at Warners, originally planned to open *A Clockwork Orange* at the end of September, but Kubrick wanted his film positioned in the prime Christmas period when the studios released all of their Academy Award hopefuls.

At the end of November 1971, Warner Bros. wanted to begin press screenings for the film. The premiere date was set for December 19, at New York's Cinema I and at theaters in San Francisco. Back in London, Stanley Kubrick was still working on the final release print of the film. Warners was prepared for *A Clockwork Orange* to receive an X rating, as the studio had for Ken Russell's *The Devils*. By November 15, Warners began running newspaper ads, radio spots, and theater trailers for *A Clockwork Orange* without a stated rating as they anxiously awaited the MPAA's verdict. Kubrick had the right to final cut. When *The Devils* received its X, Warners demanded that director Ken Russell make as many as twenty cuts of material that dealt with explicit sexual matters from his director's cut. Once the cuts were made, the X was removed. Studios were nervous about the negative impact that the X could have on box office. Columbia avoided the X rating by trimming Roman Polanski's production of *Macbeth*, as did Cinerama Releasing with Sam Peckinpah's *Straw Dogs*. Warner Bros. was not sure how Kubrick would react.

The press wanted copy on Kubrick's new film, but he would not do a press tour for *A Clockwork Orange*. Anyone interested in interviewing

Stanley Kubrick had to go to him. Warner Bros. helped to arrange time for Paul Zimmerman, Jay Cocks, and Judith Crist to meet with Kubrick. The trips were paid for by their respective bosses at *Newsweek, Time,* and *New York* magazines. When Warner Bros. realized that a print of the film would not arrive in New York on its original schedule, they paid to fly Hollis Alpert to England so he could do his cover story on Kubrick and *A Clockwork Orange* for *Saturday Review.* When Penelope Houston talked to Kubrick, the director added a feline audio element to the interview. "While we are talking to Kubrick one of his household, an enormous cat, stalks about the long table, entangling its feet in the tape recorder and purring vigorously into the microphone," Houston wrote in the London *Times'* Saturday Review. "We go on talking and the cat goes on recording its purr. And the purr on the tape seems, too, a very proper kind of Kubrick incident."

Kubrick did allow journalists and visitors into his home and office, but he still maintained a vow of silence on many matters concerning exactly how he made films—an area he considered private. He also took measures to physically conceal areas that exposed how he worked. "When I visited Stanley's house I noticed lots of Turkish towels covering one wall," Malcolm McDowell stated to Paul D. Zimmerman. "It turned out that they concealed his cross-reference system. He likes secrecy."

Victor Davis of the *Daily Express* interviewed Kubrick at a local restaurant near the director's Hertfordshire home. Kubrick entered wearing a windbreaker and ammunition boots and moved uncomfortably past businessmen drinking and talking loudly at the bar. Kubrick was in a philosophical mood and talked to Davis about the morality of *A Clockwork Orange.* "Culture seems to have no effect upon evil," Kubrick opined. "People have written about the failure of culture in the twentieth century: the enigma of Nazis who listened to Beethoven and sent millions off to the gas chambers. It's not good arguing that law and order is a fake issue raised by neo-fascist elements who want to exploit it. They may, in fact, do this but it's a real issue. Certainly one of the serious moral questions posed by *A Clockwork Orange* is whether the evil of the government's method in finding 'a cure for crime' is worse than the individual evil of Alex. Anyway, whatever I think and whatever the true nature of man may be, he has managed to survive somehow, and hopefully will continue to survive."

In London Kubrick was walking his film through the laborious process of producing a release print. As he moved back and forth from his command center at home and the labs, he found a moment to stop at North London's Golder's Green area. He had not purchased a new pair of shoes in more than a year. As he moved from shop window to shop window, he was torn between picking up a pair of the work boots that he preferred or buying more fashionable footwear, as his wife had instructed. Kubrick's uniform for the *A Clockwork Orange* set had been a pair of crumpled gray trousers, a blue single-breasted blazer, shiny at the elbows, and an olive-drab anorak. He wore his shirts loose and his pants baggy. The man who had once owned three suits now just had plain jackets hanging in his closet.

While Kubrick was searching shop windows for suitable footwear, his office was tracking him down. When he finally entered a shoe shop to his liking, the clerk asked him if he was an American. When he said yes, he was given a phone. Earlier in the day, while driving his 1967 Mercedes, he had noticed that the red warning light on the control panel began to blink. Kubrick instructed his assistant Andros Epaminondas to contact Mercedes for information on the car. While he was driving, Kubrick immediately got connected with Andros through mobile communications. In Kubrick's ultra-organized, military-esque operation he was operative 285 and Andros was operative 783. When they were connected, Kubrick ordered Andros to call Mercedes headquarters to learn what was wrong with his automobile. When Kubrick became aware that he possibly had a leak in the brake-fluid system of the Mercedes, he drove home from the shoe shop at half the already slow pace he drove at lately for safety's sake and switched to his twelve-seat Land Rover before going to the National Screenings laboratory to see the first print of the titles for *A Clockwork Orange.*

The screening went poorly. Kubrick found the blue background eating into the white letters. There was a hairline shadow on one of the title backgrounds. Kubrick's eye, like the ground glass in a camera, perceived that the whole screening was being projected out of focus. He calmly gave his notes. The lab chief replied that many of the problems stated couldn't possibly exist. Kubrick ordered another print and was promised the results the next day.

Kubrick had a personal staff of eight who carried out his precise requirements. "You see this piece of paper," Andros said to Andrew Bailey, who visited the director for an article he was writing for *Rolling Stone* magazine. "It measures six inches by four because Stanley thinks that six by four is the best size for a memo. The thing is that he's right. Sure, it can be frustrating working for Stanley, not because he cuts out personal initiative, but because he's always right. Actually, it's very rewarding working for him. I reckon on devoting some of my life to Stanley. I know it'll be worth it."

Bailey found interviewing Stanley Kubrick a challenge. The director rarely discussed what his films were about and was circumspect about works in progress. Bailey learned, as Arthur C. Clarke had, that Kubrick loved to jump from topic to topic in rapid-fire fashion. While Bailey wanted to hear about *A Clockwork Orange*, Kubrick zapped into topics ranging from the printing costs of newspapers to the defensive style of English soccer. The writer observed that many people wanted to meet Kubrick and that they had to come to him on his own timetable. Bailey found Kubrick to be polite and diplomatic.

One week before *A Clockwork Orange* was to premiere, the master negative was scratched and the color quality was not to Kubrick's specification. "The laboratory is quite capable of making dreadful mistakes," Kubrick said to Bernard Weinraub of the *New York Times*. "Just the other night I saw *Paths of Glory* on television, and the lab had printed several reels a word out of synchronization. Printing machines can make the print too dark, too light or the wrong colors. There are many variables involved."

When Kubrick discovered the negative scratch, he decided to switch labs to protect his film. He planned the move with military precision and personally drove the sixteen reels of cut original negative in his tanklike Land Rover. Like a secret service advance man, he had his film editor drive a short distance ahead of the vehicle to absorb the impact in the event of a possible crash. Kubrick remained calm in the face of stress and diversity. Ed Haben, a dubbing engineer who worked with Kubrick for ten weeks on *A Clockwork Orange*, told Paul D. Zimmerman, "He's had any number of good reasons to blow up at everyone. But he has never raised his voice, not once."

When the release print was finally ready, *A Clockwork Orange* was previewed almost every afternoon for several weeks at Theater 7 at Pinewood Studios. The film was shown to foreign distributors and others as Kubrick sat at the controls adjusting focus and sound levels. Kubrick had spent day and night personally checking the quality of each print coming out of the lab before it was okayed to be sent to theaters.

In one week fifteen screenings were held at Warner Bros., and the film was shown nine times at a large 20th Century-Fox screening room. Six previews were scheduled for Cinema I, where the film was to open in New York. As many as five thousand people would see the film before the public laid down its money at the ticket booth.

From his command post at home in England, Kubrick kept a tight watch on how *A Clockwork Orange* was being handled. In New York a press screening was scheduled at Cinema I. Kubrick knew that Cinema I projected films onto a white cement wall without a matte to surround and frame the image. Kubrick insisted on having a black matte. Pressure was put on Donald Rugoff, who owned the theater, and he agreed to paint a matte on the surface. Kubrick persistently kept track of the situation and called Dick Lederer, vice president of advertising and publicity for Warner Bros. at 6:00 A.M. Los Angeles time, asking him to keep an eye on Cinema I. In turn, Lederer sent his lieutenant in charge of publicity Joe Hyams to check on progress of the black matte. After visiting Cinema I, Hyams called Lederer and reported, "Good thing you sent me over—they were painting the matte neon orange."

The critical response to *A Clockwork Orange* was a study in extremes. Vincent Canby of the *New York Times* gave *A Clockwork Orange* a rave review, calling the film "brilliant, a tour de force of extraordinary images, music, words and feelings, a much more original achievement for commercial films than the Burgess novel is for literature, for Burgess, after all, had some impossibly imposing literary antecedents, including the work of Joyce," Canby wrote. "*A Clockwork Orange* is so beautiful to look at and to hear that it dazzles the senses and the mind even as it turns the old real red vino to ice."

Andrew Sarris, the American padrone of the auteur theory, had originally panned *2001*. Seeing it again actually caused him to reverse his opinion. Commenting on *A Clockwork Orange* in his Films in Focus column in the *Village Voice*, Sarris wrote, "But don't take my word for it. See *A Clockwork Orange* for yourself and suffer the damnation of boredom. For those who recall my partial recantation on '2001,' don't expect me to backtrack this time." In the bitterly negative review, Sarris stated: "Let me report simply that *A Clockwork Orange* manifests itself on the screen as a painless, bloodless, and ultimately pointless futuristic fantasy." Sarris closed the door on Kubrick, ending his attack by admonishing the excessive violence in the film. "What frightens me is the chaos that engulfs us all. I am tired of the cult of violence. I am tired of people smashing other people and things in the name of freedom and self-expression. But that has nothing to do with the ultimate failure of *A Clockwork Orange* as a movie. What we have here is simply a pretentious fake."

John Simon, the acerbic and articulate film critic, announced *A Clockwork Orange*'s placement on his ten worst list on the popular *Dick Cavett Show*. Writing in the *Daily News*, Rex Reed raved about *A Clockwork Orange*, calling Kubrick a genius and the film "a mind-blowing work of dazzling originality and brilliance that succeeds on many levels of consciousness." Reed proclaimed, "*A Clockwork Orange* is one of the few perfect movies I have seen in my lifetime."

When the Catholic press and conservatives attacked the violence in *A Clockwork Orange*, Burgess defended the film publicly while Kubrick remained silent. "I was not quite sure what I was defending—the book that had been called 'a nasty little shock' or the film about which Kubrick remained silent. I realized, not for the first time, how little impact even a shocking book can make in comparison with a film. Kubrick's achievement swallowed mine, whole, and yet I was responsible for what some called its malign influence on the young," Burgess wrote in his autobiography.

Kubrick utilized slow and high-speed action to stylize the violence and sex in *A Clockwork Orange*. Anthony Burgess used real and invented language to stylize his book. Kubrick used cinematic technique to transform the graphic violent and sexual acts into something other than explicit nature. "I wanted to find a way to stylize all this violence and also to make it as balletic as possible," he told Joseph Gelmis. "The attempted rape on stage has the overtones of a ballet. They move around the stage. The speeded-up orgy sequence is a joke. That scene took about twenty-eight minutes to shoot at two frames a second. It lasts on screen about forty seconds. Alex's fight with his droogs would have lasted about fourteen seconds, if it wasn't in slow motion. I wanted to slow it to a lovely floating movement."

"Telling a story realistically is such a slowpoke and ponderous way to proceed, and it doesn't fulfill the psychic needs that people have," Kubrick told Paul D. Zimmerman. "We sense that there's more to life and to the universe than realism can possibly deal with."

Alex's fantasy sequences were a challenge in adapting *A Clockwork Orange*. Kubrick turned to the movies to find images for Alex's dream state while he listened to his beloved Ludwig van. "The book describes things stylistically that I couldn't film," Kubrick told Joseph Gelmis. "I just wanted to have him visualizing some very inappropriate images one might think of while listening to Beethoven's Ninth Symphony. Violent images. The cavemen sequence came from *One Million B.C.*, the film with Raquel Welch. He would imagine things he had seen in films."

The ad campaign for *A Clockwork Orange* included an impressive theater display that featured airbrushed illustrations by artist Phil Castle and a slogan in large type proclaiming, "What's Stanley Kubrick been up to?" The bold illustrations depicted Alex with false teeth in a glass, Alex with a glass of milk, and Alex and his fellow droogs.

A Clockwork Orange opened at the Cinema I in New York and broke the box office record for a film running only six performances. A seven-day record was set at the Towne in Toronto and at the Metro in San Francisco.

A Clockwork Orange did receive the X rating from the MPAA, the dreaded letter that was used to label hard-core pornography. Dr. Aaron Stern of the MPAA rating board explained the decision by saying, "I flew to London to talk to Stanley about that X rating. At first he was angry. But I told him that we couldn't give *Clockwork* an R just because he had speeded up the camera on that ménage à trois scene, because, if we did that, that any hard-core pornographer could speed up his scenes and legitimately ask for an R on the same basis. We would have created a precedent. By the time we finished talking, Stanley saw my point." Stern was frustrated and publicly stated he wished there was a special rating category for X films of exceptional quality. This position on high-speed sex still held fifteen years later when the MPAA originally gave Spike Lee an X for his debut film, *She's Gotta Have It,* based on a pixilated love scene that contained frames of a penis.

In England the film was given a certificate by the British Board of Film Censors, which rated the film restricted to audiences under eighteen years of age. The organization had been created by the industry to monitor sex and violence and was now headed by Steven Murphy. Local authorities still had the right to control what was shown in their areas. When a Leeds committee tried to move to ban the film, Murphy wrote to them trying to defend the integrity of Kubrick's film.

A Clockwork Orange was nominated for best picture at the Academy Awards, along with *Fiddler on the Roof, The Last Picture Show, Nicholas and Alexandra,* and *The French Connection.* The majority of the 3,078 members of the Academy voted for *The French Connection,* directed by William Friedkin. Kubrick was nominated for best director and for best screenplay based on material from another medium. Surprisingly, *A Clockwork Orange* received only one nomination in the area of technical film crafts for film editor—Bill Butler. The film lost all chances for an award to Friedkin's film.

In reaction to the increase of sex and violence in movies, thirty newspapers across America developed a policy declining advertisement for any film rated X. The *Detroit News,* one of the largest papers taking this stand, announced its intentions in the March 19, 1972, edition. The paper, with a daily circulation of 65,000, stated that as of the following Sunday it would no longer "publish, display advertising—or give editorial publicity to X-rated motion pictures and those other unrated pictures which, in our judgment, are of a pornographic nature." Regardless of the copy content—ads for X-rated films would not be run in the paper. Publicity and promotion stories and reviews for these films would not be published. "In our view, a sick motion picture industry is using pornography and an appeal to prurience to bolster theater attendance: quite simply, we do not want to assist them in the process," the *Detroit News* proclaimed, and later closed by saying, "We anticipate no movie industry cleanup as a result of our decision. Although we are the largest newspaper in the country to have taken such a step we recognize that other advertising vehicles are available to the exhibitors both within and outside Detroit. Perhaps the only result will be in our own satisfaction in a modest declaration against the theory that makes hard-core sex, voyeurism and sadistic violence the prime ingredients of art and entertainment in the 1970s."

Ironically, the *Village Voice,* which did publish ads for films rated X, ran an ad for the 3D adult film *The Stewardess* right next to Andrew Sarris's negative review of *A Clockwork Orange,* which sported the headline "The Ultimate Trip—Flying Again."

Stanley Kubrick responded with the eloquence of a First Amendment defender. *A Clockwork Orange* was not named in the *Detroit News* editorial, but it was one of a handful of commercial, studio films to receive the X rating formerly given solely to explicit hard-core adult films. In 1969 *Midnight Cowboy* had been the first to receive the rating. The film won the Academy Award and sent the message that America was ready for a new kind of adult dramatic film. Ken Russell's *The Devils* and Sam Peckinpah's *The Wild Bunch,* contemporaries of *A Clockwork Orange,* had also been under the X fire. Kubrick spoke out against the attempt to censor and ban motion pictures from the public. Kubrick's letter to the editor was published in the April 9, 1972, edition of the *Detroit News.* He opened by saying that the paper's "modest declaration" was "an irrational diktat."

"In its emphasis on protection and purification, on purging the public mind of what, 'in our judgment,' are motion pictures of a pornographic nature, it recalls the words of another arbiter of public morals and national taste, who said: 'Works of art which cannot be understood and need a set of instructions to justify their existence, and which find their way to neurotics receptive to such harmful rubbish, will no longer reach the public. Let us have no illusions: we have set out to rid the nation and our people of all those influences threatening its existence and character.' "

Kubrick was quoting Adolf Hitler, commenting on a Munich art exhibition of "degenerate" art in 1937. "In this day and age, the *Detroit News* censors may feel better equipped to make such fine distinctions—though I do not envy them their task," Kubrick wrote. "But what they are doing is, in essence, the same."

Kubrick's principal argument was that newspaper advertisement was crucial to promote a motion picture, and if the public wasn't able to learn where and when a film was playing, it was—for all intents and purposes—being banned. He told the newspaper that it was violating the same First Amendment that protected its freedom to print its views. He explained that the MPAA does not condemn a film but merely identifies those films to be seen only by those over seventeen or eighteen in some states. "This category is consistent with the United States Supreme Court opinion that only the morals of minors are vulnerable and must be protected," Kubrick declared.

After his general and high-principled attack, Kubrick revealed his personal motives. "In addition to the anti-democratic principles involved in the position of the *Detroit News*, the indiscriminateness and arbitrariness of its edict is illustrated by the banning of my film, *A Clockwork Orange*, from its display advertising and editorial pages. The film has been awarded the New York Film Critics prizes for Best Film of the Year and Best Director of the Year, and it was nominated for Academy Awards as 'Best Picture,' 'Best Director,' 'Best Screenplay' and 'Best Editor,' yet the *Detroit News* censors would indiscriminately defame and discredit all X films because they do not conform to what they judge to be the standards of their readers."

Kubrick closed by saying, "High standards of moral behavior can only be achieved by the example of right-thinking people and society as a whole, and cannot be maintained by the coercive effect of the law. Or that of certain newspapers."

The outrage against *A Clockwork Orange* centered around the joy that Alex and his droogs exhibit for the pain they inflict on society. "When you ask is it right for violence to be fun you must realize that people are used to challenging whether certain types of violence are fun," Kubrick told Andrew Bailey for *Rolling Stone* magazine. "You see it when your western hero finally shoots all the villains. Heroic violence in the Hollywood sense is a great deal like the motivational researchers' problem in selling candy. The problem with candy is not to convince people that it's good candy, but to free them from the guilt of eating it. We have seen so many times that the body of a film serves merely as an excuse for motivating a final blood-crazed slaughter by the hero of his enemies, and at the same time to relieve the audience's guilt of enjoying this mayhem."

Discussion of *A Clockwork Orange* and its implications was everywhere. The *Hollywood Reporter,* best known for its "industry insider" point of view, reviewing films for their box office potential more than the social implications, actually asked Emanuel K. Schwartz, Ph.D., D.S.Sc, of the Postgraduate Center for Mental Health in New York City, to create a psychiatric analysis of *A Clockwork Orange.* Schwartz agreed with Kubrick that watching films was an experience akin to dreaming, and he called the film a folk dream. He found the film to be an important statement about man's conditioning. "It is the recurrence of peak experiences in clockwork, mechanical fashion that makes this particular film instructive," Dr. Schwartz wrote in conclusion. "The pursuit of the peak experience is the manic search for omnipotence. This leads us to the moral aspects of the film. Civilization survives in the attempt to control, to modify, to attenuate, to limit the magical, maniacal absolutism of unconscious fantasies. Whether we can introduce limits within which degrees of freedom may be enhanced, within which life may be experienced without a sense of impotence or omnipotence is a challenge to the social engineers. The fact is, however, that *A Clockwork Orange* is made of the stuff of which man is made."

Kubrick began his new relationship with Warner Bros. with terms that ensured complete control of his films. He exercised great care in the release of *A Clockwork Orange.* The director and his staff had amassed an enormous data bank dissecting the U.S. and foreign markets. Kubrick had analyzed two years' worth of the issues of *Variety* and used the industry organ to compile a list of every theater covered by its weekly gross reports. Kubrick and his staff tracked seating capacity, admission charges, films booked, and the length of play, which gave him a game plan of the best theaters for *A Clockwork Orange.* He chose each theater on the basis of a good track record for films of a similar caliber.

Warner Bros. vice president of sales, Leo Greenfield, who was in charge of domestic territories, found Kubrick's strategy to be astute and helpful. Kubrick and his staff used the same approach to determine which theaters *A Clockwork Orange* should play in international markets. Norman Katz, the chief executive of Warner International, had been in a struggle with Ted Ashley, president of Warner Bros., over the principal running of the company. In his jurisdiction, Katz rejected Kubrick's suggestions. Kubrick watched closely as *A Clockwork Orange* was put into release, and he was displeased with the way the studio was handling the film in Europe. With the same attention that he applied to the production process, Kubrick began to research how the film was playing, and he called a meeting to express his displeasure. He presented

Warner executives with computer printouts of the grosses of *2001* distributed by MGM as compared with *A Clockwork Orange* when they played in the same theaters. Even with the difference of three years, the figures proved Kubrick's point that Warners was not doing the best that it could. Kubrick demanded changes in the executives handling the film or he threatened to take the film away from Warners. The hardball tactics that Kubrick had learned on the chessboards of Washington Square Park, on the film set, and in his independent study of military history served him well as a filmmaker protecting his film.

As the fight escalated, Ashley seized the opportunity to get at Katz, siding with Kubrick based on his career domestic track record. Katz lost his job, and Kubrick solidified his position with Warners. At the Warner Communications annual meeting, Ashley called Stanley Kubrick a genius who combined aesthetics with fiscal responsibility.

In January 1972, Anthony Burgess was walking down London's Bond Street when a friend stopped him and asked why he looked so depressed. Burgess told the man he was on his way to dine with Stanley Kubrick. The friend told Burgess that *A Clockwork Orange* was the film hit of the year. "Precisely," Burgess said. "I sold the screen rights long ago for a few hundred dollars."

Kubrick gave Malcolm McDowell a Labrador retriever, and Malcolm named the pet Alex. Kubrick asked McDowell to do publicity for the film on the TV circuit. This continued while McDowell was working on his next project, *O Lucky Man!*, for director Lindsay Anderson. The actor did Kubrick's bidding, accepting awards at film festivals, where *A Clockwork Orange* was receiving accolades.

Burgess and Malcolm McDowell went on a publicity tour for *A Clockwork Orange*. Warner Bros. ensconced Burgess at the Algonquin Hotel in New York and booked him on radio and television shows to talk about the film. Kubrick stayed in England, monitoring the publicity and promotion. Arthur Bell, of the *Village Voice*, spent the day with McDowell and Burgess escorted by Mike Kaplan, who had been responsible for the Ultimate Trip campaign for *2001*. The men made the rounds, appearing on the *Today* show, where Malcolm was interviewed by a disapproving Barbara Walters, *The David Frost Show*, and *Midday* with Lee Leonard. McDowell told Arthur Bell that Kubrick was surveilling every move he and Burgess made. During their publicity day, McDowell told Bell the genesis of the notorious scene where Alex beats the writer who watches Alex sexually attacking his wife while crooning the Gene Kelly classic "Singin' in the Rain." "Stanley Kubrick asked me if I could sing and dance and I said yes, then I thought for a few minutes, then did this old soft shoe to 'la dee had had doo, la dee dah dah doo, I'm singing, just dancing in the rain'—and it fit and Kubrick said, 'We'll use it'; and that's how great moments are born."

"We tried to rehearse what was in the script and it was impossible to do," Malcolm McDowell told Nat Hentoff during a radio broadcast in 1972. "It wasn't working, the scene with the droogs rushing in and Alex grabbing hold of the manuscript and throwing it up like a mackerel or a cornflake and all the rest of it. It just didn't work. It was very flat. We sat around for three days. This shows the greatness of this man who can actually take the time. There are very few who will because they are so pressured. Kubrick was pressured but he put up a marquee in this garden for the crew to sit in, to get them out of the way while something was created on the spot. On the third day he came up to me and he said, 'Can you dance?' And I went into this soft-shoe shuffle and because I was thinking I was Alex I just automatically thought of the happiest song I know from childhood, which was 'Singin' in the Rain.' It could never have been written. This is why Stanley Kubrick is such a great director for actors, because he will allow you to create and he gives. He encourages it and he accepts what you have. If he trusts you, you're all right."

When the New York Film Critics gave *A Clockwork Orange* their awards for best film and best director, Kubrick asked Burgess to attend the ceremony at Sardi's. Kubrick telephoned Burgess in New York with the speech he wanted the writer to deliver on his behalf. Burgess listened attentively, but in front of the New York Film Critics he used more of his own words than Kubrick's.

After his New York press tour was completed, Burgess headed back to Rome, where he lived. First, he stopped in London to deliver the best film and best director plaques from the New York Critics to Kubrick. During his London stopover, Burgess was booked on a BBC radio program where *A Clockwork Orange* was bitterly attacked.

Violence in the movies became a passionate subject. *A Clockwork Orange* and Sam Peckinpah's *Straw Dogs* were often spoken about in the same breath. Both films originally received X ratings. In England, the majority of critics praised Kubrick and damned Peckinpah. Thirteen film critics wrote to the *Times* of London to condemn *Straw Dogs*, saying the film was "dubious in its intention, excessive in its effect."

"Violence itself isn't necessarily abhorrent," Kubrick told Paul D. Zimmerman. "From his own point of view, Alex is having a wonderful time, and I wanted his life to appear to us as it did to him, not restricted by the conventional pieties. You can't compare what Alex is doing to any kind of day-to-day reality. Watching a movie is like having a daydream.

You can safely explore areas that are closed off to you in your daily life. There are dreams in which you do all the terrible things your conscious mind prevents you from doing."

In October 1972 Kubrick decided to withdraw *A Clockwork Orange* for sixty days to comply with the MPAA rules about resubmitting a film for a new rating. Kubrick replaced thirty seconds of footage in two scenes that contained explicit sexual material with less-objectionable shots from the same scenes. When the MPAA saw the new version, it rated *A Clockwork Orange* R and the film was rereleased at the end of the year. The change in rating allowed Warner Bros. to book the film in many areas where X-rated films were not permitted.

On May 9, 1973, Anthony Burgess filed suit in High Court in London against Si Litvinoff and Max Raab, executive producers of the film *A Clockwork Orange*, Warner Bros., and various associated companies, alleging conspiracy to defraud the author over the motion picture rights to his novel. Stanley Kubrick was not named in the suit. Burgess, who was in New York teaching at City College, claimed that misrepresentation by Litvinoff led to his relinquishing valuable rights to his work without royalties. Burgess eventually won a percentage less than executive producers Litvinoff and Raab, payable when the film was in profit.

Although Anthony Burgess was a prolific author and composer, he was defined and best known by his novel *A Clockwork Orange*. The book had a quiet life until Kubrick's movie was released. Burgess was vilified for inflicting violence on society and causing copycats, who duplicated Alex's acts of ultra-violence in real life. In his celebrity Burgess had been propositioned by women and offered preposterous movie deals.

Stanley Kubrick's *A Clockwork Orange* brought Anthony Burgess fame not for his enormous literary and musical output but for a sole novella. The book was published in Bulgaria, Czechoslovakia, and Poland. There was also a Hebrew edition and a Russian edition for Russian-speaking émigrés. Like Nabokov, Burgess took this narrow attention in good stride, but by 1973 he was beginning to tire of having to answer for the film while Kubrick largely remained silent. "I am becoming increasingly exasperated by the assumption of guilt that it is my duty to defend the film against its attackers and not merely my book. It is surely the duty of the maker of the film to speak out for his own work," Burgess told *Variety*.

"This may not be strictly relevant, but I am inevitably somewhat tired of the general assumption that *A Clockwork Orange* is the only book I have written. I'm the author of nearly thirty books and I should like some of these to be read.

"Most of the statements I'm alleged by journalists to have made in fact have been distortions of what I have really said. This can be blamed on the difficulties of telephonic communications between Rome, where I live, and London. But it can chiefly be blamed on the scrambling apparatus which resides in the brains of so many journalists."

In 1974 Senator John Roeder of Arizona introduced a bill which became known as "The *Clockwork Orange*" bill. The legislation proposed to protect prison inmates who volunteered for therapy programs that, like the Ludovico treatment, claimed to turn violent criminals into peaceful citizens of society.

A Clockwork Orange had a chilling effect in England. Critics and community groups were appalled by the film's violence. Copycat crimes of rape and murder were attributed to it. Young men in Great Britain were seen marauding the streets dressed like Alex and the droogs.

When Arthur Bremmer was arrested after shooting Governor George Wallace while he was campaigning for president, police found a diary he had kept. "April 24 Milwaukee," Bremmer wrote. "I had to get rid of my thoughts. I went down to the zoo, down by the river, but that did not help. I saw *Clockwork Orange* and thought about getting Wallace all through the picture." He also used the term "ultra-violence," which was often spoken by Alex. Later, Bremmer's diary would be one of the influences for Paul Schrader's screenplay for *Taxi Driver,* directed by Martin Scorsese. That film led to another obsession, that of John Hinckley, who claims that he was led to shoot President Ronald Reagan after seeing Jodie Foster, who played a preteen prostitute in the film.

Violent acts that mirrored *A Clockwork Orange* began appearing in England. A seventeen-year-old Dutch girl was raped while on a camping holiday in Lancashire by a gang who chanted, "Singin' in the Rain." At Oxford Crown Court a sixteen-year-old boy obsessed with *A Clockwork Orange* was convicted and sentenced to be detained indefinitely after he kicked a sixty-year-old tramp to death. Another sixteen-year-old boy savagely beat a younger child. The attacker wore Alex's white overalls, a black bowler hat, and combat boots. Judge Desmond Bailey told the boy, "We must stamp out this horrible trend which has been inspired by this wretched film. We appreciate that what you did was inspired by the wicked film, but that does not mean you are not blameworthy." Gangs of youths strolled across Leicester Square dressed as droogs. Rapes and murders were attributed to the film's influence.

Miriam Karlin, who played the Cat Lady whom Alex smashed to death with a penis sculpture, defended the film, telling England's *Daily Mirror,* "I utterly refute the statements in court that [one of the murders] was a result of the picture. Any normal human being who had no evil intents in him or no wild desires is not going to be influenced by seeing this film."

Kubrick didn't respond to the charges that his film was inciting the youth of England to violence. Anthony Burgess, the creator of Alex and his nasty droogs, spoke out eloquently, saying to the *Times* Saturday Review in England, "Neither cinema nor literature can be blamed for original sin. A man who kills his uncle cannot justifiably blame a performance of Hamlet. On the other hand, if literature is to be held responsible for mayhem and murder, then the most damnable book of them all is the Bible, the most vindictive piece of literature in existence."

In 1974, Stanley Kubrick, concerned about all the real-life violent acts attributed to viewings of *A Clockwork Orange*, pulled the film from distribution in England, effectively placing a self-imposed ban on his work. Kubrick asked Warner Bros. to stop distributing the film in England, making it illegal to show it anywhere in the country. *A Clockwork Orange* had played at the Warner West End Cinema for sixty-one weeks, drawing record audiences: 55,716 people saw *A Clockwork Orange*, grossing £438,797. The film appeared only briefly in outlying cities before Kubrick gave Warners the word to pull it permanently. *A Clockwork Orange* had grossed $2,500,000 in England, just behind the James Bond film *Live and Let Die* and *The Godfather*.

In England, life was beginning to change—Pakistanis were being beaten by ultra-right-wing thugs, skinheads and radical trade unionists were whipping up racial and political hatred. By the end of the decade, the Sex Pistols were at the forefront of a punk movement that went beyond music into a nihilistic, angry, and violent self-immolating worldview. As the violence of *A Clockwork Orange* came off the screen and into the streets of the country where he lived, Kubrick became concerned about his family's safety and the impact that his film had on his immediate surroundings.

In August 1985 *A Clockwork Orange* was finally shown in Argentina. In 1971 the Argentine government would approve the film only if cuts were made. Kubrick refused, and the film was banned for fourteen years, until the Argentine film censorship system was dismantled. Ten Argentine presidents had been in power during the period of the ban. Kubrick insisted that the Argentines run prints with technically updated Spanish subtitles, which caused the release to be delayed for more than a year.

During the self-imposed ban, Channel 4 in England ran a twenty-five-minute documentary on *A Clockwork Orange*, which included twelve minutes and thirty seconds of the film. At Kubrick's urging, Time Warner took legal action against the broadcaster. Channel 4 said it had a journalistic right due to the "fair use" provision of the 1988 copyright act. Time Warner claimed Channel 4 had obtained the images illegally by reproducing them from an American laser disc of the film. A court of appeals ruled in favor of Channel 4.

In 1993, after being withheld from British screens for almost twenty years, the film was shown publicly, and Kubrick continued to impose his self-censorship. Twenty-nine-year-old Jane Giles, the program manager of the Scala Cinema in London, was accused of screening a bootleg copy of A Clockwork Orange. Lawyers for FACT, the Federation Against Copyright Theft, charged the program manager and projectionist with violating the Designs and Patents Act of 1988. The copyright was held by Warner Bros.

The Scala, a North London theater in King's Cross, was accused of showing the film, billed in magazine listings as "a surprise film." Giles testified she had obtained the print of A Clockwork Orange through Jean Marc Brenez, who had offered Giles the film for free. Projectionist Jeremy Cusans, who left the Scala to work for Warner Bros., reported that the theater had presented the film at least twice during the eighties. He told the lawyers and stipendiary magistrate Ian Baker of the Wells Street Magistrates Court in Central London that he had a talk with Giles about the implications of showing the film and told her that Kubrick kept a close watch on the ban, saying, "Everyone knows that Kubrick has spies all over the place who keep an eye out for his copyright." Cusans told the court that the print was supplied by a private collector who left it in the theater storeroom in 1989.

In Pittsburgh, Pennsylvania, on June 21, 1990, Michale Anderson, who had just turned eighteen the day before, was convicted of stabbing seventeen-year-old Karen Hurwitz six times in the chest with a thirty-six-inch martial arts sword. Anderson confessed to wearing a Clockwork Orange T-shirt on the day of the murder. Anderson's lawyer, Jon Botula, argued that Anderson was driven to murder by repeated viewings of the Stanley Kubrick film. As part of the defense strategy, Botula showed the jury fifty minutes of A Clockwork Orange to demonstrate the violence in the film. Deputy district attorney W. Christopher Conrad countered the argument, saying, "Even young Alex, if he saw what young Mich did, would take a lesson in 'ultra-violence.' " Opponents and defenders of the media argued over the notion of the power of the movies to incite violence.

The controversy over the sex and violence in A Clockwork Orange overshadowed Kubrick's continued mastery of the medium. More than twenty-five years since its initial release, A Clockwork Orange has not lost its visceral power. As a social document, it demonstrates that Burgess and Kubrick saw the future coming. When the film was released, the Aquarian age of peace and love was ending, and the Rolling Stones concert at the Altamont Raceway opened the door for a wave of youthful violence. In the next two decades society would see punk, skinhead, and neo-Nazi movements and violence in the inner cities—traceable to the world of Alex and his droogs.

As a cinematic experience, Kubrick's ever-blackening worldview forged with his clear visualization of Burgess's densely complex wordplay to depicting a point of view of future thugs that cannot easily be dismissed. A Clockwork Orange is structured in a continuous flow of the three parts outlined in the book. Kubrick worked in large tableaus, shooting scenes in bold master shots, with the camera tracking, moving, shooting through wide lenses that distort the images into the garish, sexual, and violent worldview of Alex. In Sam Peckinpah's seminal The Wild Bunch, the director used slow motion, intercutting, repetition, and a 360-degree wave of bloodshed to transcend the violence into a cathartic ballet of death. In A Clockwork Orange, Stanley Kubrick utilized slow motion, fast motion, and elongated cartoonlike images to transform the explicit violence and sex into a sociopolitical statement about the government's threat against personal freedom. Walter Carlos's synthesizer put the past through a magical, futuristic filter, transforming Purcell, Rossini, and Beethoven into a soundtrack for Alex's nasty and mischievous ultra-violent actions.

A Clockwork Orange was Stanley Kubrick's first truly British film. Lolita and Dr. Strangelove and 2001 had been produced in Great Britain but retained the director's American sensibilities. Kubrick's look into the near future created a backlash that ultimately caused the film to remain unseen in England for more than twenty years. The voice and vision of A Clockwork Orange remained silent, hushed by its creator, who may have felt that the film's violent power was too close to his adopted home.

Stanley and Christiane Kubrick transformed their countryside estate into a home for themselves and their children and an environmental work space for their respective professions as a film director and painter. As Stanley Kubrick continued to develop his office and film facility, Christiane Kubrick created a studio to paint in and turned the enormous land surrounding the house into a continuous garden, which would become the subject of her prolific painting career. The gardens were created by Bill Rowson, the talented greensman responsible for backlot floral feasts seen in many MGM films, under Christiane Kubrick's supervision. Rowson worked from scratch, creating a succession of panoramas dotted with little white tables and chairs that allowed the visitor to sit in the shade of a cedar tree or in front of a shimmer of flowers that embraced the spectrum of shades of a single color. "There's always something blooming here," Christiane Kubrick told Valerie Jenkins of the *Evening Standard.* "It's stacked in such a way that there's never a dead moment. One marvelous garden after another, grown specially for cutting so you don't destroy the display. Very Victorian. It's the sort of terribly rich English thing I'd only read about before and I'm still impressed with it."

The gardens featured a manmade pond built by Rowson. At first the water turned black because of an ecological imbalance, but later it became lagoon green when lilies, tadpoles, and other life-forms were added. Christiane Kubrick was well aware of the fifty-eight tadpoles in her personal pond, having done a drawing of each one. A merry-go-round that had once been part of a film set also adorned the grounds.

Christiane cut flowers and brought them into the house for decoration and as models for her to paint. She spent many hours during the day out in the gardens, and at night she watched the flaring eyes of mice-killing owls on the cedar trees from her window.

Like many in her generation, Christiane didn't feel a kinship for her homeland. She returned to Germany only when family duty called. "I go home mainly for funerals. I am attacked then by some Germans who don't understand how I can live in England, but of course today the young German is quite different." Because she had been forced to participate in the Nazi youth movement as a child and had then been disciplined by sport, she now avoided exercise, and she turned the tennis court on the grounds into a flowery orchard.

Painting out in the garden brought several problems, which motivated Christiane to create a self-contained studio where she could work. "You get exhausted carrying all the stuff out here, then flies settle on your paint and of course it starts raining," Christiane Kubrick told Valerie Jenkins of the *Evening Standard.* To paint local landscapes Christiane loaded up her Land Rover with her tools. Once she found a vista that inspired her, she often set up her easel on top of the Land Rover and painted from the aerial view. This outdoor experience had its problems as well: farmers chased her when they saw her putting a mattress down on their land, falsely accusing her of illegal dumping, and on occasion police questioned her, alleging that the Land Rover was stolen.

Christiane Kubrick converted a stable into a painting studio and a personal space that was as important to her work and life as Stanley Kubrick's office and editing rooms were to him. The large space contained favorite old furniture with polished wood, a bed for when her mother came to stay, a television, record player, brass coffeepot on a burner, a cooker, a divan covered by Liberty prints, big squashy cushions, stored canvases, easels, paints and brushes. The courtyard was filled with colorful geraniums. Jam sandwiches, a favorite snack, were fixtures in the studio. Christiane munched on the preserves spread onto bread for sustenance while contemplating a work in progress. At times, the sandwiches became part of the still-life composition and had to be replaced after nibbles had transformed their original shape. She found the tasty snack, so popular with children, to have a soothing effect when she was at a "moan and groan stage" with a painting in progress. The television was often on while Christiane painted, and it also served a dual purpose. The communication with the outside world connected her to places beyond the isolation of the estate and the communication object itself became a recurring image in her paintings. "TV sets intrigue me," Christiane told Valerie Jenkins, "because they're behind everything and they're always on at the time when I'm drawing. Especially color TV because it's such a weird intrusion. I can't get over what you can see in your own living-room among all the ordinary things."

The studio was Christiane Kubrick's domain, where she demanded as much private time as her husband. Painting with great discipline to a prescribed, strictly kept schedule, Christiane would allow interruptions only from her teenage daughters, Katharina, Anya, and Vivian. The environment that she created in her homey studio was designed to help her through creative stalemates. "When I come unstuck with a painting. I just sit and read or play music," she told Ann Morrow for the London *Times*. "It may be something the children have bought—some pop music—I can do this for hours and then go back to the problem."

Christiane Kubrick's natural beauty came through her casual artist persona. Her life as an actress flirted with glamour, but she was comfortable in a long fringe haircut, long print dresses, overalls, and functional round eyeglasses. A vivacious and buoyant person who laughs easily, she could often be seen in worn blue denim and a fishing apron loaded with pens and pencils, the tools of her trade.

When the Kubricks lived on Eighty-fourth Street in New York City, Christiane Kubrick painted the policemen, buses, and streets that made up the world around her. In England she painted what surrounded her in the rural British countryside. "In New York we watched a lot of television—we sat glued to it," Christiane told Ann Morrow. "It's intriguing the way life goes on at home uninterrupted, while shattering world events are on the TV in the living room. We are the first generation to watch astronauts over jam sandwiches."

Christiane Kubrick drew much of her inspiration for her art from a large greenhouse burgeoning with azaleas, exotic flowers, and plants. Rowson maintained the greenhouse with the same prickly care that Stanley Kubrick protected his home, also posting warning signs for visitors: "Keep door closed." "Please water sparingly." "If hot weather continues please open all windows in daytime." "Please check hose topping up pond. Water evaporating in heat." There were guidance and discipline everywhere on and in the Kubrick estate. The greenhouse, garden, home, and family were Christiane's world and her primary painting subjects. Christiane was an educated painter, but like her husband, she cringed at overintellectualized analysis of art. She avoided symbolism in her work and was influenced by French painters like Matisse and Cézanne and Vuillard, who ushered in the era of modern painting. "I went to the Art Students League in New York, and UCLA in California while I was having the children, and had a crash course in every ism there is," Christiane Kubrick told Valerie Jenkins for the *Evening Standard.* "But if I try to explain painting to Katharina, I find myself spouting asinine cliches and have to shut myself up." Katharina had aspirations of being a set designer, following inspiration of both of her parents.

Christiane Kubrick called her home a "perfect family factory." In addition to her work as an established painter, she ran the rambling household with one daily housekeeper and her children, whom she referred to as "my three slaving daughters." A film trailer sat in the driveway, and when Kubrick's crew and staff were around she made sure that everyone was fed and well cared for.

Christiane worked in her studio for prescribed, disciplined hours. She scheduled breaks for mealtimes to oversee food that she prepared in bulk like a "Red Cross cook." She managed her time strictly and would stop in between the blade strokes of cutting an onion if it was time to return to a work in progress. Christiane and Stanley Kubrick's obsession and dedication to their crafts of art and film made them respectful of the time and space needed for them to flourish. They also both shared the need for family and a warm and friendly home. Privacy was essential for both. "When Stanley is relaxed he plays chess and likes to be very quiet," Christiane Kubrick told Ann Morrow. "I am hopeless at chess. I am incapable of abstract thinking."

Stanley Kubrick was very supportive of his wife's work. *Seedboxes* was one of his favorite paintings, so he proudly put it in the film. Of course it did fit the gentle and intellectual nature of the character. Christiane Kubrick found many of the other paintings in the film that featured sexual and pornographic images to be misogynistic. The violence and sexual terror of *A Clockwork Orange* distressed her terribly. Many of the scenes made her physically ill. "That, of course, is what it's meant to do to you," she told Ann Morrow.

Christiane Kubrick had been a professional fine arts painter for nineteen years. The attention given her husband's controversial new film and the appearance of her work in *A Clockwork Orange* gave her added name recognition as a painter. "He is my greatest fan," Christiane told Ann Morrow. "The more sacchariney the picture, the better he likes it. He likes the gentle, flowery ones best, but I am frightened of being too chocolate boxy." Christiane Kubrick saw a side of her husband that the public didn't see. *A Clockwork Orange* solidified public opinion that he had a misanthropic view of the world. "Recently the local paper came to see me. It was to do with a fundraising scheme to help the deaf. Imagine what I felt next day when I saw a headline that said: 'My Husband Is Not a Beast.' It was so funny. Stanley is so gentle, such a shy and sensitive person." In February 1973 Christiane Kubrick had a London exhibition of her work. She sold thirty-nine canvases at prices from £100 to £500 each and began planning another major showing.

Christiane worked with large canvases, 48 by 72 inches, 48 by 108 inches, and alternated that with small drawings and paintings. The titles of her paintings reveal a straightforward, unpretentious artist who paints what she sees. *Beanshoots and Cucumbers, Orange Trees in Blue Pots,* and *Plants on a Red Plastic Tray* are just what the titles say they are. She has a strong sense of composition and works with vivid ochre, orange, and terra-cotta tones.

Christiane Kubrick's paintings are a record of a life shared with her husband and three daughters. An artist with a river of imagery that explores a bucolic, pastoral natural beauty, she reveals in her paintings a catalog of the life with which she and Stanley Kubrick have chosen to immerse themselves. Red roses, hedges with magpies and molehill, grass cuttings, a coral tree, alpine plants, a bowl of pansies, chrysanthemums, blue flowers, TV sets, airy, colorful tents on the lawn, cats, dogs, and family are the subjects of Christiane Kubrick's work. *Stanley* is a portrait of the film director at home as a husband and father. The 48-by-72-inch canvas features Stanley Kubrick seated in an orange chair. In the background, past orange walls, lies a winter snow and birds. Stanley Kubrick is to the right of the composition, framed by a fish tank and several unframed paintings leaning against the wall. He is looking directly at his wife. His skin is olive-toned, his hair and beard are black, his eyes are wide open and deeply lined, with arched eyebrows. He seems at peace, maybe on the verge of a soft smile, his expression intent but relaxed. *Stanley* is an opportunity to see Kubrick at rest through the eyes of someone who knows him beyond his public image as the intense, misanthropic, obsessed, and reclusive filmmaker. Stanley Kubrick also appears in *Ballynatray Rehearsal in the Rain,* which is a landscape painting featuring him wearing a parka in the rain under an umbrella and working with a figure in a black costume who looks like Reverend Runt from *Barry Lyndon.* Stanley Kubrick is arched back, looking attentively at his actor. The vista of green, gently rolling hills behind him and the road on either side of him put him in an open-air environment atypical of the countless photographs of him inside under artificial lights and the confines of a film studio. *Anya and Cats* pictures the middle daughter reading in the garden with ringlet hair, sundress, lavender jacket, and bandanna. The entire family appears in *Sunflowers and Blue Desk,* in four small gold-framed photos amid a vase of sunflowers, china, and Christmas ornaments. The painting depicts photographic images of Vivian, Anya, Katharina, with Stanley Kubrick (sans beard) on the phone, during the *Lolita* and *Dr. Strangelove* era.

Other paintings portray tents, the Kubrick cats and dogs, the greenhouse, fruit, garden, Teddy the dog, the Abbot's Mead kitchen and exterior, and a cornucopia of flowers in Cézanne, Chagall, and van Gogh–like splendor.

Christiane Kubrick is a serious painter with a conscious and vigorous style. These are not weekend still lifes but the work of an artist with a vision and meticulous technique. Working in oils on canvas with even-textured paint full of vibrant, life-affirming color, Christiane continued to explore the life around her with an affirming eye, just as Stanley continued to aim his lens at the dark side of mankind.

When not painting, Christiane worked on a puppet theater, a passion since her German girlhood. The puppets were large figures designed for a mobile theater. She created narratives and worked from a European tradition that spanned commedia dell'arte to surrealism, looked back to Grimm fairy tales, and embraced television and the cinema.

With the release of *A Clockwork Orange,* Kubrick's foray into psychological conditioning and modern morality gave way to the mannered patterning of eighteenth-century social mores.

Next, Kubrick would take a backward glance.

CHAPTER 16

Candlepower

Technology in the Service of Creativity.
—Company motto for Cinema
Products Corporation

William Makepeace Thackeray wrote *The Luck of Barry Lyndon* in October 1843. The work was published serially in *Fraser's* magazine and appeared in issues between January and December of 1844. In 1856, Thackeray significantly revised his story to be published in volume 2 of his *Miscellanies: Prose and Verse*. The story was retitled *The Memoirs of Barry Lyndon, Esq., of the Kingdom of Ireland*.

The story of *Barry Lyndon* fit neatly into Kubrick's bleak, ironic, and dark view of man. Thackeray wrote a fictional autobiography of Redmond Barry, an Irish rogue tracing his life travels as a soldier, deserter, gambler, and lover who reached the heights of society only to slowly return to where he began as petty gentry. Barry was a scoundrel and a cheat. If Stanley Kubrick could turn Alex of *A Clockwork Orange* into a screen hero for a new age, Barry was right at home with Kubrick's and society's ever-darkening worldview.

Kubrick's method of adapting Thackeray to the screen was not to create a new script fashioned on *Barry Lyndon* but to use the text of the novel to serve as continuity for the film. Then Kubrick developed the cinematic equivalent of each scene. The screenplay was just a blueprint. The film would be made with technology, art direction, and actors who would breathe life into the eighteenth-century characters on Thackeray's pages.

John Alcott was again asked to photograph a Stanley Kubrick film. "Our working relationship is close because we think exactly alike photographically," Alcott told *American Cinematographer* magazine. "We really do see eye to eye."

Barry Lyndon would be an enormous challenge cinematographically. Kubrick was unimpressed with the look of the scores of period films he had seen. He felt that the only way to capture the eighteenth century was through natural light, since it was an era before electricity. To the people in the world of *Barry Lyndon,* source light was the sun and the candle.

Kubrick and Alcott had discussed the notion of filming by candlelight during the making of *2001,* when Kubrick was considering his project on Napoleon. The fast lenses necessary to accomplish this were not available at that time and still weren't for *Barry Lyndon.*

Film speeds were still slow in the early seventies. The 50 to 100 ASA that was available did not have the latitude to allow the emulsion to be lit with the low light of a candle. Contemporary high-speed film stocks would make the feat easier, but in the early seventies Kubrick's only hope was to find a lens fast enough to photograph by the flickering flame of candlelight. Kubrick wanted to be able to capture the patina of the stately period homes he planned to shoot in.

As Kubrick pondered doing a period film, he learned the German Zeiss Company had developed very fast 50mm still-photography lenses for the Apollo space program at NASA. The availability of such lenses gave Kubrick the opportunity to push the limits of cinematography even further. Historical period films were shot with artificial light, filling in and illuminating scenes that were supposed to be lit by the candle's flame. The candles were flickering, but the interiors were overlit by multidirectional artificial light that destroyed the warm, modulating glow of actual candlelight.

To tackle the problem of shooting with candlelight, Kubrick phoned Ed Di Giulio at Cinema Products, who had gotten him the 20:1 zoom lens for *A Clockwork Orange.* "Stanley called me and said, 'I got this lens from Zeiss,' " Di Giulio remembered. "Apparently, it was intended for NASA to use as one of these satellite spy-in-the-sky-type things. It was a 50mm barrel lens, no focusing mount or anything—just an optic that was 50mm in focal length. The aperture was f0.7, which is one full stop faster than f1.0 or two stops faster than the super-speed lenses we have today, which are something like f1.2. So Stanley says, 'I've got this lens and I want to mount it on my BNC Mitchell.' I looked at the lens. The faster a lens gets, the closer the rear element gets to the film plane, and this one got within ³/₁₆ths of an inch from the film plane—that's how close it got. I said, 'Stanley, it just won't fit in there. The BNC has got two shutter blades. You've got an aperture plate on the BNC which is a substantial plate.' Stanley said, 'Well, I could take out one of the shutter blades. I don't need an adjustable shutter and maybe you could machine out the aperture plate.' 'Yes, I could do that, Stanley, but it would wreck the camera for any other application.' Stanley said, 'That's okay, let's do it.' So we made a special focusing mount for this lens. To go from near focus to infinity it took three revolutions of the barrel. We had to make the thread fine enough so you could critically focus it, because at wide open with a lens this fast, you had no chance in hell of being able to eye-focus. We were able to successfully mount up this 50mm lens. Stanley tested it and he was delighted. Then he says, 'Okay, Ed, now I want a 35mm.' So I called my old friend Dr. Richard Vetter of Todd-AO, and Dick told me that they had these Manocom adapters for projection lenses made by Cole Morgan. It's an adapter that you put on the front of a projection lens to change the focal length slightly, wider or narrower, depending on which way you put it in to fill a given thereafter. You can adapt a projection lens that maybe doesn't quite fill the proscenium, or vice versa. So I put things together and I was able to make a 75mm and a 35mm for him. Now he's got these three marvelous lenses, and he shot *Barry Lyndon* with it. I don't think they've ever been used by anybody since then. I got all kinds of calls from people, and I just kept referring them to Stanley. Of course, Stanley just treasured his own equipment and wouldn't let anybody touch it."

Kubrick had begun planning with a production designer and developed the project so the entire film could be photographed at Picketts Manor. He did not want the film to be shot in the studio. He was tired of the staid look of period films and wanted to reinvent the genre, as he had with the science fiction film on *2001*.

When the Picketts Manor concept became too limiting for the vision of *Barry Lyndon*, Kubrick contacted Ken Adam, the brilliant production designer who had created the spectacular look of *Dr. Strangelove*. *Barry Lyndon* would be a much more complex and difficult project for Adam. The designer opted for creating the interior sets of the stately period homes in the studio, but Kubrick insisted on shooting the film on location. "It always had to be a combination of exteriors and interiors but with studio sets," Adam explained. "I did that on *The Madness of King George* on a much smaller scale where the royal apartments were built at

Shepperton Studios. I tried to give them more scale by using some fantastic actual locations interiors." Kubrick remained adamant about shooting on location and became more and more obsessed with the concept of
acquiring what he called the patina of the period interiors. The candlelight would create a purity of image, combined with actual period architecture and texture. The eighteenth century could be rendered in a
painterly documentary reality. Making the task even more difficult,
Kubrick demanded locations close to his home base in Boreham Wood
just outside of London. He sent out teams of photographers to shoot
photos of all the great houses within a ninety-minute radius of his home.

   Kubrick told Richard Schickel it was "helpful not to be constantly
exposed to the fear and anxiety that prevails in the film world." He was
content living in a large manor house with two wooden walls guarding
his precious privacy. The household still enjoyed the company of six cats
and three dogs. Alexander Walker said that Kubrick was "like a medieval
artist living·above his workshop."

   Given the mandate to work strictly on location, Ken Adam had to use
the rooms of several homes to create the scope of the estates in the film.
Eventually Adam was able to convince Kubrick that he had to go further
to find the locations for *Barry Lyndon*. The search extended to Ireland.
Finding Continental buildings in Ireland was a challenge. Part of the
film took place in Germany, but Adam couldn't convince Kubrick to
shoot on location there. Finally, toward the end of the production,
Kubrick dispatched a second unit crew to Pottsdam and East Berlin to
get the German atmosphere of the period by photographing castles and
period streets.

   Kubrick never left home in England to conceive the German sequences. He studied countless photos taken on location in Germany by
teams of photographers. Kubrick determined exactly how the second-
unit crew would film the shots he wanted when they were dispatched on
location. This was the same process that he had used on *2001* for the
Dawn of Man backgrounds. Kubrick had developed an elaborate system
of utilizing a numbered and lettered grid on photographs so he could
direct his second-unit crew by phone. With mathematical precision, he
calculated a shot's composition by giving the crew the coordinates from
the photographic grid.

   The art department research on *Barry Lyndon* was massive. "Stanley
wanted to do it almost like a documentary of the period," Adam recalled.
When they began, Kubrick knew very little about the period. Adam had
a firm understanding about the art and architecture, but as time went on
Kubrick became extremely knowledgeable—absorbing mountains of de-

tails on life in the eighteenth century. "We used to photograph every location and come back and analyze the photographs," Adam explained. "We got into terrible arguments because Stanley was more attracted to Victorian interiors than the more formal, stark, eighteenth-century interiors. He would say, 'I like that wallpaper,' and I would say, 'Stanley, you can't use that wallpaper, that's Victorian.' 'Why?' Of course, in the end Stanley knew more about that period than I or probably anybody else did, because of the amount of research—the living conditions of the people, lice in their wigs, the toothbrushes they used, condoms—we went through everything to find out how those people lived." Because of the many scenes depicting gambling, research was done on period paraphernalia. "We had to make up the playing cards ourselves because they didn't have curved edges. They were very sharp and rectangular and didn't have numbers," Adam remembered. The art department also became involved with the lighting department. Adam and his staff experimented with single-, double-, and triple-wick candles to achieve the necessary intensity of light. Candelabra were designed and created to be used in the actual interior locations, and heat shields were put in place to protect the ceilings, walls, and precious oil paintings from the intense heat. Adam designed the Louis XVI–style bathtub used by Lady Lyndon and placed it in an authentic location.

Kubrick and Adam had different approaches to the art direction of *Barry Lyndon*. Adam's work method involved extensive period research on a project. He then began to interpret from his experience and imagination. As Kubrick began a meticulous study of the paintings of the period, he intended to exactingly re-create the images from the masters of the time, using the paintings to render the precise look of sets, props, and costumes. "The painstaking process of almost reproducing paintings of the period was a different challenge for me," recalls Ken Adam, best known for his interpretive visions of both period and future reality in films like his Oscar-winning *The Madness of King George* and the imaginative large-scale James Bond films.

For the costumes, Kubrick hired Milena Canonero and Ulla-Britt Soderlund. They purchased eighteenth-century clothes, which were still available in England. On the average, people were smaller in the eighteenth century, so the clothes had to be opened up and new costumes created using the same patterns. The production operated a factory at Radlet to produce the many costumes needed to populate Kubrick's time-machine visit to the eighteenth century.

The consuming job of creating the wigs for *Barry Lyndon* went to Leonard of London, who had worked with Kubrick on *A Clockwork*

Orange. Fifteen wigs were made for Ryan O'Neal alone. Leonard fashioned the hairpieces out of hair scissored from the heads of young Italian girls entering religious life. "Just think, if it hadn't been for all those young nuns, Ryan would have had to play all of his love scenes in yak hair," Leonard told journalist Thomas Wood. Leonard spent six months researching the period hairstyles that he designed for Marisa Berenson and the other women in the film. The eminent London hairdresser worked in tandem with Barbara Daly, a makeup artist who had created the droog makeup for *A Clockwork Orange* and was a darling of the London fashion scene.

Massive research was done on eighteenth-century painting. "We used the English painters like Watteau and Italians like Zoffany," Adam explained. "We used the Polish artist Chadowiecki for some of the Continental scenes." Gainsborough, Hogarth, Reynolds, Chardin and Stubbs were also highly influential on the look of *Barry Lyndon*.

Paintings were used to understand and research the period, to inform the physical look of the film, and to be part of the affluent lifestyle. The stately mansions of the eighteenth century were filled with magnificent paintings. Many of the homes were museumlike and contained extensive collections. The homes chosen for *Barry Lyndon* housed many classical paintings, which Adam and Kubrick used as set decoration. "Wilton has beautiful Van Dycks in the double-cube room, which I used again on *The Madness of King George*," Adam explained.

"Stanley has an incredible eye. Strange compositions or a strange dressing of pictures appealed to him, and he wanted to shoot that in the actual filming. We found that a lot of the paintings in the interiors were hung very high up on the wall. That appealed to Stanley—these strange things appealed to him."

Slowly, locations were found. The farmhouse where Barry's mother lived was found in the Camara mountains. Caher Castle, which was made of enormous stone walls, was selected for the Brady family luncheon. Locations for the German sequences were found at Powercourt, which had a strong German influence but was not far from Dublin and was used for the battle scenes. Dublin Castle was used for the Chevalier's home. The location where Barry meets Captain Potzdorf and his troops was a spot near Waterford and Kerkenny. Once Kubrick was settled in Ireland, he tried to persuade Ken Adam to find all the locations for the Continental sequences. Eventually Kubrick realized that the English scenes would have to be shot in England. The exterior of the Lyndon estate was shot at Castle Howard, and the interiors were a collage of Wilton, Corsham Court, and Glenum. Individual scenes taking place in specific rooms were shot at the different locations and put together in the editing room to create the extravagant and magnificent Lyndon estate. Continuity on the film was difficult. Kubrick had to keep track of the conglomeration of locations that he was using to portray a single home in the film.

To organize the location shooting, Kubrick decided that the production would have to remain constantly mobile. To keep the various departments on the road, he assigned a Volkswagen minibus to each division. Ken Adam and his art department were always on the move. "I had a drawing board in the back of my minibus, plus whatever files I needed. Stanley thought of us like Rommel in the desert," Adam stated.

The trip to Ireland involved massive planning. In meetings production managers Douglas Twiddy and Terence Clegg pressured Kubrick about details to be shipped to the locations where he planned on shooting. Kubrick tried putting off all the questions to get to other matters, but the production managers persisted. Kubrick finally agreed to address their concerns but stipulated that if there was a question they asked that he could not answer he would ring a bell and they would move on to other issues. Kubrick then set out to decide what sort of bell it should be. The production manager suggested he could get Kubrick a small servant bell. Kubrick rejected the suggestion, explaining that such a device would offend the class sensibilities of those involved in the production. The production manager then suggested a buzzer, but Kubrick found this to be annoying and instructed the production manager to give the problem to the art department, saying, "Have the art department go out and get an example of every available bell and I'll choose one." This solved the problem of the inquisitive production manager who knew that during earlier research on *Barry Lyndon* Kubrick had already sent out teams of photographers to shoot every field in Ireland that had a tree in the middle of it. When Stanley Kubrick approached something, he demanded to know all the choices before making a decision, but the bell issue was just too much for the already overworked production manager. It was the director's way of sending the message that he was in charge. Stanley Kubrick didn't like to answer questions that he didn't want to answer just yet—in fact, he liked to be the one that asked.

Barry Lyndon had the tightest security of any Kubrick project to date. All during preproduction and into production the only information available was that Stanley Kubrick was directing a movie starring Ryan O'Neal and Marisa Berenson. The title and subject remained a mystery. Speculation was that Kubrick kept this high level of secrecy because he was dealing with a piece of literary material that was in the public domain. Kubrick was concerned that the revelation that he was adapting the Thackeray novel could lead to a quick knockoff of his unprotected idea and unwanted competition at the box office. Kubrick's crypticness was so intense that he received the backing from Warner Bros. based on an outline in which names, places, and dates of the story were changed so no one could recognize the exact novel that was his source.

It was Kubrick's continuing pattern to develop screen stories from previously published material. Throughout his career he was never able to generate an original story out of his own experience. He told Richard Schickel that creating a story of life events was "one of the most phenomenal human achievements." His endless curiosity attracted him to worlds outside his experience, where he could explore through layers of detail until he hit the core.

By the end of January 1973 Warner Bros. could tell *Variety* only that the film would start shooting in England in May or June and starred Ryan O'Neal and Marisa Berenson, even though the studio was in constant contact with Kubrick. For *A Clockwork Orange* Warners had known only that it was based on the Anthony Burgess book. Kubrick did not want a unit publicist on the project. *Variety* speculated that Kubrick was filming a project previously announced by Warners, an adaptation of the Arthur Schnitzler novel *Traumnovelle,* which a press release described as a psychologically dramatic story of a doctor and his wife whose love is threatened by the revelation of their dreams. Everyone was trying to figure out Stanley Kubrick's next move.

The press was unhappy with the lack of copy fodder surrounding *Barry Lyndon* and used the occasion to take potshots at the hermitlike, reclusive, and increasingly secretive director. Kubrick was not receiving even the select journalists he had on his last films. Very few publicity stills were okayed by his office, and he had instructed the actors not to talk to the press without express prior permission. The news blackout caused rumors to circulate about all aspects of the production—from Kubrick's directorial methods to a *New York Daily News* report that the final $11 million budget had started at $2.5 million. The article portrayed Kubrick as an out-of-control auteur. Richard Schickel was one of the few journalists allowed to visit with Kubrick. Although Schickel screened the film before the majority of critics so that he could do a *Time* magazine cover story on *Barry Lyndon,* his four-hour interview was conducted under Kubrick's strictures, in the middle of the night in a fog-shrouded studio.

Kubrick was even withholding with his film's stars. Marisa Berenson, a former model who had given an impressive performance in Bob Fosse's production of *Cabaret*, committed to the film with little more information than who was directing it. "I didn't test for the part. It just came to me," she told journalist Thomas Wood. "I was sitting in my apartment in Paris one afternoon last February when the phone rang. It was Kubrick. He said he had seen my performance in *Cabaret* and asked me if I'd be available for a film later this year. 'Of course,' I replied. Then he said he couldn't tell me much about it except that the story was set in the eighteenth century and was based on a classic. But that didn't matter. After all, Kubrick was involved. That was all I needed to know, so I accepted on the spot. There was one other thing. He asked me to stay out of the sun all summer. I'm supposed to have this pallor. So when I went to Saint-Tropez for a few weeks, I kept my head under a parasol. Which was most fortuitous for me, as it made me look very mysterious and romantic."

Berenson was twenty-eight-years old, the daughter of career diplomat Robert L. Berenson and granddaughter of Elsa Schiaparelli, the Parisian designer who was the sweetheart of thirties couture. The green-eyed model was called "the most beautiful girl in the world" by *Elle* magazine and dated jet-setters David de Rothschild and automobile heir Ricky von Opel. In addition to her role in *Cabaret*, Berenson played the mother in Luchino Visconti's production of *Death in Venice.*

Ryan O'Neal was thirty-four years old. He had appeared in more than five hundred episodes of the successful landmark prime-time TV soap opera *Peyton Place*. The experience on *Barry Lyndon* was unique for O'Neal. His work in *Love Story, What's Up, Doc?* and *Paper Moon* had made him a major Hollywood star but didn't prepare him for a performance with Stanley Kubrick. "God, he works you hard," O'Neal told Richard Schickel. "He moves you, pushes you, helps you, gets cross with you, but above all he teaches you the value of a good director. Stanley brought out aspects of my personality and acting instincts that had been dormant. I had to deliver up everything he wanted, and he wanted just about everything I had. My strong suspicion [was] that I was involved in something great."

Ryan O'Neal was uncharacteristically closed-mouthed about his work on the Stanley Kubrick production. When questioned by the press as he arrived in London after shooting in Ireland he would only say, "This picture will speak for itself." Warner Bros. didn't have to be concerned about surreptitiousness because they knew little more than anyone else.

By November of 1973 *Variety* reported that John Calley, production chief of Warners, and Stanley Kubrick had agreed to suspend production of what was then being called *The Luck of Barry Lyndon*—the original title of the Thackeray story. Calley reinforced a statement from the production, indicating that filming was halted because it would intrude on homeowners who wanted to be in their homes for the holidays. Warners stated the Kubrick would commence shooting in January 1974 for an additional eight weeks of photography. The hiatus was said to add approximately $1 million to the company's budget. "It would make no sense to tell Kubrick, 'Okay, fella, you've got one more week to finish the thing,'" John Calley told Richard Schickel. "What you would get then is a mediocre film that cost say, $8 million, instead of a masterpiece that cost 11 million. When somebody is spending a lot of your money, you are wise to give him time to do the job right. The business is, at best, a crap shoot. The fact that Stanley thinks the picture will gross in nine figures is reassuring. He is never far wrong about anything." Kubrick's deal with Warner Bros. was studio financing with Kubrick reaping 40 percent of all profits.

The *Barry Lyndon* production company had been in Ireland for six months, planning and shooting, when filming was suspended. Several factors were cited as reason for Kubrick's shooting termination and the production's move to England. Dublin reports stated that the IRA had made bomb threats to the production. Although Kubrick firmly denied such reports, he did move his company out of Ireland and back to England within twenty-four hours. The production issued an official statement saying shooting had been suspended because they were not able to gain access to many of the location homes at Christmastime. During the shutdown, rumors spread through the cast and crew. Many concerned the veracity of the IRA threats. Other speculations suggested that while the director was shooting *Barry Lyndon* he was also creating battle scenes that would appear in his long-awaited epic on Napoleon. The lack of information and the thick air of secrecy inflated the expanding myth of Stanley Kubrick as the reclusive auteur.

Shooting was to resume at the start of the new year. Many inside the production conjectured that Kubrick was rethinking his film. Certainly *Barry Lyndon* went through a revision when shooting got under way again. Rather than considering this the mark of a production out of control, it could be viewed as a further sign that Kubrick was evolving his moviemaking methods. They weren't emerging full-blown, but they were meticulously crafted and examined as they were being handmade, a piece at a time. *Barry Lyndon* would reach the screen in all its glory with a disciplined, though some thought overwrought, aesthetic and concept of presenting history through the rigors of the zoom lens, candlelight, and the narrator's instructive voice. The detractors of *Barry*

Lyndon would proclaim, "When a director dies, he becomes a photographer."

Alcott and Kubrick lit entire scenes with candles. For the Lord Ludd gambling sequence, Alcott asked for metal reflectors to keep the heat of the candles from damaging the ceiling and to create an overall illumination of top light for the scene. The chandeliers held seventy candles each, giving the cinematographer the equivalent of three foot-candles of standard illumination. A foot-candle is a industry standard defining the intensity of a light on a surface where all points are at a distance of one foot from a source of one candle. The negative was pushed one full stop in development to pump the appropriate amount of light into the overall image.

Shooting at such low-light levels made it impossible to see the image through a conventional viewfinder equipped with a prism. Kubrick and Alcott adapted a viewfinder from an old Technicolor three-strip camera and mounted it on their already converted BNC Mitchell. The older viewfinder worked on a mirror principle and reflected what it saw, allowing Kubrick and Alcott to clearly view the low-light image.

The original 50mm lens made by Zeiss and adapted for cinematography by Ed Di Giulio was used for virtually all the medium and close shots. The fast lenses had very little depth of field and required careful testing and a system to keep track of the critical distances at which the lenses could retain focus. Alcott's focus operator, Douglas Milsome, was given a closed-circuit video camera to maintain accuracy. "The video camera was placed at a 90-degree angle to the film camera position and was monitored by means of a TV screen mounted above the camera lens scale," Alcott explained to *American Cinematographer* magazine. "A grid was placed over the TV screen and by taping the various artists' positions, the distances could be transferred to the TV grid to allow the artists a certain flexibility of movement, while keeping them in focus. It was a very tricky operation."

Kubrick and Alcott spent hours studying the lighting effects achieved in the paintings of Dutch masters, but they thought the style was flat and decided to light scenes from the side.

The interiors of the stately homes that encompass the world of *Barry Lyndon* were photographed to re-create the natural-light look of the period. "I've always been a natural light source type of cameraman," Alcott told *American Cinematographer* magazine. "I think it's exciting, actually, to see what illumination is provided by daylight and then try to create the effect. Sometimes it's impossible when the light outside falls below a certain level. We shot some of those sequences in the wintertime when there was natural light from perhaps 9 o'clock in the morning until 3 o'clock in the afternoon. The requirement was to bring the light up to a level so that we could shoot from 8 o'clock in the morning until something like 7 o'clock in the evening while maintaining the consistent effect. At the same time we tried to duplicate the situations established by research and reference to the drawings and paintings of that day— how rooms were illuminated and so on. The actual compositions of our setups were very authentic to the drawings of the period."

Many techniques were utilized to create the impression of natural light. The room in which Barry's son, Brian, asks whether his father has bought him a horse had five windows, with a large window in the center. Kubrick and Alcott controlled the light so it would appear to come from the center window to give the room a one-source look. Plastic material and tracing paper were put on the windows and mini-brutes were used to simulate the natural light. Every scene in *Barry Lyndon* was shot on location and inside actual homes in Ireland and the southwest of England.

Many of the estates used in *Barry Lyndon* were open to the public, and Kubrick couldn't restrict the visitors. The production was given permission to work in specific rooms which were closed off to the public who were walking past in the corridors. At times Kubrick could function only when the tours weren't running. At other times the production could shoot only during the changeover from one tour to another. In some cases Kubrick and his cast and crew had complete freedom of the location.

For several sequences, such as the one in Lady Lyndon's bedroom, for example, large rostrums were built for the lighting instruments. The rostrums could be wheeled out of the way when the crew was shooting a reverse angle that faced the windows.

A complete array of gels and filters and the technique of forced development was used to accommodate the constantly changing light conditions to maintain the look of consistent natural daylight over the long and arduous shooting schedule. The scene when Barry is ambushed by two highwaymen was shot on a day that began with full daylight. As the day progressed and the take count added up, Alcott had to utilize faster and faster lenses to match the earlier takes as the light diminished. The latter parts of the sequence were photographed with a T1.2 lens wide open.

Historically, period films relied on an assortment of diffusion filters to soften the image and create an idealized period look. Alcott and Kubrick decided not to use diffusion filters but instead employed a Tiffen No. 3 low-contrast filter and a brown net throughout the shooting. "We opted for the low contrast filter, rather than actual diffusion because the clarity and definition in Ireland creates a shooting situation that is very like a photographer's paradise," Alcott told *American Cinematographer* magazine. "The air is so refined, I think, because Ireland is in the Gulf Stream. The atmosphere is actually perfect and we thought it would be a pity to destroy that with diffusion, especially for the landscape photography."

For the wedding of Barry and the countess, Kubrick and Alcott wanted to achieve a softness that made a pictorial comment on the scene. They added an element to their low-contrast filters. "We combined them with a veil to create the kind of pictorial radiance that one associates with happiness," Alcott told Michel Ciment.

An Arriflex 35BL was used to film the majority of the production. "You've got the aperture control literally at your fingertips," Alcott told *American Cinematographer* magazine. "It's got a much larger scale and therefore a finer adjustment than most cameras. This feature is especially important when you're working with Stanley Kubrick, because he likes to continue shooting whether the sun is going in or out. In *Barry Lyndon,* during the sequence when Barry is buying the horse for his young son, the sun was going in and out all through the sequence. You've got to cater to this. That old bit that says you cut because the sun's gone in doesn't go anymore." The fine aperture adjustment of the Arriflex 35BL allowed Alcott to rapidly and precisely keep up with the changing light conditions.

Kubrick's vision of *Barry Lyndon* involved extensive use of the zoom lens. Often the camera would examine a perfectly composed image by starting on a small detail and then zooming back to a full shot. Alcott and Kubrick decided to use a Angenieux 20:1 zoom lens that Kubrick asked Ed Di Giulio to build for him. The project entailed a long series of phone calls, telexes, and letters between Kubrick, Di Giulio, and the Angenieux Corporation. Kubrick's technical acumen dazzled the engineers, who found him to be unprecedented among contemporary filmmakers.

The fluid movement of the zoom lens was achieved with a joystick control developed by Ed Di Giulio and his Cinema Products company. The device allowed Kubrick and Alcott to start and stop a zoom without the sudden jar that often occurred with motorized zoom controls. "Very few people know how to use zooms correctly," Alcott told *Millimeter* magazine. "[On *Barry Lyndon,* the] zoom enhanced the fluid look of the film and was used throughout the picture integrally and not simply as a device to speed up production." "We used the zoom a great deal," Alcott told Michel Ciment. "Each time, it became an image in itself and not, as is usually the case, a means of moving from one point in space to another. So each shot was a composition, like the zoom which moved out from the pistol duel at the river's edge. The zoom also meant that we did not depend too much on editing and so gave the whole film a kind of softness and fluidity."

The zoom technique became the movement of choice for *Barry Lyndon* and replaced the renowned Kubrick dolly and tracking shots that were so memorable in *Paths of Glory*. The use of the zoom lens became an aesthetic device that dissected the carefully framed compositions. The metaphor was one of a period painting coming to life. Staging was minimal and mannered. The repetition of the constant zooming to introduce a scene helped to transport the viewer back to the eighteenth century via the world of meticulously depicted classical paintings. As the camera eye zoomed from close to far, Kubrick expanded his exploration of the world of eighteenth-century painting not beyond the rigorous confines of the frame but by examining the depth of space in relationship to the near and far.

Kubrick continued to use video as a means of communicating between the camera and what he was getting on film. By shooting video at the same angle, Kubrick could refine his camera approach and coordinate the staging and composition in motion.

When Kubrick did choose to track the camera, it was on a grand scale. To heighten the visceral excitement of the large battle scene Kubrick planned a massive tracking shot. "We had one very long tracking shot in the battle sequence, with the cameras on an 800-foot track," John Alcott explained to *American Cinematographer*. "There were three cameras on the track, moving with the troops. We used an Elemack dolly, with bogie wheels, on ordinary metal platforms and a five-foot and sometimes six-foot wheel span, because we found that this worked quite well in trying to get rid of the vibrations when working on the end of the zoom. It seemed to take the vibration out better than going directly onto the Elemack. Virtually all closeups made from the track during that battle sequence were on the 250mm end of the zoom."

Before shooting had begun, Alcott had tested a camera traveling on a standard track and then a camera traveling on a base. Kubrick liked the results and ordered platforms to be built to run the tracks. The wooden track base was an assignment given to Ken Adam and his art department. The battle sequence took extensive pre-planning. Ken Adam created storyboards to visualize Kubrick's graphic ideas for shooting with various focal lengths. With the storyboards, Kubrick was able to plan the shots on which soldiers would wear real costumes and those on which he could use paper costumes—and eventually those long shots where he could implement dummies in the extreme distance. Lead soldiers were arranged and rearranged so that Kubrick could see his potential shots from every possible angle.

In the best sense, the glorious and beautiful cinematography in *Barry Lyndon* was a collaboration between John Alcott and Stanley Kubrick. A cinematographer working with Stanley Kubrick had to function as a co-director of photography. Both Alcott and Kubrick were involved in placement of the camera, composition, choice of lens, and physical operation of the camera.

For the cast of *Barry Lyndon*, Kubrick tapped a large group of trained stage and screen actors who were verbally adroit and experienced in the period repertoire. For the Irish sequences Kubrick drew on alumni of the famed Abbey Theater. English actors were selected for their abilities and eccentricities.

Actor Jonathan Cecil was originally contracted to play a character in the Thackeray novel whom Cecil described as "a sort of upstage, snotty, upper-class young officer." The officer is wounded, and Barry helps him up the stairs of a German farmhouse, where a young woman takes care of them. In the completed film all that remains of this segment is Barry's affair with the lonely young German woman who, with her baby, waits for her husband to return from the war.

Every supporting actor cast in *Barry Lyndon* was given a screen test. Casting director James Liggat contacted actors, many of whom Kubrick personally selected. Kubrick continued to see every movie he could to comb for new talent. Jonathan Cecil had extensive television and stage credits. During a performance of *Cowardly Custard*, a Noel Coward review in the early seventies, Cecil was told that Kubrick had been in the audience. It was essential for Kubrick to visualize each actor in the proposed role in the *Barry Lyndon* script. After seeing Cecil's screen test for *Barry Lyndon*, Kubrick told his people to advise the actor that he had the part. "It was an extraordinary experience, I can truthfully say one of the oddest I ever had in a thirty-two-year-long career," stated Jonathan Cecil, who went on to work with directors Federico Fellini, Billy Wilder, and Lindsay Anderson.

"There was a disastrous day when it was pouring as it only can in Ireland. We all arrived at this little farmhouse, which was a weather cover set, at six o'clock in the morning to find it had no roof. It was leaking, it was a ruin. So we arrived there to find Stanley and the crew all driving off in another direction to something else."

Eventually a suitable location was used to stage the farmhouse sequence and Kubrick worked with Jonathan Cecil and Ryan O'Neal to create the scene. "He tried to get us to invent something, and it was going to be quite an amusing scene," Cecil recalled. "I, as the rather supercilious young officer, was trying to seduce this German girl and in a rather boorish kind of way. Barry Lyndon, of course, made more of a success with her and I was annoyed. When I first started playing this wounded officer it was early on in the shooting. Ryan O'Neal was carrying me and I was having to act as somebody wounded. I was doing quite a lot of groaning and writhing, as I imagined somebody who had been shot in the thigh would do. Stanley said, 'That's too much. It must be more sort of British, try to act against the pain.' It actually went against the stage directions of the original script, in which the young officer although only mildly wounded, made a great song and dance about it. It was very overdramatized but Stanley didn't want that—he kept repeating to me, 'Now, remember, stiff upper lip. That's what we English call it. As I've become an older actor, I hope I realize it was much more effective doing it that way. I don't think I was overacting particularly, but I was making quite a bit of noise. Stanley watched it and I said, 'Am I codding it a bit?' Now Stanley said, 'What is this word, "cod"?' I explained that it was an old English theatrical expression which meant slightly overacting something or burlesquing it. You would say, 'He gave rather a cod performance.' It meant hamming it up. It never came to anything, because Stanley suddenly decided this whole scene was superfluous to the plot.

"Many actors were sent home, and shooting was suspended for two or three weeks. He didn't know where he was going because the Ireland scenes seemed to be going on so long, the film would have been interminable. We were all put into a hotel. There were all these actors. As Stanley worked out how he was going to re-adapt the plots and get rid of scenes, gradually more and more actors were paid off and we sat there playing Scrabble endlessly, never knowing. When I was a young actor there were these popular plays where it turns out in the end that everybody is dead—it was that kind of place. There was always a telephone call. The Irish telephone services were terrible all those years ago. You could get through to America and London with no problems, but to get from one part of Ireland to another was unbelievably difficult, and I had this crackling voice coming through, saying, 'You're still staying but could you get so and so to the phone?' Every morning I was made up and got ready for this officer, although the character no longer existed in the form that he was in the original script. Eventually I was called onto the set. I always got on very well with Stanley, who I found a most courteous and extraordinary man. I worked with Fellini on *And the Ship Sails On.* They were very different men, but they had a similar quality. When you were in their presence they would look at you as if you were the most important thing, because you were an art object, as it were, to put on the screen with possibilities of what they could do with that face.

"At weekends Stanley came into our hotel. If he would come into the bar I would flee because I couldn't stand those searchlight eyes on me. I thought, 'I'm off duty now.' He has these burning dark eyes and an immense seriousness. He was interested in every aspect, even an actor who just passed through the movie for one tiny line. He was not without humor. I look like a slightly eccentric English type and very much fitted in with that period costume. I remember him being amused at first seeing me in the costume. During the month to six weeks when I was permanently on standby, Brian Cook, the assistant director, used to ring me at my home in London and say, 'Do you know the lines?' because Stanley has a great way of thrusting lines at people. Once I was suddenly given a bit in German to do. I found it very difficult to learn it very quickly in the caravan while the makeup and all of that was going on. I wasn't very experienced at that then; I was largely a stage actor and used to having quite a time to peruse the lines. So Brian Cook would say, 'Do you know the lines?' and I'd say, 'Yes.' 'Would you be prepared to do them tomorrow if we call you?' and I'd say, 'Yes.' And Brian would say, 'Well, can we run them?' So we'd do this over the telephone. I certainly knew the lines, I can tell you. Well, for all he knew I could have had the script in my hand and could have been reading it. We went everywhere in these Volkswagen vans, from location to location even for quite short distances. When Stanley was being driven he was always working. He always had the tape on, listening to the music he was going to use, which was quite an extraordinary collection of folk music and Schubert."

For the scene as the injured officer who tried to seduce the German farm girl, Ryan O'Neal had to carry Jonathan Cecil up a wooden staircase. "We did take after take. Poor Ryan," Jonathan Cecil remembered. "He was carrying me up the staircase in a fireman's lift. It was very dangerous because it was quite slippery with moss and everything in this damp part of Ireland. We did this scene again and again. I had a speech to make. We finally got it and Stanley said, 'Cut!—Jonathan blew it, he forgot to act.' I thought, we'd done everything right. We got up the stairs, I didn't blow any lines, I got all the German right, the footfalls were right, we got into position exactly right, but I'd actually forgotten to act."

Kubrick didn't give Cecil a lot of notes. Often he would just say, "Go again" to proceed to another take. "Then one day he said to me, 'Okay, Jonathan, it looks like your part is no longer in this movie, but I like you, I think you are great. There are no other upper-class English parts in this movie. I daresay we will find something for you later on. I want you on the movie.' That was it, I was dismissed. I thought, 'Oh, well, it's very nice of him to say that.' In late October or early November I went back to England and I did a television comedy series, I did another television show, and I was in a production of *Hamlet*. I had no idea that *Barry Lyndon* was still going on. I was up in Glasgow and suddenly I got a call. Stanley rushed up his assistant, Andros Epaminondas, to do a screen test of me stripped to the waist in the hotel lounge. Andros had said to Stanley, 'Well, listen, you've got all this film of Jonathan on camera, why do you want me to go up?' Stanley with his perfectionism said, 'What are you doing on Saturday?' 'Well, nothing,' Andros said. So Andros flew up to Glasgow and filmed me in this very straitlaced hotel. I was terrified that somebody would come in and find me as this gay officer, stripped to the waist in the resident launch."

When Cecil returned to the *Barry Lyndon* set, he was still playing the obnoxious young officer that Barry uses as a conduit to escape his regiment by taking his uniform. But this time Kubrick would have him play it as a gay soldier in a love affair with another officer.

"One thing I will never forget about Stanley was the following June, months later after I said this word 'cod' he clearly filed it away in his mind, because when I was the homosexual officer in the water with the other officer, Stanley said, 'Jonathan, the way you say that, that's a bit cod.' I thought, 'What an extraordinary man.' I had used this very old-fashioned summer stock kind of actor's phrase and he had retained this and used it. I thought it was extraordinary when there must have been over a hundred actors who had gone through the film since I'd been on it."

Jonathan Cecil's new role did make it into the final version of *Barry Lyndon*. As the gay officers pine over their impending separation, Barry comes over a hill and steals one of the men's uniforms and his horse to avoid the rigors of his regiment by escaping to freedom. The camera first picks up Barry carrying water—with the off-camera voices of the male lovers as he approaches the clothes and horses. The camera continues to pan and then zooms into the water as we see the men in the near distance, then we go back to Barry as he steals their belongings. The conversation remains constant throughout the scene.

The sequence takes place on a warm day, with the men encouraged to wade in the water naked from the waist up. Kubrick chose to shoot on a day that was anything but warm. "My teeth were chattering," Jonathan Cecil recalled. "Stanley kept shouting through his megaphone, 'No, no, no. Jonathan, relax, you're warm, it's a beautiful day.'"

Compounding the situation was Kubrick's passion for shooting as many takes as he needed to find every possible nuance in a scene. "Sixty takes! I had never done that in my life," Cecil said. "It was shot from every angle. Stanley was right up on the bank and we were right below. I and my partner, the actor Anthony Dawes, were continually called throughout that summer. It was marvelous we were on the payroll. We kept being called and Stanley never quite found the location. Stanley doesn't know until he's actually there and sees the location, then he knows. I've seen him walk away from a set, although the art director has assured him that it's perfect and he's seen every kind of transparency, photograph, and slide, until he's actually there and ready to go. It wasn't until he was actually there, the actors were there, and everybody was in place in the scene that he decided this was how he wanted it. This was a very beautiful area around west of England in the countryside. We were in a river and Stanley was way up on the bank. He was shooting from a very long range. We were supposed to be standing in the water, but it was not shallow enough, so we were actually kneeling on a raft on a dinghy apparatus." The scene took a full twelve-hour day to shoot.

Kubrick demanded discipline from the highly trained actors on *Barry Lyndon.* "Stanley was very strict, in that everything was rehearsed down to the last detail and there was very little chance for the actor to vary the performance take by take," Cecil explained. "He let the camera run on Peter Sellers in *Lolita.* Leonard Rossiter, who gave an extraordinary performance as Captain Quin, was a way-out, off-the-wall actor. Stanley liked those kinds of actors. He was very strict in having everything repeated exactly. Stanley wasn't too keen on people suddenly doing something slightly different, but he made allowances for actors of this sort of eccentricity."

Kubrick continued to decide how he was going to shoot a sequence when he was on the set in front of the actors. "The toughest part of Stanley's day was finding the right first shot," Ryan O'Neal observed to Richard Schickel. "Once he did that, other shots fell into place. But he agonized over that first one. Once, when he was really stymied, he began to search through a book of eighteenth-century art reproductions. He found a painting—I don't remember which one—and posed Marisa and me exactly as if were in that painting."

O'Neal recounted a moment during a particularly difficult scene that was a breakthrough for him in understanding Kubrick's total approach to the filmmaking process. "He found a way to walk past me, giving instructions to the crew—'Let's move on to thirty-two, move those lights into the foreground' and so on—but as he passed me, he grabbed my hand and squeezed it. It was the most beautiful and appreciated gesture in my life. It was the greatest moment in my career."

Gay Hamilton, who played Barry's cousin Nora Brady, didn't meet Stanley Kubrick until she had already been cast and was on location ready to play the part. The Scottish actress came to London after attending Glasgow College. Hamilton had been a member of the Royal Shakespeare Company and had appeared in many television productions. "I knew the casting director Jimmy Liggat quite well and he called me in for an interview and he said, 'Stanley Kubrick doesn't meet anyone,'" Gay Hamilton remembered. "I was called in. There was no script. I was told to do something on video so I did *Playboy of the Western World* by J. M. Synge. That was sent off to Stanley and he said, 'Could she do something else?' I ended up doing some thing I had learned as a child and we laughed a lot. Jimmy Liggat said Stanley asked, 'if she could show her legs,' for some reason—I don't think they ever came into the picture unless perhaps a bit when we danced. I didn't meet Stanley until I had many costume fittings, which were done with great care. The underside of the materials they used looked quite faded. The shape of the costumes and the shape of the hair of my part were based on French paintings. There's a Fragonard of a girl, slightly pink-cheeked, brown hair up, with her head down reading a book. Every piece of material was shown to Stanley Kubrick, he looked at *every* costume. He was in touch with *everything*. He had advisers around him, but they had to finally show it to him and have it passed by him. There was no question that he had his finger on every single aspect of the moviemaking.

"The time I first met him I was taken to a field in Ireland. It was rather chilly. He was on a large structure filming from a height. He was looking down at me and that was my first meeting. 'Hi,' he said. 'Would you turn around?' It was extraordinary. Of course, I was extremely nervous by then, even though I had already been cast, I was already dressed and ready to go, I'd never met him. He just avoids meeting anyone unless he absolutely has to. I got along extremely well. He was nice because my part in the book is quite small and at the end he said, 'I wish she had more to do, but you know, I can't invent it.'"

Gay Hamilton had read the Thackeray novel to absorb what she could about the character. "It was not very much," Hamilton recalled. "Her hair is described as the color of carrot, which obviously wasn't me. I hoped they weren't going to do that to me. Basically Stanley gave me one note, which lasted me the whole of the shoot. English actors play restoration, so the period was familiar to me, and we play it in a mannered way. Stanley said, 'Can I talk to you a minute.' He used to take me aside and say, 'Gay, can I talk to you a minute?' He talked to me quite quietly. He said, 'You know that this character is a little flirt and she's a baddie, so you play it as sweetly as you can.' It was great. I actually have thought of that note many times since, because it was such a good note. That was hit in the head early on by him saying, 'We're playing this for real and you play it as a nice person because we know all about your character.' It was like one note that gave you a direct line of how to play the character. Of course, the narration was telling the audience about me. Occasionally he would take you aside and we would discuss something on the level of energy or emotion, but after that single note about how to play it, I didn't have too many notes from him. It's almost like we solved it and somehow the person was there.

"He was nothing but nice to me except once when I undid my hellish corset he shouted, 'Gay—you've got to have those done up by two!' but on the whole we got on extremely well. Ryan O'Neal was staying in this house near Dublin. Stanley and Ryan were always watching boxing videos because Stanley loves boxing and Ryan did as well. Of course Tatum was around at that time scampering in and out. Once I was having to try on a costume and come down and show Stanley. Stanley and Ryan were so busy watching the boxing video, I was going, 'Excuse me! Excuse me!—I'm here!' Stanley just kind of looked up and was staring at me. I said, 'Oh, you can be difficult.'

"The setups took so long—all that lighting. Stanley did an awful lot of the lighting, in close conference with John Alcott, but he was very much involved in it. Kubrick didn't go away to do something else—he was there. One day we drove around the Wickley Mountains in Ireland and did nothing the entire day. It was a long caravan—all the trailers and everyone, driving, driving, driving—we didn't shoot a single thing."

When shooting began in the fall in Ireland, the script was complete but many of the scene elements were not there. "I did get all that had been written, but there was an air of mystery shrouded around everything." For the scene when Barry and his cousin Nora Brady walk in the woods, Kubrick turned to the actors to develop the dialogue. "Stanley said to Ryan, 'This is your cousin and you're . . .'" Gay Hamilton remembers. "And he just turned to me and said, 'So what would you say at that point?' He set a scenario and we pretty well wrote the lines."

Kubrick used this same approach for the first scene between Barry and Nora in the opening of the film. We are introduced to Barry as he plays cards with his cousin Nora Brady inside a room decorated with shells. The scene was shot on location in Powercourt Mansion, just outside of Dublin. "We didn't even know we were playing cards," Gay Hamilton recalled. "We went in that place and we just sat there trying to work out how we would be. Then, suddenly, someone hit on that we might be playing cards. 'Get some cards.' There was nothing there."

Kubrick continued to work in a directorial style that included running up a lot of takes on a single setup—a philosophy that embraced the theory that film stock is the cheapest part of making a film. Kubrick was looking for a sexual tension between Barry and his cousin as she taunts him by hiding a ribbon in her bosom and daring him to find it. "There was a sort of frisson in the air at the time," Gay Hamilton recalled. "When I kiss him in the summer shell house I remember it was eight o'clock at night and we had done like fourteen takes of the kiss and Ryan said, 'I have got to get back because Tatum has a temperature!' We certainly had extremely long days from six in the morning, and we'd be driving back at something like nine at night. The days were immensely long. You drew on reserves of energy that you didn't know you had or bolstered by the Guinness by the end of the day."

Kubrick sent Gay Hamilton and Leonard Rossiter, who was playing Nora's suitor, Captain Quin, to a dancing mistress in London to learn an Irish dance that they would perform in the film. After many lessons, Hamilton and Rossiter had the dance perfected. The production was based in Waterford. Kubrick staged the scene in a field in County Clare as the townspeople watched the happy couple dance. During the filming Hamilton and Rossiter performed the dance perfectly, but Kubrick continued to shoot take after take. "We did it perfectly many times," Hamilton recalled. "We were just screaming, 'What the hell is wrong! Why is he taking this?' He didn't make it clear. He just said, 'Okay, lovely, go again.' I think he was letting us do it and do it and do it until we were doing it almost carelessly like we'd been doing that dance all of our lives. You don't want it to look as though they've just been instructed how to do that dance. We were probably doing it a bit prissily with all the steps right. Suddenly the hair was falling down and we were sweating a bit— that was intentional.

"He had a fairly devilish side to him. I was once in a long shot, the one on the hillside where I am found giving a ribbon to someone else and I'm shown up for what I am and Stanley said, and this one he did out loud, 'Gay, I can't see what you're doing. You know you're in quite a long shot here. Do it like you did your close-up so we could see what you're doing,' meaning, I'd done too much in my close-up. He was joking but quite nicely.

"He started in long shot. We did it in one that he began in long shot and then zoomed in. I remember being surprised when I saw it. I was really surprised that we were so far away at the beginning. I had no idea. It just took a very, very long time setting that shot up. Once it was set up we did it a few times but it wasn't covered by a lot of cameras. It was done on that one shot. The setup took ages. It was a lot of looking through different lenses until he finally decided how he would shoot it. I don't think he has a camera plan, that's not how he worked at all. He found the actor and got to the location, even in the shell house we were sitting there making it up on the spot and then doing it in little bits."

Kubrick operated the camera often and was demanding in the exactness of the choreography of the camera. Dolly grip Luke Quigley related one example to Bob Gaffney when they worked on a commercial together several years later. "We set up this scene and it had about eight dolly moves in it," Quigley told Gaffney. "The last move was not even an inch. We went through this take and Stanley was wearing earphones monitoring the dialogue and operating the camera." Luke dollied through the complex sequence, completing all the moves but did not do the last move. "Stanley called him on it," Gaffney related. "You know how hard it is to see the difference. Stanley was listening to the dialogue, operating the camera, and had enough sense to feel that. He wasn't counting eight moves. Stanley's whole body is tuned into this move." Kubrick's practice of operating the camera caused one of the camera operators to leave the film because he felt he was playing little of a role.

The pressure of working on location and the demands of the enormous production of *Barry Lyndon* may not have been apparent to the cast and crew who watched Kubrick confidently forge through the difficult shoot, but the film was taking its toll. A rash began to appear on Kubrick's hands and didn't dissipate until *Barry Lyndon* was complete. Although at Christiane's urging he had recently stopped smoking, he began smoking heavily again.

The actor hired for Captain Potzdorf performed the role before the cameras for almost three weeks and then Kubrick decided he wasn't working out. Kubrick did not meet or speak with the actor personally. As he had with Alex North, Kubrick avoided the confrontation and allowed staffers to tell the actor he was off the film. At one point Kubrick discussed the role of Potzdorf with Steven Berkoff, but then Kubrick recast the role, going with Hardy Kruger who had a name in Europe and America.

Filming by pure candlelight was a unique experience for the actors. "There was a fair amount of discussion going around the set about how unique it was," Steven Berkoff recalled. "I remember being fascinated that no top or fill light was used. It had to be pure candlelight so it made a unique contribution to the art of filmmaking going back to painting. The film stock was very slow and the depth-of-field was very short. Consequently there wasn't very much movement for the actors. You almost posed like for portraits. We had all these candles lit and of course, with candles for continuity unless you got going, the candles would go down. Stanley did so many takes and setups, he'd have to keep replacing the flaming candles, so the candle costs would become enormous. They were always checking to see how many candles they had. They kept taking out little books and checking the cost of the candles. It became a bit of an added strain because the candles had to be kept in continuity. A candle lasts a long time but after a couple of hours it looks different, so that was a big problem.

"I came to a big municipal building in Dublin, which they were using for the scene. There was a huge storm in Dublin and there were great arc lights outside the windows to create a feeling of daylight. This storm was lashing the building, and outside, the Irish workman were holding on to the stands for these giant lights. Inside it was a picture of serenity and calm. There were dozens of extras waiting and in the midst of all this, these guys are outside holding on to these great arc lamps. There were all these extras and all this makeup. Stanley was just quietly sitting in a corner talking to Hardy Kruger. Stanley is a fantastic kind of perfectionist. He always wants to see more. He feels something more will come out of a take if it's repeated. After a few dozen times the actor starts to get unseamed, he starts to come apart. He doesn't know if it sounds like English or Hindustani by saying the words over and over again. It certainly doesn't mean anything, because you've exhausted the association the word has for you in the mind, so it then starts to become a funny sound. Stanley has this amazing eye, a keen sharp intelligence, and he thinks something more will happen."

Steven Berkoff played Lord Ludd, a gambler and ladies' man, who plays cards against the Chevalier, a con man, played by Patrick Magee. The scene took place in an elegant room surrounded by wealthy and well-dressed men and women who watched the gambling duel. "They were shooting on Patrick first and then they could release him and I would go last," Steven Berkoff recalled. "Patrick had to say three words, those three words took all day—*all day*. Patrick had to say, 'Faites vos jeux, Mesdames, Messieurs,' which means place your bets, ladies and gentlemen—and then he deals the cards. For the first two or three takes it seemed to be okay. Pat said, *'Faites vos jeux, Mesdames, Messieurs'* with his Irish brogue—but it was all right. Then suddenly *jeux* became *yeux* which means eyes. I remember Stanley saying, 'No, it's *jeux*, Pat, *faire vos yeux* is make up your eyes.' Stanley put it gently, in an intellectual, fraternal way. So Patrick said, 'I'm sorry, Stanley, I'll get it right.' Because Pat was concentrating on saying *vos jeux*, his eye patch would wobble because his eye was blinking underneath it, but it was supposed to be a socket. So then Stanley said, 'Pat, if you could keep that eye closed because your agitation is showing and the patch is moving.' So then Pat got the patch to be still, but he said, *'Vos yeux'* because he was thinking of the patch. Then a few takes later Pat started to sweat because he was worried about the *'jeux'* and the patch. Then the cards would start to clump because the sweat from his hands was making them stick, so they had to wipe the cards. This went on for another ten takes.

"I was mainly a theater actor then, I'd been hacking it for ten years and as Stanley is doing all this I'm saying to myself, 'This isn't going to happen to me.' So I'm building up readiness like a fighter. This goes on and on and on. We have breaks and then Stanley said, 'Pat, we'll just do the close-up for *"jeux,"* then we'll do the hands separately because I know it's difficult for you.' When Stanley just shot Pat's hands, they had gotten sweaty again, so he said, 'We can't use your hands, Pat.' So I thought, 'They can't shoot his hands—what are they going to do?' So what Stanley did was he got on the phone to England and asked for a magician to come just to deal the cards. So we had a break and along comes David Berglas, who is a marvelous magician, and Stanley just photographs his hands. David's hands are beautiful and the cards swiftly leave his hand as from jet propulsion. Stanley is happy and then they go back to Pat because you see Pat's hands in the medium shot but they don't match. So Stanley says to Pat, 'You have to shave your hands, Pat,' because his hands are hairy. So Pat, who is this great star actor, a powerhouse who has worked with Peter Brook, has to adapt to the stand-in rather than putting some hair on the hands of the stand-in. But they already shot Berglas's smooth, creamy-white hands. The hands of a man who's a master of prestidigitation, and they had to shave Pat's hands. Pat came in the next day with his naked hands and he had to do *'jeux'* again. That was that, then they did the reverse on me with the girls.

"I would say to the girls, why don't you come here whisper in my ear, hold my hand, smile, be sweet, give me a little nibble on the earlobe— we just played around. I had to say a little bit of French as well, and I did it with an emphasis like the French and, of course, Stanley said,

'Perfect, perfect.' I just looked at the girls and I chucked them on the chin, I looked, I winked and played and Stanley said, 'All right, cut, that's good. Okay, Steve, we'll go again.' He was changing lenses, trying things, so I did the same thing again, we go again and Stanley said, 'Well, let's try it now a little bit closer, okay, we'll do it again.' Then he gets to eight, nine takes. 'Okay, let's try again and maybe we'll move the camera here.' I had a funny feeling that Stanley liked to see the actor break a little bit perhaps because he would see them reveal something else, they would give him something else. The cameraman was getting tired and I said to myself, 'I will never break down—never! I don't care if we sit here day and night, that camera will break, everybody will break down before I will—I will never break!'

"So we did take after take after take after take and on each take I never fluffed a word, in fact, I started to relish each take. After about twenty-five takes, Stanley said, 'Okay, we've got it.' I said, 'Oh, is that all?' That was an unforgettable day I had with him.

"Stanley has a kind of slightly rabbinical air. He has a reflective quality in his work because he's an intellectual, and intellectuals don't get riled because they spill the valuable contents of their mind—a dummy can always shout and rave because there's nothing to spill—it's empty. If you have a cup that's full, you walk gently with it.

"I saw Lord Ludd as an English fop. He was dressed with the white wig and beauty spots and lipstick. I played it with foppishness, decadence, indulgence, enormous wealth. Once I saw the costumes being designed and the effect of the makeup, I very easily got myself into that way of thinking and the role of that kind of elegant, rather sophisticated fop who loved the ladies and was a kind of Regency dandy. We rehearsed and I improvised a little bit. The scene was very largely of my own creation. By this time I got to know Stanley, he trusted me having worked with me on *A Clockwork Orange*, and he left me to my own devices."

Ryan O'Neal and Steven Berkoff had a fencing teacher to tutor them for the sequence where Barry and Lord Ludd duel to resolve the matter of Ludd's gambling debt to the Chevalier. "During the duel, I stabbed Ryan," Berkoff remembered. "They had a tiny bit of a safety tip on the sword, but because of the close-up it was a blunted end, when I made a parry I stabbed him in the knuckle. I felt very bad because he's a charming man. Stanley didn't do too many takes of the duel, but we improvised. He did a fair amount of takes but I don't think he could push Ryan too much because Ryan had so much to do and Ryan was a star, stars are treated slightly differently by all directors.

"Kubrick was articulate and communicated with everybody. He never left anybody in doubt. He was good to people, he would talk to everybody, there wasn't a person he wouldn't talk to, even the smallest actor. He had time for everyone. He would encourage people. That was his home, we were his family. He wasn't dictatorial, dogmatic, aloof, he was a human being, slightly obsessive, but deeply human about his work, about his actors and totally accessible."

Kubrick never gave his actors too much direction. He listened to suggestions and worked by having them refine their characterizations through constant searching for every nuance in the scene by shooting repeated takes. "The catch-words on the set are 'Do it faster, do it slower, do it again.' Mostly 'Do it again,'" Patrick Magee told Richard Schickel. Murray Melvin, who had been in *A Taste of Honey* and *The Devils,* played the Reverend Runt. Melvin's extraordinary face and poise had uncannily evoked the eighteenth century. In appearance he seemed to have stepped out of a Dutch master's painting onto Kubrick's *Barry Lyndon* set. Kubrick didn't press Marisa Berenson or his child actors, Dominic Savage and David Morley, but he did push the experienced actors in the cast. He shot as many as fifty takes of Murray Melvin on a particular scene. "I knew he had seen something I had done," Melvin told Richard Schickel. "But because he was a good director, he wouldn't tell me what it was. Because if someone tells you you've done a good bit, then you know it and put it in parentheses and kill it. The better actor you were, the more he drew it out of you."

Kubrick's use of such a high-take ratio was considered by many as an irrational and obsessional use of directorial power, but he firmly believed that good film actors were at their best during the actual process of making a take. "Actors who have worked a lot in movies don't really get a sense of intense excitement into their performances until there is film running through the camera," he told Richard Schickel.

For the role of Graham in the second half of the film, Kubrick cast Philip Stone, who had played Dad in *A Clockwork Orange.* Graham is a devoted servant of the Lyndon household who spends a great deal of time working on the finances, going over bills with an accountant's accuracy. Philip Stone appears in many scenes, in the background, woven into Kubrick's rich period tapestry until the very end of the film when Lord Bullingdon dispatches him. He is recruited to tell Barry the rigors of the financial deal in relation to his banishment from England and Lady Lyndon. "Graham in the wonderful *Barry Lyndon* was like a bloody extra, but then at the end in the inn after Barry had his leg shot off, I suddenly had to come up with a highly concentrated scene," Philip

Stone recalled. "Ryan O'Neal was quite surprised by my performance—
my having stood around for weeks in the background. Stanley just gave
me a wink and quietly said, 'Don't worry, Ryan, he knows how to do it.'

"Stanley is strange, dark, quiet, seems secretive and obsessive—but
who wouldn't be making films as he does. He seems to know with the
inner eye exactly where he's going. You have great trust and belief in
him. Stanley is always looking for the X-factor and he goes on until he
feels he's found it. He'd say, 'Okay, that's great! Let's go again.' Every
shot is a creation. You need a lot of patience working for him. You can be
in caravan all made up, ready to go, and you can wait for a week. Then
suddenly he comes onto you for a concentrated scene. You need nerve
working for Stanley and he can suddenly alter the dialogue on the set or
give you a lot more dialogue to learn in a quick time and you've got to
keep calm—no use losing your 'bottle.' I never did, and he just kept
coming back to me for yet another film."

Kubrick had decided on using authentic eighteenth-century music for
Barry Lyndon and not an original score. He selected Leonard Rosenman to arrange, orchestrate, and conduct the music, which would range
from classical to folk music of the period. Rosenman had been an renowned composer for film and television and had written scores for *East
of Eden, Rebel Without a Cause, The Rise and Fall of Legs Diamond,
Hell Is for Heroes, Fantastic Voyage, A Man Called Horse, Beneath the
Planet of the Apes, The Defenders, Combat, The Virginian, Kojak,* and
Marcus Welby. "Stanley called me on a Monday and said come to England on Wednesday—the picture was finished," Rosenman told an
American Film Institute seminar. "I had never done an adaptation before, and it gave me a chance to conduct the London Orchestra with
some classical pieces I was interested in. I was under no illusions that I
had any creative work to do on the film. I asked him what he had picked
out and he said, 'The first thing I want to do is to buy the theme from
The Godfather.' I said, 'Well, if you're going to do that, tell me now so I
can get the first plane out of England.' 'What's wrong with it? It's a very
beautiful theme.' I said, 'You're right, but the last time I saw *The Godfather,* it was about gangsters, not eighteenth-century aristocrats.' I listened to all the records he had, and he had picked a sarabande that had
been recorded with a harpsichord; he thought the bass would just be
marvelous for the duel scenes. He had another theme for the dying
child, which was from one of Verdi's worst operas. It was as though a
psych class had gotten together and said, 'Let's find something that will
really repel people.' I told him I couldn't go along with that and sug-

gested I do percussion, and see what it sounded like. We tried it with the London Symphony and he fell madly in love with it.

"I left after having picked out all the music and recorded it there. He then practically made a loop out of the Verdi theme and used it over and over again. If I had known he wanted that much of it, I would have orchestrated some other variations; there were five charming variations in that piece. When I saw this incredibly boring film with all the music I had picked out going over and over again, I thought, 'My God, what a mess!' I was going to refuse the Oscar. The classical music used in the film is much closer to me, because I am a pianist. I was a Bach and Haydn specialist. I picked out about half of it and he picked out about half."

The extraordinary sequence when Barry duels with Lord Bullingdon was just one line in Kubrick's screenplay reading, "Barry duels with Lord Bullingdon." The sequence took forty-two working days to edit. Kubrick had listened to every available recording of seventeenth- and eighteenth-century music, acquiring thousand of records to find Handel's sarabande used to score the scene.

As postproduction got closer to completion, Kubrick stepped up his working pace and spent as many as eighteen hours a day on the soundtrack and plotting the advertising and publicity campaigns. His devotion to his work went beyond the paradigm of the committed filmmaker. The distinction between life and work was blurred for Stanley Kubrick with his obsession for perfection and the pursuit of his evolving vision. "There is such a total sense of demoralization if you say you don't care. From start to finish on a film, the only limitations I observe are those imposed on me by the amount of money I have to spend and the amount of sleep I need. You either care or you don't and I simply don't know where to draw the line between those two points," Kubrick told Richard Schickel.

Warner Bros. saw only bits and pieces of *Barry Lyndon* during production and postproduction. The Warner executives who gave Kubrick their complete trust and financial support saw *Barry Lyndon* for the first time just three weeks before the release date. Kubrick had complete artistic control over the film. No publicity was released by the studio without his explicit permission.

In New York *Barry Lyndon* premiered on December 18, 1975, at the Ziegfeld and the Baronet Theaters. It had taken three years and $11 million to bring the three hour, four minute and four second–long film to the screen. *Barry Lyndon* was the first Stanley Kubrick feature film to be shot totally on location. The shooting schedule lasted eight and a half months. The cast and crew numbered 170, plus consultants and extras.

The advertising campaign featured the lettering used in the opening credits and title cards, an illustrated montage of scenes from the film. *Barry Lyndon* was given a limited-release pattern with plenty of room to build word of mouth.

Kubrick continued to have staffers chart box office progress so that *Barry Lyndon* could be booked into the best first-run houses in key cities worldwide. Kubrick used the system that he instituted for *A Clockwork Orange,* suggesting theater usage based on a census of previous films similar to *Barry Lyndon.* This allowed him to exercise an intelligent opinion on where to open the film.

Critical reaction to the film was mixed. Detractors continued to find Kubrick's method and strident aesthetic approach to filmmaking something to ridicule rather than to admire, but Kubrick's loyal coterie was glad to see him back. "Stanley Kubrick: proof that there are living geniuses," one fan wrote in connection with a *Time* magazine cover story on the film. "Stanley Kubrick is a cinematic Shakespeare. And I think he knows it," another wrote. The name "Kubrick" had a power to draw audiences looking for a pure cinematic experience. "Thank God Stanley Kubrick has come back to rescue all us tired victims drowning in the current movie trends," one viewer wrote, while another called Kubrick "the most innovative person to touch motion pictures since Thomas A. Edison."

Critics were less kind. Jerry Oster, writing for the *New York Daily News,* who admitted he was put off that he saw the film later than Richard Schickel and was frustrated by not being able to get a phone interview with Kubrick, said, "One is left wondering if Kubrick weren't hoist by the petard of his secretiveness. Art isn't made in a vacuum, and neither, more importantly, is entertainment. *Barry Lyndon* is an egocentric film, made by a man who has lost touch with his peers, his critics and his audience." Michael Billington of the *London Illustrated News* said, "[It is] a series of still pictures which will please the retina while denying our hunger for drama."

When *Barry Lyndon* played in New York, Warner Bros. contacted Bob Gaffney to tell him that Kubrick had requested he go to check out the projection levels and make sure the projectionist was closely watching the focus because the lenses used for the candlelit sequences had very critical focus.

Gaffney was Kubrick's operative on the East Coast; on the West Coast he turned to Ed Di Giulio. The film was about to be screened at the Cinerama Dome Theater for the Warner Bros. executives when Kubrick learned of a problem with the projection system. Apparently the equipment was not producing the correct standard of foot-candles. Fearing that the studio would not be seeing the glories of his low-light miracle, Kubrick phoned Di Giulio at home and asked him to go down and look at the problem. "At that point I didn't know squat about projectors," said Di Giulio. "Now I've learned a hell of lot more, having built a few for Showscan, but back then I didn't know beans but I wanted to do whatever I could to help Stanley out. Fortunately someone had gotten there and taken care of things, but his was the meticulous concern he had for every step of the production process right up to the screening. He is really a master of detail and concern of his art."

After the film was released, Kubrick talked to Jack Hofsess for the *New York Times* and took the occasion to explain his cinematic interest in pursuing new projects. "What happens in the film business is something like this: When a scriptwriter or director starts out, producers and investors want to see everything written down. They judge the worth of a screenplay as they would a stage play, and ignore the very great differences between the two. They want good dialogue, tight plotting, dramatic development. What I have found is that the more completely cinematic a film is, the less interesting the screenplay becomes, because a screenplay isn't meant to be read, it's to be realized on film.

"So if my earlier films seem more verbal than the later ones, it is because I was obliged to conform to certain literary conventions. Then, after some success, I was given greater freedom to explore the medium as I preferred. They'll be no screenplay of *Barry Lyndon* published because there is nothing of literary interest to read." Kubrick continued to find cinematic ways of telling stories and told Richard Schickel that movies "haven't scratched the surface of how to tell stories in their own terms."

John Alcott was named outstanding cinematographer of 1975 by the National Society of Film Critics for his work on *Barry Lyndon*. Vincent Canby in the *New York Times* said that Alcott's cinematography "transforms scene after scene into something that suggests a Gainsborough or a Watteau." Alcott won an Oscar for his extraordinary work on *Barry Lyndon*.

Ken Adam won the Academy Award for the remarkable production design of *Barry Lyndon*. The project was grueling and difficult. Kubrick's demanding work method pushed *Barry Lyndon* beyond the museum stiffness of previous period films. "He's the nearest thing to genius I've ever worked with, with all the problems of a genius," Adam recalled. "He questions everything, you have to justify that intellectually afterwards, which is not always easy if you do things instinctively. It's almost permutating to the nth degree—he's like a human computer."

Barry Lyndon was also nominated for a best picture Oscar and Kubrick as best director. In addition to art direction and cinematography, the film also won Oscars for best adapted score (Leonard Rosenman) and best costumes (Ulla-Britt Soderlund and Milena Canonero).

In 1977 Kubrick received the David di Donatello Award in Taormina, Sicily, for his direction of *Barry Lyndon.*

The candlelight photography of *Barry Lyndon* became an instant legend in the film industry. Cinematographers all over the world wanted to know about Kubrick's magic lens. When renowned cinematographer Miroslav Ondricek embarked on photographing Milos Forman's production of *Amadeus,* the Czechoslovakian master cameraman wrote to Kubrick asking if he could use the lens to shoot the world of Mozart and Salieri by candlelight. "He wrote back saying it cost him $150,000 to build the lens and that he just used it for himself," Ondricek recalled. "I understood and accepted it and started on *Amadeus* my way." In time, faster film and faster lenses caught up with Kubrick's technology, but he had set a technical and artistic standard that took a Zen-like discipline and dedication to the art of film.

Barry Lyndon opened strongly throughout Europe. The film grossed $3 million in Paris alone. Warners took advantage of the film's European popularity in their international advertising, but in the main, *Barry Lyndon* failed to live up to the box office expectations of Stanley Kubrick and Warner Bros. "*Barry Lyndon* was one of Warner Bros.' biggest grosses internationally, but not in the United States," Kubrick told John Hofsess reporting for the *Los Angeles Times.* "If business had been as good as in Europe the film would have been a great financial success."

Despite the poor reception, reevaluation has positioned *Barry Lyndon* on international best films lists. As with *2001,* on *Barry Lyndon* Kubrick was advancing his film thesis that images, sound, music, and observation of behavior could be articulated cinematically.

CHAPTER 17

"Let's Go Again"

He's kind of a dyspeptic filmmaker, a Type A filmmaker, worrying
and wanting to edit right up to the end. He's very painstaking, obviously. You know what? I think he wants to hurt people with this
movie. I think that he really wants to make a movie that will hurt
people.

—Stephen King

Stanley's good on sound, so are a lot of directors, but Stanley's good
on designing a new harness. Stanley's good on the color of the mike,
Stanley's good about the merchant he bought the mike from. Stanley's good about the merchant's daughter who needs some dental
work.

—Jack Nicholson

In 1974 while he was still working on *Barry Lyndon,* Stanley Kubrick
was sent a demo reel of a new camera device by Ed Di Giulio of
Cinema Products Corporation. Kubrick watched the reel. His cool,
methodical, logical mind processed what he was seeing. He tried to determine how what he saw was accomplished technically as his cinematic
emotions soared. The reel contained approximately twenty-four different
shots—what the industry had called "impossible shots." The camera was
constantly moving in each shot—not really moving but floating, gliding
through space with no apparent means of control. Kubrick knew it was
not on a dolly, on a track, or hand-held. The shots were too smooth for

any conventional technique. It seemed as if the lens—with no constraints—could be put wherever the operator wanted. The fluid images included the camera sailing through pine boughs in a forest, lilting over a golf course, and chasing behind a woman up the stairs of the Philadelphia museum. Kubrick had always been mesmerized by the movement of the camera. The elegant gliding camera of Max Ophuls was an early motivating force. Throughout his career Stanley Kubrick had tried to find new ways to move the camera and to explore the grammar of the motion picture.

Screening the reel was a revelation and would have a profound impact on the camera technique in Kubrick's next film. He contacted Di Giulio. With his characteristic powers of analysis Kubrick warned Di Giulio that he noticed something that might inadvertently disclose the secret of this new invention. "Dear Ed," Kubrick cabled to Di Giulio from his Hawk Films offices in London, "Mystery stabilizer was spectacular and you can count on me as a customer. It should revolutionize the way films are shot. If you are really concerned about protecting its design before you fully patent it, I suggest you delete the two occasions on the reel where the shadow on the ground gives the skilled counter-intelligence photo interpreter a fairly clear representation of a man holding a pole with one hand, with something or other at the bottom of the pole which appears to be slowly moving. But my lips are sealed. I have a question: Is there a minimum height at which it can be used?"

The mystery stabilizer turned out to be the Steadicam, which was invented and operated by Garrett Brown. It was a device that indeed did revolutionize the way films were shot. Kubrick's next film, *The Shining*, would aptly demonstrate what Garrett Brown and the Steadicam could do.

When Stanley Kubrick finished *Barry Lyndon*, he began a long process of reading in search of his next project. He was not looking for any particular genre or story. For months he pursued a method that did not follow any pattern. Often he found items of interest on the back of articles he had cut out for other reasons. He continued to read newspapers, magazines, and novels, but nothing caught his eye.

In May of 1975 Paddy Chayefsky and producer Howard Gottfried submitted to United Artists the names of directors suitable for their production of the writer's original screenplay *Network*. Many of the names—including Arthur Penn, Roman Polanski, and Martin Scorsese—were vetoed by the studio. Kubrick was one of five directors okayed by the studio. Kubrick was given a script and sent back a favorable reply, but Chayefsky, who was as much of a control freak as Kubrick, didn't want to hand his vision over to an auteur. *Network* went on to be directed by Sidney Lumet, who did a masterful job with the project.

Warner executive John Calley had read Stephen King's novel *The Shining* in galleys, and he sent a copy to Kubrick. "That was the one and only thing sent to me which has ever interested me or which I ever liked. Most of the things I read are done with the impression that after ten pages I'll drop it and stop wasting my time," Kubrick told Vincente Molina Foix. Kubrick wasn't looking for a story on the paranormal, but he had a long-standing interest in the subject. Calley knew this and thought the book would capture Kubrick's imagination.

Kubrick had never read Stephen King before Calley sent him the book, but he was attracted to the structure of *The Shining*. "I had seen *Carrie*, the film, but I have never read any of his novels. I should say that King's greatest ingenuity lies in the construction of the story. He does not seem to be very interested in writing itself. They say he wrote, read over, re-wrote maybe once and sent everything to the editor. What seems to interest him is invention and I think that is his forte."

"I thought it was one of the most ingenious and exciting stories of the genre I had read," Kubrick told Michel Ciment. "It seemed to strike an extraordinary balance between the psychological and the supernatural in such a way as to lead you to think that the supernatural would eventually be explained by the psychological. 'Jack must be imagining these things because he's crazy.' This allowed you to suspend your doubt of the supernatural until you were so thoroughly into the story that you could accept it almost without noticing."

Stephen King was becoming a phenomenon. He had written *Carrie*, *'Salem's Lot*, and *The Shining*. King and his wife, Tabitha, had three children and lived quietly in a small town in Maine. Films based on his work were being made. Brian De Palma directed a screen adaptation of *Carrie*, Tobe Hooper did a television treatment of *'Salem's Lot*, and *The Stand* was scheduled to be directed by George A. Romero. (The project took another fifteen years before it finally appeared, as a miniseries, without Romero.) When *The Shining* was released, King was thirty-two years old and had sold 22 million copies of six novels and *Night Shift*, a collection of short stories.

Historically Kubrick had been elusive in explaining his attraction to a specific story. The material had to satisfy his enormous ambitions as a filmmaker, as well as present cinematic challenges and a probable showcase for his photographic vision. It also had to stimulate his misanthropic nature. "It's very difficult to say why I finally decided upon a particular story," Kubrick told John Hofsess. "I could list the qualities it should have—a strong narrative, cinematic potential and interesting parts for the actors. But it goes deeper than merely assessing it on some point system. Certainly, Stephen King's novel had a cascade of inventions which I had not encountered before in any fiction of the genre, which tends to be built around a single idea in most other cases."

Kubrick was vaguely uncomfortable being questioned about his interest in *The Shining*, telling Jack Kroll he thought the novel to be an ingenious example of the ghost-story genre. Kroll became a minority of critics who favorably reviewed the film, saying: "The first epic horror film, *The Shining* is to other horror movies what *2001: A Space Odyssey* was to other space movies." When the critic was doing a piece on the film he continued to press Kubrick to understand what fascinated him about the King novel. "There's something inherently wrong with the human personality," Kubrick revealed to Kroll. "There's an evil side to it. One of the things that horror stories can do is to show us the archetypes of the unconscious: we can see the dark side without having to confront it directly. Also, ghost stories appeal to our craving for immortality. If you can be afraid of a ghost, then you have to believe that a ghost may exist, and if a ghost exists, then oblivion might not be the end."

The man crowned the legitimate contemporary heir to Edgar Allan Poe and H. P. Lovecraft was told that Kubrick had his staff bring him stacks of horror books as he ensconced himself in his office to read them all. Kubrick's secretary heard the sound of each book hitting the wall as the director flung it into a reject pile after reading the first few pages. Finally one day the secretary noticed it had been a while since she had heard the thud of another writer's work biting the dust. She walked in to check on her boss and found Kubrick deeply engrossed in reading *The Shining*.

King had written a screenplay adaptation of his novel for Warner Bros. before Kubrick became attached to it, but Kubrick chose not to read the script because he decided he wanted to infuse the skeleton of King's story with his own ideas.

Kubrick chose novelist Diane Johnson to work with him on the adaptation. "It must be plausible, use no cheap tricks, have no holes in the plot, no failures of motivation . . . it must be *completely* scary," Johnson said to the *New York Times*. This was Johnson's first screenplay. Kubrick had been impressed with Johnson's novels. He had begun to develop a treatment for *The Shining* when he learned that Johnson was giving a course at the University of California at Berkeley on the Gothic novel. She seemed to be the ideal collaborator for the project. After engaging in a discussion about her work, he decided to ask her to adapt *The Shining* with him. "With *The Shining*, the problem was to extract the essential plot and to re-invent the sections of the story that were weak," Kubrick told Michel Ciment. "The characters needed to be developed a bit differently than they were in the novel. It is in the pruning down phase that the undoing of great novels usually occurs because so much of what is good about them has to do with the fineness of the writing, the insight of the author and often the density of the story. But *The Shining* was a different matter. Its virtues lay almost entirely in the plot, and it didn't prove to be very much of a problem to adapt it into the screenplay form. Diane and I talked a lot about the book and then we made an outline of the scenes we thought should be included in the film. This list of scenes was shuffled and reshuffled until we thought it was right, and then we began to write. We did several drafts of the screenplay, which was subsequently revised at different stages before and during shooting."

Kubrick had liked Johnson's 1974 novel *The Shadow Knows*, the story of a woman who saw herself as the victim-to-be in a mythic detective novel. He had read about her in the *New York Times Book Review* and was familiar with her critical work. "He is the sort of person who has a penchant for critical analyses," Johnson told Denis Barbier. "He is able to pinpoint those who have this quality. I believe there is a sort of intellectual sympathy between us."

Johnson and Kubrick worked together in England for three months in 1978. Johnson stayed in an apartment in London and was driven to Kubrick's estate every day at two in the afternoon. Sitting at a big table in a large hall, Johnson and Kubrick first worked separately, outlining the film. They compared the two outlines and discussed each scene. The process was repeated two or three times as the plot line evolved. Johnson and Kubrick spent hours discussing a variety of intellectual topics. At times he would pull a book off his voluminous shelves and engage in a analytical discussion about it. Johnson found Kubrick to be a highly organized man surrounded by phones, equipment, and fine writing instruments. "He has a strong literary sense. In all respects he thinks like a novelist," Johnson told Denis Barbier. Johnson was welcomed into the Kubrick family and spent many warm evenings having dinner with Stanley and Christiane, finding Stanley to be a most affectionate family man. They talked about H. P. Lovecraft, Bruno Bettelheim's psychoanalysis of fairy tales and Freud's insights into how individuals express parapsychological experiences. Although Kubrick was making a horror movie, he

did not screen genre films with Johnson. They watched films of Jack
Nicholson, *Star Wars,* and *Leopard in the Snow,* with Keir Dullea.

Johnson and Kubrick had several copies of *The Shining,* which they
cut up into chunks and filed into envelopes marked for the individual
characters in the book.

Stanley Kubrick's relationship with Stephen King was similar to the
one he had with Anthony Burgess. Kubrick didn't want the author to
adapt his own novel but wanted King to answer questions, which ranged
from the philosophical to the conceptual, and to elaborate on the characters and plot.

"I was so flattered that Kubrick was going to do something of mine,"
Stephen King told *American Film* magazine. "The first time he called, it
was seven thirty in the morning. I was standing in the bathroom in my
underwear shaving, and my wife comes in and her eyes are bugging out.
I thought one of the kids must be choking in the kitchen or something.
She says, 'Stanley Kubrick is on the phone!' I mean, I was just floored, I
didn't even take the shaving cream off my face. Just about the first thing
he said was, 'The whole idea of a ghost is always optimistic, isn't it?' And
I said, with a hangover and one eye almost open, 'I don't understand
what you mean.' He said, 'Well the concept of the ghost presupposes life
after death. That's a cheerful concept, isn't it?' And it sounded so plausible that for a moment I just floundered and didn't say anything and then
I said, 'But what about hell?' There was a long pause on his end, and
then he came back in a very stiff voice and said, 'But I don't believe in
hell.' He doesn't believe in ghosts, either, he just found the whole concept very optimistic, which is what leads me to his version of the happy
ending for Jack Torrance—this closed loop where he is always the caretaker. He didn't seem to want to get behind the concept of the ghost as a
damned soul."

King fielded many phone calls and was granted a one-day visit to the
set. He found Kubrick to be friendly but witnessed his legendary reserve. "He's a man you can go out and have a few beers with as long as
you don't think you're going to go on and drink all night," King explained to *American Film* magazine.

Stephen King ultimately has expressed disappointment in the film but
has remained honored that such a prestigious filmmaker turned his book
into a movie. Kubrick did eliminate material and make changes. Among
the most notable were the King novel's animal-shaped hedges that came
to sinister life and could morph. Kubrick considered the idea, but the
special effects options did not satisfy his strict specifications of believability. His solution was to create a huge maze formed by a complex

arrangement of alleys and angles. The labyrinthine design had a pristine logic and offered the metaphor of entrapment and escape.

Kubrick did discuss an alternate ending with King. He proposed that the film end with the Torrance family pleasantly dining at a table in the hotel while the manager is busy greeting the new caretaker and his family. As they all walk past the diners, their eyes look right through the Torrance family, who have become invisible ghosts. King counseled Kubrick that he thought the audience would feel cheated. He kept an open mind, not concerned about Kubrick's changing the story but rather about whether the changes worked dramatically.

"Very early on, I decided the novel's ending wouldn't do," Kubrick told John Hofsess. "I didn't want the conventional ending—the big bad place burns down." Kubrick and screenplay collaborator, Diane Johnson, decided on the idea of the hedge maze which they thought would be visually exciting.

Kubrick's approach was to avoid the trappings of a typical horror film. There would be no creaking doors or skeletons tumbling out of closets. To establish believability Kubrick shot the film in what appears to be existing light without the melodramatic effects of the genre. "It's just the story of one man's family quietly going insane together," Kubrick told John Hofsess.

Kubrick cast the film while first reading the novel. Jack Nicholson was his clear choice for Jack Torrance and Shelley Duvall who he considered to be "a wonderful actress" embodied the tormented wife Wendy. "You certainly couldn't have Jane Fonda play the part; you need someone who is mousey and vulnerable," Kubrick told Hofsess.

An early treatment for the screenplay reveals that Kubrick was moving in a different direction before arriving at the plot used for the final film. In that treatment the film ends when Jack attacks Wendy from behind and she stabs him in the stomach with a knife. Jack dies and Wendy runs out when she hears the engine of a Sno-Cat. Danny has a vision of Halloran arriving and talking to Grady, who acknowledges that the chef is there to kill Wendy and Danny. Halloran becomes a lunatic savage. Wendy races through the hotel with a knife. Danny momentarily stops Halloran with his psychic power and Wendy rushes in and stabs him to death. A scrapbook on Jack's writing table contains a photograph of a New Year's celebration in 1919 with Jack in the photo. Wendy drives the Sno-Cat away with Danny. A man's hand closes the scrapbook and takes it away. A card reads, "The Overlook Hotel would survive this tragedy, as it had so many of these. It is still open each year from 5/20 to 9/20. THE END."

The treatment refers to a scrapbook that details the "lurid and sinister history of the hotel—murders, suicides and fatal accidents involving the legendary rich and famous people who have always come there." In the film the scrapbook is seen open on Jack's writing table, but it is not identified, explained, or shown in detail. The Room 217, which holds terror for Jack and Danny, is the same number as in the novel and was eventually changed to 237 in the film.

Kubrick changed the number of the room from 217 to 237. The front daytime view of the exterior of the Overlook was shot at the Timberline Lodge, near Mount Hood National Forest in Oregon. The exterior facade of the rear view of the Overlook was built on the backlot at EMI-Elstree Studios and was modeled after the Timberline Lodge. The lodge had a Room 217 but not one numbered 237. The management asked Kubrick to change the number out of concern that no one would ever want to stay in Room 217 after seeing the film. In the bathroom scene outlined in the treatment, Jack encounters the living corpse of Grady's murdered wife, but she is not first revealed as a young, seductive, beautiful, naked woman, as in the film.

Kubrick actually considered coming back to the United States to make *The Shining*. He had not shot a film in his birthplace since *Spartacus* in 1960. He called his friend and colleague Bob Gaffney and asked him if a Long Island house that he, Christiane and his daughters had lived in was available. Gaffney had recently shot a commercial on the front lawn of the estate and it was for sale. On June 5, 1977, the *Los Angeles Herald Examiner* announced that Kubrick was returning to the United States to shoot *The Shining* in Colorado. Army Archerd carried the story the next day in his Just for Variety column. The speculation was mounted on a series of notions that Kubrick always considered before and during the making of a film. Kubrick was beginning to become concerned with the growing climate of violence in Great Britain. Ultimately he decided to remain in England and bring America to him by building an American hotel on a soundstage in England.

FILM 77—a film exhibition staged in London—brought Ed Di Giulio and Garrett Brown to England. They paid a visit to Kubrick at his home in Boreham Wood and showed the director the latest model of the Steadicam that they had developed. Kubrick was in early preproduction on *The Shining*. As Roy Walker was planning the set design of the Overlook Hotel, Kubrick was interested in understanding just what the Steadicam could do so the sets could embrace the camera's ability to travel effortlessly from room to room. With the Steadicam in mind,

Kubrick began with the principle that all of the rooms of the hotel set should interconnect.

Kubrick put Garrett Brown and his Steadicam through its paces. He always had a reason for the volley of questions he pursued with someone he felt possessed valuable information. He never explained why he asked each dense and specific question, but the answer was filed away to contribute to a cinematic idea that was formulating schematically in his mind. Kubrick asked Brown to demonstrate the accuracy he could achieve with the Steadicam to hit marks in order to pull focus when working at exposures T1.4 that required critical attention to focus. As Brown hit the marks perfectly, shots inside the Overlook began to appear in Kubrick's mind's eye.

Roy Walker had been the art director on *Barry Lyndon*. Along with production designer Ken Adam, he had won an Oscar for his work on the film. Walker's work on *The Shining* confined him to the studio, but it began by his scouring America's hotels and apartment buildings. Walker went across the United States taking pictures, instructed by Kubrick to snap anything that could be used as reference. Walker had taken exacting measurements of everything he photographed so that information could be utilized in the design process. When Walker returned from his grand scout, Kubrick went over the pictures, picking out the elements and components he liked. The art department then re-created the colors and architectural elements into a combined image of the ultimate hotel.

The walls of the main room at the Overlook were filled with small framed black-and-white photographs depicting the long tradition of the hotel's hospitality and upscale guests. Kubrick went into the photographically rich archive of the Warner Bros. still photo collection of news and movie eight-by-tens and arranged them to represent the Overlook's legacy.

The bathroom where Grady and Torrance have their eerie and frightening discussion was based on a men's room in a Arizona hotel designed by Frank Lloyd Wright. Kubrick's lighting concept grew out of the same philosophy of realism as the production design. Massive wattages of artificial light were used to duplicate natural sunlight coming into the Overlook through the windows. The practical light fixtures within the hotel were given the appropriate wattage to read like source light on film. The lighting that served as the sunlight coming into the Overlook was created by first contracting the Rosco Company to make an eighty-foot-by-thirty-foot backing with a diffusion material. Sections were welded together to make a single solid backing. The lounge set had a small outdoor terrace with trees behind it. The backing was mounted behind the trees. Behind the backing were 860 1000-watt, 110-volt Medium Flood PAR 64 lamps, mounted on forty-foot tubular scaffolding at two-foot intervals. Every light could be moved individually by a control inside the set, affording the ability to shift lights during the complex movement of a Steadicam shot. The heat emitting from the unit was so intense it was impossible for anyone to walk in between the backing and the lights from one end to the other.

The acclaim for the photography of *Barry Lyndon* made John Alcott an international figure as a distinguished cinematographer. *The Shining* was shot within the confines of a studio, allowing more control for the cameraman than he had in the stately location homes on *Barry Lyndon,* but *The Shining* was as much of a challenge. The principal test of Alcott's talent was lighting the enormous set to look like a hotel lit with natural light. It took enormous candlepower—not with candles—but with powerful units of electric light. "He inspired me," Alcott said to Jack Kroll. "If Stanley was a cinematographer he'd be the most sought-after one in the world. For many films after I've worked on a Kubrick film, I'm using ideas he gave me."

Kubrick had given Alcott a copy of the Stephen King novel ten months before principal photography was to begin. Although Alcott had several other assignments, he was involved with the planning and building of the massive set—mapping the light sources such as windows and fireplaces.

Cardboard models of all the sets were built. They were created with the same colors and decor as the ones to be used in the film. Alcott made tests—lighting the models and photographing the results with a Nikon still camera in the same angles to be employed by the motion picture camera. Four months from production, Alcott continued to visit the sets as they were being constructed, surveying them each week. All of the practical lights inside the Overlook were wired as if they were actually part of the hotel. This massive job took four months of electrical wiring. The chandeliers in the main lounge and the ballroom were wired to a dimmer at a central control board. The service corridors and the main lounge were all wired, outfitted, and lit with flourescent fixtures to light the set. Transformer controls and ballasts were put in the studio corridors so they wouldn't interfere with production sound. The ever-roving lens of the Steadicam would have found any additional film lighting. For all intents and purposes, Stanley Kubrick built the Overlook as a real hotel, not a movie hotel.

The realism of the hotel set and the lighting style came from an observation Kubrick made while reading Franz Kafka. "It seemed to me that the perfect guide for this approach could be found in Kafka's writing style. His stories are fantastic and almost journalistic. On the other hand, all the films that have been made of his work seem to have ignored this completely, making everything look as weird and dreamlike as possible."

Although much of the film was shot by Garrett Brown and the Steadicam, all the lighting was within Alcott's domain. Under the watchful eye of Stanley Kubrick, Alcott constantly came up with solutions to the problems caused by the enormity of lighting a massive hotel.

This was Alcott's fourth film with Kubrick. With each film, Alcott found himself going deeper into layers of perfection, as new hurdles were overcome and bigger ones appeared. "I think that, as time goes on, Stanley becomes more thorough, more exacting in his demands," Alcott told Herb Lightman, editor of *American Cinematographer* magazine, when *The Shining* was released. "I think that one has to go away after having done a film with him, gather knowledge, come back and try to put that knowledge together with his knowledge into another film. He is, as I've said before, very demanding. He demands perfection, but he will give you all the help you need if he thinks that whatever you want to do will accomplish the desired result. He will give you full power to do it— but at the same time, it must work. Stanley is a great inspiration. He does inspire you. He's a director with a great visual eye."

Since 1969 Kubrick and Jack Nicholson had talked about working together, when the long-struggling actor broke through with his Oscar-nomination performance in *Easy Rider*. Kubrick called Nicholson "arguably the greatest actor in movies today." "I had just finished a summer's work on a script I was hoping to direct when Stanley called, out of the blue, and asked if I would be interested in working with him on his next movie," Jack Nicholson said. "I hadn't read the book, but it wouldn't have mattered. I would have done whatever Stanley wanted. Anyone would have wanted to work with him. He sent me a copy of the book. I thought it was marvelous. A great opportunity. A wonderful story. It's as simple as that. I have been quoted as saying that I must be 75 percent of every character that I play, but the truth is that I look first for something that holds my attention in the story and then for the overview of a great director. *The Shining* is a wonderful story. And although it might be my interpretation, it is Kubrick's orchestration. I am happy I have had this opportunity to try something so very different. I'm proud of the new things I've tried . . . even when they haven't come off. It's an old acting cliché, but you can only be as good as you're willing to be bad. I think this movie will be very, very good."

"I believe that Jack is one of the best actors in Hollywood, perhaps on a par with the greatest stars of the past like Spencer Tracy and Jimmy Cagney," Kubrick told Michel Ciment. "I should think that he is on almost everyone's first-choice list for any role that suits him. His work is always interesting, clearly conceived, and has the X-factor, magic. Jack is particularly suited for roles which require intelligence. He is an intelligent and literate man, and these are almost impossible to act. In *The Shining* you believe he's a writer, failed or otherwise."

Shelley Duvall was Kubrick's first and only choice for Wendy Torrance. Duvall was first discovered by another American maverick, Robert Altman, when she met the director while showing him her boyfriend's artwork in 1970. Attracted to her offbeat looks and unique contemporary Texas nature, Altman hired Duvall for *Brewster McCloud,* an equally offbeat film that suited her talents. Duvall became part of Altman's growing ensemble company and appeared in *McCabe and Mrs. Miller, Thieves Like Us, Nashville, Buffalo Bill and the Indians,* and *Three Women.*

Danny Lloyd was five and a half years old. The son of an American railroad engineer, he was selected to play Danny Torrance from an array of videotape auditions. Kubrick dispatched Leon Vitali and his wife, Kersti, to Chicago, Denver, and Cincinnati to create an interview pool of 5,000 boys over a six-month period. The three cities were chosen because Kubrick was looking for a boy who had an accent that fell in between Jack Nicholson's and Shelley Duvall's speech patterns. Vitali, who had given a riveting performance as the grown Lord Bullingdon in *Barry Lyndon,* had become a loyal and trustworthy Kubrick disciple and was given the title Personal Assistant to the Director on *The Shining.* During the production, Vitali acted as a buffer between Kubrick and the actors. A local Warner Bros. office placed newspaper ads inviting parents to submit photos and fill out applications for the film. A list was culled of around 120 boys whom Kubrick considered to have the right appearance. Kubrick was looking for a child with mobile features. He told his old friend Alexander Walker that he wanted the child's muscles connected to his nerve centers by a direct line. Vitali interviewed everyone on the list and recorded the boys performing acting improvisations on video. Kubrick reviewed the tapes and selected Danny Lloyd, the son of Jim and Ann Lloyd, who lived in a small town in Illinois.

The child employment laws in England restricted Kubrick's access to Danny Lloyd. He could keep Jack Nicholson, Shelley Duvall, and Scatman Crothers on the set for long hours to grind out upwards of half a hundred takes. Danny could be involved in the production only forty working days a year, with limited hours and a strictly observed off-the-set order by 4:30 P.M. In practical terms, all this really meant to Kubrick was a high degree of organization connected to Danny Lloyd's allotted time in front of the lens. The rules did not include rehearsal hours, so Kubrick would rehearse Danny one day and then bring him before the camera the next. Kubrick ordered a dummy to be made of the boy to use for shots when Wendy carried him. Kubrick made a wise decision in putting the nursery school–aged actor in the hands of Leon Vitali, who would give the boy his full attention. Vitali's principal assignment was to watch over Danny Lloyd and be his chaperon, friend, and direct line of communication.

Scatman Crothers got his famous nickname when in 1932 as Benjamin Sherman Crothers he auditioned for a radio show in Dayton, Ohio. The show's director told the drummer, singer, and guitar player he needed a snappier, show biz name. Crothers replied: "Call me Scatman, 'cause I do a lot of scat singing." The Scatman wrote and performed hundreds of songs and in 1948 became the first black actor on Los Angeles television. He went on to appear in many shows, including *Get Smart, Kojak, Sanford and Son, McMillan and Wife, Adam 12,* and *Chico and the Man.* Crothers became a popular character actor, appearing in *Lady Sings the Blues, Silver Streak, The Shootist, The Great White Hope,* and *Hello, Dolly!* He worked with Jack Nicholson on *The King of Marvin Gardens, The Fortune,* and *One Flew over the Cuckoo's Nest.* Kubrick selected Crothers to play Halloran, the hotel head chef with the gift to shine, the ability to communicate through ESP.

Back in the United States throughout the summer of 1978, Garrett Brown began to get occasional early morning phone calls from Kubrick in England. Amid technical questions and other data, Kubrick arranged to have the services of Brown and his Steadicam to begin in December. The plan was for Kubrick to rent the Steadicam. Brown would come to England briefly to train a Steadicam operator who would work on *The Shining.*

Kubrick's shooting schedule changed, and Brown was told his start date would be in the spring. These were heady days for Brown, as the Steadicam amazed everyone who saw the remarkable results in *Rocky, Bound for Glory,* and *Marathon Man.* His invention was beginning to revolutionize the way the motion picture camera was used and his work behind the Steadicam was making film history. Brown won the Bert Easey Technical Award given by the British Society of Cinematographers, and he decided to fly to England to accept the prestigious industry award in person. While he was in Great Britain, Brown visited Kubrick to show him the prototype of a new Steadicam model that allowed the camera to shoot at a lens height from eighteen inches to waist high. Kubrick was very pleased with the low lens shooting capability because he was about to make a film with a little boy and wanted to enter his point of view by bringing the camera down to his perspective. Kubrick took Garrett Brown on a tour of the Overlook just months before Brown would follow Jack Nicholson and company on their excursion through the hotel. As Garrett Brown walked through the cavernous kitchen and the interconnecting halls and rooms of the enormous set, he began to see tremendous possibilities to push the envelope even further than he had with Hal Ashby, John Avildsen, and John Schlesinger. Brown told Kubrick he wanted to pilot the Steadicam through *The Shining.*

Shooting on *The Shining* began in 1978, shortly after release of *Goin' South,* in which Jack Nicholson had starred and which he had directed. In what had become characteristic fashion, Kubrick released very little information about his new project to the press and to the management of Warner Bros. and the EMI-Elstree Studios, where he was going to shoot *The Shining.* A clever spokesman told *Variety,* "As befitting of any hotel, Mr. Kubrick has just hung up the 'Do Not Disturb' sign." In early 1978 the backlot of the studio, which held a street scene used for ten years to create foreign lands such as Amsterdam and Singapore was bulldozed flat so the production could construct the back facade of the Overlook Hotel and the garden maze across the way. Inside, Kubrick was using four of Elstree's nine stages.

The Shining was to be Kubrick's first film shot principally in the studio since *2001. A Clockwork Orange* was predominantly a location film, and virtually all of *Barry Lyndon* was shot on location. After toying with the idea of filming *The Shining* on location in the United States, Kubrick decided to build part of the United States in Great Britain even if it involved tearing up the backlot to do it. Kubrick's international reputation gave him status at any major studio facility—they were all too pleased just to receive a call from Stanley Kubrick.

Kubrick's persistence for perfection was notorious, but Garrett Brown got to experience it firsthand as he worked with the exacting director. On his first day, Brown performed over thirty takes, navigating his Steadicam through the vast lobby set with the grace of a dancer and the precision of a Air Force bomber pilot. The temperature on the set was pushing 110 degrees because of the 700,000 watts generated by a bank of lights. Kubrick and Alcott had devised a way to create daylight that didn't just simulate it, but duplicated the power of the sun. Eventually the air conditioning crew would figure out a way to get relief, but now

Garrett Brown was using all of his energy and skill to aim his cinematic weapon exactly where Kubrick insisted. "I quickly realized that when Stanley said the crosshairs were to be on someone's *left* nostril, that no other nostril would do," the witty Brown wrote in an article for *American Cinematographer* magazine.

Since Kubrick's early days as a still photographer, he had used a pictorial approach that centered his compositions. Centered and counterbalanced images are pleasing to the eye and respect the frame that embraces them. A centered image represents order, control, discipline, logic, and organization—the very qualities inherent in Kubrick's personality and his psyche as an artist. In the years when he was developing his skill as an image maker Kubrick spent hundreds of hours sitting over a chessboard—a visual emblem of order, with its sixty-four squares in eight rows of eight alternate dark and light blocks. The representation of a chessboard—real and symbolized—appears often in Kubrick's films. The precision of the centered image is a hallmark of almost every shot in a Stanley Kubrick film. Garrett Brown gradually reprogrammed his eye for the continual movement and reframing in his work as a Steadicam artist and learned to hit the crosshairs seen only through the lens and not by the viewer to live up to Kubrick's mandate for order and stability in his photographic work.

The technical requirements of hitting the crosshairs in the lens became Kubrick's modus operandi for doing another take and resulted in his developing the artistry of this new cinematic instrument. "A lot of that was smoke, just to have an opportunity to do another take," Brown explained. "He would admit in dailies that they were all the same, they were all good. After a while I realized that after four or five they were all perfect from my point of view and then you could concentrate on the fine points of controlling the instrument. That's where I really learned to control the damn thing. I got to the point where I could put the frame line or the crosshairs anywhere that I wanted anytime, like dance. It was great, I loved it. I loved doing fifty or seventy takes. He could not have done too many takes for me because it wasn't tiring. He did one, then you had an argument and played it back. You got a rest after every take. It was an opportunity to bear down on technique that you wouldn't find anywhere else. Half of your job is schlepping the gear through airports and then the other half is just trying to catch up with events and then make a shot based on your native abilities. If you get three takes you're lucky, but you never get this opportunity to do it and see it and do it and see it—realizing if you keep your shoulder here, this works, if you put your foot here, this works. You cultivate a muscle memory so you realize that if your hand is just at your belt and just at your breastbone, now you have exactly the boom height that you need. I was able to convert this kind of wild-haired, wing-it instrument and do it precisely."

Kubrick was not satisfied with the quality of the remote TV image that projected what the Steadicam was seeing. This prompted another series of technical and philosophical filmmaking queries that needed to be addressed. Eventually a new transmitter was cultivated to improve the video image. To establish freedom from the restrictions of the video signal, antennas were hidden behind the walls throughout the sets so that wireless video could be transmitted anywhere. Brown remarked that he immediately realized the word "reasonable" was not in the Kubrick lexicon.

The large take ratio allowed Kubrick to create a library of character reactions and emotions for any given shot. As the takes stacked up, Jack Nicholson and Shelley Duvall began to move through a range of emotions from catatonia to hysteria. Kubrick had earned the power to make films the way he wanted to make them. The way Stanley Kubrick made films gave him a myriad of choices all during the process until he signed off the release print to Warner Bros. distribution.

A day's output could be one scene or one shot. Extensive lighting tests were done before Kubrick would even begin shooting. Kubrick persisted until he felt he had gotten everything out of the scene that was there to get. He didn't begin with a preconceived idea but found what he was searching for in a series of methodical steps and inquiries as he pursued the shot.

Garrett Brown would photograph many of the shots on his feet, walking, running, and pivoting to choreograph Kubrick's elaborate long-take shooting style. Elstree Camera, under the direction of Mick Mason and Harold Payne, devised a series of custom mounts so the Steadicam could be put on wheels. A converted skateboard and a custom sackbarrel both failed their tests for mobility and precision. The solution was to use the Ron Ford wheelchair prototype developed earlier in conjunction with Kubrick. The rig allowed Garrett Brown to ride and not run, to be pushed and therefore not be winded by charging through the halls with the extra weight of his camera appendage. The Steadicam was a marvel of engineering—light enough for an operator to carry—but, as Garrett Brown later learned when actor Danny Lloyd found he could use Garrett Brown and his camera as a swing, the Arriflex BL that he used on *The Shining* weighed as much as the boy.

Garrett Brown was a striking presence on the set with his invention and his mode of cinematic expression. A tall, graceful man with a strong sense of purpose, Brown had a tremendous respect for Stanley Kubrick. As he walked, ran, glided, and on occasion seemed to fly through the Overlook set with the grace of Baryshnikov, Brown possessed the skill to put his lens wherever Stanley Kubrick wanted it and the conviction that his photographic discovery was fulfilling the expectations of the medium.

Kubrick ordered that a three-hundred-foot plywood roadway used for the camera wheelchair be entirely rebuilt three times to get it perfectly smooth. Brown, a perfectionist by most normal standards, felt he was able to complete an acceptable, printable take after the first few passes through the shot. Kubrick, on the other hand, was nothing but critical until Brown was in the take 14 range and didn't become comfortable until the slate was reading "Take 20" and above. Brown became another actor or performer on *The Shining* who would be tested by the takes-to-the-limit philosophy.

The shot where the camera follows Wendy up three flights of stairs and slows down just moving ahead of her when she sees two ghost guests in the midst of a sexual act, became one of Garrett Brown's favorites—he got thirty-six opportunities to shoot it.

Editing on *The Shining* wouldn't begin until the film was completely wrapped. On earlier Kubrick films the editing had begun during the shooting process, a standard industry practice that helps the director to see what else may be needed or what should be reshot. In addition, the editor can begin to pace the film. Kubrick was stepping ever closer to having complete and absolute control over his films in the fullest sense. Knowing he would be there through the entire postproduction process after he shot the film, Kubrick strategized that he needed at least two to three takes that fit his criterion of perfect. Watching each Steadicam take go by, Kubrick was dividing his total concentration between the performance of the actor and Garrett Brown's prowess to put the crosshairs exactly where the director wanted them. Late into the production Kubrick admitted to Brown that performance of the actors was his principal determining factor in selecting a take for the final cut, but it didn't lessen his demand for technical excellence.

The casual viewer of *The Shining* tends to think the Steadicam was used strictly for the amazing shots following Danny on his Big Wheel tricycle through the halls of the Overlook and the omnipresent force moving through the maze—but Kubrick used Garrett Brown to shoot an extremely high percentage of the film. With Kubrick's technical acumen, he quickly learned that the Stedicam was in fact so steady that it could be employed in hard-to-get-to places and could be used for a take that required the camera to be stationary. Stanley Kubrick and Garrett

Brown were both members of the society of the cinema's conceptual thinkers. A student of film, Brown understood that filmmakers were searching for ways to liberate the camera. In conceiving and inventing the Steadicam, Brown was striving to develop a device that would allow the operator to put the lens where he wanted it. Kubrick understood this and often used the head or tail of a Steadicam shot as part of a scene that was photographed predominantly with a standard stationary camera.

Brown used an 18mm Cooke lens that allowed the Steadicam to pass within an inch of walls and door frames. The wide-angle lens and unlimited mobility of the Steadicam presented a tremendous challenge for the lighting. John Alcott patiently solved every problem introduced by the omnipresent camera by designing the light to be free of shadows, emotionally correct for the scene, and often seemingly powered with the strength of the sun.

Garrett Brown followed Shelley Duvall and Anne Jackson through the hall into the living room and then held on them on the couch while they discussed Danny's condition for a half a page of dialogue. To navigate through the cavernous kitchen set filled with tables, equipment, and boxes Garrett Brown maneuvered like racing master Mario Andretti, finding the least disturbing line to take to dart through turns. By making race car turns the mode of movement, he allowed the camera to remain invisible and connected the eye to the scene. Garrett Brown squeezed through the door of the Torrance apartment in the hotel, climbed stairs up and down and served as the POV of Jack and Danny Torrance, respectively, as they entered the evil of Room 237.

The kitchen and maze sequences gave Brown the opportunity to further refine his analogy to race car driving. He constantly looked for the closest route to follow to achieve Kubrick's dynamic staging of the sequence. "The camera was never able to take what you might call the race car line through the corner," Brown explained. "The race car line is the largest radius that you can cut, therefore the closest pass to the actual corner itself you can take. I can take the lens with the least disruption so the actors are not violently wiping against the background. You have this wonderful serenity."

Brown put a bubble level on his Steadicam so that during the maze shooting he could keep the lens level and avoid the distorting keystoning of the image that so often occurs with a wide-angle lens.

Kubrick and his company checked into the Overlook Hotel set in May 1978 and occupied it until April 1979. This caused Elstree Studios to find creative ways to juggle Dino De Laurentiis's production of *Flash*

Gordon and *The Empire Strikes Back,* the second installment in George Lucas's *Star Wars* trilogy.

Kubrick maintained his customary reserve with many of the actors he was interested in. He wanted Anne Jackson to play the doctor who makes a house call to examine Danny after he has his first on-screen shining episode that gives him a glimpse into the horrific past of the Overlook Hotel.

Kubrick phoned Anne Jackson and talked to her about the role in general terms. "After we finished our conversation, I said, 'The only thing is, Mr. Kubrick, from what you tell me if it's anything to do with being murdered in a bathtub I couldn't do the part because I can't stand any kind of stabbing. I don't want to be murdered.' And he didn't laugh," Anne Jackson, stage and screen actress married to Eli Wallach, recalled. "He just said 'Oh, it's nothing like that.' *A Clockwork Orange* scared the living daylights out of me, that's why I said to him, 'Please don't have me murdered. If you're hiring me to have me murdered in the tub, I can't do it because I'll have nightmares.' "

After they talked, Kubrick told Jackson he wanted her for the role of a doctor. She was sent the Stephen King novel, and arrangements were made to fly her to London. Anne Jackson's initial impressions were that Stanley Kubrick did not look like a typical director. "He wore a lumber jacket like the boys wore in East New York when we used to ride through that area when I was a kid," Jackson remembers. "It didn't look like a grown-up man's gear and it certainly wasn't chic. He seemed to me to be a preoccupied man with a lot of things on his mind. He didn't connect easily to people. He was adamant about my costume in the film. I couldn't get out of him what he wanted the character to be like. I realized he probably didn't know until he saw what he had created."

Research had been done on what people in Colorado of a particular lifestyle would wear. Jackson was sent shopping in London with a staffer to find the doctor's house-call outfit. "We had many appointments, and the staffers kept showing Stanley clothes. They brought me a pleated skirt and a kind of doctorish-looking top. He would say, 'No, no.' That's all he said was 'No.' No to everything," Anne Jackson remembered. "Then I came in wearing a jacket and a pair of trousers that I had come over on the plane in. It's so cold when you travel on the plane. I was wearing that one rainy day in London, and Stanley said, 'That's what I want her to look like, let's get those clothes.' But he had seen them before because I didn't bring that many clothes to London, I didn't expect to be there that long.

"Then he started teaching me how to be a doctor. He invited a doctor to the set and sent me home on a weekend with a stethoscope. I said, 'I don't know what you mean, Stanley. How do I get people to practice with?' He said, 'Just ring your bell at the hotel and get the hotel personnel.' And that's what I did. I did whatever he told me to do—it was like I was hypnotized."

Jackson wanted to know if she was playing a pediatrician or a child psychologist. "I kept asking Stanley, 'How much does she know? Is she not a terribly good doctor from Colorado? How much does she know?' " Anne Jackson recalled. "Well, I would just get a look like, 'You tell me.' "

Over the weekend Anne Jackson rehearsed the scene where she sits down with Wendy Torrance and explains that Danny's episode was a normal childhood experience. The doctor then learns that Jack has a drinking problem and once hurt the boy's arm by accident. This scene was to be shot first, but in the film it would follow the doctor's examination and interview with Danny about his episode in the bathroom. The screenplay of the scene merely had the lines of dialogue, with little inkling of the character's motivation or stage directions. Shooting began, and Kubrick made several takes of the scene without saying anything to Anne Jackson. He would call for a take and then watch it on video.

"We did a shot and he said, 'Again,' and we did it again and he said, 'Again.' By the third or fourth time I started to become unnerved because I had tried different things, I didn't know what he wanted—the first one seemed to me to be on the track," Jackson recalled. "I said to him, 'How much do you want this character to know, Stanley?' He just looked at me as though 'Why do you ask questions?' I wasn't getting any satisfaction. We went on. He just kept doing it over and over again. I finally said, 'Please tell me if there's something wrong or if there's something you're missing. What is it you want, Stanley?' I did have an edge to my voice. I just said to him, 'What should I do that is different? What are you getting that you don't want?' He looked at me and I really felt like a child in school who was doing something wrong. I didn't know what it was. I felt rather good about the scene at the beginning. I thought, 'If I still haven't done what he wants after so many takes then he probably is going to fire me.' After doing it so many times I started to do suspicious things and then I started to just listen as though I didn't know what Shelley was talking about. It just created an atmosphere of tension. It went on like that and when we broke for lunch, Shelley Duvall said, 'Don't worry about it, Annie, he's done this with everyone.' Shelley gave me one of those self-help books like *Don't Say Yes When You Want to Say No*. She said, 'Here, take this book and read it.' I loved working with her, she was just so darling, kind and so talented.

"Then we came back from lunch and we did it again, I don't know how many times. I know he used the first take in the film because I remember what I had done on the first take. I know Stanley used the first take because there were many more colors in the first one than I did later, because then I was trying to correct something and I didn't know what I was correcting. Every other scene I did after that, it was one or two takes—period. After this he was very helpful to me. When I was doing the scene with Danny Lloyd, the tendency with a child is always to ingratiate yourself with them and get friendly. Stanley said, 'I don't want any of that, I want it very businesslike.' So that was helpful. I loved the fact that he sent me home with the stethoscope. I watched that doctor very carefully and watched his attitude. His attitude was exactly what Kubrick had in mind, which was a doctor who was doing good and is efficient in getting it done and not being too friendly. Most of my pediatricians were wonderful with my kids, but Stanley didn't want that."

When Anne Jackson left the studio the first day, she ran into Barry Nelson, whom she knew from New York. Jackson told him to call her when he was finished with his first day of shooting. "I wanted to warn him about what was going on," Jackson recalled. "I said, 'You call me, Barry,' and he looked at me. When he called up he knew exactly why I had said that. I said to him, 'How many takes?' and he roared with laughter. He said, 'Oh, I guess about thirty-five. But you had a scene, I had one line. I said, 'Hi ya Jack, *Hi ya* Jack, hi *Jack.*' And I said, 'What was Stanley's comment?' Barry said, 'He said I sounded like a carnival shouter.'"

The shooting on the scene in which the doctor examines and talks to Danny went swiftly. "That went so fast," Jackson recalled. "By that time the character had been established—that was the one Kubrick went with. It was just a take or two because Danny was a young child and the emphasis was on preserving his spontaneity. He couldn't work that many hours in a day. I guess the reason Stanley did the scene with Shelley first was because he wanted to get that character established and then let me work with Danny Lloyd."

The two scenes Anne Jackson had in *The Shining* took two to three weeks to shoot. "He was the most meticulous director I ever worked with. I never worked with anybody like that before. I have such admiration for him. I came with such admiration and still do. I mean even after that scene I thought, 'If he were to ask me to do another film, I'd do it.' He isn't a tyrant. Stanley is quiet. He's intimidating only because of his enormous talent and the fact that when you see his films, there's so much richness in them that you think he's probably going to be outgoing and talkative and he's not that at all."

Kubrick gradually learned to deal with the rest and food breaks required by British crews. Having started as a guerrilla filmmaker in New York, he was used to working long hours with erratic eating and sleeping patterns. The British crew regularly took their tea and bacon roll breaks. When a McDonald's opened nearby, the evening breaks began to incorporate the Big Mac, in clear violation of the culinary habits of the British crew.

In a unusual breach of intense security, Kubrick allowed his youngest daughter, Vivian, to make a documentary on the making of *The Shining*, which was aired on the BBC. The film was a rare chance to see Kubrick at work. Throughout his career Kubrick has been widely photographed by a still camera. Pictures through the years document his intense concentration, his legendary piercing eyes, and his shaggy dog appearance. Photos taken on set reveal Kubrick's hands-on approach, his leadership behind the camera, and his commanding presence on the set. The documentary format, seeing Kubrick in action, reveals him as a quiet but intense man. He is always shown in forward motion, just on the brink of impatience with those who can't keep up with him and engaged with others with whom he is in sync. His direction and suggestions are simply worded and pragmatic. His outfit for *The Shining* included a large parka and at times a blue Eisenhower jacket. Kubrick's beard sprouted out in all directions and often was reconfigured by unconscious tugs while he was deep in thought. Additional pounds had expanded his once medium-size frame to mini-Wellesian proportions, but the large, commanding presence of Stanley Kubrick taking his cast and crew into the depths of the Overlook was impressive. He appeared to be shy but focused, a man who almost always smiles when he's looking through a camera or a viewfinder. The crown of his head was almost bald, now framed by a mane of wispy hair uncontrolled by comb or brush. His glasses, aviator-style, were well crafted of high-quality ocular material. He often held his glasses in his hand as he peered through the lens looking for focus, composition, and design.

Kubrick's method of shooting take after take took its toll on the sixty-nine-year-old Scatman Crothers. One particular shot of the scene in the kitchen between Danny and Halloran discussing the shining ran up 148 takes. This was one camera position and didn't include the extensive coverage and high take ratio that Kubrick got on other angles of the same scenes. The single shot ran for seven minutes and Kubrick printed every single take. Commonly, directors will print the takes they feel are successful and leave the others to lay within the original negative. But Kubrick wanted to see every frame to search for the CRM, those critical moments that he felt gave his work directorial distinction. His years of voracious moviegoing had taught him that magic moments in films didn't come easily but only when the camera, acting, decor, content, and style aligned to create cinematic wizardry.

Kubrick relentlessly filmed forty takes of the scene when Halloran is struck with an ax by Jack Torrance. After he had axed the fatigued actor for the fortieth time, Jack Nicholson, who worked with the Scatman on many films, asked Kubrick not to continue much longer. As usual, Kubrick was more result-oriented than attentive to the human needs of the cast. Nicholson was at the height of his creative powers and had tremendous respect for Kubrick. As a director himself, Nicholson had great reverence for Kubrick's vision and agreeably submitted to as many takes as Kubrick was willing to sit for. Kubrick felt that Nicholson flourished with each plunge into new territory, encouraging him to find new colors in everything the scene called for. Nevertheless, he felt compelled to intervene on Crothers's behalf.

The process of making *The Shining* was an emotional one for Scatman Crothers. When asked by Vivian Kubrick and her documentary crew about working with Danny Lloyd, he broke down and burst into tears. "It was beautiful, just like *my son*. If you see tears, they would be tears of joy because I thank the Lord I've been here and able to work with such beautiful people. I'll never forget this."

Nicholson's scene with Kubrick veteran Joe Turkel playing Lloyd, the ghostly bartender, was shot over and over as many as thirty-six times. "Jack's performance here is incredibly intricate, with sudden changes of thought and mood—all grace notes," Kubrick said. "It's a very difficult scene to do because the emotional flow is so mercurial. It demands knife-edged changes of direction and a tremendous concentration to keep things sharp and economical. In this particular scene Jack produced his best takes near the highest number."

"Kubrick likes to do many takes. Jack Nicholson told me that on *The Shining*, Stanley sometimes did seventy or eighty takes on a set-up," John Boorman wrote in *The Emerald Forest Diary*. "When I saw the film I could see what Kubrick had been up to. He was trying to get performances that came out of extremity, exhaustion."

Nicholson was attracted to the family crisis in the Torrance family. For Stephen King it was the backdrop to set off sparks in a haunted hotel. For Kubrick and Nicholson, Jack Torrance's personal demons and the fury he inflicted on his family were the true horror of the film. Nicholson, no stranger to pathological characters, having played Randle P. Mc-Murphy in *One Flew over the Cuckoo's Nest* was attracted to Jack Torrance's psychosis. "The book had that intimation to begin with, and then I just blew it up," Nicholson said in an interview. "It's a demanding, highly difficult performance that's sort of balletic. If you ask the average person to walk down a thirty-yard hallway, they'd start fidgeting after the first ten yards, wondering where to look, but an actor has to fill the space. He has to find someplace where the style merges with the reality of the piece, some kind of symbolic design."

Actor Tony Burton was cast as Larry Durkin, the owner of an auto repair shop in Colorado who supplies Halloran with a Sno-Cat to reach the Overlook during a winter storm for the climax of *The Shining*. "The first motion picture I ever worked in was John Carpenter's *Assault on Precinct 13*," explained Tony Burton, who has appeared in many memorable films, including the *Rocky* series, *The Bingo Long Traveling All-Stars and Motor Kings*, and *Inside Moves* and the critically acclaimed television series *Frank's Place*. "At the time *Assault on Precinct 13* was running in a theater in London for years. It became a cult film. Stanley saw the film and liked it. He said he saw it as a cowboy flick, it was like they circled the wagon and the settlers were being attacked. So he liked me in the film and that's how I got the job on *The Shining*. I didn't have to read or anything. My contract was for a week. I just had two short scenes in the movie. I stayed for six weeks because Stanley and I were playing chess."

Burton arrived in London near the end of production on *The Shining*. Kubrick and his principal cast and crew had been on the film for almost a year when Burton arrived to shoot his scenes as Larry Durkin. "The first day, I wasn't working. I came to the set and while we were sitting around I got the chessboard out, set up the pieces, and started moving pieces around. That was a pleasant surprise to Stanley. He saw it and he and I ended up playing. It was right after lunch when I came in. He and I played for the rest of the day. There was no more shooting done that day. No one said, 'Come on, let's shoot this movie.' Stanley and I played two games for the rest of the day. After that I wasn't allowed on the set. They would see me at the door and say, 'Tony, please!'

"Stanley was a stronger player than I but I was strong enough to give him sufficient struggle to where he enjoyed it. I beat him in the first or second game we played, and then I didn't win anymore after that, but it was always a tight struggle. That's what he loved; I guess there was no one else around that played strong. Stanley is a very strong chess player. He talked about hanging around with Bobby Fischer and all those guys

STANLEY KUBRICK 433

in New York. Stanley stood up when he played me. He was involved in the game on a physical level, not only mentally—it was like athletics. His body psychology would change—as the fight ensued he would get more animated. Everyone knew not to bother him.

"Stanley plays a classical, conventional style. You really have to know your openings because he doesn't speculate a lot. He knows all the text-book moves, the Sicilian, the Lopez, the Larson, he *loved* to play the King's Indian. I liked to play the King's Indian in reverse, so we used to have some very interesting struggles. Stanley didn't like to trade pieces. He liked to keep the board full of possibilities and tension in the middle. Stanley waited for you to make a mistake and then he pounced on it."

For the sequence with Larry Durkin, Kubrick had scouts photograph an actual auto repair shop in the Northwest. The photographs were used to build a replica of the exterior on the backlot and an interior on the stage. Snow machines were used to make it look like Tony Burton was outside the shop during a heavy snowstorm.

As often was his method, Kubrick continued to rewrite the script for *The Shining* as the film slowly moved through production. Actors were given new pages on an almost daily basis, to the extent that Jack Nicholson gave up on his original copy and used the daily revisions as his current script. Every day Nicholson would be given new pages. He would take them and draw a line under the name of his character every time it appeared. The actor had seen Boris Karloff use this method when he worked with the horror legend on *The Raven* and *The Terror,* and Nicholson had done it ever since. Kubrick always made it clear, often through continuity person June Randall, that the pages given to the actors were not the "script" but just something to use to find the real scene with the actors, on the set, in front of the cameras, next to stacks of raw stock ready to capture what they had found.

On the set Nicholson always appeared in character. His legendary arched eyebrows, which almost matched his director's, were in constant motion up and down, left and right and expressed the playful, manic, and malevolent persona within. Holding court with the crew and addressing the visiting documentary camera of Vivian Kubrick, Nicholson displayed his devilish wit and bad boy grin. The part of Jack Torrance was extremely physical, so Nicholson often whipped himself up into a frenzy by jumping up and down, spewing bile out loud as he prepared for a take.

One of Nicholson's inspired improvisations was the now legendary "Here's Johnny!" line after he has axed in the bathroom door to get to the frightened Wendy.

Vivian Kubrick was getting an unprecedented study of Stanley
Kubrick at work on film. Kubrick used the opportunity to keep track of
his every move. "Vivian was going around shooting us making the picture
all the time," Tony Burton recalled. "She also had a little cart that she
pushed around. You would be in conversation with Stanley, some debate
or subject would come up and he would say, 'Yeah, I was talking to Jack
about that yesterday. Vivian, what was that Jack said?' And she would go
into the cart, find what the conversation was about and read it back to
him."

Stanley Kubrick's mother, Gertrude, visited her son at work during
the making of *The Shining.* Kubrick had inherited his looks from his
mother. Gert's eyes were sharp, heavily lined and punctuated with finely
arched eyebrows. An intelligent, well-spoken woman, during her stay she
quizzed her son about the methods of moviemaking.

June Randall and Kubrick's assistants worked with Nicholson and the
other actors helping them to learn their lines by reading through the
material with them so they could memorize it thoroughly. Although
Kubrick encouraged improvisation and invention when it was inspired,
he expected professionalism out of his actors. Part of the craft of acting
was learning the lines and performing them with precision. Kubrick did
not appreciate improvisation if he felt an actor wasn't word perfect on
the script first. Once that was achieved, when Kubrick felt it was appropriate for the scene, he did encourage actors, like Nicholson and Peter
Sellers, who were gifted improvisers.

"Stanley would have a dialogue coach come to my hotel, and he would
go over my lines with me," Tony Burton recalled. "Finally I had to say,
'Man, you have to quit coming up here. I don't need you. I knew my
lines when I came here,' so he quit coming."

Kubrick continued to work on the script during the shooting, typing
furiously in a improvised two-finger hunt-and-peck style on a portable
non-electric typewriter—not an electronic or digital high-tech approach
to the task. Watching Kubrick flail away at the keys, his eyes locked on
the word-forming letters and the briskly moving carriage, gives the impression that he may have been the fingers behind the sheets of "All
work and no play make Jack a dull boy" that fill the manuscript Jack
Torrance had been working on all winter. The patterns and rhythm of
words reflect Kubrick's innovative approach to screenplay format and his
obsession with symmetry, configuration, and repetition.

While directing, Kubrick got physically involved in planning a scene.
For the low-angle shot shooting up at Jack Torrance as he pleaded with
his wife to let him out of the storage room, Kubrick lined up the shot

with his viewfinder. After deciding on an extreme low-angle shooting up at Jack, Kubrick left his comfy director's chair and lay down on the floor to look up at Nicholson performing the scene above him. During the filming of the shot, Kubrick lay next to the camera operator to hold a gel over a light playing on Nicholson's manic face. To accomplish low-angle Wellesian shots Kubrick is often found lying on and rolling about the floor, shooting, assisting, and getting a direct look at his subject as the camera sees it. Kubrick's direction to Nicholson was often short and clear, such as "You couldn't find some way of not looking here and looking down as you say the line?" An intuitive actor with great command of his craft, Nicholson easily gave Kubrick what he wanted for that take and readied himself for the others.

Kubrick did not occupy his director's chair very often. He was constantly on his feet behind Brown and his Steadicam or riding the dolly or on the floor to get a direct view of what the camera was seeing if he was not looking at the video screen. Kubrick is persistent in staying a step ahead of everyone on the set. His intensity gives the impression of an inner struggle between patience and impatience. Chess taught him not to grab a piece out of emotionalism, so he stays calm on the set while constantly pushing everyone around him to be better, faster, and more perfect.

Nicholson, a veteran with so many major filmmakers, had a firm respect for Stanley Kubrick. "When I come up against a director who has a concept that maybe I don't agree with, maybe I just hadn't thought about it or whatever, I'd be more prone to go with them than my own because I want to be out of control as an actor. I want them to have the control—otherwise it's going to become predictably my work and that's not fun," Nicholson told the documentary crew.

The set pieces of Steadicam work in *The Shining* were the scenes where the lens followed Danny as he rode his Big Wheel through the rooms and halls of the Overlook. Visually, the scenes were stunning as the camera, propelled by the wheelchair rig, drove behind Danny just inches from the floor. But the sound of the plastic wheels going over wood—then rug—then wood—then rug in the main room created a visceral effect that communicated directly with the child in everyone. Conceiving just how the sequences would be shot took much trial and error. On the first attempt Garrett Brown ran after Danny's bike on foot, but the three-minute takes that Kubrick required winded the cinematographer. On foot Brown was also limited to getting the camera no lower than eighteen inches—too high to put the lens directly behind the tyke who pedaled furiously through the Overlook. The Steadicam was then adapted to the Ron Ford cinema wheelchair. Garrett Brown traveled along with the camera, controlling the leveling head. A platform was constructed so that the sound man and focus puller Douglas Milsome and others could ride on the back. Milsome, who would shoot Kubrick's next film, *Full Metal Jacket,* served as John Alcott's focus puller. The constantly moving camera was a challenge to this particular member of the camera crew. Milsome, using a wireless control, delivered razor-sharp images to his demanding director.

The weight of the rig and its occupants turned out to be too much for the original tires. One hairy excursion tearing after Danny through the halls resulted in a tire blowout that almost caused a serious crash. Solid tires were then mounted on the rig. Kubrick kept trying to find ways to duplicate takes of a given shot with regularity and precision. His solution was to mount a highly accurate speedometer, which could be monitored and used to establish the exact tempo of a given shot so Garrett Brown could perform take after identical take.

The scenes of Danny exploring the haunted halls of the Overlook with his Big Wheel allowed Kubrick to use the classic methods of silent film directors. Many of the shots didn't involve synchronized sound dialogue, so Kubrick was able to use two techniques dating back to the days of D. W. Griffith. One was to play music to establish an emotional environment for Danny Lloyd and to create a sonic atmosphere for him to perform in. Kubrick had done this skillfully on *Spartacus* and *2001.* The other classic directing tool was to talk the actor through a scene while the camera was rolling. As Kubrick shot the scene where Danny runs through the hall and hides from his raging father by getting into one of the commercial kitchen cabinets and shutting the door, he instructed Leon Vitali, who communicated with the boy directly, to tell Danny to "listen to Stanley." This single-power authority gave Kubrick direct access to the boy. Vitali was Danny's authority figure on the set; he was also the child's friend and the person who controlled his universe while he worked on *The Shining.* Once the cameras rolled, Kubrick directed Danny, yelling urgently through his electronic megaphone, "Danny, move out Danny, get out of there, look out again, Danny, get out, Danny, look back, look back, Danny, start to slow down, start to slow down, see the door, see the door, look in the cupboard, quickly, get in the cupboard, Danny!" Coincidence brought Kubrick an actor named Jack for the role of Jack Torrance and an actor named Danny for his son, Danny Torrance, but in the case of the boy it gave his performance an immediacy, since he was reacting to his birth name.

For the sequence where Jack enters the Gold Room ballroom filled with 1920s guests dancing and enjoying the festive atmosphere, Kubrick had his extras rehearse the elegant ballroom dances of the time. Kubrick watched the rehearsals carefully and personally selected the appropriate music, needle-dropping the LPs on the record player. He directed the dancers and party revelers with his megaphone, politely addressing them with information as to where to stand and how to appear to the camera. Kubrick instructed the extras not to actually talk, so as not to interfere with his sync sound take, but to mime conversation to each other. Kubrick knew from years of scrutinizing thousands of films that extras could often mime their business by nodding and using large gestures that look fake. Kubrick told them to act naturally to give the scene a chilling sense of time-tripping realism as Jack walks from the seventies into the roaring twenties.

Kubrick screened his dailies on projectors that he owned. He ordered them rebuilt on a regular basis to counteract the unsteadiness of image that comes with wear. Kubrick was especially strident about the sharpness and steadiness of his projected images. Prints were made on matte-perf film, which ensured a steady projected print. Rank Laboratories had the only printer that Kubrick felt would give him the steadiness he required. Kubrick had his staff design a master chart that gave the specification and peculiarities of every lens in his vast photographic arsenal. For years he had purchased the majority of his equipment. While others rented, Kubrick believed in ownership to secure and maintain and control the quality he demanded out of film equipment.

The sequences in the pristine and labyrinthine maze, which was adjacent to the back of the Overlook, were shot frame to frame with the Steadicam. The hedges were constructed of pine boughs stapled into place on plywood forms that patterned the maze in rows, angles, and turns that led to the center and then out again if the pathfinder took the right passages. The paths were created with gravel. A center section of the maze was built to one side of the set and wider than the rest. When cut into the film it appeared to be in the center, connected to the outer rows and angles of hedges, which all looked alike to a bewildered inhabitant. At first the maze was built with certain sections left open, but this occasionally disoriented Brown and a shot would be ruined when he pointed the moving camera toward one of the holes, destroying the maze illusion. Kubrick had an exacting overhead-view map made of the maze, which was used to get in and out and to plan his shots. Copies were given to the crew, who nevertheless continued to get lost throughout the production. Garrett Brown recalled that if you got lost and called out "Stanley!" Kubrick's laughter seemed to come from all directions inside the maze. Kubrick often remained seated at a video screen that was sent a wireless image from an antenna on a ladder. To watch the playback, Brown had to walk all the way out of the maze after walking through it to shoot the shot. To photograph the intricate sequences, Brown used a 9.8 Kinoptik lens that was twenty-four inches from the ground. The Steadicam was also used for tripod-style shots within the maze, as it saved time to have less equipment in and out of the life-size puzzle.

For the night chase in the snow between father and son that concludes *The Shining,* Roy Walker and his art department re-created the maze on Stage 1 at EMI Studios. White dendritic dairy salt and pulverized Styrofoam were used to create enough snow to duplicate the effects of a Colorado blizzard. The crew had difficulty maneuvering through the sandy texture, and it was especially arduous for Garrett Brown to trudge through the artificial snow on foot as he endlessly chased after Jack Nicholson and Danny Lloyd. For some shots his Steadicam became their view of each other during the chase, at other times Brown's lens took on the gaze of the characters themselves. Dense oil smoke was pumped into the set for eight hours a day during the shooting to create the look of fog in the quartz outdoor-style lights that were used to illuminate the snowy maze. The smoke made it difficult to breathe, especially for Brown, who was in a constant state of exertion. The crew originally wore gas masks, but Brown found that he couldn't get enough air to support running from end to end of the maze. The artificial snow was difficult to negotiate and fill lights were constantly around Brown's agile feet. These shots were the most difficult of the film. A shot traveling along Danny's feet was made at a lens height of three inches and photographed with a copy of the earliest Steadicam—made of just the camera, battery, and magazine. For the shot where Danny backs up into his own footprints and hides to fool his father, who can't figure out why the footsteps just stop, Garrett Brown wore special stilts that had Danny's shoes nailed to them so he could walk in the child's footprints.

Kubrick played music that he found appropriate on the set during the shooting of the night snow chase that climaxes the film. Personally cueing and modulating the volume, Kubrick fired vocal instructions at Danny Lloyd to keep him at the right emotional pitch. "Don't look at your hands, Danny! Don't look at your hands when you come around! Slowly. Slowly. Keep coming. More scared Danny. Now, go—run, run run!" Kubrick shouted emphatically at Danny Lloyd as he trudged through the mounds of salt and Styrofoam.

The stunning helicopter shots that open *The Shining* were shot in Glacier National Park in Montana. Kubrick dispatched a second-unit camera crew there, who reported back that the area was uninteresting. When Kubrick saw the test shots he knew that it was the perfect location but the wrong crew. He then hired Greg McGillivray, a noted helicopter cinematographer, who spent several weeks in Montana to achieve the spectacular results.

Face-to-face contact with Stanley Kubrick was becoming less frequent for anyone not directly working on one of his films or not within his well-founded intimate sphere. The world began to see Stanley Kubrick as the Howard Hughes of cinema. He rarely left his home, except to work at a nearby studio. He almost never left England. He stayed in contact with many all over the world, not to engage in small talk, a practice he neither participated in nor understood, but to get *information* and to nurture those relationships that were unconditional and firmly moored.

Security was tight on *The Shining* set, where the Do Not Disturb sign never came off the Overlook Hotel. One of the few outsiders Kubrick did see while he was shooting was his old friend journalist Alexander Walker, who had known Kubrick longer and better than almost any other film writer. Even though Walker wrote the first major study of the director, *Stanley Kubrick Directs,* and followed his career closely, Kubrick was still a partial enigma to him. Walker paid a visit to *The Shining* set and passed through the tight security that Kubrick had in place. He hadn't been officially approved in advance, but when Walker arrived, his name was given to Kubrick via two-way radio, and he received an okay from the general. Walker was provided with a map of the maze set, which detailed the exact coordinates where Kubrick was shooting at the moment.

Alexander Walker followed the intricate map and turned the corner of a hedge wall to see Kubrick standing behind Garrett Brown as they worked out a Steadicam shot. Kubrick had his hands placed gently on Garrett Brown's hips to guide him as they danced the Steadicam ballet through the maze that became one of *The Shining*'s most startling features. Walker observed that Kubrick hadn't changed much since he had seen him last. The beard was longer and Kubrick's legendary careless fashion statement had become "a standardized sort of army-surplus work and leisure getup."

Walker had been in Kubrick's presence many times over several decades, but Kubrick's eyes continued to fascinate him. "His hypnotic eyes, dominated by peculiarly strong brows, still outstare outsiders, friends, even family," Walker wrote in an article that ran in the *Los Angeles Herald-Examiner.*

In late January 1979, a week after Alexander Walker's visit, while

Kubrick was shooting on one set, a fire broke out shortly after six in the evening on an adjacent stage that contained part of the hotel. When smoke was discovered, the building was evacuated. The fire was still smoldering the next morning. The damage to the set and stage was extensive. The photographs containing classic stills from the Warner Bros.' archive were destroyed. The image of the burning photos—the black-and-white prints engulfed in flames—might have been shot in another version of *The Shining*, more appropriate to the Stephen King ending of the book than to Kubrick's cool psychic approach. The accident added three weeks to the shooting schedule, which was originally to wrap at the end of February, and pushed it to at least mid-March. EMI-Elstree's general manager Andrew Mitchell estimated the rebuilding of the stage, including a new wall and roof, at $2,500,000. *The Empire Strikes Back* production was scheduled to have the stage next, but it was then transferred to the Lee International facility in Wembley under a sublet arrangement. After assessing the damage, Kubrick and his team planned to partially duplicate the set on another stage to complete filming in that section of the Overlook.

Kubrick and his editor, Ray Lovejoy, were looking for new work methods to bring into the editing room. Well aware of leading-edge technology, he began exploring a method of employing videotape that could be applied to editing a feature film. One of the people he called was Bob Gaffney, whom he tracked down during a screening of the dailies of an Exxon commercial. Kubrick told Gaffney he wanted to learn about computer editing. Gaffney realized that the facility he was standing in had a CMX nonlinear editing system, and so he quickly found the house technical expert. Kubrick picked his brain for more than an hour.

Philip Stone was asked to make his third appearance in a Stanley Kubrick film, this time as Grady, the former caretaker, who had slaughtered his wife and two young daughters with an ax in the Overlook Hotel. Stone gives an unnerving performance in the film as a ghostly Grady, who appears to Jack as he walks out of the bar during a 1920s dance. Grady, now a waiter, spills a drink on Jack Torrance and takes him into the bathroom to clean him up. The scene takes place in a blood-red bathroom and slowly, over a long duration, the discussion turns to the evil of the hotel's past and the present evil in Jack's overheated mind. "That long scene with Grady and Jack took a long time," Philip Stone recalled. "Long takes each time. We seemed to be in that set forever. I was proud of that work. Jack Nicholson kept saying, 'You should go to the States, Phil, you'd earn a bomb.' The inner concentration and stillness came from working in Pirandello plays, long speeches lightly played, the drama of the mind, but you've got to get your balls behind the lines."

Kubrick had been tough on his principal actors. "Stanley's demanding," Jack Nicholson told Janet Huck. "He'll do a scene fifty times and you have to be good to do that. There are so many ways to walk into a room, order breakfast or be frightened to death in a closet. Stanley's approach is, how can we do it better than it's ever been done before? It's a big challenge. A lot of actors give him what he wants. If you don't, he'll beat it out of you—with a velvet glove, of course."

Kubrick was quite hard on Shelley Duvall, pushing her to the edge as Wendy Torrance is tormented by her husband's depravity. Often Kubrick would whine, "Shelley, that's not it. How long do we have to wait for you to get it right?"

Kubrick maintained a psychological advantage over Shelley Duvall by making her feel she wasn't giving him what he wanted—that she was holding everyone up. Kubrick wanted Duvall to use this harassment for her role as Wendy, but the gentle-natured actress had an idiosyncratic style that didn't flourish under personal pressure. Kubrick felt Duvall was overreacting in the scene when she hides in the bathroom while Jack threatens to ax the door down. "Shelley, the only part clearly wrong was at the end when you said, 'We've got to get him out of here.' You got strong at the end and I think it has to be a last desperate begging and I still think you shouldn't jump on every single emphatic line. It looks fake. It really does. Shelley, I'm telling you, it's too many times, every time he speaks emphatically you're jumping and it looks phoney." Duvall tried to have an impact on the lines, changing them to suit her interpretation of the character. "I honestly don't think the lines are going to make an awful lot of difference if you get the right attitude," Kubrick told Duvall. "I think you're worrying about the wrong thing." Kubrick continued to work on the attitude by maintaining pressure on the actress to portray true nervousness and fear in her situation.

To film the shot of Wendy running out of the back entrance of the Overlook, Kubrick and the crew were outside the facade built on the backlot. Kubrick directed the snow and smoke to fill the air, called for the video and film cameras to roll, and waited impatiently for Duvall to burst out of the door in desperation to escape her maniacal husband. The noise of the snow machine and a barrage of orders from Kubrick and his assistant came over the two-way radio as Duvall waited inside for her cue. Confused, Duvall never got the chance on one take to come out—because she thought she was told both to wait a minute and then to go. When Kubrick saw that Duvall was not coming out, he called cut and charged to the door. In a rare momentary display of anger he chided the actress. "There's no desperation!" he shouted. "We're fucking killing ourselves out here and you've got to be ready!" Duvall explained she couldn't understand the command over the radio, but Kubrick was interested only in Duvall's attitude as the character. "Yes, but when you do it, you've got to look desperate, Shelley, you're just wasting everybody's time now."

The process of making *The Shining* was harrowing, but ultimately rewarding for Shelley Duvall. Kubrick worked directly and easily with Nicholson, but Duvall felt she wasn't getting as much attention and wasn't given the same respect or consideration for her ideas and feelings. The stress of the long shooting schedule caused Duvall to experience health problems. The crew was attentive to Duvall when she felt dizzy and had to lie down one day, but Kubrick kept telling the actress that the attention wasn't helping her to capture the frenzied nature of a harassed wife like Wendy Torrance. "Don't sympathize with Shelley," he said. "it doesn't help you."

"From May until October I was really in and out of ill health because the stress of the role was so great and the stress of being away from home—just uprooted and moved somewhere else—and I had just gotten out of a relationship and so for me it was just tumultuous," Duvall told Vivian Kubrick's documentary camera.

Looking back on the difficult experience, Duvall told Vivian Kubrick that the end ultimately justified the means in the quality of the finished film. "If it hadn't been for that volley of ideas and sometimes butting of heads together, it wouldn't have come out as good as it did and it also helps get the emotion up and the concentration up because it builds up anger actually," Duvall said. "You get more out of yourself, and he knew that. He knew he was getting more out of me by doing that. So it was sort of like a game. You just appreciate all the pain and you always dislike whatever the cause is of pain, you always resent it. So I resented Stanley at times because he pushed me and it hurt. I resented him for it. I thought, 'Why do want to do this to me?' 'How can you do this to me?' You agonize over it and it's just the necessary turmoil to get out of it what you want out of it. We had the same end in mind, it was just that sometimes we differed in our means, and by the end the means met. I really respect him both as a person and as a director. I'm amazed, he's taught me more than I've learned on all the other pictures I've done, within one year's time on one picture.

"Stanley pushed me and prodded me further than I've ever been pushed before," Duvall said. "It's the most difficult role I've ever had to play. But Stanley makes you do things that you never thought you could do. Robert Altman says I am a changed artist since working with Kubrick. If Stanley hadn't pushed me as hard as he did, I would never have produced the performances I did. I never thought it was possible." When Altman worked with Duvall again, on his ill-fated but inspired production of *Popeye,* he noticed that the actress was transformed after suffering with Kubrick for nearly a year.

Scatman Crothers, who turned seventy when *The Shining* was released, had never heard of Stanley Kubrick until he was cast as Halloran. He found the director a force to be reckoned with. "In one scene I had to get out of a Sno-Cat and walk across the street, no dialogue. Fifty takes," Crothers recalled to Jack Kroll. "He had Shelley, Jack, and the kid walk across the street. Eighty-seven takes, man, he always wants something new, and he doesn't stop until he gets it."

"One day they were shooting a close-up of Scatman. It wasn't a dolly shot, it didn't have any camera movement," Tony Burton recalled. "Stanley shot something like a hundred thirty takes and didn't print anything. They would shoot it and Stanley would say, 'Let's go again, let's go again, let's go again.' Everybody was going crazy. 'Is it me? Is it me? Do you want me to do this. How can I help?' Stanley would say, 'Let's go again.' The next day Stanley transposed some of the lines. Scatman had eight or ten lines, so Stanley moved some of the things at the top down to the middle and moved something down at the bottom to the top. They shot it and printed in about the fourth take."

"I'm a great offstage grumbler," Jack Nicholson said. "I complained that he was the only director to light the sets with no stand-ins. We had to be there even to be lit. Just because you're a perfectionist doesn't mean you're perfect."

Nicholson accepted Kubrick's mandate to discover what could be found in the script by demanding take after take, looking for different ways of doing almost everything required. "Anything you do as many times as a successful actor you can't have one set of theories," Nicholson said to the documentary crew. "You can go for years saying, 'I'm going to get this thing real, because they really haven't seen it real.' They just keep seeing one fashion of unreal after the other that passes as real and you go mad with realism and then you come up against someone like Stanley who says, 'Yeah, it's real, but it's not interesting.'"

Tony Burton was on the set when Kubrick worked on the final shot of the film—a slow tracking shot through the lobby of the Overlook that ends on a close-up of a picture of Jack as a guest of the hotel taken in the 1920s. "They shot that for days," Burton recalls. "Stanley would just look at the monitor and say, 'Let's go again.' They couldn't get a third of the way across the lobby. It took them a week before they got a third of the way across. Stanley kept seeing bumps—he wanted it to be smooth. So they changed the cart on the dolly. Then they put it on a track. Then they took it off the track. Then they changed the wheels. Then they put some more weight on it. Then it wasn't enough weight, they put more people on it. People were hanging on to this cart trying to keep still so they could get this shot.

"I don't know how many times they shot the blood in the elevator. Somebody told me they had been shooting that ever since the shoot first started the year before. They shot it three times while I was there. About every ten days they would shoot it again and Stanley would say, 'It doesn't look like blood' and they would say, 'Well, is it the texture? Is it the color?' It would take them like nine days to set the shot up and then they would come back, the door would open, it would come out and Stanley would say, 'It doesn't look like blood.' But finally they got it."

Tony Burton's two scenes went rather smoothly. His costume was selected easily, and Kubrick didn't make excessive takes during the shooting. "He didn't direct me much," Burton recalled. "Being around him for six weeks and involved with him on the chessboard, I just kind of knew what he wanted from this character. He just wanted something very simple. Stanley was very different at different times with different people. He always liked to take people out to eat in groups, and during that time he was different from when he was over the chessboard and different from when he was on the set working. When he's on the set working he doesn't talk to anyone. He doesn't explain anything. He just says, 'Let's go again. Let's go again.' You know it's not right, but nobody knows what it is that's not right and no one knows what adjustments to make. That's what drives everybody crazy. He just says, 'Let's go again.' If it's a sixty-second scene, he may stop you in ten seconds and you say, 'Why did he stop me?' But he won't tell you. If you say, 'What is it, Stanley?' He'll say, 'That's all right, you're okay—Let's go again. Let's try it again.' You'll never know."

Throughout the film Kubrick returns to the image of the two murdered Grady girls, who appear to Danny in the halls of the Overlook. The surreal and eerie image that evokes childhood innocence and identity has its roots in two stills from Kubrick's photographic past. Biographer Patricia Bosworth in her biography of Diane Arbus points out that Kubrick may have been influenced by the famous picture Arbus shot of twin girls standing side by side. The tantalizing and disturbing photo has become most associated with the enigmatic photographer who peered into the soul of her subjects and who, in their Greenwich Village days, had taken the young Stanley Kubrick under her wing. The other image was seen through Kubrick's own lens. For the May 25, 1948, issue of *Look* magazine, Kubrick was dispatched to photograph true-life events of employees of the Electric Light and Power Companies. In the right-hand corner of the article is a photograph of two little girls, Phyllis, five years old, and Barbara, age eight, standing in front of two men who saved their lives after they were overcome by poisonous carbon monoxide fumes. The girls stand side by side, wearing similar dresses, arms fully extended downward as they hold hands. They are smiling and look directly into Kubrick's watchful eye. The father of three girls, Kubrick also spent years documenting Katharina, Anya, and Vivian with his camera. The subject was family, but the man behind the camera was always an artist first. The Grady girls stay with the viewer long after *The Shining* has unspooled. The image of two murdered girls standing side by side smiling into the camera as they court and taunt Danny Torrance resonates with a photographic history that goes beyond the imagination of Stephen King.

The Shining was also about the torment of the act of writing. Ron Rosenbaum, who wrote a profile of Jack Nicholson for the *New York Times Magazine* called the film "the first horror movie *about* writer's block." Although his celebrity rests on his work as one of America's finest actors, Jack Nicholson served as a writer on several of his early projects, writing the screenplays for *Flight to Fury, Ride in the Whirlwind, The Trip,* and *Head.* Writing informed Nicholson's acting, as did his journeys behind the camera to direct *Drive, He Said* and *Goin' South.* Working with a director like Stanley Kubrick, who confronted the writing of a scene every day with every shot, Nicholson also became involved in creating Jack Torrance's actions and behavior as a tormented writer. All good writers and actors work out of their experience, and Nicholson went to the center of his own past to create the scene in which Jack unleashes the anger he has connected to his writing frustration on his loving wife when she inquires about how his work is proceeding. "That's the one scene in the movie I wrote myself," Nicholson told Ron Rosenbaum. "That scene at the typewriter—that's what I was like when I got my divorce. I was under the pressure of being a family man with a daughter and one day I accepted a job to act in a movie in the daytime and I was writing a movie at night and I'm back in my little corner and my beloved wife, Sandra, walked in on what was, unbeknownst to her, this *maniac*—and I told Stanley about it and we wrote it into the scene. I remember being at my desk and telling her, 'Even if you don't *hear* me typing it doesn't mean I'm not *writing*. This *is* writing . . .' I remember that total animus. Well, I got a divorce."

After research and consultation, Kubrick devised a jury-rigged system employing VCRs and video monitors to make the material for *The Shining* more accessible to him and his editor, Ray Lovejoy. The system was later purchased by the celebrated film editor Dede Allen for Warren Beatty's production of *Reds,* which involved a massive amount of footage. The system allowed the Academy Award–nominated editors, Dede Allen and Craig McKay, to quickly find footage and judge performance from multiple takes by tracing a running code number.

Ray Lovejoy, who had edited *2001,* was back in the editing room with Kubrick, who—as always—took a very hands-on approach to the postproduction on his film. They worked in a cutting room in Elstree Studios. Kubrick scrupulously listened to recordings to find the music he wanted for the film. Once he settled on the composer and the specific piece, he listened to every available recording, leaving notes for his staff that often read, "Badly performed. Find another recording." Commonly, pictures are put up on the walls of an editing room to amuse visitors and break the tedium of the exacting, solitary process. Kubrick had put up a photograph of the Joint Chiefs of Staff with the handwritten comment "Shades of Dr. S."

For the music for *The Shining* Kubrick again turned to Wendy Carlos and Rachel Elkind, who had done the provocative score for *A Clockwork Orange.* Kubrick had contacted Carlos and Elkind to tell them he was interested in having them work on his new film. Kubrick's brother-in-law and executive producer, Jan Harlan, was in New York and dropped by the studio to tell them that Kubrick was making a film from the Stephen King novel and encouraged them to read it. "So the first thing we did was to run to the bookstore to get a copy of *The Shining* and we read the book," Wendy Carlos explains. After they read the novel, Kubrick contacted them again by phone from London and asked, "Do you have any ideas for music that might be appropriate for this?"

"Having seen not a foot of film, we were in the bizarre position of writing music to a novel," Carlos recalled. "We did some demo music and then we asked him, 'What have you been listening to?' and he mentioned Sibelius's 'Valse Trieste.' So we went to listen to that and a couple of other things, something by Mahler. So we used some of those as a starting point. We hired a small orchestra, brought them into our little studio, and did about a half hour of varied cues and demos. Then, we heard nothing. The next thing we hear was that they're still shooting, they haven't got anything yet for us to see, but there's a trailer, and

'Could you send us a copy of the last two cues you did on your tape?' So we sent Stanley some quarter-inch tapes and Jan came into town and said, 'Stanley wants to buy the rights to use the next to the last cue for the trailer because the film is running late and we're going to put a trailer in the theaters to keep people's attention, since we won't be out until the summer and it's winter now.'

"So they bought the rights to the one little bit of music. Then Stanley called and wanted us to plan to come to London right away at the beginning of the year. January first I got on a plane. Rachel and I met in London and got taken to Elstree Studios and were shown an incomplete film. It was up to the point when Wendy discovers that part of the Sno-Cat was removed. The film was a little on the long side. There were great gobs of scenes that never made it to the film. There was a whole strange and mystical scene in which Jack Nicholson discovers objects that have been arranged in his working space in the ballroom with arrows and things. He walks down and thinks he hears a voice. A ghost throws a ball back to him. None of that made it in the final film. We scored a lot of those, we didn't know what was going to be used for sure. So in London we saw the film as it existed.

"The next day we went up to see Stanley, and he showed us little pieces of what they were working on to finish the rest of the film—it was in very rough form. On *A Clockwork Orange* they had made us a black-and-white slop print from the work print that we could use to edit the music. I remember coming through customs in New York. Back in the seventies there was a lot in *A Clockwork Orange* that you would not necessarily have wanted a customs official to look at. They said, 'Oh, what's this?' We told him what it was. 'Oh, it's Kubrick's new one? Oh yeah, right—you go.' *Bam,* he stamped the thing and we went out.

"*The Shining* wasn't ready for us. So a week later Stanley hired a young fellow to come on a plane with a videotape of the film and bring that to us. We did an awful lot of material for *The Shining*—a ton of music. When we were in London, Stanley had wanted to know if there was anything I could think of that would apply to music about graves, death, and ghosts. I suggested *Dies Irae,* which is, of course, part of the Latin requiem mass. It always haunted me the way it haunted Rachmaninoff, like it haunted Ravel, like it haunted Berlioz. Kubrick asked me to think of a place where you could hear it, and I said, 'Well, there are some archive recordings that have the real Gregorian chants.' So I suggested the Berlioz Requiem. I told him to listen to the last movement. He got the record and he must have played it a hundred times or more and he got very wedded to it. There's a danger with any filmmaker who hears something so often that they can longer hear any variation on it. So much of the score that we went to record with the orchestra in Saint Giles Church in London was not used, simply because it didn't sound like the Berlioz Requiem. There was a ton of electronic and orchestral music I had done for that project that has never seen the light of day."

In recent years Kubrick had become more inclined to use previously recorded music in his films rather than originally composed music. Again, control was a key factor. The score for *The Shining* is an interesting blend of several atmospheric musical elements that create an aural wash that can be as successful in frightening the viewer as the visuals are. Kubrick took pieces from Ligeti and Penderecki and blended them with electronic sound design material from Carlos and Elkind to achieve dramatic and provocative results.

The soundtrack album to the film, long out of print, is a major cult item available only on vinyl and difficult to find. The album contains little of the Carlos-Elkind music, but the film utilized their sound elements, like the heartbeat soundscape. "Stanley wanted these sounds that would just sneak in and go by. He called them 'low fly-bys.' They were sounds that would sneak into you, subconsciously. In the end, the technology wasn't prepared for the richness of timbres that he was looking forward to, and that's why we tried to do some of the things with the orchestral session. Unfortunately, we went too far with the *Dies Irae,* which he then decided he didn't want to use unless it was more like the Berlioz. He was looking for low, slowly moving sounds, almost a gravissimo. This was very slow-moving material. Synchronization was not a priority for this type of music soundscape."

The opening of the film features sounds created by Elkind's voice and Carlos's realizations. Many of the wind effects come out of sound-design elements created by them. Elkind's deep contralto voice has extraordinary range, and when combined with Carlos's processing, synthesizer, and multitrack wizardry, the sounds were transformed into ethereal moments of nonverbal sounds that sent a shudder through the airwaves.

Wendy Carlos remains philosophical about working with Stanley Kubrick and demonstrates the greatest respect for his work method and body of films. "Anyone who has the chance to work with him will have a very steep roller-coaster ride and they would never forget it. It would be a marvelous experience to have in your life," Carlos reflected.

Even though *Barry Lyndon* was not a box office success in America, Kubrick and Warner Bros. devised a hardball strategy to sell *The Shining* to the theaters. After the premiere, theaters like the Sutton and the Criterion in New York were set up for the first run on May 23; bids were open for the flagship run to begin in June. The plan was to then open the film in fifty to sixty theaters in the New York metropolitan area with the same terms and conditions as the first run. Warners asked for a minimum of eight weeks and a box office split of 90 percent Warners, 10 percent to the exhibitor after the house allowance is deducted against floor or minimums, which specified three weeks at 80 percent, three weeks at 60 percent, two weeks at 50 percent and a ninth at 40 percent. Warner's was to have the discretion to chose either 90/10 minus the house allowance or take a straight percentage—whichever was greater. The studio was also asking for $50,000 in nonrefundable guarantees per screen, a plan that could get them as much as $3,000,000 payable in advance even before *The Shining* opened.

Kubrick had always opened his films slowly, carefully building word of mouth to generate interest and box office grosses. For *The Shining*, Kubrick and Warner Bros. wanted to make a big financial return fast. *2001* had cost in the neighborhood of $10 million and had taken ten years to get into profit. *A Clockwork Orange* cost $2 million and by 1978 had grossed more than $40 million but had to play off over a long time and gather a lot of repeat business before it paid its negative costs back.

The film business was changing rapidly, and Kubrick stayed on top of it. If he wanted to make productions that cost between $10 million and $15 million, he had to make the money faster and not allow the inflation and rising interest rates that affected a slow release to endanger his ability to turn a profit.

Kubrick devised his release plan a year before *The Shining* was to open. The film would open in New York and Los Angeles on Memorial Day weekend in 10 theaters and then on June 13 would open in 750 more theaters, sustained by a four-week national TV campaign concentrating on the ABC television network because Kubrick learned they had the highest ratings for the eighteen-to-thirty-four age group, a population group considered to be the best filmgoing segment. Kubrick had created an impressive trailer that showed only the Overlook Hotel elevator as a wave of blood poured out of it. The trailer ran during the all-important Christmas moviegoing season, enticing audiences with a chill for the summer of 1980. The legion of fans who wanted to know what Stanley Kubrick was up to were pleased that their nearly five-year wait was almost over. Kubrick's marketing study calculated that by the fourth week of release, 93 percent of all adults in the eighteen-to-thirty-four age group would have seen the trailer at least seven times and 88 percent of all households in America would have been exposed to the ads 10.8 times. The plan was devised to overcome any negative criticism, build an early national audience, and guarantee an early return on the reported $12 million to $18 million investment. Signet was reprinting the novel, featuring the film's logo and including scenes from the movie. The reprint was guaranteed that 1.5 million copies would be circulated in 100,000 outlets nationwide.

The MPAA gave Kubrick and *The Shining* an unusual dispensation, allowing him to print the R rating on ads for the film before officially receiving a classification. The board granted the request with the provision that the film be rated by the following Saturday, but the ads had already been scheduled for the Sunday deadlines in the *Los Angeles Times* and the *New York Times*. The delivery of the final print of the film was very close to the release date on May 23. Rumors were spreading throughout the industry that the film was heading for an X rating, as *A Clockwork Orange* originally had. Richard D. Heffner, the head of the committee that handed down the ratings, had looked at an unfinished version of *The Shining*, but the committee stated that not all the "rating relevant material" was in the print so they could not administer a final rating until they saw the completed film. Warners submitted two different versions of ads for *The Shining*, with and without the R rating symbol. If the film was not rated, they would go with the ad without the rating, but everything was on track for the R, so for the coming weekend ads the MPAA was taking the risk that Kubrick would stay in line and not move into X territory. The most recent films from a major studio to receive the X were *Emmanuelle* and *Inserts*, for sexually explicit material, and *The Streetfighter*, which received the rating based solely on its approach to violence. In covering the story, *Variety* noted that only Kubrick and Francis Ford Coppola maintained an absolute right to final cut. The MPAA did right by Kubrick's judgment, and *The Shining* passed through with an R.

Kubrick asked Saul Bass, the respected graphic artist and title designer, to design the key art to be used in the advertising campaign for *The Shining*. Kubrick had long respected Bass's work in revolutionizing title design. Working with Bass was one of the few positive experiences Kubrick had had on *Spartacus*. Bass's design was a ghostly face created with a flurry of white dots appearing in the large T and spreading throughout "The" in the title on a deep-red background. Of course, arriving at the final result was a process for Stanley Kubrick. "That was a hell of an experience," Bass recalled. "Stanley was obsessive about what he was aiming at. While it drove me nuts, I deeply respected it because that's the way I treat everybody who works for me. That took a lot of doing. Stanley pushed me very, very hard. I did three hundred drawings.

Some of them were terrific. I have the deepest admiration for that process. It's a process in which I engage when I'm doing my work. I drive myself crazy, I drive people who work for me nuts in the same way that Stanley did it to me. This is the nature of what you have to do if you want to do something good. I just loved working with him. I love his mode. He is totally in a cocoon and the cocoon is bounded by the studio and there's another cocoon at the house. Stanley travels from one cocoon to the other through a tiny little tunnel. He lives in a monastic form in his mental attitude and his emotional attitude toward what he's doing. Stanley will unhesitatingly junk things and do them over because he thinks they can be improved, changed or made better. There may be inner anguish, but he's cool outside. I admire that absorbitive, obsessive, concentrated force field that he builds around himself. He's an extraordinary guy."

The Shining opened in New York on Friday, May 23, 1980. Stanley Kubrick had worked for three years on the film. Prints of the film were not available for previews until the Wednesday before the premiere. The previews were delayed when Kubrick rejected the quality of the sound mix on the first six prints struck.

Five days later, on May 28, Kubrick ordered that an epilogue to the film be excised. In the deleted scene, Mr. Ullman, the hotel manager played by Barry Nelson, went to visit Wendy in the hospital. Kubrick had made the decision to delete the scene over the premiere weekend. "After several screenings in London the day before the film opened in New York and Los Angeles, when I was able to see for the first time the fantastic pitch of excitement which the audience reached during the climax of the film, I decided the scene was unnecessary," Kubrick told the *New York Times*. On the following Thursday, Kubrick, through Warner Bros., dispatched a film editor on each coast who would bicycle from theater to theater to remove the scene from the release print. As with *2001*, Kubrick felt he hadn't had have the time to reflect on the finished film, and when he did, he clearly saw that the epilogue wasn't necessary.

Tony Burton went to screen *The Shining* in California when the film opened and remembers seeing both of his scenes in the film. In addition to the scene where he talks to Halloran from Durkin's auto repair shop there originally was a short second scene taking place outside when Halloran arrives. As Halloran boarded the Sno-Cat, Durkin had a short dialogue with him before he drove off. The scene does not appear in the present version of the film.

Shortly after *The Shining* opened in New York, Kubrick's old friend, critic Alexander Walker, came to the studio to visit. After passing a sign that read, HAWK FILMS—KEEP OUT Walker found Kubrick among racks of film cans with a telephone at one ear and a magnifying glass clenched to his eye. In front of him was a copy of the day's *New York Times,* which had been air-dropped in, opened to a full-page ad for *The Shining.* Kubrick spoke into the mouthpiece in a chastising tone to a studio bureaucrat who apparently had not done his job properly. "Doesn't it strike you as strange that you're three thousand miles away in New York and here I am in London telling you that the one a.m. extra screening scheduled for *The Shining* has been left out of the ad in today's *Times?*"

Stephen King linked Kubrick's decision to shoot *The Shining* on a soundstage to the work of master mysterioso filmmaker Val Lewton and director Jacques Tourneur on *Cat People.* "Tourneur quite sensibly opted for the soundstage—and it is interesting to me that, some forty years later, Stanley Kubrick did exactly the same thing with *The Shining,*" King wrote in his study of the horror genre, *Danse Macabre.* "And like Lewton and Tourneur before him, Kubrick is a director who shows an almost exquisite sensitivity to the nuances of light and shadow. In 1942 Val Lewton could not shoot in Central Park by night, but in *Barry Lyndon* Stanley Kubrick shot several scenes by candlelight. This is a quantum technical leap which has this paradoxical effect: It robs the bank of imagination. Perhaps realizing the fact, Kubrick takes a giant step backward to the soundstage with his next film, *The Shining.*"

The Shining was one of Kubrick's most commercially successful films. Despite a majority of negative reviews, the film opened strong in New York and Los Angeles over the Memorial Day weekend. Terry Semel, executive vice president and chief operating officer of Warner Bros., projected the first week's gross at $1 million and called the film "the biggest opening our company has ever had in New York and Los Angeles. It's bigger than *The Exorcist,* bigger than *Superman.*" The ad campaign, the summer timing, and the marquee value of Jack Nicholson carried the film against a slew of bad reviews from the *Christian Science Monitor, Films in Review, The New Leader, New York Magazine, Newsday, Saturday Review* and the *Village Voice.* Good box office did not help *The Shining* at the Academy Awards. The film was the first Kubrick picture not to receive any Academy Award nominations in twenty-three years. The last Kubrick film to have been snubbed by the Academy was *Paths of Glory.*

Ed Di Giulio was astounded by what Garrett Brown and Stanley Kubrick achieved with the Steadicam. After seeing *The Shining,* Di Giulio wrote Kubrick congratulating him and commenting on the remarkable scenes where the Steadicam follows Danny Lloyd on his Big Wheel.

"It was like malevolent POV," Di Giulio wrote. "Evil was following the kid, evil was following the kid."

Later, when Di Giulio taught a graduate seminar in film technology at the USC film school, he always had Stanley Kubrick in his mind. "I basically told the students that no matter what they did, whether it was directing, writing, cinematography, or whatever, their palette was the technology of filmmaking. That was their artist's palette. They needed to know the technology of filmmaking like an artist has to know the tools of his trade, the pigments, dyes, and colors, so they could use them and manipulate them. To me, the consummate practitioner of that was Stanley Kubrick."

Over the years Stephen King has acknowledged that he was proud to have Stanley Kubrick make a movie out of one of his books. It certainly brought him attention and sold more books, but as a lover of the horror genre, he found that the film fell short of his expectations. "There's a lot to like about it. But it's a great big beautiful Cadillac with no motor inside," King said to *American Film* magazine in 1986. "You can sit in it, and you can enjoy the smell of the leather upholstery—the only thing you can't do is drive it anywhere. So I would do everything different. The real problem is that Kubrick set out to make a horror picture with no apparent understanding of the genre. Everything about it screams that from the beginning to the end, from plot decision to that final scene—which has been used before on *The Twilight Zone*."

The Shining was the last Stanley Kubrick film photographed by John Alcott. In 1980, when the film was released, Alcott and his wife, Sue, and son, Gavin, left England for the United States. Alcott became an American citizen and set up a residence in Studio City, California. In the United States Alcott became much in demand, photographing and directing commercials and feature films. In the American film community Alcott was a legend, as his work on *A Clockwork Orange, Barry Lyndon,* and *The Shining* set a standard of excellence in the cinematographer's art. His work on *Under Fire* and *Greystoke: The Legend of Tarzan, Lord of the Apes* underscored the talent that was all his own. Understanding the collaboration between a director and those who work with him is a mysterious notion often clouded by perceptions of the director as auteur, but one of Stanley Kubrick's true areas of genius as a film director was to work with master craftspeople like Alcott. As much as he could control his work, Kubrick could still be only as good as those around him. Time was cruel to John Alcott and did not allow him to hit the heights of *Barry Lyndon* again, one of the most beautifully photographed films in film history. In August 1986, while vacationing with his family in the south of France, he died of heart failure. John Alcott was fifty-five years old. He was scheduled to photograph David Lean's long-planned epic production of Joseph Conrad's *Nostromo*. Lean, a director who in many ways is Kubrick's landsman in conviction, control, and perfection, also died before shooting commenced.

Three years before his death, John Alcott summed up his feelings about working with Stanley Kubrick in a discussion with Herb Lightman, editor of *American Cinematographer* magazine. "I feel that when you're with Stanley the working relationship benefits from picture to picture. We've worked together since about 1965 and in working with him there is always a different outlook, a different idea: 'Let's try something different. Is there any way we can make it much better than it was before?' I feel that when you have as much time as I had on *The Shining* to make sure the sets are right and that the art director is building them to your lighting design, as well as his own design, it is a great privilege. You don't have that privilege with someone who lacks the experience and the visual perception that Stanley has. He is willing to bend over backwards to give you something you may desire in the way of a new lighting technique and this is a great help. If you have somebody who is working that way it makes the job so much easier for you. I don't think there is anything really different that has developed in our working relationship. He may be more demanding than he was before, but that makes it very easy for you when you go on to your next picture. To use an analogy in reference to our British game of cricket: it's like practicing with five wickets and playing three. You defend five and then when you come to defend three, it's much easier."

CHAPTER 18

"Has It Been Seven Years? I Never Remember the Years"

I don't know what you've read about Stanley but the impression I got was that he was this crazy lunatic who was afraid of germs and flies. It's just not true.

—Matthew Modine

As mystical as Stanley Kubrick's work can be, he's very grounded in reality.

—Tony Spiridakis

He's probably the most heartfelt person I ever met. It's hard for him, being from the Bronx with that neighborhood mentality, and he tries to cover it up. Right underneath that veneer is a very loving, conscientious man, who doesn't like pain, who doesn't like to see humans suffering or animals suffering. I was really surprised by the man.

—Matthew Modine

With the release and commercial run of *The Shining*, Stanley Kubrick fell back into his usual pre-preproduction mode. He had no definite intention for his next film, but he installed his routines—

researching, reading, screening material, and pulling out all stops to find the initial point that would culminate in his next project.

In 1982, Arthur C. Clarke published *2010: Odyssey Two,* the sequel to the *2001* novel. Clarke phoned Kubrick and joked, "Your job is to stop anybody making it so I won't be bothered." A deal was struck at MGM to make the film, but Kubrick, not one to repeat himself, turned down the project. Kubrick's lawyer, Louis Blau, negotiated with MGM for fees concerning rights to the film and footage from the original movie.

In mid-1983, Peter Hyams, director of *Capricorn One, Hanover Street, Outland,* and *The Star Chamber,* approached Arthur C. Clarke about interest in the project. "I was filled with all kinds of reservations," Hyams recalled. "The first two people I wanted to contact were Arthur Clarke and Stanley Kubrick. I had a long conversation with Stanley and told him what was going on. If it met with his approval, I would do the film; and if it didn't, I wouldn't. I certainly would not have thought of doing the film if I had not gotten the blessing of Kubrick. He's one of my idols; simply one of the greatest talents that's ever walked the earth. He more or less said, 'Sure. Go do it. I don't care.' And another time he said, 'Don't be afraid. Just go do your own movie.'" Like his idol, Hyams often photographed his own films and actually received the director of photography credit. Hyams went on to photograph and direct *2010.*

On March 10, 1984, Stanley Kubrick became a father-in-law. Katharina, age thirty, Kubrick's eldest daughter, married thirty-one-year-old caterer Philip Eugene Hobbs in the county of Hertfordshire in Saint Albans, England. Although she was the birth daughter of German actor Werner Bruhns, Christiane Kubrick's first husband, Katharina listed Stanley Kubrick, film director, as her father.

When he wasn't actively involved in production on a film, Kubrick went to the movies—rather, the movies came to him as he watched films in his personal screening room located at his compound. Kubrick's screenings weren't restricted to feature films. His viewings scanned the media, where he found examples of cinematic storytelling in seemingly unlikely venues. Stanley Kubrick was a fan of NFL football. In order to sustain his link with American culture in all its varied aspects, he asked his sister, Barbara, to tape Giants football games and send the tapes to England from her home in New Jersey. The tapes were made off the air and contained the complete game, including numerous commercials. Kubrick enjoyed the tapes and for entertainment often reran games played a year or several years before, much in the way most home viewers repeatedly watch a video of an old movie. He examined the games carefully and studied the finer points and the strategic meanings, but it was the commercials that really fascinated him. Kubrick began obsessing over the economy and physical beauty of the thirty-second spot—a form long considered mini-movies by many in the film industry, that was the polar opposite of the megaproductions *2001* and *Barry Lyndon*. When Francis X. Clines was in London to interview Kubrick for the *New York Times* concerning *Full Metal Jacket*, Kubrick was ebullient about a series of commercials he had seen on one of his football tapes. "Have you seen those Michelob commercials?" Kubrick asked Clines. "They're just boy-girl, night-fun leading up to pouring the beer, all in thirty seconds, beautifully edited and photographed." And Kubrick told Tim Cahill of *Rolling Stone* magazine, "The editing, the photography, was some of the most brilliant work I've ever seen." "Forget what they're doing—selling beer—and it's visual poetry. Incredible eight-frame cuts. And you realize that in thirty seconds they've created an impression of something rather complex." "Economy of statement is not something that films are noted for. The best TV commercials create a tremendously vivid sense of a mood, of a complex presentation of something," Kubrick told Clines. "Some of the most spectacular examples of film art are in the best TV commercials," Kubrick told Cahill. "If you could ever tell a story, something with some content, using that kind of visual poetry, you could handle vastly more complex and subtle material."

After *The Shining* was released, Kubrick considered making a film about war, a subject he had approached in *Fear and Desire* and *Paths of Glory*. He had first contacted Michael Herr in the spring of 1980. Herr was a foreign correspondent for *Esquire* magazine during the Vietnam War, from 1967 to 1968, and the author of *Dispatches*, a highly acclaimed book on his experiences in Indochina, published in 1977. Herr had worked with Francis Ford Coppola on *Apocalypse Now*, writing the narration after the director had desperately tried to make the film work as a visual and aural experience. Herr's narration, spoken by Martin Sheen as Captain Willard, entered the mind of the soldier and laid bare the insanity of the Vietnam experience. John Milius's screenplay was based on Joseph Conrad's *Heart of Darkness*, but Herr's voice-over was written from direct experience with the clashing sensibilities that reigned in Vietnam. When Herr and Kubrick met in England, the writer had spent seven years working on his book and a year refighting the war with Coppola—he had promised himself he was through with Vietnam until he was contacted by Stanley Kubrick.

In their initial talk, Kubrick and Herr discussed war, movies, and a variety of other subjects. Kubrick told Herr he was looking to make a particular kind of war film but had not yet found a story to adapt.

Kubrick had been reading and searching for a new story to make into a film. "I read. I order books from the States," he told Tim Cahill of *Rolling Stone*. "I literally go into bookstores, close my eyes and take things off the shelf. If I don't like that book after a bit, I don't finish it. But I like to be surprised."

What did Kubrick look for in a story? What attracted him to a literary work that would put him on the road to the obsessive state he often talked about? It was a question he never was able to answer specifically. Often asked why he was drawn to a particular story, he always answered in a general manner. As he got older and committed more time to the question, he likely wanted to know the answer himself. His philosophic explorations revealed the magic that Kubrick experienced when he first read a story that stimulated his imagination. "The sense of the story the first time you read it is the absolutely critical yardstick," Kubrick told Francis X. Clines. "I remember what I felt about the book. I remember what I felt in writing the script, and then I try to keep that alive in the very inappropriate circumstances that exist on a film set."

Kubrick took advantage of all that technology had to offer to communicate and receive the information which was the lifeblood of his existence, sending and receiving faxes and electronic mail. "Stanley is a great tool-using animal," Michael Herr said to describe the director who had depicted man's descendants discovering the first tool in *2001*.

Kubrick and Herr continued to talk endlessly, conversations that Herr described as "one phone call lasting three years, with interruptions."

Kubrick read the *Kirkus Reviews* religiously, scouring it for new books that interested him. The service often led him to literary works that he considered for film projects. In 1982 Kubrick first learned of *The Short-Timers* in the *Kirkus Reviews*. He perused the book and had a strong attraction to the stylistic approach. Michael Herr had received *The Short-Timers* in bound galleys and immediately thought the book was a masterpiece.

The book was a first novel by Gustav Hasford, a former Marine and military war correspondent who served in Vietnam at the height of the war. "I would say it was the story not the subject," Kubrick told Lloyd Grove for the *Washington Post*. "This book was written in a very, very almost poetically spare way. I tried to retain this approach in the film. I think as a result, the film moves along at an alarming—hopefully an alarming—pace."

Gustav Hasford was raised in rural Alabama. His long and strange journey as a writer began when he was fourteen and worked as a reporter for the *Franklin County Times* and the *Northwest Alabamian*, covering events like football games and car wrecks. In the same year he published an article about coin collecting in *Boys' Life.* Hasford didn't graduate high school but started *Freelance,* a glossy quarterly magazine for writers. He joined the Marines in 1967 when he was eighteen and was assigned to be a 4312 Basic Military Journalist with orders to go on the staff of *Leatherneck* magazine after he went to Army training school. Hasford was transferred to North Carolina, where he helped put out the base newspaper. Publishing articles about Vietnam gave him the incentive to serve a tour of duty in the war-torn country. With ten months left to serve, Hasford became a combat correspondent with the First Marine Division in Vietnam. He was stationed at Red Beach in Da Nang Bay in 1968, where he met Dale Dye, who later became technical adviser to Oliver Stone on *Platoon* and also appeared in the Academy Award–winning film. Hasford was at the Tet Offensive and received his discharge from the service in August 1968.

When Hasford arrived stateside, he learned his family was immediately moving to Washington State. Hasford settled in Kelso, Washington, got married, and lived in a cheap apartment while his wife worked at Kentucky Fried Chicken. He was a graveyard shift desk clerk in a hotel that catered to loggers and often was required to break up fights. When things quieted down after three o'clock in the morning, he read rapaciously, with a special passion for Nathaniel West. Hasford published a poem in *Winning Hearts and Minds,* the first written anthology about the war by veterans. His marriage broke up, and he came to Los Angeles with sci-fi writer Art Cover. They lived with speculative fiction master and outspoken sage Harlan Ellison. Hasford was a blunt, large, paunchy man with a high-pitched voice. Vocally, he had a hint of an Alabama accent and often wore grunt T-shirts and torn sneakers. In L.A. Hasford worked as a staff editor for adult magazines.

The initial drafts of *The Short-Timers* were developed while Hasford was still in Vietnam sitting at the typewriter writing stories as a war correspondent. Many of the characters in *The Short-Timers* were named after friends in Vietnam. The novel took seven years to write and three years to sell. It was finally published in 1979 by Harper and Row and Bantam Books. Harper had originally rejected the manuscript because it was about an unpopular subject and had been written by an unknown quantity.

The self-educated Hasford had a book collection numbering over ten thousand books, kept in storage in archive boxes numbered and cataloged by subject. The source of these extensive book compilations was shrouded in mystery. Hasford was especially fond of Depression-era

novels, books on the history of the American West, hard-boiled detective
stories, the American Civil War, Napoleon, the Alamo, Custer, the Mi-
noan civilization, Jack London, Ambrose Bierce, and Ancient Greek
coins. He wanted to write a biography of Bierce that focused on his years
as an officer, and he planned to personally walk Bierce's Civil War battlefield route.

Hasford worked as a security guard and was living in his car when a
Munich businessman with no apparent ties to the film industry optioned
the screen rights to *The Short-Timers*. Hasford took his windfall, acquired more books, and went on his first trip to Australia. When he
returned to California he learned that Stanley Kubrick owned the rights
to his first novel.

Kubrick's approach to the Vietnam War was to target the military establishment. As in *Dr. Strangelove*, Kubrick focused his attention on the
powers behind the military structure. "Vietnam was a such a phony war,
in terms of the hawkish technocrats fine-tuning the facts like an ad
agency, talking of 'kill ratios' and 'hamlet pacification' and encouraging
men to falsify a body count or at least total up the 'blood trails' on the
supposition they would lead to bodies," he told Alexander Walker.

In 1985 Kubrick formally asked Michael Herr to work on the script
for his war movie. The director had written a detailed treatment of Hasford's novel. Herr was living in England, within meeting distance of
Kubrick's home, and the two men got together every day, breaking down
the treatment into scenes. Each scene had a title card. A scene where
the platoon rested between battles was called "C-Rats with Andre." Herr
wrote the first draft of the screenplay in prose from the cards. Completed pages went out by car every afternoon and in the evening Kubrick
and Herr would discuss the work by phone.

Kubrick decided to change the title of his film from *The Short-Timers*
to *Full Metal Jacket*. The Hasford book was not a celebrated or well-
known novel as was *The Shining*, *A Clockwork Orange*, or *Lolita*, so
changing the title would not interfere with audience recognition.
Kubrick was concerned that the title would be misread as referring to
people who did only half a day's work. While going through a gun catalog Kubrick came across the phrase "full metal jacket" describing a lead
bullet encased in a copper jacket. The casing helped the bullet feed
through the rifle. The bullet was accepted by the Geneva Convention on
Warfare because it didn't expand when it entered the body.

Kubrick and Gustav Hasford had marathon telephone conversations
about the screenplay. While Kubrick continued to acquire the reputation
of being the Howard Hughes of the current cinema, he was satisfied to

communicate with those connected to his life of movies by phone, E-mail and fax.

Throughout their long involvement together, Hasford met Stanley Kubrick only once. Kubrick defied the conventional manner of collaboration on a screenplay—belying the image of the director and writer spending hours and days together, bouncing ideas off each other, with endless cups of coffee and limitless takeout. Kubrick had done that in his earlier days, hanging out with Marlon Brando and Calder Willingham and even Arthur C. Clarke, but the fifty-six-year-old Kubrick was far more insular than he had been at thirty or forty.

When Michael Herr was finished with his first draft screenplay, Kubrick rewrote the script, and then Herr reworked Kubrick's screenplay. Gustav Hasford also worked on the script in London. Kubrick continued to rewrite the script during the shooting process.

Kubrick called his perennial colleague Bob Gaffney and asked him to go to Parris Island in South Carolina. He wanted Gaffney to photograph material of the Marines in training without telling the military what the footage would be used for. When Gaffney told Kubrick the plan was unrealistic and he felt uncomfortable deceiving the United States Marine Corps, the idea was scrapped. Gaffney did go to Parris Island with a video camera—he shot a graduation to give Kubrick research and background information so he could study Marine life on a video monitor.

To cast *Full Metal Jacket,* Kubrick, through Warner Bros., advertised a national search in the United States. Ads were placed to encourage young, aspiring actors to audition. As with *The Shining* and *Barry Lyndon,* Kubrick used videotape as a means of auditioning actors. He was able to view hundreds of actors without having to meet them in person. The ads asked auditioners to dress in a T-shirt and pants and perform a three-minute acting scene appropriate to a film about Vietnam. Participants were to talk about themselves and their interests and then hold up a large card with name, address, phone number, age, and date of birth, followed by a series of close-ups, full-length shots, and examples of both profiles. The screen test was to be sent to Kubrick through Warner Bros. in England. Kubrick received as many as three thousand videotapes of prospective movie Marine grunts. Kubrick's staff reviewed all the tapes received and eliminated the ones they deemed unacceptable. Kubrick personally reviewed eight hundred audition tapes, noting that the majority of young men played guitar and were involved in body building.

In 1961 Lee Ermey, who played the drill instructor in *Full Metal Jacket,* was a seventeen-year-old Kansas farm boy who enlisted in the

Marines as soon as he graduated from high school. "I was strong. I had five brothers, and my father was a strict disciplinarian," Ermey explained to Aljean Harmetz for the *New York Times.* "I got a beating every day whether I needed it or not. And I was a good shot. I was a country boy, so I knew how to shoot." Ermey served in the Marine Corps for thirty months as a drill instructor during the Vietnam War era. His eleven-year career as a Marine came to an abrupt conclusion when a rocket exploded just north of Da Nang in 1969 while he was serving with the First Marine Division. Ermey's back and arm were riddled with shrapnel. After four months in the hospital, he used sick pay to buy a brothel on Okinawa, which he turned into a drinking club. Restless, Ermey moved to the Philippines, got married, had a short stint in college, and then appeared in television commercials as a performer selling what he called "macho merchandise"—everything from rum and watches to jeans and running shoes.

Ermey's movie career began when he met Francis Ford Coppola in 1976, while Coppola was in the Philippines to make *Apocalypse Now.* Ermey was attending college in Manila under the G.I. Bill when he was hired to play the part of a helicopter pilot. Ermey became the technical adviser on *Apocalypse Now, The Boys in Company C,* and *Purple Hearts* and was on screen in all three movies. In *The Boys in Company C* he also played a drill instructor.

Ermey first met Kubrick when he was retired on disability from the Marines and working in a factory as a quality controller. Ermey loved to be in front of a camera and asked Kubrick if he could audition for the role of Gunnery Sergeant Hartman in *Full Metal Jacket.* Kubrick told Ermey he wasn't vicious enough to play the brutal D.I. in his film. Ermey seized the opportunity to demonstrate his performance skills and keen understanding of how the Marines break down the character of their young recruits so they can properly build them into fighting men. Kubrick had been interviewing British soldiers for roles as Marines, so Ermey began to torment and humiliate the men with an onslaught of insults. Kubrick was so impressed with Ermey that he gave him the part of Sergeant Hartman. The sessions with Ermey were videotaped and used in the script. Kubrick had a transcript typed from the tape, and he used the material for Hartman's dialogue. "I was first struck by his extraordinary ability as an actor when we videotaped him interviewing British Territorial Army paratroop types who were being considered as U.S. Marines," Kubrick told Alexander Walker. "Lee lined them up like recruits who had just come off the bus into Parris Island and let go with the barrage of intimidation and insults which the occasion always brings." Kubrick compiled a 250 page transcript from Ermey's improvisations and inserted choices into the screenplay. Kubrick estimated that fifty percent of Ermey's dialogue which included lines like "I don't like the name Lawrence. Lawrence is for faggots and sailors," came from the inprovisations.

Ermey was playing the role of Sergeant Hartman out of his experience as a drill instructor. After the film was complete, he told interviewers that he didn't want to be identified with the extremity of the character, but Ermey was an equally tough D.I. in his time. "Drill instructors are very inventive," Ermey told Martin Burden. "As a D.I. I could walk down a line of recruits and drop every third or fourth one of them to his knees, and you'd never catch me at it. Just give him a little elbow, drop him like that."

Kubrick thought of drill instructors as natural actors. "Acting is an amazing, part-crazy, part-magical gift," he told Penelope Gilliatt. "An actor's power rests in his ability to create emotion in himself, and thus in the audience. The ability to cry at the clack of a clapboard is a very strange and rare talent. Of course, drill instructors can do it naturally because they're performers. And liars can do it because lying's generally important to the liar."

Kubrick used Lou Gossett's Academy Award performance as a drill instructor in *An Officer and a Gentleman* to explain to Tim Cahill of *Rolling Stone* magazine that most films pander to the audience. "I think Lou Gossett's performance was wonderful, but he had to do what he was given in the story. The film clearly wants to ingratiate itself with the audience. So many films do that."

Rehearsals with Lee Ermey took place in a fifty-foot-long rehearsal room. Kubrick's assistant Leon Vitali fired oranges and tennis balls at Ermey. "I had to catch the ball and throw it back to Leon as fast as possible and say the lines as fast as possible," Ermey explained to Aljean Harmetz. "If I were to slur a word, drop a word or slow down, I had to start over. I had to do it twenty times without a mistake. Leon was my drill instructor."

"Kubrick said I'm a super-intimidator," Lee Ermey told Martin Burden for the *New York Post*. "My dialogue coach told me I could be known in Hollywood as the rudest person in the city, that I make Don Rickles look like a Sunday school teacher."

As a former D.I., Ermey understood that the drill instructor was the person doing all the talking while the recruits just said, "Yes, sir," "No, sir." "Most films about boot camp have too much gabbing; that's why they're unreal," Ermey told Martin Burden. "But I guess the other actors feel left out if they have nothing to say. But that's the way it is—that's authentic."

Kubrick cast Matthew Modine as Private Joker, a character who, like Gustav Hasford, was a military journalist during the war. Kubrick described Matthew Modine to Alexander Walker as "the kind of baby Gary Cooper and Henry Fonda might have had." When Kubrick cast Modine, he was a fast-rising twenty-seven-year-old actor born in Loma Linda, California, and raised in Utah, who had appeared in seven films in the last four years. Modine had played a Vietnam soldier in *Birdy* and *Streamers* and had roles in *Baby It's You, Hotel New Hampshire, Vision Quest,* and *Mrs. Soffel.* Three of his four older brothers and one of his sisters served in the Vietnam War. "It was something I grew up with," Modine told Susan Linfield. "And the more that I read and the more I try to understand, the less sense it makes. I just watched the war on television. Listening to the body count—you know, listening to the score. Who was winning. It was like a baseball game. We got ten casualties, they got a hundred. Oh, we had a good day." "I was certainly old enough to understand what was going on," Modine told Caryn James for the *New York Times.* "I was probably interested in the role from having grown up with it." Modine understood the Marine philosophy of boot camp and Kubrick's concept of presenting realism and not ingratiating the audience. "You try not to color it with your opinions because boot camp isn't about characterization or personality," Modine told Caryn James. "You're taught your whole life not to hurt other people, not to kill other people; but when you go into a system like the Marines, those rules suddenly don't apply anymore.

"Joker doesn't have a name in the film. He's Private Joker from the get-go; he could be any soldier in any war. He has so many contradictions. That's what I think is great about the film. When you watch it, you don't know who to cheer for. You want to live in a world of peace, but if you scrape the veneer a little bit and get into man's psyche, he becomes an animal; there's a beast just beneath this thin facade of peace," Modine said to Caryn James.

"We called ourselves 'swinging dicks' because if you squint your eyes and look at us—everybody with their shaved heads standing at attention—we look like giant erections," Matthew Modine told Susan Linfield of *American Film* magazine. "It was humiliating, I mean, it's not pleasant getting your head shaved once a week and getting yelled at by some guy for ten hours a day.

"Everything that happens in *Full Metal Jacket* exists. The boot camp sequence is probably the most realistic portrayal of boot camp in the

Marines that's ever been put on film, with the exception of a Parris Island training film. It's not pleasant. You're not allowed an escape. The reason that Stanley's stories are shocking is because they're so truthful. He doesn't try to create some sympathy for somebody because it's a film, because he wants to win the audience over. It's not pleasant to see somebody killed. And it's not pleasant to die. Why try to make it something romantic when it's not? Maybe in all those World War II movies—because of what was happening in Europe—it was necessary to romanticize people going to fight. But to continue that romanticism is a mistake. You know, it was a tremendous thing that happened in the sixties, when people started to ask why."

Modine took the long hours and Kubrick's perfectionism in stride and respected the director's vision. "Stanley is my friend," he told Susan Linfield. "There were times when just out of pure frustration you'd get angry with Lee. But there's some kind of bonding that happens and you can't really get mad at anybody. You don't get mad at the director, because he's trying to create an art form instead of just a film. It's not like pop music, which you listen to for the summer and giggle about. It's like a piece of classical music that you're able to listen to over and over, and every time you listen, you find different nuances. That's how I feel about Stanley."

Actor Vincent D'Onofrio had learned about the *Full Metal Jacket* auditions from his friend Matthew Modine. The Brooklyn-born D'Onofrio was an athletic-looking six-foot, three-inch actor with curly dark hair who had worked in off-off-Broadway productions. D'Onofrio spent his early childhood in Hawaii and went to high school in Miami. He studied at the American Stanislavsky Theater in New York and spent three years playing theatrical roles like Murphy in *The Indian Wants the Bronx* and Lenny in *Of Mice and Men*. His first professional Broadway job was playing an Italian kid from the Bronx with a speech impediment in *Open Admissions*.

When Modine told him that the part of Private Pyle was available, D'Onofrio rented a home video camera to create his audition tape. He found a green wooden stoop that passed for the steps of an Army barrack and donned an Army cap and fatigues to perform his monologue. D'Onofrio found a speech he liked that had been written for a rookie cop, and he deleted all of the lines that referred to the police. He mailed the tape to England and received a quick response—he had secured the part. "Pyle was the hardest part to cast in the whole movie. I wanted to find new faces. We received about three or four thousand videotapes," Kubrick told Penelope Gilliatt.

When D'Onofrio was given the part, Kubrick asked the actor to gain nearly 70 pounds, bringing his weight to 280 pounds. The well-built D'Onofrio was transformed into the overweight and unfit scapegoat labeled Gomer Pyle by his drill instructor, who was bent on either breaking the young man or building him into a fighting machine Marine. "I gained weight everywhere," D'Onofrio told Leslie Bennetts for the *New York Times.* "My thighs were tremendous, my arms were tremendous, even my nose was fat. I had a tough time tying my shoelaces, but this was the only way I could play Leonard, because I had to be meekminded in the same way. Because of the weight and the fact that he was totally out of his element, Leonard's mind became weak. He was slow to start, a country bumpkin, but I don't think he was insane. What they did to Leonard was they made him into a very efficient killing machine." The physicality of the basic training sequences was a challenge to D'Onofrio. The extra weight and the unfit persona of the character made him prone to injury. While working on one of the film's obstacle-course sets, D'Onofrio injured his knee so severely it required surgical reconstruction.

With Private Pyle's visage, Kubrick added to his roster of glowering images. In *A Clockwork Orange* Malcolm McDowell as Alex penetrated the screen with a leering stare and a maniacal, head-tilted look. Jack Nicholson perfected the Kubrick crazy stare with his evil grin and deranged eyes, head slightly down, looking through the camera. Vincent D'Onofrio had his moments, watching the D.I. talk about what a Marine can do with his gun, head aslant, brows converging in symmetrical angles, mouth open, the whites of his eyes revealed below his hardened pupils. He gives a final bizarre look as Pyle sits in the latrine before killing Sergeant Hartman and then himself. D'Onofrio's gritted teeth and deranged eyes do Nicholson and McDowell proud and add to Kubrick's gallery of lunatic portraits. "That scene was very powerful," cinematographer Douglas Milsome told Ron Magid. "D'Onofrio flashes what people are now referring to as the 'Kubrick crazy stare.' Stanley has a stare like that which is very penetrating and frightens the hell out of you sometimes—I gather he's able to inject that into his actors as well."

When shooting was completed and Private Pyle had murdered D.I. Hartman and committed suicide by blowing his head off with a rifle, Vincent D'Onofrio put his full energy into returning to his former self. Shaving his head and expanding to 280 pounds wreaked havoc on the young man's psyche. "It changed my life," D'Onofrio told Leslie Bennetts. "Women didn't look at me; most of the time I was looking at their backs as they were running away. People used to say things to me twice, because they thought I was stupid." A year after being discharged from Kubrick's army, D'Onofrio, who jogged six miles a day, was back to his normal weight. His curly locks had grown back, the knee had healed, and—thanks to the good reviews he received as Private Pyle—his career had taken off.

Kubrick rounded out the cast with a strong group of young actors. For his audition Adam Baldwin submitted footage from *My Bodyguard, 3:15,* and a scene from the play *Back to Back,* about two soldiers sitting in a foxhole in Vietnam. He got the part of Animal Mother. The twenty-five-year-old six-foot, four-inch actor had admired Kubrick ever since he first saw *A Clockwork Orange, 2001,* and *The Killing.* Baldwin said he admired "the fact that he took you away from emotionally uplifting films and commercially easy choices that most other filmmakers take and that he really captures a sense of war, be it psychological war, war in space or black-comedy war like *Dr. Strangelove.* I like the way he depicted war."

Adam Baldwin also appeared in *Reckless, D.C. Cab,* and *Ordinary People.* He was first discovered by producer/director Tony Bill while he was playing ice hockey in Winnetka, Illinois. Bill cast Baldwin in his directorial debut, *My Bodyguard,* which was Baldwin's first film role.

Baldwin first read *The Short-Timers* after receiving the part and arriving in England. "The thing that really struck me about it," Baldwin said, "is it seemed to be such a tight claustrophobic picture of just these few men. It just sort of gave you that small portrait of the war and what it consisted of for these few young men, and by doing that it was antiwar statement enough for me. I'm one of those bleeding-heart liberals and any left-wing statement against war is something I agree with."

Dorian Harewood, cast by Kubrick as Eightball, had acted in *Roots: The Next Generations, The Jesse Owens Story,* and the miniseries *Amerika.* On the stage he was in *Streamers* and *The Two Gentlemen of Verona.* He was in the films *The Falcon and the Snowman* and *Against All Odds.*

Arliss Howard, who played Cowboy in *Full Metal Jacket,* was discovered by ABC Circle Films in Kansas City, Missouri, where he was working pouring concrete basements by day and appearing in community theater at night. Howard was a life member of the Actors Studio and was a theatrically trained actor. He was in the controversial miniseries *The Day After* and Jerzy Skolimowski's feature film *The Lightship.*

Ed O'Ross, who played Lieutenant Touchdown, was the son of a Pittsburgh, Pennsylvania, steelworker and a veteran of eleven years of Broadway, off-Broadway, and regional theater. O'Ross had supported himself as a jeweler, a painter, a janitor, and an engineer. He had appeared in

The Cotton Club and *The Pope of Greenwich Village* and in TV's *Moonlighting* and *Scarecrow and Mrs. King.*

Kevyn Major Howard, who played Rafterman, had worked in television for ten years in episodic series and movies made for television. He had appeared in the films *Sudden Impact* and *Death Wish II* and TV movies *Scared Straight, For Love and Honor,* and *Minnesota Strip.* He was touring Rome on a holiday when he received a frantic phone call from his agent telling him that Stanley Kubrick wanted him to play Rafterman, an innocent and naive combat photographer, in his new film.

Kubrick never allowed Lee Ermey to rehearse with the actors who played Hartman's recruits. He wanted their reactions to him to produce authentic emotions. He didn't want the young men to relate to or bond with Ermey. The result was the kind of detachment that Kubrick achieved with Danny Lloyd in *The Shining.* "It was terrifying to those actors," Lee Ermey explained to Aljean Harmetz of the *New York Times.* "My objective was intimidation. No one had ever invaded their private space. No one had ever put his head close to them. The first time I came up to Vincent, all he had to say was, 'Yes, sir' and 'No, sir' and he was so shocked he blew his lines three or four times."

Lee Ermey had a central role in the making of *Full Metal Jacket.* In addition to the role of Sergeant Hartman, which dominates the first section of the movie, Ermey was mandated by Kubrick to create a boot camp atmosphere on the set that was filled with documentary reality. The film opens with a montage of recruits having their heads shaved. After test results, Kubrick found that electric barber clippers didn't shave close enough to produce the Marine boot camp look. Ermey made a phone call to a friend at the Marine Corps training camp at the real Parris Island in South Carolina and discovered that they utilized clippers used to shear French poodles.

Kubrick continued to work with actors through indirection. He motivated them to search together with him for a scene during the filmmaking process. "My feeling is that by not telling you what he wants, you will somehow find it together," Matthew Modine told Susan Linfield. "We had a lot of talks that ranged from boxing to Greek mythology, a lot of conversations ranging from A to Z. It was great."

Modine found that although Kubrick was striving for realism in the physical details of the production, he was looking for the actors to go beyond reality. Modine discovered, as Jack Nicholson did on *The Shining,* that Kubrick looked for the multitude of choices that existed in every move and word spoken. "Stanley says, 'OK, it's real, but is it interesting?'" Matthew Modine told Susan Linfield. "Or is it more interesting to heighten reality and make it a metaphor? I mean, how does one behave when somebody puts a gun in their face? You can't say that this is 'the' real behavior. It's 'a' behavior. There are hundreds of different ways to react to having a gun put in your face. I think Stanley's interested in what reality is, but he doesn't just settle for the first thing that the actor comes up with or that he himself comes up with. He's looking for something that can be more interesting, more unusual, strange. Other film-makers don't get the time to change. They have to shoot something tomorrow, and oftentimes it's not the way they want to shoot. With Stanley, you do it the way that you want it to be, not because you're forced into making a decision based on time."

Kubrick kept the critical above-the-line positions for *Full Metal Jacket* all in the family. He was the director and producer, brother-in-law Jan Harlan was the executive producer, and Stanley Kubrick's new son-in-law, Philip Hobbs, was brought on board as coproducer.

To design *Full Metal Jacket* Kubrick hired Anton Furst, who had worked with Ken Adam on *Moonraker* and was part of the design team on Ridley Scott's *Alien*. He was the production designer of Neil Jordan's *The Company of Wolves*. The British-born designer, descended from Latvian royalty, had a European sensibility and a bold architectural style.

Full Metal Jacket was distinctly different from other films about Vietnam. It was not like *Platoon* and *Apocalypse Now*. Those films had been shot in the Philippines because the country had a jungle terrain similar to that of Vietnam. But Kubrick wasn't making a jungle combat film. The first section was Parris Island. The story of the second section of *Full Metal Jacket* took place in Hue, Vietnam, during the Tet Offensive in 1968. Researching the project was difficult. The obvious intention was to create Hue in England. Kubrick and his staff searched for information on Vietnamese signs and eventually found that the Library of Congress had microfilm editions of Vietnamese newspapers and magazines of the period. Kubrick, Furst, and the design team worked from historic news photographs taken in the Vietnamese city of Hue in 1968. They studied the photos and learned they depicted an area of the city reduced to rubble by the fighting. Kubrick and his designers used the photographs to bring authenticity to the design of the sets.

Kubrick sent his location scouts to the surrounding areas of London. He had his staff research every deserted air base in England for possible locations. Kubrick wanted to shoot the film on location to capture the required realism. The locations for the Parris Island boot camp and the Vietnam sequences were found in three different sites in northeast London within a thirty-mile radius of the Kubrick dominion. "When you think of Vietnam, it's natural to imagine jungles. But this story is about urban warfare," Adam Baldwin said to Marc Cooper of *American Film* magazine. "That's why London wasn't such a crazy location after all." Many were amazed that Kubrick shot the film on location in London. "The running gag was that Stanley had already shot the film somewhere else and when we got to London he was just going to superimpose us over it," Adam Baldwin joked.

The boot camp in *Full Metal Jacket* was built on an industrial estate at Enfield. A British Territorial Army base in Bassingbourne was used to serve as Parris Island, South Carolina. Lee Ermey consulted on the accuracy of the set as it was created and dressed.

The latrine area in the boot camp where the murder and suicide took place was designed and built on a studio stage in London. Kubrick was a slave to realistic detail except when he saw the opportunity for dramatic possibilities. The actual latrine area at Parris Island didn't have the look Kubrick wanted. "We did that as a kind of poetic license," he told Lloyd Grove. "It just seemed funny and grotesque," Kubrick said, referring to his expressionist interpretation of a Marine latrine.

For the site of the combat sequence that takes up the last section of *Full Metal Jacket,* Kubrick selected a 1930s abandoned coke-smelting plant in the East London neighborhood of Beckton on the Thames, which had been used for the remake of *1984.* Beckton had been bombed out during World War II, and much of the industrial architecture in the area had been designed by the same French architects who had worked in Hue in Vietnam. A number of the buildings at Beckton were carbon copies of the ones in the outer industrial areas of Hue.

Kubrick learned that British Gas owned the square-mile area that was in ruins and scheduled for total demolition. The area was isolated, so it could be confined in the same way as a studio backlot, except that the raw material here was real and not built from scratch like the rear exterior of the Overlook Hotel in *The Shining.* Kubrick found the location a perfect place to stage scenes taking place in Da Nang, Phu Bai, and the Imperial City of Hue which had been devastated in the Tet Offensive. He was given permission to use the area. "We had a demolition team in there for a week blowing up buildings, and the art director spent about six weeks with a guy with a wrecking ball and chain, knocking holes in the corners of things and really getting interesting ruins—which no amount of money would have allowed you to build," Kubrick told Lloyd Grove.

During the demolition, executives from British Gas brought their families out on a Sunday to watch the crew blow the buildings up. Then the set was finished off with grillwork and other architectural elements. "In this way, we achieved something unique which could not be done in any other way for any amount of money," Kubrick told Alexander Walker. "I don't think any film has ever had such vast and genuine ruins to work with—because of the isolated geography of the place we were also able to light huge fires and create giant pillars of smoke."

Anne Edwards had been involved with the Berkely Nurseries for twenty years. The company, which was founded by her former husband, supplied, leased, sold, and maintained foliage for banks and advertising, design, and computer companies. Edwards's excursion into the movies began when she received a chance phone call from Stanley Kubrick, who asked if she could supply him with sixty palm trees. "I said, 'yes,' and asked him when he needed them, guaranteeing delivery, then asked myself, 'What have I done?'" Anne Edwards told the *Observer* in London.

Edwards personally traveled to Spain and photographed three hundred separate palm trees of different varieties. Each one was identified and numbered, and the exact specifications—height, length of foliage, and circumference—were noted. Kubrick studied the photographs and selected the trees he wanted to use to re-create Vietnam in London for *Full Metal Jacket*. The North African palms Kubrick selected had been planted shortly after World War II. Then Edwards supervised the uprooting of the trees and the preparation for transportation to England. The roots of each tree were encased in plaster and the branches lashed together. The production paid £1,000 per palm, and an export permit was required to take the palms from Spain to England. The trees were searched to make sure they weren't being used to transport drugs. They were wet down daily by a fire engine hose at dockside to keep the trunks moist and the green leaves fresh. The first order of sixty palm trees required five 40-foot trailers to transport them to the location when they arrived in England. Each thirty-foot tree was in an individual builder's skip and was transported onto a low loader by a specially designed cradle.

Edwards traveled to the docks the Sunday night before her Monday deadline and was relieved to see that the five 40-foot trailers had arrived. She later learned that the palms had another visitor that night: Kubrick had come by to make sure his trees would be ready for his Vietnam in Beckton. After they arrived, Kubrick put in orders for more trees, eventually receiving almost two hundred palms. To complete the foliage, thousands of plastic plants were shipped from Hong Kong and put into place.

After working on *Full Metal Jacket,* Edwards created Palm Brokers—a company formed exclusively to serve the film and television community. Palm Brokers provided foliage for *The Secret Garden*, the James Bond film *The Living Daylights*, *The Fourth Protocol*, Spielberg's *Empire of the Sun*, and many commercials, music videos, and television shows.

For the street scenes, Kubrick brought in five thousand Vietnamese immigrants who were living in London to populate the area to look like Da Nang in 1968. To fill out the remainder of the Marine unit after casting the major speaking parts, Kubrick selected members of Britain's part-time Territorial Army, England's version of the National Guard.

The combat sequence that concludes *Full Metal Jacket* was unique in Vietnam films, which usually portrayed jungle battles in which the logistics and determination of the troops is unclear because of the quagmire nature of the war. In *Full Metal Jacket*, the battlefield is clearly delineated. "The whole area of combat was one complete area," Kubrick told Tim Cahill. "It actually exists. One of the things I tried to do was give you a sense of where you were, where everything else was. Which in war movies is something you frequently don't get. The terrain of small-unit action is really the story of the action. And this is something we tried to make beautifully clear: there's a low way, there's the building space. And once you get in there, everything is exactly where it was. No cutting away, no cheating. So it came down to where the sniper would be and where the Marines were."

With John Alcott living and working in America, Kubrick turned to Alcott's assistant, Douglas Milsome, to be the lighting cameraman on *Full Metal Jacket*. Milsome had been Alcott's focus puller on *Barry Lyndon*. On *The Shining* he was focus assistant and also shot some of the second-unit photography. Milsome had worked with Alcott for fifteen years and his untimely passing in 1986 had a strong effect. "I'd like to carry on where John stopped. I thought he was a great photographer and I learned a lot from him working with Stanley," Milsome told Ron Magid for *American Cinematographer* magazine. "The passing of John was such a blow to me that I've determined to try to perpetuate what he was trying to do."

Milsome was on *Full Metal Jacket* for a year and a half. The principal photography took a little over six months, and production was shut down for a period of five months. A great deal of Milsome's time was spent in preproduction with Kubrick. "There's always an awful lot to discuss with Stanley during preproduction because there's so much involved with his films," Milsome told Ron Magid. "They're always big subjects, so the cinematographer is often brought in quite a bit earlier than usual, not just to check the equipment but to check every single aspect of every possible situation to the *nth* degree. It involves painstaking time for discussion. He's just as methodical in his prep as he is in his shooting. Sometimes his prep takes as long as his shooting, often longer. He gives a new meaning to the word 'meticulous' and the word 'methodical.' As far as the lighting is concerned, that's open to discussion. We build models of our sets and discuss how to light them, and then we do extensive testing.

"I've actually had a lot harder time working for a lot less talented people than Stanley. He's a drain because he saps you dry, but he works damn hard himself and expects everybody else to. Sometimes it becomes a plod because it's so slow and intricate, but he loves to do things quite differently than what's ever been done before. You can't really do that sort of thing off the top of your head, so you work very hard to get it together and make something different which bears his mark. That can be a little overbearing and it tends to zap you and take up nearly all of your time. Sometimes the relationship can get a little strained because you've got to be devoted to him. You eat, drink and sleep the movie, and you're under contract to Stanley body and soul. But he allows you the time to get everything absolutely right, which is what I find so rewarding."

Milsome also observed Kubrick's distinctive use of composition as Garrett Brown experienced working with the director on *The Shining*. "Stanley's composition is very stylized. The way he places people is just amazing. You'll never find a Kubrick set-up where the actor's feet are cut off—every shot is either from the waist up or full length. Every one of his movies has that look: very square, very level and symmetrical. Things are placed exactly right every time. I use that style a lot even when I'm not working with him because that's the sort of thing that I like myself. The use of extreme wide angle lenses is distinctive, too, and allows us a great area in which to manipulate the action. We used a lot of wide angles to compose interesting shots, as well as a lot of very close angles on the same shots, and then Stanley would cut from one extreme to the other," Milsome said in *American Cinematographer* magazine.

The climax of the Marine battle with a sniper contains striking imagery. As the men were hit, Kubrick utilized slow motion. At times Kubrick had high speed cameras shooting at five times sound speed to emphasize the horror and pain of the men as they were hit with the sniper's bullet. The most chilling shot is when the sniper is revealed to be a Vietnamese young woman turning and firing on the men as they close in on her. "This wasn't just achieved by slowing the film down," Milsome revealed to Ron Magid. "We actually put the shutter of the camera out of phase with the movement of the film, which created a slight vertical strobe. As she was moving up and down and turning around, the flames seems to be standing still, and when she moved into the flames, they didn't move with her but seemed to bleed onto her face. The film is actually exposing as it's moving, which is what gives it that strobe effect. Normally, the film stops when the shutter opens, which freezes the picture, but in this case, the film's still moving while the shutter's open. Only slightly out of sync—maybe 25 percent—but it's enough to give the effect of light lasting that much longer in the shot."

For the final sequence of *Full Metal Jacket,* when the Marines march through the burning city singing the Mickey Mouse Club theme, the surrounding buildings were photographed by the light from a tank containing three thousand gallons of burning gas. Oil-burning fixtures created black smoke and a strong red glow.

Gustav Hasford made an unannounced visit to Kubrick's Vietnam location in Beckton while he was in England to make sure the film based on his novel was actually in production. "I went out to the set where Stanley was supposed to be filming in a little place called Beckton, near Essex. It's on the Thames, an abandoned gasworks. I wanted to see in fact whether the picture was being made," Gustav Hasford told Grover Lewis. "I was contemplating legal action at the time, and it would've been pointless if there were no movie. I took a couple of friends along with me. We dressed up in tiger-stripe clothes. Our idea was that they'd be shooting and we'd simply blend in as though we were extras. We went in, and this little gofer took us over to the commissary tent while somebody checked out who I was. We were having doughnuts and the gofer asked: 'Who are you? Why'd you come out here?' I said: 'Well, I'm the guy who wrote the book that this film is based upon.' His eyes lit up and he said: 'You're kidding! You're the guy? That's you?' I said: 'Yeah, yeah, I wrote the book." He said, 'Well, I want to shake your hand, because *Dispatches* is the best book I ever read.' 'Hey, I think so too,' I said."

Kubrick's longtime fascination and admiration for the silent-film era led him to his directorial approach on *Full Metal Jacket.* His desire was to have his film communicate visually and with spare, succinct dialogue. Kubrick told Francis X. Clines that he wanted the "economy of structural statement to be the nearest to silent film," because he found the dialogue of *Full Metal Jacket* to be "so almost poetic in its carved-out stark quality."

Tony Spiridakis was in England working on *Death Wish 3* for director Michael Winner when he heard that Stanley Kubrick was auditioning actors on tape for a new film. "I went down there. His assistant Leon

Vitali was running the session and he was fully booked," Spiridakis, who trained as a stage actor at the Yale Drama School, played the catcher on the Steven Bochco television series *The Bay City Blues,* and wrote and starred in *Queens Logic,* recalled. "I caught him in a break and I just said, 'Look, I'm here. I just heard about it last minute,' and he put me on at the end of the night. A couple of days later Leon called and said, 'Stanley really wants to further read you,' and that's how the whole process started. So he sent me a couple of sides for two different roles and I went back and did another audition for two different parts." Spiridakis read for the parts of Captain January and Captain Lockhart. "I auditioned a couple of times. I really liked Leon, he was great. Leon did everything. My image of Leon Vitali was that he literally had notes and phone numbers written with ballpoint pen on his skin from his fingertips to the top of his shoulders." In addition to the casting, Vitali coached the actors, ran lines, and acted as a liaison between them and Kubrick. "So believe it or not Stanley said, 'It's up to Tony, whatever he wants to do—whichever part.' I went out for coffee with Leon to sort of deliberate and we both felt that Captain January had the most impact."

Spiridakis was on *Full Metal Jacket* for five weeks. He went through the training program with Lee Ermey and the other actors who portrayed Marine recruits. "Lee was there to put the edge on, he got in our face and it was as much a psychological preparation as it was physical," Spiridakis recalled.

The screenplay to *Full Metal Jacket* at this point had a section where Private Joker went to Phu Bai to see Captain January. "There were three thirds to the film, there was the Parris Island first third—which was boot camp—and then there was the middle, which was really where the disillusionment of Joker occurred. He was disillusioned by the whole Marine Corps propaganda machine. As a journalist he was realizing that the reality of journalism was all about falsification. That was a fascinating part of the character's journey. It was a whole middle third which was not in the film. So Joker went from Parris Island—which in itself was a powerful disillusionment—right to combat craziness."

Editor Martin Hunter showed Spiridakis the scenes he was in. Captain January was a crazed officer akin to the character played by Robert Duvall in *Apocalypse Now.* "He was playing Monopoly with real money. His idea of a wonderful noble thing was to send the head of a gook back to his fiancée." Spiridakis was in two scenes. In one he plays Monopoly with Joker, and in the other they discuss body counts. The scenes with Captain January were shot in London on a set that captured the more traditional Vietnam jungle setting.

"I knew very little about Kubrick, so I was blown away that this was just a guy from the Bronx and I was a guy from Queens. It just blew my mind. I just couldn't get over that. When you get somebody as mythologically larger-than-life as is Stanley Kubrick and you find out he's from Kingsbridge Road, you just go nuts.

"I had gone back to New York and gotten tan because I was in the jungle scenes. When I got back to London Stanley was just flipping out that I was so much darker than all the other actors. The next thing I know I was shuttled back and forth to hair and makeup. They kept putting different base makeup on me and started putting moustaches on. Stanley was trying to change my ethnicity to a Puerto Rican. Finally, the Queens thing came out and I blew my top. I just said, 'Listen, I did my research, this is the way I would look if I had done two tours here!' When I got angry, I really thought I was going to be fired. I just blew my stack and Stanley looked at me, this big grin came over his face and the next day all of those actors were in tanning salons. The next morning Matt Modine said, 'Thanks a lot, I've got to get up an hour earlier and lie in a tanning salon.' Ultimately, Stanley saw it as a good idea. They had been ridiculing me because every half hour I'd come back with a new moustache. Everybody was doing little imitations: 'Captain Rodriguez, we don't need no stinkin' badges!' It was like a running gag and it was pissing me off. So I took my shot, thought it through and realized that I was right and they were wrong and Stanley agreed with me. That was big of him because he could more easily have lost me than put all these kids into the tanning salon. I fell in love with Stanley, from that moment on—we were very close, we really got along."

Kubrick shot many takes of rehearsals with the actors on video and at times edited the sequences. "If they're changing the lights and you're taking a break, he'll take you upstairs to a room and you'll watch a rehearsal," Spiridakis recalled.

"You're exhausted at the end of a day, you've really been pushed to the limit. He really gets the most out of his actors in the way that a great college basketball coach does with his athletes. He pushes you to get the best out of you. At the end you're spent, but you feel glorious.

"When Matt and I were in the scene at the Monopoly table that took place in a hut, there was an extra who was just acting up a storm. Stanley came up to me and said, 'This guy is really overacting, isn't he?' And I said, 'Well, yes, he is.' We start the next take and the next thing I know Stanley is sitting in the guy's chair acting in the scene off-camera. Stanley wanted to be there. He was really acting. It was amazing. He's such a detailed director. It felt like he jumped around and did everything. At one point in the scene he had a monitor on his lap, he had headphones on his head—he was just covered with equipment.

"After ten or twelve takes he would say, 'Let's go for a walk,' and we'd go for a walk. Like an athlete you could only go so far and then you needed to pull back. We'd talk and talk about different actors. The whole process of filmmaking was just in his blood. There are very few people you ever meet in any profession who can go as hard and yet be as centered. On one level you want to be the ultimate competitive person and on the other level you want to be a buddha and be non-result-oriented, so that's a very big contradiction—it could tear someone apart—but Stanley has that ability to go hard all the time but still be centered. He's like a kid, but sophisticated as an old wise man—he's both of those things. He would lean his head against your shoulder and close his eyes rather than go to a trailer. He's very in love with the process of acting and the physical process of filmmaking.

"He really complimented my acting and I was so touched by that. He always said, 'You remind me of somebody.' Finally, after a couple of weeks he said, 'I know who it is. If Ben Gazzara and John Cassavetes had a son—you'd be it.' I was so blown away and then after half an hour, I said to him, 'If Rasputin and Santa Claus had a son you'd be it.' That is the crossbreeding you'd have. He's got a little Rasputin in him and you definitely want to hug him. Those are the two characters—you fear one and you want to hug the other—to me that is Stanley.

"He's very funny and down to earth, telling great anecdotes about George C. Scott and pieces of equipment he invented. He said, 'You see this eye piece? I invented this and I'm not getting a penny because I didn't listen to my wife, but I put this little thing together.' "

After the film was edited, Spiridakis was cut out of it. Kubrick called Spiridakis to tell him. "He called me and said there was a fifty percent chance I would be out of the film and he was very sorry. That's how he did it—he didn't let me go to the movie and find out. I really appreciated it. A friend of mine is friendly with his daughter, and Vivian said how much her dad hated cutting me out and that he adored me. I adored him. He knew how hard it was for me to get cut out and he felt really terrible. I have a soft spot in my heart even though it devastated me. What happened was unavoidable and he was a complete gentleman. He showed that we had a connection. I couldn't have asked to be treated better than that.

"I was always fascinated by the man as a filmmaker, but as a person I just think he's much warmer than I'd heard. I just find the way they characterize him as nonsense. To me he was caring, funny, a real warm presence. With the madness of the technical part of filmmaking, he was always there with a glint in his eye. He just loved that stuff. He was like a little boy. That feeling that it was in his blood, this is what made him happy. It just emanated from him."

Kubrick's young actors functioned like a military unit. Up at dawn for a long bus ride to the location, they developed a camaraderie as they survived the tour of duty making *Full Metal Jacket*. The shooting was physically demanding, the battle sequence so realistic that actor Dorian Harewood feared that the constant intense sound of explosions and gunfire had damaged his hearing. He twice visited a doctor, concerned he had punctured his eardrums. "It was as close to war as I ever want to get," Harewood told *American Film* magazine. "And all the time, all that waiting around, turned us into a 'unit' just like in the film. There we were in army garb, rifles in our laps, in the hot weather, sitting around in the dirt and rubble and waiting and waiting, and smoking and playing cards and being away from home and our wives for months. It *was* the army!" Shooting on the film dragged on from the hot summer of 1985, which gave England the right sense of steamy heat to capture the atmosphere of Vietnam, and concluded in September 1986. In the middle of the shooting schedule, Ermey's car skidded off the road in Epping Forest at one o'clock in the morning. Ermey had broken all of his ribs on one side. Kubrick was forced to shut down production for five months because of Lee Ermey's near-fatal auto accident.

While Stanley Kubrick was directing his twelfth feature film he experienced the deaths of his parents. Gertrude Kubrick died on April 23, 1985, in Los Angeles while *Full Metal Jacket* was in the last stages of preproduction. She was eighty-two years old. Six months later, on October 19, Jacques Kubrick died in Los Angeles at Cedars-Sinai Medical Center of bacterial pneumonia. He was eighty-three years old. The Kubricks had relocated to California in 1965, where Jacques obtained a California medical license. The couple lived at 2222 Avenue of the Stars. Gertrude and Jacques were buried side by side at B'Nai Abraham Memorial Park in Union, New Jersey.

Gertrude's will left all her personal effects to Jacques. After his death, Jacques provided for the distribution of their estate according to Gertrude's wishes. Concerning their family, Gertrude acknowledged her son's success. In her will she states, "I have two children of my marriage now living, namely, Stanley Kubrick and Barbara Kroner. I have no other children. I have intentionally in the will provided only for my daughter Barbara and her issue, as my son Stanley and his issue are otherwise well provided for."

The bulk of Jacques Kubrick's estate was distributed equally among the Robert and Barbara Kroner family.

Toba Metz Kubrick Adler, whom Gertrude referred to as "my friend," was left $20,000 and two of her rings.

Their son, Stanley, was given "All awards, plaques, and other related items presented to Stanley Kubrick (in his name) which were previously given by Stanley Kubrick to decedent."

To their daughter-in-law, Christiane Kubrick, they returned "all of those paintings which she previously gave decedent."

Jacques' will returned to his granddaughter Anya Kubrick "the needle-point poem she gave to decedent at the age of eleven."

Many other personal belongings were distributed to family members and friends.

The estate also provided for the repayment of loans that Stanley had lovingly made to his father after his mother's passing.

With the loss of both his parents there was also joy in Kubrick's life. His daughter Katharina had given birth to a son, Alexander Philip Hobbs, on January 20, 1985, at St. Mary's Hospital in Westminster, making Stanley Kubrick a grandfather and his coproducer, Philip Hobbs, a father.

Kubrick conducted lengthy rehearsals with the actors and shot each scene three or four times on videotape so he could analyze it. He continued to shoot with an extremely high ratio, making as many as seventy-five takes of a shot, which Kubrick would then print and review. "Why not see it all?" Kubrick said to his actors, explaining that film stock was the cheapest part of the process.

The opening shot in the boot camp sequence was photographed twenty-five times before Ermey had his car accident. Douglas Milsome noted that after his recovery Ermey's performance seemed to improve from the ordeal of his experience.

Kubrick continued to be criticized for shooting so many takes with his actors. The astronomical take ratio on *The Shining* had quickly become legend in the industry, but Kubrick insisted it was necessary. Kubrick told Jack Kroll that what irritated him the most was the myth that he was "a mindless perfectionist who shoots a hundred takes." "It happens when the actors are unprepared," Kubrick told Tim Cahill. "You cannot act without knowing dialogue. If actors have to think about the words, they can't work on the emotion." "A lot of actors today get bad advice from teachers who tell them not to get locked into their lines," Kubrick told Jack Kroll. "So you end up doing thirty takes of something. And still you can see the concentration in their eyes; they don't know their lines. So you just shoot it and shoot it and hope you can get something out of it in pieces," Kubrick told Tim Cahill. "Now, if the actor is a nice guy, he goes home, he says, 'Stanley's such a perfectionist, he does a hundred takes on every scene.' So my thirty takes become a hundred. And I get this reputation. If I did a hundred takes on every scene, I'd never finish a film. Lee Ermey, for instance, would spend every spare second with the dialogue coach, and he always knew his lines. I suppose Lee averages eight or nine takes, he sometimes did it in three, because he was prepared."

"Stanley always has done many, many takes, but in fact, the many takes are not just repetitions of the same thing, they are often building upon a theme or idea that can mature and develop into something quite extraordinary," Douglas Milsome told Ron Magid. "The whole structure of the scene can actually change during the operation of filming it. Also, Stanley gets a lot more out of his actors after he works with them a lot longer. It's especially valuable in bringing out something in actors who may not be exactly up to the part, but Stanley works on them jolly hard until they produce the goods. That's why he's so good with actors: in the end, he'll rehearse and rehearse them until they're word perfect, and when they've got the words perfect then the rest has to happen—they then have to act. The large number of takes are mainly to get something out of the actors that they're not willing to provide right away. Of course, it's demanding on the crew as well, but it's a lot harder for the actors than it is for us. Once you've done an eight- or ten-minute scene a number of times, after take thirty or thirty-five, you're really into it. Actually it doesn't always go that many takes. There were occasions on *Full Metal Jacket* where we went a few more than twenty-five or thirty takes, but we usually didn't average more than ten to fifteen takes, although sometimes we'd go back and reshoot certain scenes later."

The music for *Full Metal Jacket* was composed by Abigail Mead. Kubrick wanted the score "to avoid any prior musical associations that conventional orchestra instruments might bring," he told Alexander Walker.

Little was known about Abigail Mead—just that *Full Metal Jacket* was her first film score and the original music was performed on a Fairlight Series III music computer. Mead's name was on the film credits and on the cover of the original motion picture soundtrack album.

As the 1987 Oscar race heated up, on January 28, 1988, an article in the *Los Angeles Times* by Robert Koehler revealed that Abigail Mead was actually Vivian Kubrick and featured a picture of Kubrick's youngest daughter, now twenty-seven and a close image of her father, sitting in her music studio. This was Vivian's third involvement in a Stanley Kubrick film. Her first was as a tyke-actress playing Dr. Floyd's daughter appearing on a videophone screen in *2001*. The second was working in the art department on *The Shining* and as director of a documentary on the making of the film. In *Full Metal Jacket,* in addition to the original score, Vivian appeared in a scene where the soldiers and the press stand over an open grave of dead Vietnamese.

Vivian Kubrick joined a select group of composers who have written original music for a Stanley Kubrick film: Gerald Fried, Alex North, Nelson Riddle, Wendy Carlos, and Rachel Elkind.

Kubrick originally ordered some Japanese drum music for the film's trailer, but he didn't like it, so he asked Vivian to come up with a piece of music for it. "He liked what I gave him so much that he asked me to do the original score," Vivian Kubrick told Robert Koehler.

Vivian decided to change her name because she wanted her work to be judged on its own merit. Her first choice for a pseudonym was Moses Lumpkin. "Stanley was horrified by that," Vivian Kubrick told Robert Koehler, as she referred to her father by his first name. "I thought of the house our family used to live in, where we had many good times, and like many in England, it had a name: Abbot's Mead. *Abbot* became *Abigail* and then Stanley had somebody look up the name's meaning. Its ancient meaning is 'a father rejoices.' He loves coincidences, and he really loved this one."

When the *Full Metal Jacket* score was presented to the music branch of the Academy of Motion Picture Arts and Sciences, it was unanimously rejected by the twenty-eight-member committee on the grounds that it did not contain a sufficient amount of original material to qualify. Composer John Addison, the committee's chairman, said, "There were key moments of the film that used pop tunes. Fifty percent was not [Mead's]. Significantly, the whole committee's feeling was that the songs played a key role in the film as the original music. What Mead wrote, while effective, didn't stand up as a substantial body of music for dramatic underscoring."

"I think it would be unfair to deem it unqualified because of the amount or percentage of music that was mine," Vivian Kubrick told Robert Koehler in Los Angeles during a phone interview from London. "I don't know if [the committee's] argument holds up. I would be surprised if there was more pop music on the soundtrack than music I wrote."

Jan Harlan, speaking as Stanley Kubrick's executive producer, and as his brother-in-law and the composer's uncle, said, "I think it's absurd to call her work not substantial enough. It's a wonderful score which advances the dramatic narrative."

The synthesizer score created atmospheric sounds that gave the sonic impression of doors swinging on rusty hinges and other environmental and interpretive effects that many found innovative, but Addison remarked, "Repeating a sequence on drums for two minutes was not especially imaginative."

Vivian sent the pages of the score to the *Los Angeles Times* to show that her original score was twenty-two minutes and twenty-six seconds and that the pop tunes ran seventeen minutes and thirty-nine seconds. These timings didn't include another four minutes of on-screen music consisting of march cadences led by Lee Ermey, leaving Koehler to surmise that this would give the committee the fifty-fifty mix they were saying excluded the Abigail Mead score from Oscar consideration.

An anonymous member of the panel told Koehler that the split sparked a closer review of the film and the final decision was based on the committee's feeling that the pop tunes dominated the overall score of *Full Metal Jacket*. In 1986 jazz musician Herbie Hancock had won the Oscar for *Round Midnight* as the best original score. Many were concerned about the win because the score was made up of Hancock's arrangements of jazz standards more than his original dramatic scoring. The 1987 rule book was revised to include the following: "Scores diluted by the use of tracked (inserted music not written by the composer) or pre-existing music" are not eligible. Addison explained, "These rules are an attempt to set guidelines to assess scores for outstanding achievement. The new rule was typical in helping to make guidelines more useful in determining excellence. [The score] may greatly please the director, but that doesn't make it a great score."

"There is no way that he would work on a film for four years and risk it all with lousy music by one of his offspring," Vivian Kubrick told Robert Koehler. "He believed in me, that I would do a good sound track." With the best music category out of the running, *Full Metal Jacket* received one Oscar nomination. Kubrick, Herr, and Hasford were nominated for best screenplay based on material from another medium.

Full Metal Jacket also featured a song score with period pop songs like "Chapel of Love," "Wooly Bully," "These Boots Are Made for Walking," and "Surfin' Bird." In classic methodical form Kubrick studied the Billboard charts of Top 100 hits from 1962 through 1968 and tried out many songs before the final edit.

The original soundtrack album contained a track titled "Full Metal Jacket," a Marine rap led by Lee Ermey that was not in the film but was released as a single. The track was produced by Vivian Kubrick and guitarist Nigel Goulding and reached number two on the British pop charts and sold well in Europe.

There were rumors that *Full Metal Jacket* had once been planned as a far more gruesome film. Several critics reported that a scene depicting a soccer match played with the head of a decapitated Viet Cong was cut from the film, but this is unsubstantiated. Robert Koehler, writing for the *Los Angeles Times,* did see the shooting script, which revealed planned violent scenes that did not appear in the finished film. Koehler reported that the script indicated that Animal Mother decapitated the sniper in the final scene. It was also reported that at a first screening of *Full Metal Jacket* actor Adam Baldwin, who played Animal Mother, was disappointed that the scene had been cut.

Julian Senior of Warner Bros. denied that the film had been altered subsequent to early screenings, but he did say that at one time the film began differently. "Originally, the film began at Joker's funeral," Senior told Koehler. "It was told in a flashback. But [Kubrick] felt it was wrong, that he'd be telling the whole story before you got a chance to see it. What's important is Joker's affirmation of life."

Gustav Hasford did not have an agent or a lawyer. Kubrick and Herr wanted Hasford to receive an additional dialogue credit. Hasford felt he contributed as much as Stanley Kubrick and Michael Herr and felt that Herr strongly objected to him receiving an equal credit on the film. "I might have made a few noises," Herr said in Grover Lewis's article on Hasford. "I suppose I felt that I'd been involved in this for such a long time. But I didn't make a terrible issue of this. It wasn't a very compli-cated matter to get me to agree to giving Gus co-credit. He must know what I think of his work. And if he doesn't I'd like him to. I always thought he should be consulted on this. Because I'm not in touch with Gus doesn't mean anything. It's not that big a deal to me. Certainly, it would have to be something a lot heavier than that to hurt a friendship."

The disagreement over the writing credits for *Full Metal Jacket* con-tinued during the shooting of the film. "For a year and a half we were in disagreement," Hasford told Grover Lewis. "From my point of view, I deserved a full credit. I heard all the arguments against my attitude from Stanley and Warner Bros. and Michael Herr, and I was never convinced their arguments were valid. I persisted until I won."

After the script was completed and the long war for the credits to *Full Metal Jacket* was over, Gustav Hasford went to Perth, Australia, to recover from his ordeal. In a letter to journalist Grover Lewis, Hasford wrote, "In the cynical world of L.A., where show 'biz' deals are conducted in the back alleys of cocktail parties like self-parodying out-takes from a comedic film noir, you might want to interject this lively note of (transitory) optimism: I won my credit battle with Stanley. I beat Stanley, City Hall, The Powers That Be, and all the lawyers at Warner Bros., up to and including the Supreme Boss Lawyer. As a little Canuck friend of mine would say: *I kicked dey butt.*

"Michael [Herr] and I got to be pretty good friends until we had the credit dispute," Hasford told Grover Lewis. "As far as I know, he's still not speaking to me. I'm speaking to him, but he's not saying anything back. As much of my work was in the screenplay as he had in, but he still seems to interpret the fact that I got a full credit as an intrusion upon his turf. Like, who is this interloper. But in fact, I worked on the screenplay for four years. I had actually written things, you know scenes and comments. I would send my work to Stanley, and undoubtedly Stanley was having Michael write the same scene. Then Stanley would work it around the way he wanted it. For some reason, Stanley had given Michael a lot of my work to look at, but I never read any of the things Michael wrote for the film. We really didn't talk about it much. I mean, we'd talk about it in general terms like, 'When is this sucker going to be finished?' I like Stanley. Stanley is funny and human and not as eccentric as he would perhaps prefer to appear. My favorite movie is *Dr. Strangelove* and *Paths of Glory* is one of the great classic war films. I'd stand Stanley a glass anytime, two, maybe."

The final screen credits for *Full Metal Jacket* read: "Screenplay by Stanley Kubrick, Michael Herr, Gustav Hasford."

In writing the foreword to the published screenplay of *Full Metal Jacket,* Michael Herr summed up his feeling about writing for Stanley Kubrick: "When *Viva Zapata!* came out in 1952, the ads featured a rave from John Steinbeck, something like, 'The greatest movie of all time.' I remember how I felt when I saw that John Steinbeck had also written the screenplay. Without the words to say it, I was shocked by the immodesty of it, the shameless conflict of interest. But I was only twelve then, and had never written for the movies. At least from the day that Stanley saw the phrase 'full metal jacket' in a gun catalogue and found it 'beautiful and touching, and kind of poetic,' he had taken the book and the script, the cast and the technicians into his obsession. We'd get out when the movie got out. Film isn't all that's released when a powerful picture is finished." Again Kubrick was using a possessive credit—*Stanley Kubrick's Full Metal Jacket*—Kubrick held ultimate claim to the film in toto.

An advertising campaign was designed with the bold and simple graphic style that Kubrick was attracted to. The ads featured a camouflaged helmet with a row of full metal jacket bullets, a peace button, and the words "Born to Kill," painted in black. Copy lines like "Vietnam Can Kill Me But It Can't Make Me Care" and "In Vietnam the Wind Doesn't Blow, It Sucks," were used to sell the film.

Full Metal Jacket gave Kubrick the forum to chide the military and the media. Not reaching for the overt black humor of *Dr. Strangelove*, Kubrick maintained a cynical level throughout *Full Metal Jacket*. A sequence in which a documentary camera crew interviews the Marines in the country gave Kubrick the opportunity to explore the way the war was perceived. He told Alexander Walker that the sequence "seemed a very economical way of stating a cross section of prevailing attitudes on Vietnam and at the same time sending up the media." The scenes that take place during editorial meetings for the Marine newspaper were created so they seemed that "they'd cooked up their news out of Hollywood movies of the 1940s," Kubrick told Alexander Walker.

Oliver Stone's career-breakthrough film, *Platoon*, was released in 1986 and won the Academy Award for best picture, best direction, best editing, and best sound just months before *Full Metal Jacket* was released. Critics and audiences compared the two films and their different points of view. *Platoon* was a more traditional war film and focused on the soldiers, the physical aspect of the fighting, and a realistic portrayal of the Vietnam experience. Previous Vietnam films, like *Coming Home* and *Apocalypse Now*, were made in direct response to the war. *Coming Home* presented the effects of the war in the United States and *Apocalypse Now* created an expressionistic interpretation of the Vietnam experience. John Wayne's *The Green Berets* was a macho, gung-ho, patriotic testament to the war. Ted Post's *Go Tell the Spartans*, made in 1978, was an early effort to deal honestly with the war and the men who fought it. Kubrick's view of the Vietnam War was linked to his perception of war in general. Like *Paths of Glory*, *Full Metal Jacket* enters the military mentality and underscores the futility and inevitability of conflict. Kubrick publicly expressed his respect for the Oliver Stone film but took the extreme position that even that brutally honest film ingratiated itself to the audience by using story elements traditional to the genre. Kubrick was often accused of alienating his audience, and in *Full Metal Jacket* he intentionally created a film that distanced itself with its cold and pedantic approach to the subject. The first section of the film was a chilling look at the creation of the soldier as killing machine, the second section was the inescapable aftermath. *"Platoon's* a good movie—ours is better," Adam Baldwin told *American Film* magazine. "Ours is sort of the 'prequel.' You see how plain young Americans are turned into individuals who are broken down, they are run ragged, they are degraded and dehumanized." Vietnam had been considered an off-limits topic by the film industry. Once the Vietnam film cycle began, filmmakers explored the myriad facets of the war. But *Full Metal Jacket* was first and foremost a Stanley Kubrick film. Again Kubrick used a genre—here the war film— to explore the basic evil in man and to satisfy his obsession with the cinematic possibilities within the conventions of the form.

Kubrick made the decision to eliminate drug experimentation from *Full Metal Jacket,* even though it had played a significant role in *Platoon* and *Apocalypse Now.* He told Tim Cahill of *Rolling Stone* magazine that drug use implied that the soldiers were out of control. His research showed that the Marines had their flak jackets buttoned, which signified they were always well prepared.

"I know there's going to be a lot of outraged and offended responses to this movie," Michael Herr said to Lloyd Grove of the *Washington Post.* "The political left will call him a fascist, and the right—well who knows? I can't imagine what women are going to think of this film."

"We're just going for the way it is," Kubrick told Grove. "I certainly don't think the film is anti-American. I think it tries to give a sense of the war and the people, and how it affected them. I think with any work of art, if I can call it that, that stays around the truth and is effective, it's very hard to write a nice capsule explanation of what it's about. I liked *Platoon,* it's very different. I think *Platoon* tried to ingratiate itself a little more with the audience. But then, I have enough faith in enough of the audience to think that they are able to appreciate something which doesn't do that. At least you're not bored. I don't know if you go to the movies a lot, but that's one of the biggest problems."

Predictably, security on the *Full Metal Jacket* set had been tight. When the film was about to be released, Kubrick did grant a few interviews that were held in the empty executive offices at Pinewood Studios in London. Always a rare interview subject, Kubrick granted them only to help promote his films. He was the master at avoiding discussion about the meanings of his work. He preferred instead that audiences experience his films as visceral and sensory experiences. His interviews were often discourses on a multitude of subjects other than film, usually a current interest or fixation.

A series of interviews around the occasion of *Full Metal Jacket*'s release provided a partial update of Stanley Kubrick as he approached completing his sixth decade and was in his third as an American in England. Francis X. Clines of the *New York Times* described Kubrick at the time of *Full Metal Jacket* as rumpled and "as lone as the night watchman." Clines found talking with Kubrick an intense experience— "Bearded and staring carefully as a question is asked, Mr. Kubrick speaks with his right hand rubbing his brow, often glancing down, like a man reciting the confiteor or handicapping the next race," Clines observed. The reporter described Kubrick's voice as having a casual New York ambience but detected "a terrible determination." When Lloyd Grove interviewed Kubrick in a boardroom at Pinewood in connection with a *Washington Post* piece on *Full Metal Jacket,* he described the director as looking shambled—wearing an ochre corduroy jacket that had a dark-blue stain in the chest area, khakis that were riding low, and wornout jogging shoes—definitely not used for running. Grove also noted there were black hairs sprouting from Kubrick's balding head and his graying beard resembled "jungle growth more than facial hair." While they talked, Kubrick often consulted his digital watch. When Tim Cahill interviewed Kubrick for *Rolling Stone* magazine, he reported that Kubrick took twenty minutes to find the executive suite at Pinewood where they were to talk. He wore the same outfit described by Lloyd Grove. Cahill surmised that the blue stain on Kubrick's ochre corduroy jacket was caused by an exploded ballpoint pen. Cahill found Kubrick to be unpretentious and captured a superb profile piece with the usually elusive and evasive director.

Kubrick told Cahill that in addition to his three golden retrievers the family now had a mutt that the director had found wandering along a road. Kubrick still wore his aviator glasses and an unfashionable heavy blue coat on location. He told Penelope Gilliatt that he remained an American, "with distance giving a better perspective." Gilliatt found Kubrick steeped in American pop culture.

Kubrick worked on *Full Metal Jacket* right up to the last moment, fine-tuning the editing and sound mix. His eleventh-hour adjustments forced Warners to push ahead screenings for critics and exhibitors.

The *Hollywood Reporter* wrote that Kubrick had rejected so many prints of *Full Metal Jacket* as they came from the lab for his approval that the original plan to open wide in twelve key markets had to be revised.

Full Metal Jacket opened June 26, 1987, to some strong reviews and a respectable box office of $5,655,225 in the first ten days. The strategy was to open the film in a three-tier release plan. Kubrick delivered his approved release print at the last minute, so Warner Bros. did not have the opportunity to preview the film widely—it relied on word of mouth to carry the unusual film over the more typical summer action and comedy fare. After the limited run at 215 theaters, the film added 635 screens and then later another 570 screens for a full national release. Kubrick continued to make iconoclastic films while striving for wide commercial success. Jack Nicholson's star power helped to sell *The Shining*. *Full Metal Jacket* featured a strong young male cast, but they lacked the box office draw of a major movie star.

Reviews were mixed, although they were better than the near disastrous reception of *The Shining*. David Steritt of the *Christian Science Monitor* called it "the most artful film yet made about the Vietnam war." *Full Metal Jacket* got favorable reviews from the *Los Angeles Times*, *Newsday*, *Newsweek*, *Time*, and *Women's Wear Daily*, mixed notices from *Films in Review*, *Jump Cut*, and negative reviews from J. Hoberman of the *Village Voice*, *Cineaste*, *Monthly Film Bulletin*, and *New York Magazine*.

Kubrick claims that his emphasis on realism and the kind of coincidence that brought him actors with the same first names as their characters on *The Shining* was responsible for what appeared to be a reference to *2001* prominently displayed in *Full Metal Jacket*. After Cowboy is shot and is dying, a concrete slab strongly resembling a monolith is visible behind him and the men who try to comfort him. Kubrick told Alexander Walker it was the result of the work done to create the rubble and told Tim Cahill that it was an accident that just happened to be there. Happenstance may have created the structure, but the prominent looming symbol stays on screen for a long duration and is apparent throughout the scene. In one shot, the men are placed so they are perfectly aligned in a position that recalls the way the apes in *2001* stood in front of the monolith. When Alexander Walker mentioned to Kubrick that the image might encourage hypotheses by critics and film buffs, Kubrick glared and said, "Critical irrelevance, you mean!"

Kubrick continued to worry about the technical standards of the theaters showing his film. He always applied the Peter Principle—if anything could go wrong it would. It perturbed him that he was labeled as an obsessional maniac when he saw his concern as pragmatic. "Some people are amazed that I worry about the theaters where the picture is being shown," he said to Tim Cahill. "They think that's some form of demented anxiety. But Lucas-films has a Theater Alignment Program. They went around and checked a lot of theaters and published the results in a report that virtually confirms all your worst suspicions. For instance, within one day, fifty percent of the prints are scratched. Something is usually broken. The amplifiers are no good, and the sound is bad, the lights are uneven . . . Well, theaters try to put in a screen that's larger than the light source they paid for. If you buy a 2000-watt projector, it may give you a decent picture twenty feet wide. And let's say that theater makes the picture forty feet wide by putting in a wider-angle projector. In fact, then you're getting 200 percent less light. It's an inverse law of squares. But they want a bigger picture, so it's dark. Many exhibitors are terribly guilty of ignoring minimum standards of picture quality. For instance, you now have theaters where all the reels are run in one continuous string. And they never clean the aperture gate. You get one little piece of gritty dust in there, and every time the film runs, it gets bigger. After a couple of days, it starts to put a scratch on the film. The scratch goes from one end of the film to the other. Now is it an unreal concern if I want to make sure that on the press shows or on key city openings, everything in the theater is going to run smoothly? You just send someone to check the place out three or four days ahead of time. Make sure nothing's broken. It's really only a phone call or two, pressuring some people to fix things. I mean, is this a legitimate concern, or is this mindless anxiety?"

Full Metal Jacket cost $17 million and grossed $38 million in the first fifty days of release. Kubrick continued to work with the film as it moved through the release process, remixing it for the European opening. Foreign box office was especially strong in Italy, France, Germany, England, and Sweden.

Lee Ermey was sent on a publicity tour for the film. As always, Kubrick kept tight control over the information revealed. When Ermey was scheduled to be interviewed by Jack Kelly for *People* magazine a memo from Edward S. Crane, a publicity manager, suggested "that there are certain areas of conversation that might be better left unreported." Crane suggested that anything negative about Kubrick fell into that domain. "I love your line that he doesn't expect anything more from the people around him than he does of himself in maximum effort and attention to detail . . . which makes for great motion pictures," Crane wrote to Ermey. "If Kelly wants Stanley's phone number, you don't have it."

Full Metal Jacket was nominated for screenplay adaptation in the year dominated by Bernardo Bertolucci's *The Last Emperor*. Before the balloting deadline, authorities in Sacramento and San Luis Obispo, California, announced they were looking for Gustav Hasford concerning allegations that the writer and hard-earned-credited scenarist had stolen hundreds of library books—a possible explanation of the magnitude of his mysterious archives. In San Clemente, California, Hasford stated that he wasn't going to the ceremonies because he disliked wearing a tuxedo. One police agency was considering the option of serving an arrest warrant to Hasford in the lobby of the Shrine Auditorium, where the ceremony was to be held.

The Vietnam cycle of films continued. *Hamburger Hill* was released, *Apocalypse Now* was rereleased in a new 70mm Dolby print, and Oliver Stone announced he was writing a sequel to *Platoon*. For Kubrick, the Vietnam War was a platform to build his ideas and feelings about the military and the war. For Oliver Stone, it was an obsession. The early announcement of a sequel to *Platoon* became a trilogy about the war— *Born on the Fourth of July*, an interpretive and powerful biography of Vietnam vet Ron Kovic, was followed by the contemplative *Heaven and Earth*—one of the few films to present the Vietnamese point of view as seen through the eyes of a Vietnamese woman. Kubrick had his own war trilogy: *Fear and Desire*, *Paths of Glory*, and *Full Metal Jacket*, made over a span of almost thirty-five years. Kubrick's obsession with the subject came from decades of fascination with military conflicts. General Kubrick imbued his organizational code of conduct and tight logistics in his films. War spoke to Kubrick, who did not believe in Anne Frank's credo that mankind was basically good. Kubrick held that evil was alive and well. A pessimist, Stanley Kubrick was drawn to the dark side of the human experience and found it thriving in armed conflict. He saw it in the spears and flaming logs in *Spartacus*, the atomic bomb in *Dr. Strangelove*, the bone weapon/tool in *2001*, the bootjacks and penis sculpture in *A Clockwork Orange*, the muskets and pistols in *Barry Lyndon*, and the ax in *The Shining*. The theme of the true evil and violent nature of man survived four decades of filmmaking for Stanley Kubrick.

In June 1988 Kubrick was the recipient of the Luchino Visconti Award for *Full Metal Jacket*, which honored his contributions to cinema during the David Di Donatello Awards ceremony in Italy.

Once the film was finished, Kubrick began to catch up with films released during the eighteen months while he had been deeply engrossed with *Full Metal Jacket*. Keeping current with the international cinema and the Hollywood movie business was essential for Stanley Kubrick. Although he remained situated at his home in England, he didn't function in a vacuum. He continued to gather information to feed his single-minded intellectual appetite. He also began to read again, in search of the next obsessional state.

Kubrick proceeded to make movies for himself and the audience, paying little mind to critics. The horrendous critical reception of *2001* and the film's subsequent box office success taught him to trust the audience. "People who didn't have the responsibility of having to explain it or formulate clear statements about it two hours after they saw the film weren't troubled," Kubrick told Francis X. Clines.

Kubrick's residence in London continued to perplex people. The public and the film community saw him as a recluse because he didn't travel and had ensconced himself at his London estate. The way that Stanley Kubrick lived was based in solid, unemotional logic. To Kubrick there were only three places in the world where he could make films—New York City, Los Angeles, and England. New York City had provided a convivial environment for the nascent filmmaker, but it lacked the technical facilities he required and demanded a frenetic lifestyle. Los Angeles had the resources but was a place he disliked intensely. Kubrick was never part of the Hollywood social or political scene and didn't fit into the mold. England had the requisite facilities, as well as the civility and privacy that he personally craved. He could make his films cheaply, without the bloated expense account budgets that Hollywood applied to load a film down and weaken its on-screen strength.

"Because I direct films I have to live in a major English-speaking production center," Kubrick told Tim Cahill. "That narrows it down to three places: Los Angeles, New York and London. I like New York, but it's inferior to London as a production center. Hollywood is best, but I don't like living there."

"I also like being away from the Hollywood phoniness," Kubrick told Jack Kroll. "When I lived there people would ask how it's going and you knew that what they hoped to hear was that you were behind schedule or had trouble with the star."

"You read books or see films that depict people being corrupted by Hollywood, but it isn't that," Kubrick told Cahill. "It's this tremendous sense of insecurity. A lot of destructive competitiveness. In comparison, England seems very remote. I try to keep up, read the trade papers, but it's good to get it on paper and not have to hear it every place you go. I think it's good to just do the work and insulate yourself from the undercurrent of low-level malevolence."

PART SIX

Infinity

CHAPTER 19

"What Has Happened to the Greatest Film Director This Country Ever Produced?"

I'm happy—at times—making films. I'm certainly unhappy not making films.

—Stanley Kubrick

Each month Stanley Kubrick isn't making a film is a loss to everybody.

—Sidney Lumet

A fter Stanley Kubrick completed nurturing *Full Metal Jacket* through its U.S. and international release, he settled back into his normal routine. Most film directors take a long vacation or holiday after finishing a film. Stanley Kubrick didn't take vacations. Following the rigors of a film in production, Kubrick engaged a standard operating procedure that remained constant. He began to check up on new releases by screening films he had missed during the last years of working around the clock on his own film. Kubrick attempted to see every film released to satisfy his deep affection for the cinema. He watched films alternately, as a fan, to gather information on technique and to study craftspeople and actors he might want to use on eventual projects. When he wasn't directly working on a film Kubrick devoted a lot of his time to reading magazines, newspapers, and books in search of his next and future films. He continued to be fascinated with chess and ordered Fritz and M-Chess software from Chess & Bridge Ltd. in London to test his skills against a computer. But Kubrick was invariably working, always developing new plans often without the awareness of the public and the press.

Stanley Kubrick releases films at long intervals and carefully proceeds with his business away from the unblinking eye of the publicity and media news frenzy. He might be misconstrued as a man out of touch and waning in his arc of influence, but as a commodity, the film director Stanley Kubrick has perpetual viability and has never fallen out of favor. Whereas many film directors of his generation have trouble getting phone calls returned, Kubrick remains a powerful filmmaking force. Actors, studio chiefs, agents, and craftspeople dream of getting a call from Stanley Kubrick. After twenty-five years, Warner Bros. continues to be his studio of choice, and the competition would jump at the chance to finance and distribute a Stanley Kubrick film.

An interlude between public knowledge of a Kubrick project and a long period of working in private have been part of the consistent Kubrick pattern for the three decades he has lived in England. Stanley Kubrick is driven by a single-minded search for the material that will satisfy the state of obsession he must reach to commit to his next film. During the years between films, Kubrick submits countless proposals to this examination. Research, plans, tests, and incessant discussions with experts inform each decision. Many projects are considered, some come close, but only those that satisfy Kubrick's literary, cinematic, philosophical, and psychological demands approach the films-in-preparation status.

In 1993, after many years of research and consideration of the options available to him, Kubrick began to move toward production of a new film. That April, *Variety* reported that Kubrick was planning to shoot a new project in Eastern Europe. Sources stated that the film would take place during the aftermath of the fall of the Berlin Wall and would center on a boy and a young woman on the road in Eastern Europe. Kubrick's office and Warner Bros. were silent and, as usual, would not confirm or deny the rumors. William Morris agent Scott Henderson confirmed that his client, Joseph Mazzello, the fine young actor who appeared in *Radio Flyer* and Spielberg's blockbuster *Jurassic Park*, had been asked to keep his summer schedule clear. The title of the project and the literary source on which it was based were secret. Mazzello and his agent did not see a script. The talented young actor appeared on TV's *Live with Regis and Kathie Lee*, where he confirmed that he was about to work with Stanley Kubrick. The only person known to have read the screenplay was Warner Bros. co-chairman Terry Semel. Kubrick would not send the script to California for fear the source material would be leaked and he would run the risk of having his story stolen or submitted as fodder for the competition. Semel was asked to fly to England, where he sat down in Kubrick's home and read the script. Reports pointed to Kubrick's interest in Julia Roberts and Uma Thurman for the part of the young woman. Scouts were sent to Poland, Hungary, and Slovakia to make inquiries about locations and facilities. The film was to have a one-hundred-day shooting schedule and possible base out of Bratislava, Slovakia. The project was on the studio schedule for Christmas 1994.

In May 1993, reports revealed that Kubrick's new film was based on Louis Begley's 1991 novel, *Wartime Lies*. The film was to take place in 1944 as a young boy, a Polish Jew, wandered the bombed-out countryside with his aunt. The shooting schedule had been pushed to September or October. Uma Thurman's agent reported he had not received a call from Kubrick's office concerning the project. Sources close to Julia Roberts confirmed she had been contacted by Kubrick, but the actress would not make a decision until she was given a script. An undisclosed Oscar-winning actress launched a campaign for the part by contacting Kubrick's office so often that staffers dubbed her "Attila the Hen."

Long interested in the subject, Kubrick had been looking for a novel on the Nazi era for more than ten years. Louis Begley's novel took place in 1939 in Poland. As the Third Reich invades the country, Maciek, the boy at the center of the story, is left an orphan dependent on his strong-willed aunt Tania. They pose as Catholic Poles watching as the Gestapo torments the ravaged Jewish community. They witness the destruction of Warsaw and escape the doomed city on a train headed for Auschwitz. They find a retreat on a peasant farm and survive the end of the war, but Maciek has not had a childhood that can help him face adulthood.

Wartime Lies is an ultimate Stanley Kubrick project. The novel was written in Maciek's voice and affords Kubrick the opportunity to tell the story in narration while showing the World War II terror through the boy's eyes. Begley's spare, poetic prose would allow Kubrick to create the haunting imagery of the nonstop, real-life terror wrought by the Nazis.

In October 1993 *Hollywood Reporter* revealed that *Wartime Lies* was to be shot on location in and around Aarhus, Denmark's second city. Shooting was to begin in February 1994. Kubrick's son-in-law, Philip Hobbs, production designer Roy Walker, and local film director Eva Bjerregaard scouted for locations to represent wartime Warsaw and Polish forests. More than two thousand photographs of the area were submitted to Kubrick for his approval. Kubrick had set up Hobby Films to produce the film, financed by Warner Brothers, which would distribute the film worldwide. The Danish Film Institute reported that it supplied Kubrick with "crates of videos of Danish feature films," possibly intended for research and casting. The crew was estimated at fifty and would also employ local technical talent in Denmark. Kubrick wrote a personal letter to Aarhus mayor Thorkild Simonsen expressing his "gratitude and relief" at having found a location and facilities to shoot his project. The central action of the film was to take place in the Warsaw ghetto, and the city of Aarhus would supply abandoned barracks and factories for Kubrick as well as facilities to house his production.

The project went through a title change. Kubrick named his new film *Aryan Papers*. Like *The Short-Timers, Wartime Lies* was not a commercially identifiable title as were *Lolita, A Clockwork Orange,* and *The Shining,* so Kubrick took the liberty of changing it.

In November 1993, Warner Bros. announced that Stanley Kubrick's next film was to be *AI*, the abbreviation for "artificial intelligence." This was reportedly a project that Kubrick had abandoned in 1991 after two years of research. At that time Kubrick had determined that the visuals for this science fiction project were beyond current special effects technology. Recent breakthroughs in computer and digital imaging as seen in *Jurassic Park* rekindled Kubrick's interest in the venture. Little information on the proposed project was released. The film would be set in the future when intelligent robots served in many capacities. The greenhouse effect had melted the ice caps, and many cities were under water. Manhattan's skyscrapers now had become monuments rearing up from the Atlantic Ocean. As far as *Aryan Papers* was concerned, Warners said that Kubrick would either produce and not direct the adaptation of Begley's *Wartime Lies* or direct it himself after completion of *AI. Aryan Papers* had been set to shoot in February 1994 in Denmark with a screenplay by Kubrick. Now the plans had shifted. When *Variety* reported the story, it had *AI* set on a post-apocalyptic New Jersey Shore.

In July 1994 *Premiere* magazine asked Cheryl Lee Terry, the numerologist for *Elle* magazine, to analyze Kubrick's handwritten signature. Terry found Kubrick to be a perfectionist, with fears and anxieties. The prominent S and K of his handwritten signature revealed him to be tenacious and obsessional. Kubrick's destiny number was eight, which Terry explained represented infinity and endowed the director with a spiritual and mystical side. Terry's perceptions closely followed Kubrick's personality, but she went out on a limb to predict that his numerology pointed toward the completion of a project in 1994 that would be considered a masterpiece. The year 1994 passed, and the world continued to wait for the next Stanley Kubrick film.

In the summer of 1995 Kubrick was reported to be talking to special effects master Dennis Muren at George Lucas's Industrial Light and Magic and to effects experts at Quantel. Rumors were spreading that *Aryan Papers* was canceled because of its similarity to Spielberg's *Schindler's List.* Likewise, *AI* had been shelved because it was too much like *Waterworld.* These theories seem unlikely since Kubrick made *Full Metal Jacket* after several major Vietnam releases, and his directorial vision on a project has never mirrored any other.

   AI was kept under the usual Kubrick top security. Rebecca Ascher-Walsh of *Entertainment Weekly* managed to get an unlisted phone number to Kubrick's office. She talked to an office assistant who introduced himself as Leon, possibly Leon Vitali. Ascher-Walsh left her number and a message. The call was never returned personally by Kubrick, and Leon "politely inquired to what criminal depths we had sunk to obtain the unlisted phone number."

   In 1995 a telephone conversation with Louis Begley, author of *Wartime Lies,* revealed little about the possibility of *Aryan Papers* or any project based on the book becoming a Stanley Kubrick film. Begley, a New York lawyer who also wrote *The Man Who Was Late, As Max Saw It,* and *About Schmidt,* had never met or spoken to Stanley Kubrick. Jan Harlan had approached Begley about the rights to *Wartime Lies* and the arrangements were made to secure the motion picture rights for Kubrick. Begley, an admirer of Kubrick's work, was not asked to write or cowrite the script.

   On December 15, 1995, the Warner Bros. News Department issued the following press release: "Stanley Kubrick's next film will be 'Eyes Wide Shut,' a story of jealousy and sexual obsession, starring Tom Cruise and Nicole Kidman. Filming was scheduled to start in London in the summer of 1996. Kubrick will produce and direct and has written the screenplay. Warner Bros. will distribute the film worldwide. Kubrick's previously announced science-fiction film, 'AI,' believed to be one of the most technically challenging and innovative special effects films yet attempted, is in the final stages of set design and special-effects development, and will follow 'Eyes Wide Shut.' "

Full Metal Jacket had been released in the summer of 1987. The *Eyes Wide Shut/AI* press release amplified the fact that it had been almost nine years since the arrival of a new Stanley Kubrick film and an announced start date was only the beginning of a shooting process that could last a year or more and a postproduction schedule that could take at least as long.

When Warner Bros. announced the production of *Eyes Wide Shut* and clarified years of rumors about *AI*, excitement spread about the director working with Hollywood's hottest couple, Nicole Kidman and Tom Cruise. On the Internet Kubrick fans argued whether the power couple was worthy of their master and word of the Kubrick-Kidman-Cruise collaboration swept through the media with no further known details.

Kubrick's directorial star had not lost any of its luster. Tom Cruise told *Newsweek* how he became involved in *Eyes Wide Shut* and described it as a psychological drama. "I got a fax one day saying there would be a script in a few months and would I be interested? It's just a damn miracle, that he wanted me and Nic to do this." Kubrick continued to attract megastars with the simple extension of an offer.

The *Hollywood Reporter* began to list *Eyes Wide Shut* as "(formerly Stanley Kubrick Untitled)" in their production listings and listed Frederic Raphael and Stanley Kubrick as the screenwriters.

Raphael is a noted novelist and screenwriter. The writer was born in Chicago in 1931 and has lived in England since early childhood. Raphael is the author of the novels *California Time, After the War, The Trouble with England,* and *The Glittering Prizes.* He has written the screenplays for *Darling, Two for the Road, Daisy Miller,* and *Far from the Madding Crowd.* He has also written plays for radio and television and has the kind of literacy and intelligence best suited to deal with Kubrick's complex method of creating a screen story, developing a screenplay during the shooting process, and evolving the structure until the postproduction process is deemed complete after exhausting all known possibilities.

An article in the January 1996 *Premiere* magazine added to the rumors surrounding *AI*, stating that the project may have been renamed *Supertoys*, based on a story by science fiction writer Brian Aldiss. The popular film magazine shared the feelings of Kubrick aficionados all over the world by saying, "For fans awaiting the first true digital work of art, the master can't reemerge soon enough." The Aldiss short story, "Super-Toys Last All Summer Long," was written in 1969 and contains the robot element of Kubrick's proposed *AI* and not the story line about the greenhouse effect and overpopulation. Alexander Walker has reported that Kubrick was interested in doing a science fiction film based on an Isaac Asimov story. Stanley Kubrick continues to keep a good secret. A look back at his previous films and their original press reports validates the director's ability to keep his work largely under wraps. The *Premiere* article continues to reaffirm Kubrick's soaring stature in the international film community. The article profiled fifteen individuals who were defining the high-tech future of the cinema. Kubrick was christened "Messiah."

It may be almost a decade since his last film was released, but Stanley Kubrick, one of the greatest film directors produced by the United States, is still out there making movies. He is living in England, doesn't travel much, doesn't do lunch, is rarely seen by an electronically connected global public, and doesn't do a film a year, or every two years, or even every three. Stanley Kubrick may not be on *Entertainment Tonight,* in the audience at the Oscars or at the Cannes Film Festival, but don't be fooled—Stanley Kubrick is still out there. He is thinking about movies, he is researching projects, he's testing technology. He's reading and reading. He's asking questions, many questions. He's looking at photographs and maps and charts. Stanley Kubrick is out there making movies. He'll be out there making movies, and international audiences will be waiting to see what he has to reveal with his cinematic imagination—until he isn't out there anymore.

Acknowledgments

I must begin by thanking Stanley Kubrick for his work and films and for providing a life filled with imagination, artistic and technical brilliance and depth. My subject has filled me with decades of wonder and increased my faith in the unlimited potential of the cinematic medium.

This is neither an officially authorized nor officially unauthorized biography. Mr. Kubrick was sent a letter asking him to facilitate access to individuals who sought his approval before they would be interviewed and for the cooperation of his office on matters of fact. This letter and copies of my books on the art of the film crafts were sent to England through the good graces of Kubrick's longtime friend and colleague, Roger Caras, currently president of the American Society for the Prevention of Cruelty to Animals. I thank Mr. Caras for his kindness in forwarding my correspondence to Stanley Kubrick. A response was not received with either a yea or nay to my requests. Mr. Kubrick has neither helped nor interfered with my efforts on this project. I thank Stanley Kubrick for not making a challenging task more difficult.

Research for this book involved primary and secondary sources in many archives, libraries, in clippings and in articles written over the course of Kubrick's career. These primary and secondary sources as well as original scholarship are identified in the chapter notes. The original interviews were conducted in person, on the phone and through correspondence with people who have known and worked with Stanley Kubrick. The insights of those who selflessly gave of their time to talk to me about Stanley Kubrick were invaluable in understanding a man and filmmaker who has become a myth to the public at large and to the international film community. Through these talks, which ranged from minutes to hours to days emerged the man behind the legend. I thank the following for their faith and trust in sharing the personal, private and professional experiences they had with Stanley Kubrick: Claire Abriss, Ken Adam, Richard Anderson, Louis Begley, Steven Berkoff, Simon Bourgin, Alice Brewer Brown, Tony Burton, Vincent Cartier, Wendy Carlos, Jonathan Cecil, Bernard Cooperman, Harriet Daniels, Jane de Rochemont, Ed Di Giulio, Keir Dullea, Gerald Fried, Bob Gaffney, Betty Garbus, Lou Garbus, Stanley Getzler, Max Glenn, Gay Hamilton, James B. Harris, Anthony Harvey, Peter Hollander, Faith Hubley, Anne Jackson, Gerald Jacobson, Loren Janes, Joseph Laitin, Robert Lawrence, John Lee, Norman Lloyd, Richard May, Robert Sandelman, G. Warren Schloat, Jr., Valda Setterfield, Howard Silver, Donald Silverman, Alexander Singer, Rose Spano, Tony Spiridakis, Harry Sternberg, Philip Stone, Richard Sylbert, Marvin Traub, Daniel Traister, Clifford Vogel, David Vaughan, and Marie Windsor.

Interviews conducted for my books on the film crafts with Ken Adam, John Bonner, Garrett Brown, Don Rogers, and Frank Warner were significant in supplying valuable information for this project.

I am indebted to those writers who came before me in examining the work of Stanley Kubrick. The following books helped fuel my insatiable thirst for information on Kubrick over the last twenty-five years and were essential in providing data, sources and solid background for my work on this biography: *Stanley Kubrick Directs* by Alexander Walker, *Kubrick* by Michel Ciment, *Stanley Kubrick: A Film Odyssey* by Gene D. Phillips, *The Cinema of Stanley Kubrick* by Norman Kagan, *Kubrick: Inside A Film Artist's Maze* by Thomas Allen Nelson, *The Film Director As Superstar* by Joseph Gelmis, *The Making of Kubrick's 2001* by Jerome Agel, *2001: Filming the Future* by Piers Bizony and *Stanley Kubrick: A Narrative and Stylistic Analysis* by Mario Falsetto. I thank all for their scholarship, insights and information.

Archives, libraries and records repositories and their staffs across the United States and in England were essential in providing valued information for my research. They include: Sam Gill, Barbara Hall and the entire staff of The Margaret Herrick Library in Los Angeles, Charles Silver and Ron Magliozzi of the Film Study Center of The Museum of Modern Art in New York, The Staff of the New York Public Library for the Performing Arts Research Collection at Lincoln Center, Stuart Ng, Archivist of the Warner Bros. Collection at the University of Southern California and the entire staff of the Doheny Library, Beverly Brannen Curator of Photography at the Library of Congress, Madeline F. Matz, Film and Television Research Librarian, Motion Picture Broadcasting and Recorded Sound Division of the Library of Congress and her staff, Alan Dein of BBC Radio, Ella Abney, librarian, Medical Society of the State of New York, Laura Tosi, librarian, The Bronx County Historical Society, James Gerlich, archives assistant, New York Hospital/Cornell Medical Center, Art and Architecture Library of Yale University, Judy Myers, the Rare Books Collection, Medical Sciences Library of New York Medical College, Lawrence Campbell, archivist of the Art Students League of New York, Jill Abraham, archives technician, Motion Picture, Sound and Video Branch, National Archives at College Park, Maryland, Richard Sydenham of the United Nations, Professor Shawn Rosenheim, Williams College, Nan Farinkoff of the California State Pharmacy Board. Karen Mix, Boston University Library, Rick Ewig, Manager, Reference Services of the American Heritage Center of the University of Wyoming, Kathy Crawford of the LaRue County Public Library, American Society of Media Photographers, Cathy Webb, Interlibrary Loan Program, Elizabeth Cornely, Periodicals and Sharon Cohen and Linda Armstrong, Reference Librarians of The Mount Vernon Public

Library, Bill Schilling, reference department of the Albany Public Library, East-chester Public Library, and the Greenwich Library in Connecticut, Sarah Lawrence College Library and the New York Public Library at 42nd Street.

My thanks to the staffs of many periodicals who supplied information concerning Stanley Kubrick and his work: Stephen Pizzello, executive editor of American Cinematographer Magazine and effects maven, Ron Magid, Roy Frumkes, editor of Films In Review, Malcolm Pein, publisher of Chess Magazine in London, the Courier-Journal in LaRue County, Charles McGrath and the New York Times Book Review for their valuable assistance in publishing my query request, Martin Singerman, Publisher of the New York Post for introduction to interview subjects, Publishers and Editors Stephen M. Samtur and Susan H. Samtur at Back in the Bronx, for providing a publication with such a wealth of information concerning Kubrick's birth borough and coming-of-age residence.

Many individuals were unconditional in their support of this book and its author and supplied essential information. I sincerely thank: Everett Aison for his mentoring, friendship, valuable information and contact with key interview subjects, Michael Brashinsky, Roberta Burrows, Paul Clemens for his extensive knowledge of Kubrick lore and for screening Vivian Kubrick's *The Making of "The Shining,"* for me, cinematographer Alan Daviau for sharing his wealth of knowledge on film history and Stanley Kubrick, Mrs. Paul Falkenberg, Dana Fishkin for his professionalism and steady support, Morton Gottlieb for talking to me about the charade parties Diane Arbus brought Stanley Kubrick to, Manil Gunawardene, personal secretary to Dr. Arthur C. Clarke and the good doctor for information and good wishes, John Joyce for his support and information on military matters, James D. LaRue, Edward Lewis, Nora Linn, Shelby Lyman for sharing his extensive knowledge about the chess world, Joel Miller Esq., Nihal of Fox Limousine Service for expert and courteous chauffeuring and information on Dr. Arthur C. Clarke and Sri Lanka, Marilyn Perlman, Bob Phillips, Charles Reynolds for sharing his extensive knowledge of still photography, Joe Rosner for his valuable publishing knowledge and information concerning *Dr. Strangelove,* film director Michael Ritchie for information on Kubrick's participation on the Lincoln *Omnibus* program, Grace Rothstein, Robert Saudek, Larry Schwartz for astute knowledge and advice on the art of archival photographs, Le See of GFI Computer Service, Fanchon Scheier, Jonathan Stern, Roseanne Spano Swider, film historian extraordinaire, Gene Stavis, for his encyclopedic knowledge on all things filmic, Ed Tassinari for detailed information on Kubrick's background in chess, Tony Walton, Freda Welsh, President, Evi Allen, Vice President of the Westport Film Society for their constant support and information concerning interview subjects, Jay Harris Esq., Max Wild Esq, Joseph Winston Esq. and Steve Siegel for his generous genealogical advice.

Many others contributed assistance much appreciated: Nina Lesser for locating a rare panel discussion recording of *A Clockwork Orange,* my colleague and friend, Ed Bowes, for video assistance, The Cinema Bookshop in London for finding rare books, Dr. Manhinderjit Singh for his wisdom and Amos Vogel for background on his groundbreaking screening venue, the legendary Cinema 16.

I thank the community of writers who continually inspire me and especially thank Jerome Agel, not only for his landmark book *The Making of Kubrick's 2001: A Space Odyssey,* but for his support and valuable research and interview leads, Patricia Bosworth for leads regarding Kubrick and Diane Arbus, John Andrew Gallagher for encouragement, support and entrée to interview subjects, Patrick McGilligan for his telephonic and written messages of support and confidence and for welcoming me into the lodge, David Weddle for leading me to valuable information concerning Kubrick and his work on the Omnibus series and for a spirited discussion about Stanley Kubrick and Sam Peckinpah and Gary Carey, an early mentor for his patience and inspiration.

Written material on Stanley Kubrick appears internationally. I would like to thank several translators for their exacting work: David Abunaw and Joseph K. Bannauti for translating several pieces on Kubrick in French, Simone Olmsted for her expertise in presenting the glorious French language as contained in personal interviews and my daughter, Rebecca Morrison, for deciphering the semi-faux Russian spoken in *2001.*

I sadly acknowledge the passing of Saul Bass, John Bonner, Vince Edwards and Herman Getter during the writing of this book. I thank them for sharing their recollections of Stanley Kubrick with me.

Several researchers uncovered valuable data and articles for my work. I thank Amanda Donnellan for her research on Kubrick's work at *Look,* Michael Pisani for locating many critical articles and John Sawyer and Jeffrey Roenning for assisting me in library research. Genealogist and researcher Estelle Guzik provided valuable background information on the Kubrick family which was essential to the development of the early section of this book. I thank her for understanding all things genealogical concerning this project.

My work as an instructor and thesis adviser for the Department of Film, Video and Animation at the School of Visual Arts in New York continues to feed my passion for film history and cinema education. I thank my Chairman, Reeves Lehmann, for his constant unconditional support of my work and for opening many doors during this project, Salvatore Petrosino, Director of Operations for his friendship, countless spirited discussions and introduction to interview subjects. I thank all of my students at SVA past and present who continue to inspire me with their enthusiasm and inform me with their thoughts. Their support and interest has helped me to see the importance of this book. So many of my students have contributed to this book by listening and sharing insights about Stanley Kubrick. I especially thank Shiho Kataoka, Adil Mohammed, Dixie Serrano and Randy Wilcox for information and research materials.

For expert and caring representation I thank Ellen Levine and the entire staff at the Ellen Levine Literary Agency, especially my original agent, Anne Dubuisson, who believed in me and this project until it found its home, and my current agent Diana Finch for her care and for piloting the manuscript through the production process. I also thank her assistant Jay Rogers for his support.

I want to thank my publisher Donald I. Fine for his belief in this project and trust in its author. My thanks to the entire staff of Donald I. Fine, Inc., my original editor Jason Poston for his editorial expertise on the early stages of the manuscript and to my current editor Tom Burke for skillful handling of the final manuscript and seeing it through the production process. I also want to thank the staff at Penguin USA for the care and expertise they have given this project.

I thank my parents Rose and Anthony LoBrutto for their love and unconditional support, my daughter Rebecca Morrison for constantly reminding me of the definition of determination and my son Alexander Morrison for sharing a cultural and artistic knowledge which is well beyond his years.

In thanking my wife, Harriet Morrison, I will try to be brief, a difficult task in acknowledging the tremendous impact she has made on my life and life's work. She has been instrumental in providing research, facts, avenues of possibility, interview subjects, reams of data and above all—good taste—in everything she has touched in relation to this project. Harriet was this book's first reader and has listened to more theories, speeches, ideas, narrative and conceptual principles connected to the life and films of Stanley Kubrick (and the cinema in general) than can be humanly tolerated by those not totally obsessed, as I am, with the subject. She has kept our lives in order and given me the ability to devote myself to this project. I thank Harriet for her literary and humane contributions and love her for selflessly seeing me through my own Ultimate Trip through the Star Gate.

Filmography

1951

Day of the Fight

RKO-Pathé, Inc., Presents *This Is America. Producer:* Jay Bonafield. *Director:* Stanley Kubrick. *Script:* Robert Rein. *Editor:* Julian Bergman. *Music:* Gerald Fried. *Narrator:* Douglas Edwards. *Running time:* 16 minutes. Black and white. *Note:* Kubrick states he photographed, edited, and did the sound editing on the film.

Flying Padre

RKO-Pathé, Inc., Presents An RKO-Pathe Screenliner. *Producer:* Burton Benjamin. *Director:* Stanley Kubrick. *Editor:* Isaac Kleinerman. *Music:* Nathaniel Shilkret. *Narrator:* Bob Hite. *Sound:* Harold R. Vivian. *Running time:* 8 minutes 30 seconds. Black and white. *Note:* Kubrick states he photographed, edited, and did the sound editing on the film.

1953

The Seafarers

Presented by the Seafarers International Union, Atlantic and Gulf Coast District, AFL. *Producer:* Lester Cooper. *Directed and photographed by* Stanley Kubrick. *Written by* Will Chasan. Technical assistance by the staff of the *Seafarers Log. Narrator:* Don Hollenbeck. *Running time:* 30 minutes. Color.

Fear and Desire

Distributed by Joseph Burstyn, Inc. *Produced, photographed, and edited by* Stanley Kubrick. *Associate producer:* Martin Perveler. *Screenplay:* Howard O. Sackler. *Music:* Gerald Fried. *Unit manager:* Bob Dierks. *Assistant director:* Steve Hahn. *Makeup:* Chet Fabian. *Art director:* Herbert Lebowitz. *Title design:* Barney Ettengoff. *Dialogue director:* Toba Kubrick. *Cast:* Frank Silvera (Mac), Kenneth Harp (Corby/General), Paul Mazursky (Sidney), Steve Coit (Fletcher/aide), Virginia Leith (The Girl), David Allen (Narrator). *Running time:* 68 minutes. Black and white.

1955

Killer's Kiss

Released through United Artists. A Minotaur Production. *Producers:* Stanley Kubrick, Morris Bousel. *Edited, photographed, and directed by* Stanley Kubrick. *Story:* Stanley Kubrick. *Music composed and conducted by* Gerald Fried. *Production manager:* Ira Marvin. *Camera operators:* Jesse Paley, Max Glenn. *Chief electrician:* Dave Golden. *Sound recordists:* Walter Ruckersberg, Clifford van Praag. *Assistant editors:* Pat Jaffe, Anthony Bezich. *Assistant director:* Ernest Nukanen. *Sound by* Titra Sound Studio. Love theme from the song "Once" by Norman Gimbel and Arden Clar. Ballet sequence danced by Ruth Sobotka. *Choreography:* David Vaughan. *Cast:* Frank Silvera (Vincent Rapallo), Jamie Smith (Davey Gordon), Irene Kane (Gloria Price), Jerry Jarret (Albert), Mike Dana, Felice Orlandi, Ralph Roberts, Phil Stevenson (gangsters), Skippy Adelman (owner of mannequin factory), David Vaughan, Alec Rubin (conventioneers), Ruth Sobotka (Iris), Shaun O'Brien, Barbara Brand, Arthur Feldman, Bill Funaro. *Running time:* 67 minutes. Black and white. *Note:* Howard O. Sackler worked on the screenplay uncredited.

1956

The Killing

A Harris-Kubrick presentation. Released through United Artists. *Producer:* James B. Harris. *Associate producer:* Alexander Singer. *Director:* Stanley Kubrick. *Screenplay:* Stanley Kubrick. *Dialogue:* Jim Thompson. Based on the novel *Clean Break* by Lionel White. *Director of photography:* Lucien Ballard, A.S.C. *Art director:* Ruth Sobotka. *Film editor:* Betty Steinberg. *Music composed and conducted by* Gerald Fried. *Wardrobe:* Jack Masters. *Special effects:* Dave Koehler. *Camera operator:* Dick Tower. *Gaffer:* Bobby Jones. *Head grip:* Carl Gibson. *Script supervisor:* Mary Gibsone. *Sound:* Earl Snyder. *Best boy:* Lou Cortese. *Second assistant cameraman:* Robert Hosler. *Construction supervisor:* Bud Pine. *Chief carpenter:* Christopher Ebsen. *Chief painter:* Robert L. Stephen. *Makeup:* Robert Littlefield. *Set decorator:* Harry Reif. *Assistant set deco-

rator: Carl Brainard. *Music editor:* Gilbert Marchant. *Sound effects editor:* Rex Lipton, M.P.S.E. *Assistant director:* Milton Carter. *Second assistant directors:* Paul Feiner, Howard Joslin. *Production assistant:* Marguerite Olson. *Propman:* Ray Zambel. *Transportation:* Dave Lesser. *Women's wardrobe:* Rudy Harrington. *Hairdresser:* Lillian Shore. *Process cameraman:* Paul Eagler. *Director's assistant:* Joyce Hartman. *Marie Windsor's costumes:* Beaumelle. *Photographic effects:* Jack Rabin, Louis DeWitt. *Sound:* RCA Sound System. *Cast:* Sterling Hayden (Johnny Clay), Coleen Gray (Fay), Vince Edwards (Val Cannon), Jay C. Flippen (Marvin Unger), Ted DeCorsia (Randy Kennan), Marie Windsor (Sherry Peatty), Elisha Cook, Jr. (George Peatty), Joe Sawyer (Mike O'Reilly), Timothy Carey (Nikki Arane), Kola Kwariani (Maurice Oboukhoff), Jay Adler (Leo), Joseph Turkel (Tiny), James Edwards (parking lot attendent), Tito Vuolo, Dorothy Adams, Herbert Ellis, James Griffith, Cecil Elliot, Steve Mitchell, Mary Carroll, William Benedict, Charles R. Cane, Robert B. Williams. *Running time:* 83 minutes. Black and white.

1957

Paths of Glory

Released through United Artists. A Bryna Productions presentation. *Producer:* James B. Harris. *Director:* Stanley Kubrick. *Screenplay:* Stanley Kubrick, Calder Willingham, and Jim Thompson. Based on the novel *Paths of Glory* by Humphrey Cobb. *Photographed by* George Krause. *Art director:* Ludwig Reiber. *Film editor:* Eva Kroll. *Music:* Gerald Fried. *Costume designer:* Ilse Dubois. *Special effects:* Erwin Lange. *Unit manager:* Helmut Ringelmann. *Assistant directors:* H. Stumpf, D. Sensburg, F. Spieker. *Script clerk:* Trudy von Trotha. *Sound:* Martin Muller. *Military adviser:* Baron V. Waldenfels. *Assistant editor:* Helene Fischer. *Camera grip:* Hans Elsinger. *Makeup:* Arthur Schramm. Produced at Bavaria Filmkunst Studios—Munich. *Camera operator:* Hannes Staudinger. *American production manager:* John Pommer. *German production manager:* George von Block. *Cast:* Kirk Douglas (Colonel Dax), Ralph Meeker (Corporal Paris), Adolphe Menjou (General Broulard), George Macready (General Mireau), Wayne Morris (Lieutenant Roget), Richard Anderson (Major Saint-Auban), Joseph Turkel (Arnaud), Timothy Carey (Ferol), Peter Capell (Judge), Susanne Christian (young German girl), Bert Freed (Sergeant Boulanger), Emile Meyer (priest), Ken Dibbs (Lejeune), Jerry Hausner (Meyer), Fred Bell (wounded soldier), Harold

Benedict (Sergeant Nichols), John Stein (Captain Rousseau). *Running time:* 86 minutes. Black and white.

1960

Spartacus

Released through Universal International. A Bryna Productions, Inc., presentation. *Producer:* Edward Lewis. *Executive producer:* Kirk Douglas. *Directed by* Stanley Kubrick. *Screenplay:* Dalton Trumbo. Based on the novel by Howard Fast. *Director of photography:* Russell Metty, A.S.C. Technicolor. Filmed in Super Technirama-70. Lenses by Panavision. *Production designer:* Alexander Golitzen. *Art director:* Eric Orbom. *Set decorations:* Russell A. Gausman, Julia Heron. *Film editor:* Robert Lawrence. *Music composed and conducted by* Alex North. *Costumes:* Valles. *Assistant director:* Marshall Green. *Main titles and design consultant:* Saul Bass. *Sound:* Waldon O. Watson, Joe Lapis, Murray Spivack, Ronald Pierce. *Historical and technical advisor:* Vittorio Nino Novarese. *Unit production manager:* Norman Deming. *Additional scenes photographed by* Clifford Stine, A.S.C. *Production aide:* Stan Margulies. *Wardrobe:* Peruzzi. *Miss Simmons's costumes:* Bill Thomas. *Assistants to the film editor:* Robert Schulte, Fred Chulack. *Score co-conducted by* Joseph Gershenson. *Music editor:* Arnold Schwarzwald. *Makeup:* Bud Westmore. *Hair stylist:* Larry Germain. *Cast:* Kirk Douglas (Spartacus), Laurence Olivier (Marcus Crassus), Jean Simmons (Varinia), Charles Laughton (Gracchus), Peter Ustinov (Lentulus Batiatus), John Gavin (Julius Caesar), Nina Foch (Helena), John Ireland (Crixus), Herbert Lom (Tigranes), John Dall (Glabrus), Charles McGraw (Marcellus), Joanna Barnes (Claudia), Harold J. Stone (David), Woody Strode (Draba), Peter Brocco (Ramon), Paul Lambert (Gannicus), Robert J. Wilke (captain of the guard), Nicholas Dennis (Dionysius), John Hoyt (Roman officer), Frederic Worlock (Laelius), Tony Curtis (Antoninus), Dayton Lummis (Symmachus), Jill Jarmyn, Jo Summers. *Running time:* 184 minutes. Color; *restored version (1992):* 196 minutes.

1962

Lolita

A Metro-Goldwyn-Mayer presentation in association with Seven Arts Productions. An Anya Production S.A.—Transworld Pictures S.A. Production. James B. Harris and Stanley Kubrick's Lolita. *Producer:* James

B. Harris. *Director:* Stanley Kubrick. *Screenplay:* Vladimir Nabokov based on his novel *Lolita*. *Director of photography:* Oswald Morris, B.S.C. *Art director:* Bill Andrews. *Editor:* Anthony Harvey. *Music composed and conducted by* Nelson Riddle. "Lolita" theme by Bob Harris. *Orchestrations:* Gil Grau. *Production supervisor:* Raymond Anzarut. *Wardrobe supervisor:* Elsa Fennell. *Miss Winters' costumes by* Gene Coffin. *Assistant art director:* Sidney Cain. *Production manager:* Robert Sterne. *Assistant director:* Rene Dupont. *Camera operator:* Denys N. Coop. *Continuity:* Pamela Davies. *Dubbing editor:* Winston Ryder. *Sound recordists:* Len Shilton, H. L. Bird. *Casting director:* James Liggat. *Makeup:* George Partleton. *Hairdresser:* Betty Galsow. *Second-unit director:* Dennis Stock. *Assistant editor:* Lois Gray. *Titles by* Chambers and Partners. Produced at Associated British Studios, Elstree, England. *Production secretary:* Joan Purcell. *Producer's secretary:* Josephine Baker. *Production accountant:* Jack Smith. *Assistant accountant:* Doreen Wood. *Secretaries:* Jack Smith, Jennifer Halford. *Second assistant director:* Ray Millichip. *Third assistant director:* Joan Sanischewsky. *Director's secretary:* Stella Magee. *Special writer:* David Sylvester. *Assistant continuity:* Joyce Herlihy. *Focus puller:* Jimmy Turrell. *Clapper loader:* Michael Rutter. *Camera grip:* A. Osborne, W. Thompson. *Second assistant editor:* W. W. Armor. *Chief draughtsman:* Frank Wilson. *Draughtsmen:* John Siddal, Roy Dorman. *Scenic artist:* A. Van Montagu. *Set decorator:* Andrew Low. *Set dresser:* Peter James. *Construction manager:* Harry Phipps. *Wardrobe mistress:* Barbara Gillett. *Wardrobe assistant:* Wyn Keeley. *Assistant makeup:* Stella Morris. *Production buyer:* Terry Parr. *Unit publicist:* Enid Jones. *Assistant boom operators:* Peter Carnody, T. Staples. *Sound maintenance:* L. Grimmel, Jack Lovelace. *Boom operator:* Dan Wortham. *Stills:* Joe Pearce. *Publicity secretary:* Amy Allen. *Cast:* James Mason (Humbert Humbert), Shelley Winters (Charlotte Haze), Sue Lyon (Lolita), Peter Sellers (Clare Quilty), Gary Cockrell (Dick), Diana Decker (Jean Farlow), Jerry Stovin (John Farlow), Suzanne Gibbs (Mona Farlow), Lois Maxwell (Nurse Mary Lore), Bill Greene (George Swine), Shirley Douglas (Mrs. Starch), Marianne Stone (Vivian Darkbloom), Marion Mathie (Miss Lebone), James Dyrenforth (Beale), Maxine Holden (hospital receptionist), John Harrison (Tom), Colin Maitland (Charlie), C. Denier Warren (Potts), Roland Brand (Bill), Roberta Shore (Lorna), Cec Linder (doctor), Isobel Lucas (Louise), Eric Lane (Roy), Irvin Allen (hospital intern), Craig Sams (Rex), Terence Kilburn. *Running time:* 152 minutes. Black and white.

1964

Dr. Strangelove or: How I Learned to Stop Worrying and Love the Bomb.

A Columbia Pictures Corporation presentation. A Stanley Kubrick production. *Producer:* Stanley Kubrick. *Associate producer:* Victor Lyndon. *Director:* Stanley Kubrick. *Screenplay:* Stanley Kubrick, Terry Southern and Peter George. Based on the book *Red Alert* by Peter George. *Director of photography:* Gilbert Taylor, B.S.C. *Production designer:* Ken Adam. *Art director:* Peter Murton. *Film editor:* Anthony Harvey. *Music:* Laurie Johnson. *Wardrobe:* Bridget Sellers. *Special effects:* Wally Veevers. *Camera operator:* Kelvin Pike. *Camera assistant:* Bernard Ford. *Production manager:* Clifton Brandon. *Assistant director:* Eric Rattray. *Continuity:* Pamela Carlton. *Dubbing mixer:* John Aldred. *Makeup:* Stewart Freeborn. *Traveling Matte:* Vic Margutti. *Sound editor:* Leslie Hodgson. *Hairdresser:* Barbara Ritchie. *Recordist:* Richard Bird. *Assistant editor:* Ray Lovejoy. *Aviation adviser:* Captain John Crewdson. *Sound supervisor:* John Cox. *Assembly editor:* Geoffrey Fry. *Main titles:* Pablo D. Ferro. Made at Shepperton Studios, England, by Hawk Films, Ltd. A Hawk Film. *Cast:* Peter Sellers (Group Capt. Lionel Mandrake/President Muffley/Dr. Strangelove), George C. Scott (General "Buck" Turgidson), Sterling Hayden (General Jack D. Ripper), Keenan Wynn (Colonel "Bat" Guano), Slim Pickens (Major T. J. "King" Kong), Peter Bull (Ambassador de Sadesky), James Earl Jones (Lieutenant Lothar Zogg), Tracy Reed (Miss Scott), Jack Creley (Mr. Staines), Frank Berry (Lieutenant H. R. Dietrich), Robert O'Neil (Admiral Randolf), Roy Stephens (Frank), Glen Beck (Lieutenant W. D. Kival), Shane Rimmer (Captain G. A. "Ace" Owens), Paul Tamarin (Lieutenant B. Goldberg), Gordon Tanner (General Faceman), John McCarthy, Laurence Herder, Hal Galili (members of Burpelson Defense Team). *Running time:* 93 minutes. Black and white.

1968

2001: A Space Odyssey

Metro-Goldwyn-Mayer presents A Stanley Kubrick Production. *Producer:* Stanley Kubrick. *Director:* Stanley Kubrick. *Screenplay:* Stanley Kubrick and Arthur C. Clarke. *Director of photography:* Geoffrey Unsworth, B.S.C. *Additional photography:* John Alcott. *Production designers:* Tony Masters, Harry Lange, Ernest Archer. *Film editor:* Ray Lovejoy.

Music: Aram Khatchaturian, *Gayane* ballet performed by the Leningrad Philharmonic Orchestra conducted by Gennadi Rozhdestvensky, courtesy Deutsche Gramophon. Gyorgy Ligeti, *Atmosphères,* performed by the Southwest German Radio Orchestra conducted by Ernest Bour; *Lux Aeterna,* performed by the Stuttgart State Orchestra conducted by Clytus Gottwald; *Requiem,* performed by the Bavarian Radio Orchestra conducted by Francis Travis. Johann Strauss, The "Blue Danube," performed by the Berlin Philharmonic Orchestra conducted by Herbert Von Karajan, Courtesy Deutsche Grammophon. Richard Strauss, *Also Sprach Zarathustra,* performed by the Berlin Philharmonic Orchestra conducted by Karl Bohm. *Special photographic effects* designed and directed by Stanley Kubrick. *Special photographic effects supervisors:* Wally Veevers, Douglas Trumbull, Con Pederson, Tom Howard. *Wardrobe:* Hardy Amies. *First assistant director:* Derek Cracknell. *Special photographic effects unit:* Colin J. Cantwell, Bruck Logan, Bryan Loftus, David Osborne, Frederick Martin, John Jack Malick. Technicolor. Metrocolor. *Camera operator:* Kelvin Pike. *Art director:* John Hoesli. *Sound editor:* Winston Ryder. *Makeup:* Stuart Freeborn. *Editorial assistant:* David De Wilde. *Sound supervisor:* A. W. Watkins. *Sound mixer:* H. L. Bird. *Chief dubbing mixer.* J. B. Smith. *Scientific consultant:* Frederick I. Ordway III. Filmed in Super Panavision. Made at MGM British Studios, Ltd., Boreham Wood, England. In Cinerama. Distributed by MGM. *Cast:* Keir Dullea (David Bowman), Gary Lockwood (Frank Poole), William Sylvester (Dr. Heywood Floyd), Daniel Richter (Moon-Watcher), Leonard Rossiter (Smyslov), Margaret Tyzack (Elena), Robert Beatty (Halvorsen), Sean Sullivan (Michaels), Douglas Rain (voice of HAL 9000), Frank Miller (Mission Controller), Vivian Kubrick (Dr. Floyd's daughter), Alan Gifford (Poole's father), Penny Brahms (stewardess), Bill Weston, Edward Bishop, Glenn Beck, Ann Gillis, Edwina Carroll, Heather Downham, Mike Lovell, John Ashley, Peter Delmar, David Hines, Darryl Paes, Jimmy Bell, Terry Duggan, Tony Jackson, Joe Refalo, David Charkham, David Fleetwood, John Jordan, Andy Wallace, Simon Davis, Danny Grover, Scott Mackee, Bob Wilyman, Jonathan Daw, Brian Hawley, Laurence Marchant, Richard Wood. *Running time:* 139 minutes. Color.

1971

A Clockwork Orange

Warner Bros. presents A Stanley Kubrick Production. *Producer:* Stanley Kubrick. *Executive Producers:* Max L. Raab, Si Litvinoff. *Associate Pro-*

ducer: Bernard Williams. *Assistant to the producer:* Jan Harlan. *Director:* Stanley Kubrick. *Screenplay:* Stanley Kubrick. Based on the novel by Anthony Burgess. *Lighting cameraman:* John Alcott. *Production designer:* John Barry. *Editor:* Bill Butler. *Electronic music composed and realized by* Walter Carlos. Symphony No. 9 in D Minor, Opus 125, by Ludwig van Beethoven; Overtures to *The Thieving Magpie* and *William Tell* by Gioacchino Rossini; recorded by Deutsche Grammophon Gesellschaft. *Pomp and Circumstance* Marches No. 1 and 4 by Edward Elgar, conducted by Marcus Dods. "Singin' in the Rain" by Arthur Freed and Nacio Herb Brown, from the MGM picture, performed by Gene Kelly. "Overture to the Sun," composed by Terry Tucker. Song: "I Want to Marry a Lighthouse Keeper," composed and performed by Erika Eigen. *Costume designer:* Milena Canonero. *Consultant on hair and coloring:* Leonard of London. *Sound editor:* Brian Blamey. *Sound recordist:* John Jordan. *Dubbing mixers:* Bill Rowe, Eddie Haben. *Art directors:* Russell Hagg, Peter Shields. *Wardrobe supervisor:* Ron Beck. *Stunt arranger:* Roy Scammell. *Special paintings and sculpture:* Herman Makkink, Cornelius Makkink, Liz Moore, Christiane Kubrick. *Casting:* Jimmy Liggat. *Location manager:* Terence Clegg. *Supervising electrician:* Frank Wardale. *Assistant directors:* Derek Cracknell, Dusty Symonds. *Construction manager:* Bill Welch. *Prop master:* Frank Bruton. *Assistant editors:* Gary Shepherd, Peter Burgess, David Beesley. *Camera operators:* Ernie Day, Mike Molloy. *Focus puller:* Ron Drinkwater. *Camera assistants:* Laurie Frost, David Lenham. *Boom operator:* Peter Glossop. *Grips:* Don Budge, Tony Cridlin. *Electricians:* Louis Bogue, Derek Gatrell. *Prop men:* Peter Hancock, Tommy Ibbetson, John Oliver. *Promotion coordinator:* Mike Kaplan. *Production accountant:* Len Barnard. *Continuity:* June Randall. *Hairdresser:* Olga Angelinetta. *Makeup:* Fred Williamson, George Partleton, Barbara Daly. *Production secretary:* Loretta Ordewer. *Director's secretary:* Kay Johnson. *Production assistant:* Andros Epaminondas. *Location liaison:* Arthur Morgan. *Technical adviser:* John Marshall. *With special acknowledgment to:* Braun AG Frankfurt, Dolby Laboratories, Inc., Kontakt Werkstaetten, Ryman Conran Limited, Steinheimer Leuchtenindustrie, Temde AG. Made at Pinewood Studios, London, England, at EMI-MGM Studios, Boreham Wood, Herts., England, and on location in England by Hawk Films, Limited. Distributed by Warner Bros. A Warner Communications Company. *Cast:* Malcolm McDowell (Alex), Patrick Magee (Mr. Alexander), Michael Bates (chief guard), Warren Clarke (Dim), John Clive (stage actor), Adrienne Corri (Mrs. Alexander), Carl Duering (Dr. Brodsky), Paul Farrell (tramp), Clive Francis (lodger), Michael Gover (prison governor), Miriam

Karlin (Cat Lady), James Marcus (Georgie), Aubrey Morris (Deltoid), Godfrey Quigley (prison chaplain), Sheila Raynor (Mum), Madge Ryan (Dr. Branom), John Savident (conspirator), Anthony Sharp (minister), Philip Stone (Dad), Pauline Taylor (psychiatrist), Margaret Tyzack (conspirator), Steven Berkoff (constable), Lindsay Campbell (inspector), Michael Tarn (Pete), David Prowse (Julian), Jan Adair, Vivienne Chandler, Prudence Drage (handmaidens) Richard Connaught (Billyboy), John J. Carney (C.I.D. man), Carol Drinkwater (Nurse Feeley), Virginia Wetherell (actress), Gillian Hills (Sonietta), Katya Wyeth (girl), Barbara Scott (Marty), Barrie Cookson, Gaye Brown, Peter Burton, Lee Fox, Shirley Jaffe, Neil Wilson, Craig Hunter, Cheryl Grunwald. *Running time:* 137 minutes. Color.

1975

Barry Lyndon

Warner Bros. presents. A Film by Stanley Kubrick. *Producer:* Stanley Kubrick. *Executive producer:* Jan Harlan. *Associate producer:* Bernard Williams. *Director:* Stanley Kubrick. *Written for the screen by* Stanley Kubrick. Based on the novel by William Makepeace Thackeray. *Photographed by* John Alcott. *Production designer:* Ken Adam. *Editor:* Tony Lawson. *Music adapted and conducted by* Leonard Rosenman. From works by Johann Sebastian Bach, Frederick the Great, George Friedrich Handel, Wolfgang Amadeus Mozart, Giovanni Paisiello, Franz Schubert, Antonio Vivaldi. Irish traditional music by The Chieftains. Schubert Piano Trio in E-flat, Op. 100, performed by Ralph Holmes, violin, Moray Welsh, cello, Anthony Goldstone, piano. Vivaldi Cello Concerto in E minor, Pierre Fournier, cello, recorded on Deutsche Grammophon. *Hairstyles and wigs:* Leonard. *Costumes designed by* Ulla-Britt Soderlund, Milena Canonero. *Art director:* Roy Walker. *Assistant to the producer:* Andros Epaminondas. *Assistant director:* Brian Cook. *Sound editor:* Rodney Holland. *Sound recordist:* Robin Gregory. *Dubbing mixer:* Bill Rowe. *Assistant editor:* Peter Krook. *Sound editor's assistant:* George Akers. *Second unit cameraman:* Paddy Carey. *Camera operators:* Mike Molloy, Ronnie Taylor. *Focus puller:* Douglas Milsome. *Color grading:* Dave Dowler. *Camera assistants:* Laurie Frost, Dodo Humphreys. *Camera grips:* Tony Cridlin, Luke Quigley. *Gaffer:* Lou Bogue. *Chief electrician:* Larry Smith. *Production managers:* Douglas Twiddy, Terence Clegg. *Assistant directors:* David Tomblin, Michael Stevenson. *Unit managers:* Malcolm Christopher, Don Geraghty. *German production manager:* Rudolf Hertzog. *Location liaison:* Arthur Morgan, Col. William O'Kelly. *Set dresser:* Vernon Dixon. *Assistant art director:* Bill Brodie. *German art director:* Jan Schlubach. *Property master:* Mike Fowlie. *Property man:* Terry Wells. *Property buyer:* Ken Dolbear. *Construction manager:* Joe Lee. *Painter:* Bill Beechman. *Drapesmen:* Richard Dicker, Cleo Nethersole, Chris Seddon. *Wardrobe supervisor:* Ron Beck. *Costume makers:* Gary Dahms, Yvonne Dahms, Jack Edwards, Judy Lloyd-Rogers, Willy Rothery. *Hats:* Francis Wilson. *Wardrobe assistants:* Gloria Barnes, Norman Dickens, Colin Wilson. *Makeup:* Ann Brode, Alan Boyle, Barbara Daly, Jill Carpenter, Yvonne Coppard. *Hairdressing:* Susie Hill, Joyce James, Maud Onslow, Daphne Vollmer. *Producer's secretary:* Margaret Adams. *Casting:* James Liggat. *Choreographer:* Geraldine Stephenson. *Production accountant:* John Trehy. *Production secretaries:* Loretta Ordewer, Pat Pennelegion. *Assistant accountants:* Ron Bareham, Carolyn Hall. *Continuity:* June Randall. *Gambling adviser:* David Berglas. *Historical adviser:* John Mollo. *Fencing coach:* Bob Anderson. *Stunt arranger:* Roy Scammell. *Horsemaster:* George Mossman. *Wrangler:* Peter Munt. *Armourer:* Bill Aylmore. With special acknowledgment to Corsham Court, Glastonbury Rural Life Museum, Stourhead House, and the National Trust, Castle Howard. Lenses for candlelight photography made by Carl Zeiss, West Germany. Adapted for cinematography by Ed Di Giulio. Special sound assistance: Dolby Laboratories, Inc. A Peregrine film. Distributed by Warner Bros. A Warner Communications Company. Made on location in England, Eire, and Germany by Hawk Films, Ltd., and re-recorded at EMI Elstree Studios, Ltd., England. *Cast:* Ryan O'Neal (Barry Lyndon), Marisa Berenson (Lady Lyndon), Patrick Magee (The Chevalier), Hardy Kruger (Captain Potzdorf), Steven Berkoff (Lord Ludd), Gay Hamilton (Nora), Marie Kean (Barry's Mother), Diana Koerner (German Girl), Murray Melvin (Reverend Runt), Frank Middlemass (Sir Charles Lyndon), Andre Morell (Lord Wendover), Arthur O'Sullivan (highwayman), Godfrey Quigley (Captain Grogan), Leonard Rossiter (Captain Quin), Philip Stone (Graham), Leon Vitali (Lord Bullingdon), Dominic Savage (Young Bullingdon), David Morley (Little Brian), Roger Booth (George III), Norman Mitchell (Brock), Pat Roach (Toole), Anthony Sharp (Lord Harlan), Michael Horden (narrator), John Bindon, Billy Boyle, Jonathan Cecil, Peter Cellier, Geoffrey Chater, Anthony Dawes, Patrick Dawson, Bernard Hepton, Anthony Herrick, Barry Jackson, Wolf Kahler, Patrick Laffan, Hans Meyer, Ferdy Mayne, Liam Redmond, Frederick Schiller, George Sewell, Roy Spencer, John Sullivan, Harry Towb, John Sharp. *Running time:* 183 minutes. Color.

1980

The Shining

Warner Bros. presents A Stanley Kubrick Film. *Executive producer:* Jan Harlan. *Producer:* Stanley Kubrick. *Director:* Stanley Kubrick. Based on the novel by Stephen King. Produced in association with The Producers Circle Company, Robert Fryer, Martin Richards, Mary John. *Screenplay:* Stanley Kubrick and Diane Johnson. *Photographed by* John Alcott. *Production designer:* Roy Walker. *Film editor:* Ray Lovejoy. *Music:* Béla Bartók, *Music for Strings, Percussion and Celesta,* conducted by Herbert Von Karajan, recorded by Deutsche Grammophon; Krzysztof Penderecki; Wendy Carlos and Rachel Elkind; Gyorgy Ligeti. *Costumes designed by* Milena Canonero. *Production manager:* Douglas Twiddy. *Assistant director:* Brian Cook. *Steadicam operator:* Garrett Brown. *Helicopter photography:* Macgillivray Freeman Films. *Personal assistant to the director:* Leon Vitali. *Assistant to the producer:* Andros Epaminondas. *Art director:* Les Tomkins. *Makeup:* Tom Smith. *Hairstyles:* Leonard. *Camera operators:* Kelvin Pike, James Dewis, *Second-unit photography:* Douglas Milsome, Macgillivray Freeman Films. *Focus assistants:* Douglas Milsome, Maurice Arnold. *Camera assistants:* Peter Robinson, Martin Kenzie, Danny Shelmerone. *Grip:* Dennis Lewis. *Gaffers:* Lou Bogue, Larry Smith. *Sound editors:* Wyn Ryder, Dino Di Campo, Jack Knight. *Sound recorders:* Ivan Sharrock, Richard Daniel. *Dubbing mixer:* Bill Rowe. *Assistant editors:* Gill Smith, Gordon Stainforth. *1920s music advisers:* Brian Rust, John Wadley. *Assistant directors:* Terry Needham, Michael Stevenson. *Makeup artist:* Barbara Daly. *Continuity:* June Randall. *Production accountant:* Jo Gregory. *Set dresser:* Tessa Davies. *Construction manager:* Len Fury. *Titles:* Chapman Beauvais and National Screen Service. *Property master:* Peter Hancock. *Decor artist:* Robert Walker. *Second assistant editors:* Adam Unger, Steve Pickard. *Color grading:* Eddie Gordon. *Hotel consultant:* Tad Michel. *Casting:* James Liggat. *Location research:* Jan Schlubach, Katharina Kubrick, Murray Close. *Production secretaries:* Pat Pennelegion, Marlene Butland. *Producer's secretary:* Margaret Adams. *Production assistant:* Emilio Dalessandro. *Engineering by* Norank of Elstree. *Wardrobe supervisors:* Ken Lawton, Ron Beck. *Draughtsmen:* John Fenner, Michael Lamont, Michael Boone. *Property buyers:* Edward Rodrigo, Karen Brookes. *Video operator:* Dan Grimmel. *Boom operators:* Ken Weston, Michael Charman. *Drapes:* Barry Wilson. *Master plaster:* Tom Tarry. *Head rigger:* Jim Kelly. *Head carpenter:* Fred Gunning. *Head painter:* Del Smith. *Property men:* Barry Arnold, Philip McDonald, Peter Spencer. With special acknowledgment to Timberline

Lodge, Mount Hood National Forest, Oregon. Continental Airlines. State of Colorado Motion Picture Commission. KBTV Channel D. Denver, WPLG Channel 10 Miami, KHOW Radio Denver, Harrods of London, American Motor Company, Carl Zeiss of West Germany, National Vendors, Music Hire Group LTD., Cherry Leisure (U.K) Ltd. Filmed with Arreiflex cameras. A Peregrine film. Distributed by Warner Bros. A Warner Communications Company. Made by Hawk Films, Ltd., at EMI Elstree Studios, Ltd., England. *Cast:* Jack Nicholson (Jack Torrance), Shelley Duvall (Wendy Torrance), Danny Lloyd (Danny), Scatman Crothers (Halloran), Barry Nelson (Ullman), Philip Stone (Grady), Joe Turkel (Lloyd), Anne Jackson (doctor), Tony Burton (Durkin), Lia Beldam (young woman in bath), Billie Gibson (old woman in bath), Barry Dennen (Watson), David Baxt (forest ranger 1), Manning Redwood (forest ranger 2), Lisa Burns (Grady daughter), Louise Burns (Grady daughter), Allison Coleridge (secretary), Burnell Tucker (policeman), Jana Sheldon (stewardess), Kate Phelps (receptionist), Norman Gay (injured guest). *Running time:* 142 minutes. Color.

1987

Full Metal Jacket

Warner Bros. presents A Stanley Kubrick Film. *Executive producer:* Jan Harlan. *Producer:* Stanley Kubrick. *Co-producer:* Philip Hobbs. *Associate producer:* Michael Herr. *Director:* Stanley Kubrick. *Screenplay:* Stanley Kubrick, Michael Herr, Gustav Hasford. Based on the novel *The Short-Timers* by Gustav Hasford. *Lighting cameraman:* Douglas Milsome. *Production designer:* Anton Furst. *Editor:* Martin Hunter. *Original music:* Abigail Mead. *Costume designer:* Keith Denny. *Special effects senior technicians:* Peter Dawson, Jeff Clifford, Alan Barnard. *Assistant to the director:* Leon Vitali. *Sound recording:* Edward Tise. *Boom operator:* Martin Trevis. *Sound editors:* Nigel Galt, Edward Tise. *Dubbing mixers:* Andy Nelson, Mike Dowson. *Re-recording:* Delta Sound, Shepperton. *Special effects supervisor:* John Evans. *Casting:* Leon Vitali. *Additional casting:* Mike Fenton and Jane Feinberg, C.S., Marion Dougherty. *Additional Vietnamese casting:* Dan Tran, Nguyen Thi My Chau. *First assistant director:* Terry Needham. *Second assistant director:* Christopher Thomson. *Production manager:* Phil Kohler. *Unit production manager:* Bill Shepherd. *Production coordinator:* Margaret Adams. *Wardrobe master:* John Birkenshaw. *Wardrobe assistant:* Helen Gill. *Co–makeup artists:* Jennifer Boost, Christine Allsop. *Dialogue editor:* Joe Illing. *Assistant sound editors:* Paul Conway, Peter Culverwell. *Montage editing engineer:* Adam Watkins. *Video operator:* Manuel Harlan. *Camera trainees:* Vaughn Matthews, Michaela Mason. *Editing trainee:* Rona Buchanan. *Hair by* Leonard. *Art directors:* Rod Stratford, Les Tomkins, Keith Pain. *Set dresser:* Stephen Simmonds. *Assistant art directors:* Nigel Phelps, Andrew Rothschild. *Technical adviser:* Lee Ermey. *Art department research:* Anthony Frewin. *Armourers:* Hills Small Arms, Ltd., Robert Hills, John Oxlade. *Modeler:* Eddie Butler. *Prop master:* Brian Wells. *Construction manager:* George Crawford. *Assistant construction manager:* Joe Martin. *Prop buyer:* Jane Cooke. *Color:* Rank Film Laboratories, Denham. *Steadicam operators:* John Ward, Jean-Marc Bringuier. *Follow focus:* Jonathan Taylor, Maurice Arnold, James Ainslie, Brian Rose. *Grip:* Mark Ellis. *Camera assistant:* Jason Wrenn. *Chief electrician:* Seamus O'Kane. *Helicopter pilot:* Bob Warren. *Continuity:* Julie Robinson. *Production accountant:* Paul Cadiou. *Assistants to the producer:* Emilio D'Alessandro, Anthony Frewin. *Producer's secretary:* Wendy Shorter. *Production assistant:* Steve Millson. *Assistant accountant:* Rita Dean: *Accounts computer operator:* Alan Steele. *Production runners:* Michael Shevloff, Matthew Coles. *Nurses:* Linda Glatzel, Carmel Fitzgerald. *Special computer editing programs:* Julian Harcourt. *Unit drivers:* Steve Coulridge, Bill Wright, James Black, Paul Karamadza. *Helicopter:* Sykes Group. *Laboratory contact:* Chester Eyre. *Louma crane technician:* Adam Samuelson. *Louma crane and montage video editing system:* Samuelsons, London. *Aerial photography:* Ken Arlidge, Samuelsons Australia. *Optical sound:* Kay-Metrocolor Sound Studios. *Sound transfers:* Roger Cherrill. *Titles:* Chapman Beauvais. *Catering:* The Location Caterers, Ltd. *Transport:* D&D International, Daven Croucher, Ron Digweed, Chalky White. *Facilities:* Willies Wheels, Ron Lowe. *Unit transport:* Focus Cars. *Action vehicle engineer:* Nick Johns. *Chargehand prop:* Paul Turner. *Standby props:* Danny Hunter, Steven Allett, Terry Wells. *Propmen:* R. Dave Favell Clarke, Frank Billington-Marks. *Dressing props:* Marc Dillon, Michael Wheeler, Winston Depper. *Supervising painter:* John Chapple. *Painters:* Leonard Chubb, Tom Roberts, Leslie Evans Pearce. *Riggers:* Peter Wilkinson, Les Pipps. *Carpenters:* Mark Wilkinson, A. R. Carter, T. R. Carter. *Plasterers:* Dominic Farrugia, Michael Quinn. *Stagehands:* David Gruer, Michael Martin, Stephen Martin, Ronald Boyd. *Standby construction:* George Reynolds, Brian Morris, Jim Cowan, Colin McDonagh, John Marsella. *Cast:* Matthew Modine (Private Joker), Adam Baldwin (Animal Mother), Vincent D'Onofrio (Private Pyle), Lee Ermey (Gunnery Sergeant Hartman), Dorian Harewood (Eightball), Arliss Howard (Private Cowboy), Kevyn Major Howard

(Rafterman), Ed O'Ross (Lieutenant Touchdown), John Terry (Lieutenant Lockhart), Kieron Jecchinis (Crazy Earl), Bruce Boa (Poge Colonel), Kirk Taylor (Payback), John Stafford (Doc Jay), Tim Colceri (Doorgunner), Ian Tyler (Lieutenant Cleves), Gary Lanon (Donlon), Sal Lopez (T.H.E. Rock), Papillon Soo Soo (Da Nang hooker), Ngoc Le (VC sniper), Peter Edmund (Snowball), Tan Hung Francione (Arvn Pimp), Leanne Hong (motorbike hooker), Marcus D'Amico (hand job), Costas Dino Chimona (Chili), Gil Kopel (Stork), Keith Hodiak (Daddy Da), Peter Merrill (TV journalist), Herbert Norville (Daytona Dave), Nguyen Hue Phong (camera thief), Duc Hu Ta (dead N.V.A.). Parris Island recruits and Vietnam platoon: Martin Adams, Kevin Aldridge, Del Anderson. Philip Bailey, Louis Barlotti, John Beddows, Patrick Benn, Steve Boucher, Adrian Bush, Tony Carey, Gary Cheeseman, Wayne Clark, Chris Cornibert, Danny Cornibert, John Curtis, Harry Davies, John Davis, Kevin Day, Gordon Duncan, Phil Elmer, Colin Elvis, Hadrian Follett, Sean Frank, David George, Laurie Gomes, Brian Goodwin, Nigel Goulding, Tony Hague, Steve Hands, Chris Harris, Bob Hart, Derek Hart, Barry Hayes, Tony Hayes, Robin Hedgeland, Duncan Henry, Kenneth Head, Liam Hogan, Trevor Hogan, Luke Hogdal, Steve Hudson, Tony Howard, Sean Lamming, Dan Landin, Tony Leete, Nigel Lough, Terry Lowe, Frank McCardle, Gary Meyer, Brett Middleton, David Milner, Sean Minmagh, Tony Minmagh, John Morrison, Russell Mott, John Ness, Robert Nichols, David Perry, Peter Rommely, Pat Sands, Chris Schmidt-Maybach. Al Simpson, Russell Slater, Gary Smith, Roger Smith, Tony Smith, Anthony Styliano, Bill Thompson, Mike Turyansky, Dan Weldon, Dennis Wells, Michael Williams, John Wilson, John Wonderling. *Music:* "Hello Vietnam," performed by Johnny Wright, courtesy of MCA Records, Written by Tom T. Hall, Unichappell Music, Inc., Morris Music, Inc.; "The Marines Hymn" performed by The Goldman Band, courtesy of MCA Records; "These Boots Are Made for Walking," performed by Nancy Sinatra, Courtesy of Boots Enterprises, Inc., written by Lee Hazelwood, Criterion Music Corp.; "Chapel of Love," performed by The Dixie Cups by arrangement with Shelby Singleton Enterprises c/o Original Sound Entertainment, written by Jeff Barry, Ellie Greenwich, and Phil Spector, Trio Music Co., Inc., Mother Bertha Music, Inc.; "Wooly Bully" performed by Sam the Sham and the Pharaohs, courtesy of Polygram, a Division of Polygram Records, Inc., written by Domingo Samudio, Beckle Publishing Co., Inc.; "Paint It Black," written by Mick Jagger and Keith Richards, performed by the Rolling Stones, produced by Andrew Loog Oldham, courtesy of ABKCO Music and Records, Inc. Cameras by Arri Munich. Fairlight Digital Audio-Post Music System.

Lexicon: Time Compression/Expander. With grateful acknowledgment to: Depot Queens Division Bassingbourn, PSA Bassingbourn Barracks, British Gas PLC North Thames, The Vietnamese Community, National Trust Norfolk. A Natant Film. Filmed on location and at Pinewood Studios, Iver, Bucks. Distributed by Warner Bros. A Warner Communications Company. *Running time:* 116 minutes. Color.

Notes

In the half century since Stanley Kubrick began his professional career, his name and his works have been mentioned in hundreds of newspapers, magazines, and books. Space does not allow the listing of all. I gratefully acknowledge those before me who have written about Stanley Kubrick. Your work has greatly benefited me and has enlightened my work on this biography. I refer the reader to the excellent *Stanley Kubrick: A Guide to References and Resources,* by Wallace Coyle, for further interest. I am also in debt to the many critics and theorists who have written about the films of Stanley Kubrick. Their writings helped me to develop my own thinking on the subject and have opened paths of exploration. The following were key sources in the researching and writing of this book. My apologies for any omissions or errors. As has often been said, a biographer benefits from the kindness of strangers. My thanks to all the strangers who have become friends through their contributions to this work.

Prologue: The Myth of the Reclusive Auteur

Letter from Jim Coleman to Walter Scott, "Walter Scott's Personality Parade," *Parade* magazine, *Newsday,* February 25, 1996, p. 2.

Part One 1928–1948: The Bronx

Chapter One: "Stanley Was Only Interested in What He Was Interested In"

Genealogy information concerning the Kubrick, Perveler, and Metz families was gathered from the following sources: United States Petitions for Naturalization, State of New York, New York City Hall of Records, Social Security Death Indexes, 1920 Census Records, NYC, Birth Certificates, New York City Hall of Records, Health Department/City Clerk, NYC Hall of Records, New Jersey State Department of Health, and U.S. Petition for Citizenship.

Information concerning Jacques Kubrick's medical career was obtained from Rare Books Collection, Medical Sciences Library of New York Medical College, Medical Directory of New York, New Jersey, and Connecticut 1935–1936, 1963–1964.

Background on Lying-In Hospital is from New York Hospital Archives.

Background on July 26, 1928, is from *New York Times.*

Background on 2160 Clinton Avenue, 1131 and 1135 Grant Avenue, 1414 Shakespeare Avenue, and 1873 Harrison Avenue was obtained from research visit and photographs taken on 3/23/96, the Bronx Address Directory, and the Bronx County Historical Society.

Information concerning SK's school career came from school records, W. H. Taft High School yearbooks, author's interviews (hereafter AI) with Bernard Cooperman, Lou Garbus, Betty Garbus, Herman Getter, Robert Sandelman, Alexander Singer, Rose Spano and Daniel Traister.

Background on Martin Perveler is from California State Pharmacy Board, Los Angeles County Superior Court Divorce Records, Harriet Morrison's interview with David Niemerow of Cal-Oaks Pharmacy.

Information on the Graflex camera is from *Life Library of Photography.*

Background on the Grand Concourse and 2715 Grand Concourse is from author's interviews with Donald Silverman, Cliff Vogel, and Stanley Getzler.

Information on SK and Marvin Traub friendship is from author's phone conversation with Marvin Traub, author's interviews with Donald Silverman, Cliff Vogel, and Harriet Daniels.

Background on the Loew's Paradise is from Theater Files, the Bronx County Historical Society.

SK's photograph of newsstand after FDR's death is from *Look* magazine, 6/26/45.

Information concerning SK's relationship with Aaron Traister is from AI with Lou Garbus, Betty Garbus, and Daniel Traister.

SK's photographs of Aaron Traister appeared in *Look* magazine, 4/2/46.

Recollections of friendship between Gertrude Kubrick and Rose Florio is from AI with Rose Spano.

SK's *Look* magazine photostory "A Short Short in a Movie Balcony" appeared in *Look,* 4/16/46. Background is from AI with Bernard Cooperman.

SK photographing Taft High School cheerleaders is from AI with Claire Abriss.

SK and Alexander Singer at Taft High School is from AI with Alexander Singer.

Information on Howard O. Sackler at Taft is from school records and Taft High School yearbooks.

SK and Herman Getter at Taft is from AI with Herman Getter.

Information on Toba Metz's school career is from school records and Taft yearbooks.

"Why Still Photographers Make Great Directors," by James Monaco, *Village Voice,* 12/22/75, was helpful background for discussion of still photographers who became film directors.

Gardner Cowles and the creation of *Look* magazine is from *The Look Book.*

Stanley Kubrick's work as a still photographer for *Look* magazine in this period appeared in the following issues: 1/8/46, 6/11/46, 7/23/46, 8/20/46, 9/3/46,

9/17/46, 10/10/46, 11/26/46, 12/10/46, 3/4/47, 3/18/47, 8/5/47, 1/6/48, 1/20/48, 3/2/48, 3/16/48, 3/30/48, 4/27/48, 5/11/48, and 5/25/48.

Information on Arthur Rothstein's film book collection is from author's phone conversations with Grace Rothstein and Beverly Brannen.

SK's candid photography technique on NYC subway and work at *Look* magazine were discussed in AI with G. Warren Schloat Jr.

Part Two 1948–1956: New York

Chapter Two: Photographed by Stanley Kubrick

Information concerning the marriage of Stanley Kubrick and Toba Metz is from marriage certificate records, City of New York, and Commissioner of Deeds, Mount Vernon, New York.

Information on Barbara Kubrick's school career is from Adelphi College.

Stanley Kubrick's work as a still photographer for *Look* magazine in this period appeared in the following issues: 6/8/48, 8/3/48, 8/17/48, 10/12/48, 1/18/49, 4/26/49, 5/10/49, Father's Day issue 1949, 7/14/49, 8/2/49, 8/16/49, 9/13/49, 9/27/49, 10/25/49, 11/8/49, 12/6/49, 1/3/50, 1/17/50, 2/14/50, 3/14/50, 4/11/50, 5/9/50, 5/23/50, 6/20/50, 7/18/50, 8/1/50, and 8/15/50.

Information concerning SK and Diane Arbus is from *Diane Arbus,* by Patricia Bosworth and letter to author from Patricia Bosworth.

"Nothing is ever the same . . .": *Diane Arbus,* Aperture Monograph.

"It was tremendous fun . . .": *Kubrick,* by Michel Ciment.

Chapter Three: "He Now Understands That It's Directing He Wants to Do"

Epigraphs: "Stanley came in prepared . . .": AI with Vincent Cartier.

Information on Alexander Singer's graduation is from Taft yearbook 1945.

Background concerning Alexander Singer and art and filmmaking ambitions, notebook and production of *The Iliad,* MGM, Dory Schary, exploring NYC art film scene with SK, goal to be film director, SK goal to be cinematographer, job at Time Inc., decision to make short film with SK, planning of short, cost of a *March of Time* segment, SK choosing "Prizefighter" as basis of short, shooting second camera on *Day of the Fight,* SK desire for original score on DOF and meeting Gerald Fried, financing and cost of DOF, SK photographing Singer wedding, is from AI with Alexander Singer.

"At 17 I decided . . . ," "He was very polite . . . ," "I'd take Stanley . . . ," "It's about some teenagers . . . ," "I will never forget . . . ," "We had a notion . . . ," "I was very proud . . .": AI with Alexander Singer.

Background concerning Singer and Kubrick production of *The Iliad,* SK reading classic literature is from AI with Faith Hubley.

"Stanley would walk around . . .": AI with Faith Hubley.

History of *The March of Time* is from *The Film Encyclopedia,* by Ephraim Katz.

Background concerning SK choosing "Prizefighter" as basis of short, SK and

Walter Cartier, death of WC, Roland LaStarza fight film, Cartier brothers, WC
fight career, SK working with WC on *Day of the Fight,* SK working with
Cartier brothers in their apartment, the Steak Joint, WC's religious practices,
Saint Jude medal, brothers playing chess, SK joining chess club and playing at
Washington Square Park, date and location of Cartier/James fight, Montgom-
ery Clift considered as narrator for DOF, WC forty-seven-second knockout of
Joe Rindone, WC entertainment career, SK advising WC about his son's ca-
reer, is from AI with Vincent Cartier.

SK's photostory "Prizefighter" appeared in *Look* magazine, 1/18/49.

SK's photostory "The Day of the Fight Is a Long One" appeared in *Look* magazine, 2/14/50.

Bernard Cooperman asked to do sound for *Day of the Fight* is from AI with
Bernard Cooperman.

"Walter had a high regard . . . ," "Stanley was quiet . . . ," "Walter would
say . . ." "He would get from you . . . ," from AI with Vincent Cartier.

"I was a cameraman . . .": *The Film Director as Superstar,* by Joseph Gelmis.

"I did everything . . .": *Stanley Kubrick: A Film Odyssey,* by Gene D. Phillips.

Results of D'Amico/Cartier, Mangia/Cartier fights are from *Look,* "Prizefighter,"
1/18/49.

Synopsis of *Day of the Fight* is from author's screening of film. Background
concerning Gerald Fried and SK's desire for original score on DOF, meeting
SK, spotting and recording music for DOF is from AI with Gerald Fried.

"I was a handball partner . . . ," "That was a joint decision . . .": AI with
Gerald Fried.

General background on Walter Cartier: Various obituaries.

Opening and release of DOF: *New York Times,* 4/26/51.

Chapter Four: "He Was Like a Sponge"

Synopsis of *Flying Padre* is from author's screening of film.

"It was at this point . . .": *The Film Director as Superstar,* by Joseph Gelmis.

Background concerning Richard Sylbert is from *By Design: Interviews with Film
Production Designers,* by author.

"A guy comes to see me . . .": AI with Richard Sylbert.

"He was like a sponge . . .": AI with Faith Hubley.

Production background of *The Seafarers* is from *Stanley Kubrick: A Film Odyssey,* by Phillips.

Synopsis of *The Seafarers* is from author's screening at the Library of Congress.

Chapter Five: "It Took Stanley Kubrick, Is What It Took"

Epigraphs: "There have been no wasted people . . ." AI with Faith Hubley;
definition of existentialism, Oxford American Dictionary.

Background concerning SK and Richard de Rochemont is from AI with Jane de
Rochemont and de Rochemont papers at University of Wyoming.

"He was a wonderful man . . . ," "I was brought east . . . ," "The first episode . . . ," "Rebiere went down to Hodgenville . . . ," "Kubrick shot silent material . . . ," "In these interviews . . . ," "So he shoots all of the material . . .": AI with Norman Lloyd.

"Dick was always interviewing people . . . ," "You know we're really Dick's children . . .": AI with Jane de Rochemont.

Information concerning Martin Perveler's financial background and living in California is from Los Angeles County Superior Court Divorce Records.

Background concerning Martin Perveler's attempts to get SK to sign exclusive contract is from AI with Alexander Singer.

"Okay, that's the way you want it . . . ," "I was a snotty kid . . . ," "Out front there were . . .": AI with Alexander Singer.

Information concerning 2/26/51 agreement between SK and MP on *The Trap* (later *Fear and Desire*), "a one-man band . . . ," and background on Virgina Leith, budget details of F&D from "Kubrick-Financial Resume," RdR involvement with musician's union, Omnibus *Lincoln* series, Marcel Rebiere photographing *Lincoln,* second-unit material directed by SK for *Lincoln,* SK in Hodgenville, Kentucky, for *Lincoln,* production background on *Lincoln,* SK casting children in Hodgenville, *The Trap* title history, review of *Shape of Fear* (*Fear and Desire*), Perveler, SK, and RdR agreement, Joseph Burstyn and SK, RdR essay on SK is from de Rochemont papers at University of Wyoming.

"The entire crew of *Fear and Desire* . . .": *Stanley Kubrick Directs,* by Alexander Walker.

Description of Toba Metz at the time of *Fear and Desire* is based on photographs in *Kubrick* and *Stanley Kubrick: A Film Odyssey.*

Description of Mexican laborers working on F&D is based on photograph in, *Kubrick.*

"The first time . . .": *The Film Director as Superstar.*

Background concerning Gerald Fried, recording and scoring of F&D, is from AI with Gerald Fried.

"The music was supposed to mourn . . .": AI with Gerald Fried.

Background concerning SK and Omnibus *Lincoln* series is from *"If They Move . . . Kill 'Em!"* by David Weddle; phone conversation with David Weddle; *Stages,* by Norman Lloyd; AI with Norman Lloyd; Library of Congress; correspondence to author from Michael Ritchie and letter to author from Robert Saudek.

Background on Norman Lloyd and Marcel Rebiere photographing *Lincoln,* second-unit material directed by SK for *Lincoln,* SK casting children in Hodgenville, casting *Lincoln,* Marian Seldes sending press clippings is from *Stages* and AI with Norman Lloyd.

Information concerning SK in Hodgenville, Kentucky, on *Lincoln* is from *Courier-Journal* in LaRue County, Kentucky, and Harriet Morrison phone conversations with James D. LaRue and Kathy Crawford, LaRue County Public Library.

Background on SK casting children for *Lincoln* in Hodgenville is from AI with Alice Brewer Brown.

"A couple of people . . .": AI with Alice Brewer Brown.

SK future plans after *Fear and Desire* is from *New York Times*.

Background on SK and Joseph Burstyn is from AI with Faith Hubley; *Dame in the Kimono*, by Leonard J. Leff and Jerold L. Simmons; and *The Censorship Papers*, by Gerald Gardner.

"He's a genius . . .": AI with Faith Hubley.

"An American art picture . . ." is from the de Rochemont papers at University of Wyoming.

Information on F&D's Legion of Decency Certificate, preview, and *Variety* review is from the MPAA files at the Margaret Herrick Library.

Information on F&D at the Guild Theater in NY, SK publicity photographs is from AI with Alexander Singer.

The Wallace Markfield review of *Fear and Desire* appeared in the *New Leader*.

"There are too many . . .": James Agee from Film Forum 2 publicity notes.

Synopsis of *Fear and Desire* is from author's screening of the film at New York's Film Forum and Fear and Desire press notes.

SK letter to Joseph Burstyn is from *The Cinema of Stanley Kubrick*, by Norman Kagan.

Information concerning F&D not shown for forty years is from "A 'Lost' Kubrick Unspools," by Thelma Adams, *New York Post*, 1/14/94, "A Young and Promising Kubrick," by Janet Maslin, *New York Times*, and John Powers, *New York* magazine, 1/24/94.

"Pain is a good teacher . . .": *New York Times Magazine*, Joanne Stang, 10/12/58.

"I just didn't have . . ." *The Film Director as Superstar*.

Information concerning print of F&D at Eastman House and screening of film at Telluride Film Festival is from "A 'Lost' Kubrick Unspools," by Thelma Adams, *New York Post*, 1/14/94.

Information concerning the re-release of F&D at Film Forum is from Film Forum schedule.

"He considers it . . .": "A 'Lost' Kubrick Unspools," by Thelma Adams, *New York Post*, 1/14/94.

Chapter Six: Guerrilla Filmmaking

Epigraphs: "Black and white are colors . . .": *Painting with Light*, by John Alton, University of California Press, 1995. "Many people have asked me . . .": AI with Marie Windsor; "Just as a man . . ."

Background on Ruth Sobotka, background on Valda Setterfield, David Vaughan's role as choreographer and actor on *Killer's Kiss*, Alec Rubin, SK filming DV and AR running down Times Square, is from AI with David Vaughan.

"Ruth tried very hard . . . ," "We used to go . . . ," I had to sit in the back . . . ," "It had to be a solo . . . ," "It was a freezingly cold

night . . . ," "Alec was more of an actor . . . ," "We had to not . . .": AI
with David Vaughan.

Background on Valda Setterfield is from AI with Valda Setterfield.

"She was wearing . . .": AI with Valda Setterfield.

Letters: SK to Richard de Rochemont, 4/22/54, RdR to SK, 4/28/54, are from de
Rochemont papers at University of Wyoming.

Norman Lloyd asked to appear in *The Nymph and the Maniac (Killer's Kiss)*,
Lloyd at La Jolla Playhouse is from AI with Norman Lloyd.

"Stanley is on the phone . . .": AI with NL.

Background on Alexander Singer's work as unit still photographer on *Killer's
Kiss* is from AI with AS.

Background on Nat Boxer's work in production sound on *Killer's Kiss* and "We
were in some loft . . ." are from an interview with NB in *Filmmaker's Newsletter.*

Background on Peter Hollendar, Titra Films, SK editing *Killer's Kiss* at Titra, SK
telling PH Ruth Sobotka was a Jewish refugee is from AI with Peter Hollendar.

Background on Titra Films, SK editing *Killer's Kiss* is from AI with Max Glenn.

"I worked for Titra . . .": AI with Max Glenn.

"He amplified and enlarged . . .": AI with Alexander Singer.

"Titra was a very nice place . . . ," "One day Stanley came in . . .": AI with
Peter Hollendar.

Information on SK and Ruth Sobotka marriage is from Surrogate's Court—N.Y.
County—Probate—Letters of Administration.

Information on Toba Metz Kubrick's marriage to Jack Adler is from motor vehicle records.

"To the best of my belief . . .": *Stanley Kubrick Directs.*

Background on film noir is from *The Film Encyclopedia,* by Ephraim Katz; *Film
Noir,* by Alan Silver and Elizabeth Ward; and "Notes on Film Noir," by Paul
Schrader, *Film Comment* 8, no. 1 (Spring 1972).

Background on scoring of *Killer's Kiss* is from AI with Gerald Fried.

"I was working . . .": AI with Gerald Fried.

Background on Marshall Chess Club and New York chess scene is from AI with
Gerald Jacobson and Shelby Lyman.

SK as member of Marshall Chess club, "We played a few times . . . ," "There
were tables . . .": AI with Gerald Jacobson.

Part Three 1956–1960: Hollywood

Chapter Seven: Harris-Kubrick

Background on Alexander Singer and James B. Harris meeting in the Signal
Corps, Singer and Harris making a film, Lucien Ballard screening SK feature
films, decision to send LB to Bay Meadows racetrack, and results, AS to Bay
Meadows, results, method, AS phones SK from Bay Meadows, screening of

AS footage, SK using 25mm lens for tracking shot, set up of tracking shot is from AI with AS.

Background on Alexander Singer and James B. Harris meeting in the Signal Corps, Flamingo Films, Singer and Harris making a film, SK and JBH meet a second time, SK and JBH meet at Flamingo Films, forming of Harris-Kubrick Pictures, JBH inquiring about rights to *Clean Break,* Jaffe Agency, buying rights to *Clean Break,* JBH meeting with Bob Benjamin, SK tells JBH about Jim Thompson, Harris-Kubrick hires JT, JT screenwriting format for *The Killing,* JT credit on *The Killing,* adaptation of *Clean Break,* JBH and SK bring *The Killing* script to United Artists, SK and JBH send script to Jaffe Agency with list of actors, JBH brings script to Jack Palance, Bill Shiffren calls JBH, JBH and SK tell UA they secured Sterling Hayden, researching location, decision to film in LA, Chaplin Studios, budget and financing of *The Killing,* preview of *The Killing,* trying to re-edit film, *The Killing* shown to Max Youngstein, SK and JBH get an agent, taking out a trade ad, SK taking publicity pictures, creating ad and bringing it to MY, running ads, Youngstein's reaction, release of *The Killing,* UA distribution is from AI with JBH.

"I was a little nervous . . . ," I was impressed with this guy . . . ," "He said, 'I really don't . . . ," "I said, 'The first thing . . . ," "I immediately went to Scribners . . . ," "I called Stanley . . . ," "It just happens . . . ," "That's impossible, we're going to . . . ," "Boy, we were excited . . . ," "I called him . . . ," "I represent Sterling Hayden . . . ," "We said, 'Guess what . . . ,'," "I knew before . . . ," "Bill Shiffren, Sterling Hayden's agent . . . ," "The book was that way . . . ," "We couldn't get ourselves . . . ," "We proudly showed . . . ," "Are you guys crazy . . . ," "He screamed at me . . . ,": AI with James B. Harris.

Background on SK meeting Bob Gaffney is from AI with Bob Gaffney.

"My brother Jimmy was conned . . .": AI with Bob Gaffney.

Background on Louis de Rochemont: *The Film Encyclopedia,* by Ephraim Katz, and AI with Bob Gaffney.

"I realized Jimmy . . . ," "In 1956, Stanley . . . ," "Stanley and Jimmy looked at it . . . ," "I preset my exposure . . . ," "I got the footage . . . ," "I couldn't wait . . . ," "Stanley set up . . . ," "The Mitchell viewfinder . . .": AI with Alexander Singer.

"Probably the most chilling . . .": SK blurb on *The Killer Inside Me,* by Jim Thompson (Vintage Crime, 1991).

Background on Jim Thompson receiving additional dialogue credit on *The Killing,* Thompson family reaction, adaptation of *Clean Break, I Stole $16,000,000* is from *Savage Art,* by Robert Polito.

Background on Ruth Sobotka's ballet and design career, betting-window plates named after friends, breakup of SK marriage to RS, RS friendship with DV after marriage to SK is from AI with David Vaughan.

Background on Lucien Ballard, "It was just my style . . ." is from *Behind the Camera,* by Leonard Maltin.

Background on the Hughes Brothers and *The Killing* is from *"Three Moods Prevail in Dead Presidents,"* by author, *American Cinematographer,* September 1995; AI with Albert Hughes, AI with Lisa Rinzler.

Background on SK shooting hand-held camera, Kola Kwariani, Vince Edwards getting part is from AI with Vince Edwards.

"I knew Jimmy Harris . . .": AI with Vince Edwards.

Background on Marie Windsor is from *The Film Encyclopedia,* by Ephraim Katz, and AI with MW.

"Stanley saw a movie I made . . . ," "It was very hard . . . ,": AI with Marie Windsor.

Background on storyboards for *The Killing* is from AI with Marie Windsor.

Background on scoring of *The Killing* is from AI with Gerald Fried.

"We call it a dogfight . . .": AI with Gerald Fried.

"At twenty-seven . . .": "The New Pictures," *Time* magazine.

"We are all used . . ." *New York Times Magazine,* Joanne Stang, 10/12/58.

"I gathered from her . . .", "You don't have to . . .": AI with David Vaughan.

Chapter Eight: "This Is Stanley Kubrick"
Epigraphs: "The opening looked like . . .": AI with Keir Dullea, "I'd call Stanley . . .": AI with Richard Anderson.

Background on Dore Schary is from *The Film Encyclopedia,* by Ephraim Katz.

Background on Schary's interest in buying *The Killing* from United Artists, Schary signing Harris-Kubrick to MGM, SK and JBH looking for project about war, SK rereads *Paths of Glory,* sends it to JBH, JBH and SK agree to send POG to Schary, DS not interested in POG, Harris-Kubrick interest in *The Burning Secret,* MGM and Harris-Kubrick deal, SK bringing in Calder Willingham, selling idea of using Willingham to Schary, CW on *The Bridge on the River Kwai,* MGM's 9–5 mentality, Willingham writing *The Burning Secret* screenplay, Jim Thompson writing *Paths of Glory,* not meeting MGM deadline, Schary fired, Harris-Kubrick dismissed from MGM, Harris calls Schary in NY, Harris-Kubrick shift to POG, finishing script, SK takes photo for script cover, JBH approaches UA with POG, script rejected by UA, Harris-Kubrick told project needs a star, Harris-Kubrick approach Kirk Douglas with POG, Harris-Kubrick approach Gregory Peck, GP turns down POG, Harris-Kubrick difficulty finding a star for POG, Kirk Douglas comes back, background on Ray Stark, meeting between Harris-Kubrick, Lubin, Douglas, and Stark, details of contract, Harris-Kubrick move into Bryna offices, budget, fees, and percentages of POG, decision to shoot POG in Germany, multipicture contract with Bryna, Harris-Kubrick signs, SK admiration for Max Ophuls, SK dealing with Adolphe Menjou after filming many takes, difficulty in filming final meal sequence, actor who died on screen earlier used for ending, Harris-Kubrick approaches actors for new projects, development of TV series with Ernie Kovacs, *The German Lieutenant, I Stole $16,000,000* is from AI with James B. Harris.

"I'd like MGM . . . ," "He said after . . . ," "I remember being called in . . . ," "We would like . . . ," "I got him out of . . . ," "But what was . . . ," "This was like . . . ," "The killer was . . . ," "We're going to stay . . .": AI with James B. Harris.

Background on Kirk Douglas and Bryna Company, Harris-Kubrick approach KD with POG, KD not available, KD brings POG to UA, budget, fees, and percentages of POG, KD reaction to rewritten screenplay of POG is from *The Ragman's Son,* by Kirk Douglas.

"Stanley, I don't think . . . ," "He had revised it . . . ," "As I had predicted . . .": *The Ragman's Son,* by Kirk Douglas.

Background on SK researching World War I photographs at Los Angeles Library, Simon Bourgin, is from AI with Simon Bourgin.

Background on Richard Anderson is from AI with Richard Anderson and *The Film Encyclopedia* by Ephraim Katz.

"He came up to my apartment . . . ," "He read a lot of . . . ," "Stanley said, 'Wait a minute . . .'," "Max Ophuls died today . . . ," "After a couple of takes . . . ," "He said, "Here's where . . . ," "The trench was gruesome . . . ," "Stanley said, 'Dick, . . .'," "Stanley said to me . . . ," "I'll be very interested . . .": AI with Richard Anderson.

Background on Kubrick's voracious reading habits, RA asked to be dialogue coach on POG, production sound recording on POG, shooting opening scene, tribute to Max Ophuls, RA first day as Saint-Auban, digging trenches for POG, shooting tracking shots, SK on dolly during trench sequences, Auban's reaction to explosions, filming execution sequence, use of long lenses, RA approach to execution scene, Adolphe Menjou working with Charlie Chaplin, RA meeting AM after POG release, difficulty in filming three prisoners discussing their fate, SK losing his temper, is from AI with Richard Anderson.

Background on SK admiration for Max Ophuls is from AI with Alexander Singer.

Background on Bavaria Film Studios, use of German policemen as actors, SK working with German crew, location for no-man's-land, Ludwig Reiver, Baron Otto Waldenfels, transforming pasture to battlefield, special effects, Erwin Lange, explosion techniques is from POG press notes.

"The Germans were superb . . . ," "We had six cameras . . . ," *Stanley Kubrick Directs,* by Alexander Walker.

Background on cinematographer George Krause is from *Elia Kazan: A Life,* by Elia Kazan, and *Kazan on Kazan,* by Michel Ciment. "Kubrick's cinema is . . .": "Why Still Photographers Make Great Directors," by James Monaco, *Village Voice,* 12/22/75.

"We worked for a month . . . ," "We had 600 soldiers . . . ," "You let the character . . . ," "Intuition is the thing . . ." are from Simon Bourgin interview with SK, which appeared in *Newsweek* unsigned.

"Unflinchingly like a weapon" is from Peter Cowie.

Background on Adolphe Menjou and George Macready is from *The Film Encyclopedia,* by Ephraim Katz.

Background on Christiane Kubrick is from *Christiane Kubrick Paintings*, introduction by Marina Vaizey (Warner Books, 1990), "Christiane Kubrick: Flowers and Violent Images," by Ann Morrow, *London Times*, 2/5/73, and "The Flower-Filled World of the Other Kubrick," by Valerie Jenkins, *Evening Standard*, 9/10/72.

"I remember we had . . . ," "When I was at Salem . . .": "Christiane Kubrick: Flowers and Violent Images, by Ann Morrow, *London Times*, 2/5/73.

"It added up to a child's . . .": "The Flower-Filled World of the Other Kubrick," by Valerie Jenkins, *Evening Standard*, 9/10/72.

Background on scoring POG is from AI with Gerald Fried.

"There are certain places . . . ," "Either I was so good . . .": AI with Gerald Fried.

"An almost perfect . . .": AI with Simon Bourgin.

Background on Joseph Laitin, "I wrote and narrated . . . ," JL meets and interviews SK, "He finally arrived . . . ," "He dressed like . . . ," JL unable to sell article on SK, JL interview with SK for radio show, description of radio program, is from JL letter to author and AI with JL.

The description of SK's voice is based on listening to tape of Joseph Laitin radio documentary for CBS.

"Some younger people . . . ," "This is Stanley Kubrick . . . ," CBS radio documentary.

Letter from SK to Joseph Laitin is from JL personal correspondence.

Information on Gertrude and Jacques Kubrick's move to Englewood Cliffs, New Jersey, Jacques' earnings and car is from Bronx County Court papers.

European reaction to POG, foreword to the film, Truffaut remarks, POG not presented to French censorship board, POG in Berlin, reaction of General Geze, reaction of French soldiers, banned in Europe, Italian critics, Churchill's reaction, POG release in France is from various articles appearing in *Variety*.

Letters: 1/7/58 A. Joseph Handel to SK, 1/8/58 SK to AJH, 1/15/58 AJH to SK, 8/10/58 SK to Richard de Rochemont, 8/18/58 RdR to SK are from de Rochemont papers at University of Wyoming; de Rochemont's fondness for the novel *Lolita*, "Dick liked the novel . . ." is from AI with Jane de Rochemont.

"Stanley wrote to me . . .": AI with David Vaughan.

Chapter Nine: "This Isn't Working, Stanley"

Title from line attributed to David Seltzer in *Brando*, by Peter Manso.

Several excellent books were crucial in my understanding Kubrick's work with Marlon Brando on *One-Eyed Jacks* and Sam Peckinpah's role in the project, and they also served as valuable research material for this chapter: *Brando*, by Peter Manso; *Brando*, by Gary Carey; *Brando: Songs My Mother Taught Me*, by Marlon Brando with Robert Lindsey; *"If They Move . . . Kill 'Em!": The Life and Times of Sam Peckinpah*, by David Weddle; and *Bloody Sam: The Life and Films of Sam Peckinpah*, by Marshall Fine.

Background on Harris-Kubrick's relationship to Marlon Brando, SK asked to direct *One-Eyed Jacks* by MB, JBH renegotiates Bryna contract, JBH discovers *Lolita* novel, Vladimir Nabokov, contacting Putnam, Calder Willingham tells SK about *Lolita*, SK and JBH read *Lolita*, getting screen rights to *Lolita*, Irving Lazar's interest in Harris-Kubrick's making a film out of *Lolita*, Harris deal with Lazar, financing *Lolita* is from AI with James B. Harris.

"Stanley is unusually perceptive . . . ," *New York Times Magazine,* Joanne Stang, 10/12/58.

"One night we . . .": Weddle.

"I cracked the book . . .": AI with James B. Harris.

"Marlon screwed it up . . . ," "Marlon taught me . . .": Fine.

Background on Lewis M. Allen's offer to buy screen rights to *Lolita* is from *BFI Film Classics: Lolita* by Richard Corliss.

"You've gotta have faith . . . ," "She can't act . . . ," "We gotta get rid of Kubrick . . . ," "With deep regret . . . ," "If he had hired . . .": Manso.

Background on *Lolita* is from *Vladimir Nabokov: The American Years,* by Brian Boyd, *BFI Film Classics: Lolita* by Richard Corliss.

Kubrick and family at South Camden Drive in California is from Registrar-Recorder/County Clerk, Birth, Death and Marriage Records, Los Angeles, California.

SK's black Mercedes is from "Tell Me, Who Is Kubrick?" by Hollis Alpert, *Esquire,* July 1958.

Chapter Ten: "He Never Really Would Agree to the Concept That This Was His Movie"

Epigraphs: "Stanley is a very monastic . . .": AI with Saul Bass, "He'll be a fine director . . .": *The Ragman's Son,* by Kirk Douglas.

Kirk Douglas's superb autobiography, *The Ragman's Son,* was key in providing background, insights, and production details into the making of *Spartacus* and the producer/actor's relationship with Stanley Kubrick.

Tony Curtis: The Autobiography, by Tony Curtis with Barry Paris, is a wonderfully candid memoir, which was critical in providing information on the making of *Spartacus* and Stanley Kubrick's work on the film.

Also helpful were Universal's extensive press notes on the film.

Background on Harris-Kubrick's work on *Lolita*, Harris-Kubrick decides that SK directing *Spartacus* good for company, JBH renegotiating with Kirk Douglas, JBH and SK working on *Lolita* out of *Spartacus* bungalow is from AI with James B. Harris.

Background on Dalton Trumbo and *Spartacus* is from *Additional Dialogue,* by Dalton Trumbo.

Background on the blacklisting period in Hollywood is from *Naming Names,* by Victor Navasky; *The Hollywood Writer's War,* by Nancy Lynn Schwartz, completed by Shelia Schwartz; *The Inquisition in Hollywood: Politics in the Film Community, 1930–1960,* by Larry Ceplair and Steven Englund.

Background on Saul Bass, SB relationship with Kirk Douglas and Edward Lewis, scouting locations, design concept for gladiator school, sets built prior to SK, personnel discharged, storyboards of final battle, budgets, reconceived battle scene, screening classic battle scenes, SB credit on the film, meetings with Edward Muhl and SK, meeting SK for first time, preproduction, SB and Elaine Bass creating title sequence is from AI with Saul Bass.

Background on SK learning he's hired to direct *Spartacus* and "I'm starting tomorrow . . ." is from AI with Richard Anderson.

"I was the only one . . . ," I simply took . . . ," "Look, Golitzen feels . . . ," "I talked to him . . . ," "Saul, five minutes? . . .: AI with Saul Bass.

Background on Anthony Mann's work for *Spartacus* opening scene not reshot is from AI with Robert Lawrence.

Background on stunt team and stunt work on *Spartacus* is from AI with Loren Janes.

Information on the birth of Anya Kubrick is from Registrar-Recorder/County Clerk, Birth, Death, and Marriage Records, Los Angeles, California.

Background concerning SK working with Charles Laughton and Laurence Olivier and scientific magazines in SK bungalow are from AI with Norman Lloyd.

Alexander Golitzen's recollections of working in Spain on *Spartacus* were from the Oral History Collection at the Margaret Herrick Library.

Background on SK's method of assigning numbers to extras is from *Life* magazine article on *Spartacus*.

Alexander Singer's observations on the set of *Spartacus* are from AI with AS.

"Stanley wouldn't you feel . . . ," "That story was sold . . . ," "In the nearly . . . ," "You don't have . . .": *The Ragman's Son,* by Kirk Douglas.

Background history of postproduction of *Spartacus,* Howard Fast in editing room, SK relationship with Russell Metty, temp music, SK in editing room is from AI with Robert Lawrence.

"If you ever get . . .": AI with Faith Hubley.

"There was a lot of film . . . ," "What's this! . . . ," "I used to sleep . . . ," "You know what would be fun . . .": AI with Robert Lawrence.

"boisterous, red-faced man . . . ," "His greatest effectiveness was his . . .": *Tony Curtis: The Autobiography.*

Background on Alex North working on score to *Spartacus* and "I had the greatest . . ." is from *Knowing the Score: Notes on Film Music,* by Irwin Bazelon.

Background on Frank Warner working on *Spartacus* sound team and "Stanley Kubrick was the first . . ." is from AI with Frank Warner for *Sound-On-Film.*

Background on John Bonner working on *Spartacus* sound team, Murray Spivak's work as re-recording mixer, and "I would start at 6 o'clock . . ." is from AI with John Bonner for *Sound-On-Film.*

Background concerning the state of film sound re-recording in 1960 is from *Sound-On-Film,* by author.

Background on Murray Spivak's work as re-recording mixer on *Spartacus* and Don Rogers's work on the sound team is from AI with Don Rogers for *Sound-On-Film.*

Information on the birth of Vivian Kubrick is from Registrar-Recorder/County Clerk, Birth, Death, and Marriage Records, Los Angeles, California.

Information on Oscar nominations and awards for *Spartacus* is from *Inside Oscar,* by Mason Wiley and Damien Bona.

"*Spartacus* is the only film . . .": *Stanley Kubrick: A Film Odyssey.*

Part Four 1960–1964: England

Chapter Eleven: "How Did They Ever Make a Movie out of *Lolita*?"

Several books were essential in understanding the events surrounding the Harris-Kubrick production of Nabokov's *Lolita: BFI Film Classics: Lolita,* by Richard Corliss; *Vladimir Nabokov: The American Years,* by Brian Boyd; *Lolita* the novel, and *Lolita: A Screenplay,* by Vladimir Nabokov; *The Celluloid Sacrifice* and *Peter Sellers: The Authorized Biography,* by Alexander Walker; *Peter Sellers: The Mask behind the Mask,* by Peter Evans; *Shelley II,* by Shelley Winters; *Before I Forget,* by James Mason; *Dame in the Kimono,* by Leonard J. Leff and Jerold L. Simmons; and *The Censorship Papers,* by Gerald Gardner.

Background on the Motion Picture Association of America Code Seal is from the MPAA files at the Margaret Herrick Library.

Background concerning Warner Bros.' interest in Harris-Kubrick production of *Lolita,* Harris-Kubrick's motivation for Nabokov getting solo credit for screenplay, James Mason approached and turns down role of Humbert Humbert, SK and JBH approach Laurence Olivier to play Humbert during production of *Spartacus,* David Niven and Marlon Brando approached to play Humbert, plan to presell foreign territories, JBH meets with Kenny Hyman, Mason becomes available, deal with United Artists, decision to do film in England under the Eady plan, Shelley Winters and the cha-cha scene, Mr. Haze played by Raymond Anzarut (production supervisor of *Lolita*), Nelson Riddle scoring and recording music for *Lolita, Lolita* theme song, Elliot Hyman and Ray Stark, negotiating with the Legion of Decency and Monsignor Little, getting the Code Seal, Nabokov reaction to *Lolita* given to JBH, production schedule and budget, is from AI with James B. Harris.

"You couldn't make it . . .": Corliss.

"I knew Elliot from the old days . . . ," "You're killing Elliot . . .": AI with James B. Harris.

Background on the Eady plan in England is from *Hollywood England* and *National Heroes,* by Alexander Walker.

Marie Windsor offered role in *Lolita* is from AI with Marie Windsor.

Background on the search for an actress to play Lolita, "We had a desperate search . . . ," "From the first . . . ," is from Jack Hamilton, *Look* magazine.

Background on Sue Lyon is from *The Film Encyclopedia,* by Ephraim Katz, and Jack Hamilton, *Look* magazine.

"When Peter was called . . .": *Peter Sellers: The Authorized Biography,* by Alexander Walker.

"The most interesting . . . ," "Sue Lyon he directed very carefully . . . ," "Shelley Winters was very difficult . . . ," "He'd say, 'Now I want this scene . . .' " is from interview with Oswald Morris, by Bob Baker and Markku Salmi, in *Film Dope*.

"Kubrick understood . . . ," "I can't believe you can't . . . ," "Peter, you explain . . .",: *Shelley II*.

Background on Gilbert Taylor and Oswald Morris is from The Film Encyclopedia by Ephraim Katz.

Background concerning Bob Gaffney's second-unit work on *Lolita*, BG telling SK about *The Magic Christian*, by Terry Southern, is from AI with Bob Gaffney.

Background on Anthony Harvey is from *Directors on Directing*, by John Andrew Gallagher, and AI with Anthony Harvey.

"I really loved . . . ," "Anyway, after about . . . ," "These things come out . . .": AI with Anthony Harvey.

"He gave me the MI-5 treatment . . .": *Directors on Directing*, by John Andrew Gallagher.

Background on SK and Anthony Harvey in the *Lolita* cutting room, AH and assistant available in NY to work on *Lolita* for Code Seal, AH overseeing print production and checking on box office is from AI with Anthony Harvey.

Bernard Herrmann approached to score *Lolita* is from *A Heart at Fire's Center: The Life and Music of Bernard Herrmann*, by Steven C. Smith.

Canon John Collins asks British Board of Censors not to give *Lolita* a Certificate is from *Variety*.

Information on Oscar nominations for *Lolita* is from *Inside Oscar*, by Mason Wiley and Damien Bona.

"I wasn't able to . . .": SK to Gene D. Phillips.

"The surprise of *Lolita* . . ." is from Pauline Kael.

"Stanley Kubrick began . . .": Godard, *Godard on Godard*, translated by Tom Milne (Viking 1972).

Public reaction to *Lolita* ran in the *New York Herald Tribune* Sunday, July 15, 1962.

Kubrick family living at 239 Central Park West, Christiane Kubrick studying at the Art Students League is from the Art Students League records.

"She was one . . . ," "I didn't like watercolor . . . ," Christiane in Sternberg's Art Students League class is from AI with Harry Sternberg.

"Had I realized . . . ," *Newsweek*, 1972.

Richard de Rochemont encouraging SK to film *Lolita* and "Stanley never gave . . ." is from AI with Jane de Rochemont.

"If one of the new young . . ." is from *Before I Forget*, by James Mason.

Background on Adrian Lyne's remake of *Lolita* is from *Hollywood Reporter*, 7/6/95, and Liz Smith column.

Chapter Twelve: "Do You Think This Is Funny?"

Peter Sellers: The Authorized Biography, by Alexander Walker, and *Peter Sellers: The Mask behind the Mask,* by Peter Evans, were extremely helpful in researching this chapter.

Background on Harris-Kubrick deal with Ray Stark and Seven Arts, SK in England doing postproduction, SK and JBH working on *Red Alert* screenplay, end of Harris-Kubrick Pictures, JBH on West Coast, *The Passion Flower Hotel,* JBH directing career, is from AI with James B. Harris.

SK interest in thermonuclear war is from author's interviews with David Vaughan and James B. Harris.

"We started to get silly . . . ," "The only way this thing . . .": AI with James B. Harris.

SK's description of *Dr. Strangelove* is from *New York Times,* 12/31/62, by A. H. Weiler.

Background on Terry Southern is from *The Film Encyclopedia,* "The Hot Day Terry Southern, Cool and Fatalistic, Strode In," by Jeff MacGregor, *New York Times,* 11/12/95, *Hollywood Reporter,* 10/31/95, and Terry Southern *New York Times* Obituary, 10/31/95.

"Stanley's so steeped . . . ," "My mind is working . . . ," He'll pour himself a drink . . . ," SK impressing British crews, SK changing telephone number: Elaine Dundy, *Glamour* magazine, April 1964.

Background on Richard Sylbert and SK planning production design of *Dr. Strangelove* in NY and "I've got a terrific script . . ." is from AI with Richard Sylbert.

Background on Richard Sylbert's career is from *By Design: Interviews with Film Production Designers,* by author.

Information on MPAA and *Dr. Strangelove* and letters between SK and Geoffrey Shurlock are from the MPAA files at the Margaret Herrick Library.

Background on Ken Adam and the production design of DS, Peter Sellers wearing a prosthetic nose as Mandrake, casting Slim Pickens, Adams redesigning bomb bay set, sets built at Shepperton, London Airport, and IBM, no cooperation from U.S. military, realistic technology, instrument panels, B-52 models, the War Room maps and floor, designing missiles, President Reagan inquiring about White House War Room, "Stanley said to me . . . ," "Gee Ken, it's great . . . ," "Stanley is a brilliant cameraman . . . ," "I know this cowboy . . . ," "I was desperate . . . ," "It was so amazing . . . ," "I had no idea . . . ," "You must be joking . . . ," is from *By Design,* by author, and AI with Ken Adam.

Background on James Earl Jones and DS, casting George C. Scott, Lieutenant Zogg questioning mission, lines taken away from Jones, JEJ not getting reply from SK, and "I'll take the black one too . . ." is from *Voices and Silences,* by James Earl Jones and Penelope Niven.

"I got a call . . ." and Pickens first arriving in London is from *New York Times.*

Background on Slim Pickens is from Katz, *The Film Encyclopedia.*

Background on Wally Veevers is from *Movie Magic,* by John Brosnan.

"My first day . . ." and "Stanley is very meticulous . . .", "I find his films . . . is from *Movie Talk,* by David Shipman.

Background on George C. Scott is from Katz, *The Film Encyclopedia.*

"The only thing that . . ." is from Jack Piler in *Variety.*

"He's the hardest worker . . .": *The Mask behind the Mask,* by Peter Evans.

"During shooting many substantial . . . ," "It was too farcical . . . ," "My idea of doing it . . ." is from SK to Gene D. Phillips.

Background on *Dr. Strangelove, Red Alert,* and *Fail Safe* is from the article *Everybody Blows Up!* by David E. Scherman.

Background on Anthony Harvey's editing *Dr. Strangelove,* comedy philosophy, cut of bomb-run sequence disappears and is recut, SK debut canceled because of JFK assassination, "I would sit with him on the studio floor . . . ," "Strangelove certainly . . . ," "The Boulting brothers. . . ."

Background on Winston Ryder is from *Sound-On-Film,* by author.

SK at Columbia publicity office and "Short, dark, pudgy . . ." is from AI with John Lee.

SK didn't feel the Kennedy assassination affected DS and "There is absolutely . . ." are from column by Eugene Archer.

Background on the shooting of the pie-throwing segment and "The early days . . ." is from "The Ending You Never Saw in 'Strangelove,'" by Peter Bull, *New York Times,* 1/9/66.

Background on SK idea to run lyrics of "We'll meet again" over bomb footage is from "The Bomb and Stanley Kubrick," by Lyn Tornabene, *Cosmopolitan,* November 1963.

SK putting friends in preview audience, "I said they won't . . ." is from AI with Bob Gaffney.

Bosley Crowther pan of film and Lewis Mumford's reaction are from the *New York Times.*

Reactions to *Dr. Strangelove* by Elvis Presley, Steven Spielberg, and Oliver Stone are from " 'Dr. Strangelove' Turns 30. Can It Still Be Trusted?" by Eric Lefcowitz, New York Times, 1/30/94.

Oscar background on *Dr. Strangelove* is from *Inside Oscar,* by Mason Wiley and Damien Bona.

Background on SK reaction to *The Loved One* ad is from "Kubrick Threatens Suit on 'Strangelove' Writer," by Lee Mishkin, *New York Morning Telegraph,* 8/12/64.

Background on Christiane Kubrick at the Art Students League is from the Art Students League records.

United Nations plans to do film with SK is from the New York Times and Harriet Morrison interview with Richard Sydenham.

"I always wanted to get Stanley . . ." is from AI with Peter Hollander.

Background on thirtieth anniversary print of *Dr. Strangelove* is from the Film Forum schedule notes.

"Dr. Strangelove Revisited" aired on ABC's *Nightline,* 11/10/95.

Russell Baker's comments on *Dr. Strangelove* appeared in *New York Times*, 11/14/95.

Part Five 1964–1987: Isolation—Solitude—Hermitage

Chapter Thirteen: The Ultimate Trip

The title for this chapter was inspired by the Mike Kaplan advertising campaign for *2001*.

Epigraphs: "Among the younger generation . . .": *This Is Orson Welles*, by Orson Welles and Peter Bogdanovich, edited by Jonathan Rosenbaum; "He's made a transplant . . .": AI with Faith Hubley.

Several books were instrumental in my understanding of the creation and production of *2001* and provided valuable research material for this chapter: *The Making of Kubrick's 2001*, by Jerome Agel; *2001: Filming the Future* by Piers Bizony; the novel *2001: A Space Odyssey*; short story "The Sentinel," *The Lost Worlds of 2001* and *Report on Planet Three* by Arthur C. Clarke; *Film Guide to "2001: A Space Odyssey,"* by Carolyn Geduld; and *Odyssey: The Authorized Biography of Arthur C. Clarke*, by Neil McAleer. Herb A. Lightman's article "Filming 2001: A Space Odyssey," which appeared in *American Cinematographer* 49 (June 1968), contained important technical and aesthetic information. Jeremy Bernstein's wonderful profile of Stanley Kubrick and the making of *2001*, "How about a Little Game," *New Yorker*, 11/12/66, contains valuable details and information on Kubrick and *2001*, which informed the writing of this chapter.

Background on Alexander Walker in SK apartment in 1957 and "Are you making . . ." is from Alexander Walker.

"Why waste your time? . . . ," "This one was aimed at . . . ," "Even from the beginning . . . ," "Arthur and Stanley . . . ," "I said, it would be a disaster . . . ," "I took the treatment . . . ," "I said, Hey, Arthur . . . ," "Stanley asked me . . . ," "Stan and I used . . . ," "The longest flash forward . . . ," "There was a lot . . . ," "Okay, I'll buy it . . . ," "I tore up one . . . ," are from *Odyssey: The Authorized Biography of Arthur C. Clarke*, by Neil McAleer.

The physical description of SK in 1964 was based on various photographs of the director taken during this period.

"Had the vaguely distracted . . . ," "One of the English science-fiction writers . . . ," "With such a big staff . . . ," "At this stage . . . ," "The problem is to find . . . ," "Maybe the company . . . ," "I take advantage . . . ," "We're looking for . . . ," are from "How about a Little Game," by Jeremy Bernstein, *New Yorker*, 11/12/66.

"Most astronomers, and other . . . ," "It's simply an . . . ," are SK talking to William Kloman, *New York Times*.

"a glittering, roughly pyramidal . . ." is from the short story "The Sentinel," by Arthur C. Clarke.

Background on film at New York's 1964 World's Fair is based on author's recollections of the event.

Background on Christiane Kubrick talking to Harry Sternberg about SK, "I looked forward . . . ," and "The inventiveness of this man's . . ." is from AI with Harry Sternberg.

Background on HAL and IBM, Ernest Shackleton, BG work on 2001, SK shooting bone shot, shooting Moon-Watcher smashing bones, SK deciding on aspect ratio, SK quizzing BG, special effect used on terrain footage, shooting terrain footage, reason for SK not flying, BG as SK press representative, SK giving BG Bosley Crowther review of *Citizen Kane* for Orson Welles, "I remember there was one . . . ," "He operated the camera . . . ," "I said, you've . . . ," "I almost got killed . . . ," "Stanley was furiously digging . . . ," is from AI with Bob Gaffney.

"It was an amazing . . ." is SK to Alexander Walker.

"We lived on . . .": "Christiane Kubrick: Flowers and Violent Images," by Ann Morrow, *London Times*, 2/5/73.

Information on Jacques and Gertrude Kubrick moving to the West Coast, Dr. Kubrick's California medical license, and membership in American College of Gastroenterology is from the Medical Society of the State of New York.

Background on Ken Adam approached by SK to design 2001 and his decline is from AI with Ken Adam.

Background on Wally Veevers and Tom Howard is from *Movie Magic*, by John Brosnan.

Background on Douglas Trumbull is from *American Cinematographer*, October 1969.

Background on Geoffrey Unsworth is from *By Design*, by author, AI with Tony Walton and Katz.

"The ending was altered . . . ," "I don't like . . . ," "Maybe next time I'll show . . . ," is from *The Making of Kubrick's 2001*, by Jerome Agel.

Background on the characters of Poole and Bowman, Keir Dullea, research given to KD and Gary Lockwood, Nigel Davenport on 2001, Derek Cracknell reading HAL's line, SK directorial manner, SK intensity on set, KD doing stunt through airlock, working in centrifuge, KD and GL starting camera inside centrifuge, rotating sets, shooting Poole eating, improving on script, Bowman and Poole in hub hatchway, wearing Velcroed shoes, redesign of shoes, working with actors, SK dinner parties, Parker Brothers game designed for 2001, shooting scenes with HAL, reaction of British crew to SK, shooting stuntmen on wires, shooting KD in pod, playing *Antarctica Suite*, KD shaking his body, shooting close-ups of KD eye, makeup, original script of Victorian room scene, SK not ever discussing meaning of 2001, Dullea at Washington premiere, KD watches Neil Armstrong walk on the moon with Arthur C. Clarke, is from AI with Keir Dullea.

"This man looked . . . ," "When I read the screenplay . . . ," "We had our . . . ," "That was good, let's try another . . . ," "I adored Stanley . . . ," "Somebody would come . . . ," "When we were filming . . . ,"

"He's a very quiet man . . . ," "Stanley is a true . . . ," "It was a little like . . . ," "The brain room . . . ," "But you know . . . ," "The most beautiful . . . ," "They had some . . . ," "That was a little scary . . . ," "Never!, he *never* . . . ," "I was blown away . . ." are from AI with Keir Dullea.

Background on Gary Lockwood and Nigel Davenport is from Katz.

"There are certain . . ." is from *New York Times*.

"It was like watching . . . ," "It was a novel thing . . . ," "There were basically . . ." is from "Filming 2001: A Space Odyssey," by Herb A. Lightman, *American Cinematographer* 49 (June 1968).

"Must keep away . . ." is from Arthur C. Clarke.

"The next time . . . ," "You just get carried along . . . ," "Stanley inspires people . . . ," "Stanley's a genius . . . ," "Stanley sat up all . . . ," "I was present . . . ," "Arthur has a tremendous ego . . . ," "2001, I see it every week," are from *2001: Filming the Future*, by Piers Bizony.

Background on video assist is from forthcoming book of interviews with cinematographers by author.

Background on death of Ruth Sobotka is from AI with David Vaughan and *Variety* obituary, 6/21/67.

Background on rear screen photography is from *By Design*, by author.

Background on Fairchild-Hansard technique is from *King Vidor on Filmmaking*, by King Vidor.

"Somebody said that man . . ." is SK to Gene D. Phillips.

Shooting the Star Gate sequence, "I met the . . ." is from *Sight & Sound*, May 1995.

Background on original score and Alex North is from liner notes to *Alex North's 2001: The Legendary Original Score*, world premiere recording, National Philharmonic Orchestra, conducted by Jerry Goldsmith, Varese Sarabande, 1993.

Ray Lovejoy promoted to edit 2001, Anthony Harvey moves on to directing is from AI with Anthony Harvey.

Information concerning another composer originally hired to score 2001 and "Then Stanley called me in New York . . ." are from *Knowing The Score: Notes on Film Music*, by Irwin Bazelon.

"I remember seeing . . ." is from *Film Score: The Art and Craft of Movie Music*, by Tony Thomas.

"I don't regard . . ." is SK to Henry T. Simon for *Newsweek*.

"a film that is so dull . . .": Stanley Kauffmann, *New Republic*.

"It is morally pretentious . . .": Arthur Schlesinger, Jr., *Vogue* magazine.

"2001 is not the worst . . .": Peter Davis Dibble, *Women's Wear Daily*.

"The movie is so completely absorbed in its own problems . . .": Renata Adler, *New York Times*.

"It's fun to think . . .": Pauline Kael.

"On the deepest . . .": SK to *Rolling Stone* magazine.

"Capable of making . . ." is from *I, Fellini*, by Charlotte Chandler.

"So you see . . ." is from *Encountering Directors*, by Charles Thomas Samuels.

"As the Western declined . . ." is from *The Emerald Forest Diary,* by John Boorman.

IBM reaction to *2001* is from AI with Faith Hubley.

Oscar background on *2001* is from *Inside Oscar,* by Mason Wiley and Damien Bona.

Background on *2001* at 1969 Moscow Film Festival, "I'll be watching . . ." is from *I'll Be Watching . . . ,"* by Joyce Haber, *Los Angeles Times.*

"Jacques Kubrick audits Jerome Agel lecture at Sherman Oaks Experimental College" is from *Variety,* 3/21/73.

"As soon as I . . .": James Cameron to Syd Field. "*2001* is the reason . . ." Ray Lovejoy to Syd Field.

"I discovered that there . . ." is from *Working in Hollywood,* by Alexandra Brouwer and Thomas Lee Wright.

Background on the *2001* parody in *Minnie and Moskowitz* is from *American Dreaming: The Films of John Cassavetes and the American Experience,* by Raymond Carney.

Background on the parody of *2001* in *Coogan's Bluff* is from *Negative Space,* by Manny Farber.

2001's influence on David Bowie's *Space Oddity* is from *Alias David Bowie: A Biography,* by Peter and Leni Gilman.

Influence of Jordan Belson and the Whitney brothers on *2001,* "Strongly reminiscent of . . ." and "This becomes a dizzying . . ." is from *Expanded Cinema,* by Gene Youngblood.

"Why do we go back . . ." is from Ray Bradbury.

Chapter Fourteen: "He Is Napoleon Really, Isn't He?"
The title for this chapter comes from AI with Gay Hamilton.

Epigraphs: "It would have been . . .": AI with Bob Gaffney; "I found him a likable man . . .": AI with Jonathan Cecil.

For this chapter I have drawn heavily on Joseph Gelmis's interview with Kubrick that appeared in his superb collection *The Film Director as Superstar.* The interview took place after the release of *2001,* when Kubrick was deeply involved in researching and planning his still unrealized film project on the life of Napoleon. The Gelmis interview is the only extended record of Kubrick discussing his ideas for the epic film. I am also indebted to Bob Gaffney, who so graciously sat down with me and shared his recollections of his work with Kubrick on this project, among many other topics. Patrick McGilligan's insightful biography of Jack Nicholson, *Jack's Life,* and *Jack Nicholson: Face to Face,* by Christopher Fryer and Robert David Crane, were very useful references in understanding Nicholson's participation in the project. Anthony Burgess's witty and literate memoir, *You've Had Your Time: The Second Part of the Confessions,* was instrumental in understanding the writer's role in the proposed film.

Background on the life of Napoleon is from *The World Book Encyclopedia.*

SK counting soldiers in a painting to determine troop size is from AI with Keir Dullea.

"It's a novel . . ." is from a Sheila Weller article in the *Village Voice.*

Napoleon: A Novel in Four Movements was published by Knopf in 1974.

"As rare as . . ." is SK to Gelmis in *Newsday.*

"I plan to do *Napoleon* next . . ." is SK to Penelope Houston in *Saturday Review.*

Talk on set of *Barry Lyndon* about shooting battle scenes for *Napoleon* is from AI with Jonathan Cecil.

"Stanley Kubrick—I feel obligated . . . ," *Variety.*

"I've invested a lot . . ." is from Ron Rosenbaum profile of Nicholson in the *New York Times Magazine.*

Shadows on a Wall is a novel by Ray Connolly published by St. Martin's Press in 1994.

Chapter Fifteen: Ultra-Violence

Epigraphs: "He is everything . . .": Malcolm McDowell to Kitty Bowe Hearty in *Premiere* magazine, "*A Clockwork Orange* is . . .": Luis Buñuel, "I hate reading . . .": Paul Cook in article by Tony Parsons, *The Times Saturday Review,* England, 1/30/93.

Several books and articles were essential research for this chapter and were instrumental in my understanding of the background concerning Anthony Burgess's extraordinary novel *A Clockwork Orange* and the making of Kubrick's screen adaptation: the novel *A Clockwork Orange; You've Had Your Time: The Second Part of the Confessions,* by Anthony Burgess; the Malcolm McDowell profile in *Burke's Steerage,* by Tom Burke; *Stanley Kubrick's A Clockwork Orange Based on the Novel by Anthony Burgess,* by Stanley Kubrick; and "A Clockwork Utopia: Semi-Scrutable Stanley Kubrick Discusses His New Film," by Andrew Bailey, *Rolling Stone,* no. 100, 1/20/72.

For background on Christiane Kubrick, her life at home in England, and her work as a painter, I've drawn heavily on *Christiane Kubrick Paintings,* introduction by Marina Vaizey (Warner Books, 1990); *Christiane Kubrick: Flowers and Violent Images,* by Ann Morrow; *London Times,* 2/5/73; and "The Flower-Filled World of the Other Kubrick," by Valerie Jenkins, *Evening Standard,* 9/10/72.

"It was the most painful . . ." is Anthony Burgess to Sheila Weller in the *Village Voice.*

"The book had . . . ," "It's very pleasant . . . ," "The laboratory is quite . . ." is SK to Bernard Weinraub in *New York Times.*

"The story has . . . ," "I wanted to find . . . ," "I just wanted to . . . ," is SK to Joseph Gelmis.

"My problem, of course . . . ," "One doesn't find . . . ," "While we are . . ." is SK to Penelope Houston.

"Although a certain . . . ," "Telling me to take a vacation . . . ," "Chess masters will sometimes . . . ," "He's had any . . . ," "Telling a story realistically . . . ," "Violence itself isn't necessarily . . ." is SK to Paul D. Zimmerman in *Newsweek*.

Background on the style of SK screenplay to *A Clockwork Orange* is from author's examination of the first-draft screenplay at the Margaret Herrick Library.

"*A Clockwork Orange* employed . . ." is John Alcott to *American Cinematographer*.

Background on SK technical innovations and equipment used on CO, "Stanley just calls . . ." is from AI with Ed Di Giulio.

Background on Liz Moore designing Korova Milkbar tables is from Bizony.

"I scratched the cornea . . ." is from *The Ragman's Son*, by Kirk Douglas.

Background on Steven Berkoff, CO set, "Stanley was incredibly gentle . . . ," "He offered me . . ." is from AI with Steven Berkoff.

Background on Philip Stone, "Suddenly Stanley asked me . . ." is from letter to author from PS.

"The basic equipment I use . . ." is from *Stanley Kubrick Directs*.

Background on Walter Carlos, Wendy Elkind, scoring CO, "Stanley was fascinated . . ." is from AI with Wendy Carlos.

"When I visited . . ." is from *Newsweek*.

Victor Davis's impressions of SK at the time of CO. "Culture seems to have . . ." is from *Daily Express*.

Background on previews for CO is from *Variety*.

Background on painting matte on wall of Cinema One in New York is from *You'll Never Eat Lunch in This Town Again*, by Julia Phillips.

"brilliant, a tour de force . . ." is from Vincent Canby's review of CO in *New York Times*.

"But don't take my word . . ." is from the Andrew Sarris review of CO in *Village Voice*.

John Simon announces CO one of the ten worst films of the year on the Dick Cavett show; "Stanley Kubrick asked me . . . ," is from a *Village Voice* article by Arthur Bell.

"a mind-blowing work . . ." is from Rex Reed in *New York Daily News*.

Background on the advertising campaign for CO is from the Warner Archive at USC.

"I flew to London . . ." is from *Hollywood on the Couch*, by Stephen Farber and Marc Green.

Background on British Board of Film Censors giving CO a certificate and Steven Murphy is from *National Heroes*, by Alexander Walker.

Background on CO and the Oscars is from *Inside Oscar*, by Mason Wiley and Damien Bona, and *Hurricane Billy*, by Nat Segaloff.

Background on *Detroit News* position on X-rated films is from *Detroit News*.

Background on mainstream films rated X is from *Dame in the Kimono*, by Leonard J. Leff and Jerold L. Simmons, and *The Censorship Papers*, by Gerald Gardner.

SK letter to the editor of *Detroit News* was published 4/9/72.

Background on SK and Warner Bros. is from *Variety*.

"I sold the . . ." is from *Time*, 1/17/77.

"We tried to rehearse . . ." is from *Sound on Film* broadcast, April 1972, Erwin Frankel productions.

SK withdraws CO to get new rating is from *New York Times*, 8/25/72.

"I am becoming . . . ," "This may not be . . . ," "Most of the statements . . ." are from *Variety*, 8/22/73.

"A Psychiatric Analysis of Kubrick's 'Clockwork Orange,'" by Emanuel K. Schwartz, was in *Hollywood Reporter*, 1/31/72.

Background on Arizona's Roeder Bill is from article by Nick DiSpoldo in New York Times, 6/20/74.

Background on copycat violence and CO is from Victor Davis, *Daily Express*, January 1972; Tony Parsons, *Times Saturday Review*, 1/30/93; and "The Clockwork Killer," by Edward Laxton in *Daily Mirror*, 7/4/73.

Arthur Bremmer and CO, "April 24 Milwaukee . . ." is from Joseph Gelmis in *Newsday*.

Miriam Karlin's reaction to CO copycat crimes in England is from article by Edward Laxton, *Daily Mirror*, 7/4/73.

SK pulls CO from distribution in England is from William E. Schmidt, *New York Times*, 2/6/93.

CO box office figures in England is from *London Times*, 1/18/73.

CO shown in Argentina—*Variety*, 8/14/85.

Background on Warner's versus Channel 4 in England is from *Variety*. SK and Warner's versus Jane Giles is from William E. Schmidt, *New York Times*, 2/6/93, and Kathy Marks, *Independent*, 2/5/93.

Chapter Sixteen: Candlepower

Epigraphs: "Technology in the service of creativity": AI with Ed Giulio.

Several articles were instrumental in providing research and details into the making of *Barry Lyndon* and were relied upon for the writing of this chapter: "Barry Lyndon Par for the Kubrick Course," by Thomas Wood; "Kubrick's Grandest Gamble," by Richard Schickel, *Time*, 12/15/75; "Photographing Stanley Kubrick's Barry Lyndon," by Herb Lightman, includes interview with John Alcott in *American Cinematographer* March 1976; "Two Special Lenses for Barry Lyndon," by Ed Di Giulio, *American Cinematographer*, March 1976; and "How I Learned to Stop Worrying and Love Barry Lyndon," by John Hoffess, *New York Times*, 1/11/76. I have also drawn on Michel Ciment's insightful interview with John Alcott, which appears in *Kubrick*.

Background on William Makepeace Thackeray is from the introduction to the World's Classics edition of *Barry Lyndon* by Andrew Sanders, published by Oxford University Press (1984).

Background on SK method of adapting the novel *Barry Lyndon* is from author's interviews with Gay Hamilton and Jonathan Cecil.

Background on Ed Di Giulio and Cinema Products' work on *Barry Lyndon*, SK use of the zoom lens, EDG checking projection for BL at Cinerama Dome theater, "Stanley called me and said . . ." is from AI with Ed Di Giulio.

Background on Ken Adam's work for *Barry Lyndon* is from *By Design*, by author and AI with Ken Adam.

"Like a medieval artist . . ." is from Alexander Walker.

Background on SK and production manager, "Have the Art Department . . ." is from *The Emerald Forest Diary*, by John Boorman.

Warner Bros. knowledge of SK production of BL while shooting and SK production of *Traumnovelle* is from *Variety*.

Background on Ryan O'Neal and Marisa Berenson is from Katz.

Suspension of production on BL is from *Daily Express* and *Variety*, 11/28/73.

Background on revision of BL during suspension, casting English and Irish actors for BL is from author's interviews with Gay Hamilton, Steven Berkoff, and Jonathan Cecil.

"When a director dies . . ." was originally said by John Grierson. In his autobiography, *Fun in a Chinese Laundry,* director Josef von Sternberg refutes this theory and presents a philosophy that can be well applied to the work of Stanley Kubrick: "With few exceptions, the central force of the motion picture, the director, is not a master of photography, which is the principal element in the transfer of his vision to the screen. The director is at the mercy of the camera. It writes its own language, it transliterates all that is fed into it, and when the director does not control the principal tool of his craft, he has surrendered his most important function."

"Very few people . . ." is from *Millimeter.*

Background on Jonathan Cecil working on BL, actor playing Potzdorf for three weeks before being released, "A sort of upstage . . . ," It was an extraordinary . . . ," "There was a disastrous day . . . ," "He tried to . . ." is from AI with Jonathan Cecil.

Background on Gay Hamilton's work on BL, "Stanley Kubrick doesn't meet . . ." is from AI with Gay Hamilton.

SK operating camera, working with Luke Quigley, BG checking projection focus in New York for BL is from AI with Bob Gaffney.

Background on Steven Berkoff working on BL, "There was a fair amount . . ." is from AI with Steven Berkoff.

Philip Stone playing Graham in BL, "Graham in the wonderful Barry Lyndon . . ." is from letter to author from Philip Stone.

Leonard Rosenman's musical work on BL, "Stanley called on me . . ." is from his interview in *Film Makers on Film Making: The American Film Institute Seminars on Motion Pictures and Television,* Vol. 1. Edited by Joseph McBride. J. P. Tarcher, Inc., Los Angeles, 1983.

"One is left . . .": Jerry Oster, *New York Daily News,* 12/21/75.

"[It is] a series . . ." is from Michael Billington in *London Illustrated.*

"transforms scene after scene . . ." is from Vincent Canby in *New York Times.*

Oscar nomination and award information on *Barry Lyndon* from *Inside Oscar,* by Mason Wiley and Damien Bona.

"SK wins David of Donatello Award" is from Gregg Kieslay, *Los Angeles Times,* 6/13/77.

SK and Miroslav Ondricek, "He wrote back . . ." is from an interview with Miroslav Ondricek from forthcoming book of interviews with cinematographers by author.

Chapter Seventeen: "Let's Go Again"

Epigraphs: "He's kind of a dyspeptic filmmaker . . .": *Movie Talk,* by David Shipman; "Stanley's good on sound . . .": *Chambers Film Quotes,* compiled and edited by Tony Crawley.

Vivian Kubrick's penetrating documentary, *The Making of The Shining,* which aired on BBC on 10/4/80, is a rare, if not unprecedented, opportunity to see Stanley Kubrick at work. This thirty-three-minute, twenty-eight-second documentary was instrumental in providing texture, background, and details on Kubrick's production of *The Shining* and the inner core of his work methods. Garrett Brown's article "The Steadicam and The Shining," which appeared in *American Cinematographer* in August 1980, was extremely valuable in understanding the Steadicam's important role on *The Shining* and Brown's work on the film. Additional material on Garrett Brown and the Steadicam comes from my interview with him for a forthcoming book of interviews with cinematographers. "Photographing Stanley Kubrick's *The Shining,*" an interview with John Alcott by Herb Lightman in *American Cinematographer,* August 1980, was key in providing background and details on Alcott's work on the film.

"In all things . . . ," "It's very difficult . . . ," "Very early on . . ." are from John Hofsess, *New York Times,* 6/1/80.

Background on SK and the demo reel of the Steadicam is from author's interviews with Garrett Brown and Ed Di Giulio.

Background on *Network* and SK is from *Mad as Hell: The Life and Work of Paddy Chayefsky.*

John Calley sending the galleys of *The Shining* to SK, SK and Jack Nicholson, JN intervening for Scatman Crothers, JN and Danny Lloyd, JN attracted to family crisis in *The Shining,* JN writing background, "Jack's performance here . . . ," "The book had that intimation . . . ," are from *Jack's Life,* by Patrick McGilligan.

Background on helicopter shots in *The Shining,* "I thought it was one . . . ," "With *The Shining* . . . ," "I believe that Jack": Ciment.

Background on Stephen King and *The Shining,* "Tourneur quite sensibly . . . ," is from *Danse Macabre.*

SK hard on Shelley Duvall, Robert Altman's reaction to SD, *The Shining* editing room, "The first epic horror film . . . ," "There's something inherently wrong . . . ," "He inspired me . . . ," "In one scene . . . ," "I'm a great off-stage grumbler . . . ," is from Jack Kroll, *Newsweek,* 5/26/80.

SK reading *The Shining,* "I was so flattered . . . ," "He's a man you can . . ." is from Harlan Kennedy in *American Film* magazine.

"It must be plausible . . ." is from Diane Johnson in *New York Times.*

SK reading *The Shadow Knows,* by Diane Johnson; SK hearing about DJ, SK and DJ working together, "He is the sort . . ." is from Denis Barbier.

Description of Kubrick's early treatment of *The Shining* is based on reading the treatment in the Warner Archives at USC.

SK considering return to U.S. to shoot *The Shining* is from AI with Bob Gaffney, *Los Angeles Herald Examiner,* 6/5/77, and Army Archerd, Just for Variety, 6/6/77.

Background on Garrett Brown and Ed Di Giulio visiting SK to demonstrate the Steadicam is from AI with Ed Di Giulio.

Background on Roy Walker is from research for *By Design* by author.

Background on the stills used on the walls of the Overlook is from Alexander Walker's article in the *Los Angeles Herald Examiner.*

Background on Shelley Duvall, the first and only choice for Wendy, Scatman Crothers, Robert Altman's reaction to SD, "Arguably the greatest actor . . . ," "I hadn't read . . ." is from *The Shining* press notes.

Tight security on *The Shining,* "As befitting of any hotel . . ." is from *Variety,* 6/14/78.

Background on SK working with Anne Jackson, "After we finished . . ." is from AI with Anne Jackson.

Background on SK concept of the Critical Rehearsal Moment, Alexander Walker's visit to *The Shining* set, "a standardized sort . . ." is from *Los Angeles Herald Examiner,* 5/23/80, and Alexander Walker.

"Kubrick likes to do many takes . . ." is from *The Emerald Forest Diary,* by John Boorman.

Tony Burton on *The Shining,* shooting final shot, deleted scene, "The first motion . . . ," "Stanley would have . . . ," "One day they were shooting . . . ," "He didn't direct me much . . . ," is from AI with Tony Burton.

Jack Nicholson's improvisation of "Here's Johnny" line is from Jamie Wolf, *American Film,* January–February 1984.

Fire on *The Shining* set is from *Variety,* 1/3/79.

SK looking for new editing technology is from AI with Bob Gaffney.

Background on Philip Stone in *The Shining,* "That long scene . . ." is from letter to author by Philip Stone.

"Stanley's demanding . . ." is from Janet Huck.

Origins of image of the Grady sisters is from *Diane Arbus,* by Patricia Bosworth, and Kubrick's photo in *Look* magazine, 5/25/48.

Background on Jack Nicholson as a writer. "The first horror movie *about* writer's block," "That's the one scene . . ." is from "The Creative Mind of Jack Nicholson," by Ron Rosenbaum, *New York Times,* 7/13/86.

Background on Jack Nicholson, JN as writer, *Jack Nicholson: Face to Face,* by Christopher Fryer and Robert David Crane.

Video editing system used on *The Shining* is from *Selected Takes,* by author.

Scoring *The Shining,* "So the first thing . . ." is from AI with Wendy Carlos.

Warner release strategy for *The Shining* is from *Variety, New York Times,* 6/1/80, and *Los Angeles Times,* 6/1/80.

MPAA and *The Shining* is from Todd McCarthy, 6/14/80.

Saul Bass's work on *The Shining* key art, "That was a hell . . . ," is from AI with Saul Bass.

Opening previews delayed is from *New York Times*, 5/23/80.

Epilogue cut, opening box office, is from Aljean Harmetz, *New York Times*.

"Doesn't it strike you . . ." is from *"It's Only a Movie, Ingrid,"* by Alexander Walker.

Background on reviews for *The Shining* is from *Film Review Annual*.

"I basically told . . ." is from AI with Ed Di Giulio.

Stephen King's reaction to *The Shining* is from *American Film*, 1986.

Background on John Alcott is from obituaries in *Hollywood Reporter* and *New York Times*.

Chapter Eighteen: "Has It Been Seven Years? I Never Remember the Years"

"Has it been seven years . . . ," and epigraphs, "I don't know . . . ," "As mystical . . .": AI with Tony Spiridakis.

Several articles and books were instrumental in my understanding this chapter on *Full Metal Jacket*, Kubrick's film of the Gustav Hasford novel, *The Short-Timers: Full Metal Jacket: Cynic's Choice*, by Ron Magid, which includes a perceptive interview with Douglas Milsome, appeared in *American Cinematographer*, September, 1987; "Winner of the Filmic Palm," *Observer*, 2/28/88; "The Rolling Stone Interview with Stanley Kubrick," by Tim Cahill, *Rolling Stone*, 8/27/87; "Stanley Kubrick's Vietnam," by Francis X. Clines, *New York Times*, 1987; "Kubrick Does Vietnam his Way," by Lloyd Grove of *Washington Post*, as it appeared in *Boston Globe;* "Matthew Modine Plots the Course to Character," by Caryn James, *New York Times*, 9/27/87; "*Jacket* Actor Invents His Dialogue," by Aljean Harmetz in the *New York Times*, 6/30/87; "Lee Ermey: Marine Right to the Corps," by Martin Burden, *New York Post*, 7/2/87; "Stanley Kubrick's War Realities," by Alexander Walker, *Los Angeles Times*, 6/21/87; "Was 'Full Metal Jacket' Even Bleaker before Trims?" by Aly Sujo; "The Trauma of Being a Kubrick Marine," by Leslie Bennetts, *New York Times*, 7/10/87; "Finding Their Way to Oscars' 'Shrine', by Martin Kasindorf, *Newsday*, 4/11/88; "Stanley Kubrick Wants You," *Video*, May 1984; "Light at the End of the Tunnel," by Marc Cooper, *American Film*, June 1987; "The Several Battles of Gustav Hasford," by Grover Lewis, *Los Angeles Times Magazine*, 6/28/97; the novel *The Short-Timers*, by Gustav Hasford; "Heavy Metal," by Penelope Gilliatt, *American Film*, September 1987; "The Gospel According to Matthew," by Susan Linfield, *American Film*, October 1987; "Controversy Dogs 'Jacket' Score As It's Barred from Oscar Race," by Robert Koehler, *Los Angeles Times*, 1/28/88; and the published screenplay for *Full Metal Jacket*, by Stanley Kubrick, Michael Herr, and Gustav Hasford, with a foreword by Michael Herr, published by Knopf, 1987.

Background on *2010* and Peter Hyams is from *Odyssey: The Authorized Biogra-*

phy of Arthur C. Clarke, by Neil McAleer, and *The Odyssey File,* by Arthur C. Clarke and Peter Hyams.

Information on marriage of Philip Hobbs to Katharine Kubrick is from marriage certificate, General Register Office, County of Hertfordshire, District of St. Albans, England.

Background on Michael Herr is from *Apocalypse Now* playbill, 1979.

Background on Bob Gaffney shooting background research footage for SK on *Full Metal Jacket* is from AI with Bob Gaffney.

"Lee lined them up . . . ," "a mindless perfectionist . . . ," "A lot of actors . . . ," reasons of SK living in England, "I also like being . . ." is from Jack Kroll.

Background on Adam Baldwin, "The fact that he took . . . ," "The thing that really . . .": *New York Times,* 9/4/87.

Background on Dorian Harewood, Arliss Howard, Ed O'Ross, and Kevyn Major Howard is from *Full Metal Jacket* press notes.

Background on Anton Furst is from research for *By Design,* by author.

Background on Tony Spiridakis, his work for *Full Metal Jacket,* "I caught him . . ." is from AI with Tony Spiridakis.

Information concerning the death and wills of Jacques Kubrick is from Los Angeles County Superior Court—Probate Records.

Information concerning the birth of Alexander Hobbs is from General Register Office, England.

Oscar background on *Platoon* and *Full Metal Jacket* is from *Inside Oscar,* by Mason Wiley and Damien Bona.

Screenings for *Full Metal Jacket* pushed up was reported in *Variety,* 6/10/87.

Revising the release plan for FMJ was reported in *Hollywood Reporter.*

Background for release pattern and box office for FMJ, authorities looking for Hasford, is from Martin Kasindorf, *Newsday,* 7/8/87.

Background on reviews for *Full Metal Jacket* is from *Film Review Annual.*

Background on Lee Ermey's publicity tour for FMJ and "That these are certain . . ." is from Warner Archive at USC.

SK recipient of Luchino Visconti Award is from *Hollywood Reporter,* 6/6/88.

Part Six: Infinity

Chapter Nineteen: "What Has Happened to the Greatest Film Director This Country Ever Produced?"

Title is from Jim Coleman letter to Walter Scott. "Walter Scott's Personality Parade," *Parade* magazine, *Newsday,* February 25, 1996, p. 2.

Epigraphs: "Each month Stanley Kubrick . . ." is from "A Genius Who Lives by Night," by David Gritten, *Daily Telegram,* 3/23/93.

SK ordering computer software from Chess and Bridge, Ltd., in London is from Harriet Morrison's phone conversation with Malcolm Pein.

Background on SK production of *Wartime Lies* is from "Kubrick, Like Clockwork, Has a Secret," by Leonard Klady, *Variety,* 3/20/93; "Kubrick Telling

Lies in Aarhus," by Keith Keller, *Variety*, 10/5/93; "Kubrick's Got His Next Pic," by Leonard Klady, *Variety*, 4/5/93; "Julia Roberts, Again," *People* magazine,

5/11/92; *Variety*, 5/11/93; "Kubrick's Rubic of Silence Kept Up," *London Times*, 4/13/93; and "Gleaming the Kube," *Hollywood Reporter*, 4/24/92.

Joseph Mazzello talking about working with SK is from *Live with Regis and Kathie Lee*.

Background on *AI* "Politely inquired to . . ." is from "Kubrick's Next," by Rebecca Ascher-Walsh, *Entertainment Weekly*, Summer Double Issue, 1993.

Background on Cheryl Lee Terry's analysis of SK's handwriting is from "Sign of the Times," *Premiere*, July 1994.

Background on Louis Begley and SK's production of *Wartime Lies* is from AI interview with LB.

"Stanley Kubrick's next film will be . . ." is from Warner Bros. News Department press release, 12/15/95.

"I got a fax . . ." is from *Newsweek* reported in *People* magazine, 6/10/96.

Background on Frederic Raphael is from *The Film Encyclopedia*, by Ephraim Katz.

Background on *AI*, "For Fans Awaiting . . ." is from *Premiere*, January 1996.

Alexander Walker reporting about SK doing sci-fi film based on Isaac Asimov is from "A Genius Who Lives by Night," by David Gritten, *Daily Telegram*, 3/23/93.

Selected Bibliography

Agel, Jerome. *The Making of Kubrick's 2001*. New York: Signet, 1970.

Bach, Steven. *Final Cut: Dreams and Disaster in the Making of Heaven's Gate.* New York: William Morrow, 1985.

Balio, Tino. *United Artists: The Company That Changed the Film Industry.* Wisconsin: University of Wisconsin Press, 1987.

Bazelon, Irwin. *Knowing the Score: Notes on Film Music.* New York: Arco, 1975.

Bizony, Piers. *2001: Filming the Future.* London: Aurum, 1994.

Boorman, John. *The Emerald Forest Diary.* New York: Farrar, Straus and Giroux, 1985.

Bosworth, Patricia. *Diane Arbus.* New York: Knopf, 1984.

Boyd, Brian. *Vladimir Nabokov: The American Years.* Princeton: Princeton University Press, 1991.

Brando, Marlon, with Robert Lindsey. *Brando: Songs My Mother Taught Me.* New York: Random House, 1994.

Brouwer, Alexander, and Thomas Lee Wright. *Working in Hollywood.* New York: Crown, 1990.

Burgess, Anthony. *A Clockwork Orange.*

———. *Napoleon Symphony: A Novel in Four Movements.* New York: Knopf, 1974.

———. *You've Had Your Time: The Second Part of the Confessions.* New York: Grove Weidenfeld, 1990.

Burke, Tom. *Burke's Steerage.* New York: G. P. Putnam's Sons, 1976.

Carey, Gary. *Brando.* New York: Pocket Books, 1973.

Caute, David. *Joseph Losey: A Revenge on Life.* New York: Oxford University Press, 1994.

Ciment, Michel. *Kubrick.* New York: Holt, Rinehart and Winston, 1984.

Clarke, Arthur C. *2001: A Space Odyssey.* New York: Signet, 1968.

———. *The Lost Worlds of 2001.* New York: New American Library, 1972.

———. *Report on Planet Three.* London: Victor Gollancz, 1973.

Corliss, Richard. *BFI Film Classics: Lolita.* London: BFI, 1994.

Coyle, Wallace. *Stanley Kubrick: A Guide to References and Resources*. Boston: G. K. Hall, 1980.

Curtis, David. *Experimental Cinema*. New York: Universe Books, 1971.

Curtis, Tony, and Barry Paris. *Tony Curtis: The Autobiography*. New York: William Morrow, 1993.

De Vries, Daniel. *The Films of Stanley Kubrick*. Grand Rapids, Mich.: Eerdmans, 1973.

Douglas, Kirk. *The Ragman's Son*. New York: Simon and Schuster, 1988.

Evans, Peter. *Peter Sellers: The Mask Behind the Mask*. Englewood Cliffs, N.J.: Prentice-Hall, 1968.

Falsetto, Mario. *Stanley Kubrick: A Narrative and Stylistic Analysis*. Westport, Conn.: Praeger, 1994.

Farber, Stephen, and Marc Green. *Hollywood on the Couch*. New York: William Morrow, 1993.

Fine, Marshall. *Bloody Sam: The Life and Films of Sam Peckinpah.*New York: Donald I. Fine, Inc., 1991.

Fryer, Christopher, and Robert David Crane. *Jack Nicholson Face to Face*. New York: Evans and Company, 1975.

Geduld, Carolyn. *Film Guide to "2001: A Space Odyssey."* Bloomington: Indiana University Press, 1973.

Gelmis, Joseph. *The Film Director as Superstar*. Garden City, N.Y.: Doubleday, 1970.

Godard, Jean-Luc. Translation and commentary by Tom Milne. *Godard on Godard*. New York: Viking, 1972.

Hasford, Gustav. *The Short-Timers*. Harper and Row, 1979.

Hirsch, Forster. *The Dark Side of the Screen: Film Noir*. New York: Da Capo, 1981.

Jones, James Earl, and Penelope Niven. *Voices and Silences*. New York: Charles Scribner's Sons, 1993.

Kagan, Norman. *The Cinema of Stanley Kubrick*. New York: Holt, Rinehart, and Winston, 1972.

Katz, Ephraim. *The Film Encyclopedia*. 2d ed. New York: HarperCollins, 1994.

King, Stephen. *The Shining*. New York: Doubleday, 1977.

————. *Danse Macabre*. New York: Everest House, 1981.

Kolker, Robert Philip. *A Cinema of Loneliness*. New York and Oxford: Oxford University Press, 1988.

Kozloff, Sarah. *Invisible Storyteller: Voice-Over Narration in American Fiction Film*. Berkeley, Los Angeles, and London: University of California Press, 1988.

Kubrick, Christiane, and Marina Vaizey. *Christiane Kubrick Paintings*. New York: Warner, 1990.

Kubrick, Stanley. *Stanley Kubrick's A Clockwork Orange Based on the Novel by Anthony Burgess*. New York: Belard-Schuman, 1972.

———, Michael Herr, and Gustav Hasford. *Full Metal Jacket*. New York: Knopf, 1987.

Kubrick, Vivian. *The Making of The Shining*. BBC.

Lewis, Jerry. *The Total Film-Maker*. New York: Warner, 1971.

Lloyd, Norman. *Stages*. New York: Limelight Editions, 1993.

LoBrutto, Vincent. *By Design: Interviews with Film Production Designers*. Westport, Conn.: Praeger, 1992.

———. *Selected Takes: Film Editors On Editing*. New York: Praeger, 1991.

———. *Sound-On-Film: Interviews with Creators of Film Sound*, Westport, Conn.: Praeger, 1994.

Maltin, Leonard. *Behind the Camera: The Cinematographer's Art*. New York: Signet, 1971.

Manso, Peter. *Brando*. New York: Hyperion, 1994.

Mason, James. *Before I Forget*. London: Hamish Hamilton, 1981.

McAleer, Neil. *Odyssey: The Authorized Biography of Arthur C. Clarke*. London: Victor Gollancz, 1992.

McBride, Joseph. *Film Makers on Film Making: The American Film Institute Seminars on Motion Pictures and Television, Volume One*. Los Angeles: J. P. Tarcher; Boston: Houghton Mifflin, 1983.

McGilligan, Patrick. *Jack's Life*. New York: W. W. Norton, 1994.

Nabokov, Vladimir. *Lolita*. New York: Fawcett, 1959.

———. *Lolita: A Screenplay*. New York: McGraw Hill, 1974.

Phillips, Gene D. *Major Film Directors of the American and British Cinema*. London and Toronto: Lehigh University Press, 1990.

———. *Stanley Kubrick: A Film Odyssey*. New York: Popular Library, 1975.

Polito, Robert. *Savage Art*. New York: Knopf, 1995.

Rosenthal, Alan, ed. *New Challenges for Documentary*. Berkeley: University of California Press, 1988.

Samuels, Charles Thomas. *Encountering Directors*. New York: G. P. Putnam's Sons, 1972.

Seydor, Paul. *Peckinpah: The Western Films*. Urbana: University of Illinois Press, 1980.

Shipman, David. *Movie Talk: Who Said What about Whom in the Movies*. New York: St. Martin's, 1988.

Silver, Alan, and Elizabeth Ward. *Film Noir*. New York: Overlook, 1979.

Simmons, Garner. *Peckinpah: A Portrait in Montage*. Austin: University of Texas Press, 1976.

Sitney, P. Adams, ed. *Film Culture Reader*. New York: Praeger, 1970.

Smith, Steven C. *A Heart at Fire's Center: The Life and Music of Bernard Herrmann*. Berkeley, Calif., 1991.

Taylor, John Russell. *Directors and Directions: Cinema for the Seventies*. New York: Hill and Wang, 1975.

Thomson, David. *Overexposures*. New York: William Morrow, 1981.

Trumbo, Dalton. *Additional Dialogue*. New York: Evans and Company, 1970.

Walker, Alexander. *The Celluloid Sacrifice*. London: Michael Joseph, 1966.

———. *National Heroes: British Cinema in the Seventies and Eighties*. London: Harrap, 1985.

———. *"It's Only a Movie, Ingrid": Encounters On and Off Screen*. London: Headline, 1988.

———. *Peter Sellers: The Authorized Biography*. New York: Macmillan, 1981.

———. *Stanley Kubrick Directs*. New York: Harcourt Brace Jovanovich, 1972.

Weddle, David. *"If They Move . . . Kill 'Em!": The Life and Times of Sam Peckinpah*. New York: Grove, 1994.

Wiley, Mason, and Damien Bona. *Inside Oscar*. 4th updated ed. New York: Ballantine, 1986.

Wilson, David, Editor. *Sight and Sound: A Fiftieth Anniversary Selection*. Faber and Faber in Association with BFI Publishing, 1982.

Winters, Shelley. *Shelley II*. New York: William Morrow, 1984.

Youngblood, Gene. *Expanded Cinema*. New York: E. P. Dutton, 1970.

Other titles of interest

STEVEN SPIELBERG
A Biography
Joseph McBride
544 pp., 44 photos
80900-1 $16.95

SKYWALKING
The Life and Films of George Lucas
Updated Edition
Dale Pollock
approx. 364 pp., 28 photos
80904-4 $15.95

THE ADVENTURES OF
ROBERTO ROSSELLINI
Tag Gallagher
852 pp., 107 illus.
80873-0 $24.50

HOW I MADE A HUNDRED
MOVIES IN HOLLYWOOD AND
NEVER LOST A DIME
Roger Corman with Jim Jerome
256 pp., 39 photos
80874-9 $14.95

PAPPY
The Life of John Ford
Dan Ford
368 pp., 38 photos
80875-7 $15.95

AMERICAN SILENT FILM
William K. Everson
473 pp., 159 photos
80876-5 $17.95

THE AMERICAN CINEMA
Directors and Directions, 1929–1968
Andrew Sarris
393 pp.
80728-9 $14.95

BILLY WILDER
Updated Edition
Bernard F. Dick
192 pp., 25 photos, film stills, and
frame enlargements
80729-7 $13.95

BUSTER KEATON:
CUT TO THE CHASE
A Biography
Marion Meade
464 pp., 51 photos
80802-1 $16.95

CHAPLIN
His Life and Art
David Robinson
896 pp., 185 illus.
80600-2 $22.95

THE CINEMA OF ORSON WELLES
Peter Cowie
262 pp., 131 photos
80201-5 $14.95

COPPOLA
A Biography
Updated Edition
Peter Cowie
352 pp., 89 photos
80598-7 $14.95

CRIME MOVIES
Carlos Clarens
Updated by Foster Hirsch
376 pp., 212 illus.
80768-8 $15.95

THE DARK SIDE
OF THE SCREEN
Film Noir
Foster Hirsch
229 pp., 188 photos
80203-1 $17.95

FILM AS FILM
Understanding and Judging Movies
V. F. Perkins
New introd. by Foster Hirsch
204 pp.
80541-3 $12.95

FELLINI ON FELLINI
Federico Fellini
192 pp., 35 photos & film stills
80673-8 $13.95

THE FILMS IN MY LIFE
François Truffaut
368 pp.
80599-5 $14.95

FRITZ LANG
Lotte Eisner
420 pp., 162 photos
80271-6 $15.95

GODARD ON GODARD
Critical Writings by
Jean-Luc Godard
Edited by Tom Milne
292 pp., photos
80259-7 $13.95

HITCH
The Life and Times of
Alfred Hitchcock
John Russell Taylor
336 pp., 31 photos
80677-0 $14.95

AN ILLUSTRATED HISTORY OF
HORROR AND SCIENCE-FICTION
FILMS
The Classic Era, 1895–1967
Carlos Clarens
New introduction by J. Hoberman
328 pp., 135 illus.
80800-5 $14.95

INNER VIEWS
Filmmakers in Conversation
Expanded Edition
David Breskin
409 pp.
80801-3 $15.95

JOHN FORD
Joseph McBride and
Michael Wilmington
234 pp., 104 photos
80016-0 $11.95

MY WONDERFUL WORLD
OF SLAPSTICK
Buster Keaton and
Charles Samuels
282 pp.
80178-7 $13.95

THE NAME ABOVE
THE TITLE
An Autobiography
Frank Capra
Foreword by John Ford
New introd. by Jeanine Basinger
534 pp., 111 photos
80771-8 $18.95

NEGATIVE SPACE
Manny Farber on the Movies
Expanded Edition
Manny Farber
New preface by Robert Walsh
416 pp.
80829-3 $15.95

AN OPEN BOOK
John Huston
443 pp., 97 photos
80573-1 $14.95

ORSON WELLES
Revised and Expanded Edition
Joseph McBride
320 pp., 64 pp. of illus.
80674-6 $14.95

A TALENT FOR TROUBLE
The Life of Hollywood's Most
Acclaimed Director, William Wyler
Jan Herman
544 pp., 33 photos
80798-X $16.95

THIS IS ORSON WELLES
Orson Welles and Peter Bogdanovich
Edited by Jonathan Rosenbaum
New introd. by Peter Bogdanovich
592 pp., 93 illus.
80834-X $19.95

TRAMP
The Life of Charlie Chaplin
Joyce Milton
604 pp., 35 illus.
80831-5 $17.95

UNDERGROUND FILM
A Critical History
Parker Tyler
New introd. by J. Hoberman
New afterword by
Charles Boultenhouse
287 pp., 67 film stills and
frame enlargements
80632-0 $13.95

Available at your bookstore

OR ORDER DIRECTLY FROM

DA CAPO PRESS

1-800-242-7737
FAX 1-800-822-4090